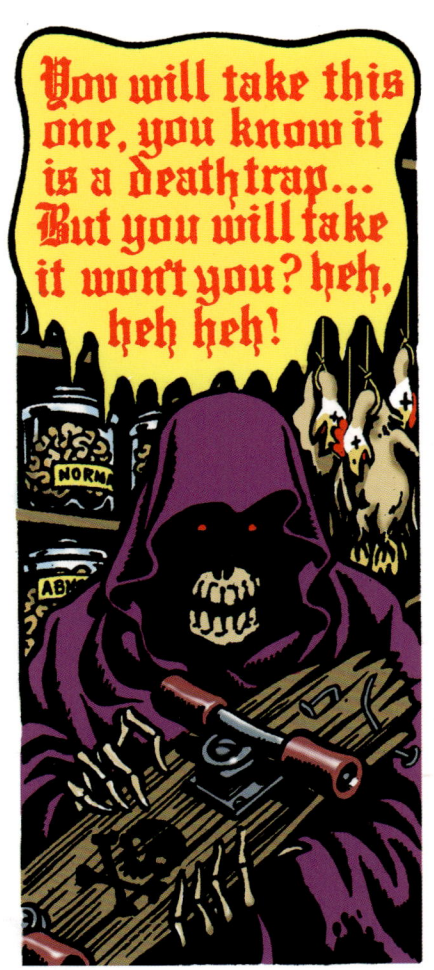

SURF SKATE & ROCK ART of JIM PHILLIPS

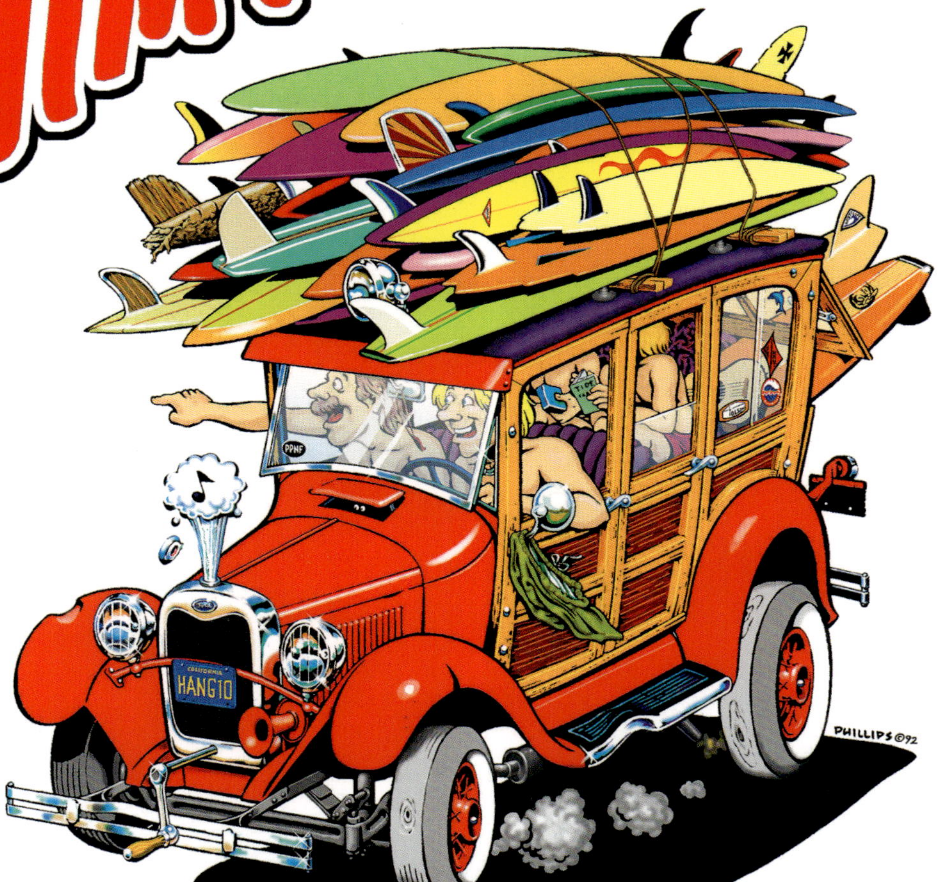

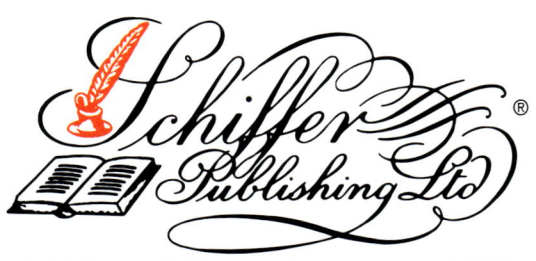

40 Years of Surf, Skate and Rock Art

Schiffer Publishing Ltd

4880 Lower Valley Road · Atglen, PA 19310

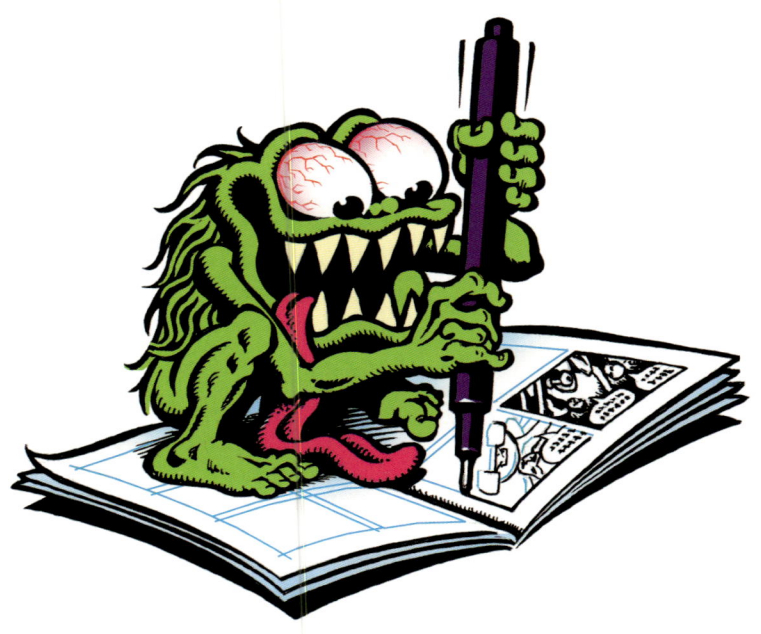

Published by Schiffer Publishing, Ltd.
4880 Lower Valley Road
Atglen, PA 19310
Phone: (610) 593-1777; Fax: (610) 593-2002
E-mail: Info@schifferbooks.com
Web: www.schifferbooks.com

For our complete selection of fine books on this and related subjects,
please visit our website at www.schifferbooks.com. You may also write
for a free catalog.

Schiffer Publishing's titles are available at special discounts for
bulk purchases for sales promotions or premiums. Special editions,
including personalized covers, corporate imprints, and excerpts, can
be created in large quantities for special needs. For more information,
contact the publisher.

We are always looking for people to write books on new and related
subjects. If you have an idea for a book, please contact us at proposals@
schifferbooks.com.

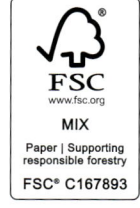

FSC
www.fsc.org
MIX
Paper | Supporting
responsible forestry
FSC® C167893

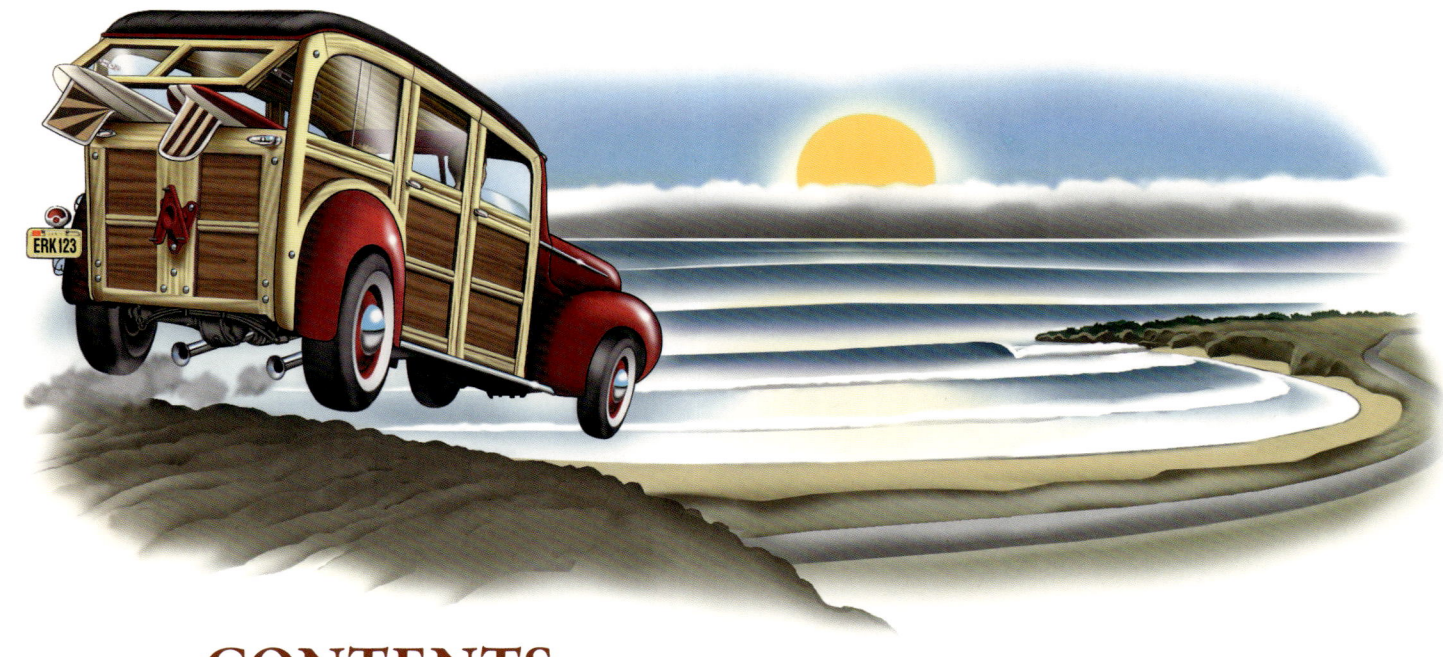

CONTENTS

CHAPTER I 9
ENERGIZED: 1944 to 1961
Some Portraits From the Young Man as a Promising Artist

CHAPTER 2 21
ON THE ROAD: 1961 to 1969
Childhood to Manhood, Santa Cruz to Mexico to Florida

CHAPTER 3 41
ROLLING: 1970 to 1977
Roots of Skateboarding

CHAPTER4... 101
THE ROARING 80s: 1979 to 1989
Screaming Icons of Infamy

CHAPTER 5 133
BACK TO THE FUTURE: 1989 to 2002
Jimmy Rocks Digital

Jim Phillips Jr... 201

Index 206

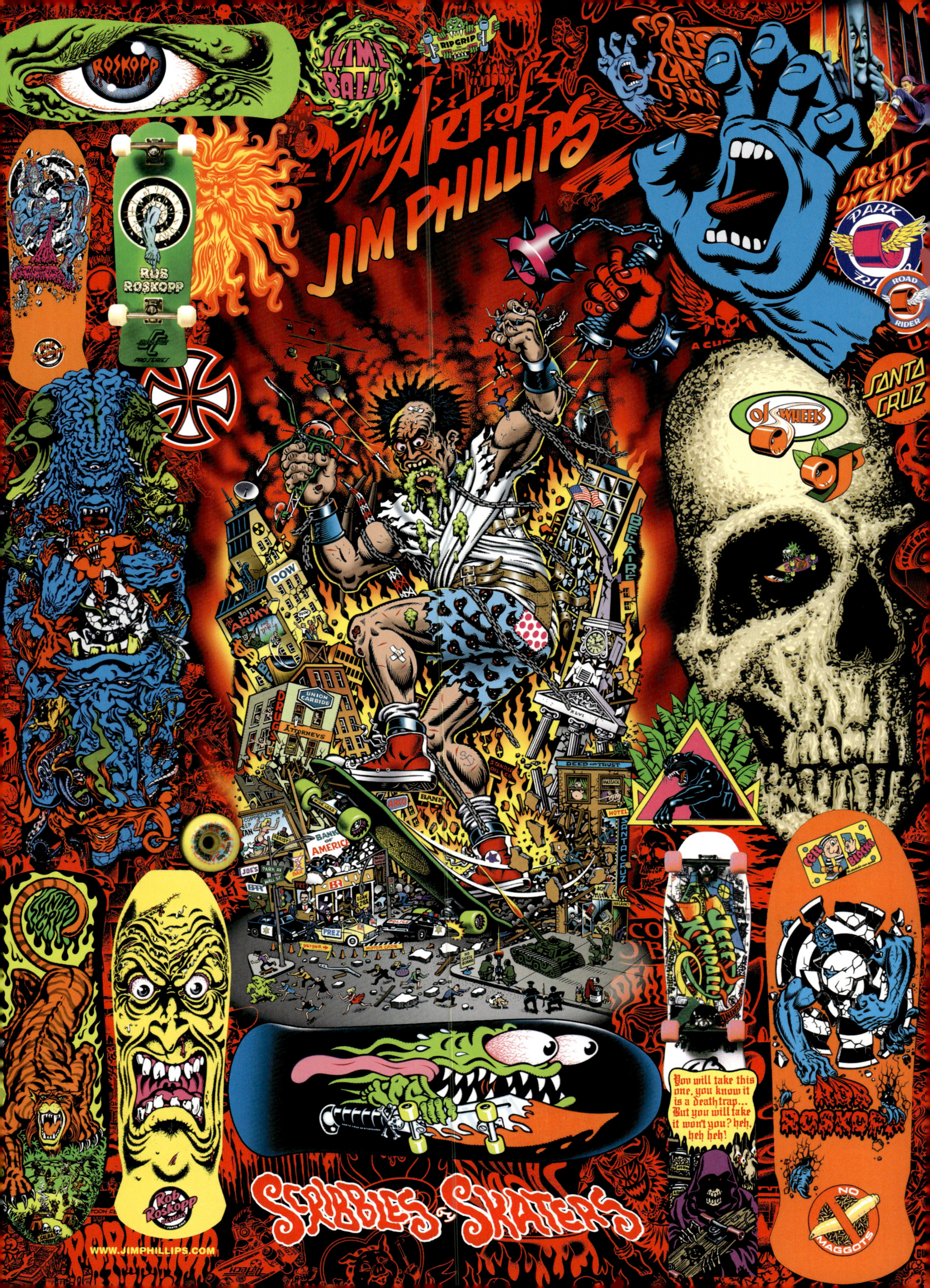

FOREWORD *by Rich Novak*

I first met Jim Phillips in the late '50s at Pleasure Point. A couple of buddies and I were getting out of the water, and at that time you could go out at Pleasure Point and not see another surfer all day. Jimmy and a few of his friends were coming down the cliff with their boards. They asked if it was OK for them to surf there. We said no, for no apparent reason other than we didn't like other people surfing there; we thought at the time that it was a secret spot. We exchanged some words about territory and about Jimmy and his buddies surfing there, but Jimmy ended up going out. After that, we spent many years surfing together.

Later, as I got to know Jimmy better, I began seeing his art. He would draw surf characters and cartoons that were emblematic of the times: little characters surfing or driving around in funky cars. Later, as I look back, I realized he was an artist and so I became a collector. To this day, he always seems to come up with a drawing or a picture or some memorabilia from the surfing past in Santa Cruz.

In the early '60s I worked at Olson Surfboards. George Olson wouldn't promote me until I flunked the draft. Upon accomplishing that task, I became a partner. George had hired Jimmy as glasser, and I think he eventually became the glosser. The rest of the '60s went by really fast. We surfed, partied and traveled, and I would only get glimpses of Jimmy's art. Most of what I saw were reflections of the times and characters of that era.

At the end of the '60s, Jay Shuirman, Doug Haut and I started NHS Inc. We were making surfboards and selling reinforced plastics (raw material for boats and surfboards) for a surfboard label called Solar Surfboards, a parallel brand for Haut Surfboards' gulf and east coast dealers. This marked the start of my relationship with Jimmy's commercial artwork. From there, Jimmy's graphics became the mainstay for the Fiberglas Works and many other industries in Santa Cruz.

Unfortunately, the Fiberglas Works went bankrupt soon after, and they threw out a lot of Jimmy's work. We got wind of this and went dumpster diving. We were able to salvage a great amount of art, and Jim Byberg was in the dumpster with us fighting for as much of it as he could. Thus began my Jim Phillips art collection.

We were put into a bind after the downfall of the Fiberglas Works, because they owed NHS a lot of money for raw materials. We had to scramble to pay our debt to our vendors. This pushed us into the skateboard business. We started Santa Cruz Skateboards as an offshoot of Santa

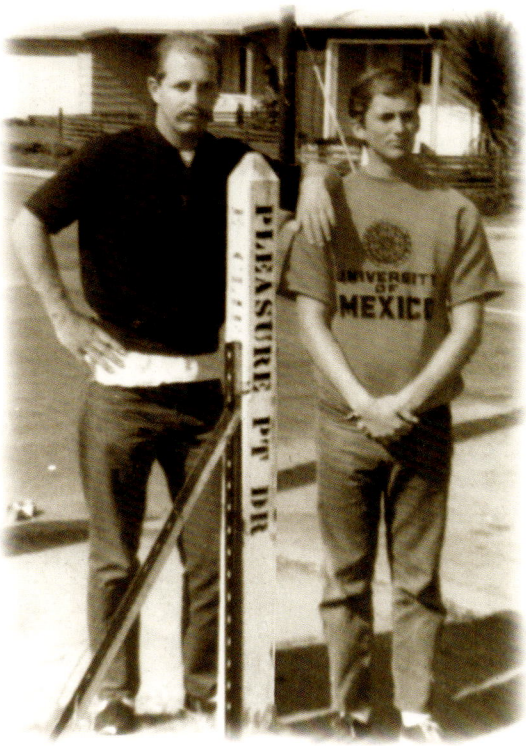
Rich Novak and Jimmy Phillips, 1963.

Cruz Surfboards. We had Jimmy do some basic graphics and ad work, but we were being very conservative in the message we were trying to get across. This was a reflection of our history in the surfboard business, and of our attempts to learn how to do business in general, especially such a new business as skateboards. Shortly thereafter, we started a wheel line call Road Rider, the first precision bearing skateboard wheel. Road Rider launched us into a whole new way of marketing and presenting our products, and this is where Jimmy's ideas began to work.

By the end of the '70s, we were rolling. We had Road Rider, and we started the Independent brand. Jimmy was the creator for our icons, ads, and graphics. He pushed to put more art onto the skateboard, but we were reluctant to try. We'd use stripes and checkers, but nothing too radical. For my part, I would always try to get Jimmy interested in just doing art. To me, Jimmy was a mix of Escher and Dali. His work was detailed but could be very abstract, and you always had to look deep into the art to find some hidden message, or as we called it, "the Pope in the pizza."

In 1979, my partner Jay Shuirman died of cancer, and the skateboard business died at the same time, leaving us in pretty bad shape. Jimmy plugged away for me, mainly just to survive, and I slowly worked my way back into the market during the '80s. This is when Jimmy's art really started to click. He created the first graphics on skateboard wheels, and he was finally given the chance to project the images he wanted onto skateboards. He did everything, nothing was off limits. His art was the right art at the right time for the right market. His creations were all over the world. The skateboard community would wait with anticipation for the next set of graphics.

I still would try to commission him to do some fine art for me, but he was always too busy. He did do a painting of a woodcutter for me, and for the longest time this was the only solid piece of his art that I owned.

The '80s finally came to an end. We were all way overworked, and our nerves were stretched to the limits. Jimmy and I parted ways for awhile, but a few years ago I finally was able to get him to just paint. His recent work portrays some of our past surf history; other stuff is just whatever is on his mind. I always thought it was fantastic. I am very fortunate to have been a part of Jimmy's life, and I must have been chosen to be able to have so much of his great art around me. This book is long in coming, and it reflects both an era and the life of the greatest artist I know. ENJOY

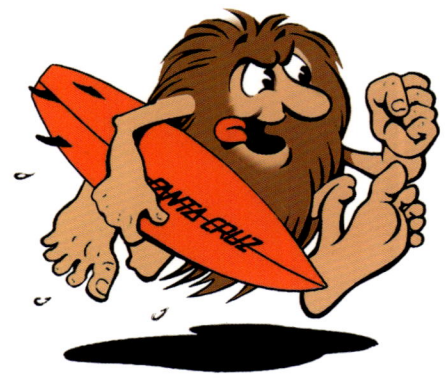

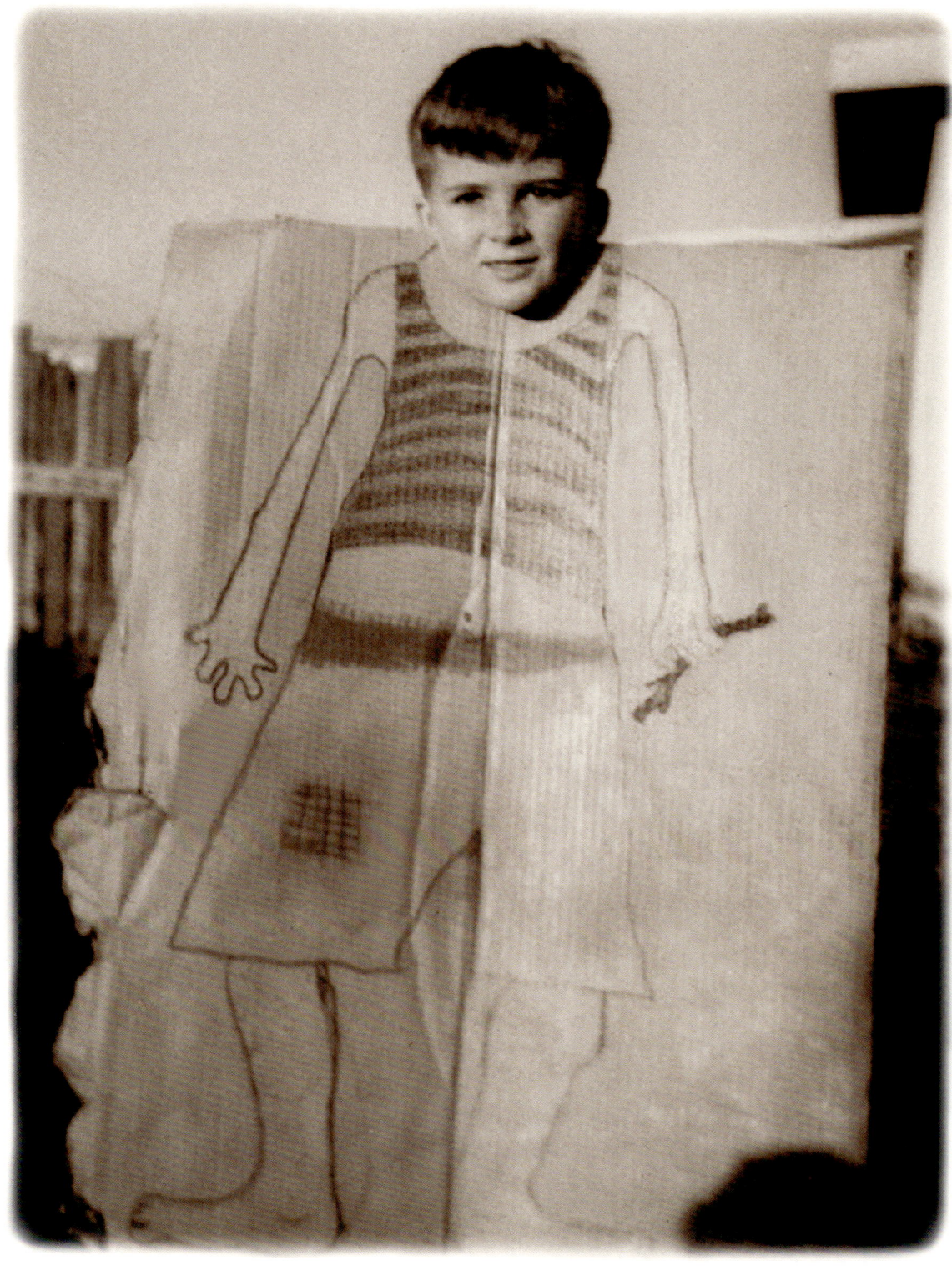

Jim, age 8, with his handmade cardboard cutout.

CHAPTER 1

ENERGIZED: 1944 to 1961

Some Portraits From the Young Man as a Promising Artist

Every artist dips his brush in his own soul,
and paints his own nature into his pictures.
-Henry Ward Beecher

Jim Phillips inks his pens in the black oil pan of a '48 Packard woody, and colors with the palette of Northern California. Phillips' blackline sketches vibrate with the energy of men and machines: a thrumming V8 powering a woody wagon, the blatty torque of a juiced-up chopper, the humping lines of a winter west swell, the happy, sunburned faces and endorphined brains of the surf stoked and the gently jazzed. God given or man made, Phillips energizes his outlines then colors them with a brush swirled in the blue winter skies of the Monterey Bay, the green, kelpy waves of Steamer Lane and the orangy-red sunsets of the Pacific west.

If it's not pretentious to mention Da Vinci and Phillips in the same sentence, where Da Vinci drew inspiration from Florence and Milan, Phillips draws his from California, specifically Northern California, and more specifically, Santa Cruz, California.

Phillips drew his first breath in San Jose but will probably draw his last in Santa Cruz, a coastal town on the northern tip of the Fertile Crescent of the Monterey Bay. Santa Cruz is unique along the California Coast; a Northern California town with its feet in the tingly cold Pacific but its face looking up and south, into the sun. In the lush Santa Cruz microclimate, palm trees just get along with the pines, and people try to do the same. Santa Cruz is one of the most beautiful, and expensive, places to live in the United States, and anyone who spends a day there will understand why. Squinting south into the sun, Santa Cruz enjoys a million-dollar view across the Monterey Bay, up the cornucopia of the Salinas Valley and along the dry, Steinbeck mountains of the Santa Lucia Range. The Monterey Bay is one of the most fertile places on earth by land and sea, and part of that bounty is the surf that sweeps into the bay from the north and west in the winter, and the south in the summer.

Santa Cruz is Surf City North, where people of every description get away from the shady turf by catching green, kelp-tinged waves in the cold, briny surf. If it's okay to put Phillips and Da Vinci in the same sentence, then it's fair to say that Phillips is to Santa Cruz what Warhol was to soup cans, Big Daddy was to hot rods and Rick Griffin was to mystic eyeballs. Santa Cruz is Jim Phillips' muse, and Jim Phillips is Santa Cruz' champion.

Phillips' talent is natural, nurtured by nature. The images that flow from his "own soul" down through his fingertips and onto the page are drawn from what is around him. But the talent comes from within and before the cradle. The Phillips' talent is hereditary and if you need proof, all you have to do is climb Jim Phillips' family tree and look at all the pretty pictures hanging off the branches.

One of Phillips' earliest influences was his grandfather, Henry C. Hall, a career educator who began teaching in Half Moon Bay circa 1910 and worked his way through a principal's position in San Bruno and superintendent of schools in San Mateo, then a Ph.D. at Stanford and a position at the University of San Francisco. Henry Hall taught history, but he practiced art. He dabbled in painting and was serious in ceramics. The inherent ability is there in his work, and he not only passed on the art talent that flows through grandson Jim, but helped ignite it in Jim's youth.

Grandpa Hall's sister Mary did pen and ink drawings of flappers living the ritzy life, reminiscent of Charles Gibson's work. Mary lost a leg to a San Francisco streetcar as a child, which may have inspired many of her beautiful fashion figures of the early 20s to be balanced on one leg. Henry Hall's wife Edna said of Mary, "Even though she died young, Mary was a talented musician, artist and a fine, fun-loving person."

Edna Hall had an artistic bent as well. She created leaf-shaped dishes, and molds of the Madonna. Together, Henry Hall and Edna created their own little work of art, Edna May, whose talent tended toward music more than painting or drawing or ceramics. In the mid-30s, Edna May was a schoolteacher in Pescadero, a small town between San Francisco and Santa Cruz that is still rural in the 21st Century, and must have been a real outpost 70 years ago. Edna May was living with family friends across the street from Pescadero Elementary School when she met a 20-something bus driver named Ray.

Raymond L. Phillips was a Wisconsin boy who suffered ear problems from the cold climate. In 1927, at age 17 he offered to join the Army if they would guarantee him service in a place where fish didn't freeze in rainbarrels. The Army honored their promise and sent Ray to Hawaii. In peacetime the pen is mightier

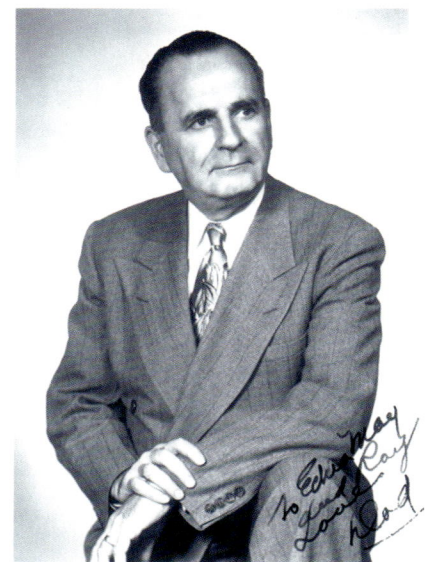

Henry C. Hall

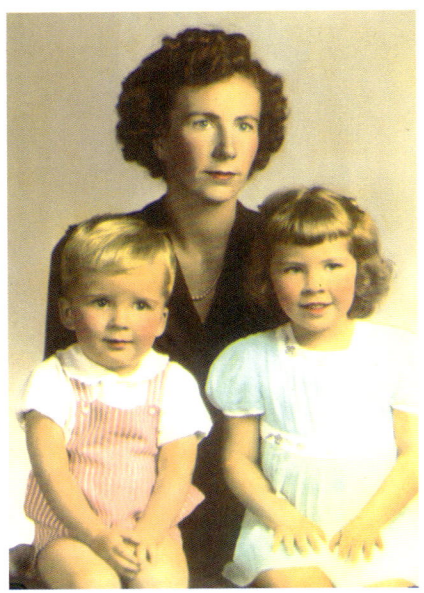

Edna May, Jim & Ann Phillips

Raymond L. Phillips

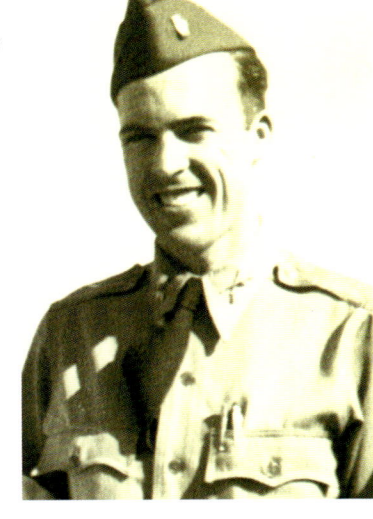

than the sword. Phillips had typing and shorthand skills due to a high school teacher's particular interest in him, which garnered him immediate and frequent promotions. Raymond Phillips' duties afforded him the luxury of cruising the South Shore in a dual-ignition Nash Roadster with Waikiki's first built-in car radio. He drove a Harley Davidson around the island, and even tried a little surfing on the South Shore and at Sunset Beach.

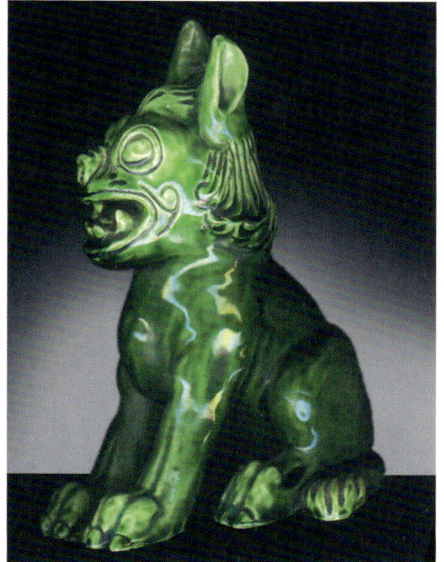

Chinese Dog ceramic by Henry C. Hall

1948

During the late 30s in California, Phillips was taking a break from the service and working as a Greyhound bus-driver on a route that took him from San Mateo over hazardous mountain roads to Highway One. He passed through Pescadero on his route, where he made the acquaintance of a certain schoolteacher named Edna May Hall. Phillips opened the bus door, symbolically speaking, winked at Edna May and said, "Hop in, baby. Let's go." She did. Ray and Edna married in 1941, and then Ray re-enlisted to fight the war.

Jim Phillips was born two years after his sister Ann, on October 24, 1944, in San Jose because of the proximity of a doctor in the family, his grandfather's brother. Jim's artistic talent began to sprout early. His first drawings had a lot of pumpkins in them, possibly because he spent a lot of time in the vicinity of Half Moon Bay, The Pumpkin Capitol of the World, and also because Jim's birthday was a week before Halloween. Phillips was well into drawing cars by the age of 5, but also birds and ships and family portraits.

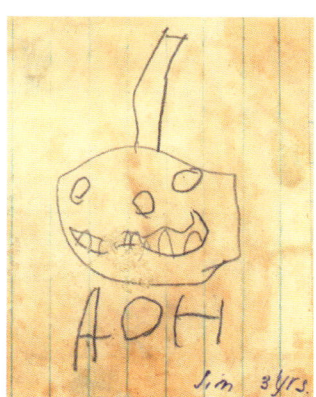

One of Jim's first drawings, 1947.

Below: An early car drawing, 1950.

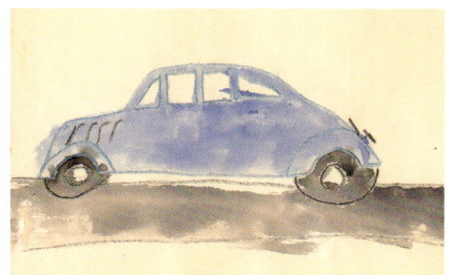

Ray Phillips was career Army and always on the move, marching ahead of his family, who followed dutifully, in formation, to Panama, North and South Carolina, Richmond, California, Oakland, California and Salt Lake City. Jim attended eight different schools by the second grade and he will admit that he never recovered. Perhaps the trauma of all this early childhood moving helps explain Phillips' obsession with drawing. Since he didn't stay anywhere long enough to make friends, he entertained himself with cartoons.

Mary Hall's pen & ink drawings from 1923

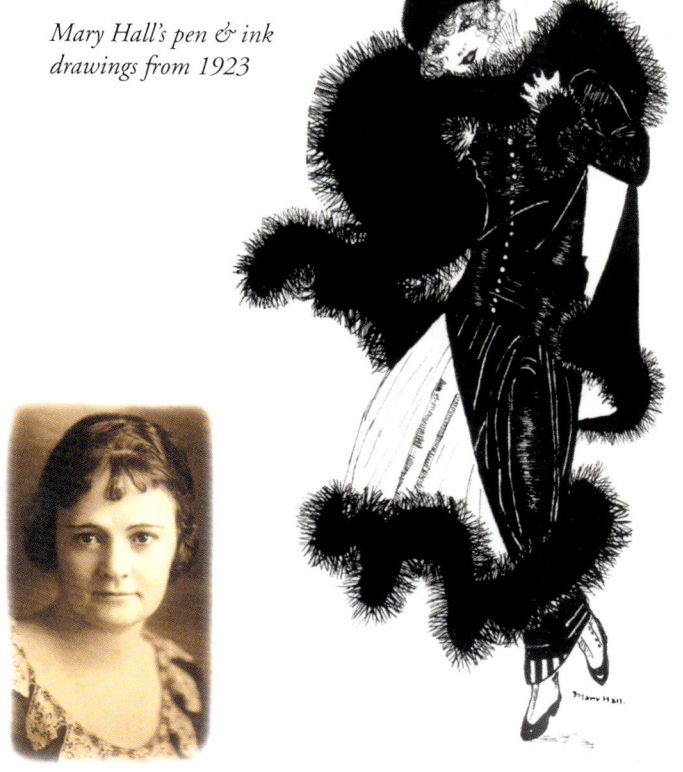

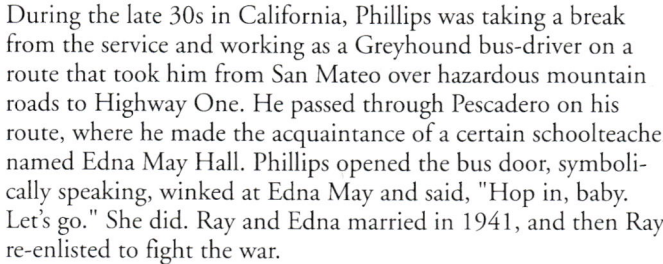

Mary Hall

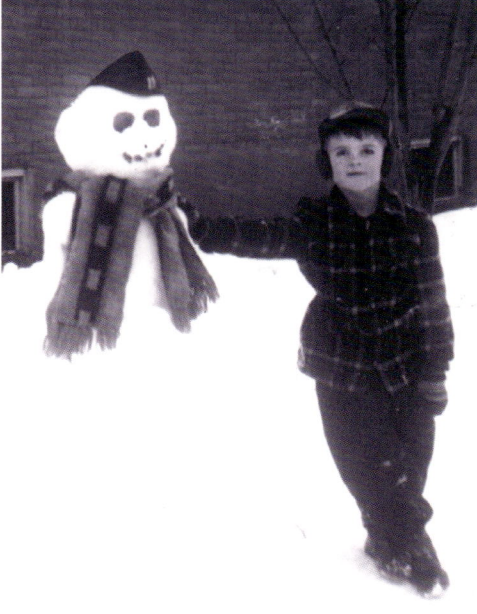

Fort Douglas, Utah 1950

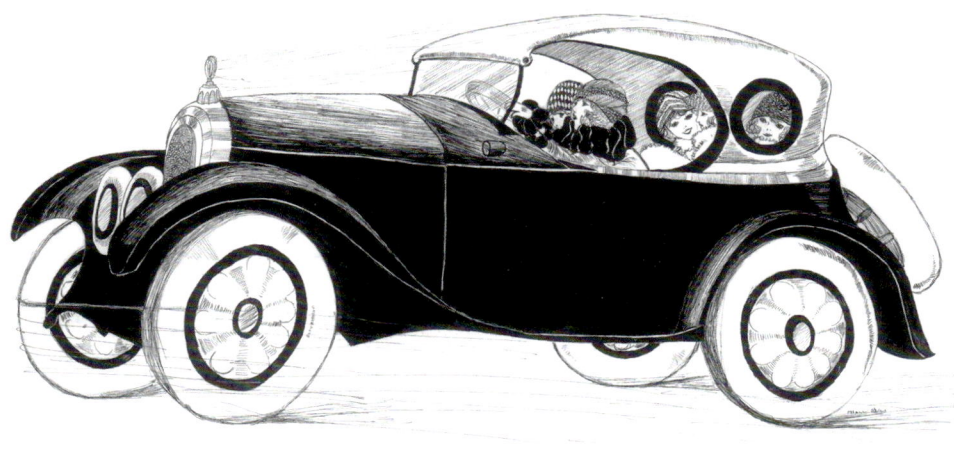

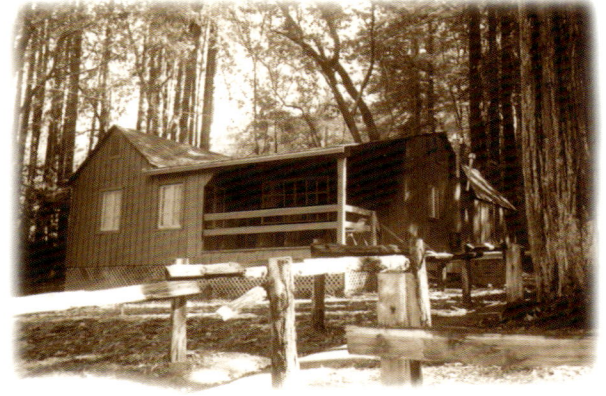

Some of Phillips' happiest times were spent drawing at "The Cabin," on an acre in the mountains near Pescadero. The land was a gift from Doc Hoffman, a surly German physician who practiced medicine on Jim despite losing his license when he spoke out about World War II. Henry Hall had used his credentials and good standing to keep Doc Hoffman out of jail, and Doc returned the favor by deeding the acre of land to the Hall family. Jim and his sister Ann loved the peace and quiet and stability of the cabin; the simple life-style of kerosene lamps, outhouse and woodstove. They were California hillbillies and loved it.

At age six, Jimmy received a present from Grandpa Hall, *Pen Tips on Cartooning*, a how-to published by Speedball Pen Company. The book had line drawings of cartoon figures and faces, thick and thin lines, with the type of pen shown drawing the different lines. Jim practiced drawing the cartoons shown in that book, helped along by drawing games with his Grandpa Hall. He would draw something and then Jim drew something and they took turns, mostly adding to the previous draw. These sessions, and Grandpa's extraordinary ability to communicate, piqued Jim's imagination and set him on the road.

In 1951, Raymond Phillips, now an Army Captain stationed at Ft. Douglas, near Salt Lake City, was called to fight in Korea. He asked his wife where she wanted to live and as family history has it, Edna asked to be blindfolded and given a map to point to. She could have pointed at Fallon, Nevada or Omaha, Nebraska, but fickle fortune put her finger directly on Santa Cruz. Edna must have peeked, as she had often vacationed there with her parents, and everyone who visits Santa Cruz falls in love with the area.

For the first time in his 7 years of life, Jim Phillips had a permanent home, on 26th Avenue, a block from the Pacific Ocean. After all of that moving, Phillips was thoroughly neurotic and like most transient kids, he kept himself entertained and sane with fantasies. He learned to draw, inspired by Krazy Kat and Ignatz and Offisa Pup, and Felix the Cat and Donald Duck and everything from Disney Studios. Phillips looked forward to visits to his grandparents' house in San Bruno, as they got all the San Francisco stations on TV. Phillips had *carte blanche* to Crusader Rabbit and Mighty Mouse, Flash Gordon and Superman. Back in rural Santa Cruz, all Phillips could get on TV were endless Felix the Cat reruns.

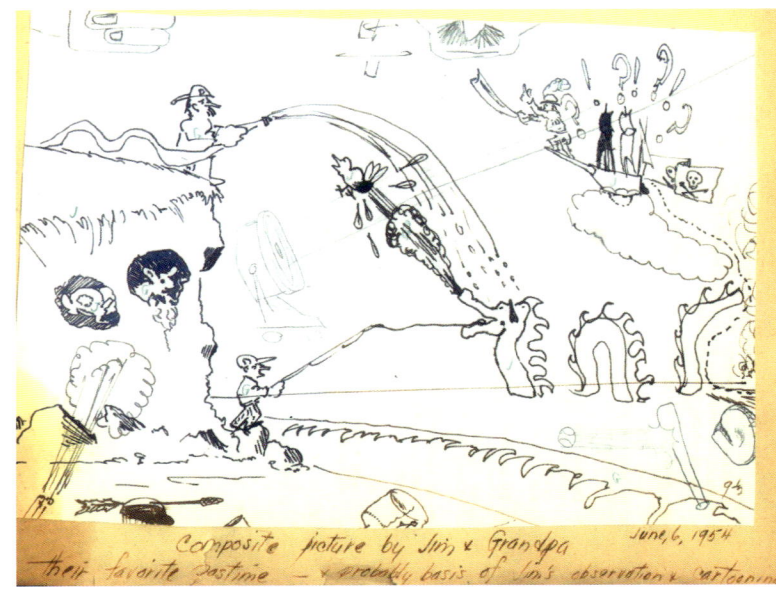

One of many drawings Jim made with his grandfather by taking turns and adding to each others' work. Written below by Jim's mother in the family scrapbook: "June 6, 1954 - Composite picture by Jim & Grandpa - their favorite pastime - & probably (the) basis of Jim's observation & cartooning."

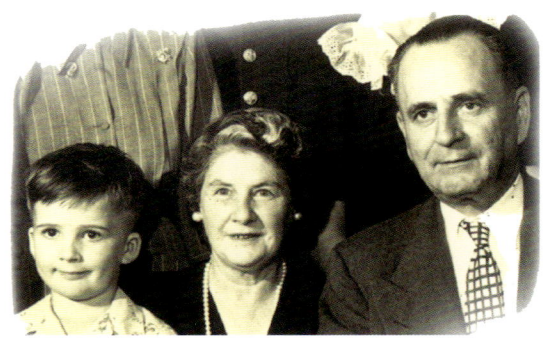

Jim with Grandma & Grandpa Hall

The Phillips' home on 26th Avenue was a two-bedroom bungalow. Ann got the bedroom and Jim was given a small space behind a hutch off the kitchen and later a small trailer which was musty, but Jim's own space. At night he listened to *The Red Blanchard Show* on his first radio, where he was exposed to a new form of music, rock & roll. Blanchard was a zany DJ who injected funny sound effects to his routine, between records. Grandpa Hall took Jim and his sister to San Francisco to be in the studio audience during a live show. By day Jim had easy access to the world's greatest bane for childhood jitters: the ocean. In the early 50s, very few people used the beach at 26th Avenue, but Jim and his sister were there all the time. They called it "Our Beach."

By 1955 Ray Phillips had returned from Korea, Edna was teaching at Soquel Elementary and the Phillips moved into a bigger house off 35th Avenue, at Pleasure Point. The fields above the ocean were rural back then, and their knotty-pine, ranch-style house was surrounded by open fields. Jim joined the Boy Scouts and played Little League and splashed in the ocean whenever he could. It was a great place to grow up.

Top left: The family cabin at Pescadero, Ca.

Bottom left: 26th Ave. home, Santa Cruz, 1951

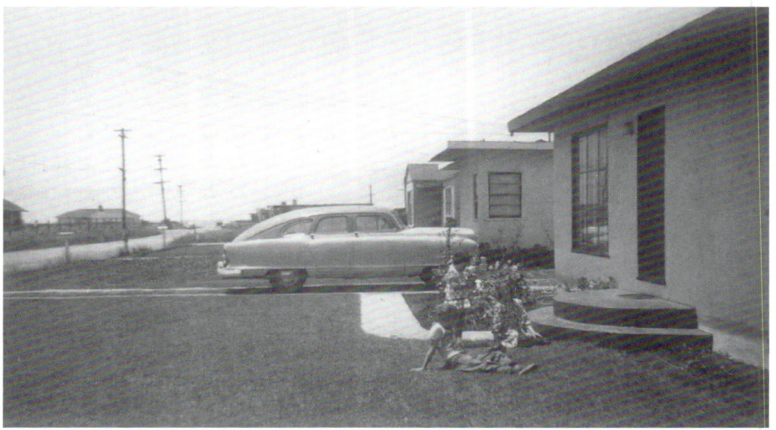

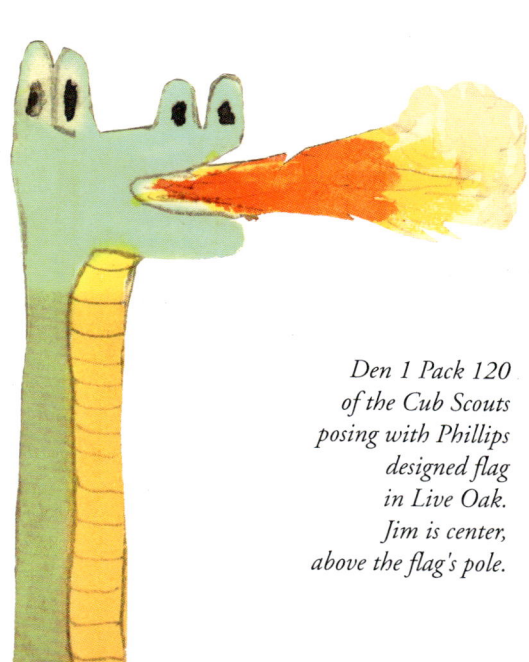

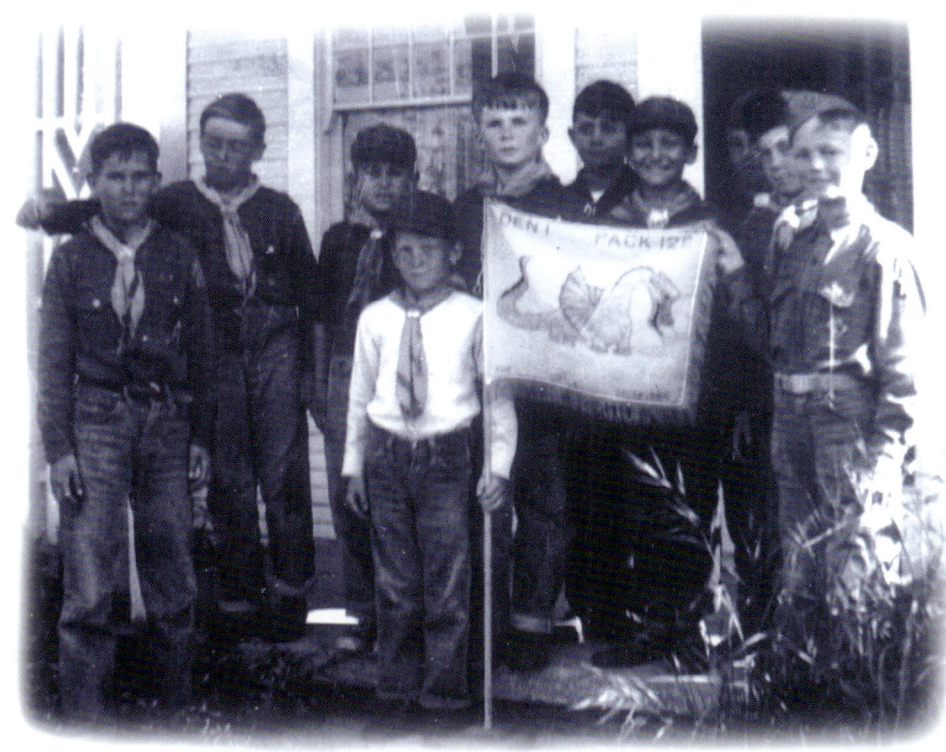

Den 1 Pack 120 of the Cub Scouts posing with Phillips designed flag in Live Oak. Jim is center, above the flag's pole.

"Jungle Newspaper" Eight page Dreadful Dragon comic book circa 1953.

Dreadful Dragons

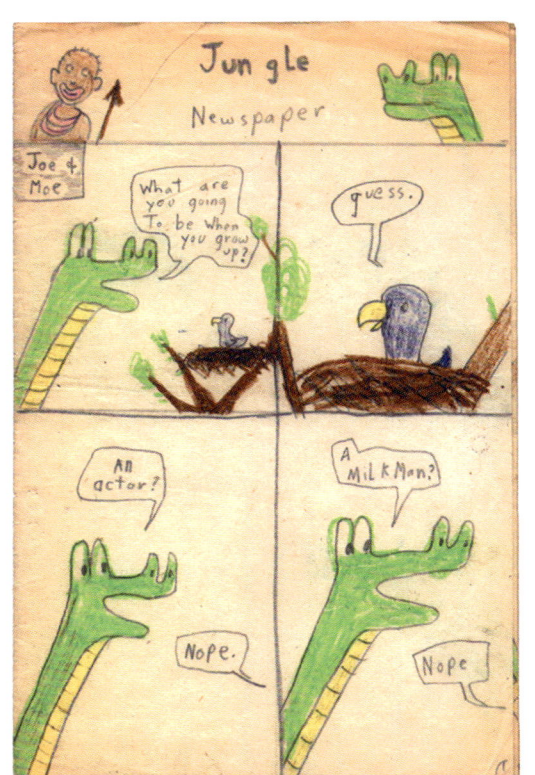

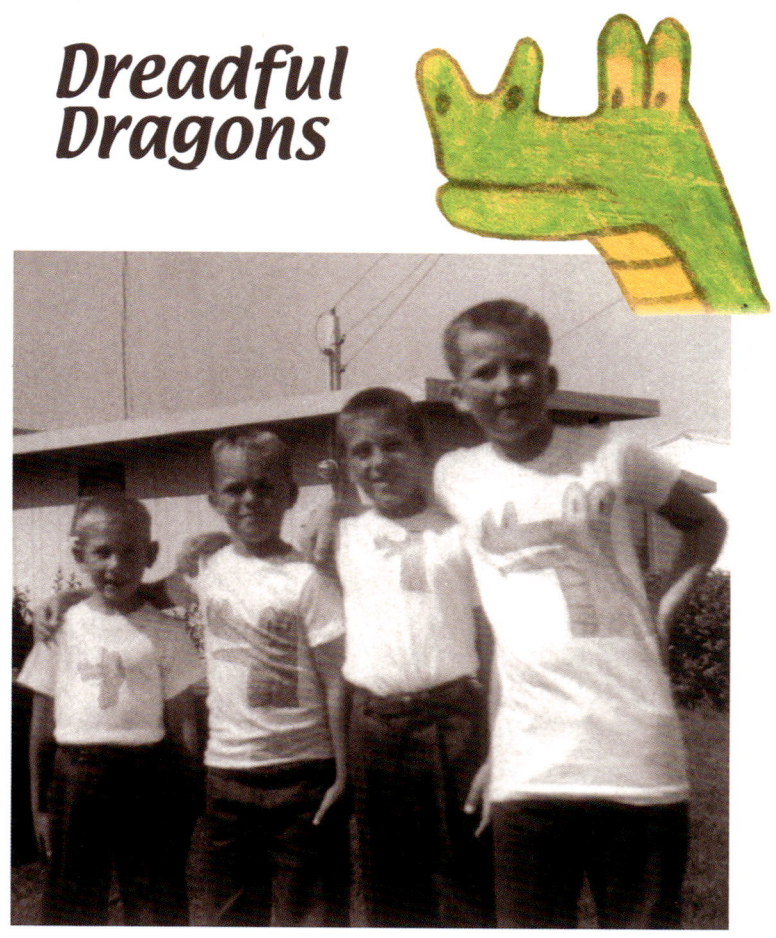

Jim was known as Big Jim in the 26th Avenue neighborhood. He talked Little Jim and Mediumsize Jim, shown here, into forming a club called the Dreadful Dragons. Phillips hand-drew the club t-shirts modeled here by members.

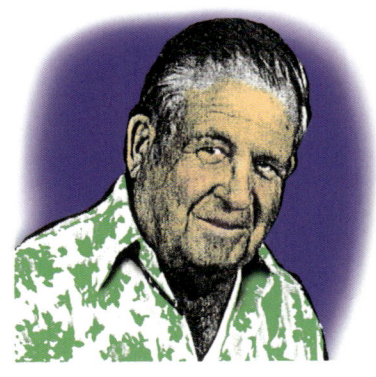

Ralph Gray Studio

In 1955, Edna enrolled Jim in free children's art classes at Ralph Gray Studios, a hole-in-the-wall storefront studio on Seabright Avenue, which was paint-spattered, littered with drawings, painted cutouts, drawing boards and art tools. It was a forerunner of a lot of studios and glassing rooms Jim would work in during later years. Ralph Gray was the cousin of Harold Gray, the creator of *Little Orphan Annie*. Ralph had some success in the 30s with political cartoons and a syndicated strip called *Dozey Dinkel*. When Phillips was his student, Gray was busy doing large cutout elves and fairies for Santa's Village, which was going up near Santa Cruz. Ralph Gray held his drawing classes out back in the uncut grass under the few apple trees that survived in the Seabright area. Phillips and the other students were allowed to draw whatever they wanted, and Gray would wander around and give advice.

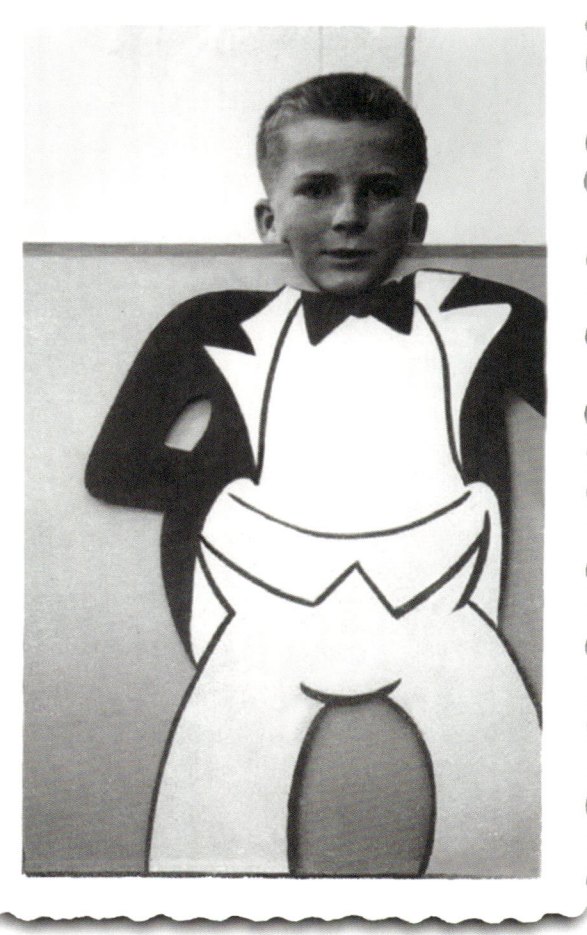

Jim posing behind a cartoon cut-out at KSBW TV Studios, 1956.

Sometimes Gray took the kids on field trips to visit Hank Ketcham at the Dennis the Menace studio in Monterey, or to KSBW TV 8 in Salinas. On one TV trip, Ann and Jim were chosen to represent the Ralph Gray Children's Art Classes. Ann did some yo-yo tricks, while Jim and Freddie Gray drew on a large easel, on live TV. Jim drew a character called Dudley, he refers to as "just a dumb-looking guy." Jim was terrified to draw on live camera, but it was also an intoxicating experience for him.

Ralph Gray was everywhere in Santa Cruz during the 50s, as Jim Phillips' work is now, and a comparison of the two shows a direct influence. Ralph's artwork was always accompanied by his quality hand-lettering, which is always more pleasing than type. Ralph Gray's tutoring and work had a profound effect on Jim, and you can see it to this day.

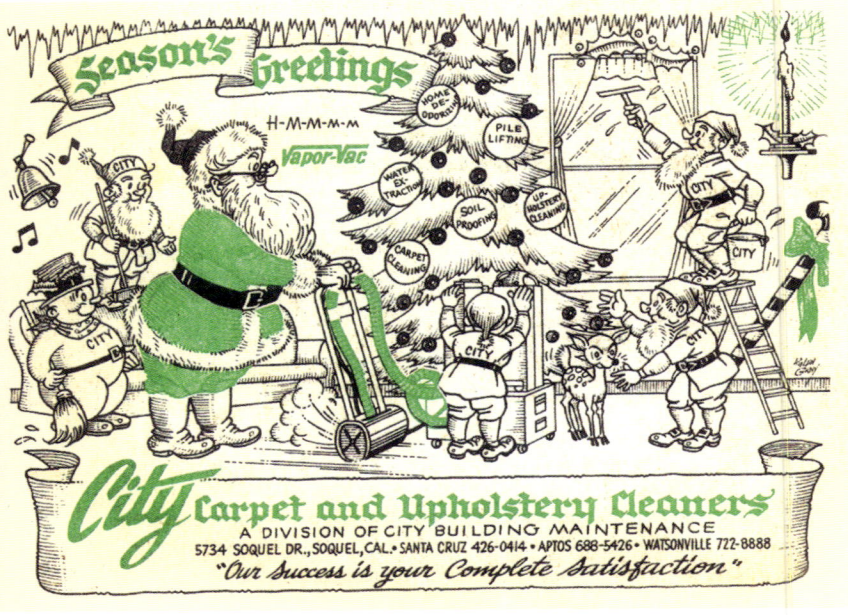

A sample of Ralph Gray's imaginative cartoon ad work showing his hand lettering.

One of Gray's editorial cartoons.

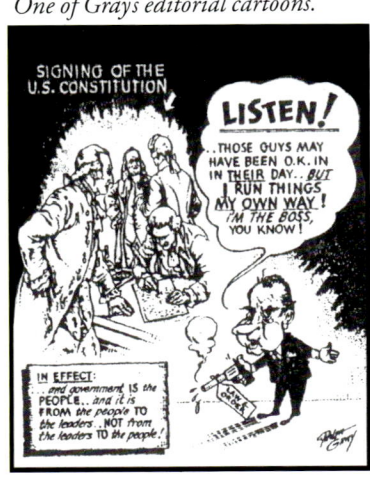

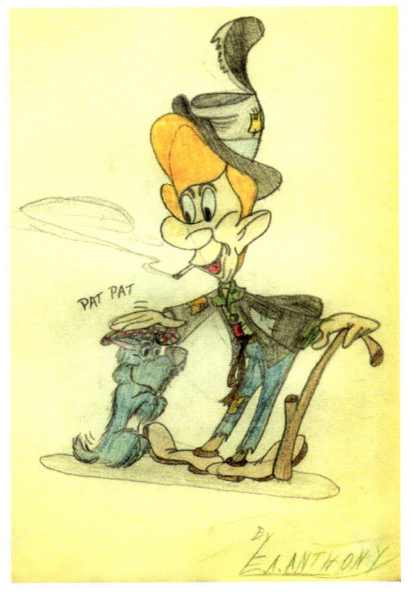
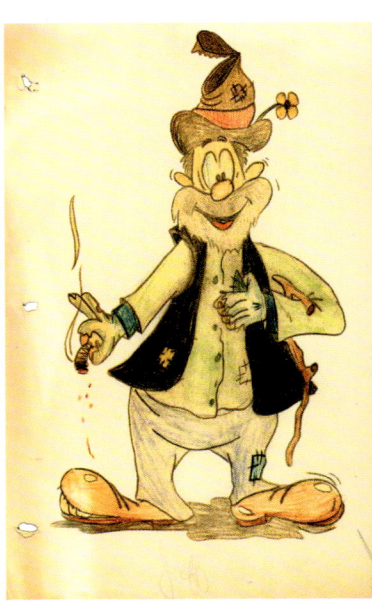

Hobo characters by Earl Anthony (right) and Jim (left).

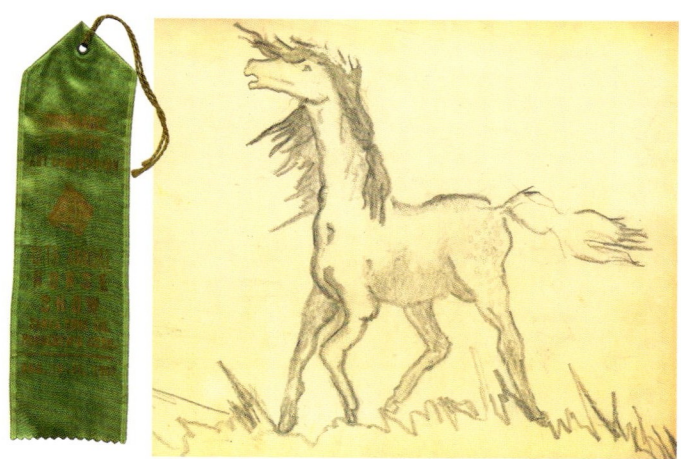

While at Ralph Gray Studios, Phillips progressed from drawings to animation, inspired by another young artist named Earl Anthony. Earl was a little guy with black rim glasses, and he was a Disney fanatic. He even carried a little plastic Jiminy Cricket in his shirt pocket. Ten years old and he already wanted to work for Disney Studios! Earl got Jim into doing art on acetate cells, which was the standard for animation then. You'd do the ink on one side and the color on the other. Earl was the one who told Jim where to buy his first bottle of India ink, pens and holders, which were available at the small neighborhood Opal Cliffs Drug Store. Earl had a table in his room so Jim wanted a table in his room. He drew a hobo character, so Jim drew a hobo character. Earl Anthony was a major influence on Jim, but a few years later he took his own life with a hose, car and garage. In her grief, his mother used the same things to do the same thing. One can only imagine, if he had lived, what creations he would have made from such a fertile mind.

hearings inspired the Comics Code Authority. *Mad* reprinted all the EC *Mad* stories in paperback and Jim bought all four of them, right off the paperback rack. The panels were chopped up and they didn't have color, but he didn't care, he felt that the graphic, black and white style of Wally Wood and Bill Elder were dynamic and didn't need color to carry the images.

Phillips attended Live Oak Elementary School from the second to the seventh grade, and then transferred to Branciforte Junior High for the eighth and ninth grades. Phillips was an edgy student, and attributes a lot of his early drawing success to the boredom and frustration of sitting in class with a pencil and paper in his hand: "Not enough can be said for the value of grade school for an artist," Phillips has said, "not so much for the learning, but for being given paper and pencil in a boring atmosphere." School desks were drawing tables to Jim in those days. In seventh grade, his teacher, Mrs. Elliott, let him work on art projects in lieu of studies. Maybe she thought he was hopeless, or maybe she thought he had talent. One project was drawing a chronicle of Jim's Dudley character in various costumes of history. She must have thought it was an instructive level he could handle. For a few weeks, Phillips was asked to paint earth and oceans on a four-foot globe while everyone else had to study. It was good to be an artist in Mrs. Elliott's class, and being an artist was a good thing to be in Mr. Eggert's Journalism class, too. Phillips says he thought Journalism would be easy.

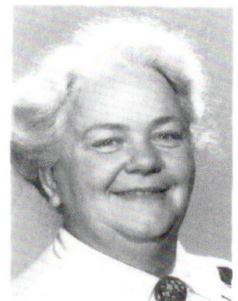

Above: Mrs. Elliott.

Left: Jim's Dudley character, as Elvis. Pen and ink on acetate cell layered over magazine photo.

By the mid-fifties, Jim was hitting teen years and drawing the things that preoccupied teens: cars, cowboys, ships, cars, girls and cars. Around this time, Ann Phillips corrupted her little brother with *Mad Comics* and *Mad Magazine*, and opened up a whole new world of satirical humor to the impressionable Phillips. Ann brought home a few copies of the older, smaller EC *Mad* comic books that were printed around 1952, but were run out of business by the Joseph McCarthy hearings. That's how times were back then: A comic book could get blacklisted! The *Mad Magazines* were funny but *Mad Comics* were edgy, and had a biting satire that was new in American culture. The McCarthy

Horse drawing, won honorable mention from the Horsemen's Assn. 1957

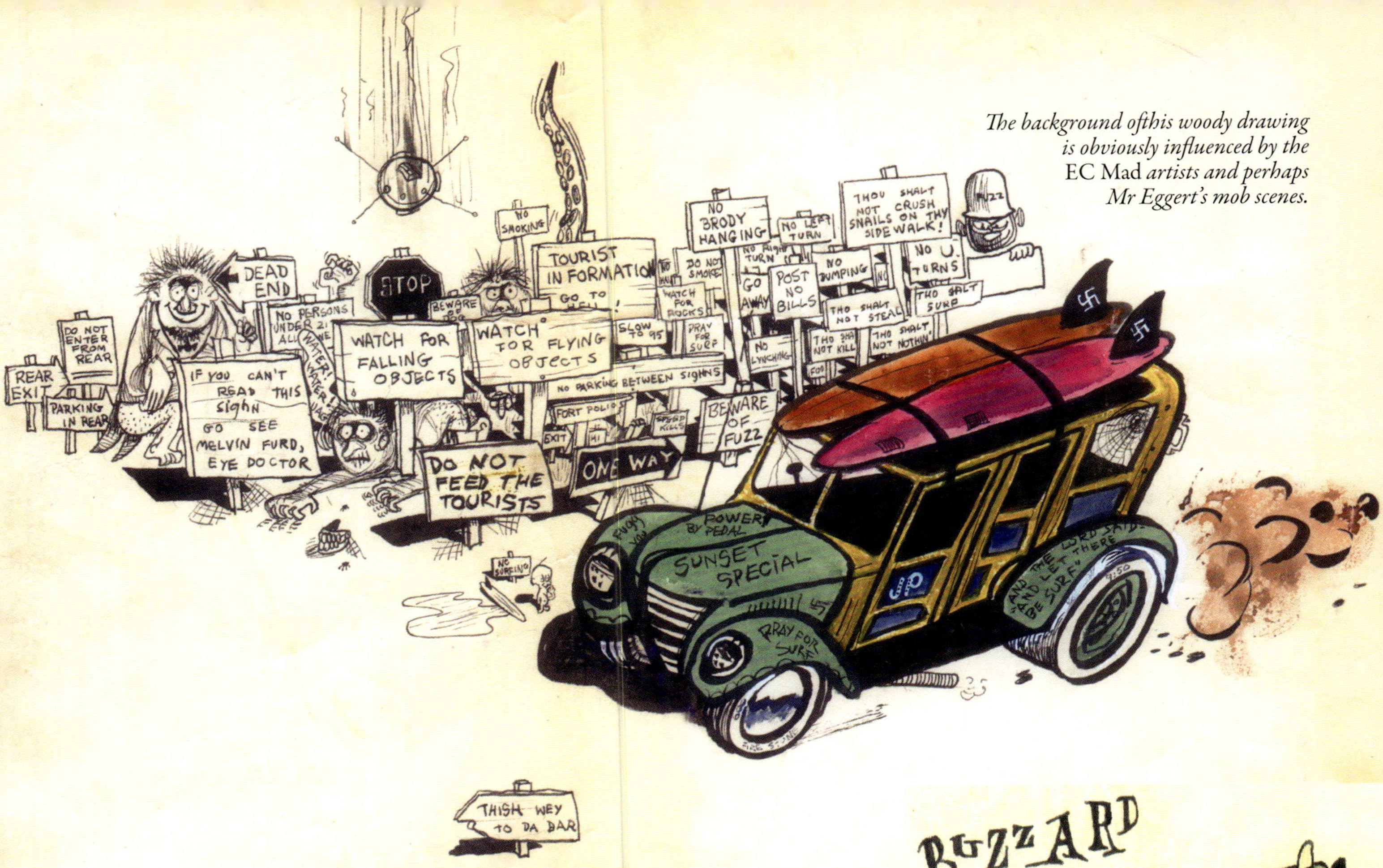

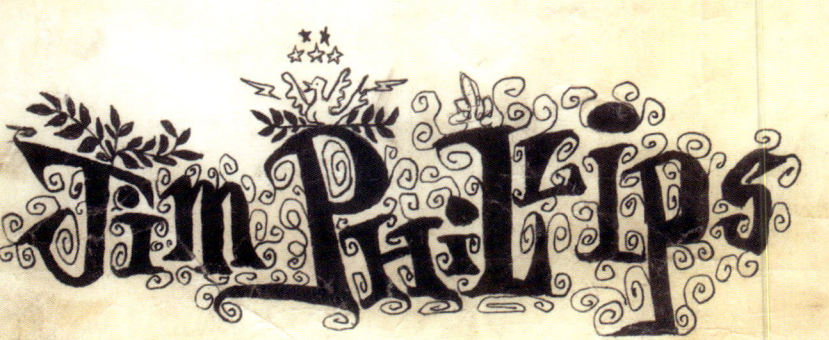

The background of this woody drawing is obviously influenced by the EC Mad artists and perhaps Mr Eggert's mob scenes.

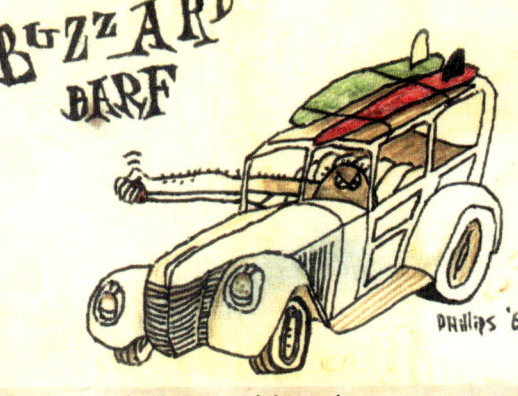

Buzzard Barft t-shirt escaped the rag drawer. The skewed appearrancence is a result of roller tipped fabric ink tubes on jersey which tended to stretch

Jim Phillips

But Journalism was writing; taking a list of facts and; organizing stories from them. Immediately Jim knew he couldn't cut it, but Mr Eggert had his eye on the doodles Phillips was trying to hide. Jim figured he was cooked when the teacher looked down and asked what he was doing. "Can you do mob scenes?" he asked. Jim was surprised and replied, "Like they do in Mad Magazine?" Eggert nodded, and Jim said he could, and pretty soon he was doing cartoons for the Branciforte Bee. Phillips started by making the mob scene Eggert wanted and went on winging it.

One of Mr. Eggert's thrills was for Jim to draw a monthly lampoon of one of the other teachers. One of the first victims was the woodshop teacher, Mr. Joe Merkel, who was a little heavy-set and spent summers working as a park ranger. Mr. Eggert dubbed him Moe Jerkel, and Jim drew him to look like Smokey the Bear lighting a cigarette and tossing the match over his shoulder into a pile of moonshine jugs. What fun! Just like Mad Magazine! And just like Mad Magazine, after another few caricatures, the Branciforte Junior High administration blacklisted the feature. Phillips continued to cartoon and earned A's in journalism from Mr. Eggert. Mr. Eggert was right up there with Mrs. Elliott as an inspiring teacher for Jim.

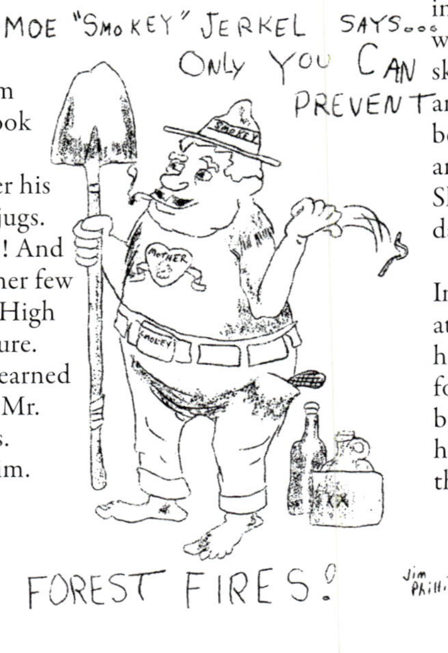

Full page illustration for Branciforte Bee, 1958. Refer to page 207 for Bee cover art.

You can't go too far in Santa Cruz without bumping into the ocean. Jim and his sister had played at the beach as kids. Down at the end of their beach was the Sunny Cove. Kids from Live Oak School would go there, so Jim began hanging out there. The surf breaks between two cliffs which keep the current from running, so it was a good swimming and bodysurfing hole. Jim did what a lot of Santa Cruz kids did, progressing from bodysurfing and inner tubes to skimboarding to surfing. They had a wide area where the water came in about an inch deep, a good skimboarding zone. Jim bought a piece of marine-grade plywood and shaped his own board. It had a square tail and a round bevelled nose. He painted it all black with red hot-rod scallops, and small white pinstripes around the scallops. Skimboarding was "cool," and Jim spent hours and days doing it down at the Sunny Cove.

In junior high school, a classmate of Jim's who lived at Pleasure Point asked him to paint something on his surfboard. Jim painted a monster with a long forked tongue within a circle on the nose of his board. It was then that Jim got serious about getting his own surfboard. Phillips painted a monster, but then surfboards became a monster he had to own.

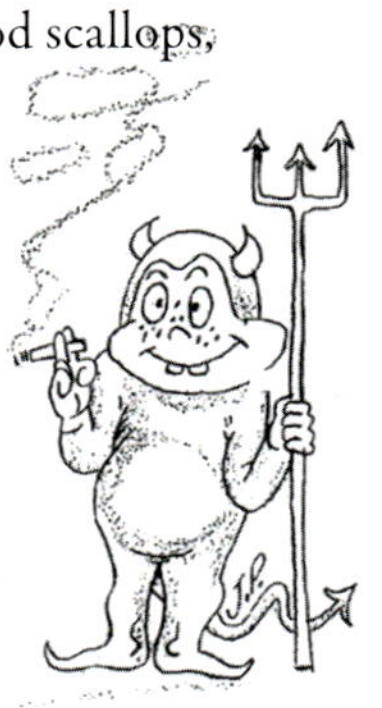

Illustration for Branciforte Bee, 1958.

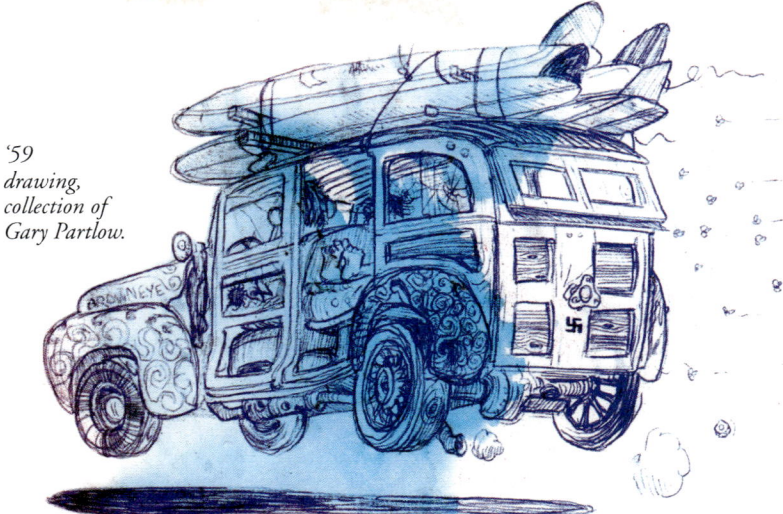

Jim Phillips was a surf-stoked Opie during the late 50s. With money saved from his paper route, he paid $70 to the Rauen brothers on the Westside for a new, nine-foot Mako balsawood "Pig." It had a transparent, red and clear "abstract" of colored resin, blended nose to tail, and a resined mahogany skeg. He began surfing at Cowell's at age 15, when there were few other guys in the water. In the late 50s, surfing was pursued by only a few, on big, clunky boards with no wetsuits or leashes. Santa Cruz had all the advantages of geography and climate and waves that it has now, but without the crowds. The real problem was finding someone to surf with. Surfing was fun and Jim was out in the sun every day.

DAVEY SULTZER: *"We decided we were going to have a surf club when we were prepubescent adolescents. We named it the Gremlin Society. Jimmy drew each t-shirt one by one, freehand. We used to hang out in his bedroom at his parents' house. There were alot of his drawings, great caricatures of people we knew, surfing. I remember sitting on his bed, when he was doing the gremlin t-shirts."*

BIG JOHN EVENSON: *"I remember back then, Jimmy's room being filled with art projects, like chopping and channeling model cars, and making his own body filler out of glue, because you couldn't buy it. He won a model contest downtown. You could hardly walk into his room without going through a maze of drawings and one-of-a-kind t-shirts in progress."*

Phillips' classroom daydream doodles of the time featured and combined his two preoccupations: surfing, hot rods, surf cars, woodies and surf hot rods. Phillips had a pig of a surfboard and he started thinking it would be nice if he had something to cart it around in. From his youth at the cabin in Pescadero, Jim remembered a line of about a dozen discarded Model T's lined up against a fence on the property. He went up to Pescadero hoping to score something to turn into a hot rod. But neighbor Mr. Hyman had died, and the old cars were gone.

BIG JOHN EVENSON: *"During this time Big Daddy Ed Roth was becoming popular. I believe his art had an influence on Jimmy: there were flaming eyeballs, Rat Fink, and monsters, not that Jimmy needed much help. While everyone else was drawing stick men, Jimmy was doing intricate, three-dimensional street scenes."*

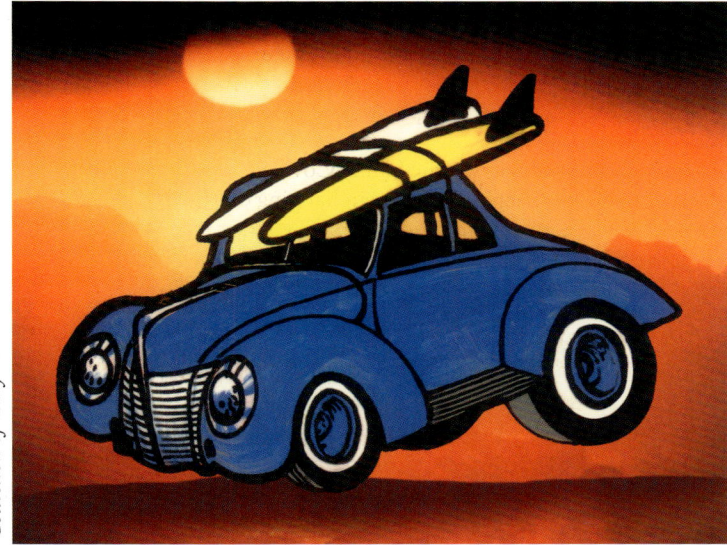

'40 Ford pen & ink drawing on acetate, layered over magazine photo, 1959.

Phillips drew a lot of cars and drew on a lot of them. He pinstriped some cars and was paid to do it, and scalloped an entire '55 Ford. Big Daddy Ed Roth was in his prime at the time, and that inspired Phillips to do a few monsters on dashboards. But Phillips was torn between the shady turf and the sunny surf, and

the ocean tide was a powerful pull. Drawing hot rods and pinstriping the real thing became a little too "ho-dad" for a surfer. Back then, surfers didn't have the money for hot rods. They drove old woodies or station wagons, decorated only with wax and resin drips and rust. This duality inspired Phillips to take a plastic model kit of a Model A, cut the body off and build a woody body onto it using balsawood. He painted the body red like his later woody logo, stained the door panels dark brown and varnished the wood clear. His hybrid model won first prize from a Pacific Avenue hobby shop. But it was the other model Jim submitted as a joke that got attention. It was mostly different-colored plastic stems that model parts come attached to, glued together with other weird spare parts and a pair of legs sticking out from under. It looked bizarre, but that's what got the press photo in an art magazine, not the woody.

BIG JOHN EVENSON: *"We used to skateboard on two-by-fours. We called them bunboards because you could bust your buns. Later, it became known more as the skateboard. I had this t-shirt that Jimmy painted with a purple mouse and the name 'Ambrose,' but one day I decided to push the envelope on the bunboard. I was going down Vine Hill Road, clocked at about 35mph. The road tar had softened and rippled up like a wash board; I went into a high speed wobble and tried to run, but after two giant steps, I did a big endo and broke my wrist. What really bummed me out was getting the t-shirt torn up. My wrist was broken and I had a cast on my arm, a pure white canvas begging for paint, so down the street I go to Jimmy's house. Jimmy paints a masterpiece, on the full length of my forearm, a surfboard with one of his many characters of inimitable style, only he made him butt naked with only a few warts and hairs. It was beautiful, I was proud. I went home to show my mom; she came apart. 'You can't go to church like that!' She made me go back to Jimmy's and he painted a pair of flowered baggies over the offending area."*

Jim continued his quest for a ride. At 15 he was still too young to drive, but he wanted to get the whole thing rolling in anticipation of the day. The first car he bought was a '29 Model A that he found in an orchard in Soquel. Phillips was too young to drive but that was okay because it didn't run. The boys that sold it to him must have chuckled at getting $15 out of Jim, because the rusted coupe body was sitting in a heap to the side. There were no fenders either, just the cowling with windshield sitting up on the frame, and a raggedy seat. There was no hood over the four-banger engine but it still had a grille shell with a radiator on it. The wire-rimmed wheels all had air. Jim left the body in the orchard and had someone tow him home. Jim remembered that it was a great feeling to steer the car during the tow home, but that was the closest thing he ever got to driving it. Phillips tried to turn the art of his winning plastic model into reality, but it was much, much harder. He tried to build the wooden body on the back of his Model A, but reality, he would learn, was more complicated and difficult than art.

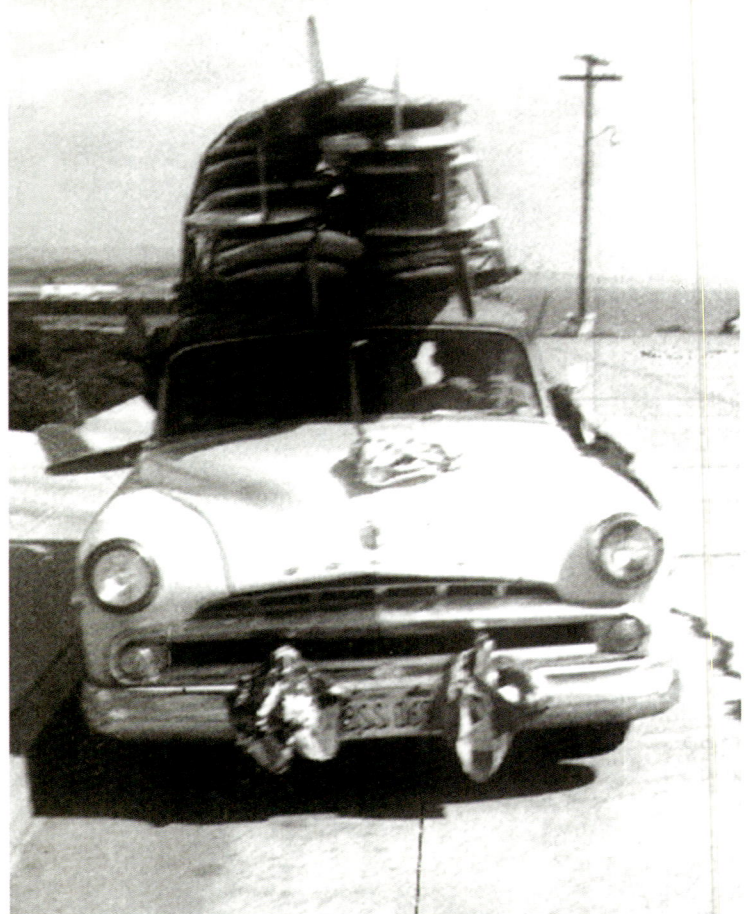

Jim's 1951 Dodge stacked with 19 surfboards and loaded with 19 surfers. Photo by Bob Biddle in front of his house at Cowell's Beach, circa 1962.

Jim began getting rides to school with Big John Evenson, a tall kid who lived around the corner. He got the old '46 Ford woody that was in tall grass in a backyard down the street, the one Jim daydreamed about fixing up, but Evy actually did it, he was quite mechanically adept. Evy and Jim would bring their boards and go surfing after school. It was a lot cooler getting rides to and from school in John's woody instead of riding the bus or hitchhiking, as Jim often did, to avoid riding the school bus. As Davey Sultzer recalls, "We used to cruise around with Big John in his woody, on Friday nights, goin' out and raising hell, sneaking into the drive in, stuff like that."

BIG JOHN EVENSON: *"When I first met Jimmy, he lived about two blocks from me. I was a junior at Santa Cruz High, Jimmy was a sophomore. I had a driver's license and wheels. Not just any wheels, but a '46 Ford woody. Every school morning I picked him up. His mother always gave him fifty cents to eat at the cafeteria. Down on the corner, we could get gas for twenty cents a gallon, and by the end of the week we had enough gas to take a safari to some faraway place like Carmel or Carpenteria."*

Phillips was tutored in the art of restoring old cars by Big John. Jim handed tools to Big John as he revived a 1935 Ford delivery-sedan. Dave Stearns, who bought it from John's painter uncle, hired Jim to paint surfing murals on the panels. Jim painted a large wave on each side, with what he calls goofy-looking guys surfing all over them. Stearns got a new car, and offered Jim the '35 for $35. Jim was afraid to ask his parents if he could buy it, because he didn't have a license, and never actually got the '29 running. But he loved that car! It was perfect for carrying surfboards. Jim bought it on the sly and left it out in the empty field in back of his house where some of Big John's other relics languished without notice. The first thing Jim did was primer over the surf murals. He said he liked them when it was someone else's car, but not when it was his. A couple of times when his mom was at work, he sneaked it out and drove around. The little flathead V8 purred, and it had the old floorshift tranny. He drove it to school one day, still without a license, and talked his way out

of a small accident at lunchtime. He was deathly afraid of getting a ticket, and having his scheme exposed so he started sneaking out at night, under cover of darkness. After everyone was asleep, Jim would push it down the driveway and start it up down the street. He was excited to drive his little car around and was getting bolder. One night he had a friend staying over. They stuffed their beds like *Escape From Alcatraz* and snuck out the window, drove around for hours, and came back to find the bedroom light on and mom fuming. She ordered Jim to sell his beloved car, and made him go to church the next morning, as he had been skipping. He walked sadly down the tracks to Saint Joseph's in Capitola, his last attendance for a long time. He got $15 for the '35, and a broken promise for $45 more. Later, Jim saw it parked on a street with the grille smashed, and after that, stacked on top of other wrecks at Speckman's, the seediest wrecking yard in town, on a rainy day.

As time went by, Phillips got a legitimate driver's license and wanted a legitimate car. His grandparents offered their '51 Dodge sedan for $200, and Phillips said nix, but thanks. He wanted a Ford or a Chevy, and not a four-door granny-cruiser with a visor! But when they offered to give it to him for free, it was an offer he couldn't refuse. The car was only 10 years old but to Jim it was a relic. A geek car. That '51 Dodge put him at the bottom of the gene pool at school, but at the beach it was cool. He soon realized it was cool for surfers to have uncool, decrepit vehicles. This was the era of *Rebel Without a Cause*. Surfers would have car fights sometimes, and sometimes the peace of Pleasure Point would be disturbed late at night as two cars grinded and scraped until there was a fatal ramming. Then the drivers would go back into a house and drink more beer. One day Jim was driving when one of the "old guard" came by in an old, black Packard woody, even the wood panels were painted black. As soon as he recognized Jim he drove over to ram him, which was his way of saying hello. Fortunately the street was wide enough for Jim to get out of his way. Back then, cars that had run their course went off the cliff, from The Hook to Ano Nuevo. There are still rusted hulks under the sand at The Hook from back in the day. One of those is Jim Phillips' '50 Plymouth.

JIM RAUN-BYBERG: *"I remember the first time I came to Pleasure Point in the early 60s. The guys that ran the point told us where we could surf, if we wanted to keep breathing. They said we could go down to Shark's Cove. At that time, Sharks Cove was pretty much Jimmy's territory, and I remember as a kid watching him surf there. He was absolutely an inspiration to all of us young guys, and watching him practice his flying kickouts which were incredibly intimidating. It kept a lot of people away from him, so he could catch waves all by himself, rather than them losing any of their bodyparts."*

This was the late 50s when beach boys were still Hawaiian guys who worked the tourists at Waikiki Beach. Surf music was instrumentals from Dick Dale and the Del Tones and The Ventures. "Surf music didn't have vocals back then, and there was none of that 'two girls for every guy,' stuff," Phillips said. To get surf music, people in Santa Cruz tuned into KRLA, all the way from Pasadena. They didn't play surf music in Santa Cruz. The KRLA reception was weak, but it was listenable, and back then at Jim's age it was coming from a different world. When KRLA announced a *Puff the Magic Dragon* contest, Phillips sent a colored drawing of Puff loaded with surfboards and surfers riding on top. He forgot all about it, until he was on a surf trip to Southern California, listening to KRLA. They announced his name as one of the winners and that his drawing would go on exhibit at the Cinnamon Cinder nightclub in Long Beach. Jim was 17 and for him it was cool to hear his name mentioned every half an hour, and so far from home, the kind of thing that made being an artist attractive.

Artist's recollection of the KRLA, Puff the Magic Dragon entry.

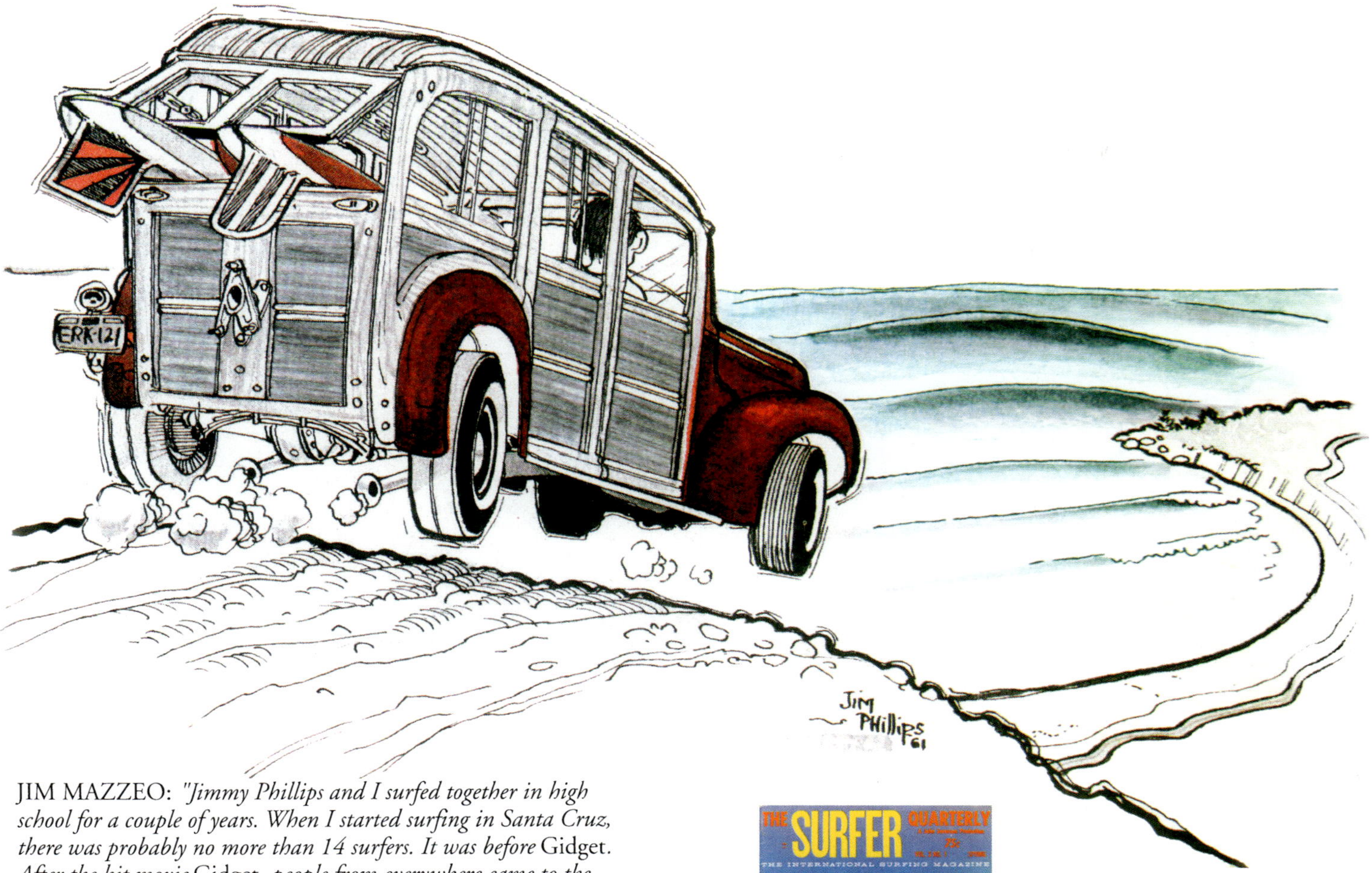

The illustration shows a woody wagon signed "Jim Phillips '61"

JIM MAZZEO: *"Jimmy Phillips and I surfed together in high school for a couple of years. When I started surfing in Santa Cruz, there was probably no more than 14 surfers. It was before* Gidget. *After the hit movie* Gidget, *people from everywhere came to the beach. After that, surfing got popular. Jimmy had been surfing longer than me, and was better than I was. We had a whole history in high school when I would come over and hang out. We would hop in old cars and drive up and down the coast and go surfing. We would take surf trips in my '47 Ford 3/4 ton panel truck, my grandfather's old furniture refinishing truck."*

DENNIS CONQUEST: *"Santa Cruz has a knack for producing artists. Through the years some really great artists have developed there; Steve Desmond, Al Palm, and my old friend Jimmy Phillips. Jimmy is a few years younger than I am, but he always made an impact on all of us. I admired his artist's abilities and his personality right from when I first met him. When he was about 16 years old he drew a series of surfing portraits of a bunch of us. Many of us who got their picture done lived at a house called the Topaz house: Gene Williams, Jeff Thomsen, Doug Haut, and myself. He's a bit of a legend amongst his friends. He's become a substantial surf artist, one of the best. I feel lucky to be one of those that Jimmy did a drawing of. Too bad Jimmy never did one of himself hanging ten at Shark's Cove."*

Phillips attended Santa Cruz High from sophomore to senior. He was introduced to different mediums - paint, airbrush, scratchboard - in Ross Jones' art class. They got into everything in Mr. Jones' class, but Jim mostly used pen and ink with watercolors. He remembers Jones painting in the back of the room while the students worked, rambling about "man's inhumanity to man." This was 1960 and Mr. Jones was an inspiration and another good influence on Jim's art.

SURFER Magazine was started as an art project by a young southern Californian named John Severson in 1959. The first issue was printed to accompany one of Severson's 16 mm surf films, and it all took off from there. By 1961, *SURFER* was a quarterly that featured art and cartoons from Severson, Rick Griffin and photographers from up and down the California coast.

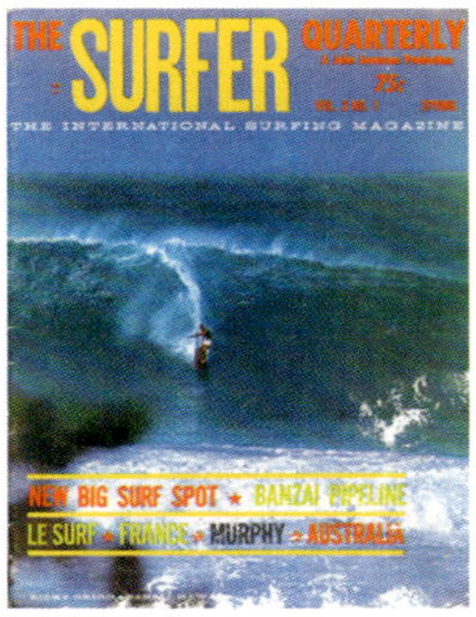

Phillips' Woody featured as honorable mention winner in Surfer Quarterly Magazine Volume 3 Number 1, Spring, 1962.

When the magazine promoted a "surf car cartoon contest," 17 year old Phillips thought he had something to offer. He submitted an energized cartoon of a blatty, '39 Ford Wagon literally flying down a hill toward energized swells breaking off an empty point. He signed the sketch "Phillips '61" and sent it in. Severson gave the woody drawing an Honorable Mention and prominent half-page placement in the bible of the sport. Jim didn't think much of his chances at this kind of thing, but then there it was! Phillips was a mini-celebrity in Santa Cruz. Being in *SURFER* reinforced the things he liked about being an artist.

JOHN SEVERSON: *"I remember it was the whole SURFER staff who did the picking. The winners were selected based on ideas as well as cartoon skill. Phillips' was picked because it was a well-drawn woody and had a reckless bounce to it as it cleared the hill. It was fun, had a nice detail to it, and added the element of surf."*

Getting into *SURFER Magazine* in any way is always a big deal, and that woody marked the beginning of a long career as an artist, but also the end of a long, blissful, all-American 50s childhood. Phillips, the surf-stoked Opie, was about to turn 18 and leave school in 1962. A dangerous age for a dangerous age.

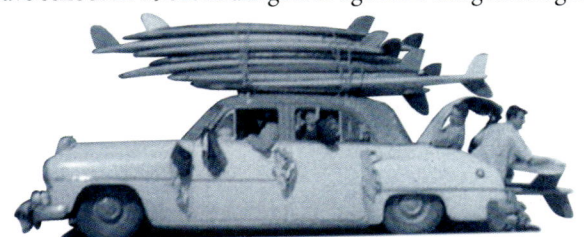

Side view of Jim's '51 Dodge with 19 boards and 19 surfers, 1962.

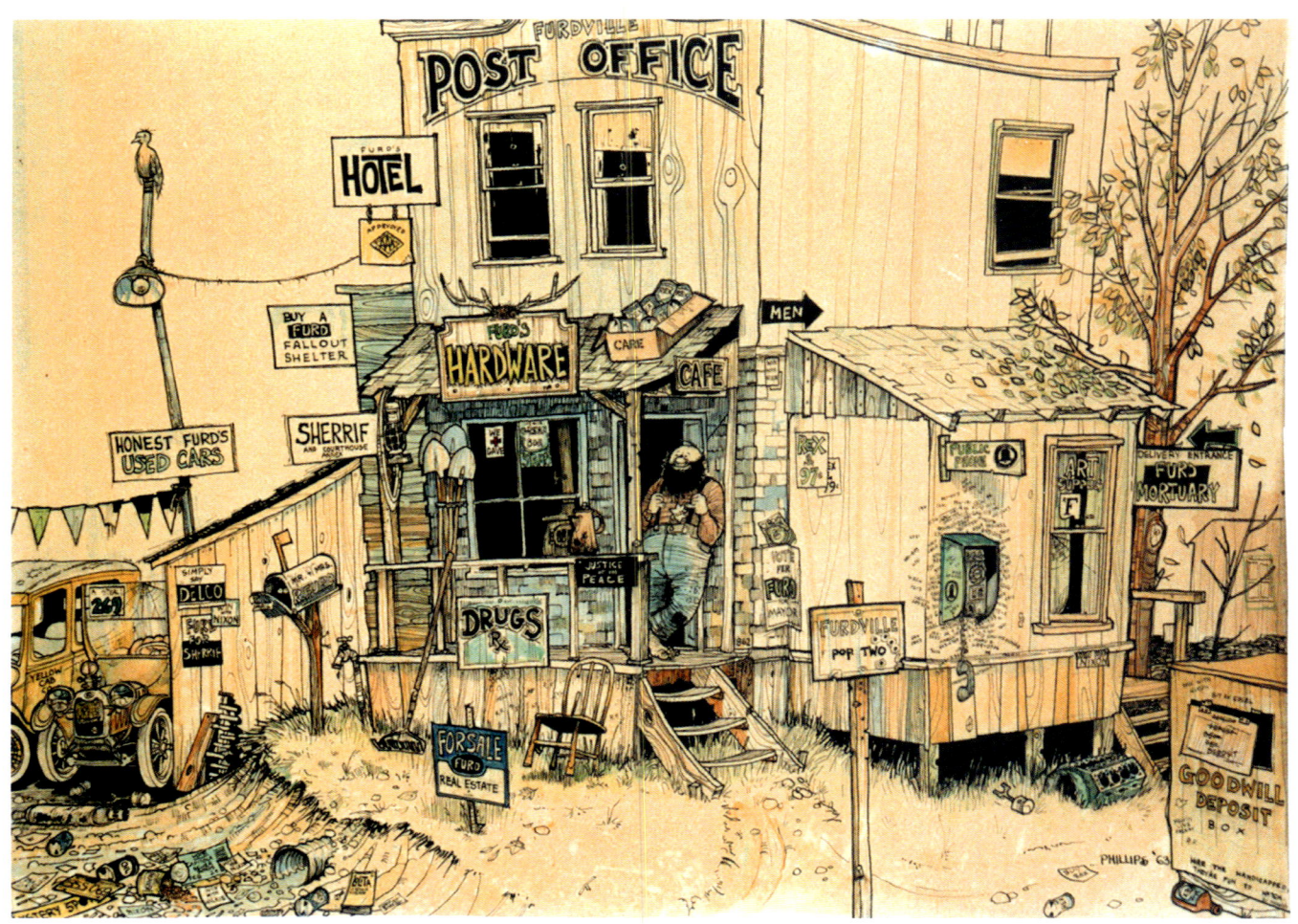

Furdville, pen & ink, 16"x20", 1963. Created in Mr. Jones' art class at Santa Cruz High.
Collection of Steve Fithian, Spain.

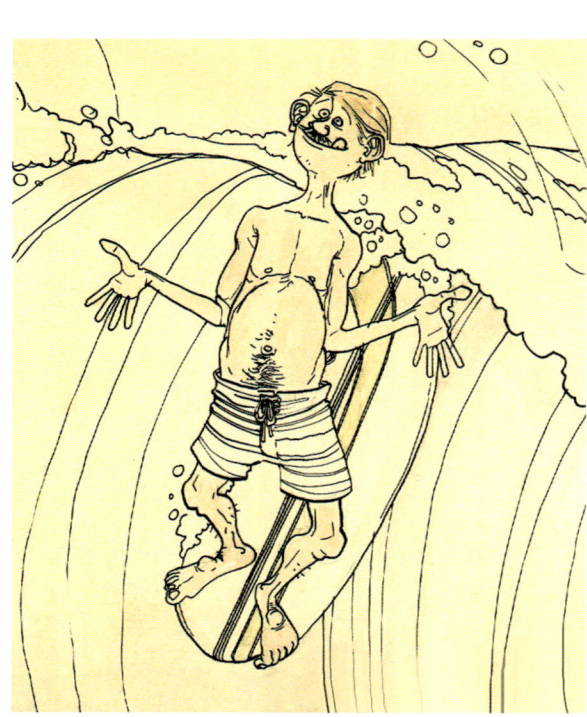

Dennis "Murphy" Conquest caricature, circa 1961.
Collection of Dennis Conquest, New Zealand.

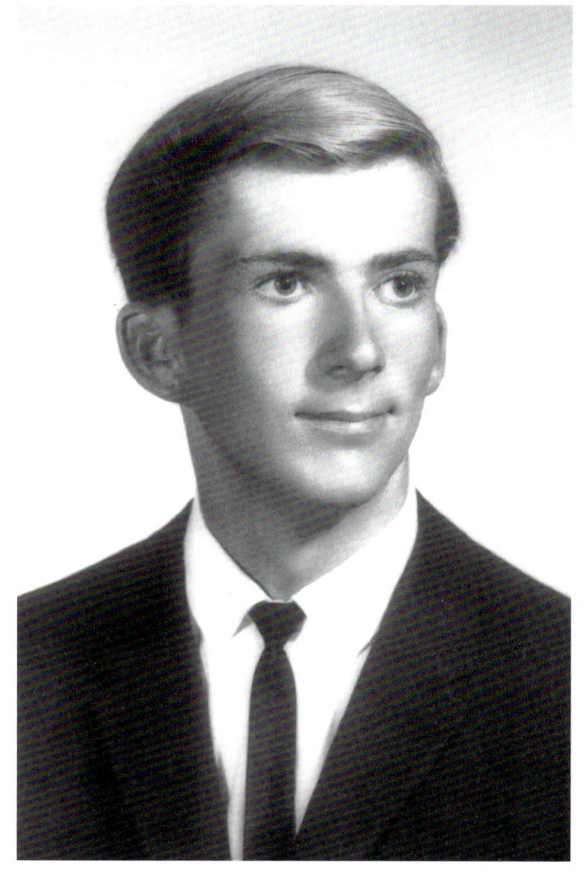

Jim's senior photo, 1963, Soquel High School.

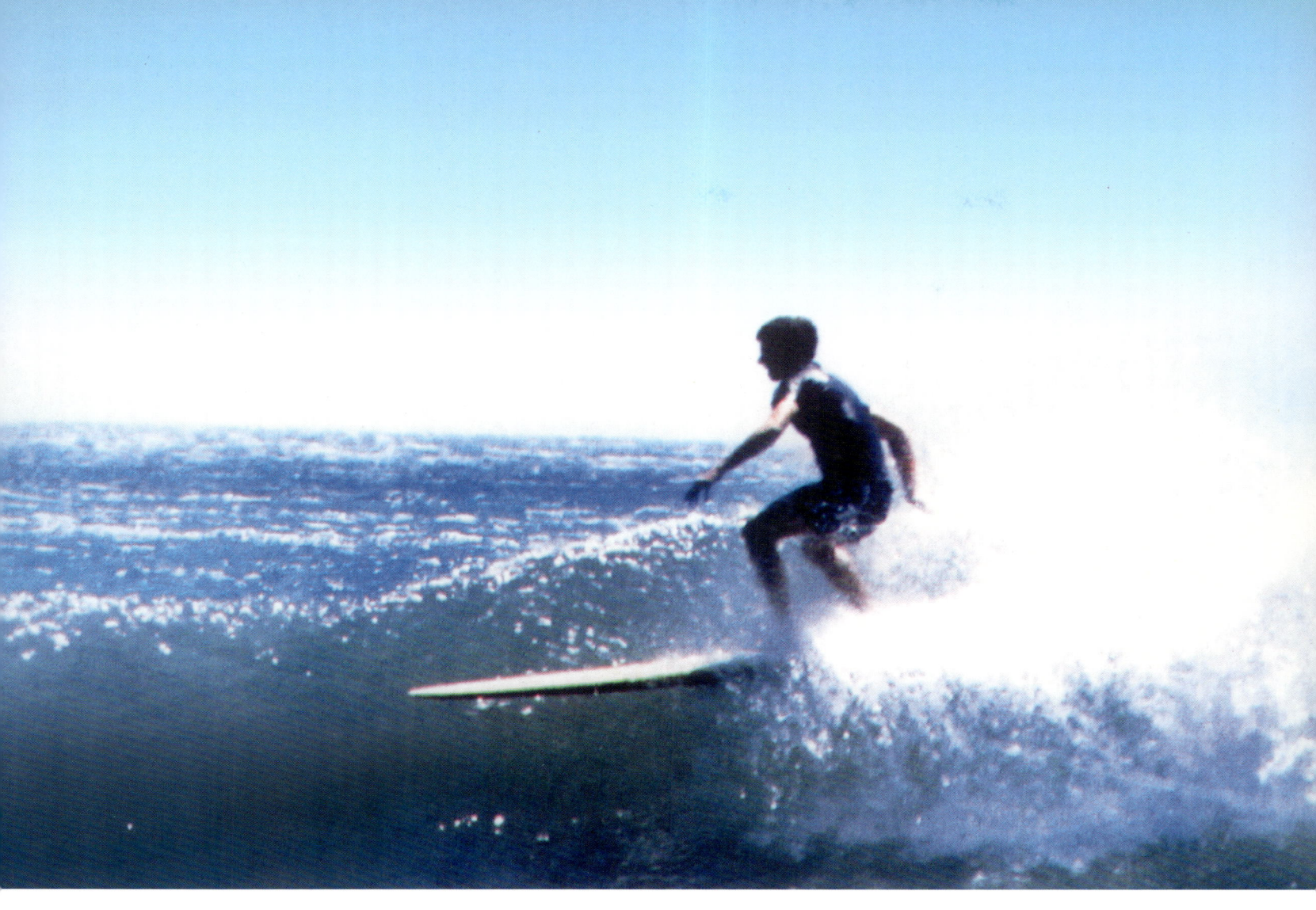

CHAPTER 2

ON THE ROAD: 1961 to 1969
Childhood to Manhood, Santa Cruz to Mexico to Florida, Kennedy to Nixon.

Every child is an artist.
The problem is how to maintain the art when you become an adult.
-Pablo Picasso

The Sixties? Jim Phillips was there, man, surfing and surviving. From the surf-stoked Opie of the 50s, the 60s turned Phillips into a Kerouac/Guthrie/Gump hybrid, a mostly-broke, usually-paranoid, high-school dropout psychedelic hippie. Jimmy was a little bit Woody Guthrie, riding the rails for adventure, and then he was a little bit Arlo Guthrie, getting anything he wanted and doing what he wanted. Phillips was 18 in 1962, a dangerous age for a very dangerous age. There were dangers and distractions overseas, but also down the street, down south, south of the border and across the United States.

Jim Phillips went through the 60s like Forrest Gump, sometimes on the fringe of the action, sometimes caught in the crossfire. Phillips went through the 60s like Jack Kerouac. He was *On the Road*, burning to know what was out there beyond the horizon, up the Salinas Valley, over the hills and far away. Phillips didn't really know where he was going, but he got there the best he could, hopping freight cars to southern California, hitchhiking and driving beaters deep into Mexico, crisscrossing the United States with one eye out for work and the other in the rearview mirror. The Sixties? Phillips went through like a motorcyclist riding through a tunnel of flame. Somehow he survived and in the process began to find himself as an artist.

Jimmy Phillips at the Wild Hook, Santa Cruz, circa 1961. Photo by Bob Richardson.

Phillips' high school career ended as it began: with a fracture. Where he was dragged through eight different schools to begin his education, it took Phillips two high schools and a college try to finish it. And he never did get that diploma. Phillips failed to graduate from high school in 1962, because of, in his words: "Perfect six-foot Shark's Cove with no one out!" Jim was surfing while the world went by, along with his class of '62 appointment to graduate. In those days, before the small craft harbor was built in Santa Cruz, the road to school went right past the River-mouth, and of course, Jim and his buddies always had boards in the trunk.

DAVEY SULTZER: *"Jimmy had a car called 'the Delightful Dodge.' When we were on our way to school at Santa Cruz High, we'd have to go by the Rivermouth, and if there were waves, I mean real waves, there was no question of going to school. I don't know how many times that happened, countless times. I don't remember anyone else being out at eight in the morning either, it was absolutely perfect! Surfing was totally different than it is now. The weekends weren't even crowded. I remember summer days with Jim and I and a few others, on hot summer days, surfing perfect waves at Shark's and the Hook....just lying on the beach and surfing!"*

What else could a poor boy do? Imagine Santa Cruz in the early 60s, before the Beach Boys and Frankie and Annette and everybody had an ocean, across the USA. Surfing was still a shadow pursuit in the early 60s for those who wouldn't realize until much later how good they had it. Imagine Santa Cruz with all of the advantages of location and geography and swell but few of the population density problems of the 21st Century. Crowds? Traffic? Parking lots? None of it. "You could have had a picnic on East Cliff Drive in the middle of the day and not been interrupted by a single car," is how Peter Van Dyke described Santa Cruz from the 50s into the 60s.

Phillips made another attempt to graduate in 1963. He attended Soquel High to catch up, but his daily watery habit had devoured his will. His counselor pleaded with him, "Jim! Just attend every day for the last two weeks and we'll give you a diploma!" The next day had unbelievable surf; Shark's Cove, six foot, no one out. Jim says his head spins when he looks back at his failing twice, but at the time, he says he felt helpless, as if locked in the grip of a drug.

Phillips' art ability got him hired as a surfboard glasser at O'Neill's Surf Shop in 1962, and then his surfing habit got him fired. O'Neill surfboard shaper George Olson hired Phillips because he thought an artist would have the "good hands" necessary to create a solid finish on a surfboard. Glassing was okay but Jim envied the glossers, because they were able to use color and create designs. Jim's job at O'Neills' was also sacrificed to the surf. He had been cutting work for some time when Jack O'Neill came to him, and said, "Jimmy, you're a month late for work. If you want the job then be here tomorrow!" The next day Shark's Cove had perfect six-foot waves with no one out. George eventually opened his own shop, Olson Surfboards, with partner Rich Novak, and hired Phillips as his glasser.

And then there was art. The Honorable Mention in the Surf Car Contest had given Phillips some credibility as an artist, but it didn't stretch too far. Being a published cartoonist was a stoke for him, but it also established his standing as an artist. He submitted new cartoons to some new surf magazines, thinking Rick Griffin had *SURFER* covered. Walt Phillips' *Surfing Illustrated* featured some Phillips cartoons, as did *Surfing International*. Jim Phillips met Walt Phillips while hanging out at Gene Van Dyke's 38th Ave. beach house. Gene's brothers, Peter and Fred, were big-wave pioneers, guys who had been the first to surf Steamer Lane through the 50s on crummy boards with no wetsuits or leashes, then moved on to pioneer the giant surf of the North Shore of Oahu in the 60s. Fred was featured frequently in Walt Phillips' *Surfing Illustrated Magazine*. Jim was sitting on Gene's steps, in the sun, watching the surf with Walt, when he told Jim he liked his cartoons. Walt asked Jim if he could come up with a feature cartoon story, about two or three pages, like Griffin was doing with *Murphy*. Jim was elated to get the assignment, but in those days, surfing ruled his life. That means surfing, not necessarily surf cartooning. When Jim wasn't glassing surfboards, he spent his free time at the beach, relatively a million miles away from a drawing table. Then there were parties almost every night. Soon, in the glare of life, it became evident to him what had happened with his art - nothing. The fact is, Jim regrets not making more of Walt's offer. Later in life, the experience would have been an asset, as *Murphy* was for Griffin.

No scholar, Phillips was at least civic-minded. In 1962, Jimmy and friends founded the Pleasure Point Surfing Association, a loose affiliation of surfers imitating what was going on beyond Point Conception. The purpose of the PPSA was competition, to compete with all of the surf clubs down south, but they also took pride in Pleasure Point. The PPSA showed their pride by planting the first ancestral garbage cans along the point, and Phillips and his surf buddies formed a sort of vigilante posse to make sure any and all visitors showed respect by land and sea. One of the founding members, Davey Sultzer offers this assessment, "For its time, PPSA was a really cool organization, we did some slick stuff. We did the Surf Fair, the Miss California Parade, and there

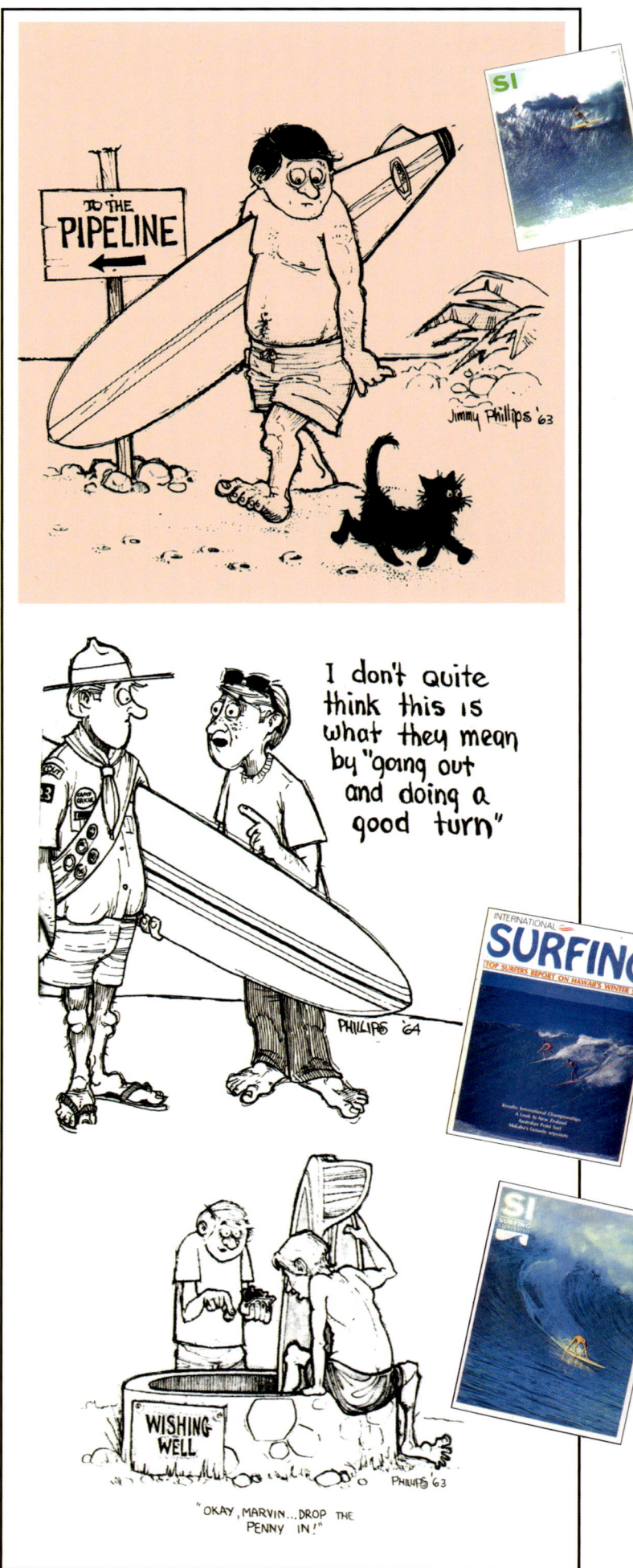

Above: Cartoons published in surfing magazines.
Top: Surfing Illustrated, *Vol 2, #2, April/May, 1964.*
Center: International Surfing, *Vol 1, #3, Spril, 1965.*
Bottom: Surfing Illustrated, *Vol 1, #3, Summer 1963.*

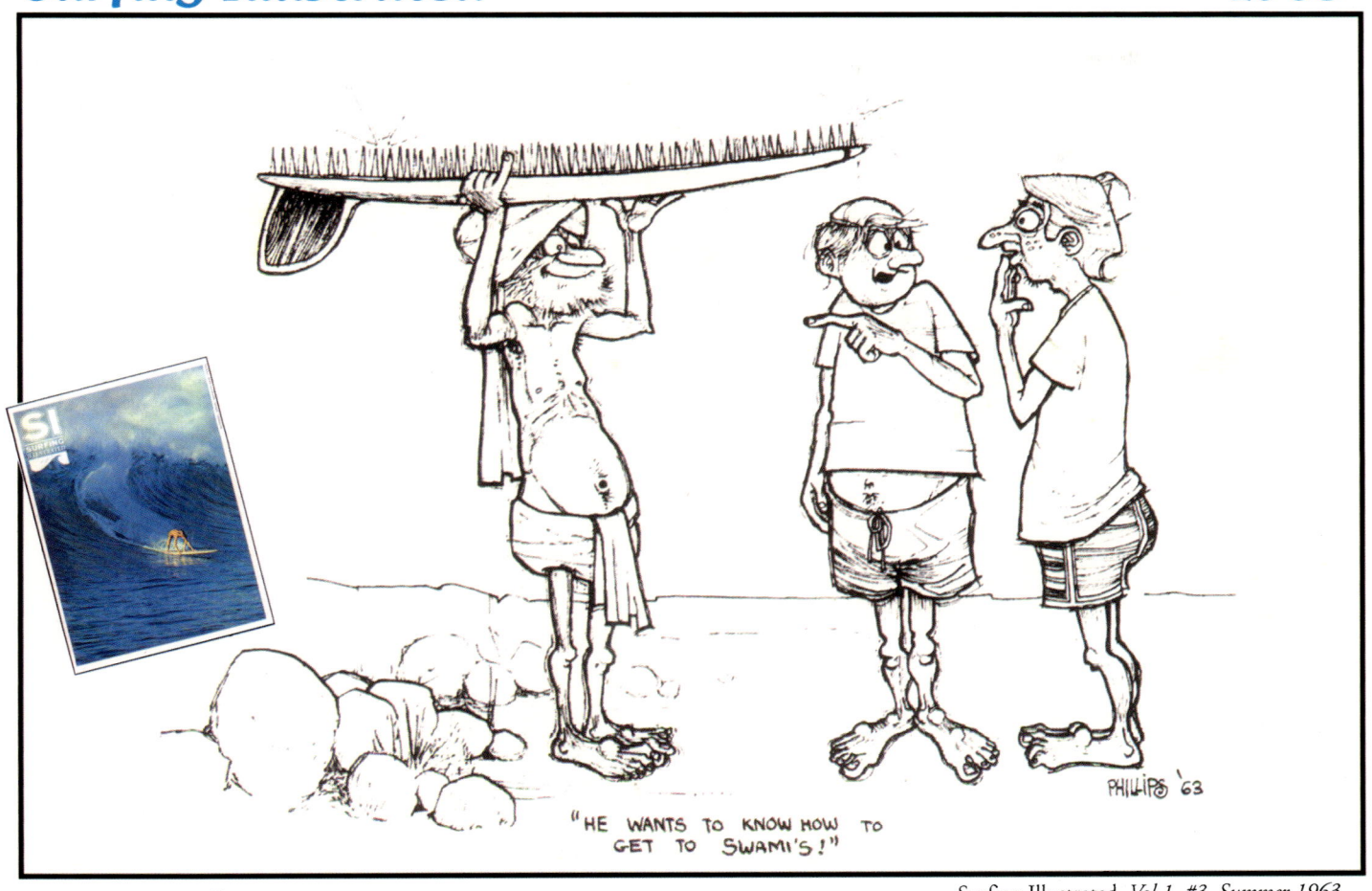

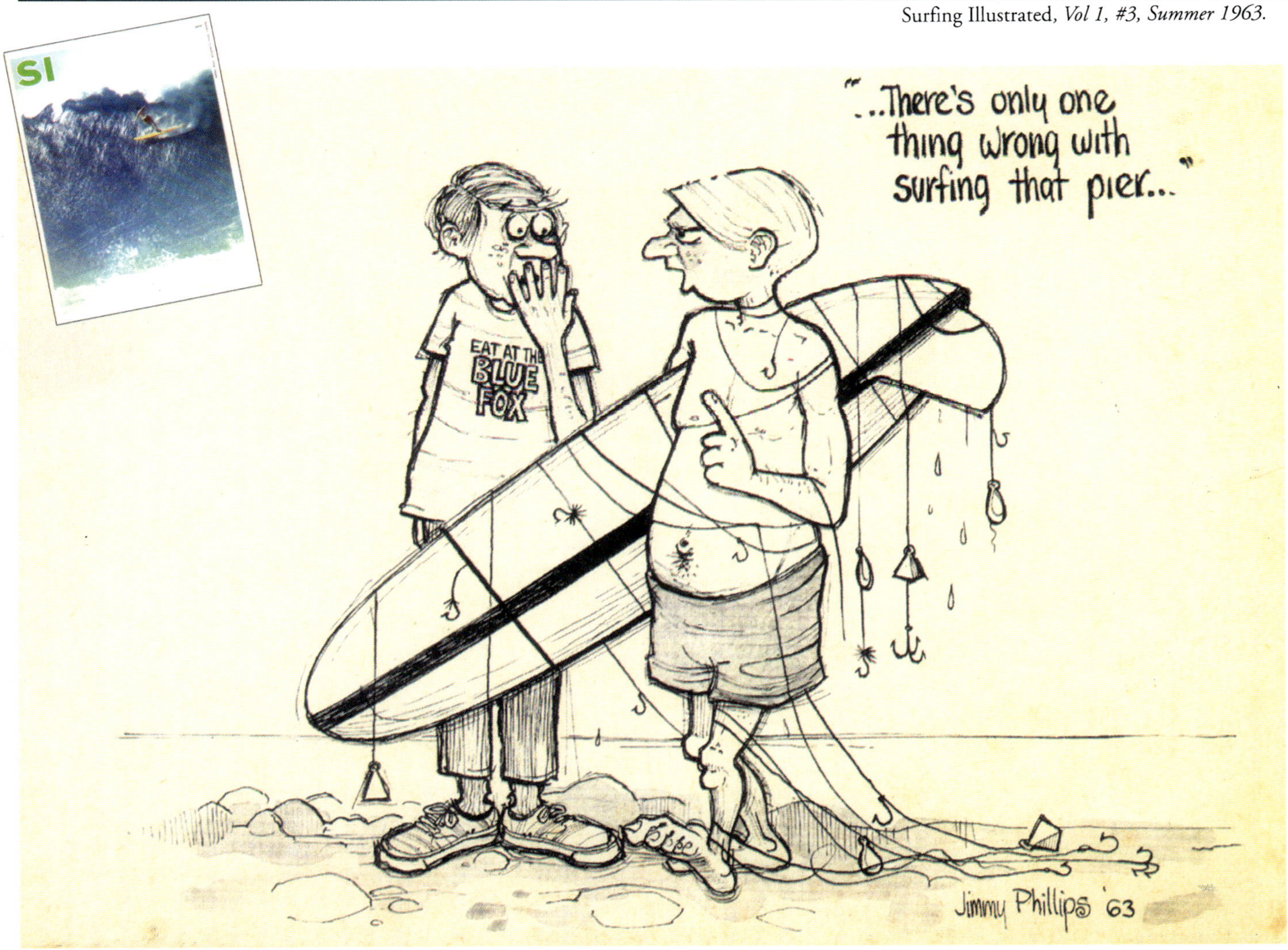

Surfing Illustrated, *Vol 1, #3, Summer 1963.*

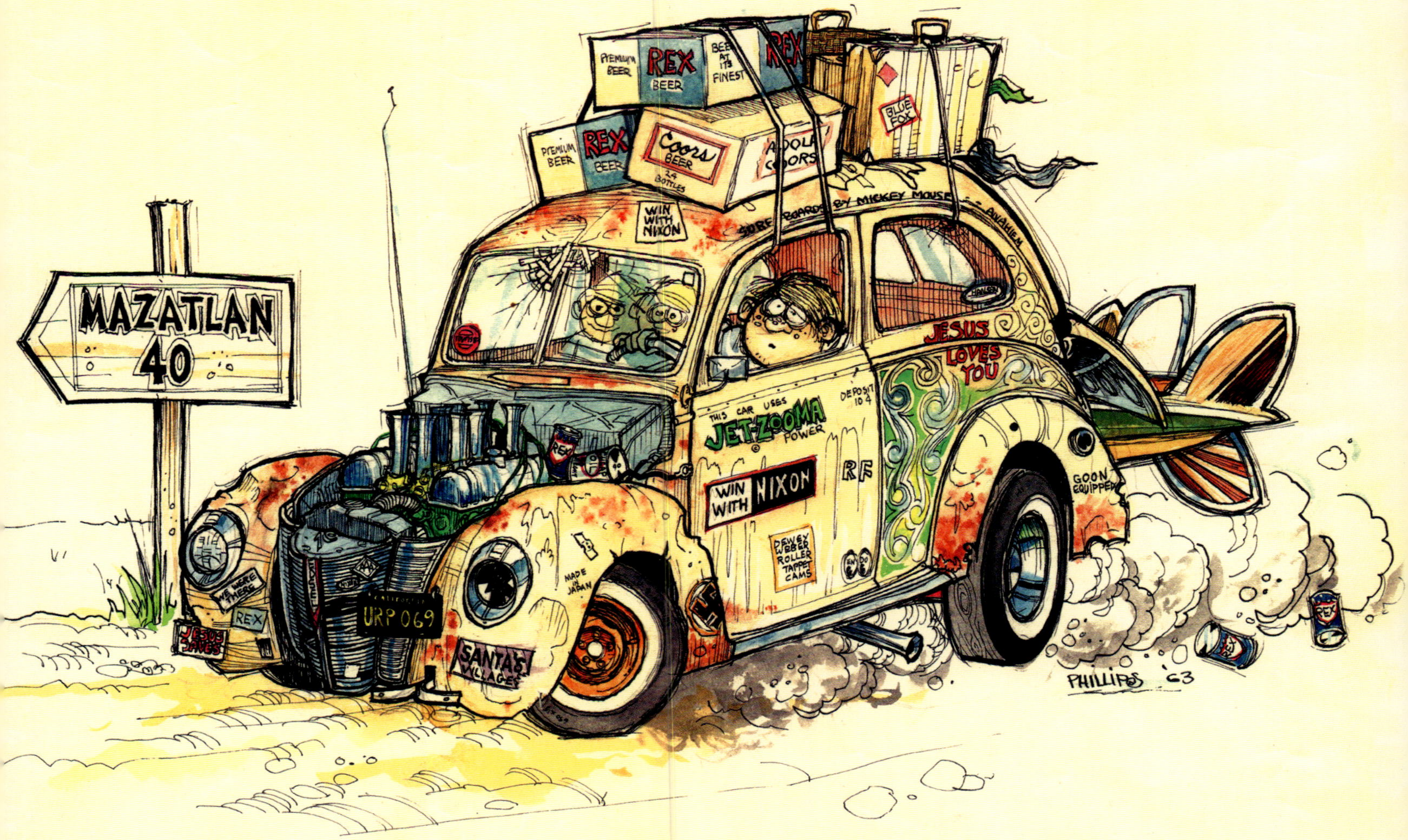

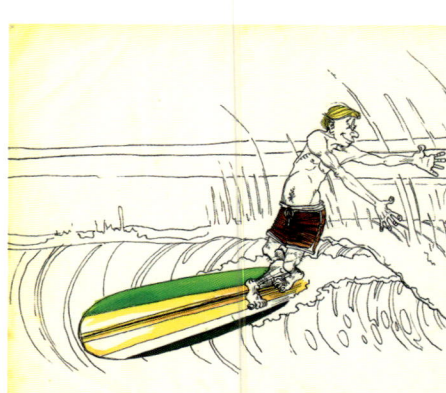

Ron Parker collection

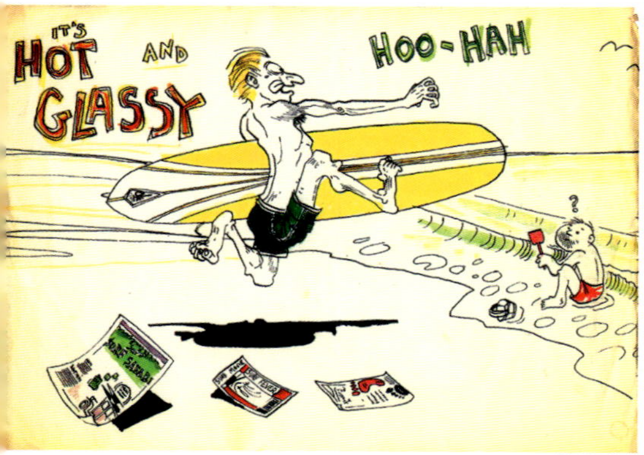

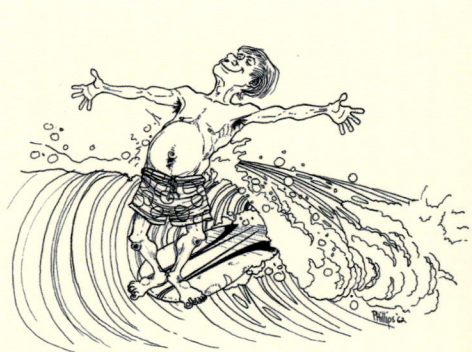

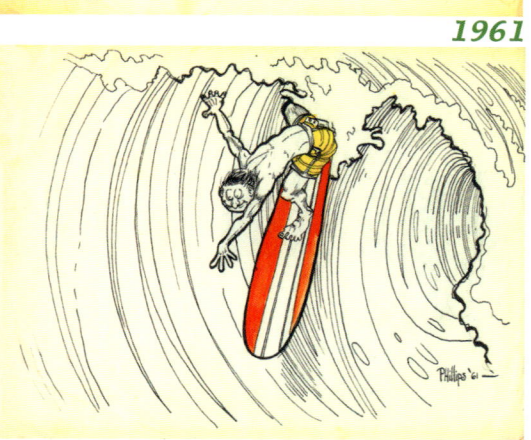

1961

1961

1962

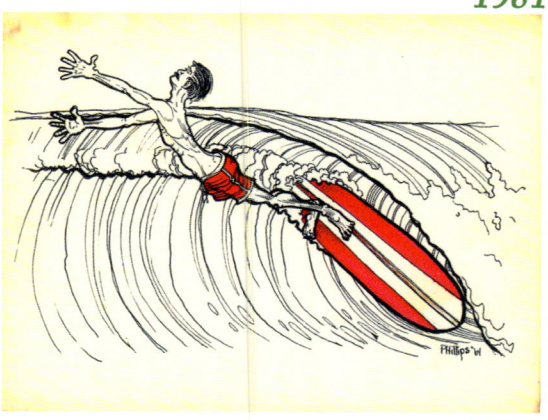

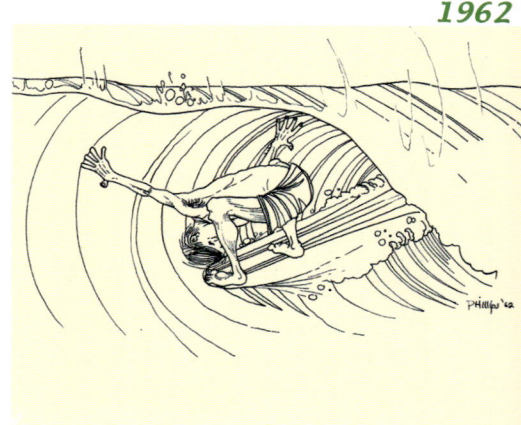

1961

1961

1962

24

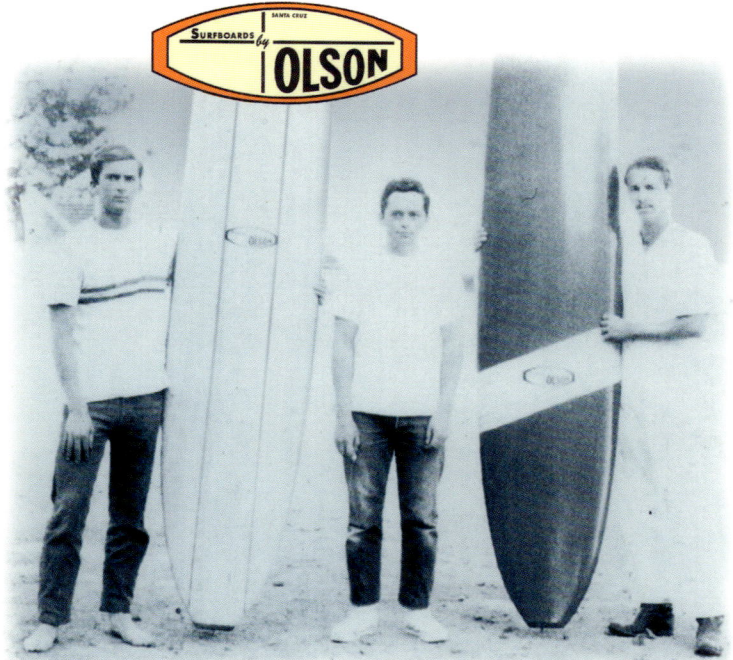

Olson Surfboards shop crew, 1964.
Jimmy Phillips, George Olson, Gary Benson.

were a lot of cool people in that club. It rocked!" At Steamer Lane on November 29, 1964 the surf club won first place at the First Annual Northern California Surfing Club Invitational against such clubs as Pedro Point, Hope Ranch, West Wind, North Side, South Peninsula and East Cliff. This was the early 60s and it was sometimes hip to be square. In the Summer of 1965, the PPSA entered a float in the Miss California parade on Beach Street in Santa Cruz. Led by Phillips as Art Director, they built a giant, crepe-paper trash can on Tom Kienholz's VW bug which proclaimed, "Keep Your Beach Clean." The PPSA float won first place in the Club Division.

Another local institution was the Pleasure Point Night Fighters, a bene-vigilante group with roots in the 1920s. The locals then formed because the Santa Cruz Fire Department refused to go out to Pleasure Point at night. A group of locals became the PPNF to fight fires or whatever other fights presented themselves. It was during that time that heroic stories and legends were established. Later, during the late 50s "Pleasure Point Night Fighters!" was a rallying cry, like a rebel yell, used by a very loose affiliation of rascals and rowdies, who Phillips looked up to. Always quick to apply his talent where it was appreciated, Phillips got to work to give the PPNF what modern marketing dingalings call "identity." As a joke in 1964, Phillips designed

some PPNF calling cards which listed satellite offices in Tijuana and Bitahoche, Arizona. They didn't have a use for the cards really, but a guy who wasn't a member found a dastardly application. Anytime he stole money from a valley's car - he called it "Seeing Uncle Fred" - he would leave a PPNF calling card where the money had been.

Jan and Dean wrote *Surf City* in 1963. Some say they wrote the song about Huntington Beach, but it could just as easily have been about Santa Cruz. Two girls for every guy was a bit of a stretch, but they really were either surfin' or partyin'. Phillips spent a lot of time hanging out at the "Harbor House" on 5th Avenue, during a time when the Yacht Harbor was under construction. The Army Corps of Engineers didn't know it, but they were creating one of the world's best man-made waves. Jim and Tom Keinholz surfed the harbormouth as the sandbar started to build. Jim remembers the cranes carrying huge, four-ton jack pods over their heads as they surfed. Phillips also remembers the Harbor House as, "a raging party house." It was rented by some PPSA members: Tom Keinholz, Rick Metzger and Dave Puissegur. During the summer, there was a party almost every night. Tony Hill's band would set up and play. More than once the police would sweep through and throw everyone they could catch into the paddy wagon.

TONY HILL: *"We would bring our little rock and roll band down from playing San Francisco. That was my first encounter with wild parties in Santa Cruz, and then for the next year or two we were having parties at the Harbor House a couple times a month. We didn't get paid, we did it for chicks and beer. Police would show up at four in the morning. People would be sitting on the roof throwing beer bottles on the roofs of the cop cars. The police usually knew everyone and called people by name. It seemed rowdier then, more rowdy with the human touch, and without the violent touch."*

When they weren't rocking with Tony's band, sometimes Phillips and his friends would drive down south, other times they would jump freights and cast their fate to Southern Pacific. They usually got the bright idea at a party. Someone would say "Let's go south!" They drove over to the rail yard in San Jose and jumped on a train. Open freight cars were good, but the best were auto-paks, which carried new cars. If you got the right car, you had the keys and a heater and a radio and a plush ride way up high, with the best view in the world. Some of the trains went along the coast, right along Point Conception and the Hollister Ranch. Some trains would go inland and they would oversleep and end up in Glendale. It was beautiful and dangerous and stupid and great and a lot of things. But that was the 60s and that was being 18.

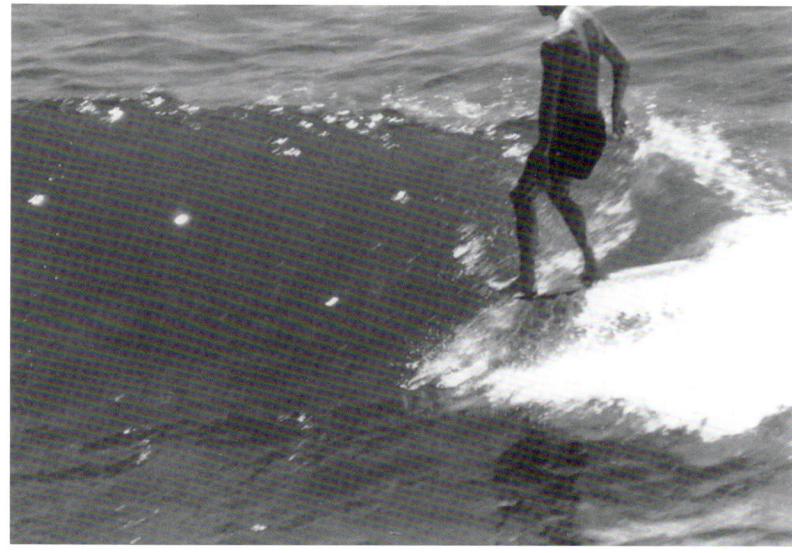

Jim Phillips loses his head at the Hook, 1963. Photo by Bob Richardson.

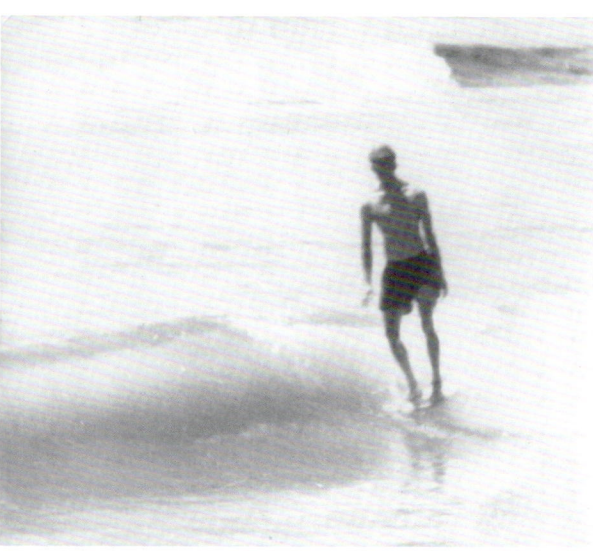

Hanging ten at 38th Avenue, summer '62. Photo by "Satch" Basinger.

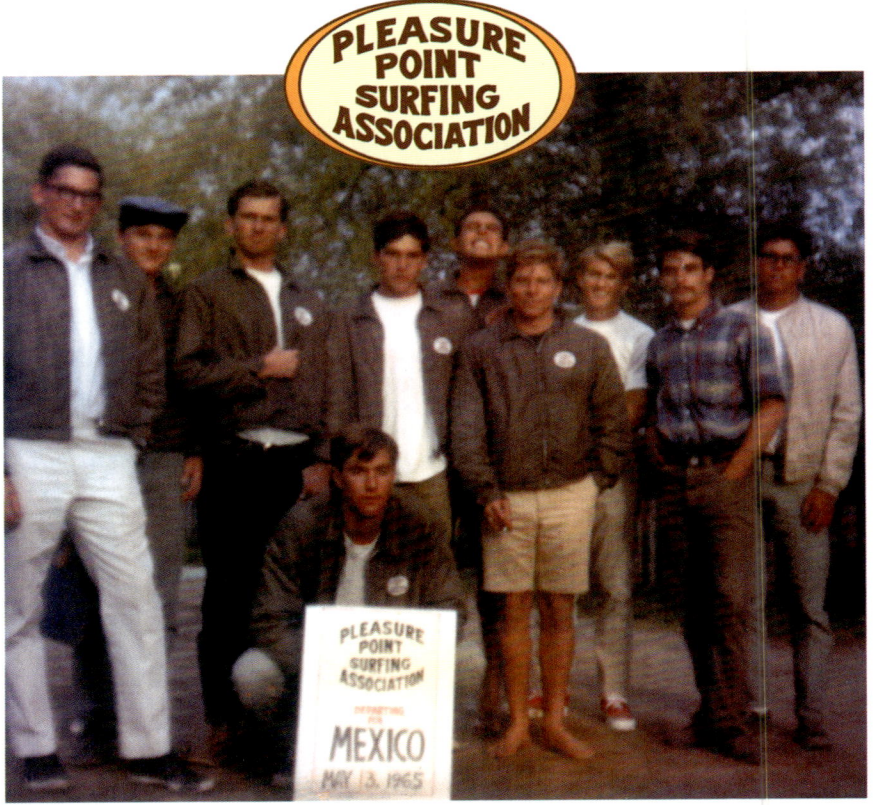

PPSA members pose before trip to Mexico, May 1965.
Gene Hall, Little Joe Harris, Jim Phillips, Gary Venturini (sitting)
Tony Mikus, Davey Sultzer, Leo Gurno, Tom Kienholz, Rick Metzger,
Keith Monroe (other members not present).

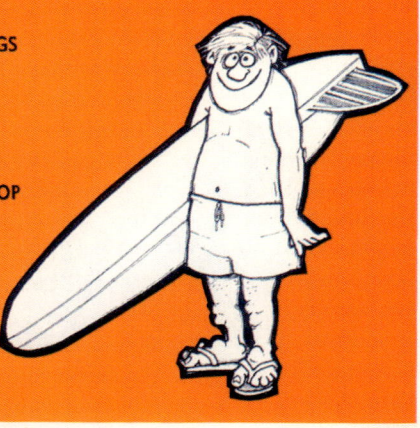

FIRST ANNUAL NORTHERN CALIFORNIA
SURF FAIR

- PRIZE DRAWINGS EVERY HOUR
- DANCING
- MOVIES
- SURFBOARD SHOP DISPLAYS
- SURF CLUB DISPLAYS
- PLUS MANY OTHERS

Presented by the

PLEASURE POINT SURFING ASSOCIATION

SANTA CRUZ CIVIC AUDITORIUM

Donation $1.50 ENABLING PATRONS TO LEAVE AND RETURN AT WILL

APRIL 15, 1965 • 10 A.M. – 12 MIDNITE
DURING EASTER VACATION

Surf Fair poster by Phillips, 1965. Sentinel Printers.

Santa Cruz Sentinel   Sunday, February 23, 1964

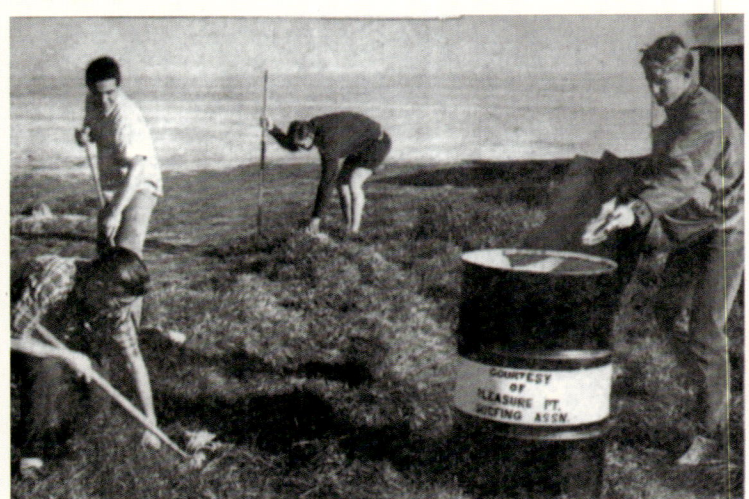

Surfers At Work

"Surfers have decided to improve their public relations via the rake and shovel method on the vacant lot leading to the beach at Pleasure Point and East Cliff drives. A group got together to form the Pleasure Point Surfing Association with a view to cleaning up the cluttered lot and placing trash cans. Main purpose of the organization: 'To improve the problems involving surfing and to promote a good relationship between the surfer and the community.' Hard at work this week were (from left) Rick Metzger, Davey Sultzer, Jimmy Phillips and Tom Kienholz. Joe Kienholz is president of the new association. Phillips is secretary and Gary Benson, treasurer. A planning committee is made up of Sultzer, Tom Kienholz and Dave Puissegur. Besides placing three trash cans the boys are policing the area in cooperation with the Santa Cruz county sheriff's office."

- Santa Cruz Sentinel, Sunday February 23, 1964

PPSA patches,
Top version,
Dave Puissegur
found "a little old lady
on Seabright Ave."
to make the first patches,
circa 1963.
Lower version,
patches ordered
from a patch company.

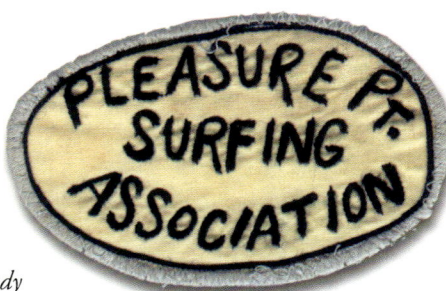

Pleasure Point
Night Fighter
business card,
1963.

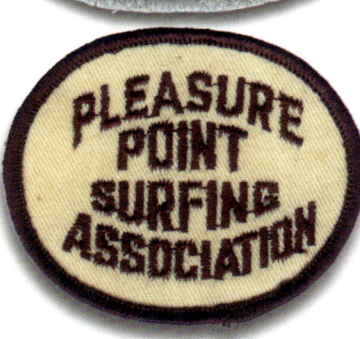

PLEASURE POINT
NIGHT FIGHTERS
MAIN OFFICE
BLUE FOX
TIJUANA

PLEASURE POINT
CALIFORNIA

JOINT OFFICE
BITAHOCHE
ARIZONA

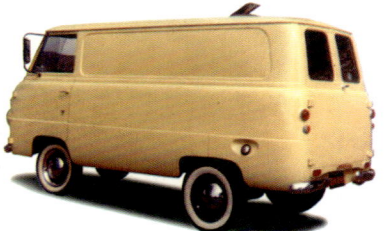

Thames Freighter 800

TONY HILL: *"I was living across the street from Jim. He always had something going on, like painting outside on the beat up van if I remember right. The first time I saw his art was a woody he had drawn then. Now I've been to Europe and around the world, and whenever I mention that I'm from Santa Cruz, people will ask if I know Jim Phillips. If you talk about Santa Cruz, Jimmy's name seems to pop up."*

Harry Conti recalls stories about Jimmy's Thames Freighter, "His yellow van was infamous! Phillips rolled it a few times, one time right in front of his mother who happened to be driving by. But they weren't hurt, just got out and tipped it back up, said 'Hi mom,' and drove off."

Phillips gave that elusive diploma one more college try by attending Cabrillo Junior College in 1964. He shared a house near the school in Aptos, up Trout Gulch Road with Rod Russell, more commonly known as Stickman, but best intentions fell into old patterns and he excelled in the art classes and cut everything else. "Cabrillo had some excellent art teachers, including Dave McGuire and Don Thompson," recalls Phillips. It was Thompson who encouraged Jim to send a portfolio to the California College of Arts and Crafts. Jim didn't think much about it until he won the scholarship, then it was decision time: To leave Santa Cruz and the surf and the friends and parties, and to go to the city on some quest to become an artist? The night Jim won the scholarship, he gave it deep thought and decided that he was essentially an artist, and that surfing must fall by the wayside. It was a bitter pill, but he knew he had to become something more than a surfer to survive.

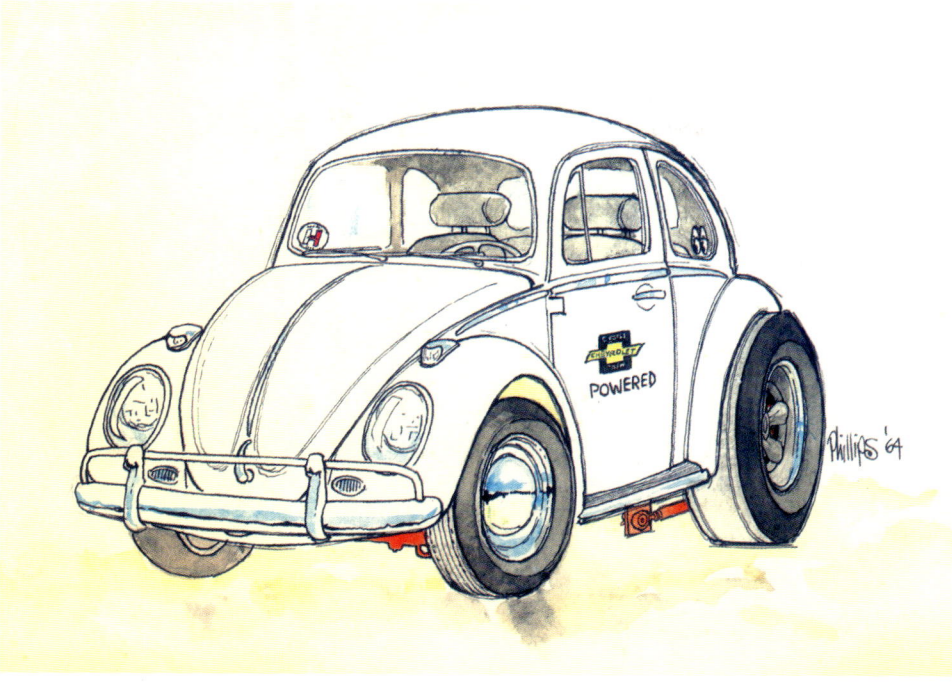

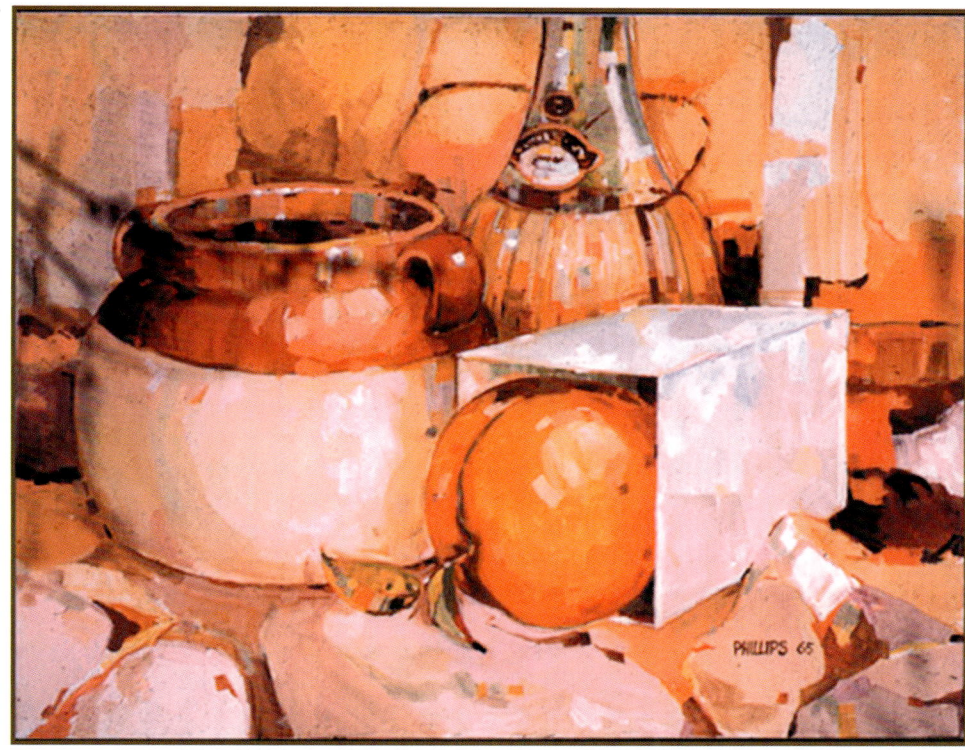

Top: VW Bug, 1964, home drawing.

Middle: Still Life, oil on canvas, 48"x36." Phillips' first oil painting from Dave McGuire's class at Cabrillo College, 1965.

'51 Ford, acrylic on art board, 20"x9", a field painting from Don Thompson's drawing class at Cabrillo College, 1964.

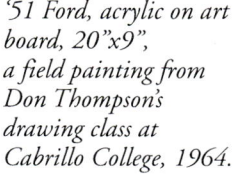

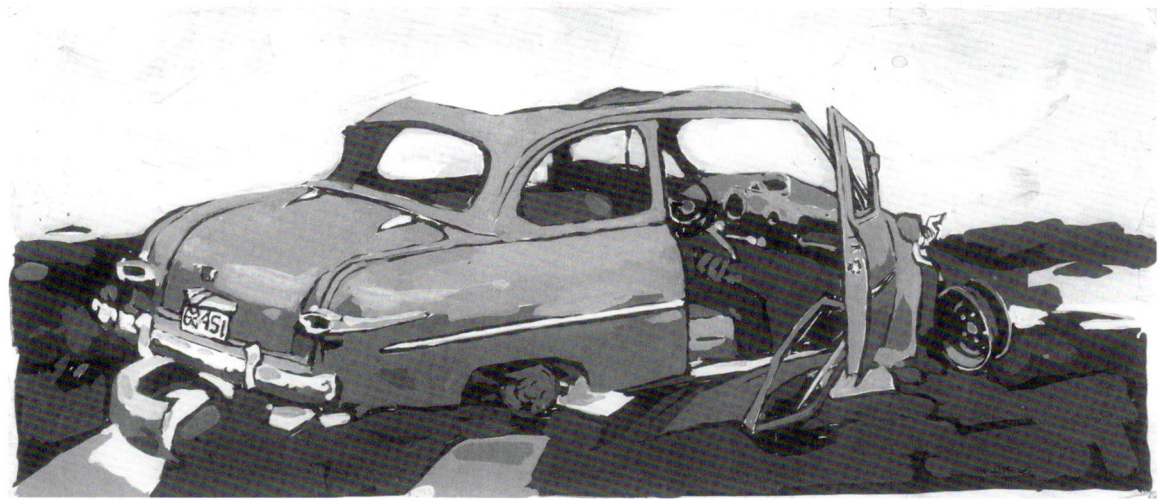

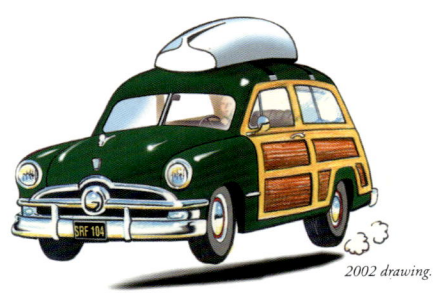

2002 drawing.

In September of '65, Phillips packed his art materials inside his '49 Ford woody, and strapped his eight-foot Jester dinghy to the roof and drove over the hill and inland to the big city of Oakland. While still in sight of the San Francisco Bay, Oakland was a long way from the quiet, coastal town of Santa Cruz.

The California College of Arts and Crafts is still there, on the corner of Broadway and College. Phillips rented a third-story apartment from a little old lady in Piedmont for seventy dollars a month. Away from the distractions of perfect, six-foot Shark's Cove and perfect six-foot Rivermouth, Phillips was free to work all day, study all night and he excelled. He says he enjoyed the courses and teachers and did well, earning A's in all his art classes. At CCAC, Jim was exposed to art, art history, different methods and mediums, but also to the big world outside of Santa Cruz. He was getting an education in the best sense of the word.

To connect with the ocean, Phillips sailed his Jester dinghy made at the Olson shop. Sailing around the Oakland estuary, dwarfed by giant container ships, he "asserted" his right of way, as he had the sail - with the Emerald City skyline of San Francisco and the Golden Gate off to the west. For Christmas break 1965, Phillips drove to Florida to visit friends, because he'd been feeling a little lonely in Oakland in between all the schoolwork and art. That loneliness began to change when he got back for the second semester. Phillips bumped into an old surfing friend named Jim Mazzeo who was serving in the Coast Guard in Martinez.

JIM MAZZEO: *"I heard Jimmy was going to Arts and Crafts and sought him out, it didn't take long. He was living in this nice clean little attic above this nice clean little old lady. He had a nice pad and I would go over there and hang out and play these two albums. One was* I Talk With the Spirits *by Roland Kirk. We listened to those over and over, and those songs are emblazoned into my brain. Even when I did rock and roll concerts and light shows years later, I still remember Roland Kirk. I whistle those songs subconsciously when I'm doing stuff."*

Mazzeo was living almost directly across the street from CCAC in a psychedelic pad called The Palace. Mazzeo was an artist, and he had an artists' pad.

JIM MAZZEO: *"The Palace was Benewigg's Palace. Benewigg was this old lady who rented out her College Avenue apartments to California College of Arts and Crafts art students. I wallpapered my entire apartment with big giant billboard advertisements, most were misprints, blurry and doubled over dots perfectly psychedelic. I made chandeliers out of paper bags, put colored tissue paper and shellac on all the windows and over my TV set. We did all this on a budget of zero dollars."*

The Palace was a hangout for characters like Mitchell Rose and Harvey Cohen. Harvey was into Yoga, was vegetarian, and he inspired Jim's interest in both. He introduced the Yoga to Jim, including the five famous Yoga teachers who were revered. Jim read about Parmahansa Yogananda, and his teacher Sri Yukeswar, and then Meher Baba, Babachrist and Jesus. This was how he became attracted to Jesus at that time, around his 21st birthday.

He began to let his hair and beard grow and started a few paintings in his apartment that had religious imagery influenced by a Catholic childhood. It seemed to be an extension of the deep need he felt at that time for understanding the reason for existence.

CCAC was work, but it wasn't all work and no play. Davey Sultzer recalls, "I used to go up to stay at Jimmy's apartment in Oakland occasionally, to spend the weekend. There was always a lot of our surfing friends that would show up there: Metzger, Stickman, Canty, Maz, and others."

Phillips seemed to start a Santa Cruz clique in Oakland which attracted surfing buddies like Steve Canty, who came to room with Phillips for the second semester at CCAC. "Stickman" moved into the basement apartment, and John Manwarren moved in across the street. As a key connection to future events, Steve was into scrounging dusty antiques from attics in some old Oakland houses up on that hill - without notifying the owners. Jim was afraid of trouble, and warned Canty, and then kindly asked him to leave. Canty answered an ad for a room for rent at a house in Berkeley. That's where Santa Cruz met Bakersfield. Steve moved there and Jim visited, and that's when Jim met George Davis, and Jeff Blackburn. Jeff was a musician who had recently released a record under the name Blackburn and Snow. After a few months, Canty wound up moving into an apartment across the street from Jim with Brian McMahan, one of the Berkeley housemates. Phillips began hanging out there, until one night, cops bust in, looking for stolen antiques and whatever else. Phillips was arrested and spent a night in jail. They found the antiques and pot that didn't get flushed, but Phillips was released the next day when it was made clear he wasn't involved in the antiques.

Phillips only lasted one year at California College of Arts and Crafts, but he took away lessons that still serve him, 40 years later. He says he learned two great things in Oakland: how to paint in oil with materials made from scratch, and anatomy. Jim says he had one of the best anatomy teachers in the world. His name was Mr. Jaque Fabert. He looked in his late 40s then. He wore an artist's smock every day, with a big bow in front. A large man, he had a big goatee shaved to a square below his mouth, giving him a powerful square jaw, which would have given him a very stern look even if he wasn't angry-looking all the time. A deadly serious artist, Jim says he never saw Mr. Fabert crack a smile. On a blackboard he would methodically outline the whole

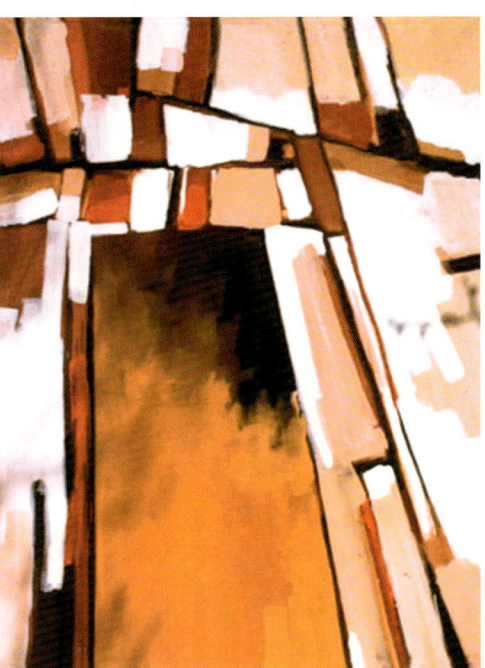

The Door, oil on canvas, 1965, approx. 36"x28". This photo by Jim's mom, represents the only remaining example of his work from CCAC, as most of his art school porfolio was lost in Mexico and elsewhere.

human form with all its organs in just a minute. Mr. Fabert would give out his grades in front of the whole class, and it was embarrassing to the first and suspenseful to the rest, nervously waiting for the ax to fall. Jim was the last person in the class to get his grade. Mr. Fabert criticized him for being absent so much, and gave him the coveted final A.

Phillips passed a lot of different kinds of tests in Mr. Fabert's anatomy class, including one test at the beginning that he seemed to single out for Jim alone. Anatomy means nude models and one day a model came to class. She was an exceptionally beautiful model, and Mr. Fabert announced that fact. You understand Jim was a red-blooded young man of 20. "I looked away when she started to undress and pose, because that's the sexy part," Phillips recalls, "and I was a very serious student of art then. Once the models are posed it's not so erotic, it's just art. So then I started my drawing while Mr. Fabert walked toward the back of the room, turned around and announced, 'Mr. Phillips! May I see *your* drawing?' This obviously meant I would have to walk across the semicircle of students seated around the model. As I did I couldn't help but notice everyone's attention to my situation, and to my anatomy. But I was a serious student, and proved it by not having to walk across the room funny." Mr. Fabert may have given Jim the A just for that.

Toward the end of the school year at CCAC, Phillips was still getting good grades, but he was struggling financially and feeling homesick. When the CCAC administrators discovered he didn't have a high school diploma, they told him he'd have to earn one at Oakland High night school, or his scholarship would be revoked and all of his hard work that year would be marked incomplete. They weren't interested in the GED test that Jim had passed back home the previous summer.

Phillips returned to Santa Cruz for the summer of 1966, and was offered room and board on Jeff Thomsen's "surfboard farm" in Soquel. In exchange for feeding the farm cats, Jeff gave him a bare room up in the old, dried-up water tower. Jim found an old stained-glass window that was deep red, and installed it in his dark little room. Phillips spent the summer glassing surfboards and doing art wherever he could.

JOHNNY RICE: *"The glass shop that Jeff had was just up a small road from my shop. The glass shop was an old house, and a barn with a water tower. In the house the glossing and sanding was done and in the barn was the glass shop. I didn't have a compressor at that time, so Jimmy would walk the boards down to the gas station and blow off all the shaped blanks, then walk them back up to glass. He lived in the water tower, and put a window in using red glass. Only Jimmy would do that. He painted the inside with all different colors and of course he had all his art work around. I've known Jimmy for many years, and he's always been an incredible artist."*

JEFF THOMSEN: *"Jim discussed influences on his art. I already knew about Escher and Dali, but he got to the heart when he talked about all the Disney artists. Those were truly the guys. No one else in*

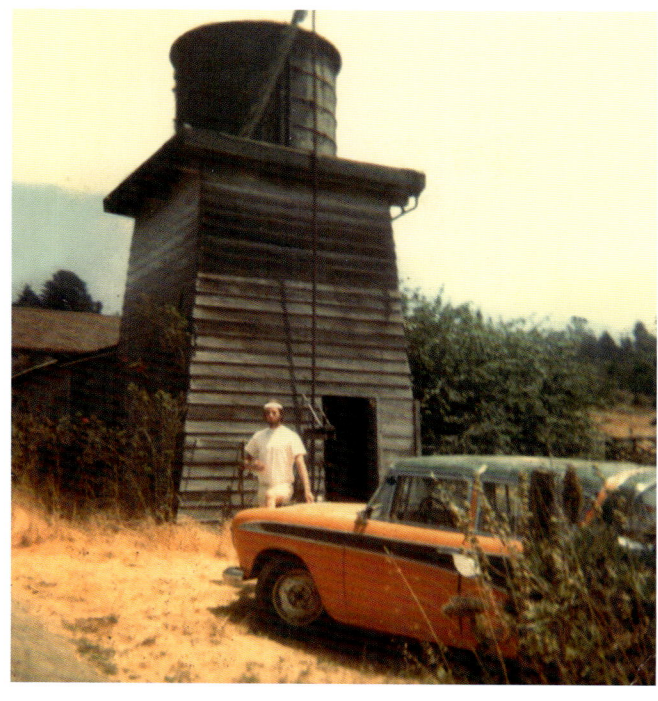

this universe could've dialed in on Porky Pig's doorknob that went 'CLICK', and later focused on it and went 'UNCLICK'. That's talent and unfailing attention to the smallest details. I don't think many people ever saw that but Phillips did, and pointed it out to me."

JIM MAZZEO: *"Jimmy lived in a water tower on an old chicken farm that Jeff Thomsen had. He put in a big red window that was psychedelic, as if Jimmy Phillips was in one of the weirdest places on earth. After visiting him, the Coast Guard no longer allowed me to go to Santa Cruz. I got in trouble mostly for showing up late."*

Mazzeo came to the Thomsen Fiberglass surfboard farm one day and gave Phillips his '48 Pontiac coupe, which had been banned from the Coast Guard station. The motor in Phillips' woody had long since burned up getting to art school and back through the long, hot valley. Maz had begun a dayglo psychedelic paint job on the Pontiac when got it banned by the base.

JIM MAZZEO: *"That Pontiac was given to me for my birthday by Mitchell Rose when I was in the Coast Guard. He was a great pen and ink artist, drawing elaborate and wonderful stuff, and so I guess he knew I didn't have a car. Anyway, Mitchell ended up giving me this car. It was a '48 Pontiac with dull gray paint. Steven Canty wrote on the back in white letters 'PELIGRO' which is Spanish for danger, and he put a big peace sign on it. Then the Coast Guard wouldn't let me drive the car on base or allow me to park it there. Rather than fix up the Pontiac, it was easier to give it to Jimmy. He painted the inside white, and then yellow and orange and red fluorescent spray paint, and colors which would light on fire when the sun would hit through the windows. It glowed on the inside like a nuclear reactor going down the road."*

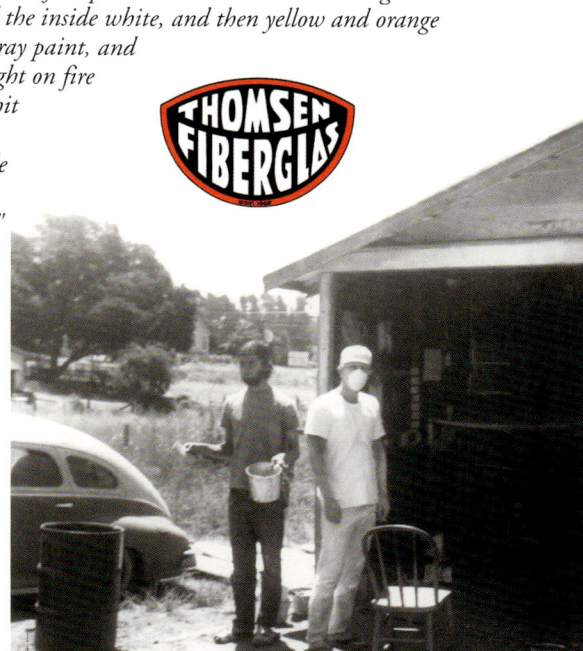

Top: The water tower at Thomsen's.
Left: Phillips pauses between glassing.

Bottom: Phillips, left, holding squeegee and bucket, and Jeff Thomsen with sanding mask, 1966.
Inset: Thomsen logo, by Jim.

There is something about Santa Cruz that echoes the Clash lyric, *Should I Stay or Should I Go Now?* On the one hand, anyone who leaves Santa Cruz eventually returns, realizing there are few better places in the world. And yet people from Santa Cruz are relentless travelers. There is something about the layout of the town, tall mountains behind, open mouth of the Salinas Valley to the southeast, and the long ocean horizon that lures Santa Cruz people into going over those mountains or up that valley or across the horizon and off the edge of the earth.

While living on the farm as summer came to a close, Phillips wondered what he would do with himself: Go back to Oakland and heap all the night school classes on top of his art classes? Or something else? Rick Metzger came by offering an "all expenses paid" trip to Mexico. Jim abandoned the psychedelic Pontiac, his job and everything he had built for himself on the farm, leaving for Mexico with all the money he had on him, three dollars.

Phillips' stories about his travels through Mexico in 1966 and 1967 are perilous and worth a few volumes themselves. He was long on hair and short on money, hitchhiking with a lot of nerve and little Spanish, going anywhere and nowhere and having trouble getting there.

Mexico beat him and blessed him. He was arrested, starved, fed, watered, rained on, nearly drowned, frowned upon, hassled, frozen, mugged, boiled, busted, and disgusted. The Mexicans thought Phillips was a bandito, Fidel Castro, Jesus, a bum, an artist, a friend and an enemy. Old ladies fed him, young men robbed him, banditos abused him, and cops hassled him. On his first trip he went through Mazatlan, where he befriended shoeshine kids and learned to hustle. To earn a few pesos, he attempted to sell paintings in the parks of Mexico City, but was turned away by the police.

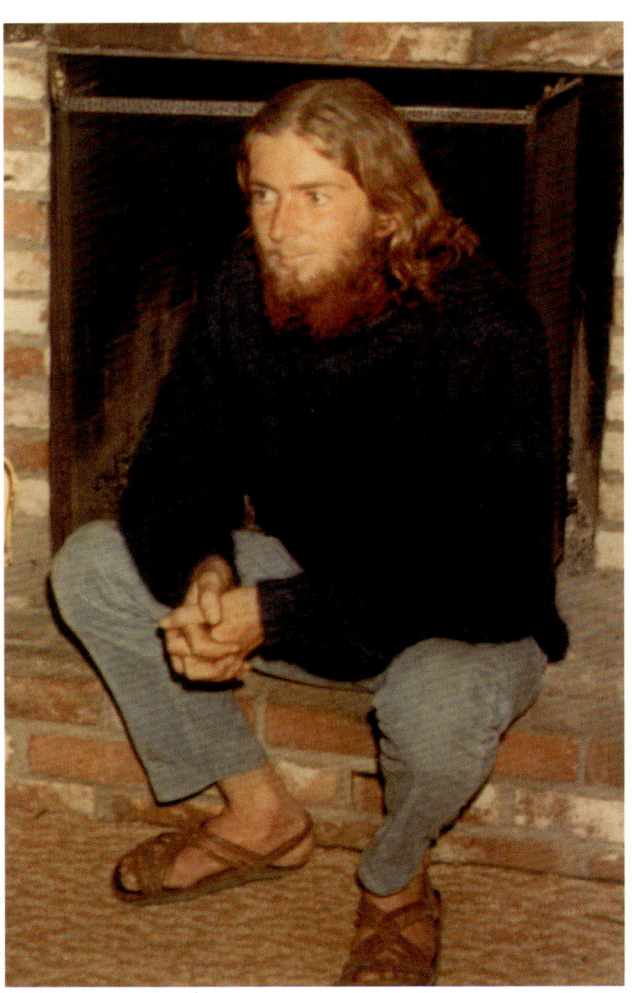

Photo taken by Jim's mother on his return from Mexico, December 1966.

The "all-expenses paid" trip promised by Metzger turned out to be paid by Mexico, and Phillips finally made it back to the border after a grueling hitchhike through the Sonora Desert. In Ventura he was arrested for a previous hitchhiking warrant. The jailer was itching to cut off Phillips' Jesus locks and maybe do other nasty things, but the Judge heard Phillips' stories about hitching through Mexico, and figured he'd suffered enough and let him go.

In Santa Barbara Phillips hopped a boxcar that took him along Point Conception and all the way to Gilroy. From there it was a short hop over the Santa Cruz Mountains, to the nearest thing Phillips could call home. Filthy from the grueling trip and unable to get rides, he ate dried walnuts and apples as he walked 20 miles over Hecker Pass to Watsonville, then a short ride that took him to Santa Cruz. But not for long.

Three days after he arrived back in Santa Cruz, Phillips was off to Mexico again, this time in a car with Steve Canty. They headed south in an old Studebaker that came with "7th Avenue," the house Ernie Keller had rented and shared with artist Ron Lafond, George Davis and the the Berkeley crowd.

Phillips must have been wondering why, oh why, was he going back to a place where he had suffered so much. On the way down Jim and Steve stopped and painted on their car. It got colorful by the time they got to Southern California. Near the Salton Sea they were pulled over by cops who were acting on an all points bulletin for Ken Kesey, who was on the lam at that time. They looked like Kesey, but they weren't Kesey, so the cops let them go.

They weren't quite Kesey but they were a little cuckoo and they were flying. This trip to Mexico wasn't as eventful as the first, but who needs events on the road? They got *La Turista* pretty bad and by the time they got to Mexico City they were out of money and out of gas. Back on foot, Phillips and Canty fell in with two Americans from Haight Ashbury, Boz and Cricket, who were staying in a huge, unfurnished cement house owned by Merry Prankster Neal Cassady. They didn't believe it until they saw an elaborate chemistry lab in the kitchen and a '57 DeSoto registered to Cassady in the carport.

Phillips painted some canvases hoping to sell them for gas and road money, but he was disappointed when told that Americans weren't allowed to make money in Mexico. Phillips and his partner parted company in Mexico City as Steve had decided to hitch home, and then, unable to endure, Jim finally hitched away leaving behind his paintings, drawings, portfolios, and the painted Studebaker in the carport alongside the DeSoto. Many days later in Tequila, Phillips got lucky hitchhiking when along came an old surfing friend, with seven people and a surfboard in a Hillman convertible. Jim sat on the rear fender all the way to Mazatlan, where some of the others got out and he got a ride all the way to San Clemente. He stayed with some friends in San Clemente, and then started hitchhiking north, finally getting a ride in the back of a pickup to Santa Cruz, and then offered a porch to share with Einer Paulson's monkey at 7th Avenue.

ERNIE KELLER: *"Seventh Avenue was a historic 1870 Victorian, and a house where hippies came and went. The windows had the original red and blue stained glass above each window, so when we pulled the shades down it made natural black light. Jimmy painted murals on the walls on his stays there. My favorite was the giant Zig Zag man painted over the mantle on a space that was the exact proportion as a pack, including the sides; also, Jim's mural in the monkey room, and his painting on the refrigerator gave the house lots of color."*

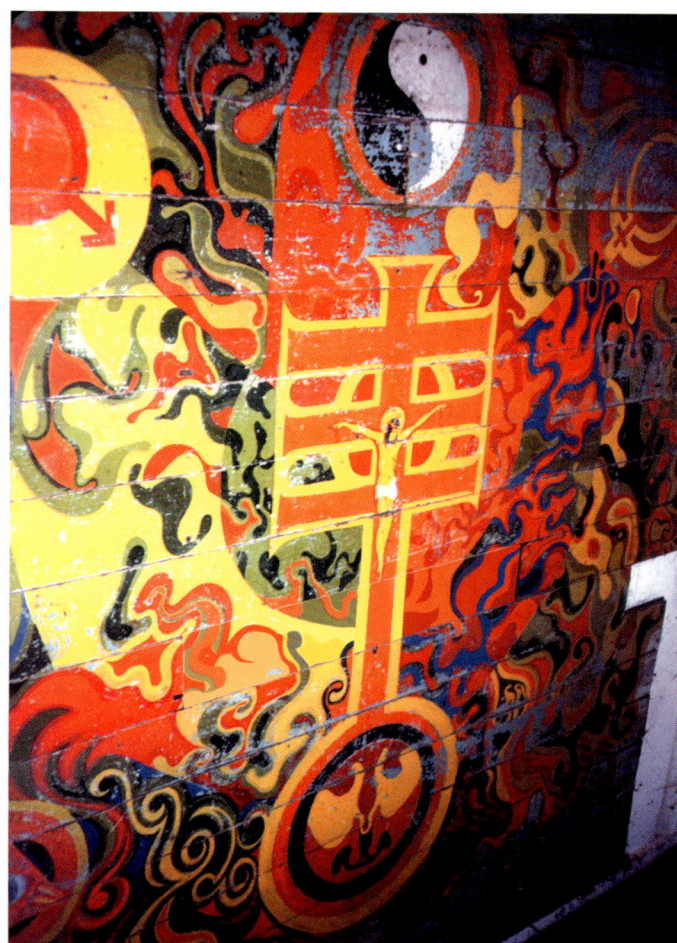

7th Avenue Monkey Room mural, enamel, 1966. Brian McMahon happened by the house during its demolition in the late 60s. He managed to save the mural by rushing in front of the jaws of a bulldozer which was about to rip the wall down. Later, while in storage, the mural endured a muddy flood in Soquel. It is shown in this photo, reassembled in a shed on the Phillips' property.

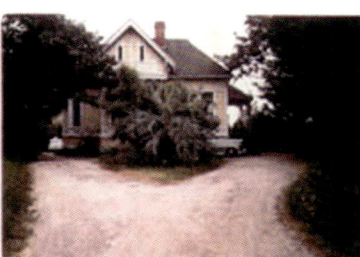

Left: 7th Ave. house from Soquel Ave.

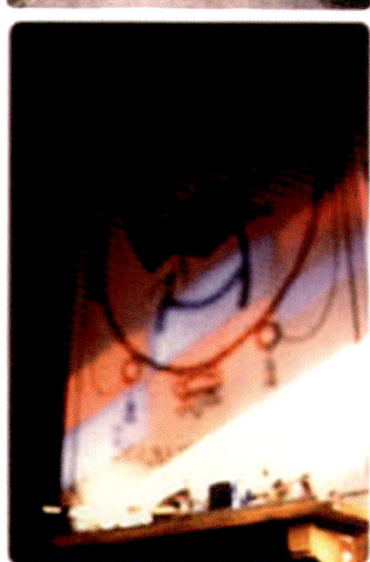

Light from the red and blue windows is cast across the Zig Zag mural at the 7th Avenue dining room, 1966.

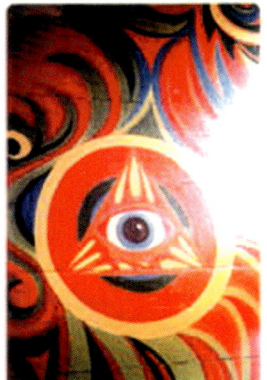

Original detail from Monkey Room mural.

Photos: Courtesy of Ernie Keller.

A "smoothie," the 7th Ave. refrigerator, in Phillips' enamels, with Iris Paulson in the foreground, January 1967.

JEFF THOMSEN: *"Jimmy mentioned something that struck a chord, from years ago while he was in lessons with Ralph Gray. It was Jimmy's grandfather, to the effect that they built on one another's drawings. Later, when Jim and Steve Canty lived in the tall Victorian by the cork oak on the corner of 7th Avenue, he worked on a painting with Steve and called it 'Dual-Expressionism.' Man, what a term to tickle the artsy-fartsy gallery crowds! Good one dude! Jim was an influence on him. Canty's style was influenced by him, with different touches. He never got a handle on Jim's eye for detail. The other guys went their own ways, Jim Byberg, John Hara, Bill Ballentine...but whether he knows it or not, elements of Jimmy's style found their way into the work of those guys even if they never knew. I don't know if others ever knew or cared, but I did."*

It wasn't long before Phillips was off again with friends who stopped by on their hitchhiking trip to San Diego, chasing down a rumor of the mystery ship *Call Me Free* that needed a crew for Tahiti. The ghost ship was just that, so Phillips and his friend Mitchell Rose painfully made their way north to North Beach, where Mitchell had an apartment. Phillips was wandering and lost, but in San Francisco he blundered into what would become the first step in a lasting career: the making of psychedelic posters. Mitchell was kind enough to let Jim stay in his North Beach apartment. Mitchell was a TV advertising artist from New York who had stayed at Maz's for a few weeks when he arrived in California to retire. He had a drawing board, pens and ink in his apartment. To show his gratitude he wanted to make a drawing for Mitchell. The pen and ink drawing was *Dr. Mota's Medicine Show*, an old truck painted up like a medicine show wagon, with a lot of herbal references. A guy named Harvey Cohen was also staying there with his girl, Dawn "who he found in a fog," and the next morning, he suggested that Jim take the art down to the *Oracle*, which was publishing Summer of Love type stuff out of the Haight Ashbury. Editor Allen Cohen asked Jim do a split-fountain rainbow coloring, which was his first color separation. *Oracle* art director Gabe Katz gave Jim a piece of rubylith and told him what to do with it. They published *Dr. Mota's Medicine Show* in the February 1967 issue, and it was made into a poster in 1968. He didn't get any money from the *Oracle* then, and the few other art jobs he managed to get could not provide enough, even for a vagabond with scarcely a bottle of ink, a pen and two pencils.

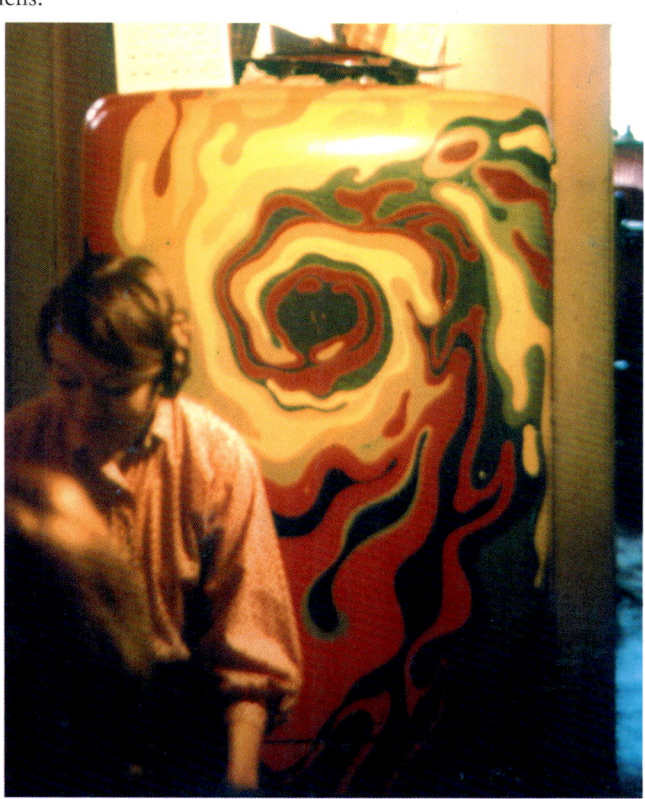

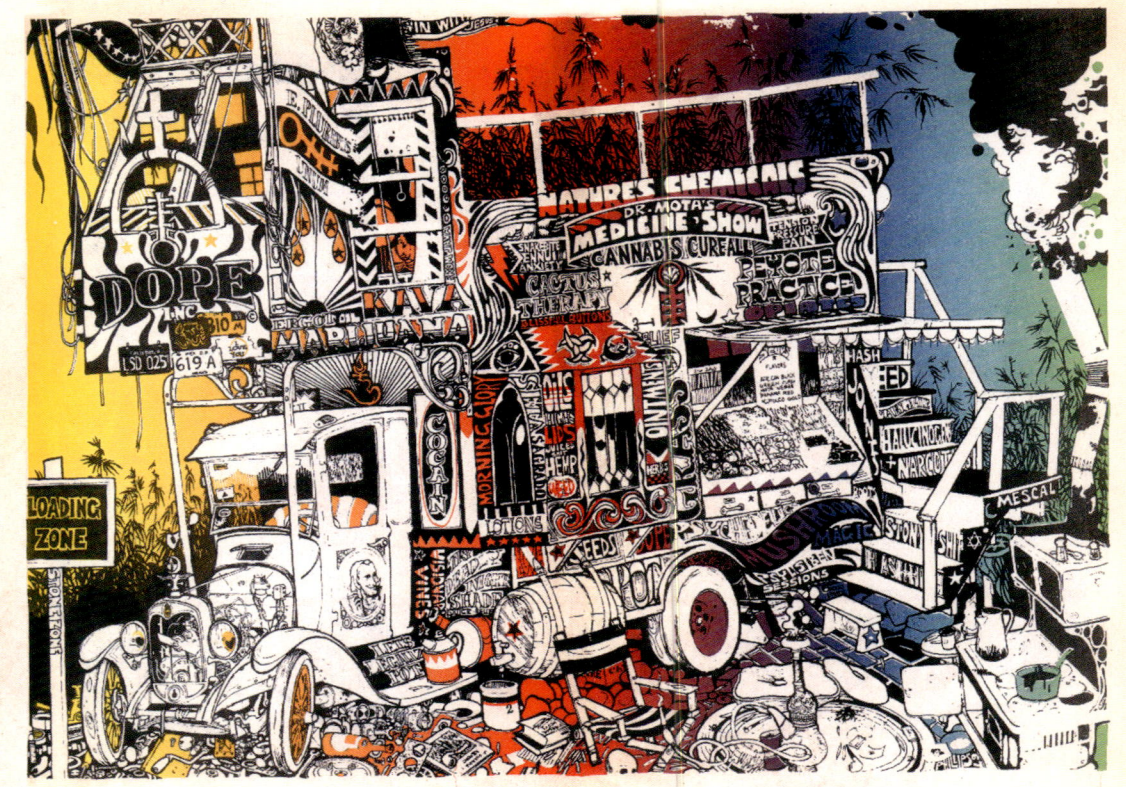

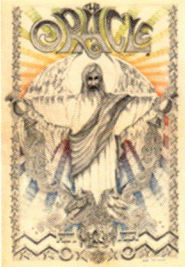

Dr. Mota's Medicine Show, a satire of the drug culture, by Jim Phillips, 11"x15", in Oracle No. 6, February 1967.

Phillips then bumped into Michael Brown, another friend of Maz's from CCAC, who offered an unfurnished house on Pine Street to sit while he went to New York. Phillips accepted the offer in trade for illustrating the walls of the classic old Victorian. He also got a few small jobs: illustrating three menus for a North Beach restaurant, and some low-paid drawings that a neighbor signed his own name to and submitted to the *Oracle*. Life was hard, Phillips was poor.

Back in the 60s, people seemed to give away cars like we 21st Century citizens give away business cards. Mitchell offered Phillips a '55 Ford wagon on its last legs, called Eddy, which Phillips gratefully accepted and drove down to Moss Beach. There he stayed at Sandy Vickers' who had an airplane at Half Moon Bay Airport and wanted a psychedelic paint job on it. Phillips toyed with opening a small art shop in Moss Beach. There was a tiny storefront in front of his small room in the basement, and he started calling it "Moss Beach Arts." Jim painted it up and went so far as to get a stack of *Oracles* to sell.

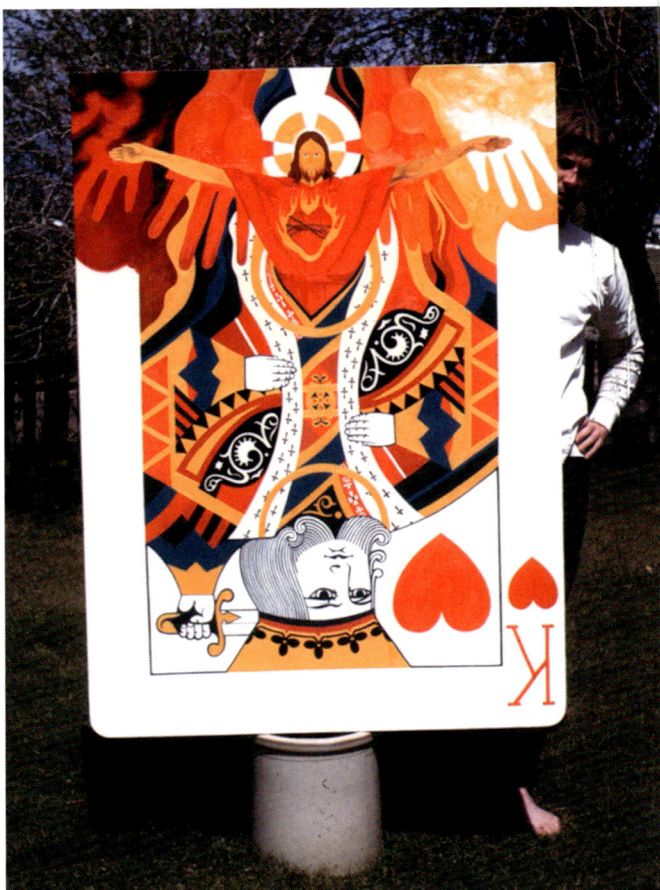

King of Hearts, oil on canvas, 36"x60", 1967.

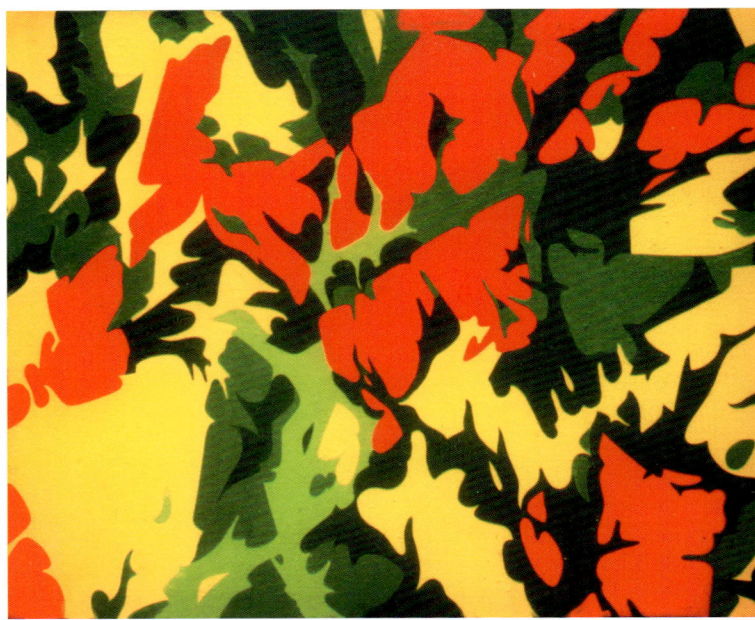

Trees, acrylic on canvas, 22"x28", 1967.

But he was dirt poor and it was unrealistic for him to attempt such a venture. The cold coastal winds of February kept Jim from working on the plane. Pretty soon Eddy died, and Jim's life seemed dead. He felt that he had hit bottom. Jim cut his long hair, and moved back to his mom's where his bedroom was still intact. He stayed locked up in his old bedroom, painting large canvases of Christ in oil. He also painted canvases in acrylics on the patio, tracing the tree shadows as they changed with the movement of the sun, but Jim was lost and basically miserable.

Then Jim got a call from Jeff Thomsen. Jeff asked if he wanted a job glassing at what must have been at the time, the largest surfboard factory in the world, Oceanside Surfboards, in Cocoa, Florida. Phillips borrowed seventy dollars from his mom for plane fare and was waiting for Jeff at the factory door the next morning. That job got Jim back on his feet. He bought a '55 Chevy panel truck for seventy-five dollars and occasionally painted on it. After awhile he got a letter from Jim Mazzeo, who got an address from Jim's mother. Since getting discharged, Maz had been touring with rock bands and doing light shows across the Midwest. They kept in touch with letters. A few months went by, and Maz called and asked if Jim would be interested in a studio art job doing rock posters for a psychedelic rock club called The Crosstown Bus in Boston. Maz said, "It's a Family Dog type deal!" That was all Jim had to hear, being a faithful patron of the Family Dog's Avalon Ballroom during his Oakland and San Francisco times. He didn't offer his artistic services back then, but inwardly he longed to be involved in the "family" like that seemed to be.

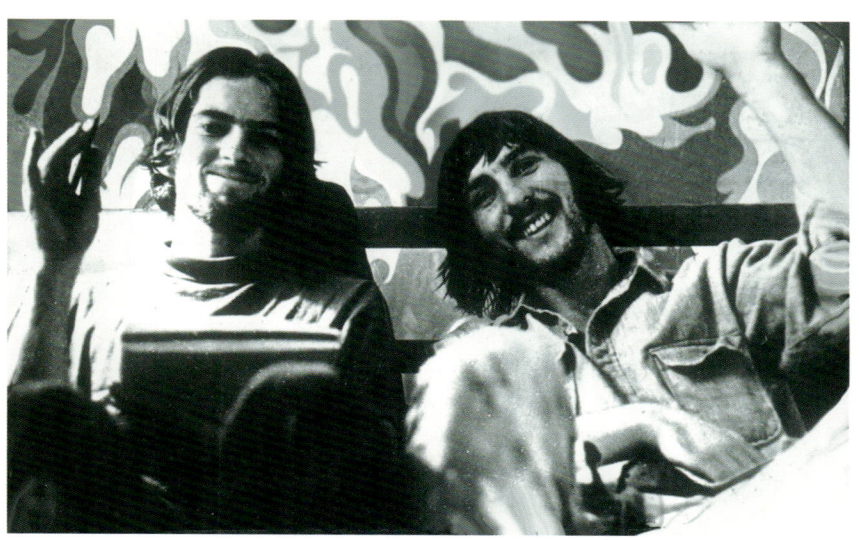

Jim Phillips & Jim Mazzeo at their Ashford St. apartment in Boston, 1967. The three-story house was offered by Crosstown Bus patron "Joe the landlord" in exchange for painting on the walls.

Jim finished work that day at Oceanside, which was Friday and payday. The boss, Willie Fineburg, looked at him funny as he said "I'll see you tomorrow, right?" as if he knew something was up. Jim just smiled, knowing if he told him about the offer, Willie would demand notice or sweet talk him into staying. Jim was a power glasser, and he knew he was depended upon, but was determined to go to Boston immediately. Jim got his few belongings from the cheap little motel room he lived in out on the mosquito swamps where Fineburg's shop was located, and drove his psychedelic truck nonstop for three days, except for a few hours in South Carolina where he crawled in back and caught a little sleep. As soon as Jim drove into Boston he called Maz. Maz came down to meet me with Ian Heim, one of the owners, in a big flashy convertible. Phillips followed Maz to the club where he was immediately pressed into service, painting the entrance of the club from flat black to psychedelic.

DOLLY PHILLIPS: *"I was living in an apartment on Peterborough St. off Kenmore Square, right around the corner from the Museum of Fine Arts, the Gardner Museum and Fenway Park in Boston. My friend and roommate Lori was seeing a guy she had bumped into at Harvard Square, who said he would be working a lightshow at a new rock & roll club in Boston called the Crosstown Bus that was just about to open. He invited us over to the club to check it out and I became a regular part of the scene, helping paint the walls psychedelic colors, and later working the ticket booth. We enjoyed watching from the upstairs art studio as different bands auditioned in the large auditorium. About a week later Jim Mazzeo showed up, and with his lightshow experience, was hired to take over as lightshow director. Jimmy arrived a week or so after that. He looked like a true hippie and a real artist. Although he was tired and bedraggled, he got right into his first assignment, which was painting the stairway up to the ballroom. I was assisting the art director paint psychedelic designs on the stairway. We had started at the top of the stairs and when Jimmy came in they told him to start painting at the bottom. It was sort of a race to the middle, where Jimmy and I met."*

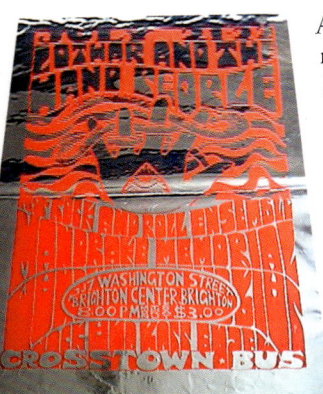

Mylar version of the Lothar poster, 1967. Courtesy of Maria Lewis.

After a few days Jim was assigned his first rock poster by the art director, James McCracken, who was also letting him and Maz stay at his house. McCracken was a master silkscreener. He asked Jim for art for *Lothar and the Hand People*, for the grand opening show for the club. He processed Phillips' drawing into a 35 inch format, and Jim helped while "Mac" printed it into a day-glo red and yellow silkscreened beauty.

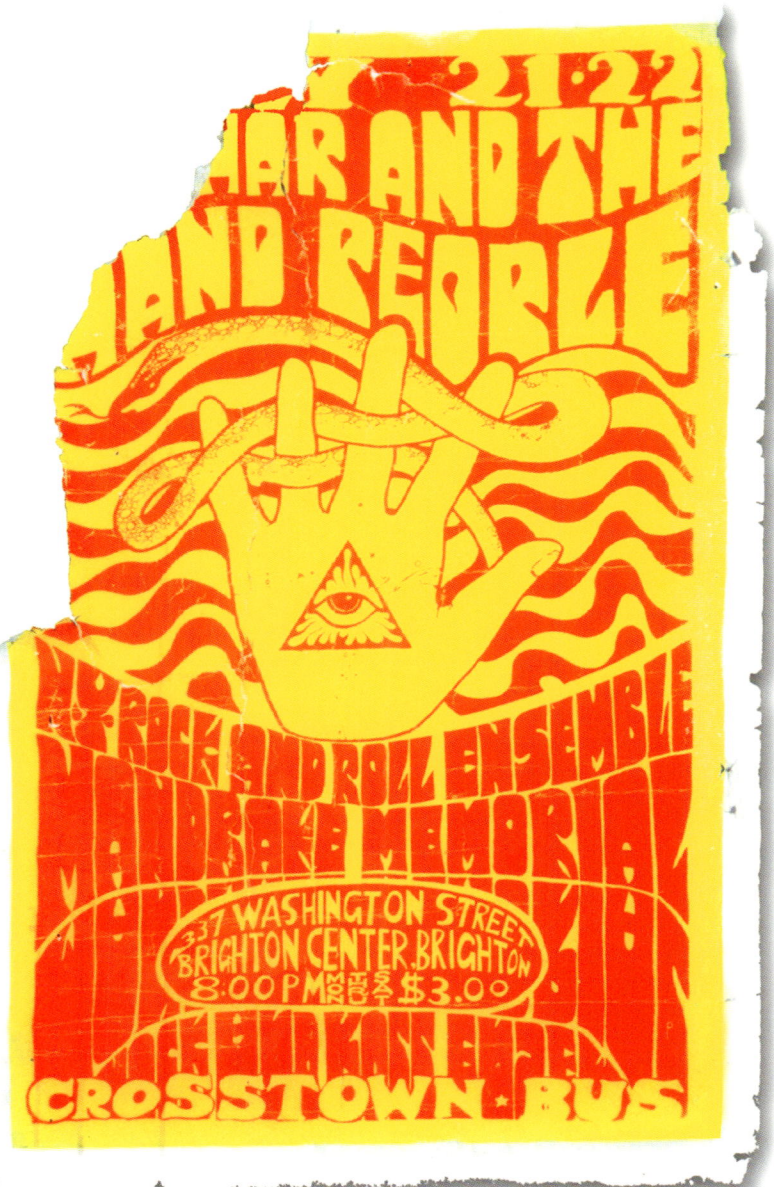

Jim's first rock poster was for Lothar & the Hand People, *silk screened, 23"x35", 1967. Some of these large posters were used on sandwich boards worn by a few club ladies around Harvard Square and Cambridge as advertising.*

33

JIM McCRACKEN: *"I was traveling with Joanne around the country selling posters at Student Unions at colleges. Joanne ran into this guy from Boston University and he said they were looking for someone to do the graphics at the Crosstown Bus. I met up with those guys and I started doing it. I liked Jim's work a lot. He and Maz stayed with us there in Cambridge. It was really great those guys showed up because it was more than I could do by myself. The posters were great. A great time, beginning of the opening up of consciousness and the wildness and freeness of the sixties and seventies. It was fun. Too bad it was so short-lived, I guess everyone was going some direction or other, but it was great that it happened at all."*

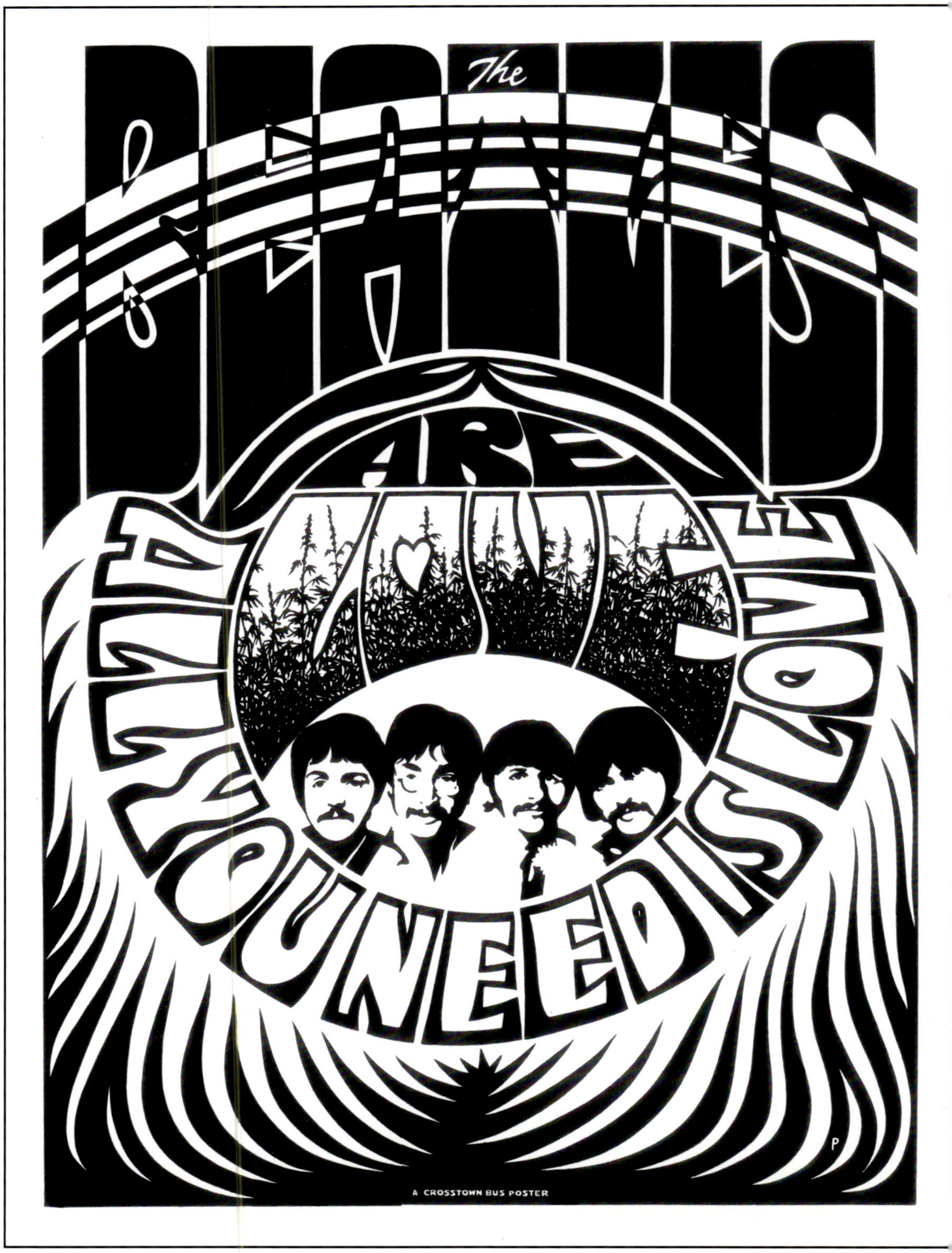

JIM MAZZEO: *"Jim McCracken is one of the greatest artists I'll ever know. I mention the same thing in Neil Young's book too. Mac was living with his old lady, a gal named Joanne, they had two kids and one on the way. She used to go down to the college with him to silkscreen postcard-sized 'accidental images,' which were accidentally very psychedelic. Mac drank a lot and he'd be pretty much drunk and working and creating stuff that was incredible and it blew my mind. Joanne was in the family way and she tried to turn Mac's work into money to pay the rent and food and stuff. She met Ian and those guys who then put Mac in charge of producing posters for the club. Mac was into doing some posters, but didn't want to get stuck doing all the posters. So I saw an opportunity to get Jimmy up there. I remembered his incredible pen and ink drawings, in addition to his art school work, amazing stuff, and you know that's the kind of stuff I wanted in our posters. I've been calling on Jimmy for posters ever since."*

Phillips' second poster was for the Doors' first east coast appearance. He was helping Maz with the lightshow, and worked the liquid crystal overhead projector and slide projectors for that show. Jim Morrison glared at Jim when one of his slides malfunctioned and bright, white light flooded the singer. Jim's big moment with Jim. The famous Boston disc jockey Arnie Ginsburg was at the show. He climbed up to the lightshow booth and introduced everyone to Bobby Gentry, who had the big hit then, *The Tallahachee Bridge.* Dolly recalls, "Maz asked me if I wanted to help in the light booth. It was a big thrill to be doing a light show, it was so much fun bouncing the liquid crystals to the beat of the music and nice to be working next to Jimmy for the first time."

Beatles promotional silk screen edition, 22"x28", a Crosstown Bus poster, 1967, commisssioned by Arnie Ginsburg.

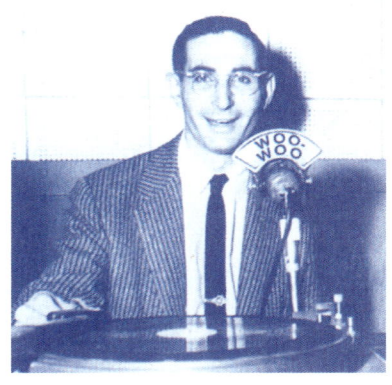

Arnie "Woo Woo" Ginsburg, a popular Boston DJ during the late 50s and early 60s'.

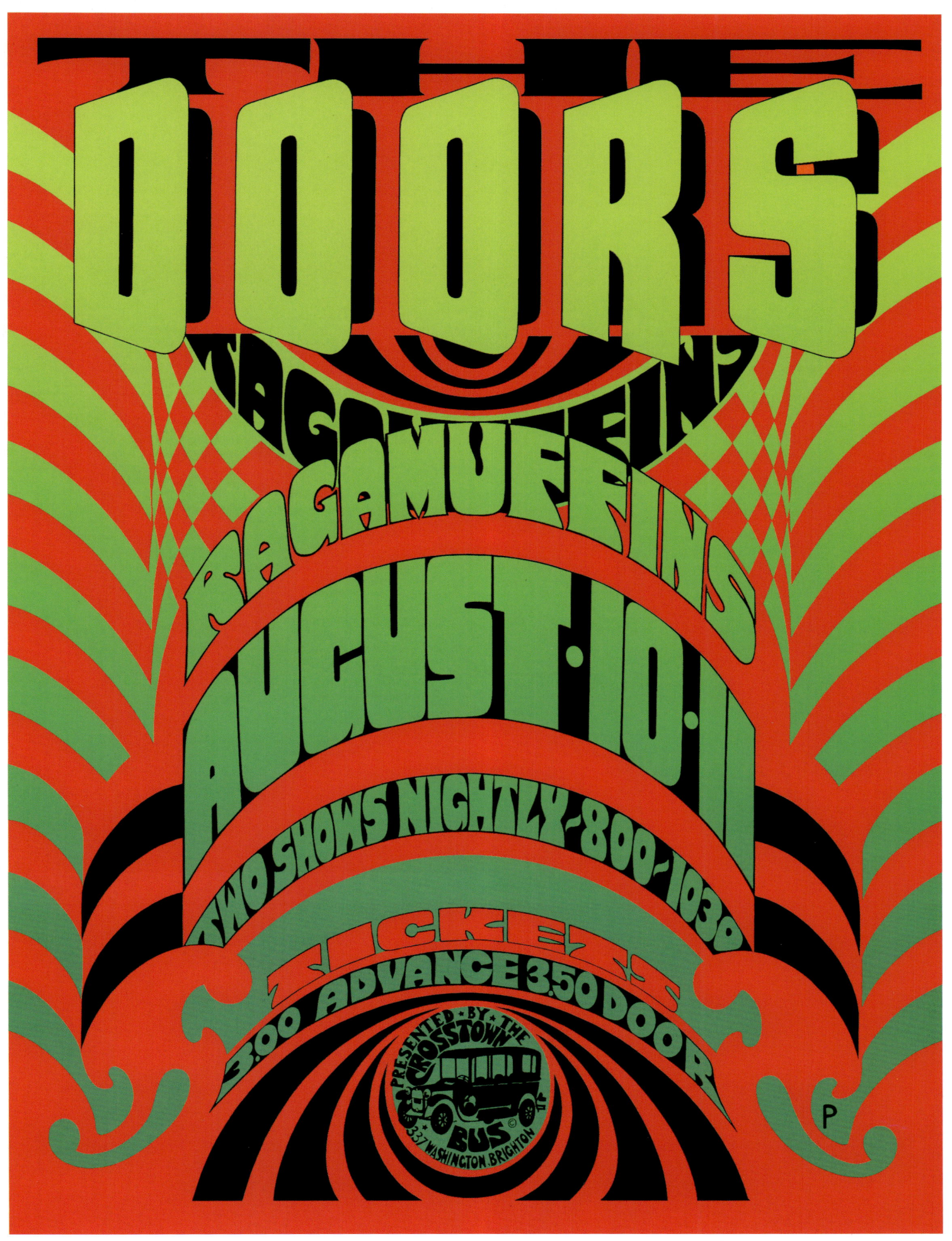

The Doors, 8"x10", Crosstown Bus Poster, 1967.

JIM MAZZEO: *"The carousel slide machines went on their own. The Liquid projectors took two people, and another couple to take a break now and then. Jimmy loved doing those liquid projections. We would play in yellow and mineral oil, with yellow food color origin, and two or three clock crystals to create a good squeegee effect. We'd have two different images laid out on the overhead projectors, like a peace symbol and a Zuni sun sign, with the peace symbol on the outside and the sun on the inside, one would be yellow and the other red, and we'd overlay on each other and just have fun. One guy would follow the drums."*

A big night in Boston. Jim Phillips had Forrest Gumped his way directly into the middle of the sixties, doing lights for The Doors and getting frowned upon by the Lizard King. The world was turning pretty fast and the work kept coming. Phillips was commisioned to do a *Beatles Are Love, All You Need is Love,* poster by Arnie Ginsberg. He obliged, and helped McCracken run off a hundred silk screen posters in black ink. At the end of the run Jim took off his shirt and printed it. That was the only copy of rhe poster he retained, and 25 years later the ragged t-shirt was the basis of a limited-edition second printing.

Mazzeo recalls, "I did all the light shows, but Wes Levine did the mylar sections, and the mylar cave with the strobe-lights and chrome mylar bags on the walls. The walls would expand and move like you were on acid. I liked that part. He was like a hip New York designer kind of guy that those rich guys knew. He didn't get a whole lot of money for his contribution. The same with us, which is why they gave us places to live and restaurant tabs and stuff."

JOE "CAP" CAPUOZZO: *"The Crosstown Bus......Ah yes, I remember it well....I was driving down from Vermont in a '51 Ford Vicky, with a couch in the trunk, headed for my New York apartment when I decided to make a brief stop in Boston to visit this banjo player, Mike Kropp, that I knew from Denver. I heard on the grapevine that he'd thrown in his lot with two partners on a club in Brighton, near Boston. It was a cool, huge brick hall in an old Polish/Bohunk neighborhood with neat houses, great hardware stores and luncheonettes, diners, and weird stores and great girls ... Who wouldn't stop there? Next thing I knew 1 was offered a job as a 'Lighting technician,' but the job entailed much more, as shall be revealed...I ran the strobe light intensity in the strobe room as well as played the color organ from a platform and table located on a rear balcony, and also did some carpentry work to make these very hot lights legal for the fire laws. I was also an "advance man" dealing with incoming bands and their managers, sound men, and finding out their requirements, electrical and otherwise. Also worked with McCracken doing drive-around publicity for The Doors' concert, playing their records at top volume from roof-mounted loudspeakers atop a beat, but rust free, Corvair van. I remember playing the color organ during the Doors concert and it was real amazingly oscillating ambiotic ... The Doors ... The drums ... The Bus.... The Cross... The Town .... The lights... The colors.... The girls .... The clock crystals lighting the stage .... So, I was offered thisjob as lighting technician and assistant carpenter. The pay was supposed to be seventy per night and all the cheeseburgers you could sign for at the luncheonette across the street where the club had a tab. Never did get fully paid but the girls there were great n' cute n' cuddly. So I took the job and soon realized this Crosstown Bus scene was becoming like a magnet! Out of Michigan came artist Jim McCracken. Up from Cocoa Beach in a vintage Chevy panel comes California artist/designer/conceptualizer Jimmy Phillips fresh from painting surfboards and changing the face of history in Florida. Out of the west coast came Jim Mazzeo, pop entrepreneur, artist, lighting magician, managerial detail smoother, and from the surrounding neighborhoods and suburbs came nubile, sexy beautiful girls to the club, some were dancers ..... who wouldn't stay? So....I stayed. Then the magnet became stronger. ..people from Manhattan who owned huge companies became interested. .. .. people*

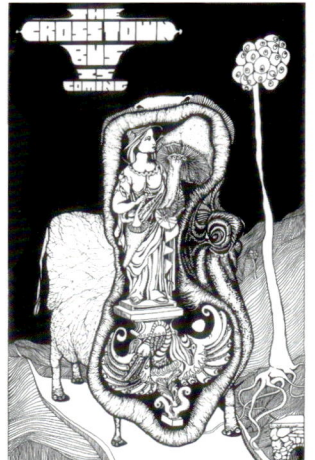 

Crosstown Bus poster art by art directorJim McCracken, 1967. Courtesy of "Cap" Capuozzo.

from England, Europe, even showed up ... Bands from Colorado, bands from Liverpool, bands from London, bands from Germany via Holland by way of LA. Next thing, local hustlers, parasites, criminals and people who don't drive Chevys showed up. And you know when people who don't drive Chevys show up, the end is near. The Crosstown Bus closed, the Beatles were up for sale and the intensity was dying down in Boston. The Crosstown Bus was only around for a short time but the few of us who took that brief, wild, spiritual ride will never forget it. It was the ultimate bus trip, and that's trip with a capital T"

JIM MAZZEO: *"Crosstown Bus was owned by three wealthy, spoiled rich kids, sort of halfheartedly, kind of into it, but no dedication or the drive to follow through. The Crosstown Bus stayed open for less than six months. I think it closed because of the fire department. At first, they had to pay off two firemen. One policeman showed up at the opening night to get their money. This is the Boston rip-off payola scam, and so they started to pay those guys, and as more people came, and the Doors came, and the club was creating a stir, and becoming a real place, they had to pay off like four cops and eight firemen. It was like $1500 a week, and back then that was a lot of money. That's why the Crosstown Bus got shut down."*

The Crosstown Bus rocked all summer long, but suffered from poor attendance on weeknights because of its location in the Brighton districr. By the end of the summer there had been some shows that bombed, one night's receipts were stolen and it all closed in September of 1967. It wasn't a total loss though, as Phillips followed the family tradition of courting. You might say that he opened his car door, and said "Hop in baby, let's go" to that cute ticket-taker named Dolly.

An adventurous gal from Waltham, a suburb of Boston, Delores Marie Gorgone was working days as a secretary at Geoscience in Cambridge. At night she was helping out at the Crosstown Bus. Dolly had just gotten back from three months in Florence. She said, "I didn't need much convincing. It was California Dreamin' and the Summer of Love, and Jimmy."

Dolly hopped in and got a three week, cross-country taste of La Vita Phillips. They left The Crosstrown Bus with a couple hundred dollars and a handshake. Dolly and Jimmy headed for California in his psychedelic panel truck, which they named "Poor Truck" because of the rust and the funky condition. The colorful truck was turned away at the Canadian border in upper New York state, but got through at Niagara Falls.

DOLLY PHILLIPS: *"Jimmy's old truck was something 1 had never seen before, even in Harvard Square. It had a wild psychedelic paint job, and big letters on the back proclaiming the second coming of Jesus. I wouldn't have 'hopped in' with just anyone, but my better judgement told me Jimmy was someone I could trust, and it turned out I was right."*

They were going to take the northern route west, but gas became too expensive and it was cold, so they headed south. They had a little accident in Sioux City and bought the guy off with one of the two $100 bills Jim had. The victim later tried to sue, but they were turnips and had no blood. Poor Truck barely made it over the Continental Divide in Colorado, but three weeks after leaving Boston they rolled into San Francisco, straight to the Haight Ashbury, where the Summer of Love was still in full bloom!

Back in Santa Cruz with a gal in tow, Phillips couldn't just flop anywhere. He and Dolly ended up on "The Farm," a rabbit farm commune in Soquel that George Davis was heading with Sandy Kelly, her kids and a half dozen other people. To warm his welcome and earn his keep, Phillips painted a life-sized Spiderman on the living room wall. Dolly and Jimmy moved into a small room with a wood stove, and Jim turned a detached shed into a nice studio with a woodstove, and a wooden floor radio from surf buddy Denny Cox that cost two dollars at the Goodwill.

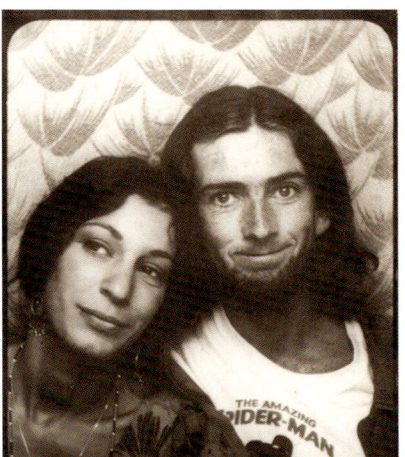

Dolly and Jim, photo booth at Woolworths, Santa Cruz, 1967

This was 1967. The Monterey Naval Post-Graduate School was advertising a religious art show on the radio, and Phillips remembered the large canvas he had painted at his mom's, a big painting of Christ he called *King of Hearts.* Jimmy and Dolly strapped the canvas to the roof of Poor Truck, "like the *Beverly Hillbillies,"* drove it down around and through the Fertile Crescent of the Monterey Bay and entered it in the show. Two weeks later they returned to Monterey to check out the show. They walked in and found Jim's canvas and were shocked to see a blue ribbon on it. Phillips had won first prize! Someone asked if Jim was the artist, and when the crowd of judges came over and got a look at him, they almost fell over.

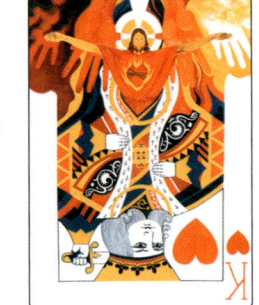

King of Hearts won first prize at the Fifth Annual Monterey Naval Post-Graduate School religeous art show, 1968

They were outraged that an apparent "hippie" had won! The head judge walked away, but a priest stopped him and took the prize money envelope out of his hand and gave it to Jim. He was later approached by a dealer and agreed to let the canvas be shown at a Cannery Row gallery for a month.

The San Francisco art and music scene was still raging into early 1968 and Gabe Katz, the *Oracle* art director, contacted Phillips to

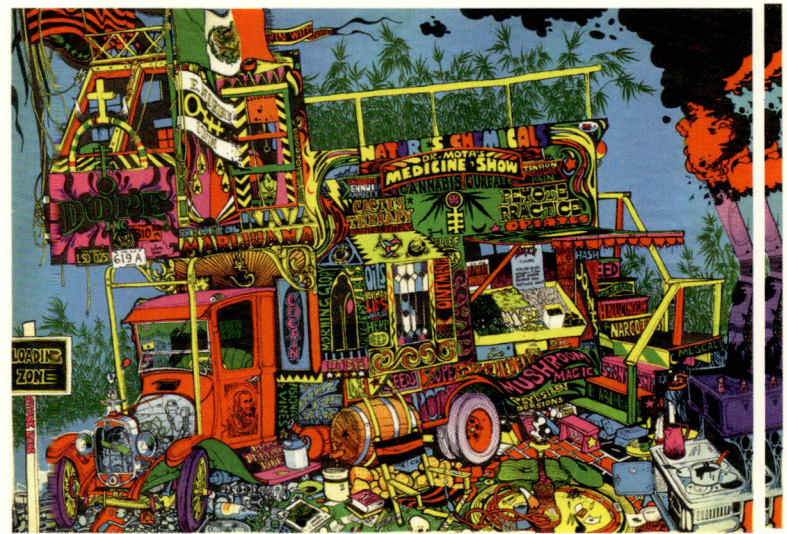

In 1968 Exoterica published a full color 28"x21" poster version of this work which originally appeared in the 1967 San Francisco Oracle.

turn *Dr. Mota's Medicine* Show into a poster. Phillips got another introduction into the world of mass printing. They enlarged the art by 200% and Katz showed Jim how to do a "blue-line" color separation, which turned out to be the first of Jim's full-color separations. Cal Litho was doing a lot of rock posters for the Avalon Ballroom then, and they printed the Dr. Mota poster. Jim met artist Alton Kelley there while working side by side on the light table.

While visiting some hippies in the Haight Ashbury, Phillips approved of the idea of color TV with the dials tuned to make the colors go all out of whack like the hippies had it. He came up with a plan to do his own poster to pay for one for the farm. Since religious themes and satire seemed to be an obsession for him, he combined the two in a play on *The Last Supper.* Jesus was there, and the disciples were the famous cartoon characters he loved. That poster was going to raise the $400 for the color TV. Phillips bounced around trying to get it printed. A poster company in Berkeley got all the way to making bluelines when they backed out when suddenly Cal Litho said they were too religious! Jeff Blackburn visited the farm often, and took Jim up to meet Reggie Williams who ran the Straight Theater on Haight Street in San Francisco. Williams printed the poster, but it wouldn't sell, not even in Berkeley, and the farm never got a color TV.

REGGIE WILLIAMS: *"That summer, Jim Phillips, the fabulous artist who did* Dr. Mota's Medicine Show *then created* The Next Supper, *a wonderful five-color piece of print-ready art that freaked out printers and poster publishers alike. After wide rebuke, he sought me out, bringing the 32" x 25" original to my house. As Caitlin and I saw him for the first time coming up the hill to our pad in Larkspur, he looked like Christ with similar hair, beard, and vibrant demeanor.* The Next Supper *has many of modern life's dilemmas wrapped in a comic format, presented in the context of* The Last Supper. *Here Christ is surrounded by comic heroes while a mob is breaking in the back door under the cross and a paisley roof sky dotted with flying saucer light fixtures, Picasso's* Guernica, *and the California Bear Flag. All the characters and icons were so prevalent in our common mind, they seemed to become universal symbols and copyrights did not concern us. We loved it. I hocked my MGB to raise the capital, then Jim and I went to get it printed. Jim's first choice, and several other litho houses, showed us the door. We finally prevailed upon a printer willing to overcharge us. Hogan Kaus printed 5000 and we distributed them for pennies above cost.*

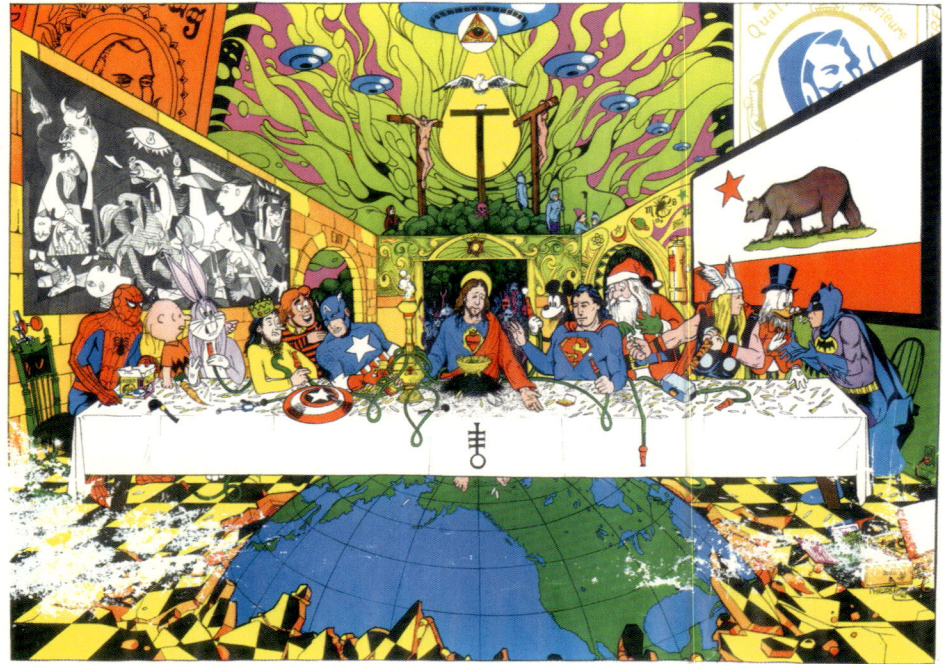

The Next Supper *poster, published by the Straight Theatre, March 1968, 32"x23". This misunderstood poster was widely rejected.*

These rare posters, unfortunately, were printed on acid-rich paper which decomposes at the first sign of moisture and many have suffered untimely ruin. I think this poster is classic art and a reprint would do great today with a wider open market, perhaps with altered or generic characters."

No color TV. How about kids? Whenever Dolly and Jim went out in Poor Truck they took George and Sandy's kids, Tamsen and Conner, with them, and maybe some of the other kids from the farm. Davey Sultzer recalls, "I remember seeing Jimmy and Dolly at the Hook. It was the first time I met Dolly and they had about three or four kids with them. I thought they were hers." Everyone thought the kids were Jim and Dolly's, even Jim's mother thought they were Dolly's, and it made Jim and Dolly want a family of their own.

One week after Jim's 23rd birthday, he and Dolly attended a Halloween party and two days later they were married. Just wanting a simple ceremony, they looked up the Justice of the Peace in the phonebook. His name was Reverend Mahood. They made an arrangement to meet at the Saint George Hotel downtown, and brought Stickman, Sandy and Farm resident Iris Paulson as witnesses. They announced themselves at the front desk and then waited in the lobby. The elevator doors opened and Reverend Mahood came out and looked aghast. He wasn't prepared for hippies in far-out wedding garb. He said, "I won't do it!" and stepped back into the elevator. Stickman pressed him and said "What's your number Reverend? I'm turning you in!" but the elevator doors closed and he was gone. They were on the sidewalk when Stickman said, "It's okay, I know a Boo Hoo!" Jim and Dolly didn't have a clue what a Boo Hoo was, so they followed his car until they passed a little picturebook white church in Soquel. They stopped there and the kindly old pastor was happy to perform the ceremony. Facing uncertainty after depleting their savings they sold Jim's Jester sailboat. Good Friday came, and it was very good; they both got tax refunds. Phillips called Willy Fineburg in Florida to ask for a glassing job. Jim and Dolly immediately packed and drove back to Florida. They left George and Sandy the *King of Hearts* painting in lieu of anything else they could offer. They had let them stay on the farm for months without asking for anything in return.

Six months after Jim and Dolly had driven across country in Poor Truck, they were driving back across the country as man and wife, in a '56 Chevy, which was traded for a drawing. Pretty soon

Dolly was setting up a decent house in Eau Gallie, Florida, and Jimmy was working 12 hours a day, six days a week glassing surfboards at the Fineburg's Oceanside plant.

James Jesus Phillips was born in Melbourne, Florida on December 23, 1968, and came home on Christmas Day. Dad was still glassing surfboards furiously, but he really just wanted to do art. Frustration is the mother of invention sometimes and it was Phillips' pent-up art ability that began expressing itself in a new technique for coloring surfboards. He was looking for new ways to add color to a surfboard and came up with a great new idea: painting directly on the foam, on a shaped deck, before glassing. What sounds retro here in the 21st Century was cutting edge in 1968. Jim ran a series of tests using the ends of blanks, then used various types of paint and glassed them to see the result. Spray paint worked great and resin didn't hurt it. He created some stencil designs to spray through onto the foam, with mass production in mind. Then after the board was laminated and sanded he outlined the design with India Ink. Jim did Superman, Goofy Donald Duck because they were simple and it all needed to be done inexpensively. The boards went to Ron Jon's showroom in Cocoa Beach but sales were weak. They were too different. Ron Jon suggested that Jim make template type tape designs like what was happening in gloss

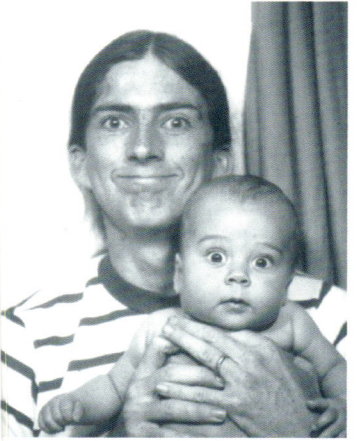

Phillips and Son, 1968.

coats at that time, but Jim lost interest and continued with glassing. That would have been the end of it until the boss' wife Marjane became intrigued with the concept and brought an airbrush to work. She created a great picture of Jesus on a deck using acrylic paint. When the glosser saw it he asked Jim to do template designs like Ron Jon suggested. Jim said no, knowing it would probably mean less pay, but encouraged the glosser to do it, essentially the same thing he did in glossing, except on foam. Those designs sold better and better until they were copied by other shops in town. The boards were shipped around the world and the new method spread to other places. In a few years, surfboard airbrush became the major art form of the medium.

After twelve months in Florida, Phillips got tired of working in the heat and humidity and long hours and he and Dolly decided to take baby Jimbo back to Santa Cruz. They bought a Saab. Phillips had painted some designs on it, but painted them over with two-tone, except the Donald Duck on the door. The Saab had just three cylinders and the back was chickenwired for their three cats. The little Saab could hardly get up the driveway and out, but it pulled a U-Haul trailer and the whole family all the way to California

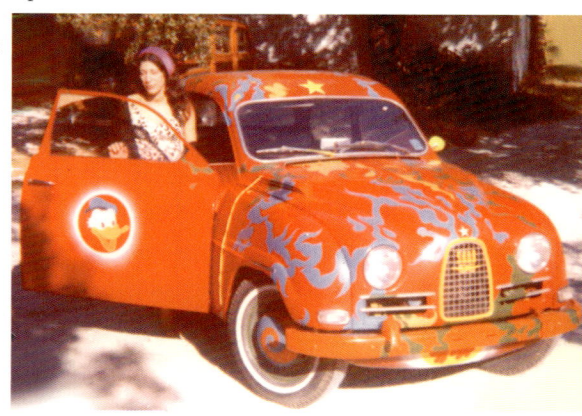

Dolly steps into painted Saab, Eau Gallie, Florida, 1968.

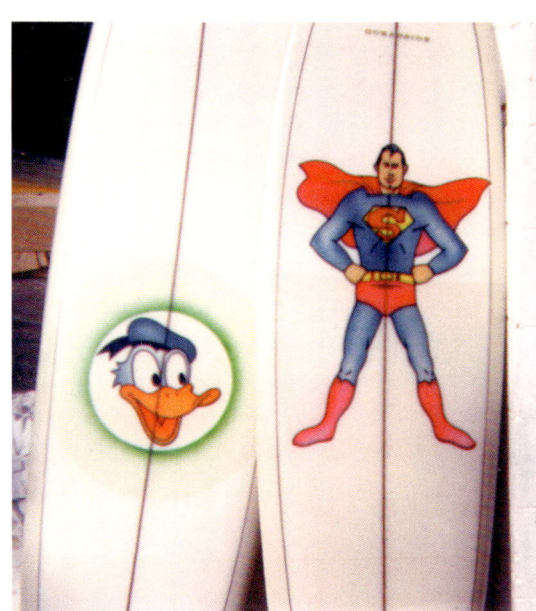

Phillips experimented with sprayed paint on foam at the Oceanside Surf factory in Cocoa, Florida, 1968.

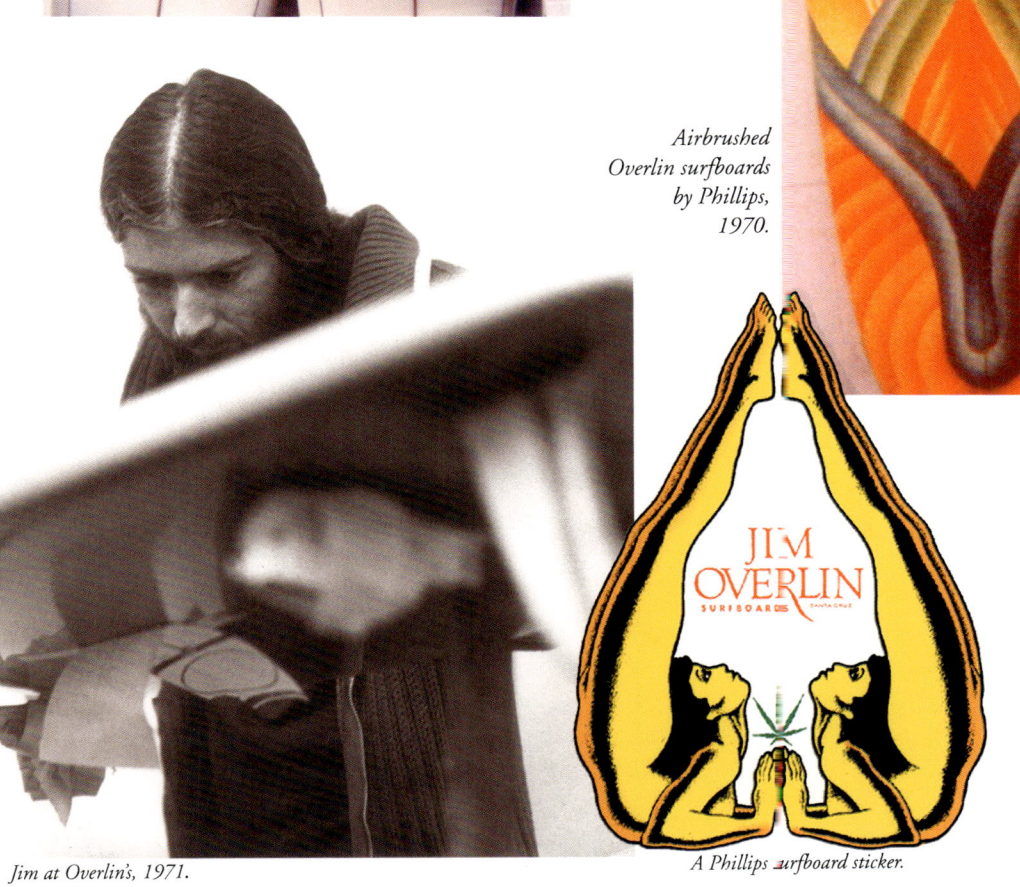

Airbrushed Overlin surfboards by Phillips, 1970.

Jim at Overlin's, 1971.

A Phillips surfboard sticker.

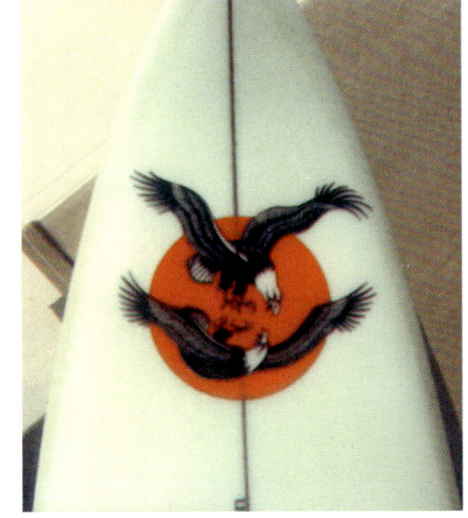

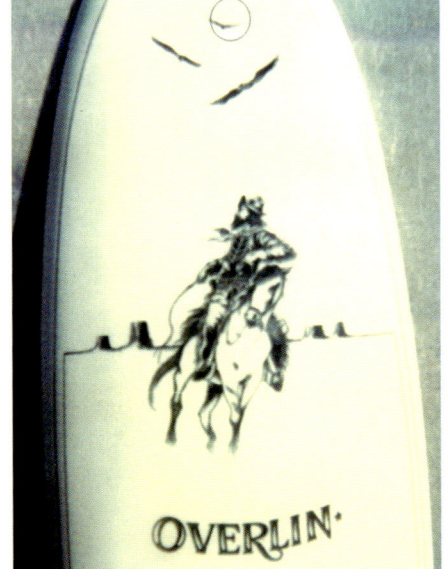

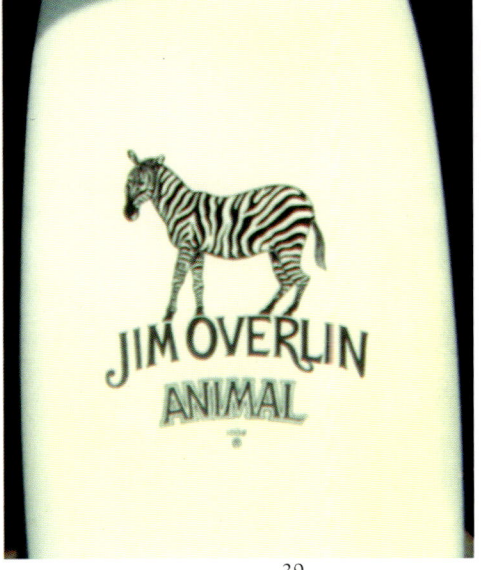

JIM OVERLIN
ANIMAL

OVERLIN·

39

Some of the hundreds of surfboard pen & ink and scratchboard drawings done at the Jim Overlin surfboard shop in Santa Cruz in 1970.

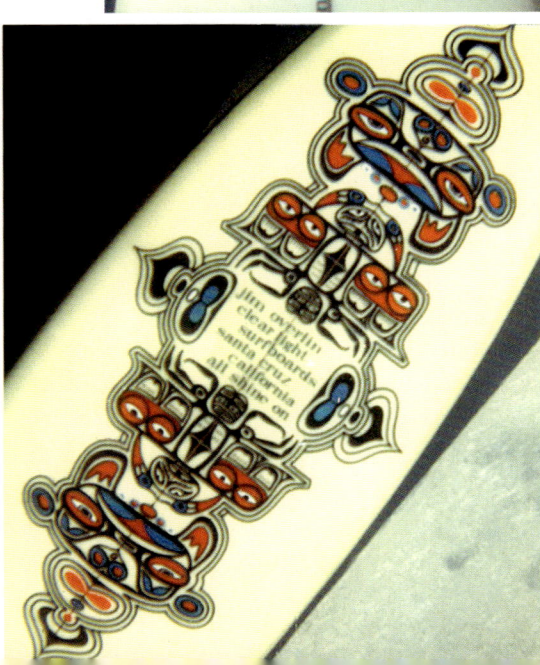

making it through rain and snow and sleet and 100 degree weather in the desert. But they made it.

In the fall of 1969, Phillips was offered a glassing job at Scofield Surfboards in Santa Cruz. Phillips brought the airbrushing techniques from Florida and made a couple of Superman designs on surfboards. One of those boards became a favorite street display for rentals at Otto's Surf Shop, down by Cowells. Otto's was there forever and when Otto died, his obituary photo showed him standing next to the Superman surfboard.

Scofield's surf shops came and went and so did the jobs there.

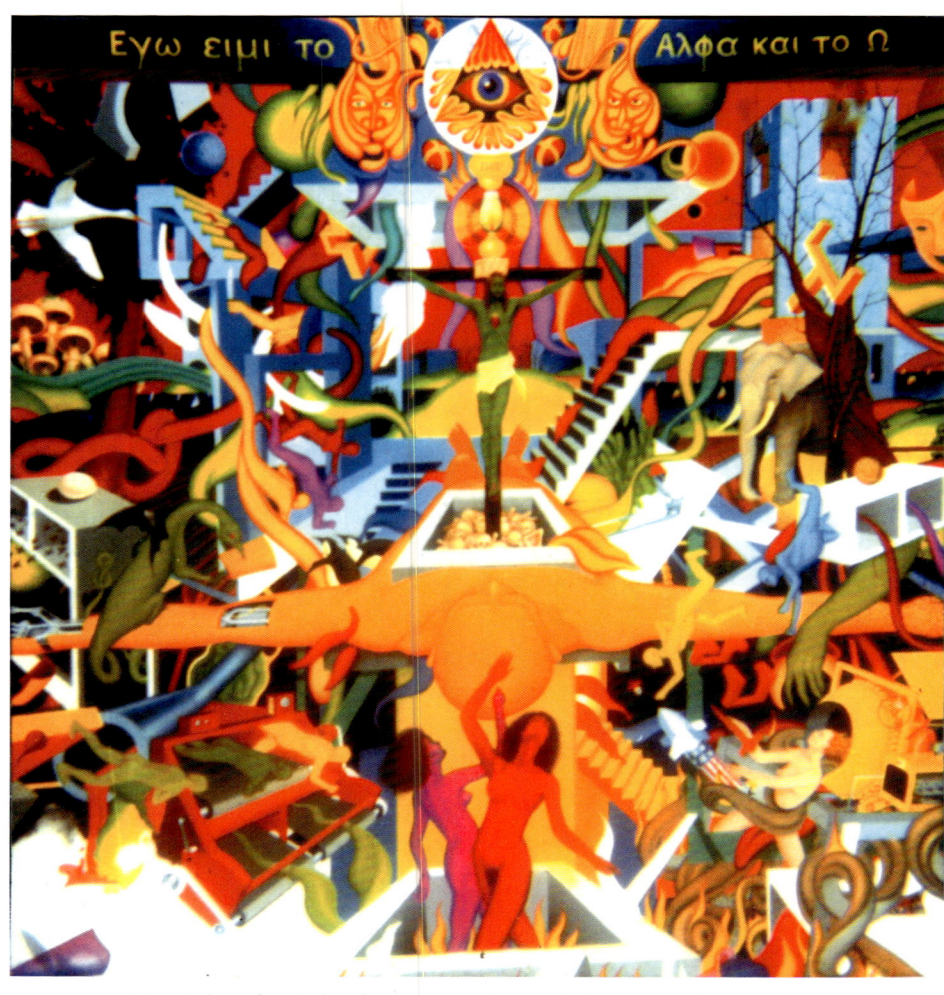

Untitled, unfinished, oil on canvas, 6'x6', 1970. Stolen a few years later.

When this version of Scofield Surfboards closed down, it was bought by Jim Overlin who offered Phillips a job as a glosser. Overlin was an aggressive manufacturer who brought one of the first shaping machines to Santa Cruz and shipped a lot of boards to the Florida market.

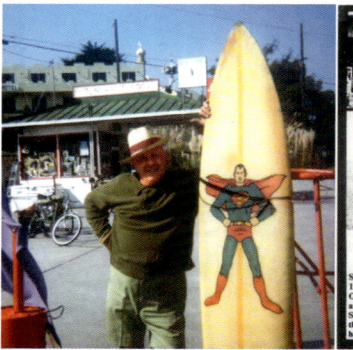

Otto with his favorite rental display.

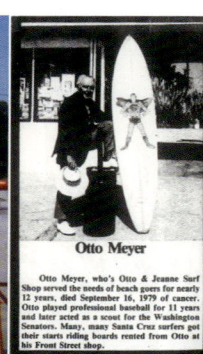

Otto's obituary.

Phillips was doing a lot of "pinlines," the fashion at the time, which required an ink line running along the tape edge. Phillips discovered that a sanded board made a good canvas for India ink, so he brought some Speedball pens and began hand-drawing the Overlin label on the deck with calligraphy. That transformed into drawings, to go under the gloss coats. Beatle portraits were popular and it earned Phillips a dollar extra. He did naked ladies, Mayan birds, Eskimo gods, cowboys, cartoons, all sorts of stuff, mostly pen and ink on the sanded deck, with a little colored resin. Then Jim talked his way into higher paying designs and began a series of boards using scratchboard technique. He scratched the ink with a trim knife blade just like scratchboard. It was a new medium, it looked like scrimshaw. Soon Jim was allowed to ink full-time, without having to do the gloss coats at all. He was set up in a little room with three sets of stands, a stool and classical music.

It was now the fall of 1969, and the decade was coming to an end. It had been a long decade for the world and a long decade

for Jim Phillips, but Phillips was doing better. By the fall of '69 he was set up in a nice little house with a nice little family and a nice little job in a nice little Santa Cruz that is a little hard to imagine now. There was no traffic jam up to Freedom Boulevard every day, and you could buy an entire house for much less than a 21st Century down payment.

In the summer of 1969, Phillips' grandmother convinced Jim and Dolly to take a look at a house next to the one his mother and stepfather were buying for a rental. The house next door was for sale for a whopping six thousanddollars. Phillips took a tour with the owner and he and Dolly liked the funky little place, and liked the large backyard because they wanted to garden. They bought the house in the Live Oak area of Santa Cruz with a small nest egg from Florida for a down payment. Jimmy Phillips ended a wandering decade as a homeowner, with one stipulation: His grandmother demanded that he sign a contract to secure a loan, and when she whipped it out, the contract stated that, "I, Jim Phillips, agree not to paint the house psychedelic."

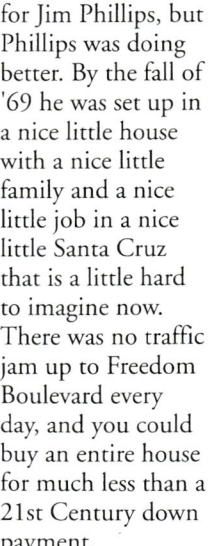

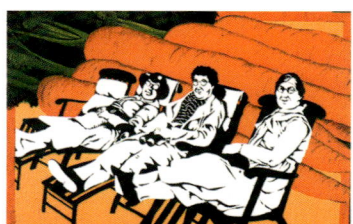

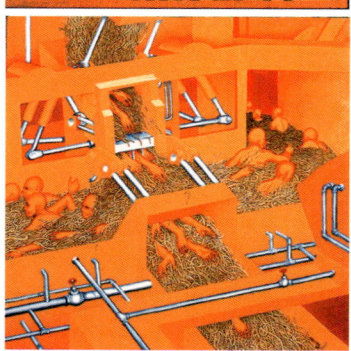

Top: Carrot Ladies, 18"x12", mixed media on canvas, 1969. Bottom: The Spaghetti Factory, 14"x14", oil on wood panel, 1969.

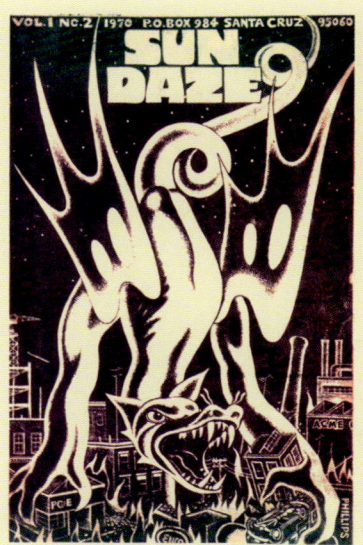

Sun Daze, newspaper cover, 1970. This alternative paper was the forerunner of the Good Times and others.

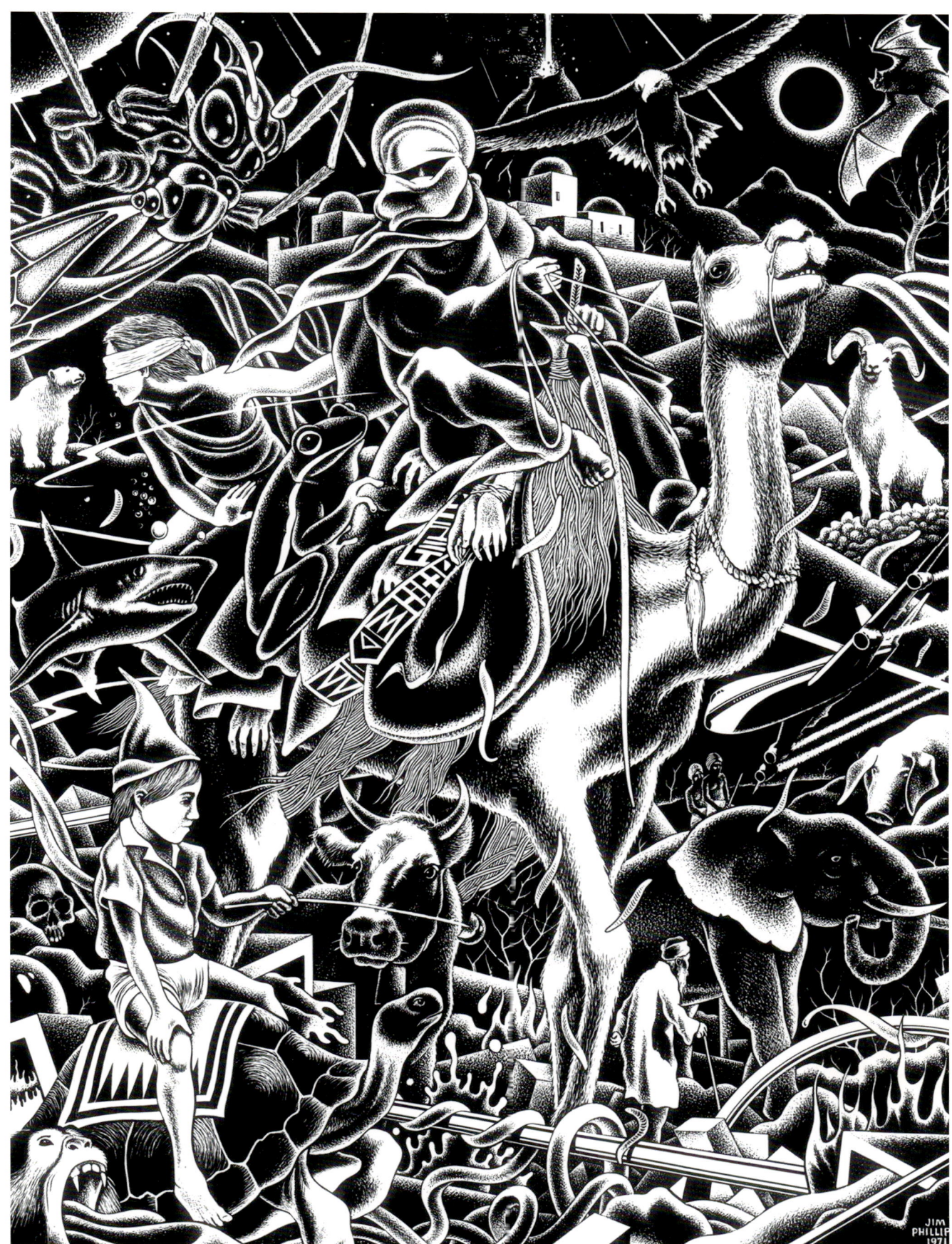

The Camel, *scratchboard, 17"x13", 1971.*

CHAPTER THREE

ROLLING: 1970 to 1977

Roots of Skateboarding

Ever see *The Graduate*? That 1967 movie starred Dustin Hoffman as Benjamin Braddock, a 20 year old Berkeley graduate unsure what to do with himself. At his graduation party, Braddock is cornered by a family friend named Mr. McGuire who offers some friendly advice. "I just want to say one word to you... just one word. Plastics. There is a great future in plastics." Well Benjamin Braddock isn't so sure about that. But Braddock wasn't a surfer or a skateboarder. Frank Nasworthy was. And so was Jim Phillips.

In 1970, Frank Nasworthy visited a friend at a plastics factory in Purcellville, Virginia and saw a line of urethane wheels made for Roller Sports, a chain of roller rinks. When Nasworthy discovered the wheels would fit on his Hobie skateboard, he developed a

41

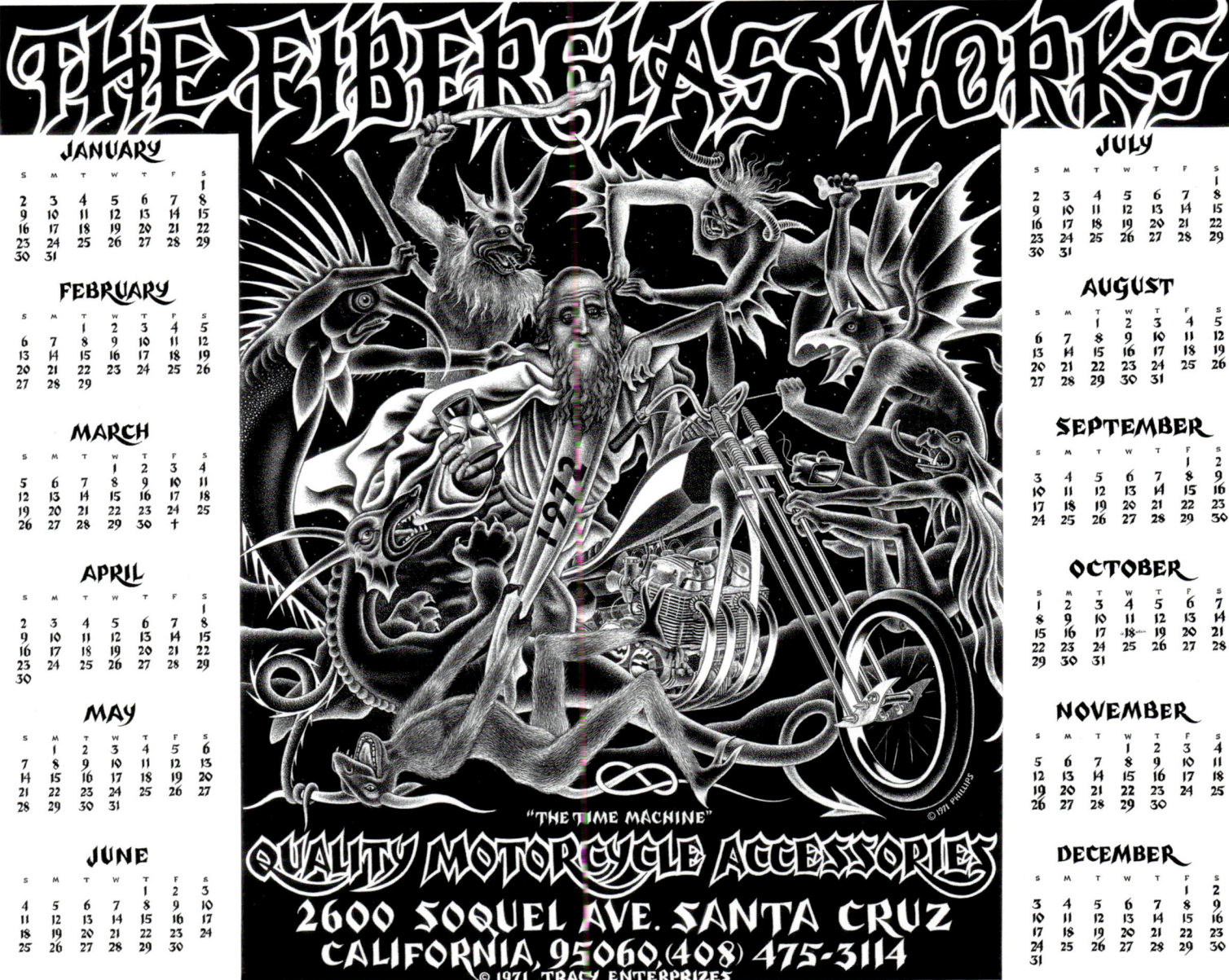

Temptation of St. Anthony, *Fiberglas Works 1972 calendar, scratchboard 22"x28", 1971.*

skateboard wheel made from urethane that would have made Mr. McGuire proud. Nasworthy marketed his new urethane rollers as Cadillac Wheels, and they were a sensation. Where clay and metal wheels stopped dead on kidney stones, it took a decent-sized rock to stop a Cadillac. They rolled faster and lasted longer, and now all of those pools and drainage pipes and park benches and Terra Terrible that skateboarders had been damaging themselves on for years were now Terra Radical. To make the next 30 years of skateboard history a short story, the loose bearings of Cadillac Wheels begat sealed bearings and Road Riders and they begat about three dozen different kinds of wheels and five dozen kinds of trucks and millions of skateboard decks. Skaters rode pools, then skate parks until skate parks went bust because of liability. Then skate took to street and eventually made the X Games.

Where was Jim Phillips during all of this? He was rolling with it. Like all surf-stoked California kids, Jim Phillips had been a bun-boarder during the 50s and a sidewalk surfer during the 60s, and when urethane hit in the early 70s, Phillips got swept into the revolution like Forrest Gump.

Phillips came into the urethane revolution from an oblique

angle, on the back of a Harley Chopper. In 1971, Phillips was working as an artist and glosser at Overlin's Shop on Swift Street. He was content with his work, doing scratchboard art on surfboards, with that work inspiring other larger pieces, in his happy home in Live Oak.

During the late 60s, an O'Neill's Surf Shop glasser named Tracy Nelson began making fiberglass molds for motorcycle tanks as a sideline. This was during a time when the Hell's Angels were at their peak, and on a Saturday night there would be dozens of Harley choppers lined up along Beach Street, in front of the Boardwalk. This was a time when the dirt bike world was a United Nations of CZ, Montessa, Husqvarna, Puch, Bultaco and other exotic labels from all over the world. This was a time when guys would field-strip Honda 750s and take them mountain-climbing at Hollister Hills Motorcycle Park. They were primitive motorcycle times compared to now, but the motorcycle market was Heavy Metal, primed for some *Fantastic Plastic*.

Tracy's products were successful enough that he gave notice at the Surf Shop and opened his own shop in a small shed nearby and dubbed it The Fiberglas Works. Tracy's forceful

42

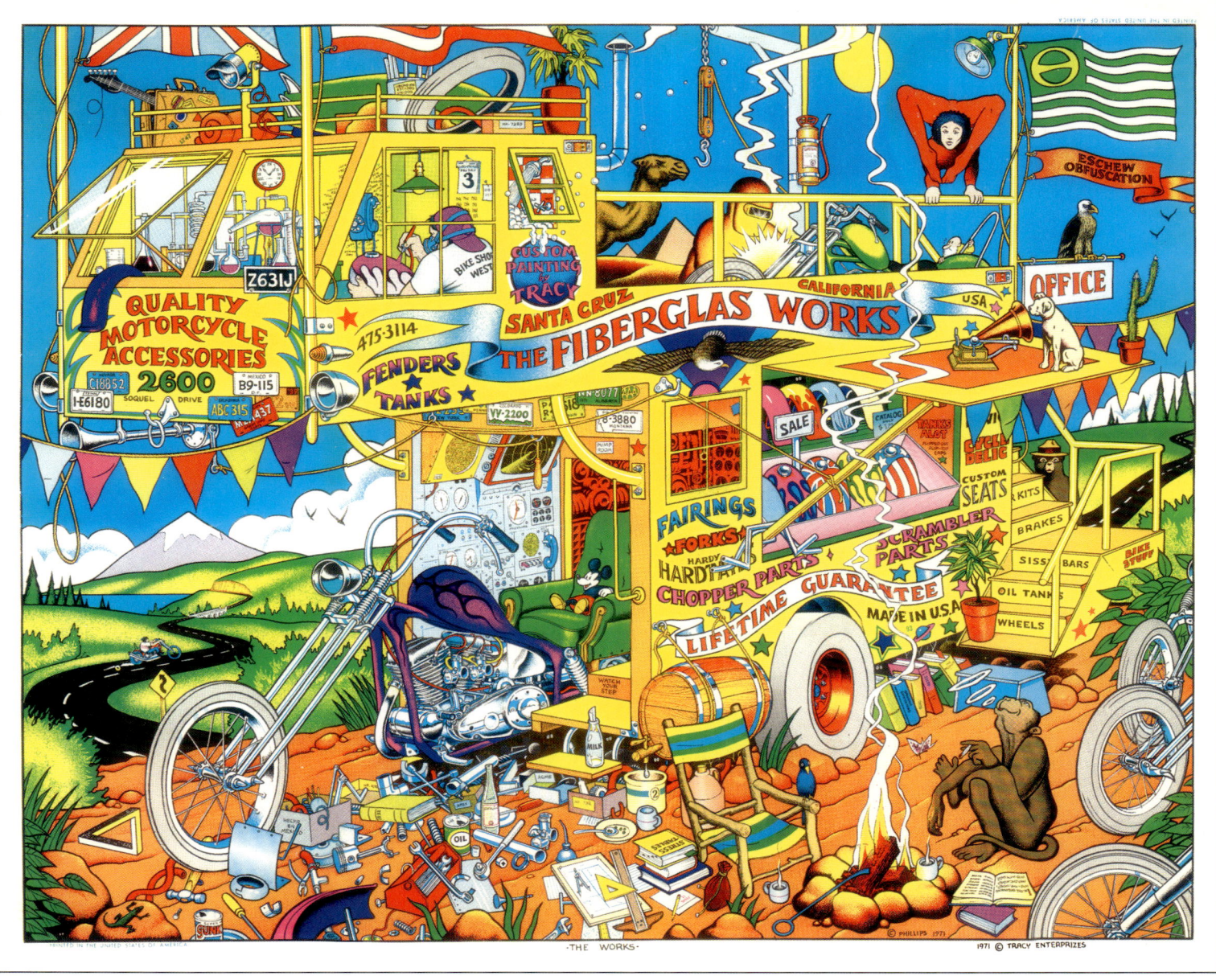

The Works, *pen & ink, blue line mechanical separations, 23"x29", 1971. Printed at Cal Litho, S.F.*

sales skills and marketing genius were becoming evident, as others in the industry began to take notice. Tracy Nelson was way ahead of his time, making gas tanks and futuristic cowlings and wind screens from fiberglass, and plastics for the motorcycle market that weren't available elsewhere.

Around 1971 Tracy located to a much roomier shop. It was formerly an old neon sign shop near 7th Avenue, with enough warehouse space to hire a dozen or so workers, glassers, sanders, custom painters, office workers, and salesmen. Tracy realized that graphics would enhance his advertising and turned to Jim Phillips. Tracy called one day and ordered a 22"x28" full color poster. Tracy had seen Jim's *Medicine Show* poster and he asked for a poster that recycled the motif, a traveling medicine wagon, into a motorcycle parts wagon. Phillips went right to work on the pen and ink drawing. Tracy gave free rein on the content, so Jim added lots of sight gags and humorous details. In one window you could see Tracy airbrushing a chopper tank.

As soon as *The Fiberglas Works* poster was finished, Tracy ordered another without skipping a beat. It was the Fiberglas Works 1972 calendar which seemed to herald great things to come. Tracy let Jim decide what to draw, so he created a takeoff on Albrecht Durer's *Temptation of St. Anthony,* which showed St. Anthony calmly riding a chopper, besieged by demonic monsters.

Soon after the posters were printed, Tracy offered Phillips a full-time studio artist job at a new factory which he had just moved into, a spacious plant on Ingalls Street. Tracy walked into the Overlin surfboard shop where Jim was doing pen and ink drawings on surfboard decks, and asked "Hey Jimmy, do you want to make more money in my new art department a few blocks away?" Jim was fairly content doing surfboard art, but the raise in pay was irresistible. Business was skyrocketing and Tracy needed an illustrator to draw ads and brochures. Tracy asked Jim to work for the new art department as a full-time illustrator. It offered a step-up in pay, and the studio art job was a relief after so many years of resin odors. Tracy had a great sense of humor and the motorcycle market was used to wildness, so it was fertile ground for art. It was to be a turning point for Jim, to leave the surfboard industry after ten years, and become a commercial artist in advertising. But it turned out to be a godsend, a full time art job in a real ad agency. Geoff McCormack, an old surfing friend, was the advertising director there, and Phillips was given pens and a drawing table and asked to crank out motorcycle illustrations. Geoff wrote ad copy, ordered typesetting and did layout. Jim learned ad skills from Geoff, like the tricky methods of type specifying which were vital in that day, and photo masking and scaling. They worked well together.

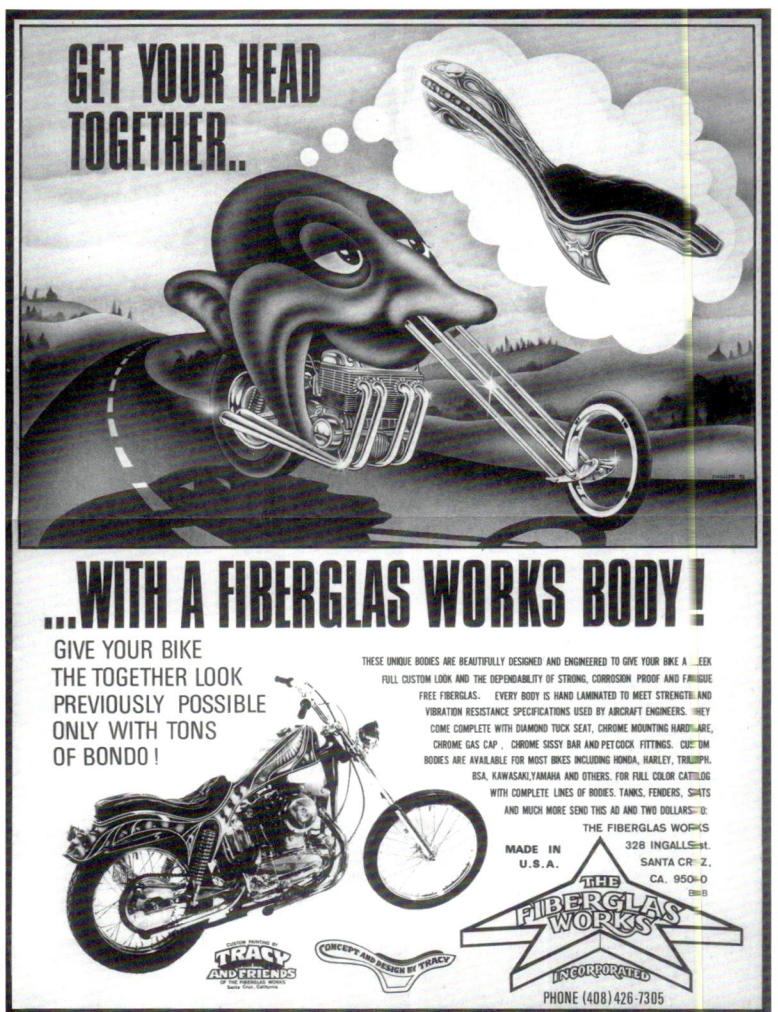

One of many full page ads for motorcycle magazines.

The Fiberglas Works business really began to erupt, and as his business began to take off, Tracy Nelson was featured in a national Bank of America TV commercial as a successful young entrepreneur who was benefitting from a B of A loan package. It was their attempt at reaching out to the youth culture in a time of dissension including the torching of the B of A bank branch in Isla Vista, near Santa Barbara.

Tracy opened Bike Shop West, a custom chopper showroom on Water Street, in the building which now houses the Staff of Life health-food store. It was "trick" as Tracy would say, with lots of chrome and metal-flaked accessories showcased with radically stretched and chopped hogs. Phillips designed the outdoor sign logo, and it became another sign of Tracy's evolving empire.

One of Jim's first assignments was to create a new logo. Tracy asked for a star, squashed and with an edge as if it were at an angle. A red star with the words "The Fiberglas Works" emblazoned across it was made into stickers for product identity, but they wound up on every VW woody and any other kind of surf buggy in the county. During the early 70s, a Tracy's Fiberglas Works star on the back window of a Chevy van or on the rear fender of a Harley Chopper was the equivalent of a 21st Century Pack Your Trash Sticker or Screaming Blue Hand. Tracy's was everywhere in town and Phillips got his first taste of ubiquity.

Eventually McCormack went on to other things and was replaced by another of Jim's old surfing buddies, Jim Raun-Byberg. Byberg had an enlarged funny-bone and he added another dimension to the production and made it a relaxed and fun place to work. Byberg was adept at utilizing some of Phillips' off-the-wall creations that no one quite knew what to do with. He recalled, "Jimmy made this monstrous mega-machine cycle drawing. He was about halfway through, when he suddenly got up and left. I located him out in the parking lot sitting in Rosie, his truck, and asked him what was going on. He said he was frustrated because he had this big drawing but didn't know what to do with it. Then I remembered this dry mailer I was laying out and got an idea." Byberg changed the ad copy to "Moonlight Jungle Cruise sale," and showed Jim where his drawing would go. At first people scratched their heads about it, but the reaction was the wildness of the image attracted the dealers' attention and resulted in more sales. That sort of influence added momentum to Jim's creativity, and was one of the ways that helped expand Tracy's advertising effectiveness.

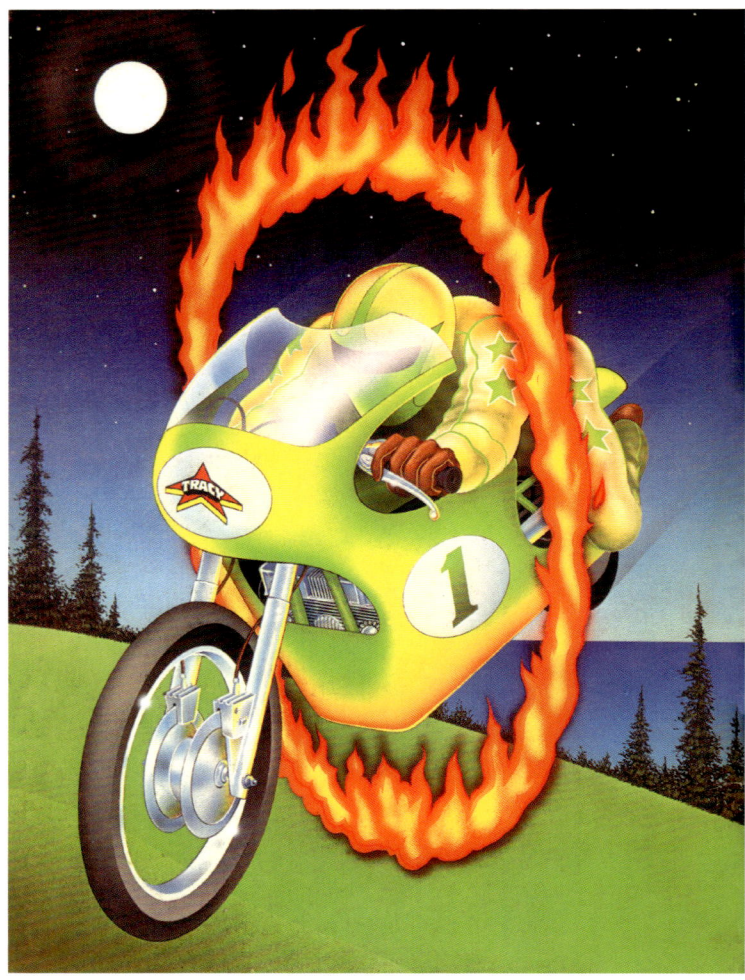

Ring of Fire, *Tracy catalog back cover, airbrush, 1972.*

Tracy's Fiberglas Works

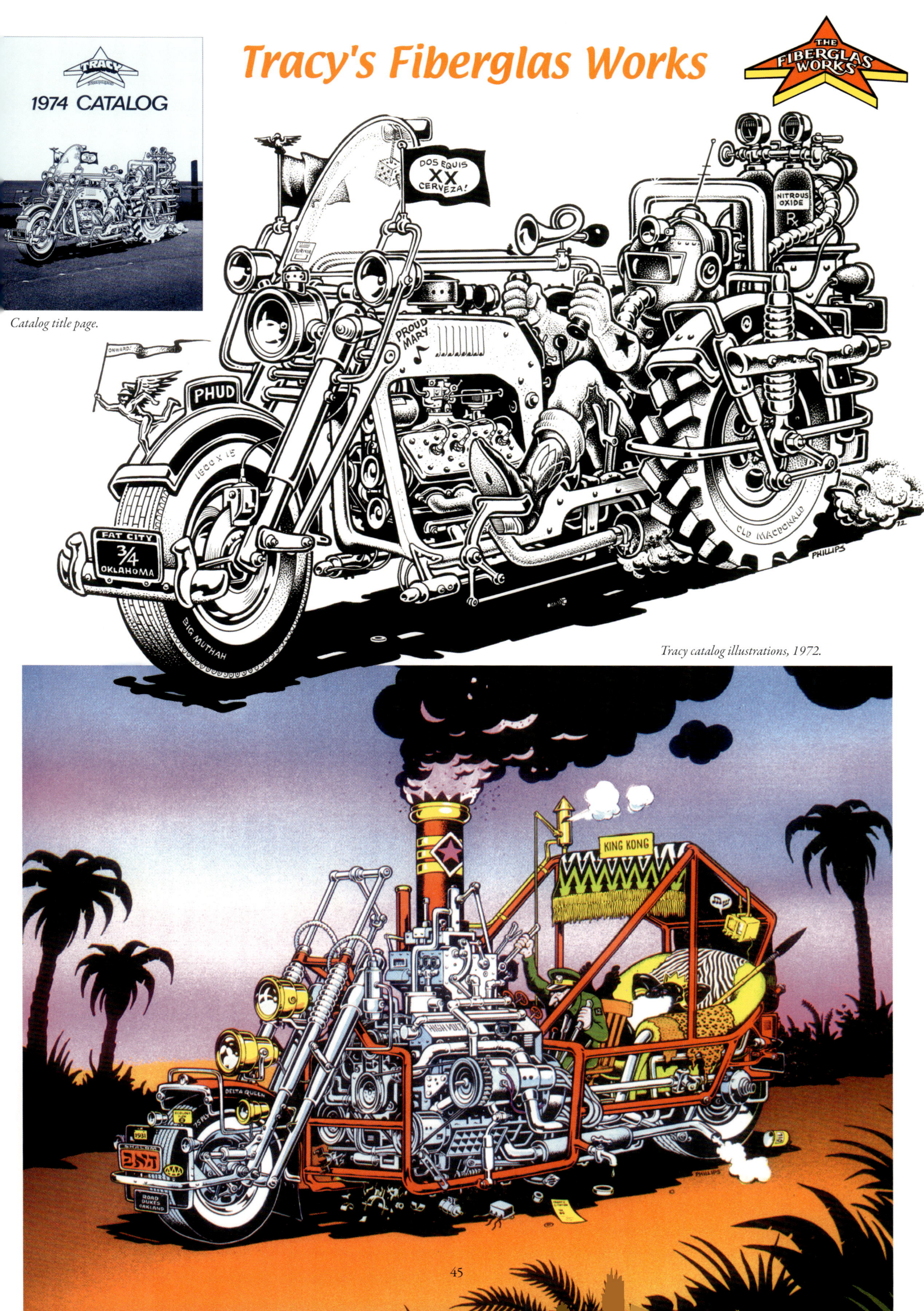

Catalog title page.

Tracy catalog illustrations, 1972.

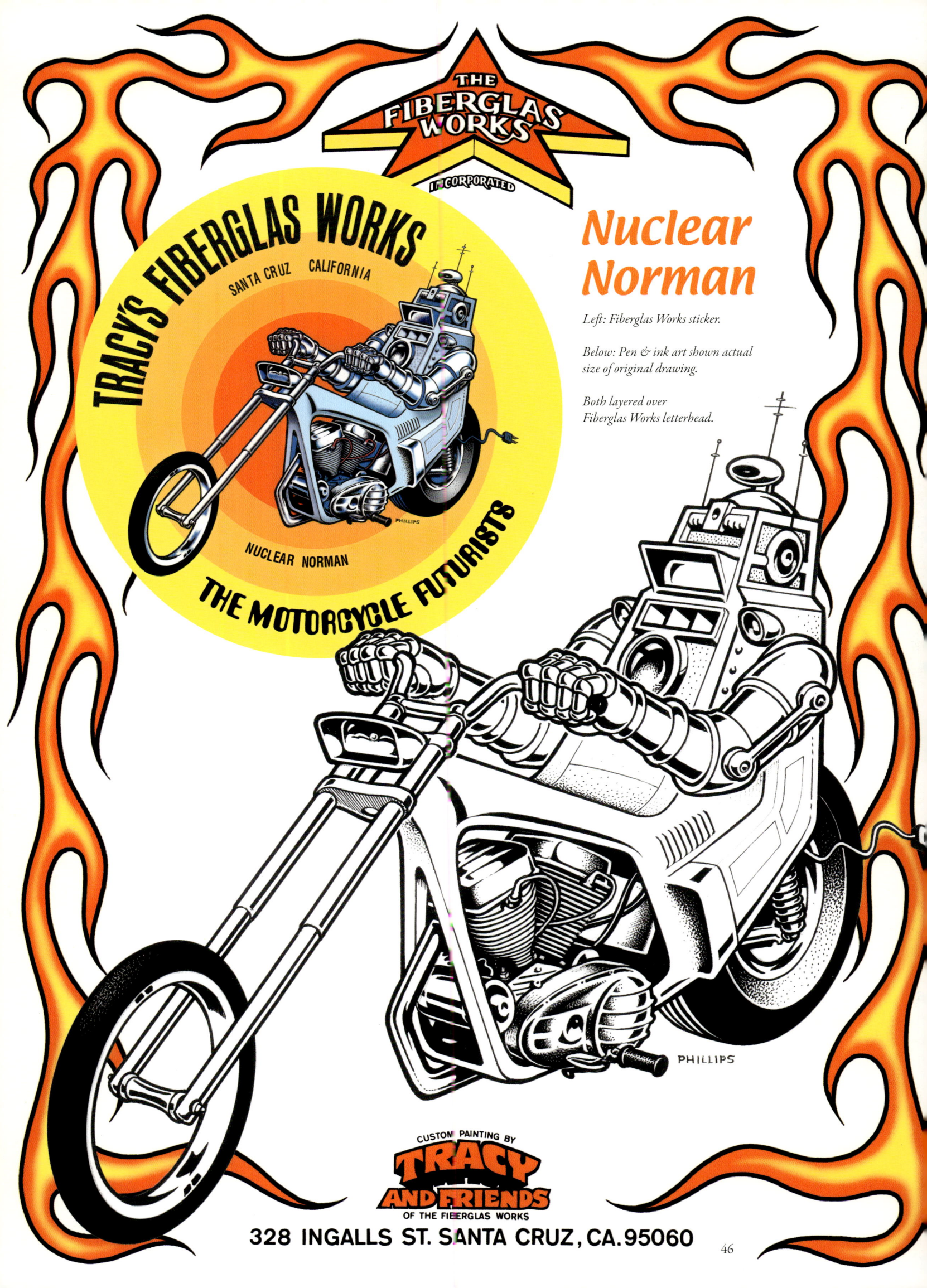

Nuclear Norman

Left: Fiberglas Works sticker.

Below: Pen & ink art shown actual size of original drawing.

Both layered over Fiberglas Works letterhead.

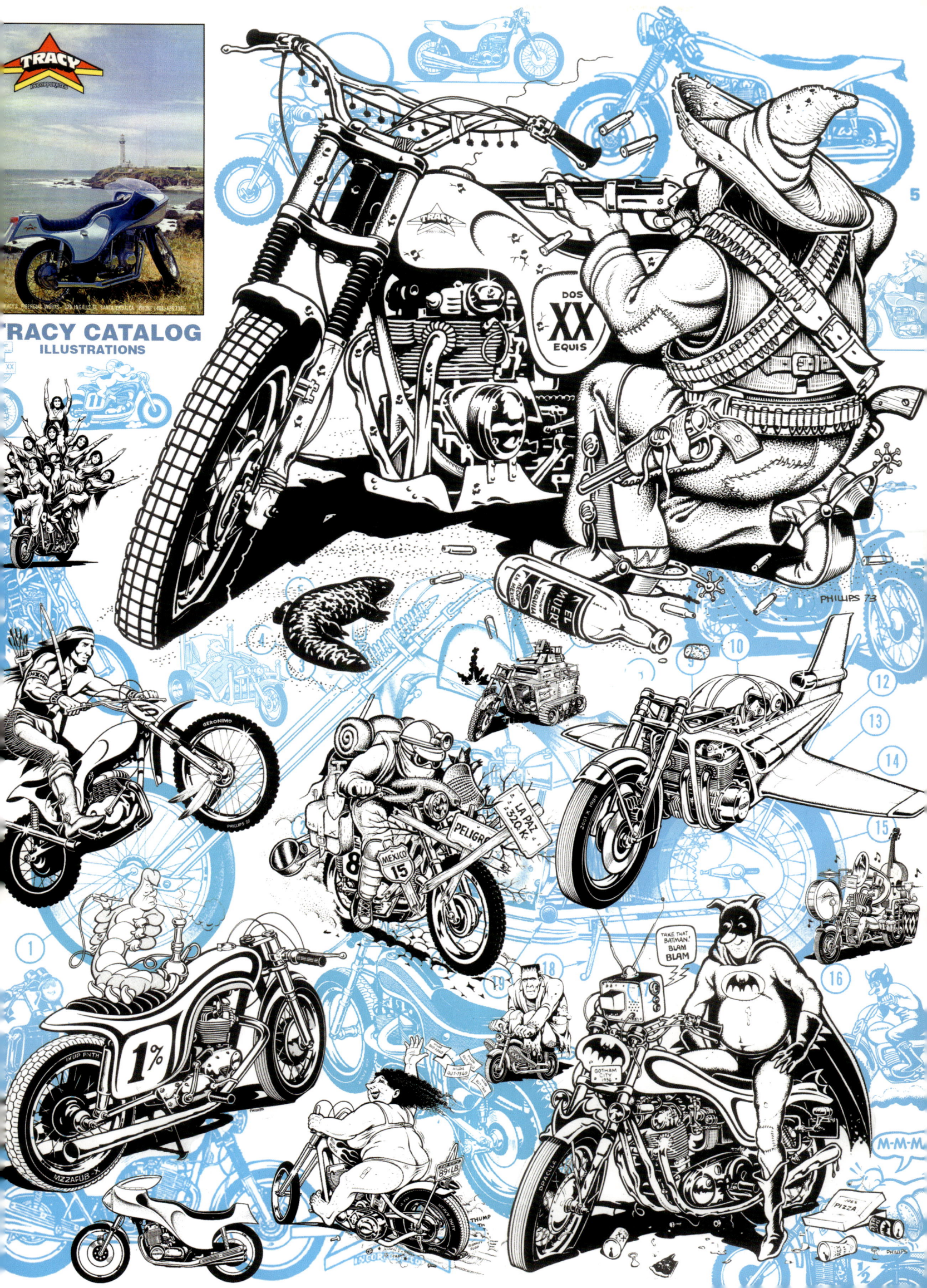

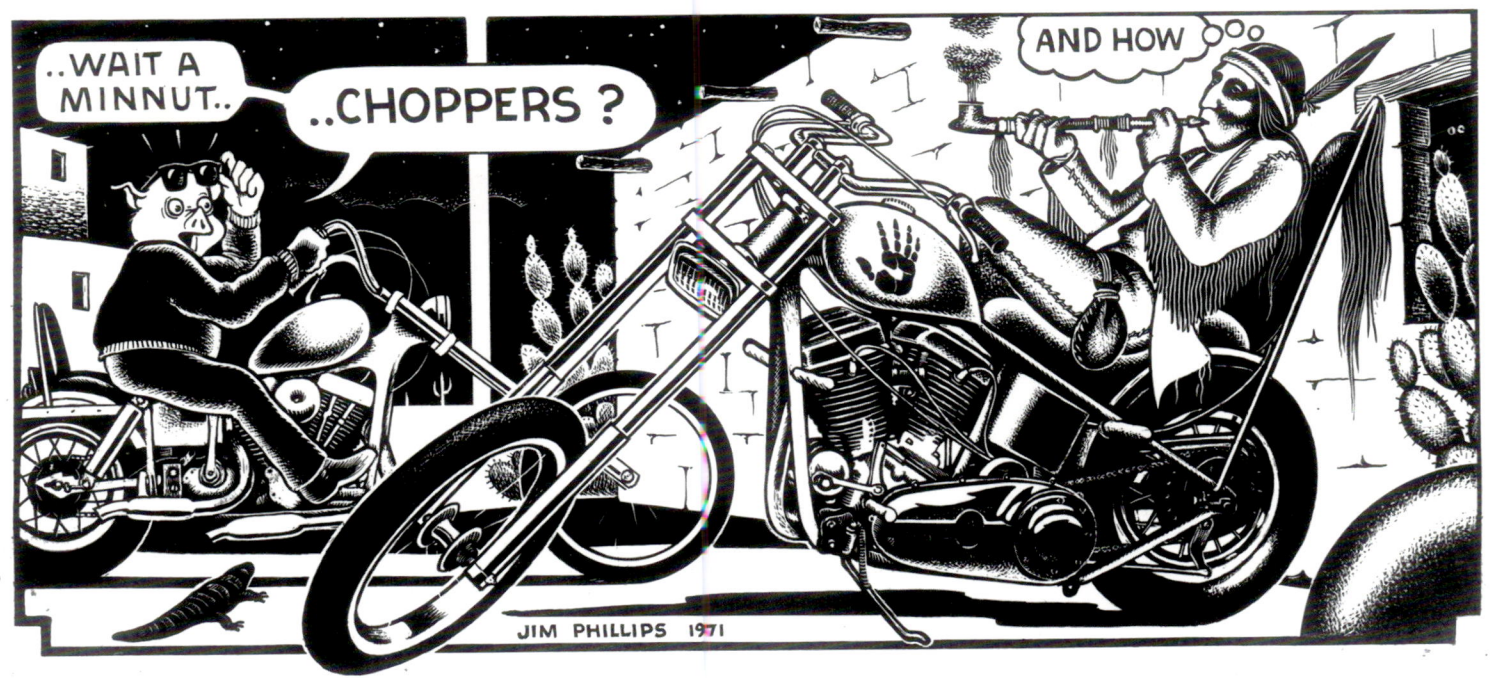

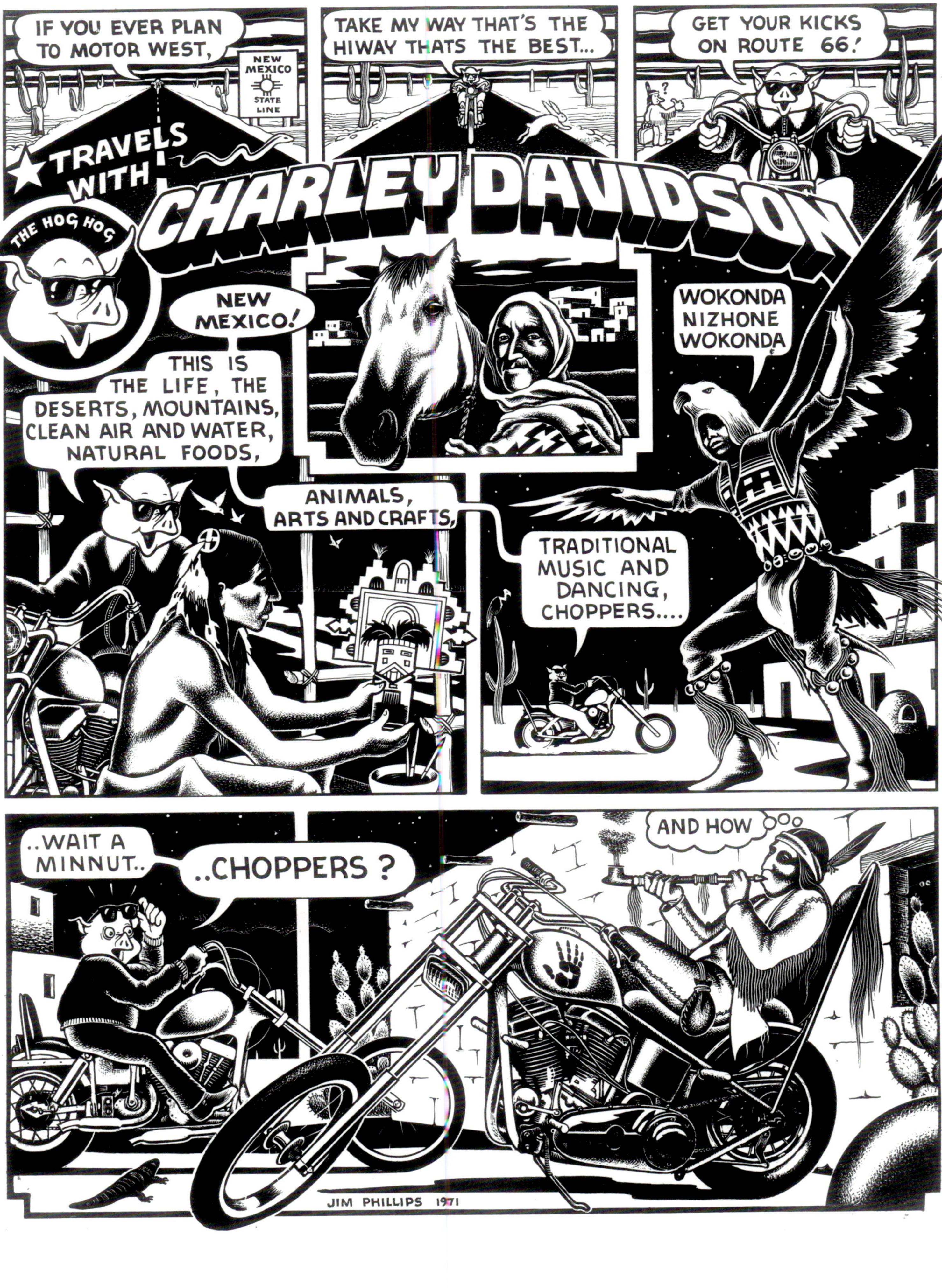

Phillips was drawing nonstop, trying to keep up with the incredible number of products, the demand and the sales. He worked on illustrations for ads and brochures, but most of the time he created motorcycle cartoons for the Tracy parts catalog. Tracy wanted art on every page, and that was Jim's job. He was fairly free to draw what he wanted, so he drew every imaginable kind of motorcycle, and every sight-gag he could think of.

Tracy's Fiberglas Works was a business phenomenon that flamed out as fast as it started. Sometime in 1973, Tracy's beautiful wife Randy was killed in a horrible car crash on Highway 17. Tracy was devastated, and in his grief the business foundered. "Tracy lost it," Phillips said. "He lost his business and he lost everything." Byberg adds, "When Tracy's went down the tubes, all the money was gone. It was so devastating to the B of A loan officer that he suffered a fatal heart attack!" Randy's death was also a personal blow for Jim, who knew Randy from Live Oak Elementary, and as one of the kids that hung out down at the Sunny Cove.

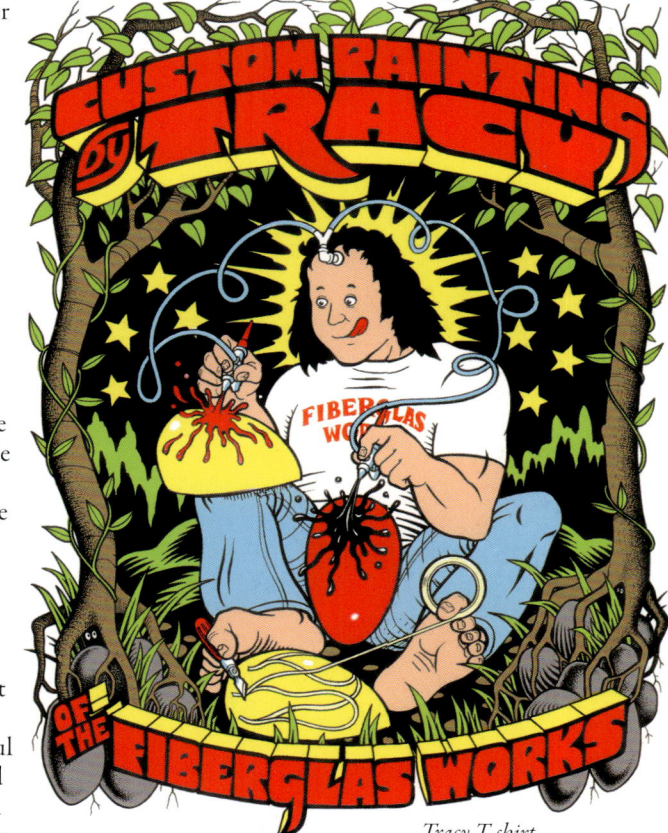

Tracy T-shirt

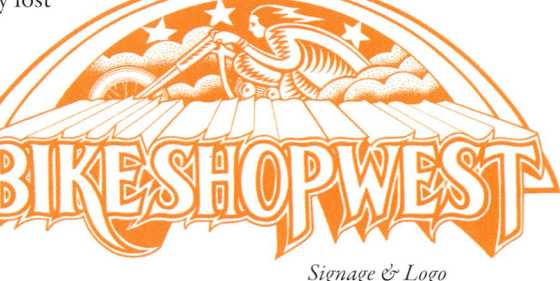

Signage & Logo

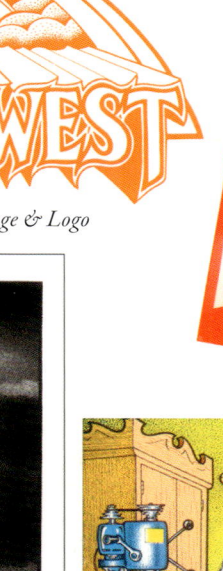

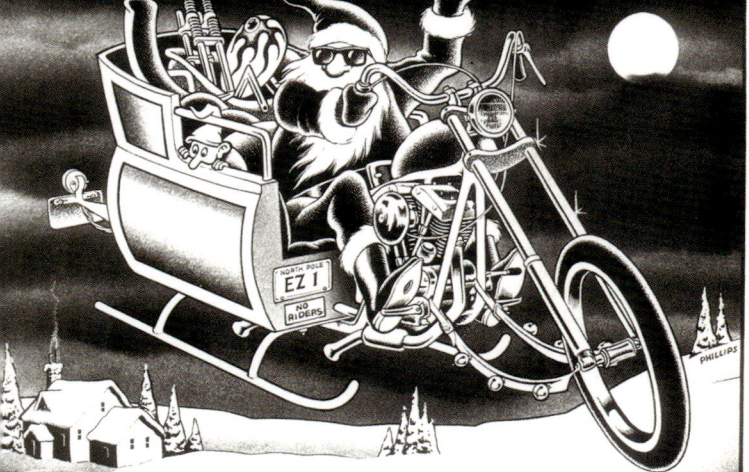

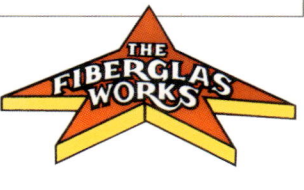

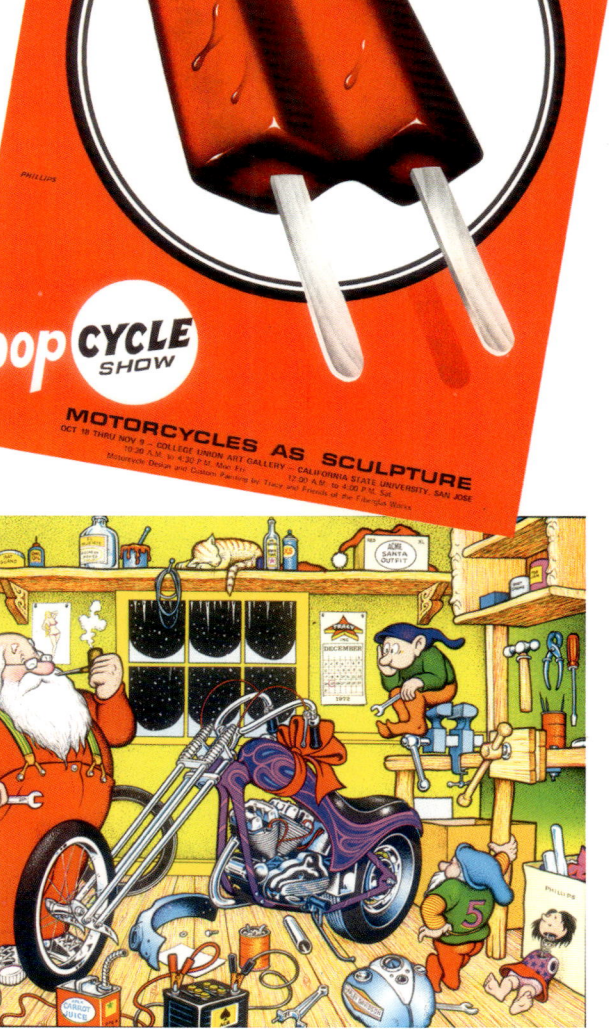

Top right: Catalog page.
Middle right: Poster for Pop Cycle Show at San Jose State College, 1972.
Bottom: Tracy Christmas cards, 1971 & 1972.

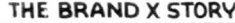

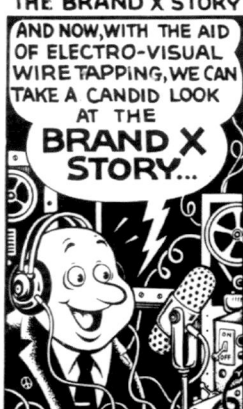
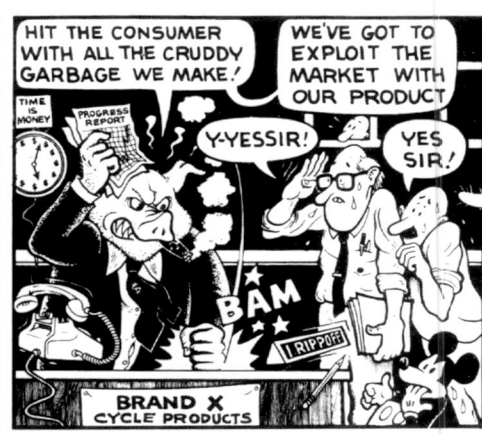
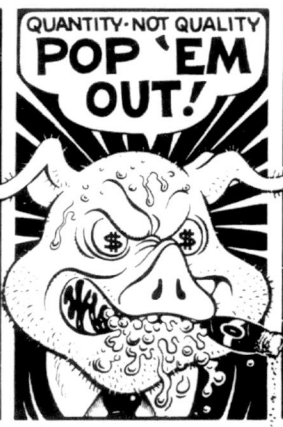
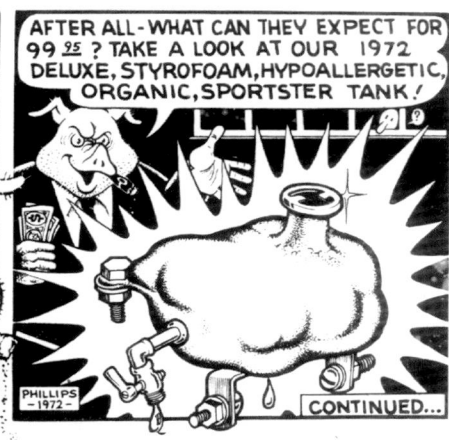

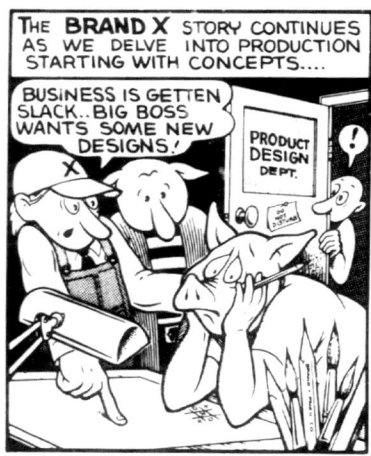
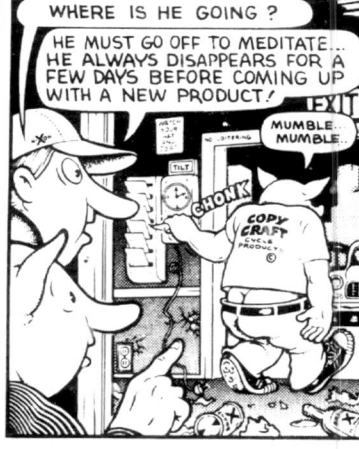
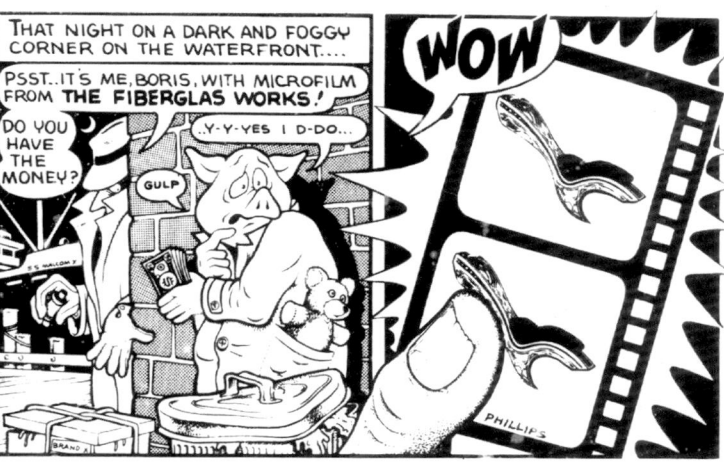

THE BRAND X STORY

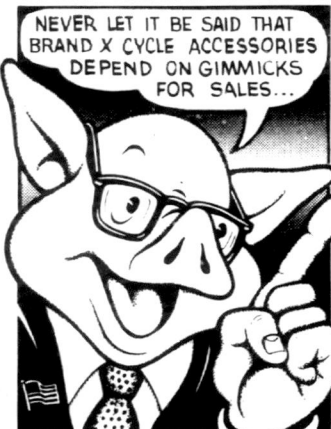
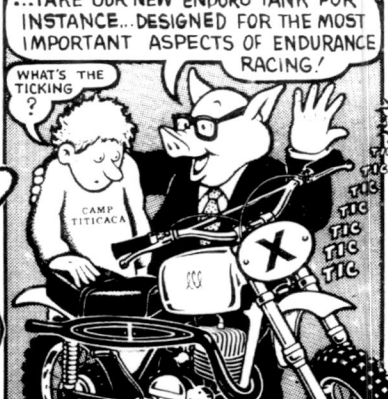
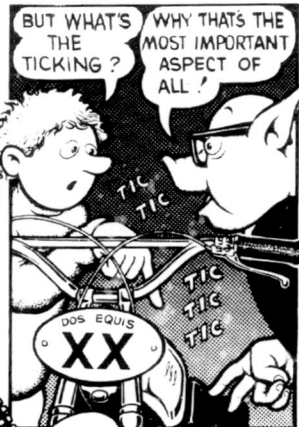
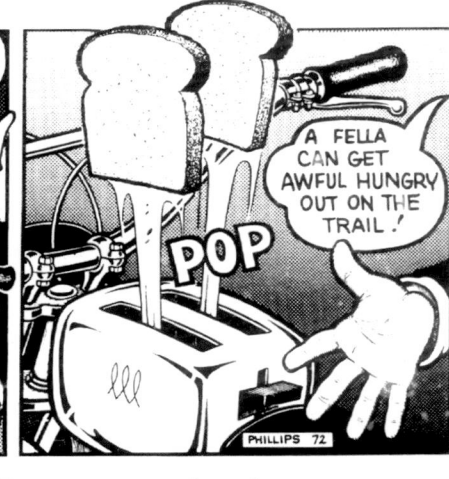

Brand X comic strips appeared in each issue of Tracy's Dealer News *direct mailers.*

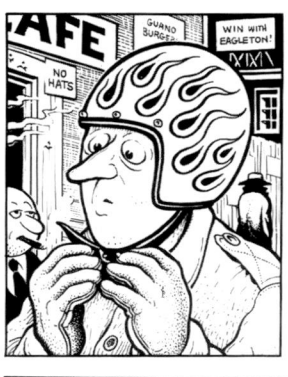
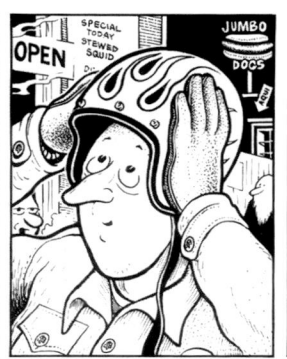
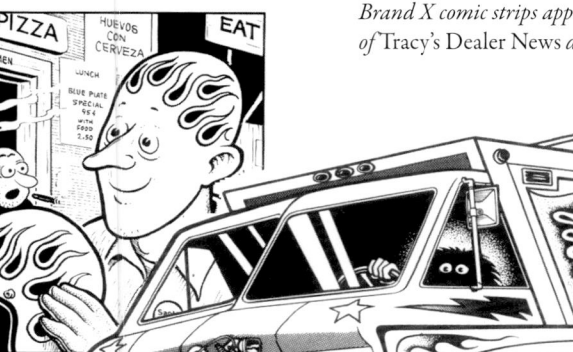

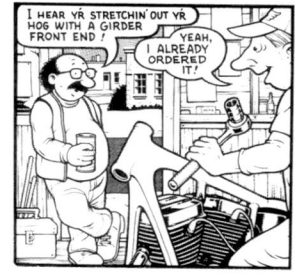
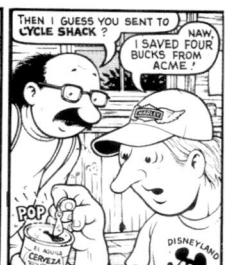
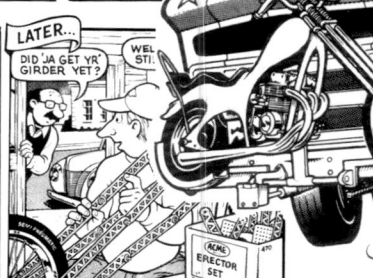
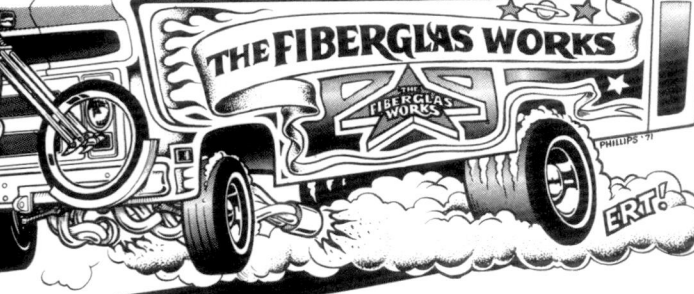

Tracy painted his real motor home to match Jim's cartoon version.

50

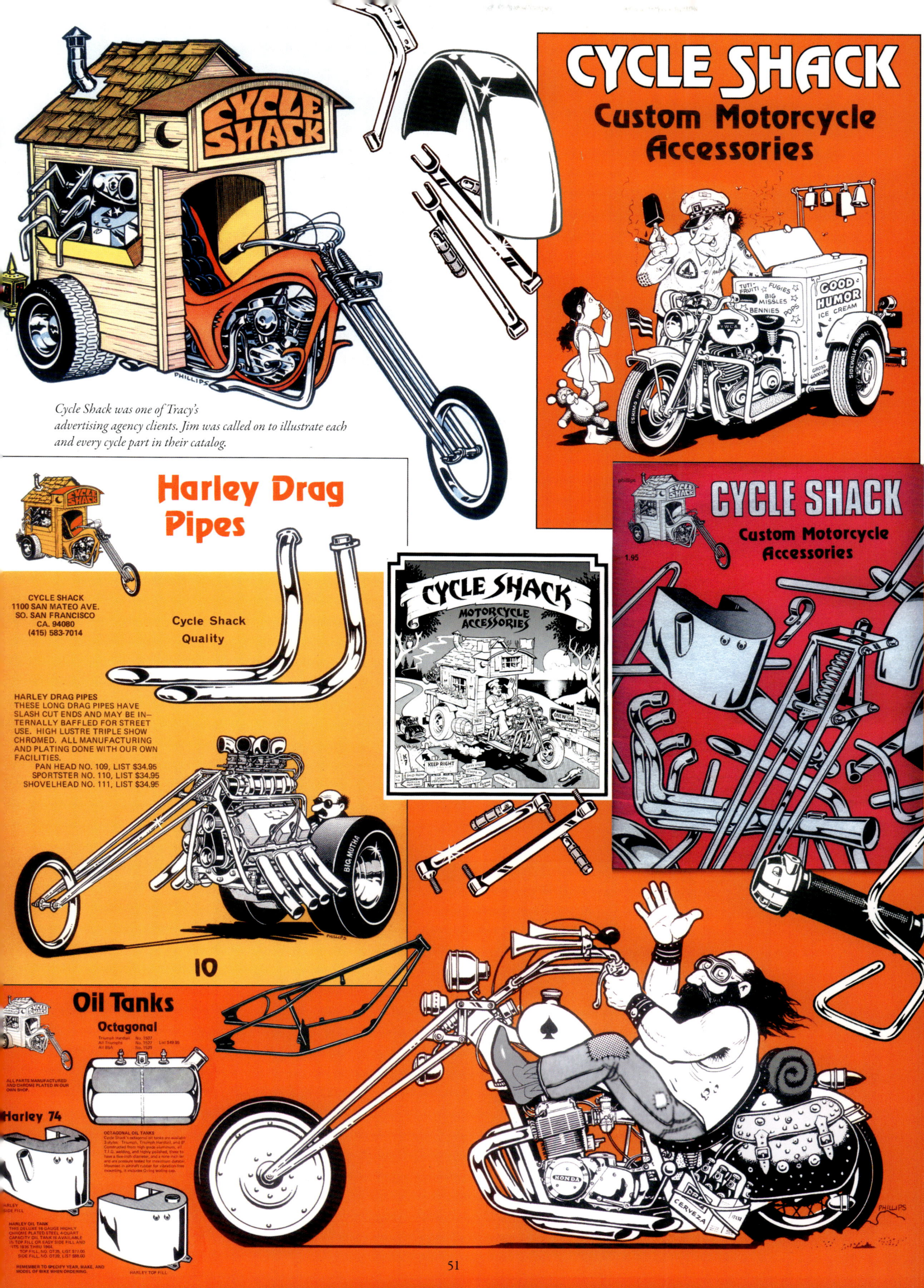

CYCLE SHACK
Custom Motorcycle Accessories

Cycle Shack was one of Tracy's advertising agency clients. Jim was called on to illustrate each and every cycle part in their catalog.

Harley Drag Pipes

CYCLE SHACK
1100 SAN MATEO AVE.
SO. SAN FRANCISCO
CA. 94080
(415) 583-7014

Cycle Shack Quality

HARLEY DRAG PIPES
THESE LONG DRAG PIPES HAVE SLASH CUT ENDS AND MAY BE IN—TERNALLY BAFFLED FOR STREET USE. HIGH LUSTRE TRIPLE SHOW CHROMED. ALL MANUFACTURING AND PLATING DONE WITH OUR OWN FACILITIES.
  PAN HEAD NO. 109, LIST $34.95
  SPORTSTER NO. 110, LIST $34.95
  SHOVELHEAD NO. 111, LIST $34.95

CYCLE SHACK
MOTORCYCLE ACCESSORIES

CYCLE SHACK
Custom Motorcycle Accessories

10

Oil Tanks
Octagonal

Triumph Hardtail	No. 1537	
All Triumphs	No. 1532	List $49.95
All BSA	No. 1526	

ALL PARTS MANUFACTURED AND CHROME PLATED IN OUR OWN SHOP.

Harley 74

OCTAGONAL OIL TANKS
Cycle Shack's octagonal oil tanks are available 3 styles. Triumph, Triumph Hardtail, and 8" Constructed from high grade aluminum. All T.I.G. welding, and highly polished, these to have a low-inch diameter, and a nine inch length are produced for maximum clarity. Mounted in aircraft rubber for vibration free mounting, it includes O-ring sealing cap.

HARLEY OIL TANK
THIS DELUXE 16 GAUGE HIGHLY CHROME PLATED STEEL 4 QUART CAPACITY OIL TANK IS AVAILABLE IN TOP FILL OR EASY SIDE FILL AND FITS 1936 THRU 1964.
  TOP FILL, NO. OT35, LIST $11.00
  SIDE FILL, NO. OT39, LIST $98.40

REMEMBER TO SPECIFY YEAR, MAKE, AND MODEL OF BIKE WHEN ORDERING.

HARLEY SIDE FILL

HARLEY TOP FILL

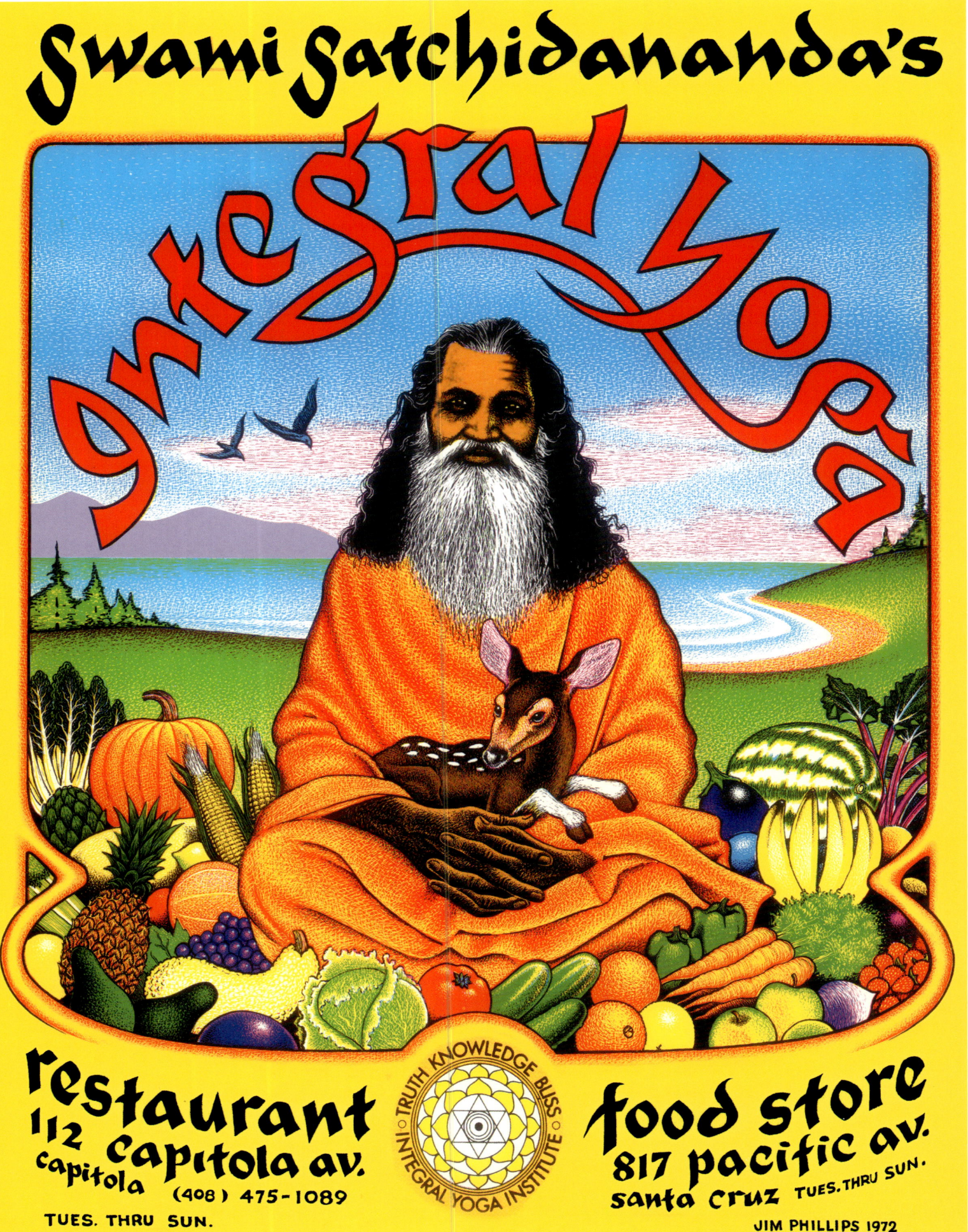

Swami Satchidananda's food store poster, scratchboard, 13"x10", 1972. Printers at Cal Litho accommodated Jim's experiment providing him with "blue lines"
on scratchboard panels, thus enabling the artist to render each color with scratchboard technique, printed at Cal Litho, S.F.
Original art: Collection of Larry Williams.

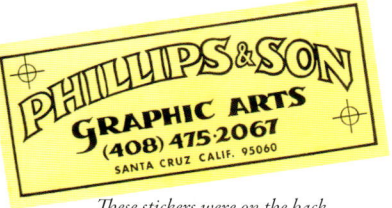

These virulent end times for The Fiberglas Works signalled for Phillips to start his own art business. He had plenty of studio experience, skills in ad work and contacts with typesetters and photostat houses, so he decided to go free-lance.

Jimmy took his work home with him, and stayed there. The little house in Live Oak was quiet and had enough space for a small studio: He drew on a Hamilton Oak professional drafting table given to him by Steve Scofield, with the legs cut down for comfort. As a reminder of his blessings, a framed copy of Hienrick Hoffman's classic painting of Jesus praying at Gethsemane hung over the table. Phillips' blessings were simple, but comfortable. He had a nice home and a nice wife and a nice son and a decent little free-lance business. He burned the Midnight Ink, listening to classical and rock music, enjoying Santa Cruz in the early 70s, a very different world from now: Jim never worked without music. Family, warmth and music.

Phillips has always been a better artist than a businessman but he did the best he could to promote himself. He began with a simple business card, "Jim Phillips and Son Graphic Arts," with a cartoon of himself at the drawing table, working. That was Jim's art imitating Jim's life, because work was what he did, as much as he could. He explained that it was easy for him to become a workaholic then. He'd often work into the night, putting more work into a job than he was getting paid for, but enjoying the work. Work generated more work, and word of mouth became his way of advertising.

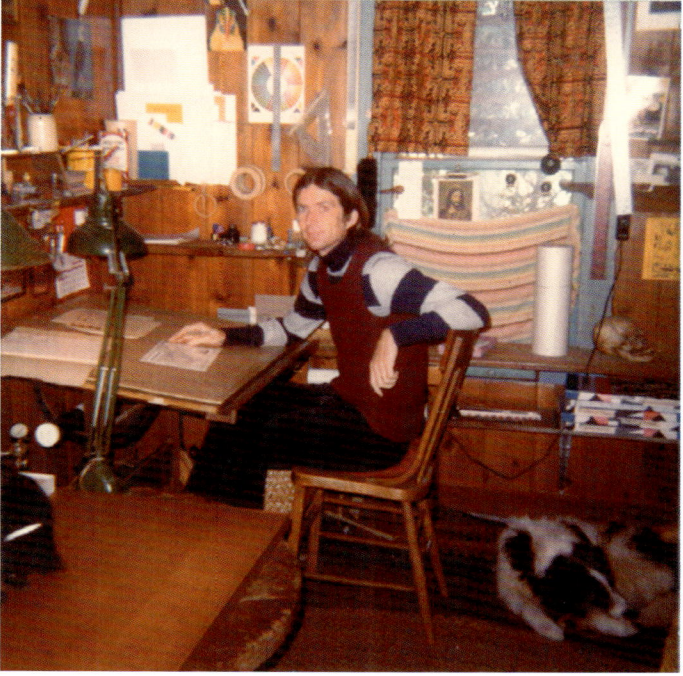

Phillips at the drawing table in his home studio. Prune the dog was brought home as a puppy from the shop clean-up kid at Scofield's surf shop.

local community activist Gary Patton involved to help. We also called Jimmy to see if he could create a poster to advertise the surf movies. He jumped right on the project and stayed up all night to complete the poster on a very short deadline. He never charged us a penny for his work. Because the poster was so cool, it helped draw a lot of people to see the surf movies, and we were able to raise the money we needed for legal fees. Jimmy was instrumental in helping us stop the building of the convention center which would have been a scenic and ecological disaster."

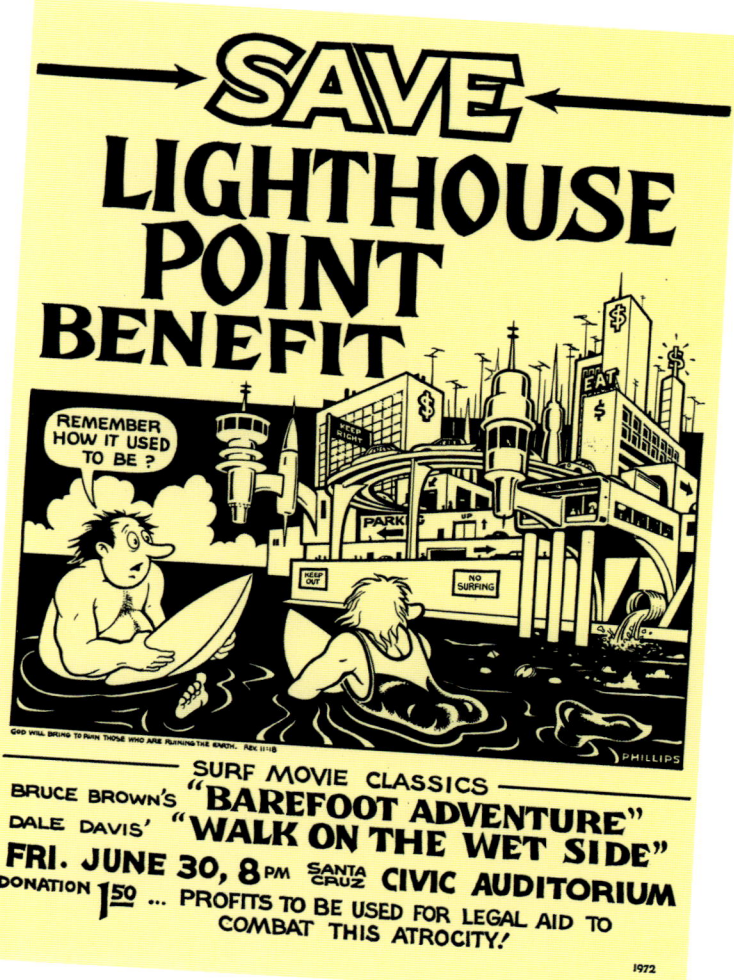

Things were slow at first. As Andy Warhol said, "An artist is someone who produces things that people don't need, but for some reason, think it would be good to have." Phillips was producing something that people really didn't need, but he was also charging money for it. There were times when he had trouble making the mortgage to his grandmother but they eventually caught up, paid her off with interest and had her over once a week for cards before her passing

These stickers were on the back of Phillips' art boards during the 70s.

KENNY STOCKS: *"Not only is Jimmy Phillips a gifted artist, he's also a sensitive and caring person who has always been there to help his friends. He's a rare person in that he used his artistic gifts to help whenever he could, becoming involved in projects to help the environment and social causes, especially surfing.*
In the early 1970's, an investment group tried to purchase Lighthouse Field at Steamers Lane with the intent of building a convention center. Building on this coastal property would prevent people from surfing there, and would destroy the natural beauty of this pristine spot. Mitch Lachman and I showed rare surf movies donated by Bruce Brown, at the Santa Cruz Community Center to raise money for the legal fees to fight the construction. We got

1972 benefit poster

53

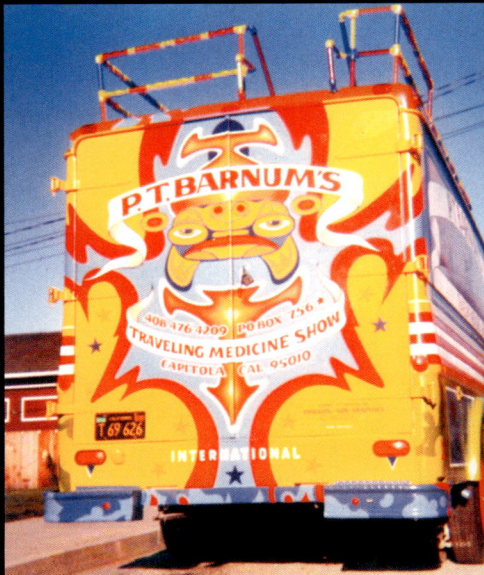

The work came from wherever. Phillips had long experience painting cars, and in the 70s, the streets of Santa Cruz were lined with funky Volkswagens and pickup trucks, and not the bourgeois buggies of the 21st Century.

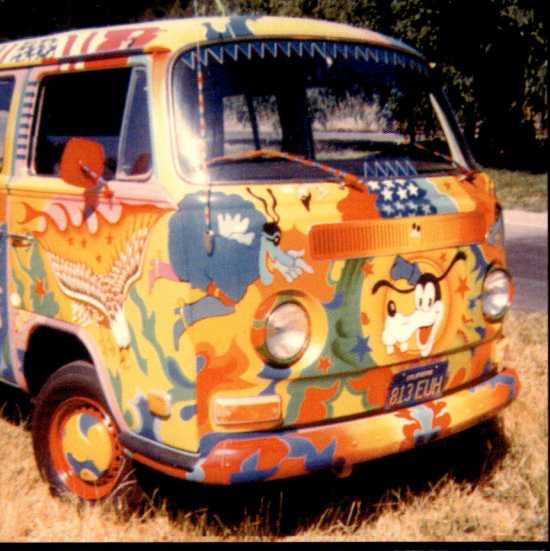

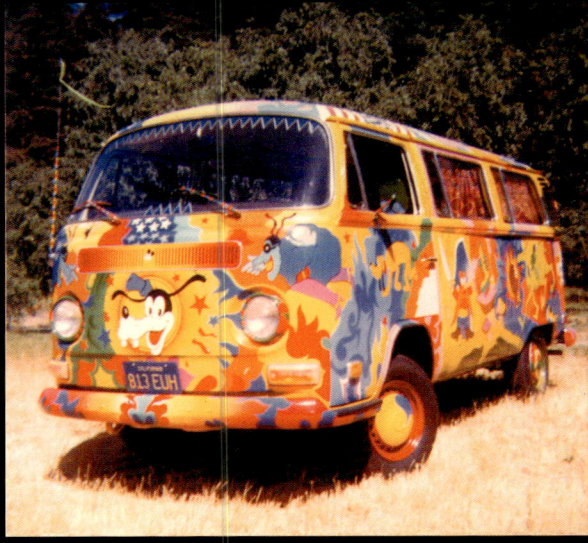

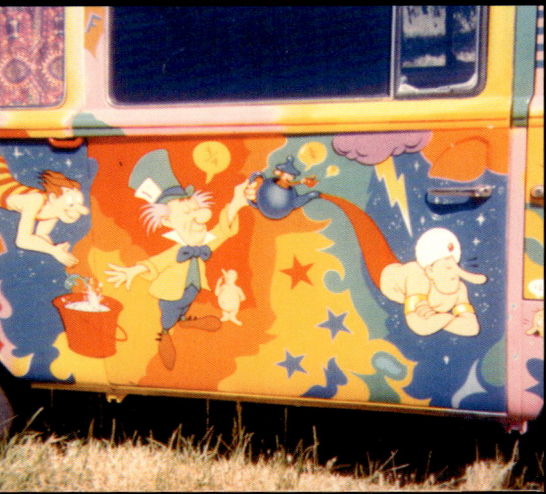

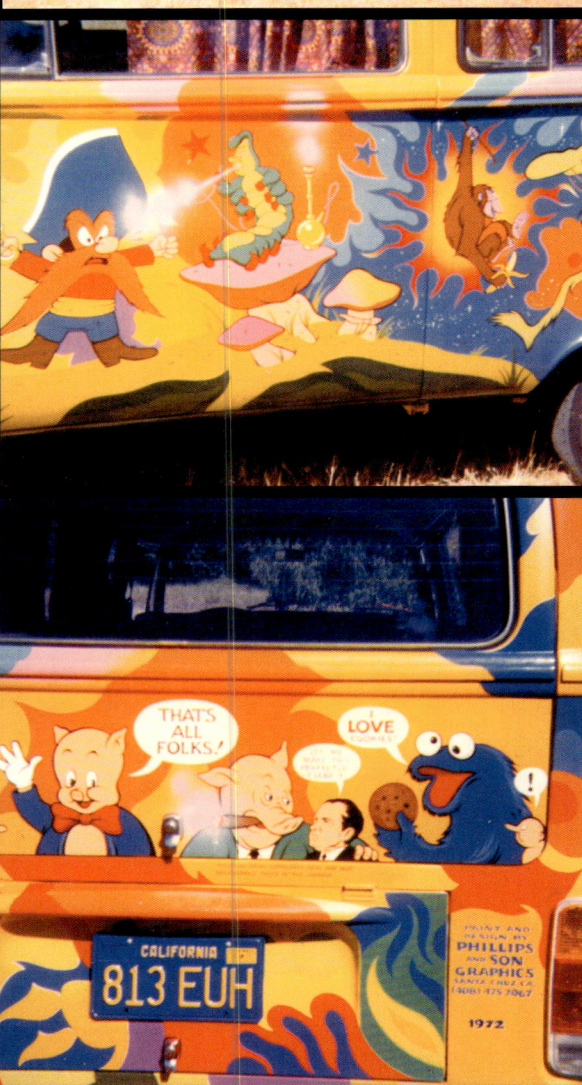

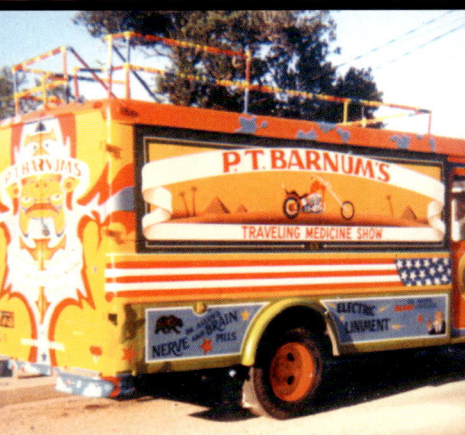

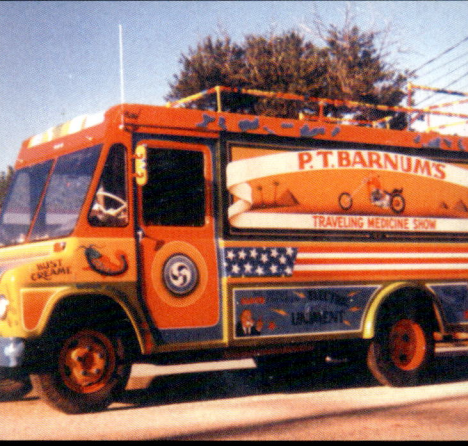

Customizing paint jobs was the thing to do, and Jim Phillips did a lot of them. He revived his car painting work with a sales van for a former Tracy's Fiberglas Works salesman who was branching out on his own. That led to a Volkswagen bus painted nose to tail with *Alice in Wonderland* characters and Blue Meanies. That bus attracted the attention of Wes Behel Volkswagen in Sunnyvale, and Phillips got a corporate job: a Captain America motif on a Volkswagen bug for the showroom. He went over the hill and was told to pick any of the new bugs.

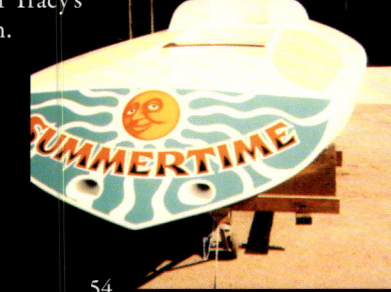

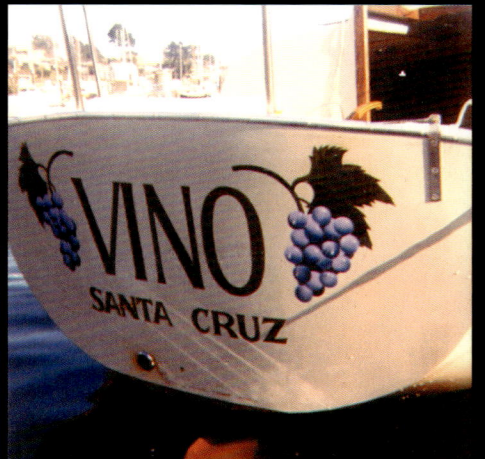

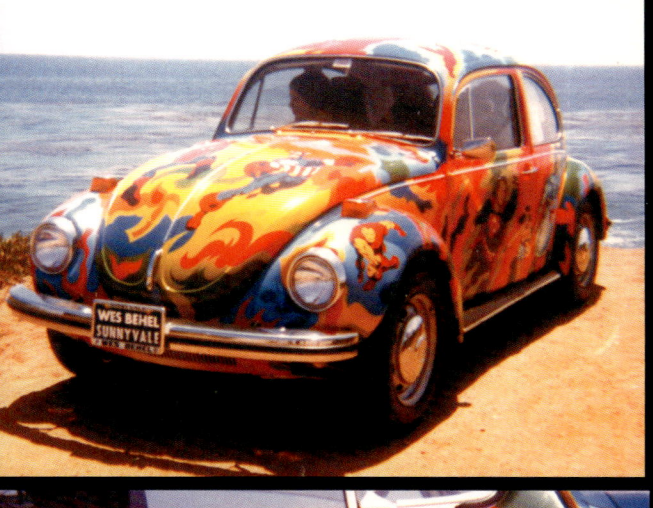

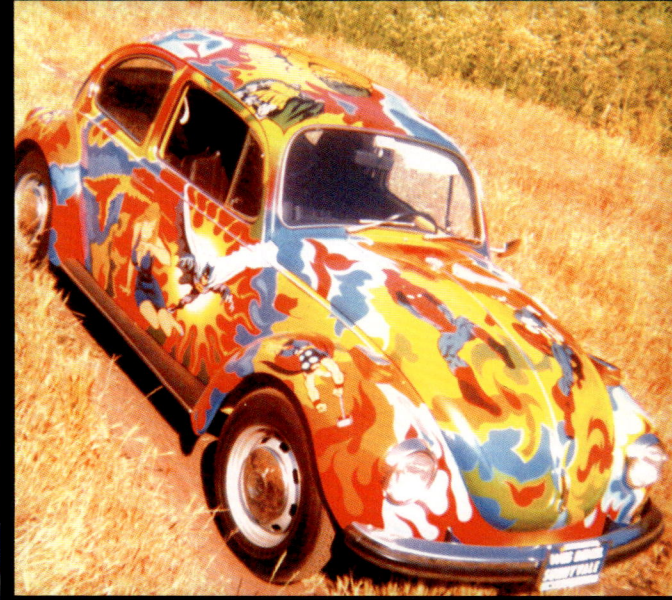

Phillips chose one with a light yellow paint job because it would easily take colors. He painted superheroes all over it: Wonder Woman, Spiderman, the Hulk and a dozen others. Dolly helped. It took three days to paint.

Phillips painted cars for $300 a pop back then, and his clients got their money's worth. The painted cars were very visible on Santa Cruz streets that didn't have half of the 21st Century traffic, and they attracted attention. Writing in the *Santa Cruz Sentinel*, Don Righetti noticed Phillips' designs: *"There are a lot of homemade imitations of Phillips' unique auto treatments running around Santa Cruz streets. But there's no mis- taking a real Jim Phillips car, it's like passing a psychedelic light show. Running throughout all variegated color and design is a kind of maniacal cohesiveness that makes the cars into a genuine artwork and gives them a weird kind of beauty. Phillips calls cars 'smoothies' because the brush glides so easily on their surfaces. Refrigerators, he adds, also make pretty good smoothies, although it is difficult to imagine what kind of kitchen decor a Phillips refrigerator would complement."*

A Volkswagen bug painted by Phillips for Wes Behel Volkswagen, 1972

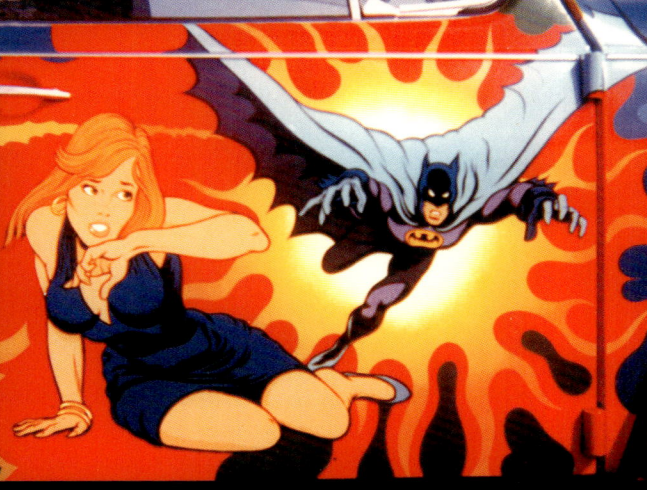

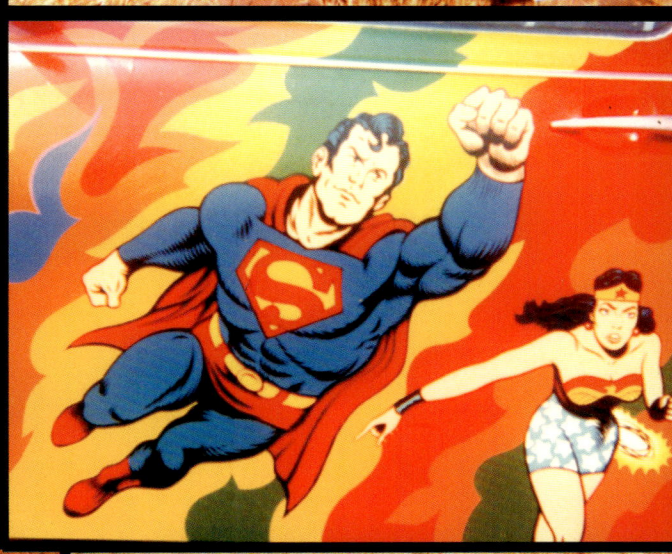

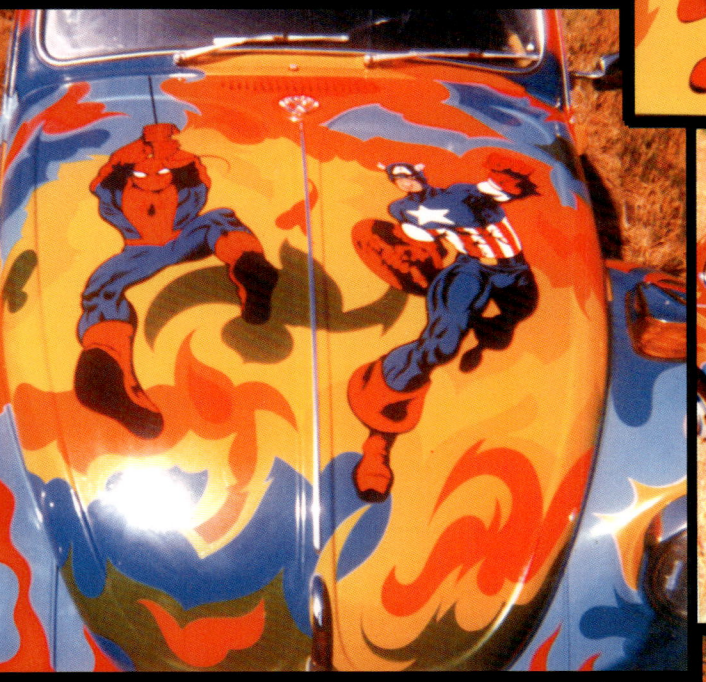

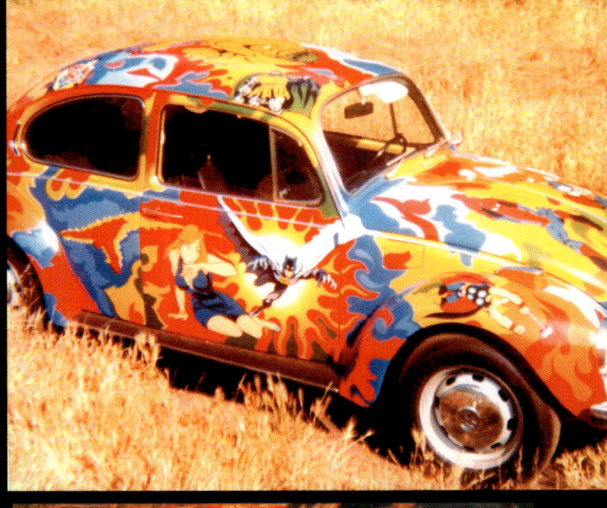

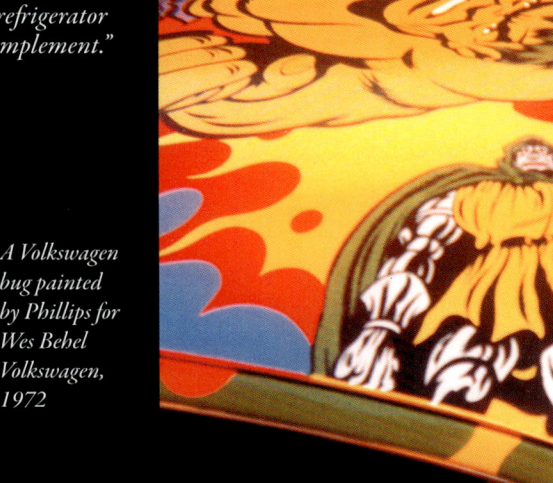

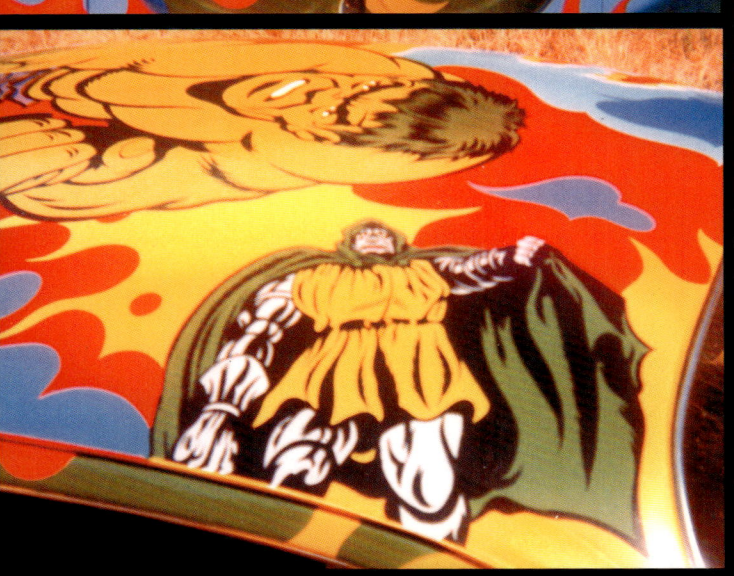

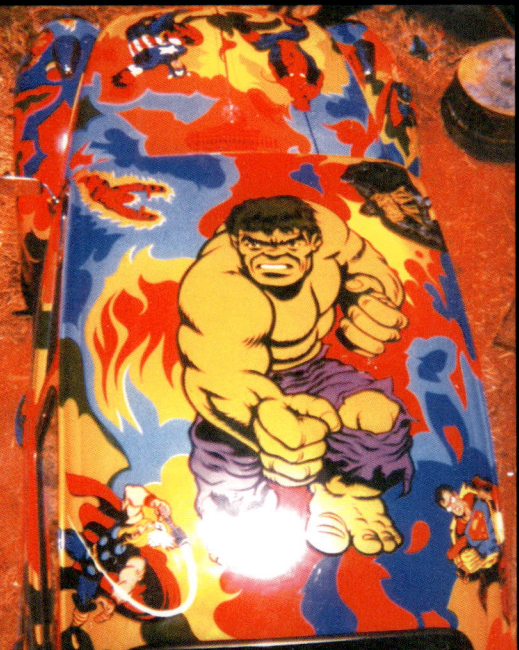

Health foods

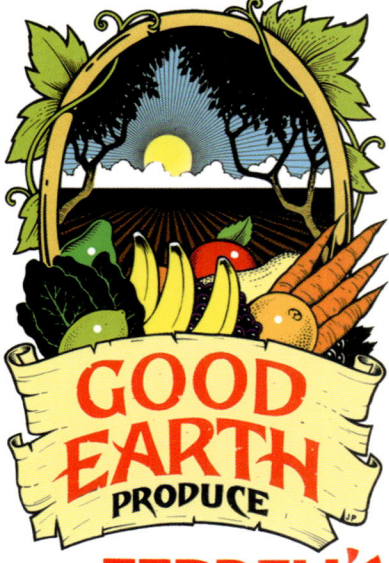

GOOD EARTH PRODUCE

FERRELL'S

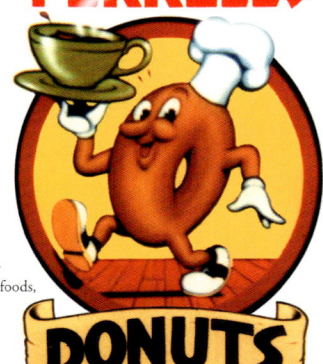

Mostly health foods, that is.

DONUTS

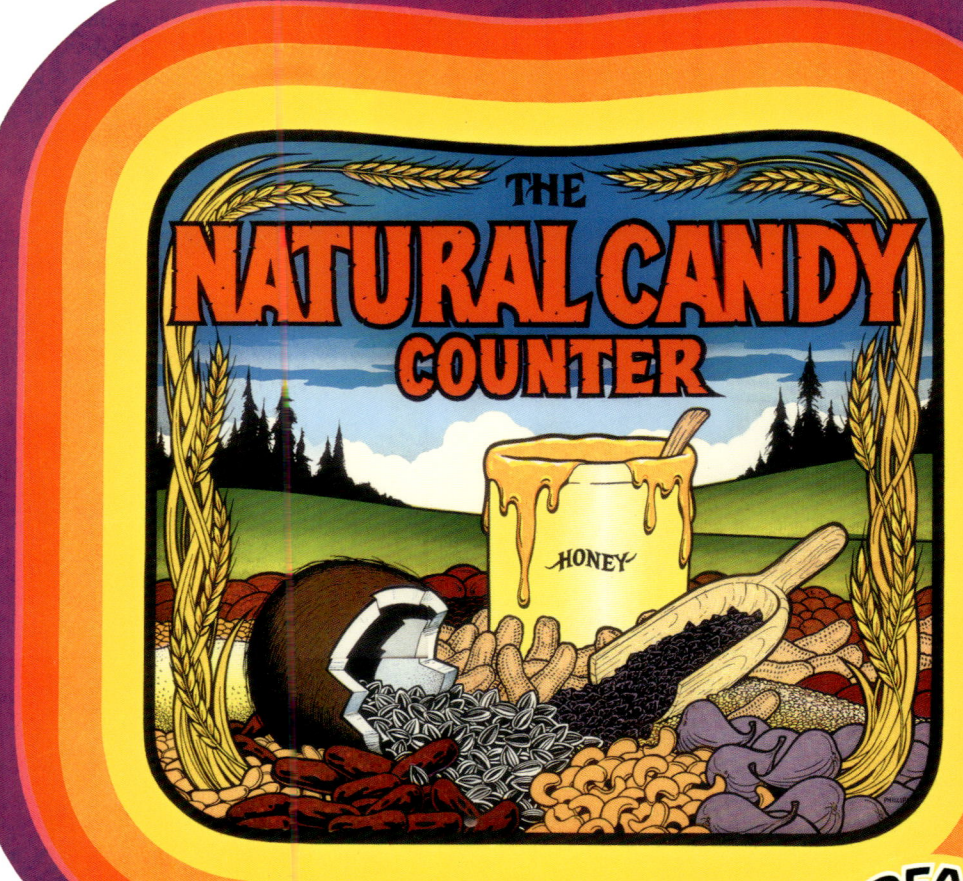

THE **NATURAL CANDY** COUNTER

HONEY

THE BREAD SHOP
No Sugar or Salt added
The Original CRUNCHY **GRANOLA** No Preservatives

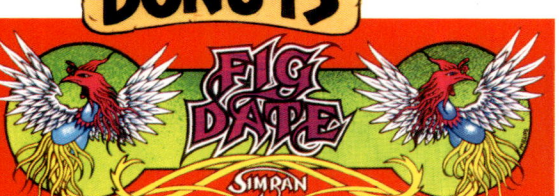

FIG DATE SIMRAN
NET WT. 8 oz

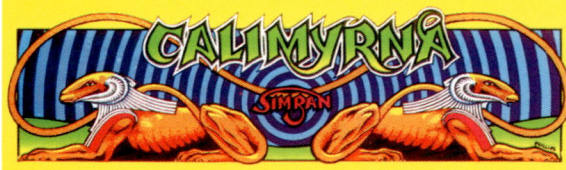

CALIMYRNA SIMRAN
NET WT. 8 oz

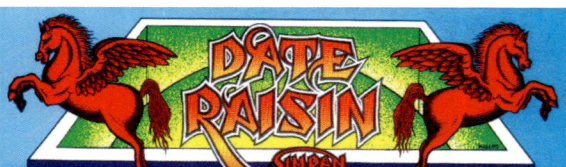

DATE RAISIN SIMRAN
NET WT. 8 oz

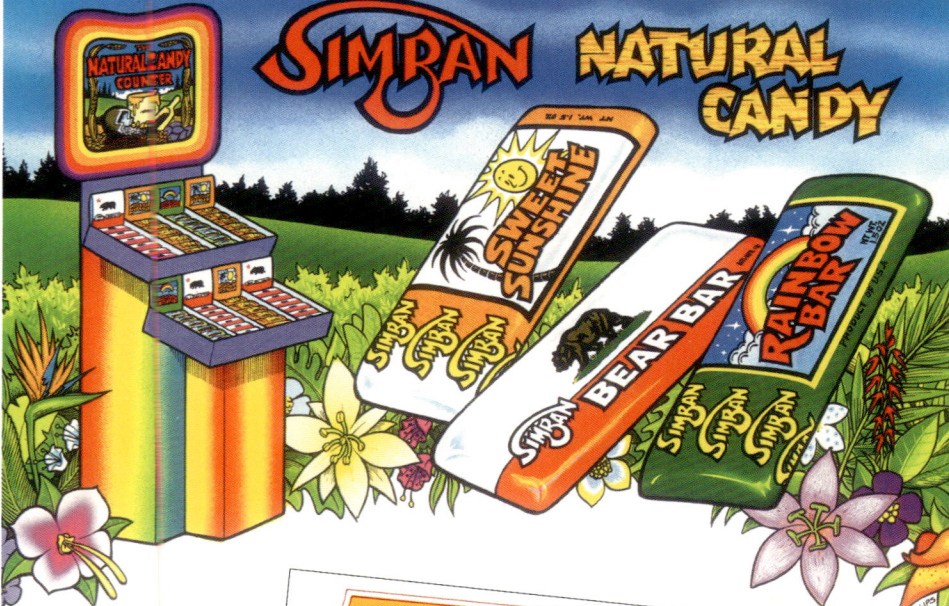

SIMRAN NATURAL CANDY

NATURAL CANDY COUNTER

SWEET SUNSHINE

BEAR BAR

RAINBOW BAR

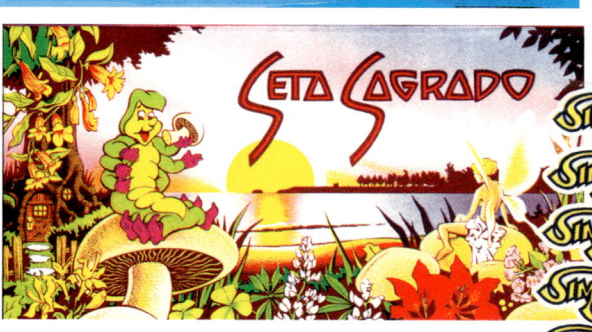

SETA SAGRADO

SIMRAN SIMRAN SIMRAN SIMRAN SIMRAN SIMRAN SIMRAN SIMRAN

Various food labels for Harmony Foods, Simran and others, circa 1973.

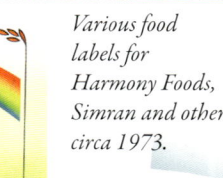

HARMONY BRAND
MOUNTAIN WILD FLOWER
RAW 100% PURE **NATURAL**
HONEY
U.S. CHOICE LIGHT AMBER
Unfiltered-Uncooked-Undiluted
NET WT. 5 LBS.
SOLD BY HARMONY FOODS • SANTA CRUZ, CA 95060

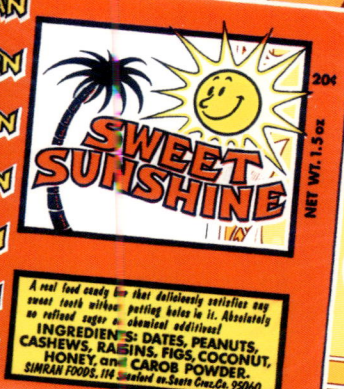

20¢
SWEET SUNSHINE
NET WT. 1.5 oz
A real food candy bar that deliciously satisfies any sweet tooth without packing holes in it. Absolutely no refined sugar or chemical additives!
INGREDIENTS: DATES, PEANUTS, CASHEWS, RAISINS, FIGS, COCONUT, HONEY, and CAROB POWDER.
SIMRAN FOODS, 114 Stanford av. Santa Cruz, Ca. 95060

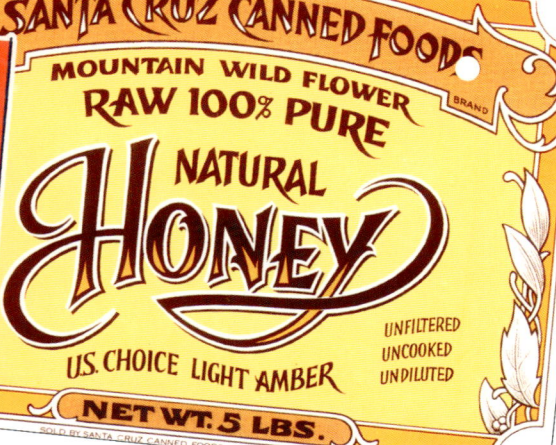

SANTA CRUZ CANNED FOODS
MOUNTAIN WILD FLOWER
RAW 100% PURE
NATURAL
HONEY
BRAND
U.S. CHOICE LIGHT AMBER
UNFILTERED
UNCOOKED
UNDILUTED
NET WT. 5 LBS.
SOLD BY SANTA CRUZ CANNED FOODS • SANTA CRUZ, CA 95060

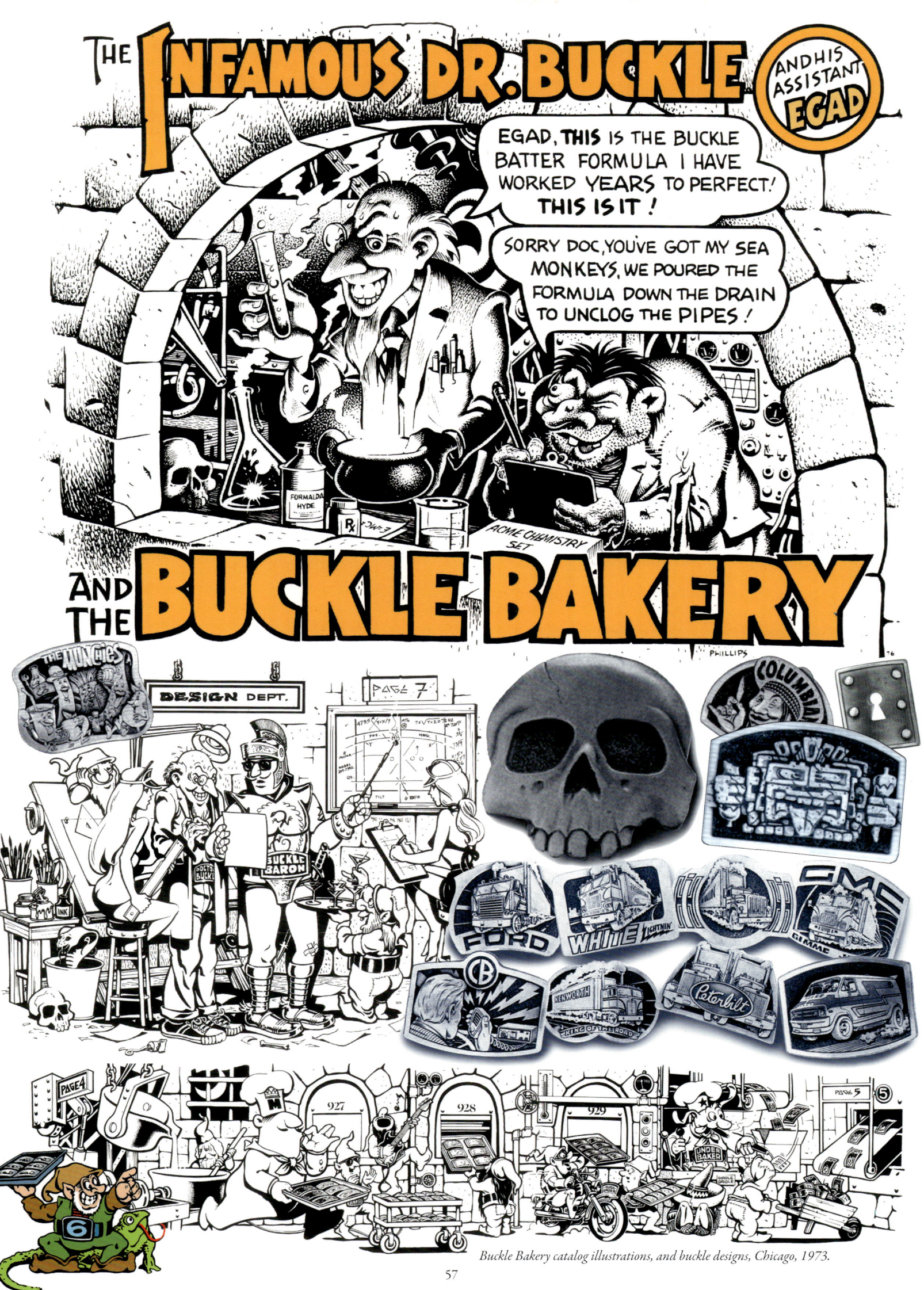

Buckle Bakery catalog illustrations, and buckle designs, Chicago, 1973.

That Sentinel article, along with his Tracy's work, helped drum up some business for Phillips. He picked up a couple of health food companies who needed packaging, labels and advertising. A company in Chicago had him design belt buckles and illustrate a catalog, and they flew Jim and Dolly out to Chicago to work at a buckle booth at a Renaissance Fair. Jim did a few posters, but work was slow, especially during winter. Phillips did some projects to occupy time between jobs. He started a comic book story. *The Hitchhiker* was about someone who gets a ride and discusses salvation with the driver. There was a lot of 'Jesus People' material around at that time. He received a call from Craig Yoe from Akron, Ohio, using a number that Rick Griffin had given. Yoe was doing some Jesus People publications, along with artwork by Rick Griffin, like the cover for Yoe's Jesus Loves You magazine. Craig was a zany cartoonist himself, and he wanted to publish some Jesus comic books.

Rick Griffin is the artist Phillips is most compared with. They were operating in the same era and in the same worlds, Griffin doing his famous Murphy cartoons for *SURFER Magazine* and then moving into psychedelic rock posters. Jim Phillips and Dolly met Rick Griffin at his home in 1967. They were introduced by a publisher who was considering marketing Jim's comic-troversial *The Next Supper* poster. Griffin remembered Jim's *Surfing Illustrated* cartoons, and he liked *The Next Supper*. Rick connected to Jim in a Christian sort of way. That Griffin connection found a publisher for Phillips' comic story, which was published as *Eternal Truth* by Sonday Funnies Comics.

KENT "WEBSTER" SHELLEY: *"In 2001 I took a long shot and asked Christian Comics International if they knew of a Phillips who put out a Christian comic in 1973 with a character named Webster Crotchit in a story called* The Hitchiker, *and they connected me with Jim. That comic was the answer to The Freak Brothers and Zap comics of that time. Anyway, many years ago, I borrowed an original copy from a friend and copied it before giving it back. I taught Junior and Senior High Sunday School for 10 years. The Name of my class? 'The Excellent Adventures Of Webster Crotchit.' A short history of how the work started a whole teaching ministry: Back then, I was one of the early 'Jesus Freaks' as they (and we ourselves) used to call us. I still love Jesus and 'Yes' I am still a 'freak!' The Hitchiker was created for the street people and Jesus freaks for that time. I was rather a 'different' kind of teacher with different methods. The pastor gave me full reign and the parents were too scared to come into my room. You see, I built that Sunday school around the 'Street Jesus' I had met back in the late 60's & 70's. The Hitchiker was placed in my hands at just the right time back then. I blew up three important pages. Those were always permanent fixtures on the wall and they were always the first thing people would come into the room and read. To this day my closest friends still call me 'Webster' or 'Web.' And one thing that even the Christian-raised kids know as I drilled it into them is, "There's a little bit of Webster in all of us." If the comic did not exist, I wouldn't have taught. My co-teacher Dave Zolman agreed that if there was no Webster there would not have been 10 years of Sunday school."*

Phillips and Dolly fell in with a "Jesus People" church in Felton called The Christian Community. Rollin Dingman was a deacon and he lined Jim up with a long job. At the time, the basketball player Jerry Lucas was a memory lecturer who had devised a method

Christian Community logo

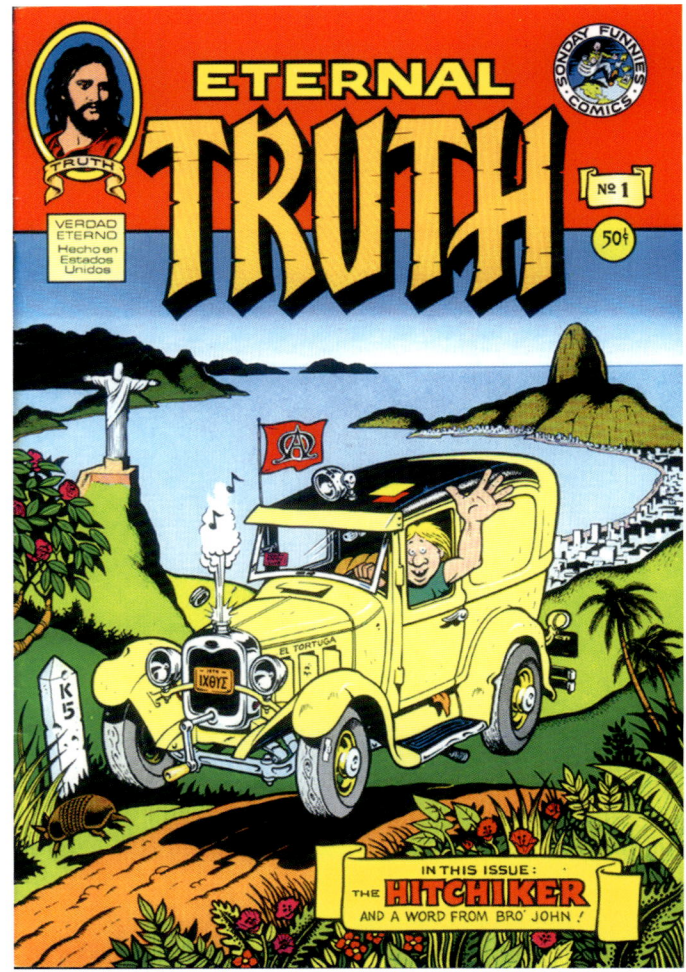

Eternal Truth was published by Sonday Funnies, Akron, Ohio, 1974.

of memorization, called The Lucas Method, where symbols represented words. You would string those cartoons together to form a message. A pair of bulls was parables. A puzzle was apostle. A bee on a leaf was belief. Lucas wanted to interpret the New Testament into symbols. Jim's assignment was to draw it. Rollin would then ink his pencils. The job stretched out over the months.

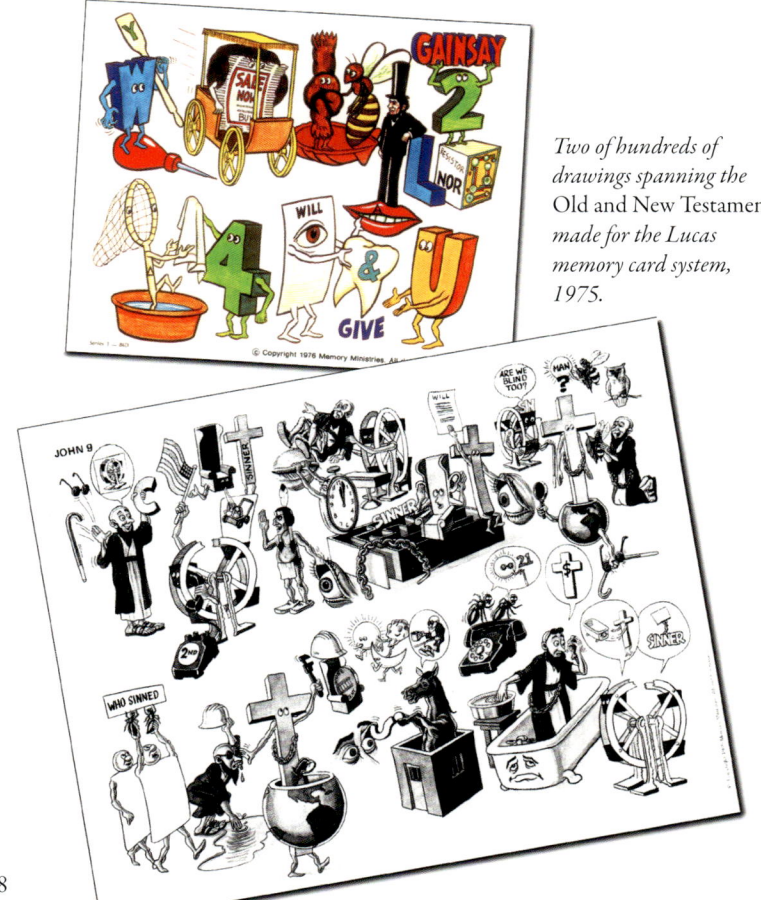

Two of hundreds of drawings spanning the Old and New Testament made for the Lucas memory card system, 1975.

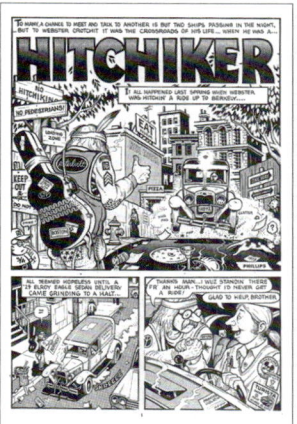
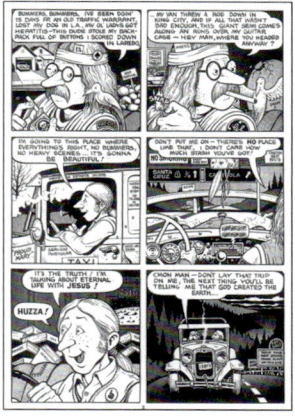
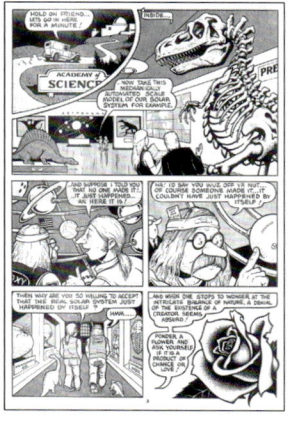
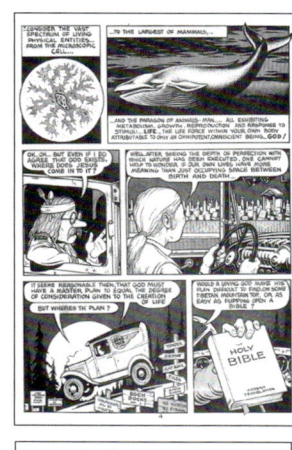

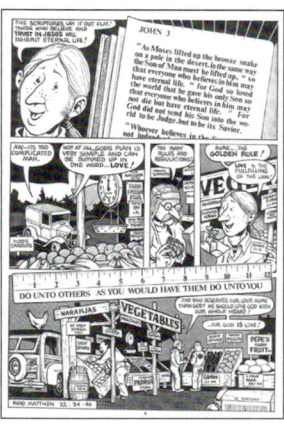
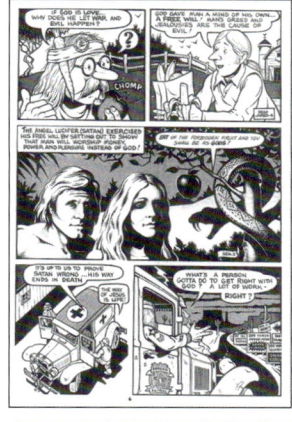
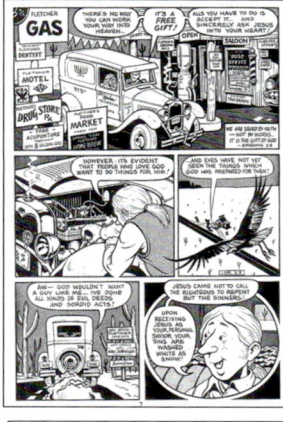
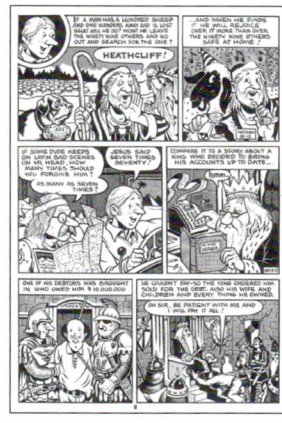

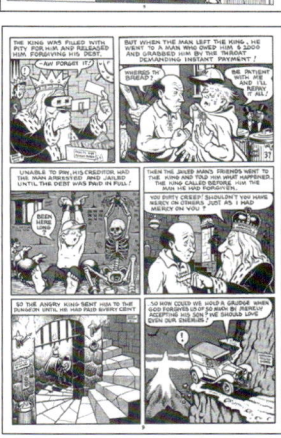
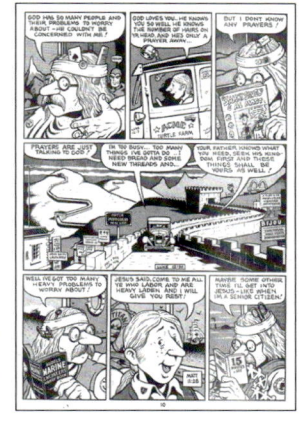
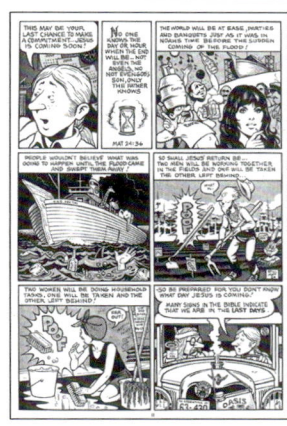
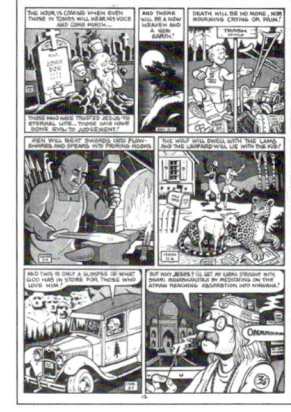

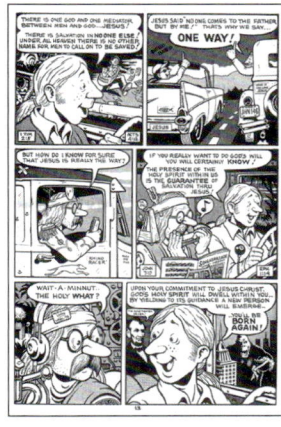
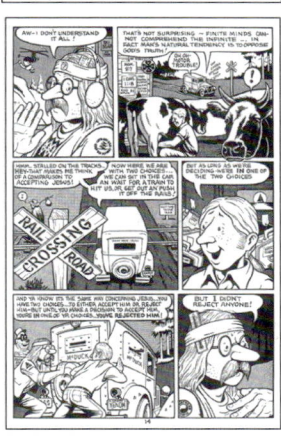
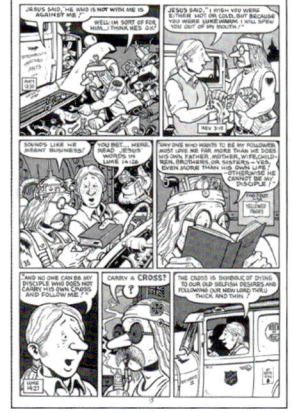
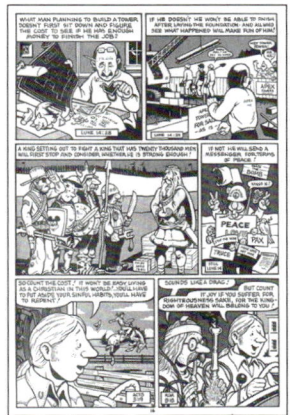

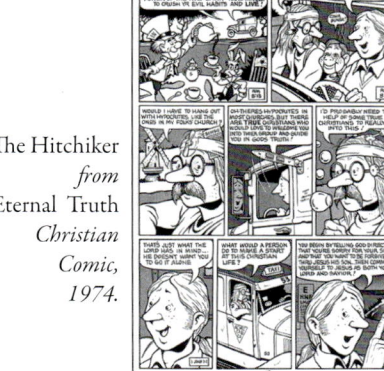
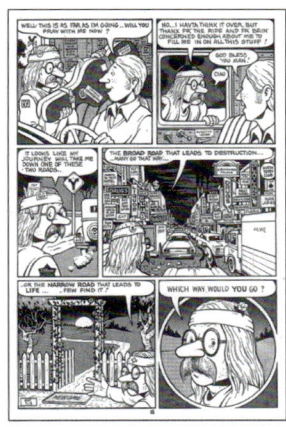
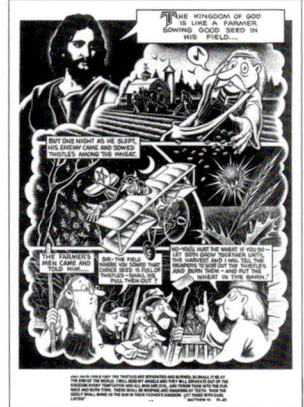
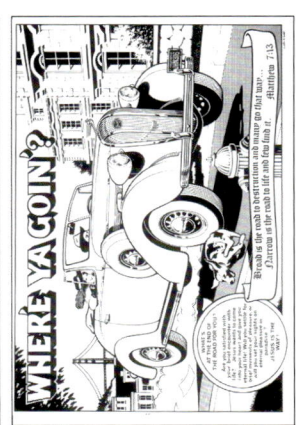

The Hitchiker *from* Eternal Truth *Christian Comic,* 1974.

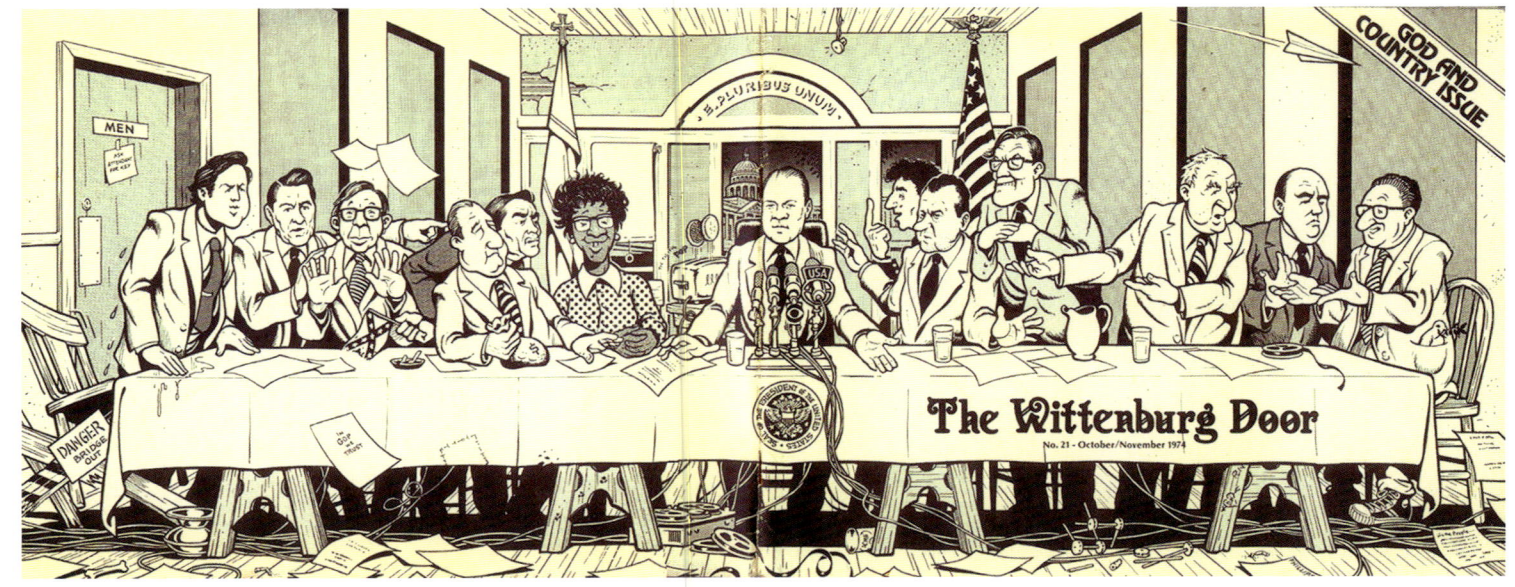

The Wittenburg Door magazine cover 1974

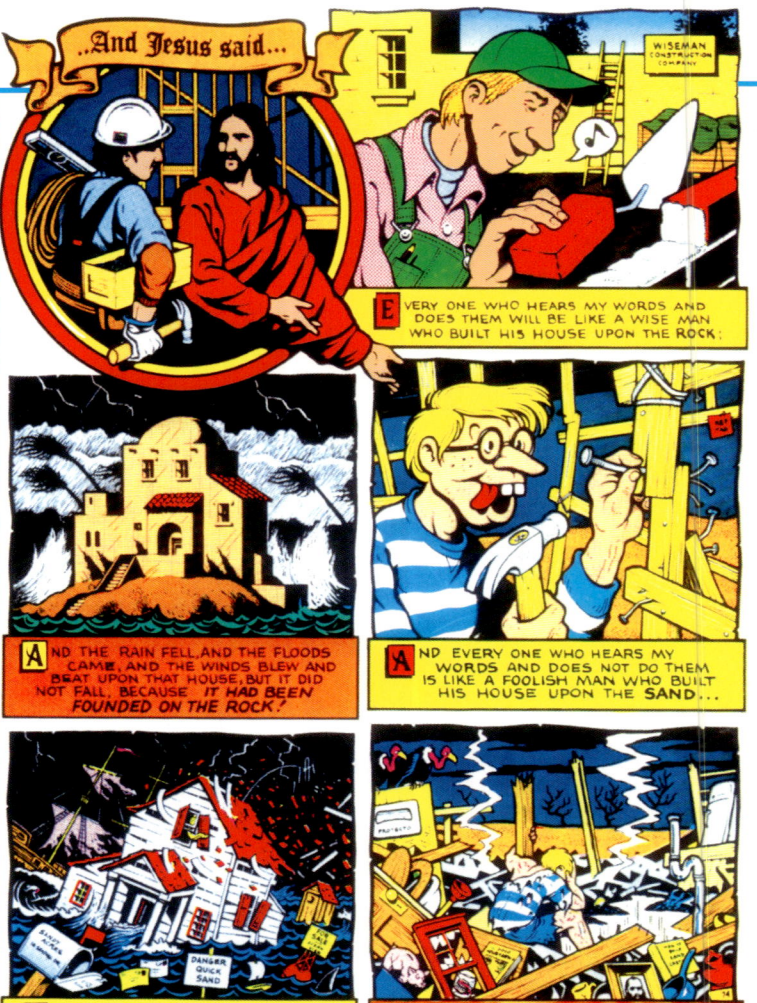

Eternal Truth *comic book back cover color separated with bluelines.*

BLUE LINES

Most of Phillips' color work during the seventies was colored using "blue lines," a mechanical color separation technique, and a welcome alternative to overlays. It gave the artist an artboard to use ink or Zipatone for each color. To make blue lines, printers reproduced the pen and ink drawing in light (non-repro) blue onto three art-board plates, one for each color, red, yellow and blue. The blue line color separation was invented by Cal Litho printers of San Francisco, according to president Lou Longwenus, who has kept the recipe classified. Phillips persuaded Longwenus to make a set of scratchboard blue lines, a method found in an old commercial art book. But obtaining blue lines in San Francisco was costly and time consuming, so Phillips experimented with different ways to make blue lines. Along the way he checked with his old teacher Ralph Gray, who had used a similar technique using photostats: make four stats, and then add or subtract from each one according to the color. But Jim didn't get free filmwork at Ray's Photo Engraving like Ralph, so the cost of stats could cost as much as Cal Litho blue lines. Jim experimented and discovered an excellent way to make blue lines, and used home-made boards after that. His recipe is provided here.

Materials: A film positive of the pen and ink graphic with registration marks; a piece of plate glass and a piece of 3/4 inch plywood, both as large as the art; three pieces of artboard to size (coated board was used); a bottle of blue Pelikan ink, and an airbrush.

Method: Spray an even coating of blue ink on each of the three art board plates, let dry. Place the film positive on one of the plates, place the plate glass on the film positive, and place them all on the wood. Place in full mid-day sun for one to two hours. You will see that the ink has faded, remove plate and repeat for the two other boards. Attach or ink registration marks to blue lines.

BLUE LINES

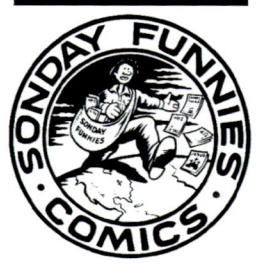

Black

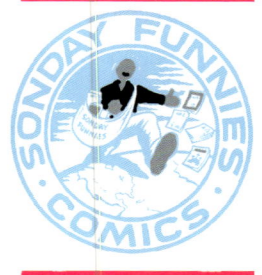

Yellow

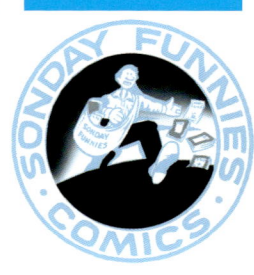

Magenta (red)

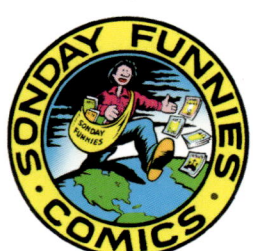

Cyan (blue)

4C

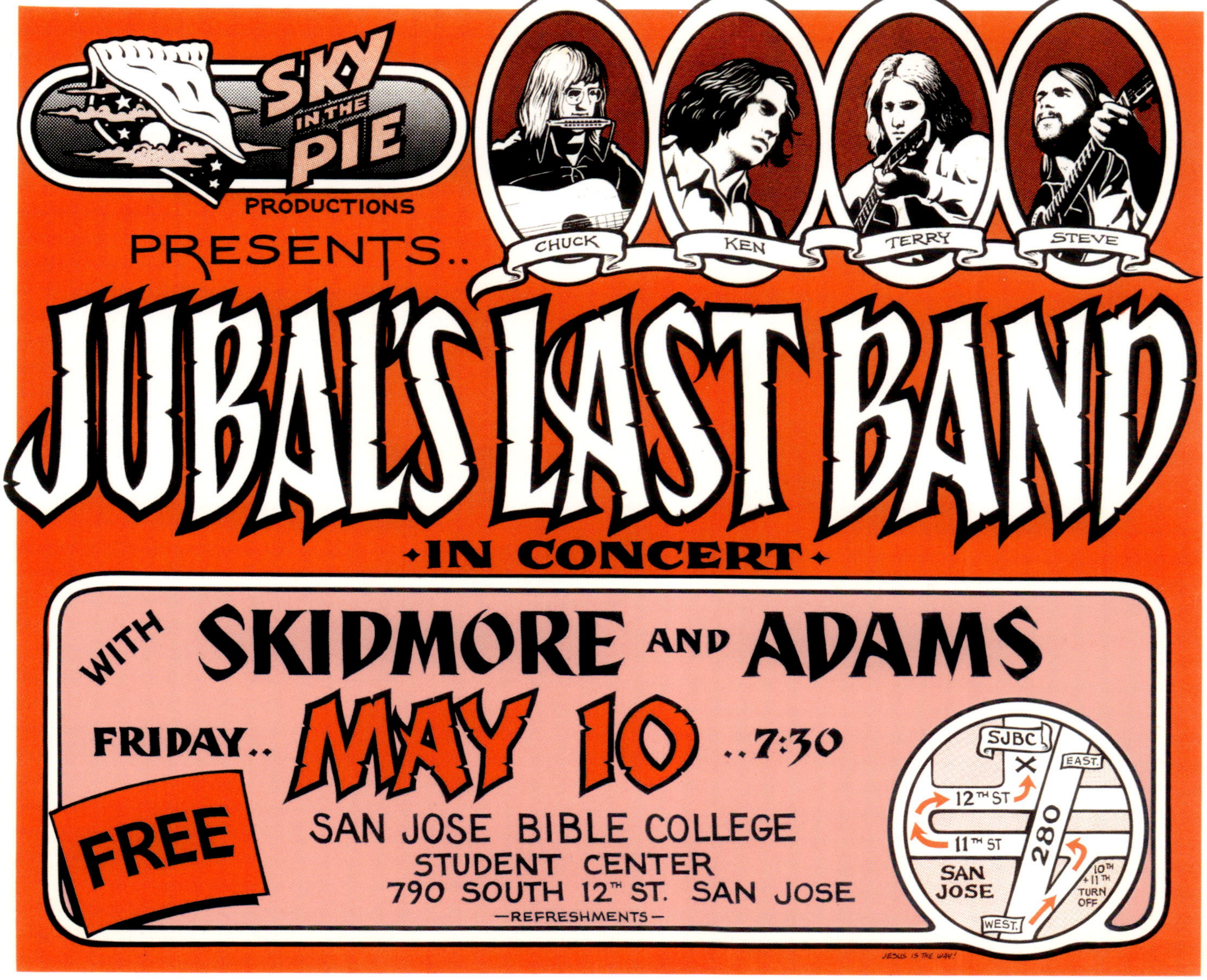

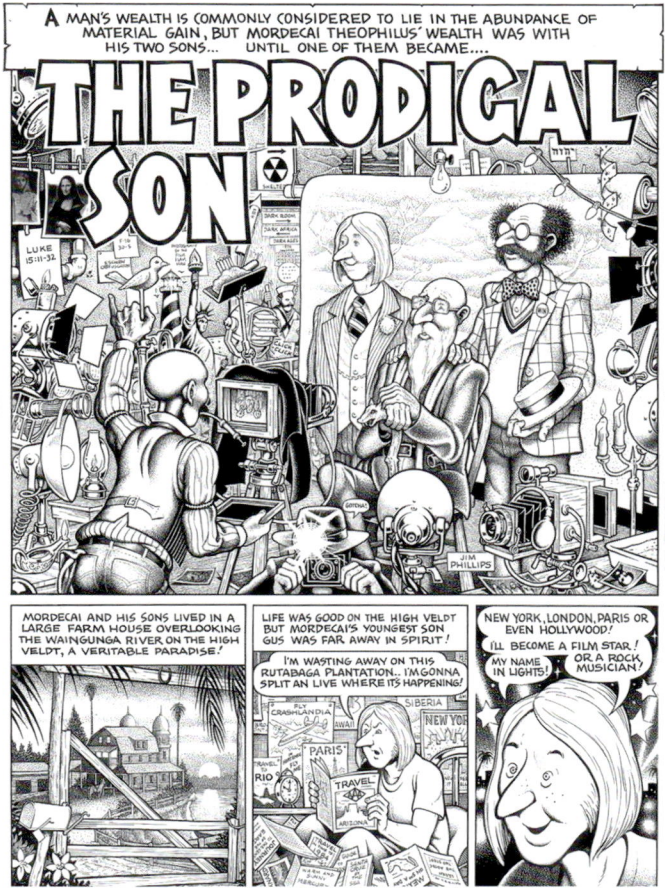

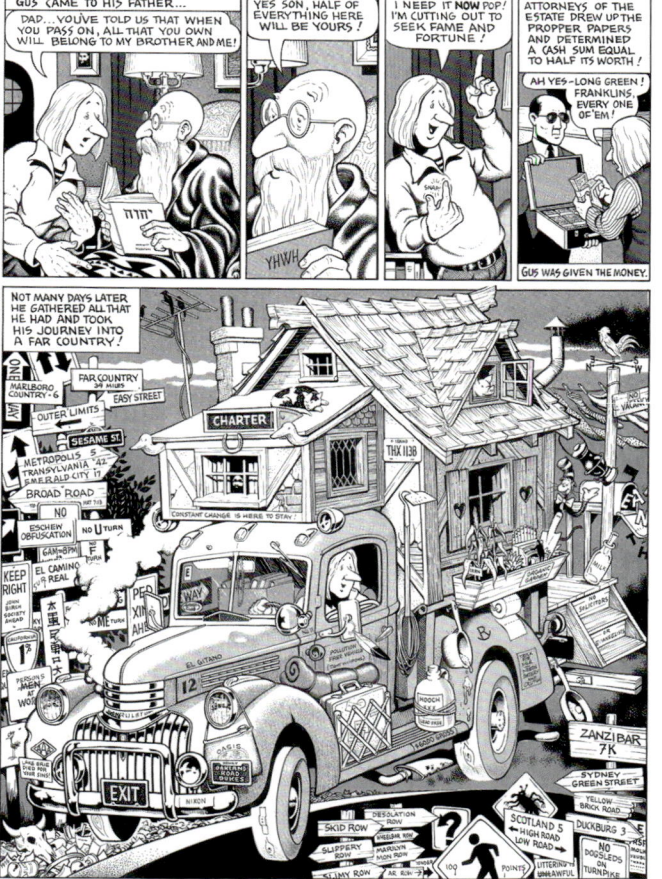

Wheels for Safety

SAFETY IS OF THE LORD

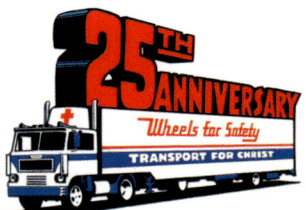

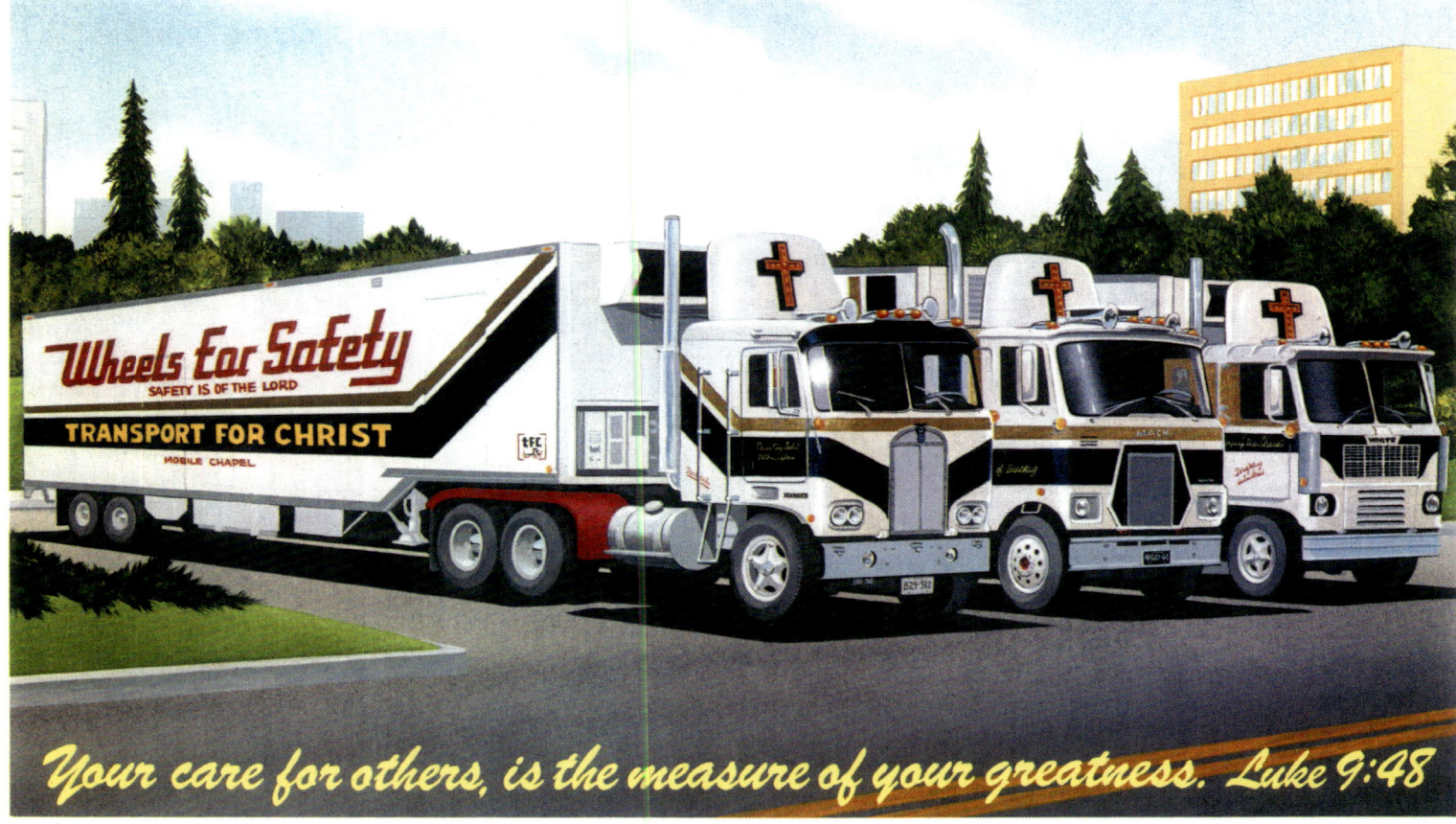

Your care for others, is the measure of your greatness. Luke 9:48

Wheels for Safety, *1976 calendar, airbrush on Cresent board, 1975.*

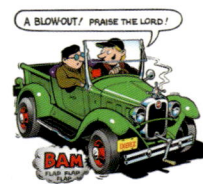

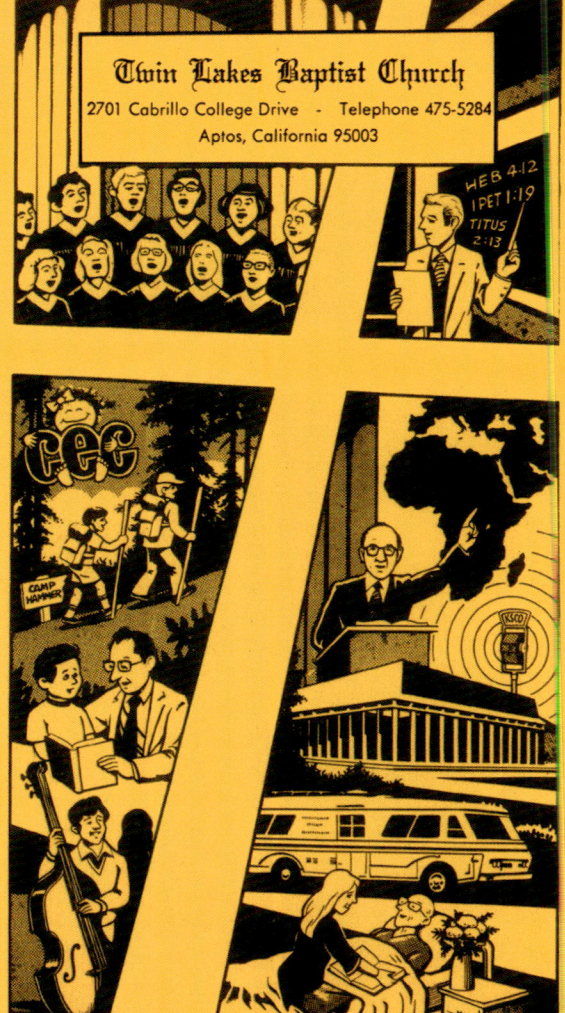

Twin Lakes Church weekly bulletin, 1970s

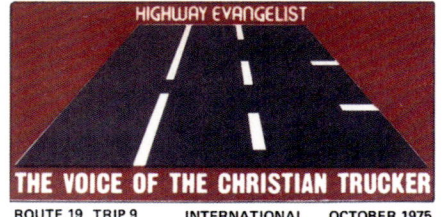

TRUCKER'S SKILL SAVES CHILD!

ROUTE 19 TRIP 9   INTERNATIONAL   OCTOBER 1975

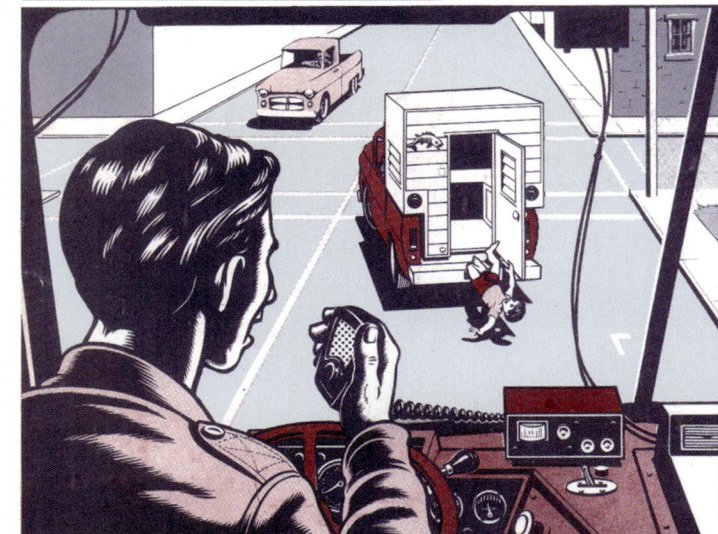

C.B. PROVES ITS WORTH ONCE AGAIN

"Breaker, breaker, how about a base? I have an emergency."

"Go ahead, you've got your base."

This is the way it was for Ron Clark, owner and operator of his own rig. Ron was headed east on the Ohio Turnpike about 12:00 midnight, when he noticed a Chevy crew cab with a camper, travelling in front of him. Nothing seemed unusual about the truck, but as he watched intently, he noticed a small child open the rear door and fall out.

Because of his skill as a truck driver,

Ron was able to bring the big rig to a halt in seconds. Without a moment to waste, Ron jumped from the rig to assist the child. He did not know what he would find as he walked toward the small, still figure. Would he find a child badly mangled, or possibly dead? To him it seemed like a nightmare. As he neared the body, the child reached out and spoke to him. Being surprised that the boy was conscious, with no visible signs of a fall, he knelt by him. The boy's first words were not of concern for himself, but of the trucker. He asked

Ron, "Are you a Christian?" Ron noticed the deep concern the boy had for him, so he replied, "Yes, I am a Christian." Immediately the boy was relieved. By this time another trucker had stopped to assist, but everything was under control.

It was learned later by Mr. and Mrs. Danston, parents of the boy, that David was asleep in the camper and while sleepwalking, he had crawled over his brother, opened the rear door and fallen out. While David was falling, he noticed the truck

(Continued on back page)

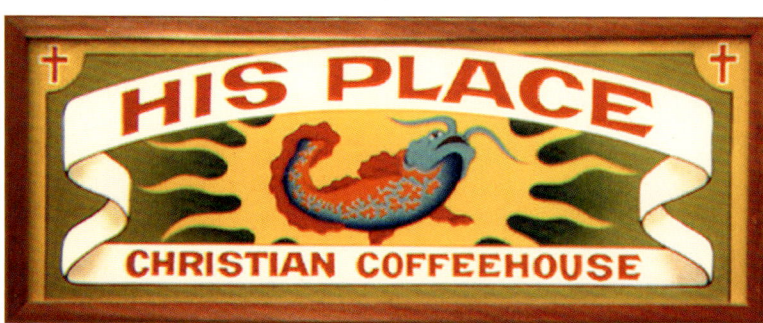

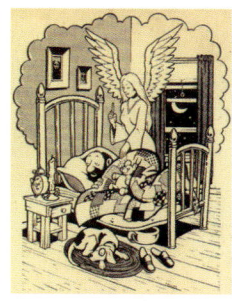
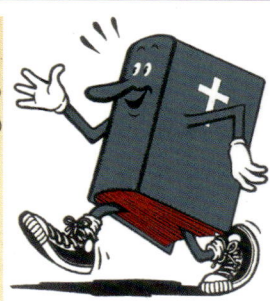
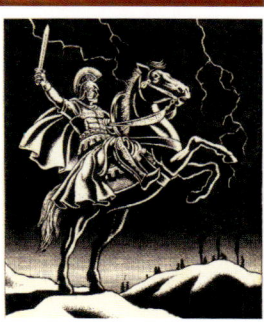

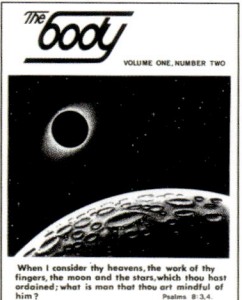
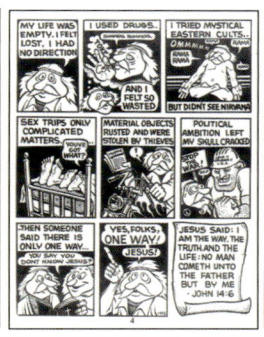
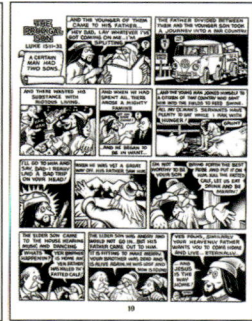

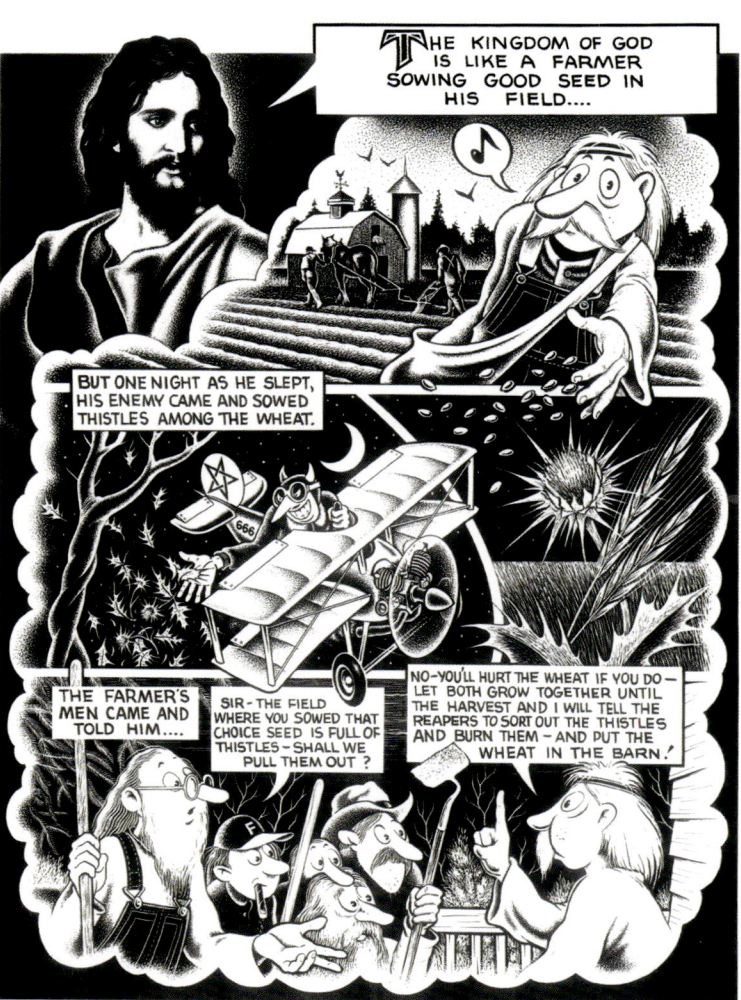

Off-campus living not quite what you expected?

SAN JOSE STATE UNIVERSITY HOUSING OFFICE

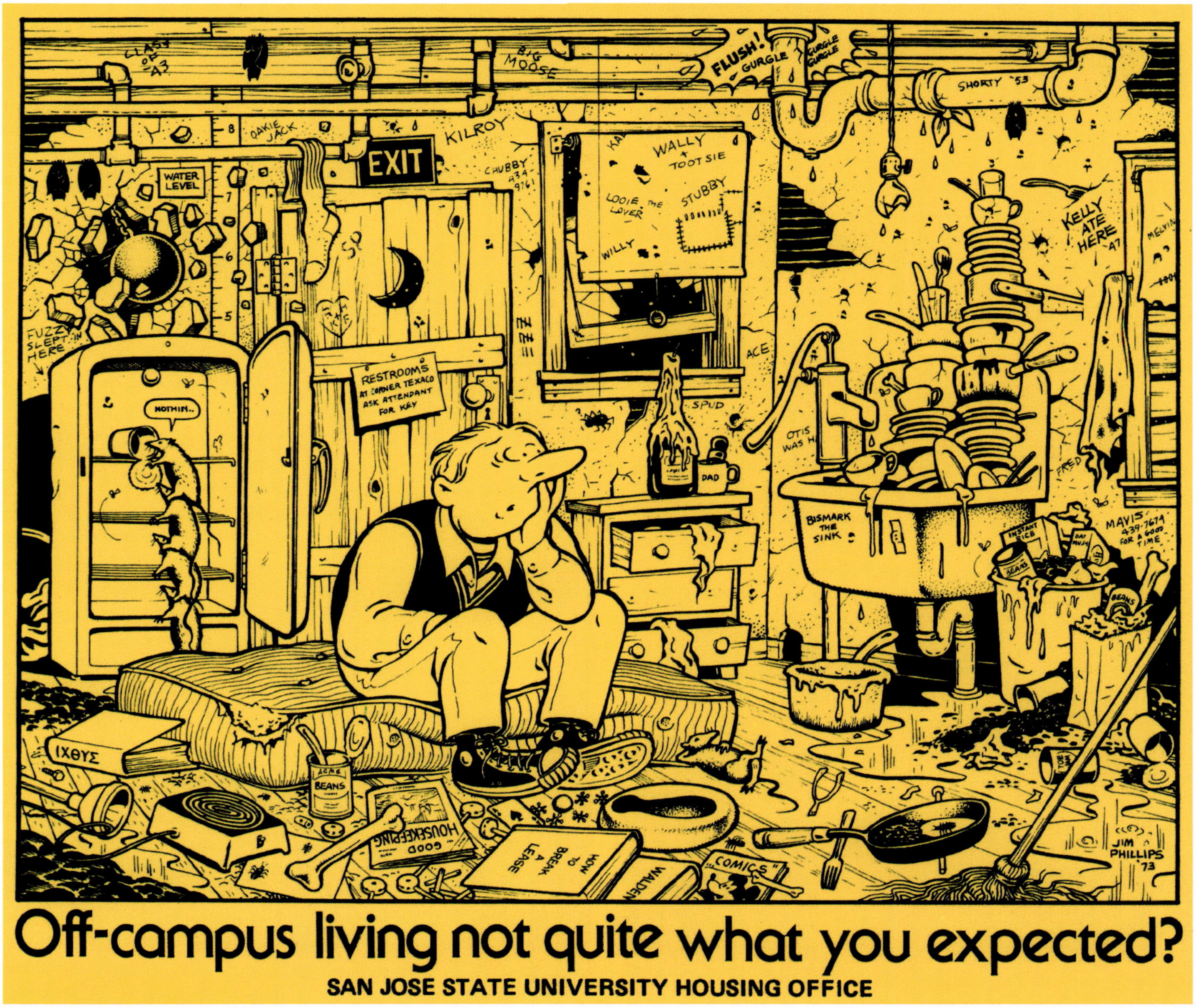

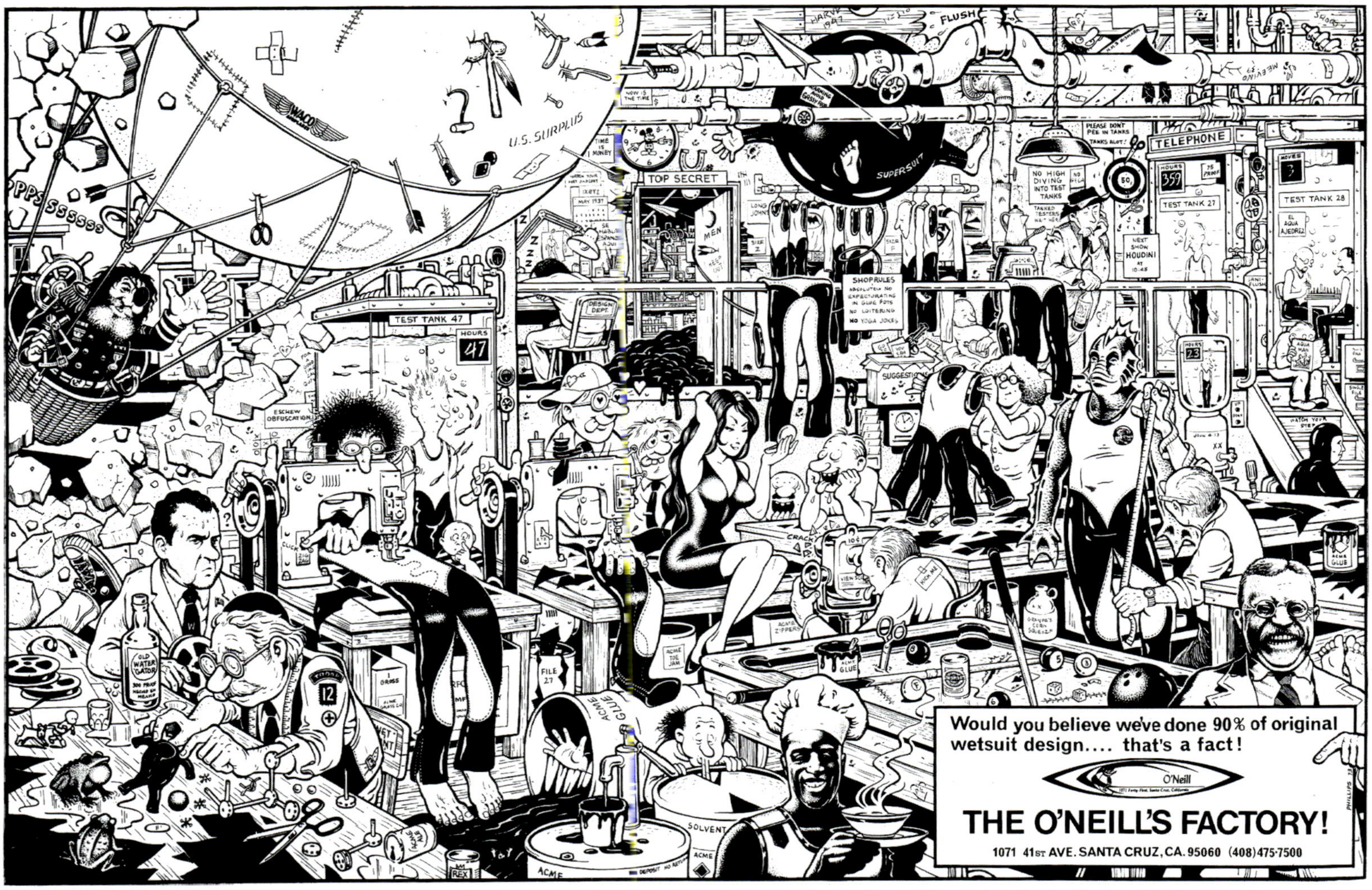

The O'neill's Factory appeared as a two-page ad in Surfer Magazine, Vol.14, No.6, March 1973. *It clearly shows influence from Wally Wood, Bill Elder, and Mr.Eggert.*

DREW KAMPION: *"Phillips' brilliant over-the-top vision of a glue-intoxicated O'Neill wetsuit factory c.1970 was a cartoonist's "Last Supper" drawn with exquisite graphic literalism underpinned with decidedly Daliesque nuances evocative of some dreams I've had. In short, the artist captured a time, place, and psychic space with impeccable acuity and wit. But then, that's what Jim Phillips does."*

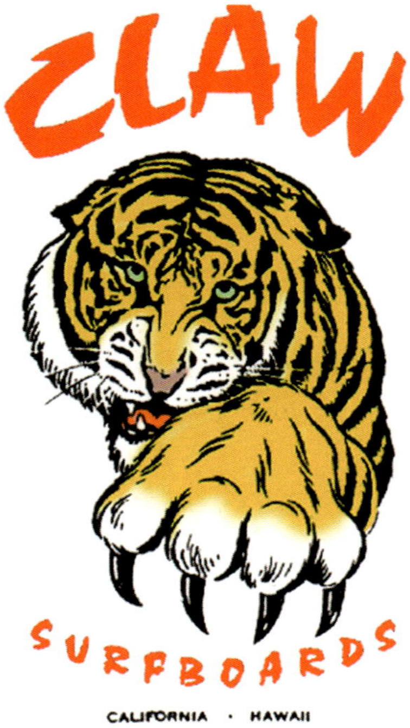

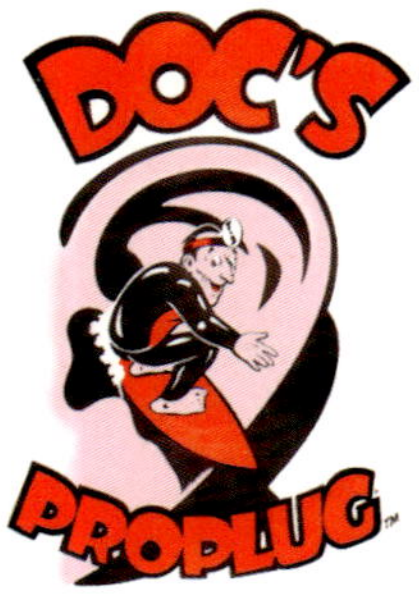

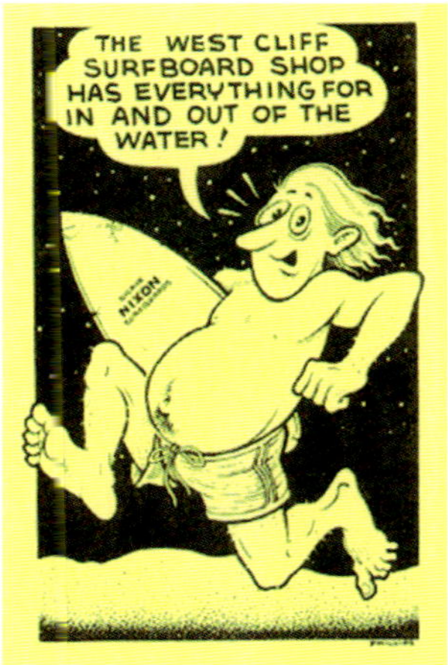

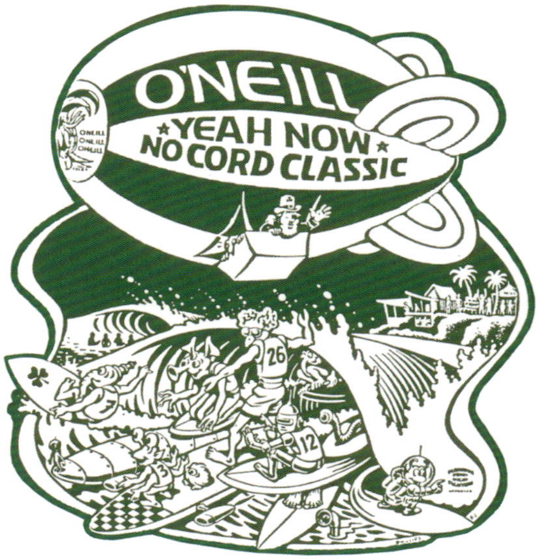

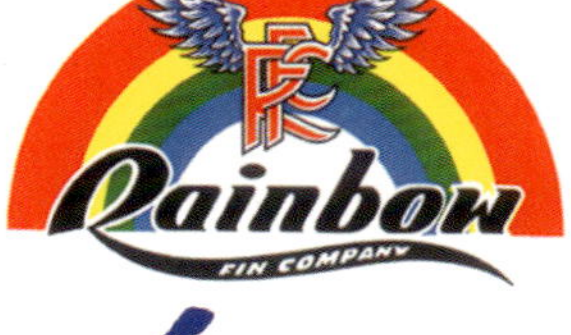

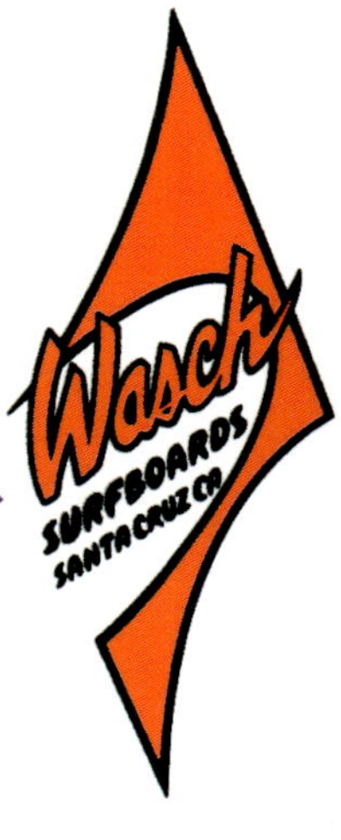

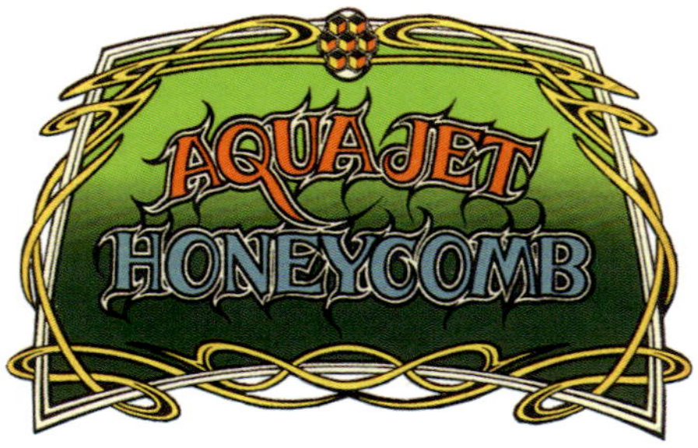

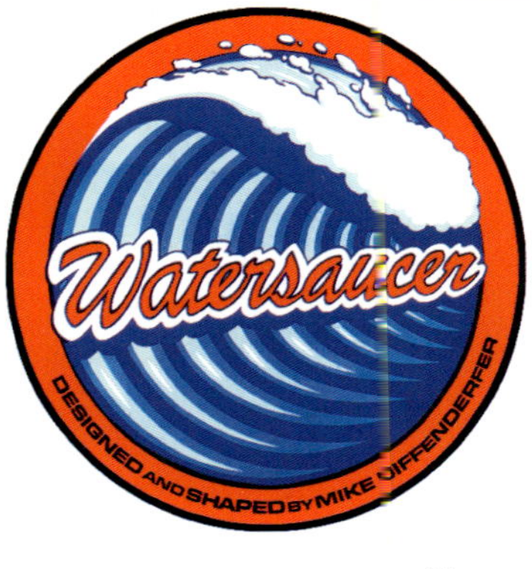

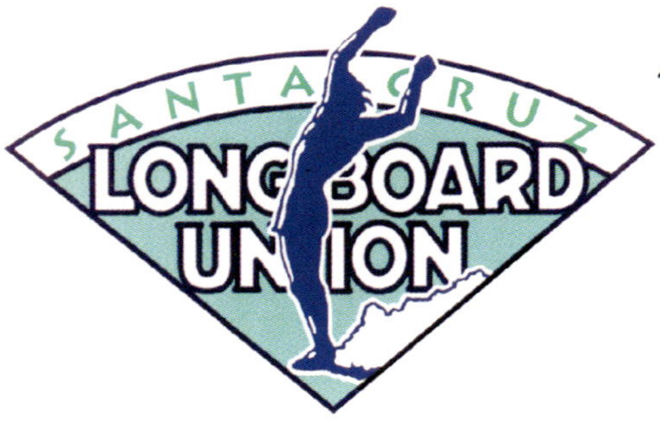

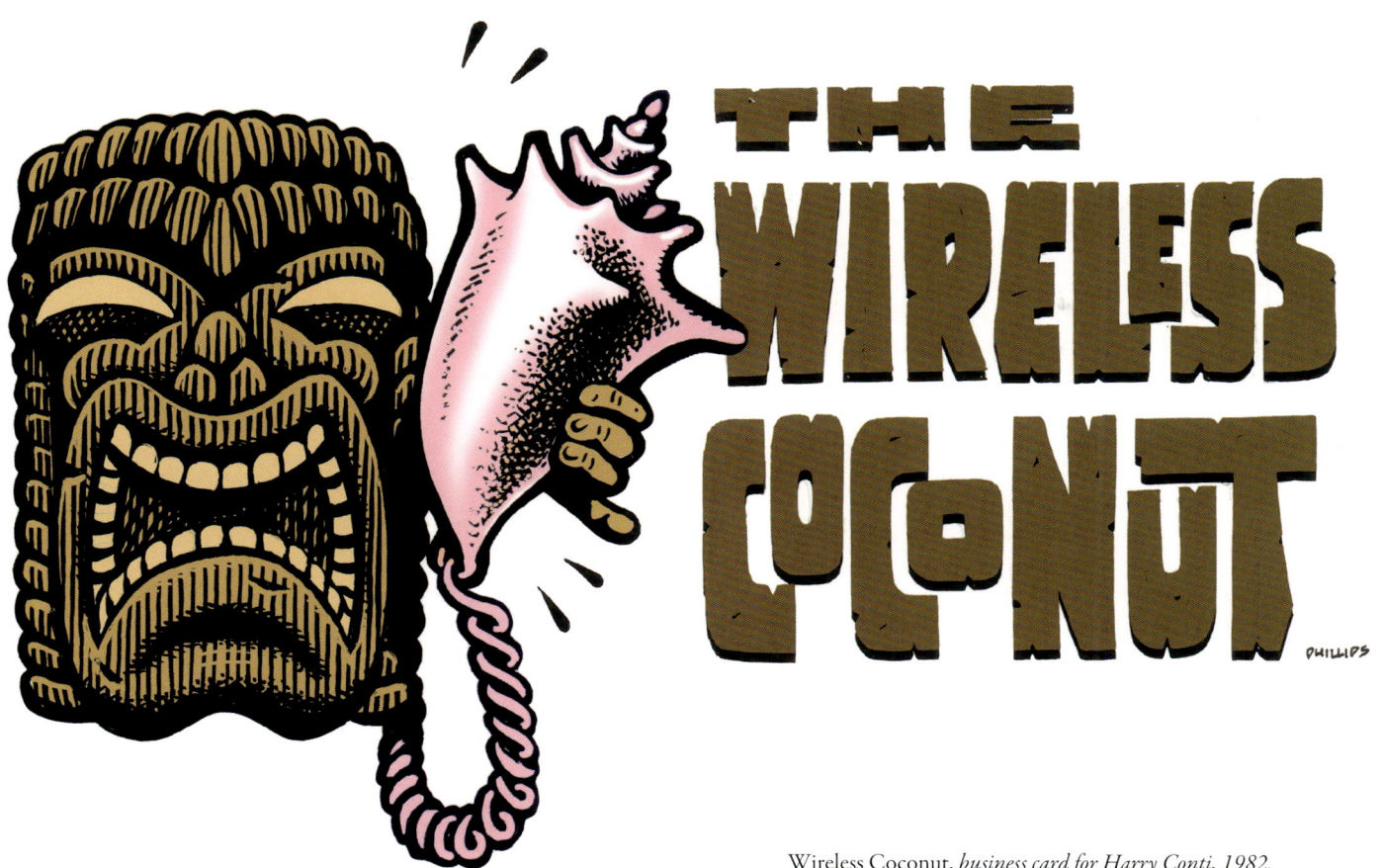

THE WIRELESS COCONUT

PHILLIPS

Wireless Coconut, *business card for Harry Conti, 1982.*

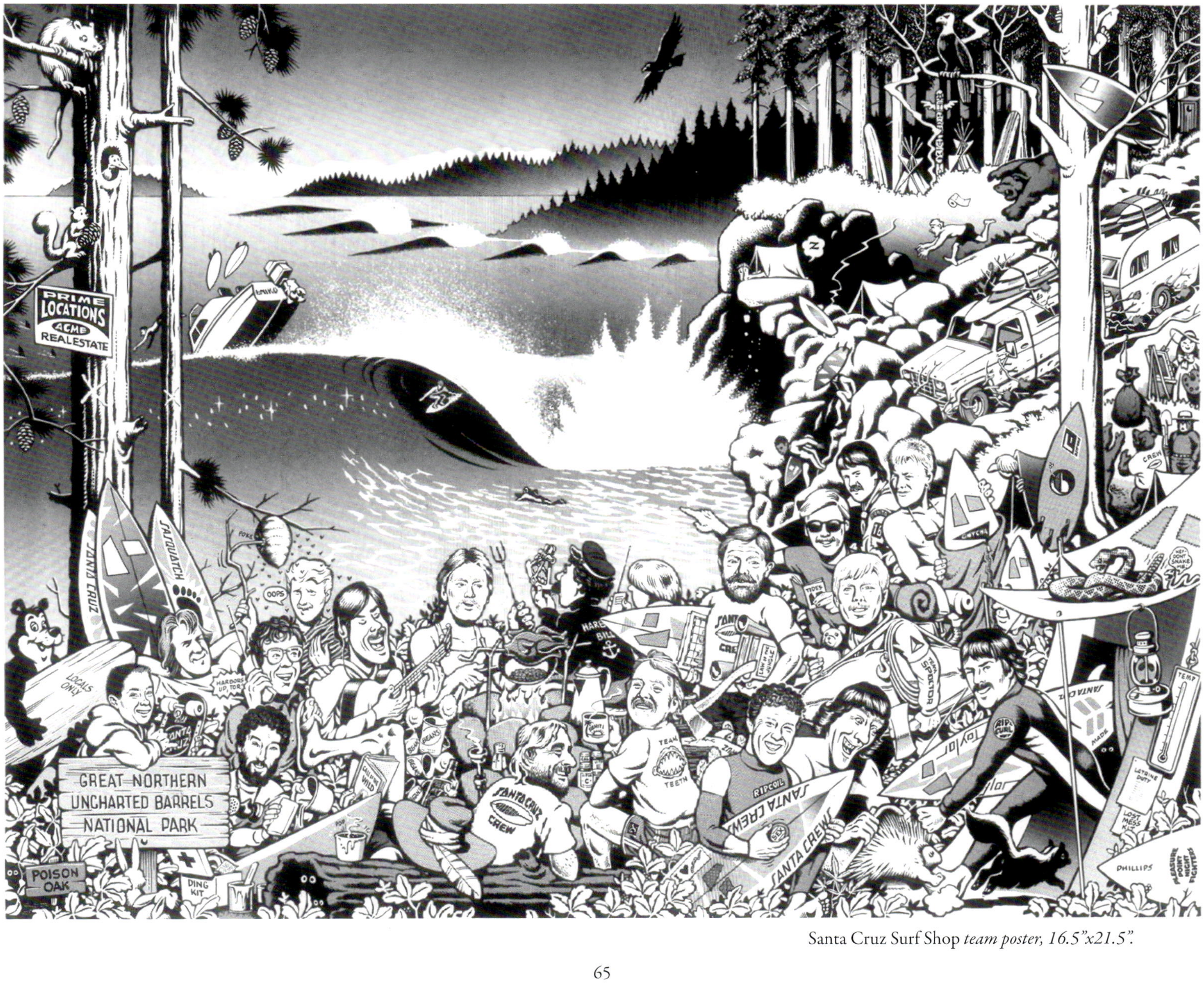

Santa Cruz Surf Shop *team poster, 16.5"x21.5".*

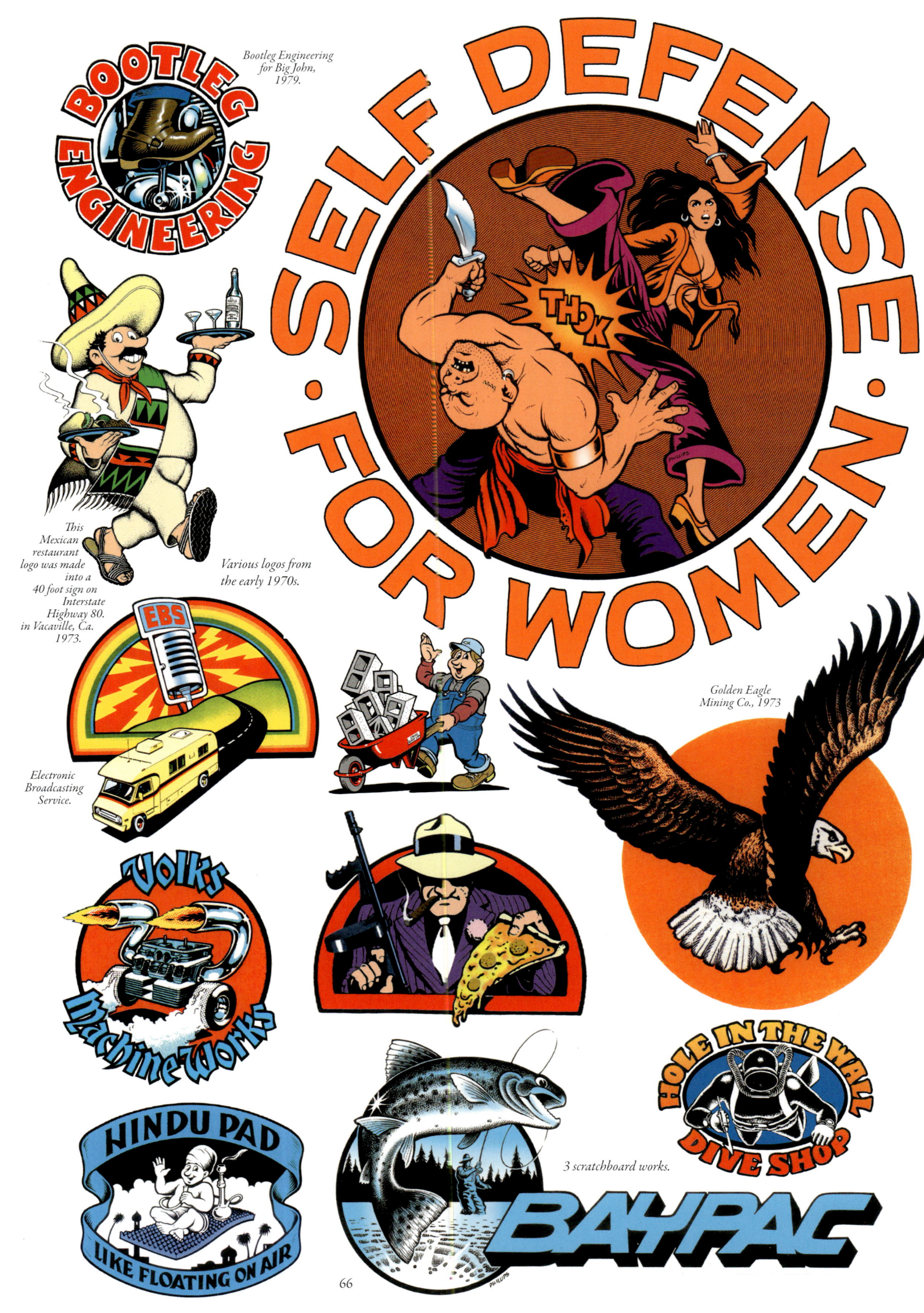

Bootleg Engineering for Big John, 1979.

SELF DEFENSE · FOR WOMEN ·

This Mexican restaurant logo was made into a 40 foot sign on Interstate Highway 80. in Vacaville, Ca. 1973.

Various logos from the early 1970s.

Electronic Broadcasting Service.

Golden Eagle Mining Co., 1973

3 scratchboard works.

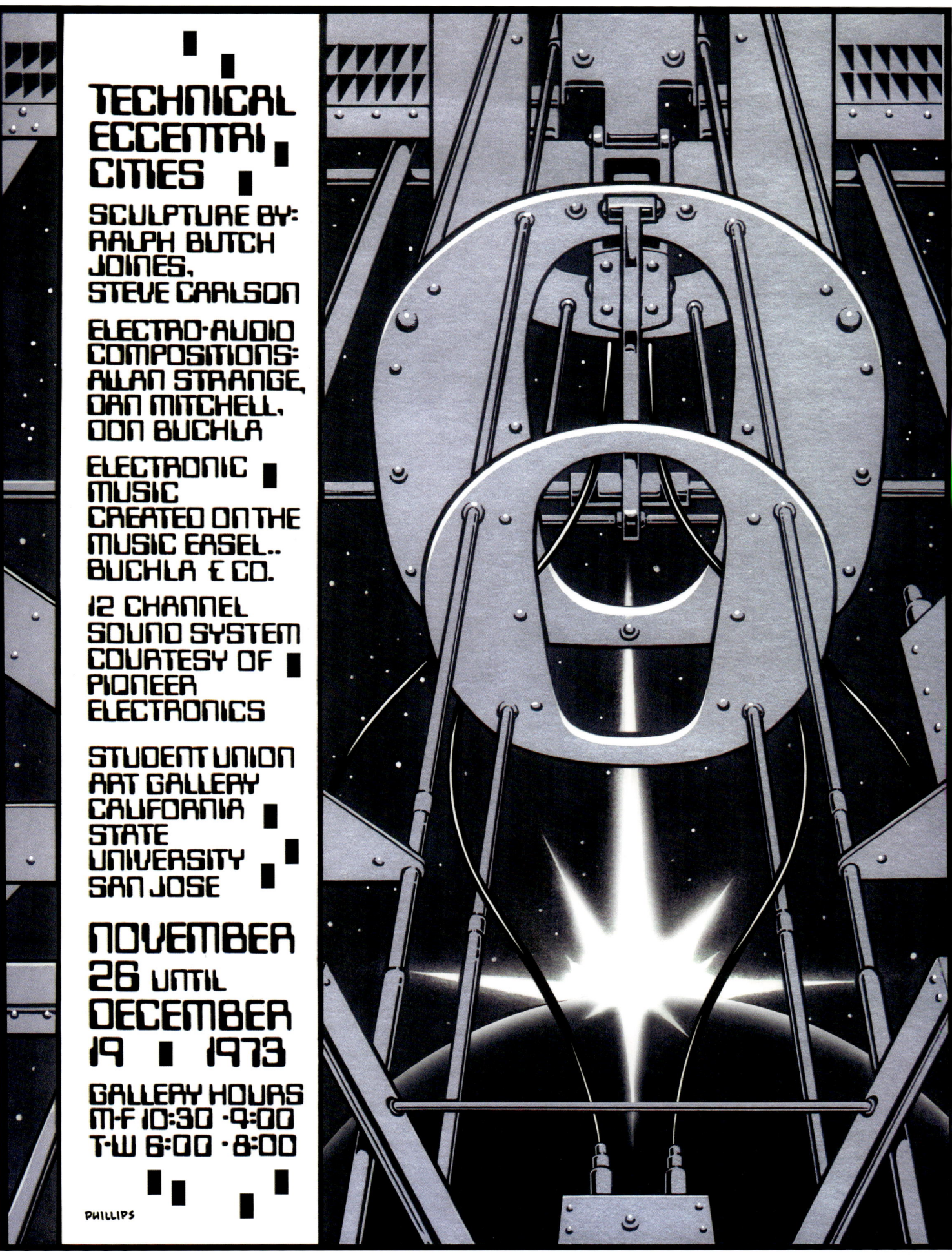

TECHNICAL ECCENTRICITIES

SCULPTURE BY:
RALPH BUTCH
JOINES,
STEVE CARLSON

ELECTRO-AUDIO
COMPOSITIONS:
ALLAN STRANGE,
DAN MITCHELL,
DON BUCHLA

ELECTRONIC
MUSIC
CREATED ON THE
MUSIC EASEL...
BUCHLA & CO.

12 CHANNEL
SOUND SYSTEM
COURTESY OF
PIONEER
ELECTRONICS

STUDENT UNION
ART GALLERY
CALIFORNIA
STATE
UNIVERSITY
SAN JOSE

NOVEMBER
26 UNTIL
DECEMBER
19 1973

GALLERY HOURS
M-F 10:30 -4:00
T-W 6:00 -8:00

PHILLIPS

BUCHLA & CO. *"TECHNICAL ECCENTRICITIES"* at San Jose State University, Nov. 1973, 8.5"x11" - early electronic music.
Printed white (ink) & black, on silver stock. Printed in San Jose, Ca.

67

PLASTICS
The Urethane Revolution

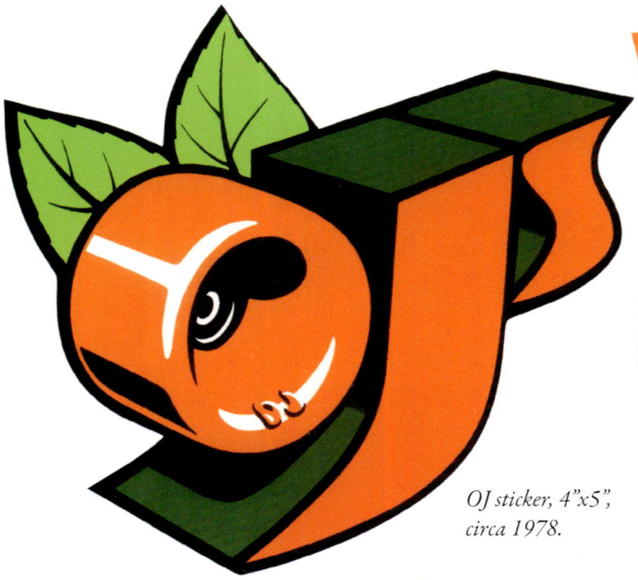

ROAD RIDER WHEELS

OJ sticker, 4"x5", circa 1978.

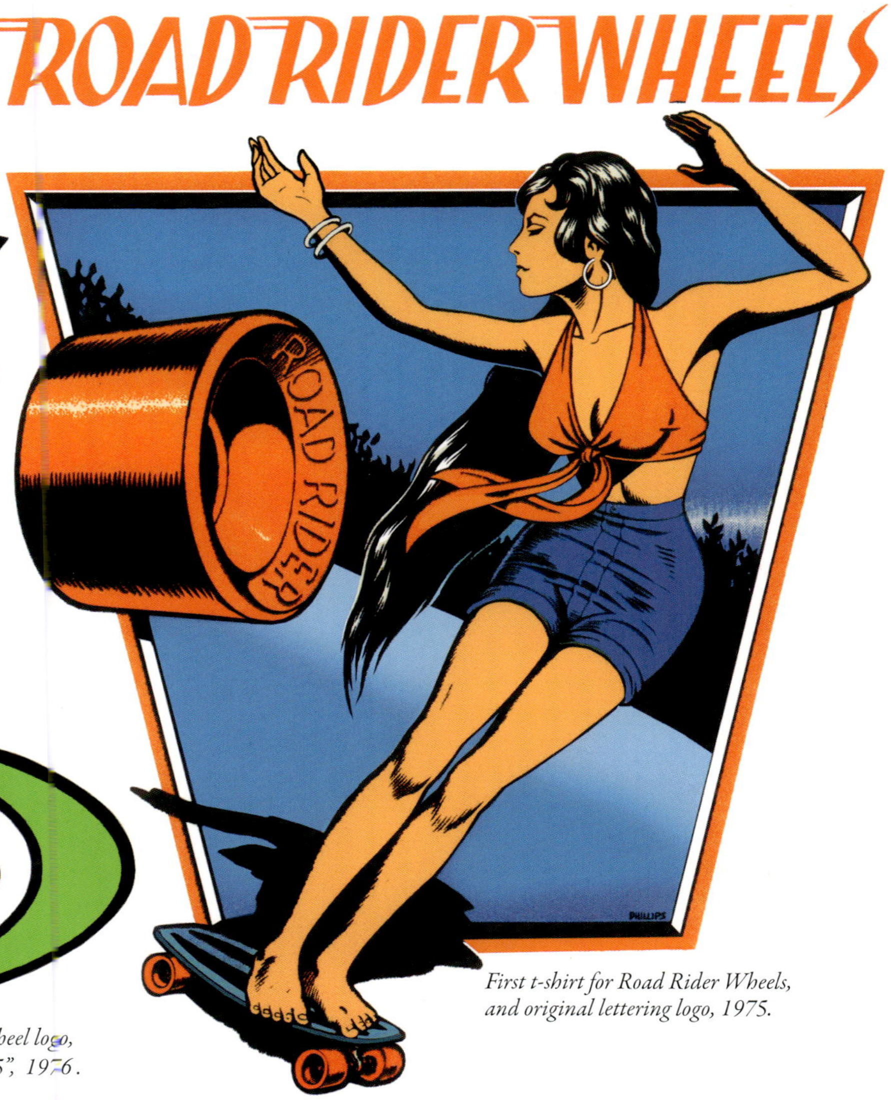

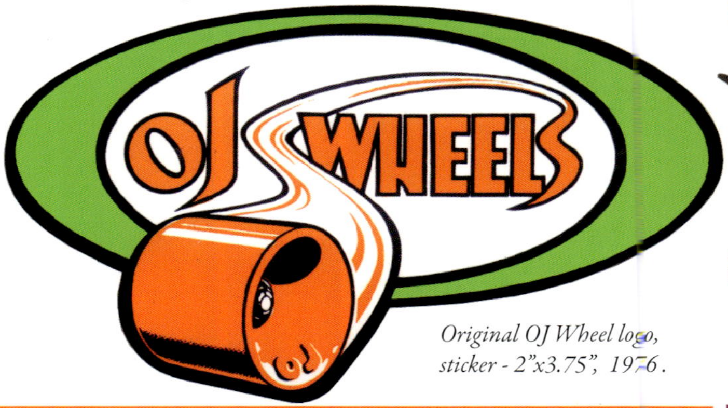

Original OJ Wheel logo, sticker - 2"x3.75", 1976.

First t-shirt for Road Rider Wheels, and original lettering logo, 1975.

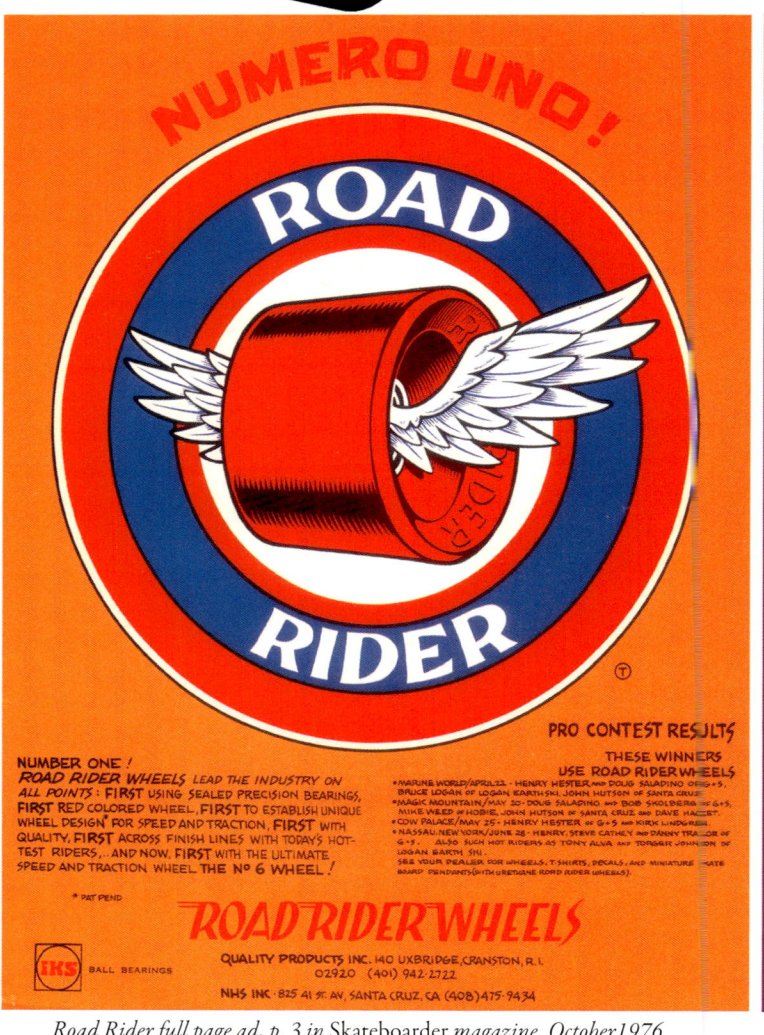

NUMERO UNO!

ROAD RIDER

PRO CONTEST RESULTS

THESE WINNERS
USE ROAD RIDER WHEELS

NUMBER ONE! *ROAD RIDER* WHEELS LEAD THE INDUSTRY ON ALL POINTS : FIRST USING SEALED PRECISION BEARINGS, FIRST RED COLORED WHEEL, FIRST TO ESTABLISH UNIQUE WHEEL DESIGN* FOR SPEED AND TRACTION, FIRST WITH QUALITY, FIRST ACROSS FINISH LINES WITH TODAY'S HOTTEST RIDERS,.. AND NOW, FIRST WITH THE ULTIMATE SPEED AND TRACTION WHEEL, THE N° 6 WHEEL !

* PAT PEND

ROAD RIDER WHEELS

IKS BALL BEARINGS   QUALITY PRODUCTS INC. 140 UXBRIDGE, CRANSTON, R.I. 02920 (401) 942-2722. NHS INC · 825 41 ST. AV, SANTA CRUZ, CA (408) 475-9434

Road Rider full page ad, p. 3 in Skateboarder *magazine, October 1976.*

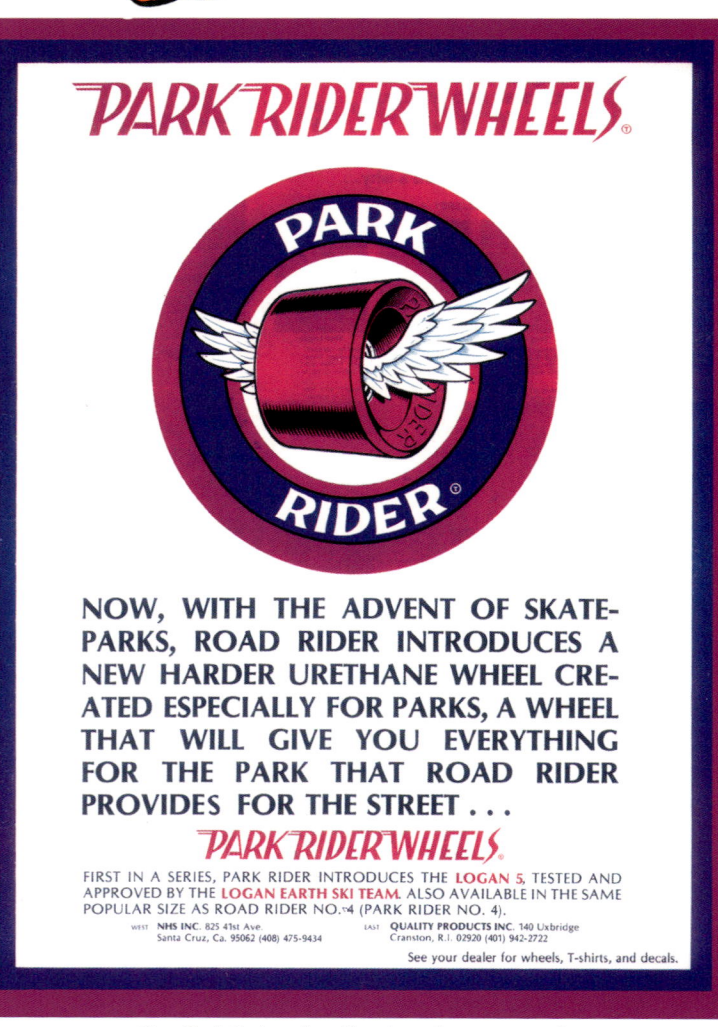

PARK RIDER WHEELS

PARK RIDER

NOW, WITH THE ADVENT OF SKATE-PARKS, ROAD RIDER INTRODUCES A NEW HARDER URETHANE WHEEL CREATED ESPECIALLY FOR PARKS, A WHEEL THAT WILL GIVE YOU EVERYTHING FOR THE PARK THAT ROAD RIDER PROVIDES FOR THE STREET ...

PARK RIDER WHEELS

FIRST IN A SERIES, PARK RIDER INTRODUCES THE **LOGAN 5**, TESTED AND APPROVED BY THE **LOGAN EARTH SKI TEAM**. ALSO AVAILABLE IN THE SAME POPULAR SIZE AS ROAD RIDER NO. 4 (PARK RIDER NO. 4).

WEST **NHS INC.** 825 41st Ave.
Santa Cruz, Ca. 95062 (408) 475-9434   EAST **QUALITY PRODUCTS INC.** 140 Uxbridge,
Cranston, R.I. 02920 (401) 942-2722

See your dealer for wheels, T-shirts, and decals.

First Park Rider ad, in Skateboarder, *circa 1976.*

SANTA CRUZ SKATEBOARDS

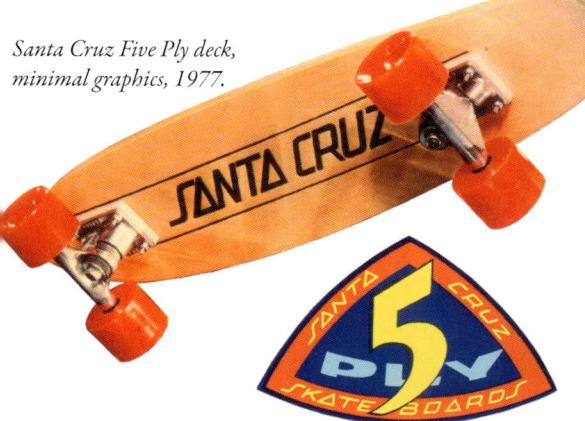

Santa Cruz Five Ply deck, minimal graphics, 1977.

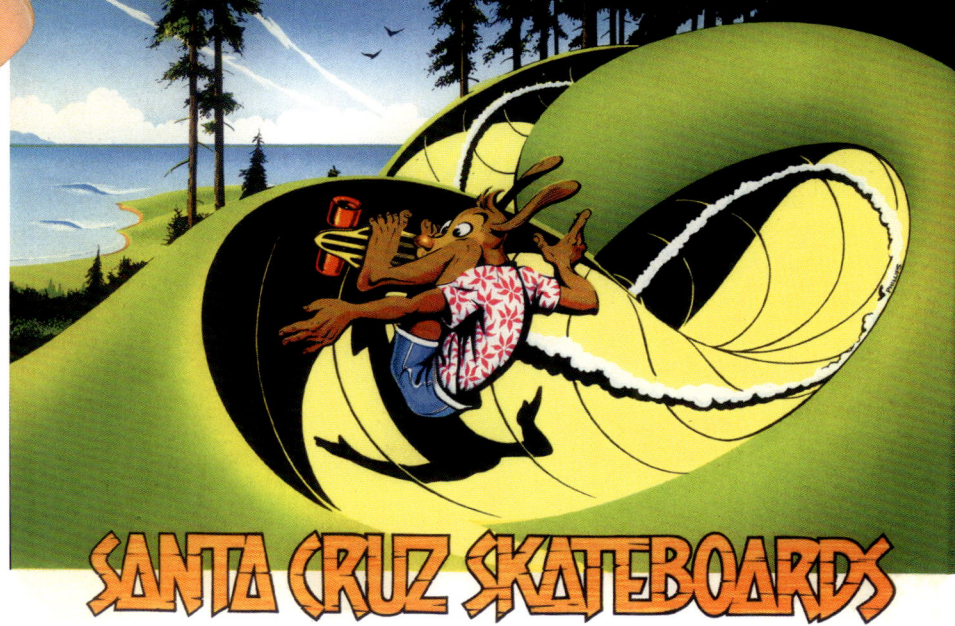

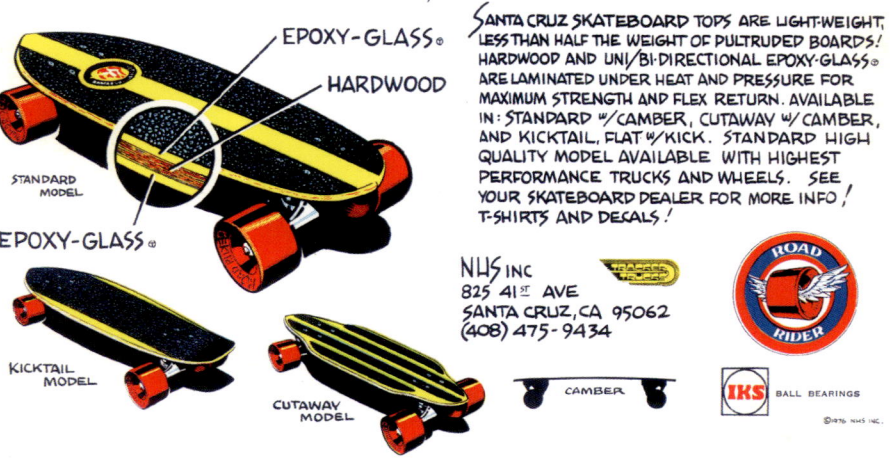

Ad work appearing in Skateboarder Magazine *1976. Drawing the products allowed for advance advertising.*

One door slams in your face and breaks your nose like Maxwell Smart, another door swings open wide to reveal King Tut's Tomb. By 1977 the skateboard revolution was... rolling. The first Cadillac Wheels ad appeared in *SURFER Magazine*, and *Skateboarder Magazine* was reborn for the Summer of '75. The cover of that issue showed a graceful kid about halfway up a vertical, eight-foot dry swimming pool wall. What seems primitive by 21st Century standards was revolutionary in the 70s. Technology had removed the fear of skidding to a stop on kidney stones, and all that weird terrain - swimming pools, drain pipes, drainage ditches - that skateboarders had been eyeing for years, was now accessible.

In Santa Cruz, Phillips was well-acquainted with Rich Novak, Doug Haut and Jay Shuirman, the N, the H and the S in NHS. Phillips knew all of these guys from surfing around Pleasure Point. They were all a few years older than Phillips and some had taken advantage. When Jim was a gremmie at Pleasure Point, Novak tried to kick him off the beach when he first surfed there. Shortly after, Jim gained acceptance when Shuirman stood up for him against some valley goons. Jim later worked for Novak who was a partner with George Olson in '63 at Olson Surfboards.

In the early 70s, Novak, Haut and Shuirman formed a company called NHS to sell fiberglass and resin and other materials to all the Santa Cruz surf shops, Tracy's Fiberglas Works and anyone else who needed plastics. They were living up to Mr. McGuire's prediction, and they were perfectly positioned when the urethane revolution hit.

Cadillac Wheels were a revolution, so to speak, but their loose bearings were still funky. NHS distributed Cadillac wheels, but were challenged into innovation when Jay Shuirman dumped a barrel of 100,000 ball bearings onto the floor of the NHS warehouse. What a mess. There had to be a better way. That better way walked in the door soon after in the form of Tony Roderick, a salesman from a Rhode Island company

called Quality Products. Mr. Roderick held in his hand a sealed bearing from a Hoover vacuum cleaner, and wondered if there might be some kind of application in skateboard wheels. Novak and Shuirman smiled quietly to themselves. They, too, opened the door to their car, and said "Hop in baby, let's go!" to Quality Products.

At the time, Novak and Shuirman had a small office in the back of Santa Cruz Surf Shop. Their sealed-bearing wheels would be called Road Riders, but they needed some "identity." Their desks were side by side and they had the habit of talking into the phone at the same time for sales calls. Phillips got one of those double-voiced calls. In 1974 Novak and Shuirman called about doing some ads and t-shirts for their first skateboard products. Phillips' first skate art was for Road Rider Wheels. He gave the wheels wings, no doubt because they flew with those sealed bearings.

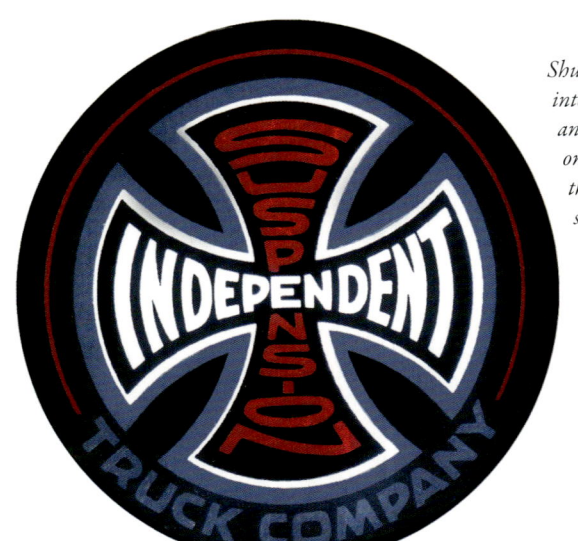

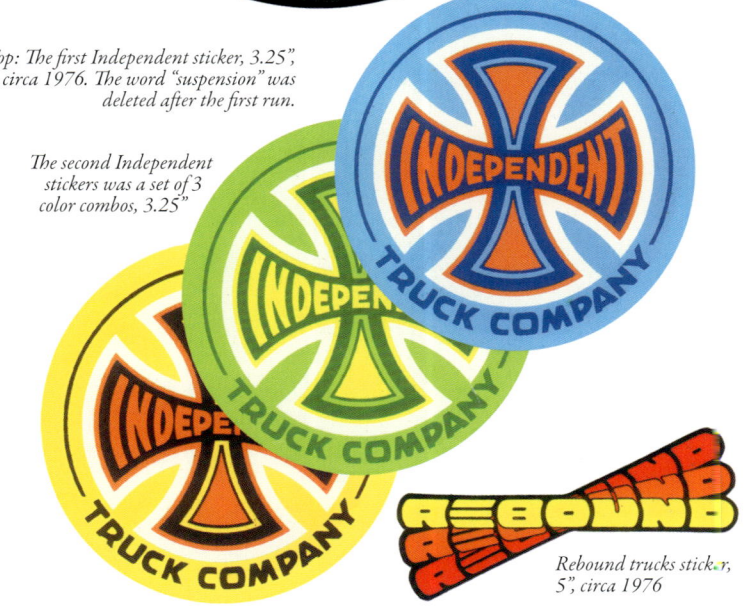

Top: The first Independent sticker, 3.25", circa 1976. The word "suspension" was deleted after the first run.

The second Independent stickers was a set of 3 color combos, 3.25"

Rebound trucks sticker, 5", circa 1976

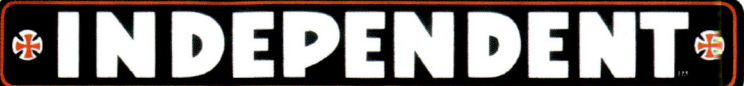

Independent bar 4.5"sticker designed to fit fit trucks, also 9", circa 1976.

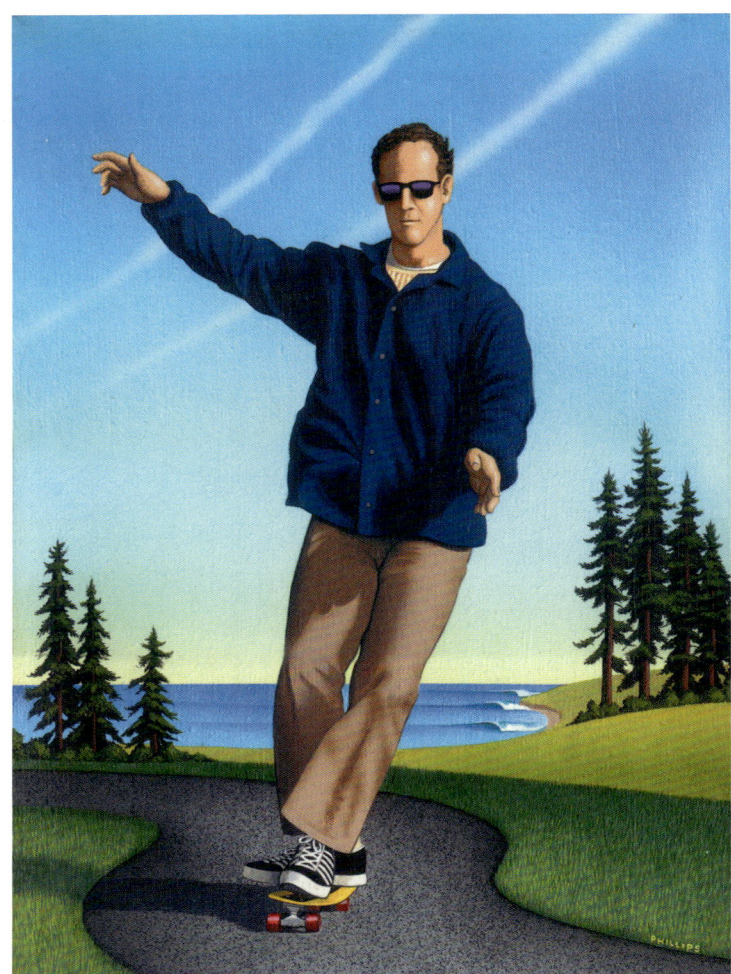

"JAY", acrylic on canvas, 12"x18", Mar 1999, memorial portrait of Shuirman, co-founder of NHS and Santa Cruz Skateboards.

Road Riders were red but sold in the black and that inspired Novak, Haut and Shuirman to start Santa Cruz Skateboards in 1975. They moved from a desk in a little room in the back of Santa Cruz Surf Shop, to the upper floor of the old Sprouse Ritz building on 41st Ave., near Pleasure Point. When Jim first started working for NHS, the company consisted of the two partners and a secretary. They had Jim do the original Road Rider logo, and there were also ads and brochures. The skateboard market was heating up. Skateboarder Magazine was reborn in 1975, published by SURFER Magazine. Severson was no longer associated with SURFER or Skateboarder, but Jim soon was. He did many colorful ad artworks in those publications.

Road Rider wheels pushed skateboarding into the stratosphere. They begin with Road Rider #2 then added #4 and #6 and a Henry Hester model for slalom. When parks came in vogue in 1976, they introduced a pink, Park Rider model. Phillips' first full-page ad for Road Rider wheels appeared in October, 1976. The graphics were typically Phillips - colorful and bulging with energy - and the lettering harked back to the days of Ralph Gray Studios, when Phillips' mentor would hand-letter everything himself. The copy on that first Road Rider ad was the shape of Screaming Things to come: "Numero Uno! ROAD RIDER

WHEELS lead the industry on all points: FIRST using sealed precision bearings. FIRST red colored wheels. FIRST to establish unique wheel design for speed and traction. FIRST with quality. FIRST across finish lines with today's 'hot-test' riders. And now FIRST with the ultimate speed and traction wheel, the No. 6 wheel!" That first Road Rider ad touted all the winners who used Road Rider wheels and at the bottom two companies were mentioned: Quality Products and NHS.

Santa Cruz Skateboards' first full-page ads appeared in that same issue and they were typically Phillips and typically low-key. The graphics were energized and colorful, and the copy was bashful: "LAMINATED UNDER HEAT and PRESSURE! "

Skateboarding took energy, all the energy Phillips had, and then some. There was as much work as he could do, and plenty of demand to have it fast. The large amount of work paid on an hourly basis, and added up to the Phillips family getting ahead of the bills and getting the house paid off.

Cell Block riser pads sticker, 4"x 2.35", circa 1976

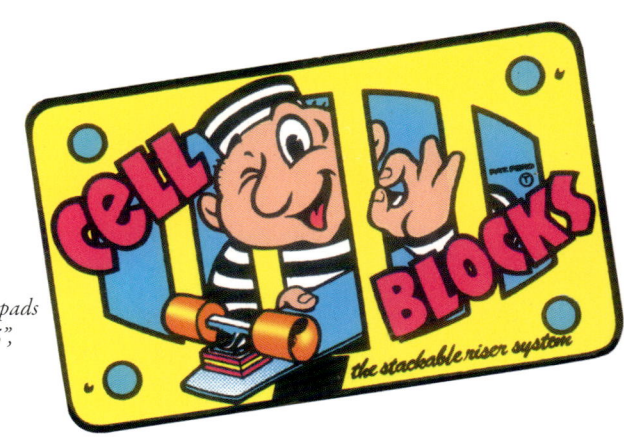

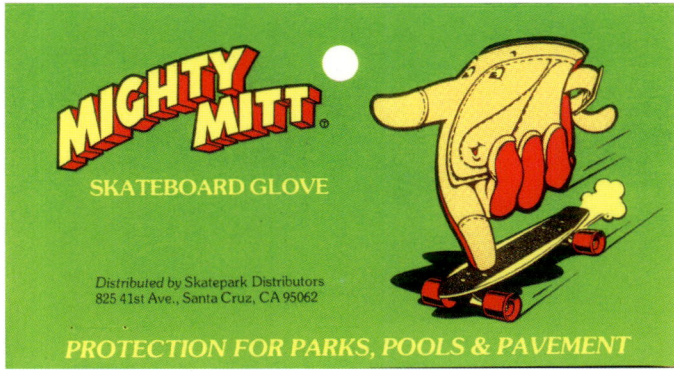

It was surfing that launched Phillips' art career, and skateboarding that began to threaten it. When Jim started work for Santa Cruz skateboards, he got a board with the first of the great new urethane wheels, and one for young Jim who was about 8 then. They terrorized parking lots and shopping centers. There weren't any NO SKATEBOARDING signs back then, and hardly anyone paid any attention to skateboarders. When Dolly went to some new shopping center, big and little Jim would skate all over it while she shopped. Over the next few years Jimbo grew older and their skating improved, and Jim started doing riskier maneuvers in the Harbor High parking lot. One day while he was doing a lay back, he fell and bent his drawing finger, hyperextending it backwards. It wasn't his worst skateboard injury up till then, except for the fact that his family depended on that finger! The demand for skateboard graphics was getting heavy at that time and it was vital that he maintained his vigorous drawing schedule. The finger was okay after a few days, and Jim cooled off on total aggro skating.

JIMBO PHILLIPS: *"When my dad started doing skateboards I remember him bringing home two brand new complete Santa Cruz skateboards, with Road Rider 2's and 4's. Needless to say we started skating all the time: We skated schools, malls, parking lots, anything cement and we would never see other people skating unless we went to Soquel Skate park or Frederick Street. But then one day Big Jim had a big spill. We were bombing the hill behind Harbor High. I was at the bottom already and here comes my dad 'hauling' then when he got to the bottom he hit a pebble and did the Pete Rose slide."*

Santa Cruz innovated Road Rider wheels and five-ply decks, and in 1976 Jay Shuirman led the innovation in skateboard trucks. The first Independent Truck ads were simple, a rad skate shot and some hypey type and that Independent logo, courtesy of Jim Phillips who had to stick up for the visual correctness of his historically un-PC logo. Since skateboarding was sidewalk surfing, he drew from the history of surfing and brought back the Surfer's Cross, except rounded. They didn't quite want it. It was "Too Nazi." Not for the first or last time, Phillips had to do some convincing to put across one of his ideas. He found fire-fighter logos that featured the Iron Cross, and topped that off with a cover of *Time Magazine* which featured a photo of the Pope with an Iron Cross pattern on his robe.

With a little help from On High, Phillips convinced them, and Independent adopted what is perhaps Phillips' most ubiquitous logo. Go around the world and you will see a Screaming Hand on a feral hut in Indonesia or a Pack Your Trash sticker flashing on the oar of a paddle in equatorial Brazil or a Santa Cruz sticker on the back of a taxi in Santa Cruz, Mexico, but it is that Independent Iron Cross logo that you will see from Moscow to Maine, Peru to Poughkeepsie.

By 1978, Santa Cruz Skateboards was booming, but beginning to feel a little pressure from Down South. Dogtown and Powell were beginning a design push that produced "pig boards," decks that were as wide as 10 inches, and a perfect canvas for graphics. Up to this point, Santa Cruz decks were pretty Plain Jane, mostly featuring simply the "Santa Cruz" lettering logo. Toward the end of the decade, skaters began plastering their decks with stickers and logos and their own graphics, and Phillips began to push for doing his own graphics on the wider decks. As always, it was a battle, and as usual, Phillips won. Jim wanted to do graphics on decks from day one, but eventually it was other marketing forces that enabled it. It started slow, the Steve Olson and Duane Peters models had some checkerboards and stripes, requested by the skaters, but the first real graphic was a generic deck with a winged dragon holding a ball with the round-dot Santa Cruz logo on it.

After that came the Stinger. The graphic breakthrough came on strong with the first Roskopp deck, which later evolved into a series of many decks.

In 1980, *Skateboarder Magazine* folded into *Action Now Magazine*, which lumped skating in with other shady turf sports like BMX, cool sports like surfing and semi-cool board sports like sailboarding and snowboarding. Skate parks were hit with liability problems and when they tried to pass those costs onto young skaters, young skaters passed and took to the street. There was a big skateboard industry shake-out at the end of the 80s, and millions were lost where millions had been made.

Of the original founders of NHS, Doug Haut had gotten out of the business in the early 70s to devote himself to making surfboards. Jay Shuirman and Rich Novak took the business into the promise of much, much bigger things around the corner. Tragically, Jay Shuirman passed away from leukemia in 1979. One of the founding fathers of NHS wouldn't live to see the success of the business he had founded. Phillips was devastated, "I went in, concerned about an ad deadline." Rich told Jimmy that Jay had died. "I knew Jay was ill, but didn't know he had leukemia." After he heard the awful news, the ad deadline seemed insignificant, and he just went home. At the date of Shuirman's death, NHS employed a half dozen workers, still operating out of the Sprouse-Ritz building, and Phillips was working for them nonstop, mostly out of his home. This was the end of the 70s, but the beginning of the Boom Decade. And somewhere, Mr. McGuire was smiling quietly to himself while Benjamin Braddock, like a lot of others, was kicking himself. "Plastics!"

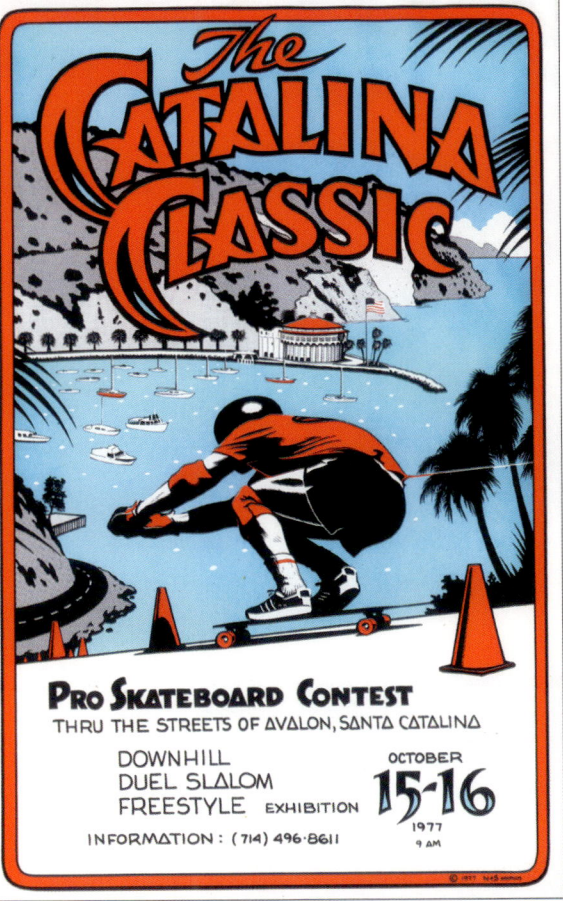

Gypsy Sky - *Santa Cruz, 14"x20", Quick Print, 1973.*
Bonnie Raitt - *Santa Cruz, 11"x17", Pilot Press, 1976.*
Maria Muldaur - *Santa Cruz, 11"x17", Pilot Press, 1976.*

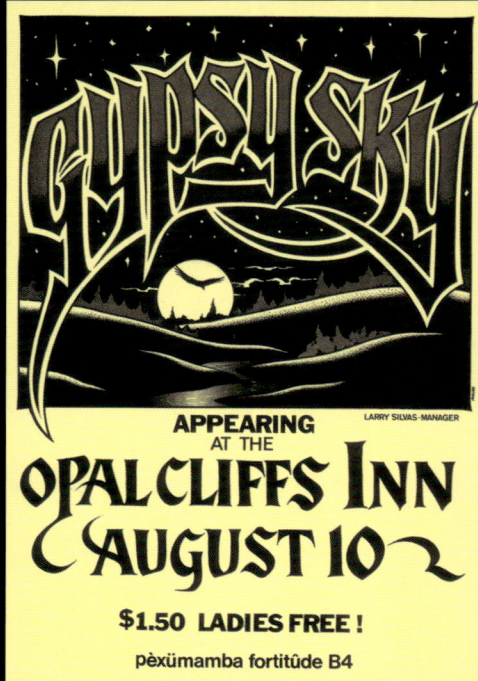

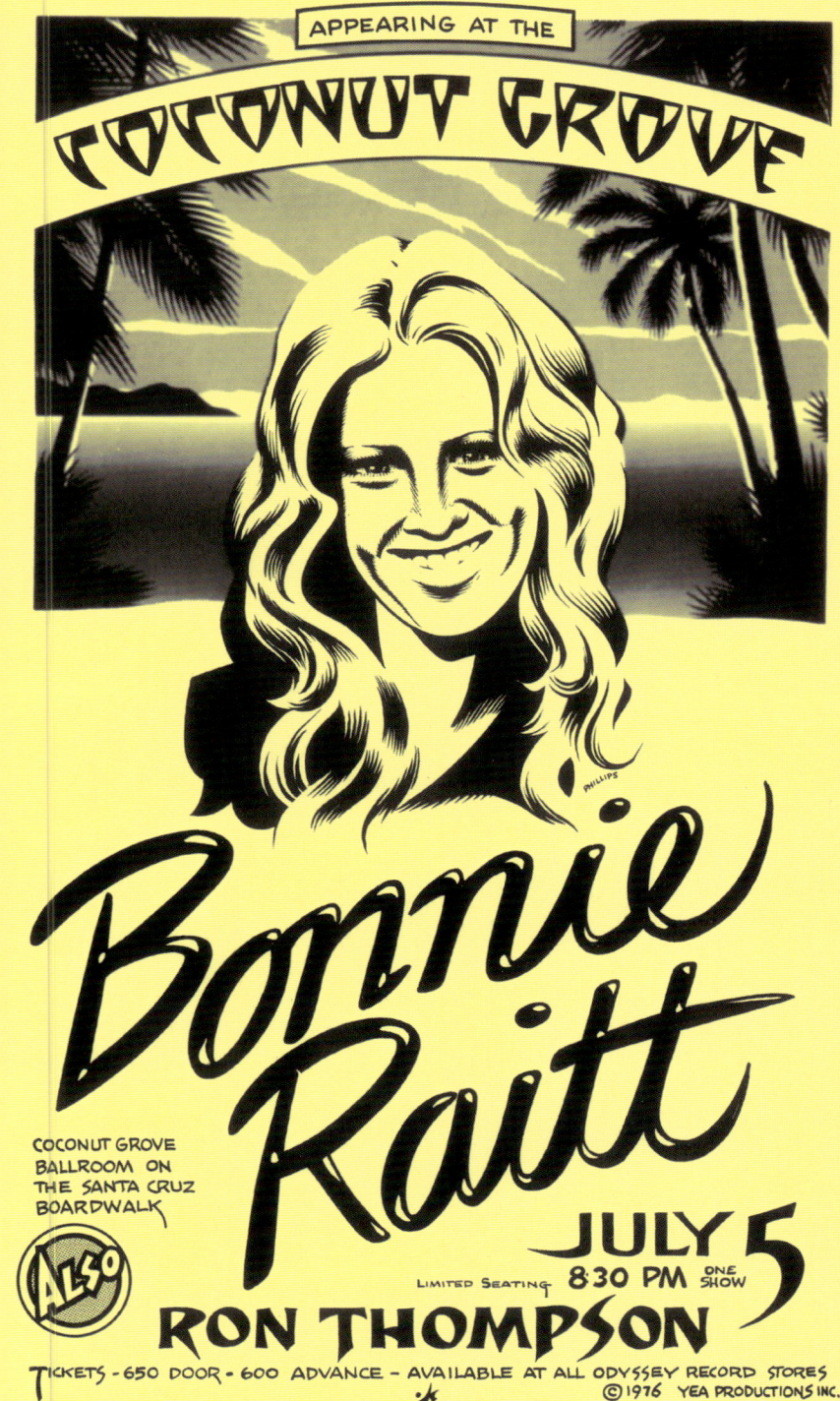

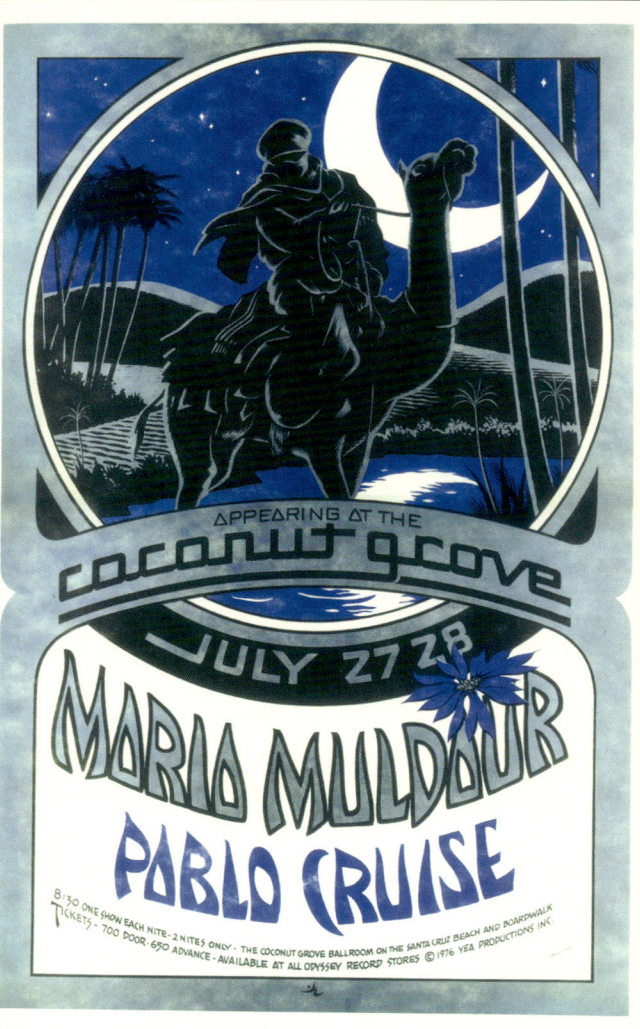

In June of 1976, Phillips took a "nuisance job" from Geoff McCormack, who had been the Art Director during the wonder years at Tracy's Fiberglas Works. McCormack had a free-lance business going, and handed off a $50 concert poster to Phillips. It was a Bonnie Raitt poster for the Coconut Grove, produced by Yea Productions. The job was simple but the budget was low. Jim did a pen and ink portrait of Bonnie, and Yea stapled them onto poles all over town. Then Yea Productions called with another poster order. This was for Maria Muldaur at the Coconut Grove. The repeat order got Jim thinking that maybe it was an opportunity, in a wave of music nostalgia from the 60s, that he could ride. Jim put a lot more into the new poster, even though it was derivative of his Camel scratchboard, because of *Midnight at the Oasis*. This poster would have a second color. Jim used a deep blue for the midnight effect. He had his artists' equity in the poster and expected a quality product from the printers, Pilot Press. The owner of Pilot was the son of one of the old photo engravers in town, who did all of the printing plates when they were still made of lead. They knew Ralph Gray, and liked Jim. But there was a devil. A printer's helper is called a devil, and this one was named Harold. Harold got a bright idea, to use up an old pile of parchment paper that was lying around in the shop. Printing on parchment gave the poster splotches, and dampened Jim's hope of making something out of the job.

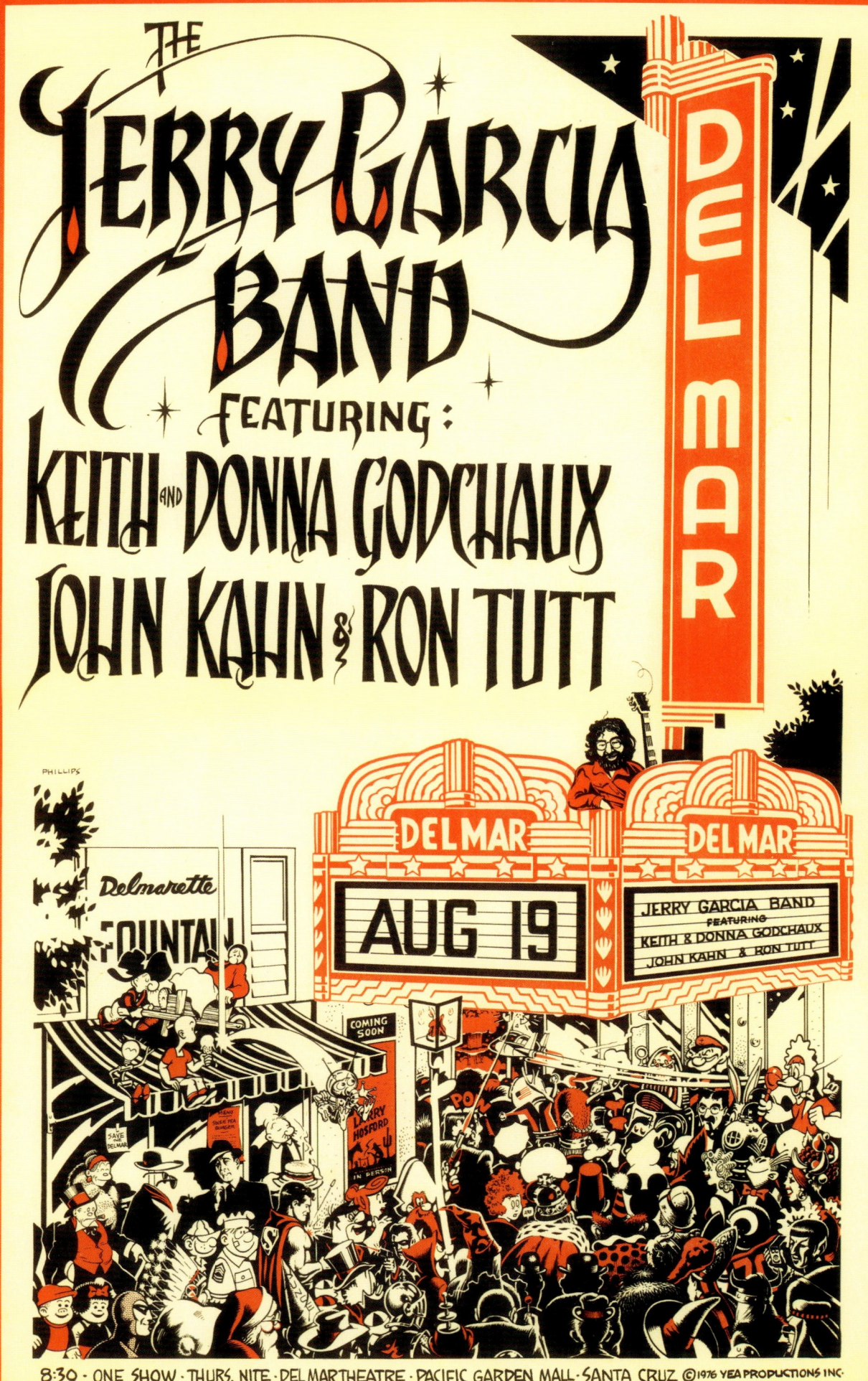

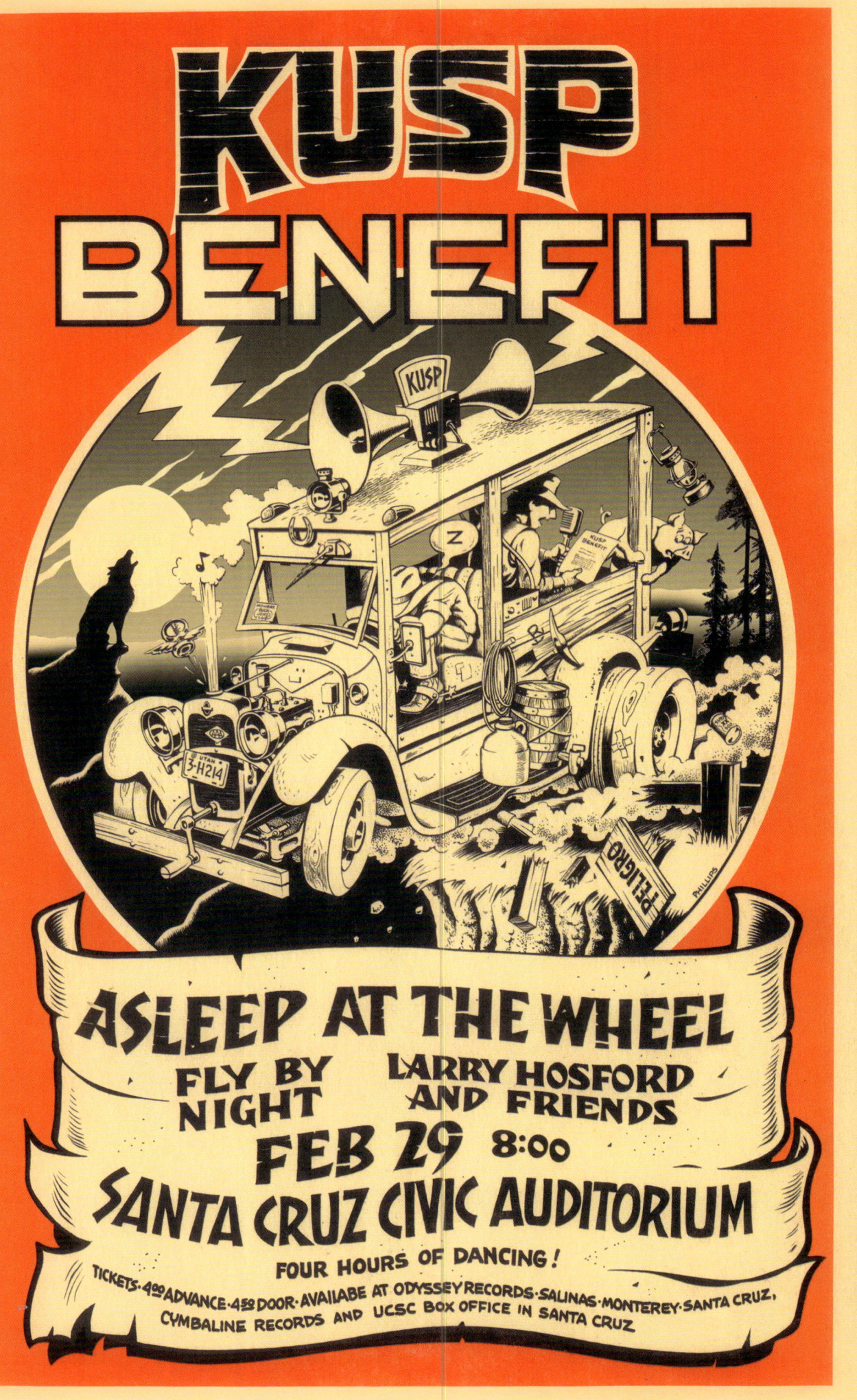

A month later Yea called again. This time they wanted a two-color poster for the Jerry Garcia Band at the Del Mar Theater. Jim knew this was his chance to show what he could do, so he sketched a crowd going into the theater: one of Mr. Eggert's classic 'mob' scenes. Humphrey Bogart and Dr. Livingston were in the crowd, with many other cartoon and comic characters. Jerry Garcia was sitting in the marquee looking down on the crowd. Another bummer besides the measly pay was the tight deadline. It takes someone to plan enough in advance to get the dates finalized, have the art done, get the printing done and get them distributed at least a weekend ahead of the show. There is usually a shortfall somewhere, and it often falls on the artist to make up lost time

KUSP Benefit poster 11"x17", Quality Offset, 1977.

by rushing. Jim attacked the Garcia poster aggressively in order to squeeze everything he wanted into it in the time allotted, working late hours for several days.

Because of Harold's past casual use of old parchment, Jim decided to look for another printer and went to Quality Printing, on Brommer Street. Quality Offset Printing was near his house and they had printed the old Phillips & Son cards. This press house incident in 1976 would later turn out to have another connection for Phillips that would revive his rock poster art twenty years later.

The midnight oil and the elbow grease congealed together nicely, and got Phillips what he wanted: recognition and work. People noticed the Jerry Garcia posters, and some people noticed how hard Phillips was working, amazed that anyone would work that hard on an artwork for poster pay.

Phillips returned to one of his favorite childhood motifs, pumpkins, for his next job, a Halloween poster for The Catalyst, a popular club downtown. During the 70s, The Catalyst was one of the more popular clubs in California. Major bands would kick off their tours at The Catalyst and it

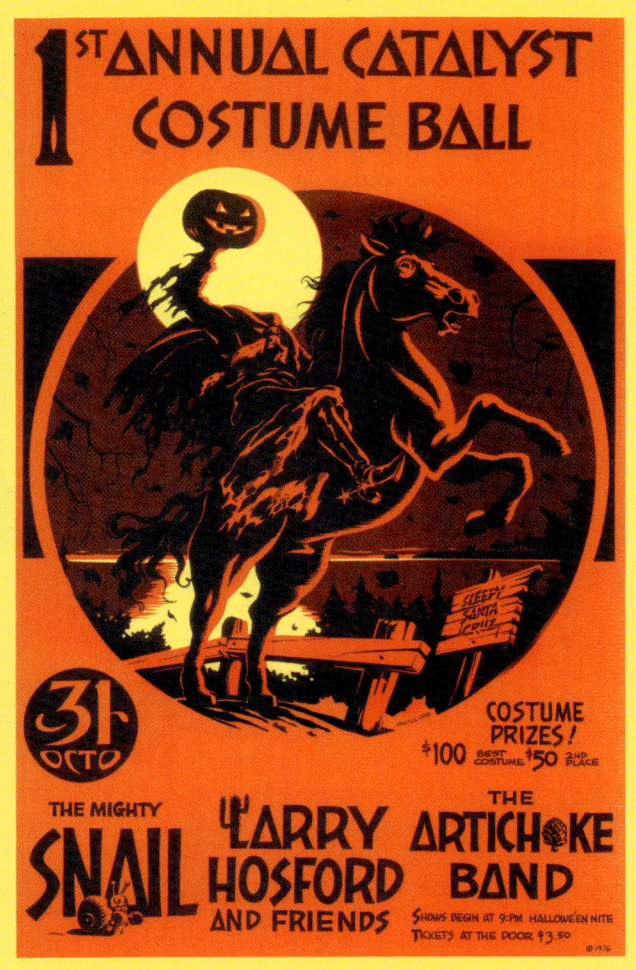

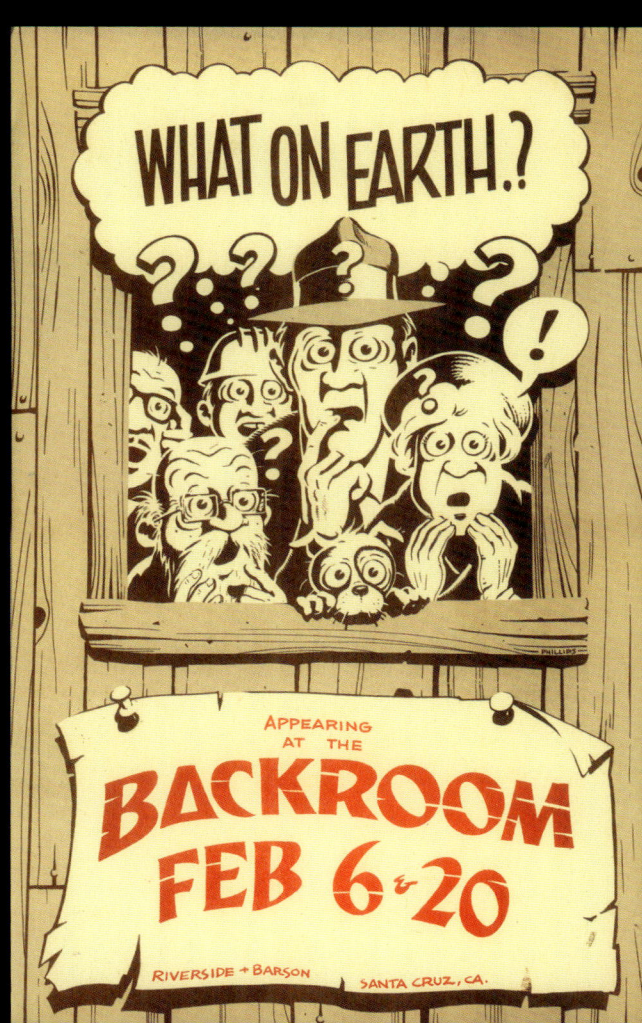

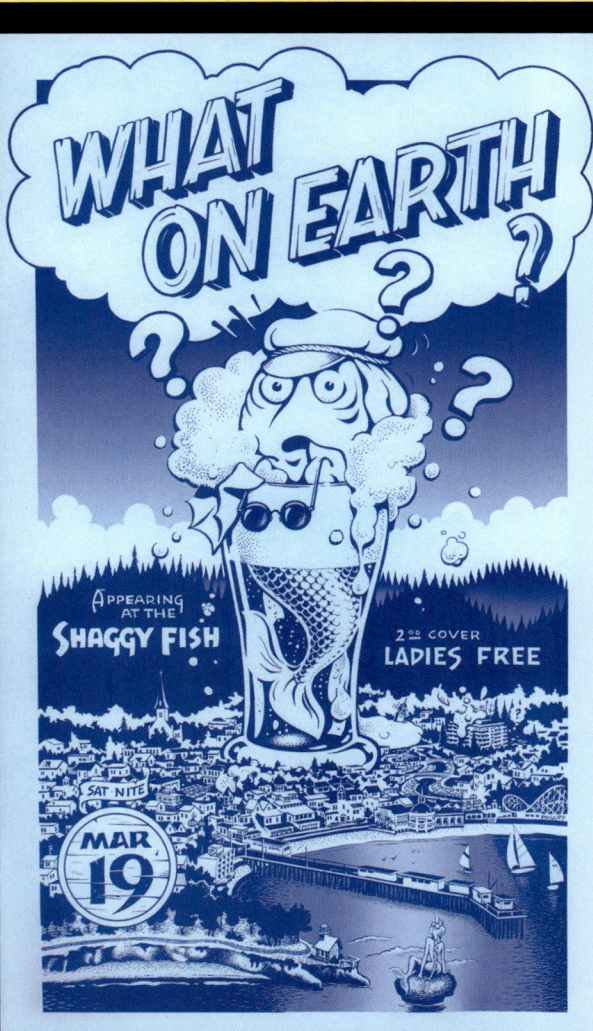

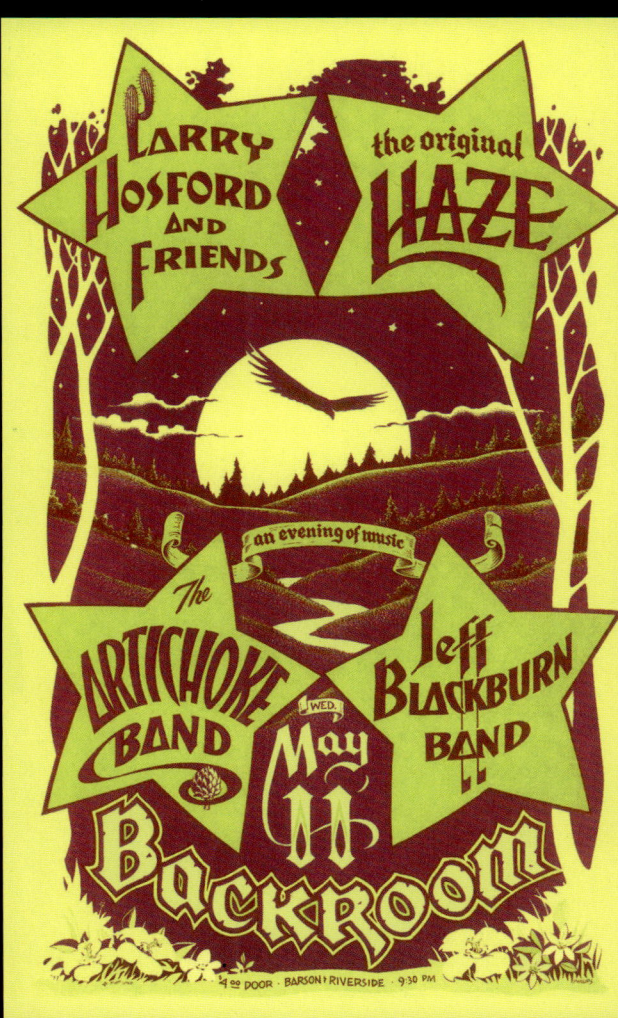

Top and clockwise: Catalyst poster, 11"x17", Quality Offset, 1976.
What on Earth at the Backroom poster, 11"x17", Quality Offset, 1977.
What on Earth at Shaggy Fish poster, 8.5"x14" Quality Offset, 1977.
Hosford, Haze, Buck & Chokes, Backroom poster, 11"x17", Quality Offset, 1977.

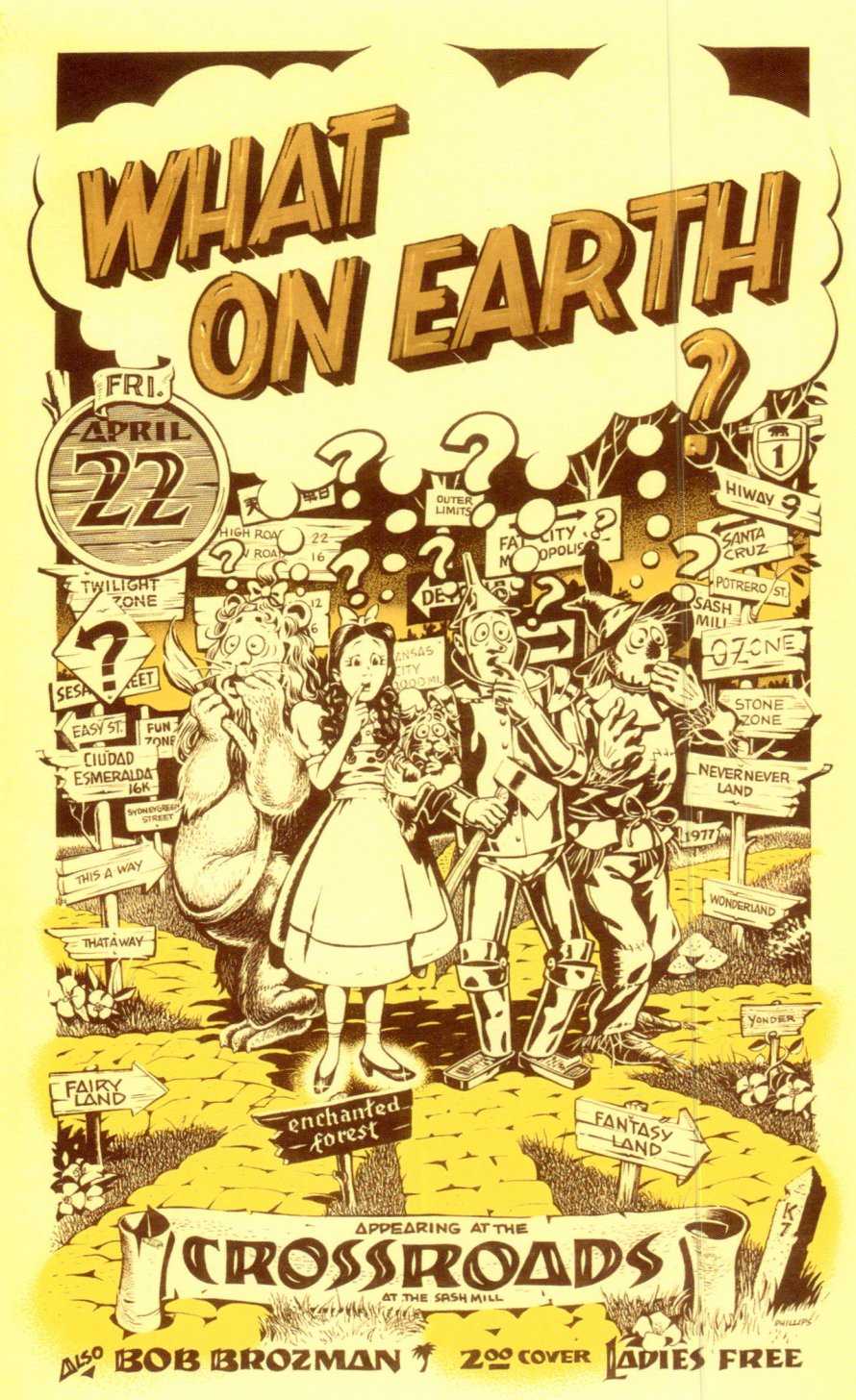

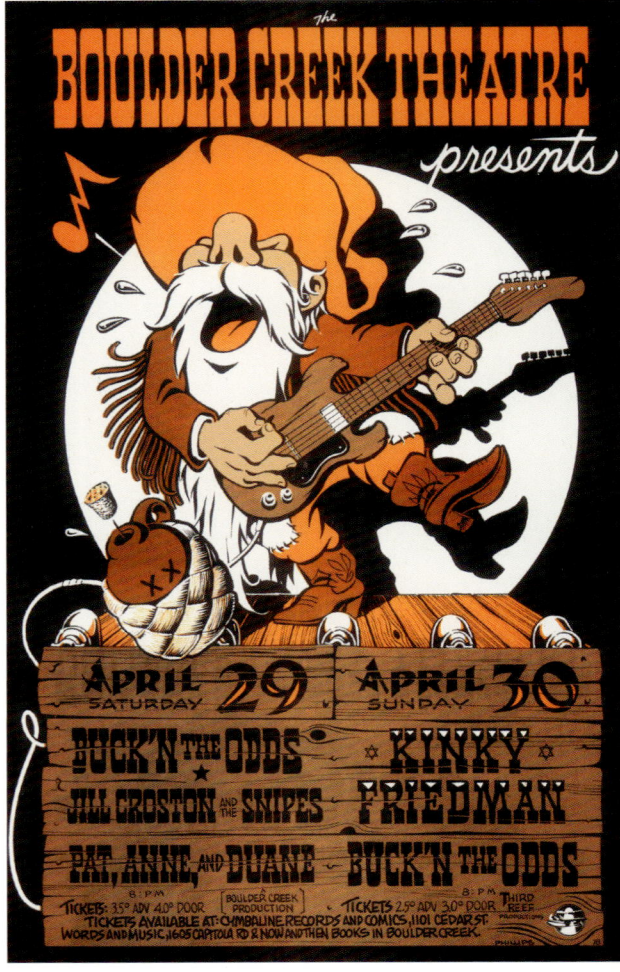

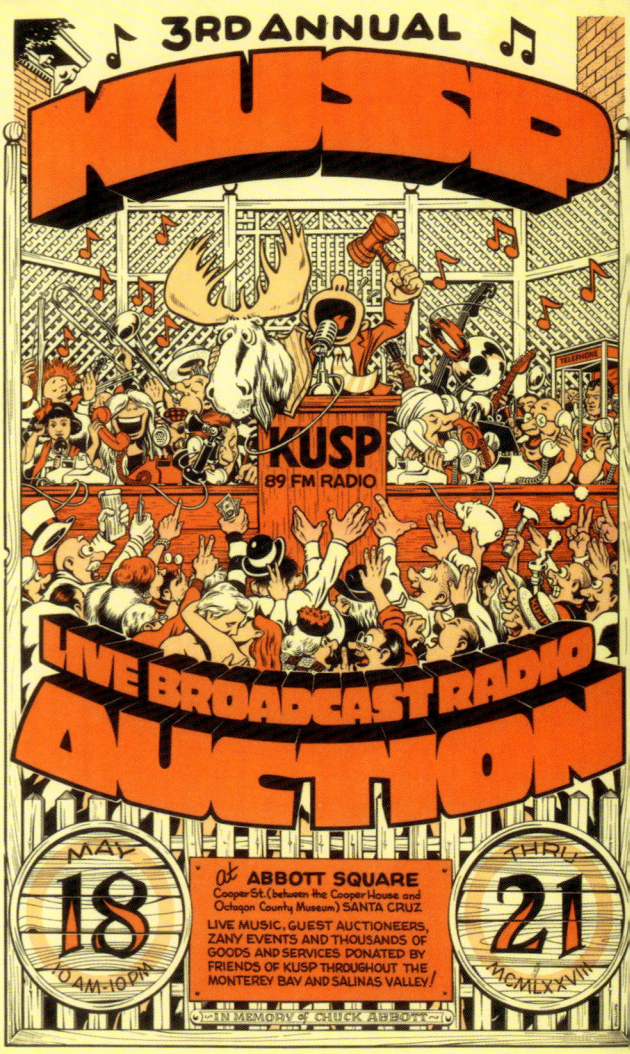

Above: What on Earth, *8.5"x14", 1977, Quality Offset printing.*
Top right: Boulder Creek Theatre, *7.25"x11", 1978, Third Reef Productions (Maz), Quality Offset.*
Right: KUSP Auction, *11"x17", 1977, Live music radio broadcast, Quality Offset printing.*

seemed like anyone who was anyone played there at some time: The Police, The Talking Heads, Devo, Neil Young, The Tubes, Stray Cats. The Catalyst Halloween party was one of the best parties of the year, during a time when Santa Cruz went berserk for the colorful holiday. Phillips' Halloween Ball poster featured a headless horseman rearing back on a ghostly charger.

Santa Cruz has at least a half-dozen "alternative" newspapers and magazines here in the 21st Century, but in the 70s *Good Times* was the father of all these weeklies. If the Catalyst was the happening club then *Good Times* was the happening thing to read, an alternative to the *Santa Cruz Sentinel*. *Good Times* ran ads for all the concerts at The Catalyst and the Civic Auditorium, and these ads all began to feature Jim Phillips' artwork. For the second but not last time in his life, Phillips was ubiquitous in Santa Cruz, on every telephone pole and every newsstand, all over town. His concert posters were in *Good*

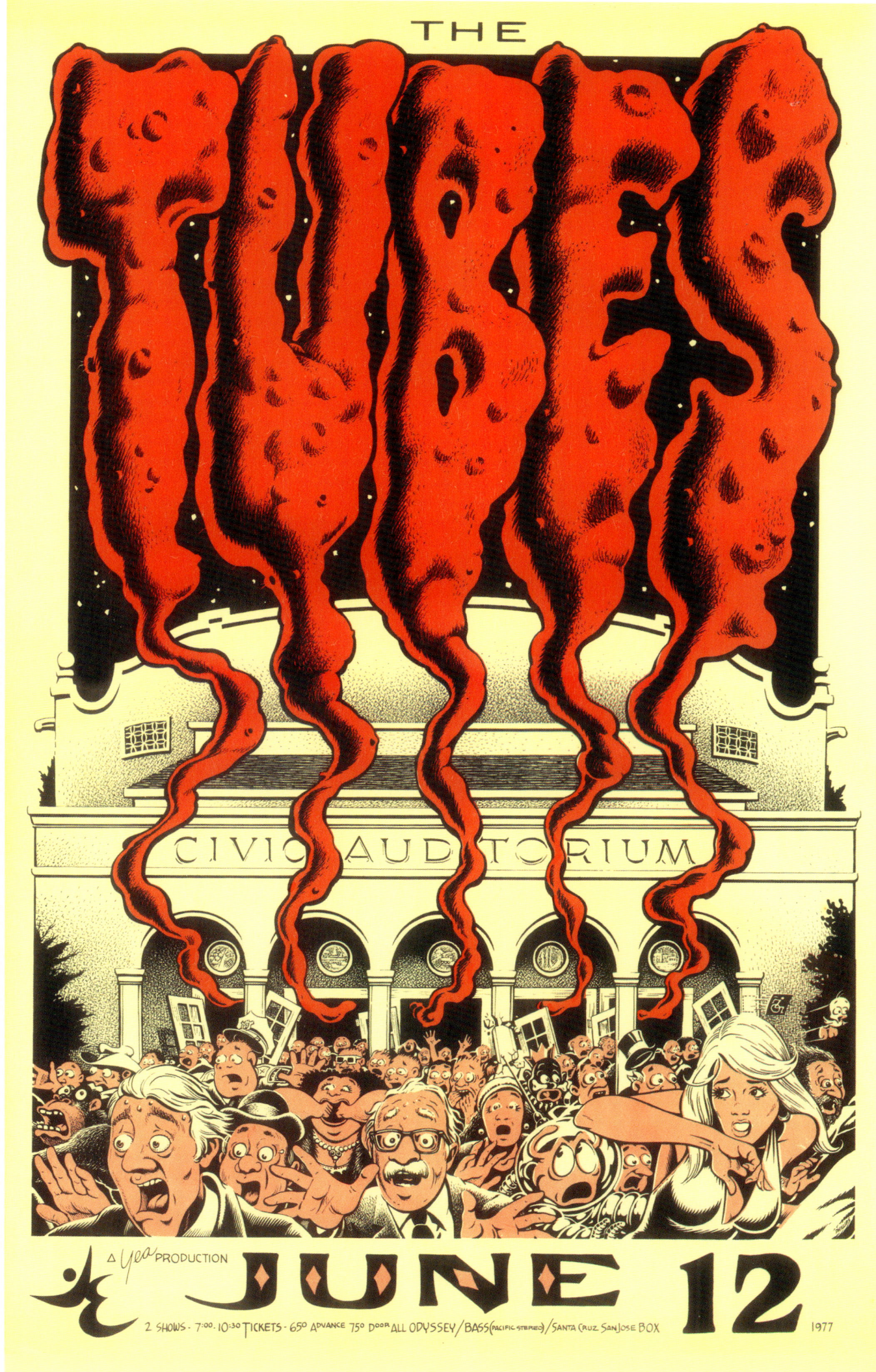

Tubes poster, 1977, 11"x17", Quality Offset.

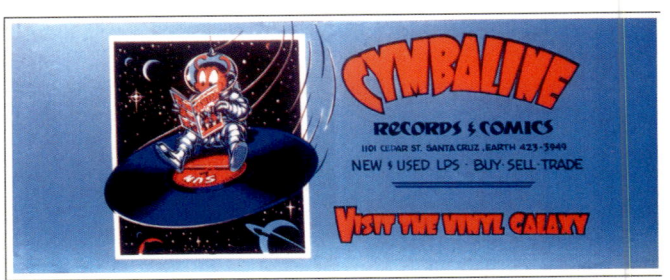

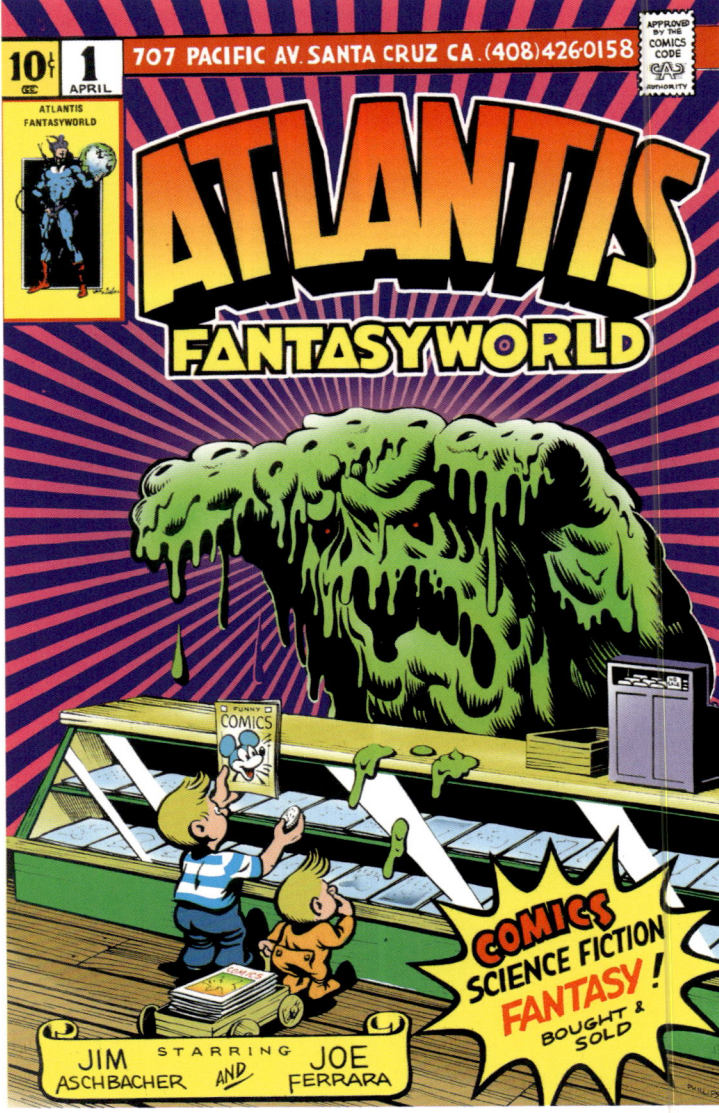

Atlantis Fantasyworld ad, circa 1978.
Top: Cymbaline city bus display card, 11"x28", 1976.

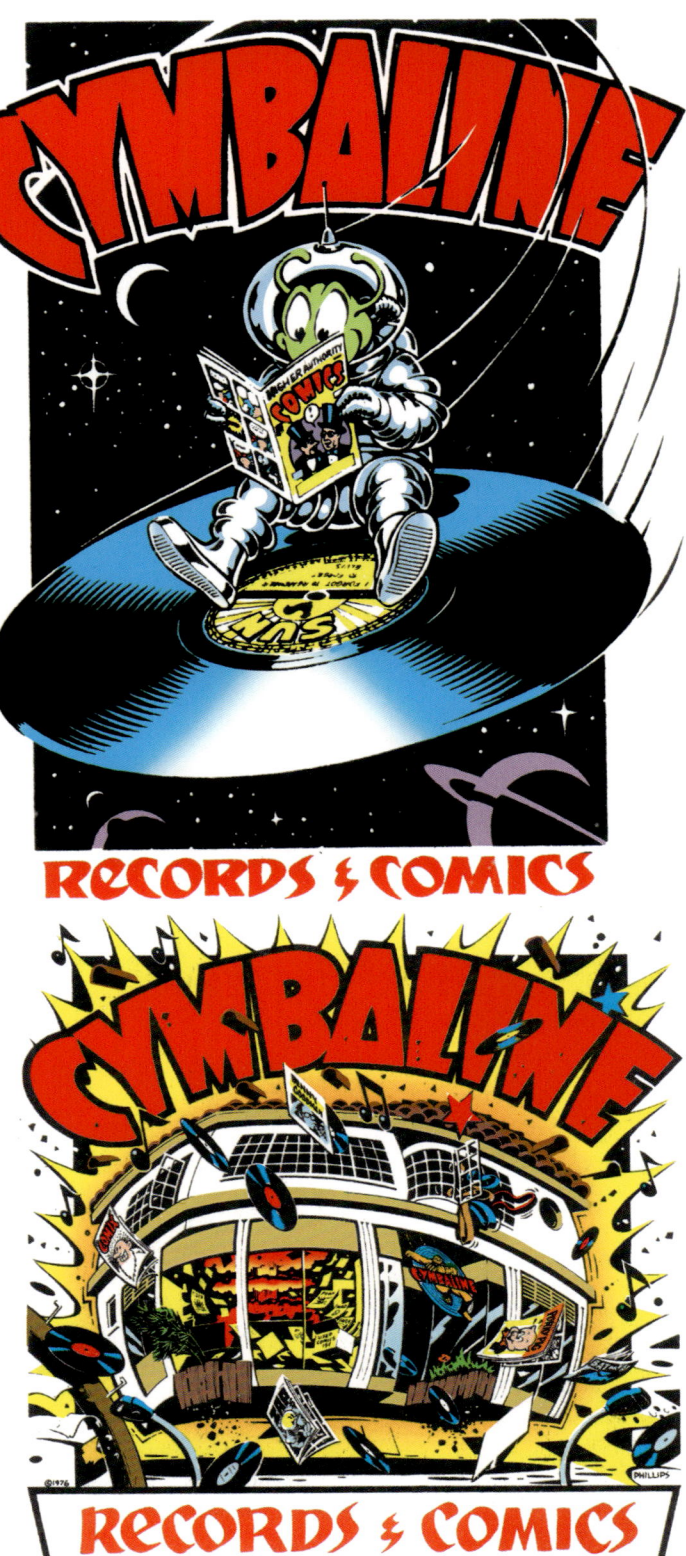

Cymbaline Records and Comics logos and ads, 1976.

Times and he did a logo for Cymbaline Records which had a little spaceman riding on a record. "Sparky the Space Gremlin," appeared in several other posters and comics in the years to come.

From the concert posters and Good Times and Cymbaline, Phillips began to be "in there" in Santa Cruz in the early 70s, and that generated other work and the ball started rolling. The Catalyst Halloween poster caught the attention of Pete Simmons, who took it to his brother Willie, who was a drummer for a band called What On Earth? Willie called the next day and ordered a logo, and then a series of posters. Phillips' logo was a barn window and a bunch of people looking out with "What on Earth?" looks on their faces. That logo was the basis of their first poster, for a show at the Backroom on December, 1976. Willie

was kinder and easier to deal with than the Yea guys. Phillips and Simmons became good friends. He pulled Jim and Dolly out of their shells and got them out to the clubs. They danced to the band's music, and it was a good time. Willie ordered a rash of other posters over the next few years, and the band became closely identified with Phillips' art.

WILLIE SIMMONS: *"What on Earth? was a Santa Cruz Rock and Roll band formed in 1976. I was the manager and drummer for the band. We were thinking about a band logo when my brother Pete said 'Look no more, you've got the best artist in the west right here in Santa Cruz.' He showed me one of Jim Phillips' posters he'd taken off a telephone pole, and before I knew it I was thumbing through the phone book looking for Jim's number. I commissioned*

Jim to do a logo for the band which we could put on a t-shirt. Jim created the people looking through the window with that 'What on Earth?' expression. Due to the band's humble means, we recycled this first piece of art on different posters with different dates. We followed this poster with the Shaggy Fish venue, and then The Crossroads which had Dorothy, Tinman, Scarecrow and Lion all wearing that 'What on Earth?' look. Later posters became more elaborate as we were able to afford more colors. We gave Jim full reign on subject matter. The only thing I would tell him was the name of the place we were playing and the date. We (the band) were like kids at Christmas time waiting to see what Phillips was going to come up with next. I never asked Jim what to draw, I would just tell him the date of the gig, and which venue it would be at. He never ceased to amaze me with the end product. It always amazed me how fast Phillips worked. In more than one case I would call or go see Jim, tell him the date and place we'd be playing, then he'd call me the next morning and tell me to come over and see the poster. I know Jim Phillips' art work brought many smiles to many faces here in Santa Cruz. Over the years I was in numerous bands, and one of my great joys in entering a new band was 'Oh-Boy, a new Phillips logo!' To this day, it is still a thrill to go over to Jim's and see what he's working on."

Daddy-O logo, 1977,
a consolation for being bumped
by the band Ducks
on request by Neil Young.
(retro-color)

Not for the first nor the last time, Jim Phillips' work inspired a little controversy. The *Santa Cruz Sentinel* came out with a front page story about the "trashy" rock and roll posters stapled to the telephone poles all over town. Right at the top was a large photo of a telephone pole with posters plastered all over it, and a Jim Phillips' What on Earth? poster the most prominent. But people pretty much ignored the Sentinel, and the postering of Santa Cruz continued every time there was a surf movie or a rock concert in town.

WILLIE SIMMONS: *"It became a challenge to find places to put up the posters where they would last more than a couple hours. We would go out and put up a couple hundred posters in a day, and by that evening you'd be lucky to find a dozen left up. People were collecting them like crazy! That's when Jim and I started numbering the backs of the posters. We would try to save the first 50, he'd get odd numbers and I would get the even numbers. Then of course we had all these people who had their own certain number that they had to have each time a new poster came out. Not only the people in town were collecting Phillips posters, it seems other artists were collecting Jim's ideas and putting them on their own posters. I don't know if that was flattering or frustrating for Jim. At least myself and Phillips fans knew who the originator was."*

KUSP Radio asked Jimmy to do a benefit poster. He agreed as his contribution to the newly-emerging, noncommercial station that Jim listened to daily and nightly while he worked in the peace and quiet of his Live Oak home. They asked Jim to do a poster for Asleep at the Wheel, so he did his classic, Woody-Off-the-Cliff for the benefit. A few months later they offered a paying job for their May radio auction poster. Jim calls his cartoon of the auction, "Moose head on the block."

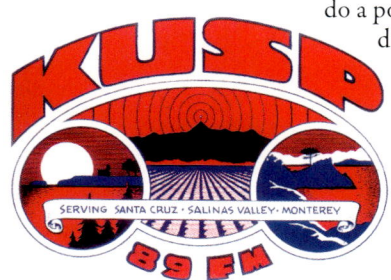

KUSP logo, 1976

Yea Productions called Jim for another poster, and the price was still only fifty bucks. It was for Atlanta Rhythm Section, the last live show at the Del Mar before they turned it into a multiplex. Jim didn't knock himself out for this one, considering the budget. But they must have liked it because they ordered a Tubes poster for June, 1977. He knocked himself out on this one, with giant letters blobbing out of the Civic Auditorium, and the crowd running and screaming. A lot of people [including the editor of this book] consider this one of Jim's classics.

In 1977, Neil Young slouched into Santa Cruz and hooked up with some friends to form a band called Ducks. One of Phillips' friends, Jim Mazzeo, was Neil Young's manager at the time and he hooked up Phillips with a Santa Cruz institution that rocked the town all summer long. "Maz told me I was now the 'band artist' and I accepted," Phillips said. Jeff Blackburn was in the band along with Bob Moseley of Moby Grape and Johnny Craviatto, another old friend. They had an old farmhouse at Pleasure Point called Duck's Landing and they played top secret gigs all around town. Neil Young drove his '40 Packard Woody to all his gigs, and was followed by his semi-rig and recording studio. They had Jim draw up some *Good Times* ads about local dates. Then Neil wanted a poster, an art print that would be sold at the Box Office instead of displayed on telephone poles. The only catch was, Neil didn't want his name on it. Or the venue or the dates. The poster was supposed to pay whenever it cleared the printing costs. Jimmy and Dolly made a Ducks banner and gathered cattails for the stage. An article on Jim's posters in Good Times was postponed a week to put a Ducks story on page one. The following week Phillips was featured as a front-page story, "The Best Illustrator in Town." They used *The Camel* on the front page, and a few of Jim's drawings inside. Jim felt embarrassed by "The Best" title, but things were heating up pretty good for his art.

THE CARTOON WORLD OF JIM PHILLIPS
By Dan Coyro
From The Good Times, September 8, 1977

You've seen his poster illustrations all over town-from the corner telephone poles, to the new kiosks on the Mall. And though his drawings are stapled with dozens of other handbills, Jim Phillips' posters for local rock groups such as What on Earth, Larry Hosford, and most recently, The Ducks, are truly pieces of art among the toss-away flyers. In almost all of his rock posters and other commercial pieces, there are several well-recognized traits. The most obvious is Phillips' cartoon style-about 95% of his work, he says, is done with a crow quill pen (one that is dipped into the ink). He says the biggest influence over his style is "anything Walt Disney has ever done. He's my main man," adds Phillips. "He inspired me in my early years... my formative years." Bill Elder (an illustrator who worked with Mad Magazine*) is the source of inspiration for Phillips' offbeat humor, another trademark of his drawings. For instance, Phillips was commissioned to do a poster in 1976 for the Jerry Garcia concert at the Del Mar Theater. He drew a crowd scene jamming into the doors of the theater and the cast of characters included Groucho Marx, Superman, Fred Flintstone, Popeye, Santa Claus and Yosemite Sam, while Jerry Garcia sat on top of the theater marquee. Early this summer, Phillips was commissioned again by the same production company, Yea Productions, to illustrate a poster for the Tubes concert at the Civic. This time, Phillips depicted Pandemonium, crowds screaming and streaming from the movie,* The Blob, *where the theater audience ran in a panic from the advancing, monsterish goo.*

At the bottom, right-hand corner of The Tubes poster you can see even the wheelchair sign is scooting away from the walls in terror of The Tubes. Detail is another of Phillips' strong suits. In this respect his work exists on at least two different levels. Phillips draws the basic information such as name, dates and place very boldly. Up close, you can see the incredibly busy scenes with characters interacting in countless subplots. Another important and obvious trait of Phillips' work is his compulsion to draw Santa Cruz people against local landmarks. Phillips says there are so many beautiful vistas here he can't help but include them in his drawings. Some of his favorites are the Twin Lakes beach, the harbor jetty, and Lighthouse Point. These have been put into dozens of Phillips' illustrations.

Jim Phillips has lived in Santa Cruz most of his 32 years. In fact, his eight-year-old son Jimmy goes to the same elementary school (Live Oak) that Phillips attended. Jim first started taking drawing lessons when he was 10, from Ralph Gray, an illustrator who's worked locally for many years. Gray, who also was a big influence on Phillips, is the illustrator who drew, among countless other things, the dancing milk bottles on the Linda Vista Market. After attending Cabrillo College, Jim won a scholarship to study fine art at the California College of Arts and Crafts. Then he worked briefly in Florida and Boston, before returning to Santa Cruz in the mid-Sixties. He began working at a custom motorcycle parts business known as the Fiberglas Works, which later became Tracy Inc. There, he illustrated catalogues and ads with an old surfing buddy and artist illustrator, Jim Raun-Byberg. Byberg says he and Phillips had a passageway from their office to the roof and the two of them would sit up on the roof bagging rays while they drew. "Not only is Jimmy the best illustrator in town," says Byberg. "He's also a conceptualist-probably the best I've ever encountered. I wish someone would discover him and put him in a gallery where he belongs." Bill Prochnow, another prominent graphic artist and illustrator in Santa Cruz agrees with Byberg that Phillips is the best illustrator in town. Right now, Phillips' bread and butter account is his work for Santa Cruz Skateboards, where he designs and draws the ads that go into the national skateboard and surfing magazines. But he also has four or five other steady accounts which keep him working steadily from his living room studio, in addition to his favorite jobs-posters and ads for music events and rock bands. Jim's rock posters must be a release for him because while the scenes are chaotic, his personal life is quiet to the point of being reclusive, and he doesn't even care that much for rock and roll. He draws his concert posters while listening to classical music. "There's a real challenge in doing posters because there are deadlines you have to meet," says Phillips. "And I also usually have all the freedom I want in drawing them."

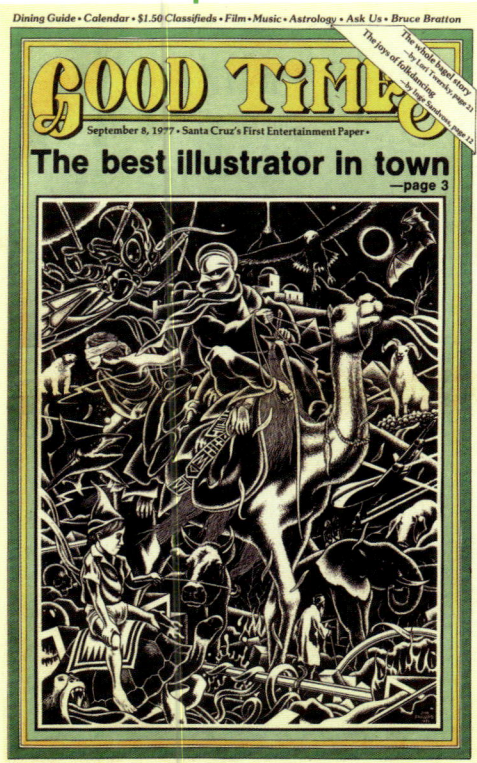

Phillips was still turning out What on Earth? posters, and he did a set of three which he still considers some of his finest work. One of the posters featured a witch for a Halloween party with Moby Grape and What on Earth? at the Boulder Creek Theater October, 1977. Yea Productions called again and ordered a Country Joe McDonald poster, then a Jesse Colin Young poster a few weeks later. Jim put a lot into the portrait of Country Joe, but still didn't get much respect from Yea. He did the minimum amount on Jesse although it still turned out to be an adequate poster, considering the pay.

Yea quit calling for a couple of months, and then ordered a Tubes poster for a Valentine's Day concert at the Del Mar Theater for 1978. Jim knocked himself out more than ever on this one, which means he worked around the clock for about four days, stopping only to eat and get a few hours of sleep. This series of posters stretched Jim's endurance beyond previous limits.

A manager at A and M Records in Hollywood called Jim and ordered a couple of blobs of "whatever The Tubes lettering was made from." Phillips' blobs were featured on a billboard up at Sunset and Vine for a month.

The posters were very gratifying, but all for $50. Jim was tired of it. "I got another call from Yea. Another poster. Another fifty bucks. 'Listen,' I said. 'I've knocked myself out for you guys, and met all your deadlines. Don't you think I should get more than just starting pay? I need more, like maybe seventy bucks.' The loud reply echoes in Jim's mind, "What? You won't do a poster for fifty bucks?" He hung up on Jim, and that was the end of his Yea posters, and shortly after, the end of Yea Productions.

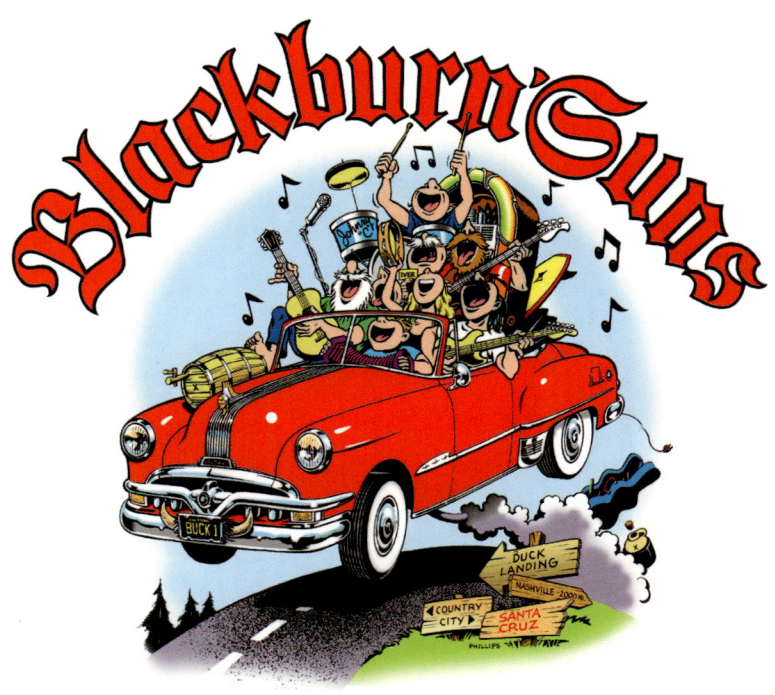

Above; T-shirt design for Jeff Blackburn's jukebox restoration company, 1977.
Opposite page: Ducks *poster 1977, 22"x28", numbered,* Quality Offset *printing*

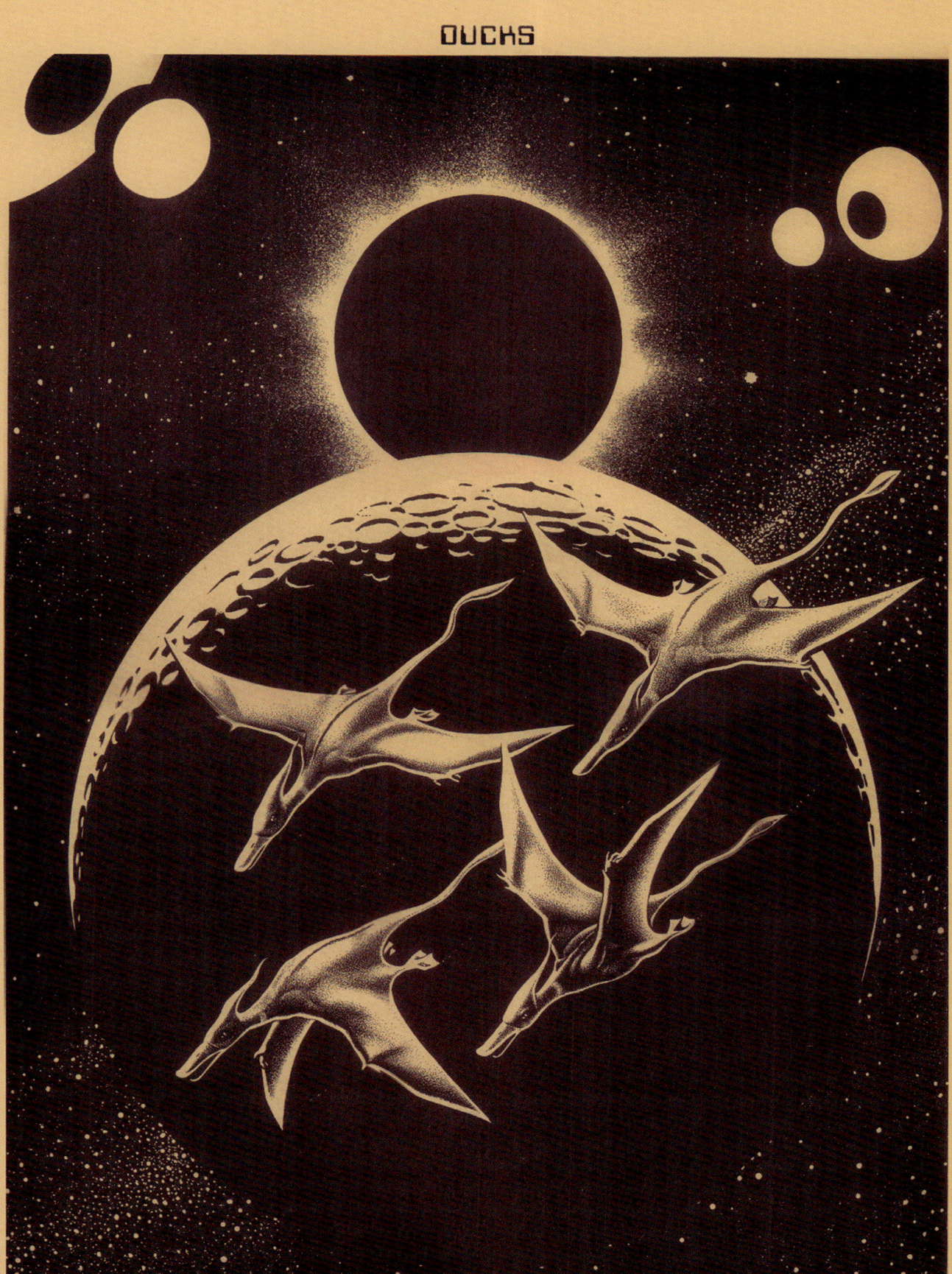

THE MIGHTY

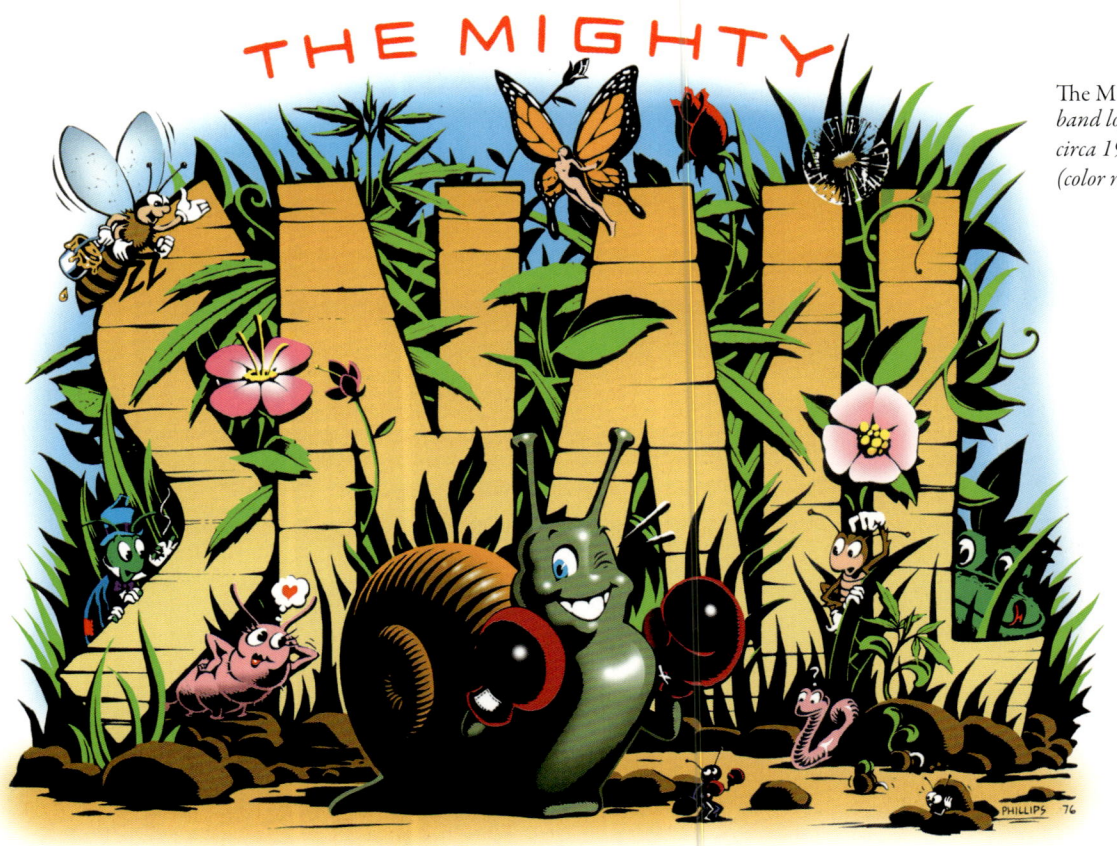

The Mighty Snail,
*band logo and T-shirt design,
circa 1977.
(color restored)*

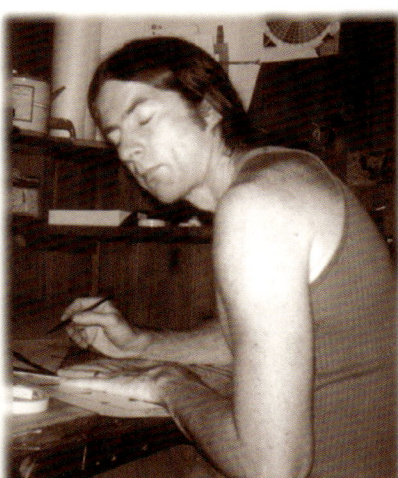

*Top left: Artist asleep at the pen, 1977.
Bottom: The Pen, Hunt 107,
and ink drawing shown actual size.*

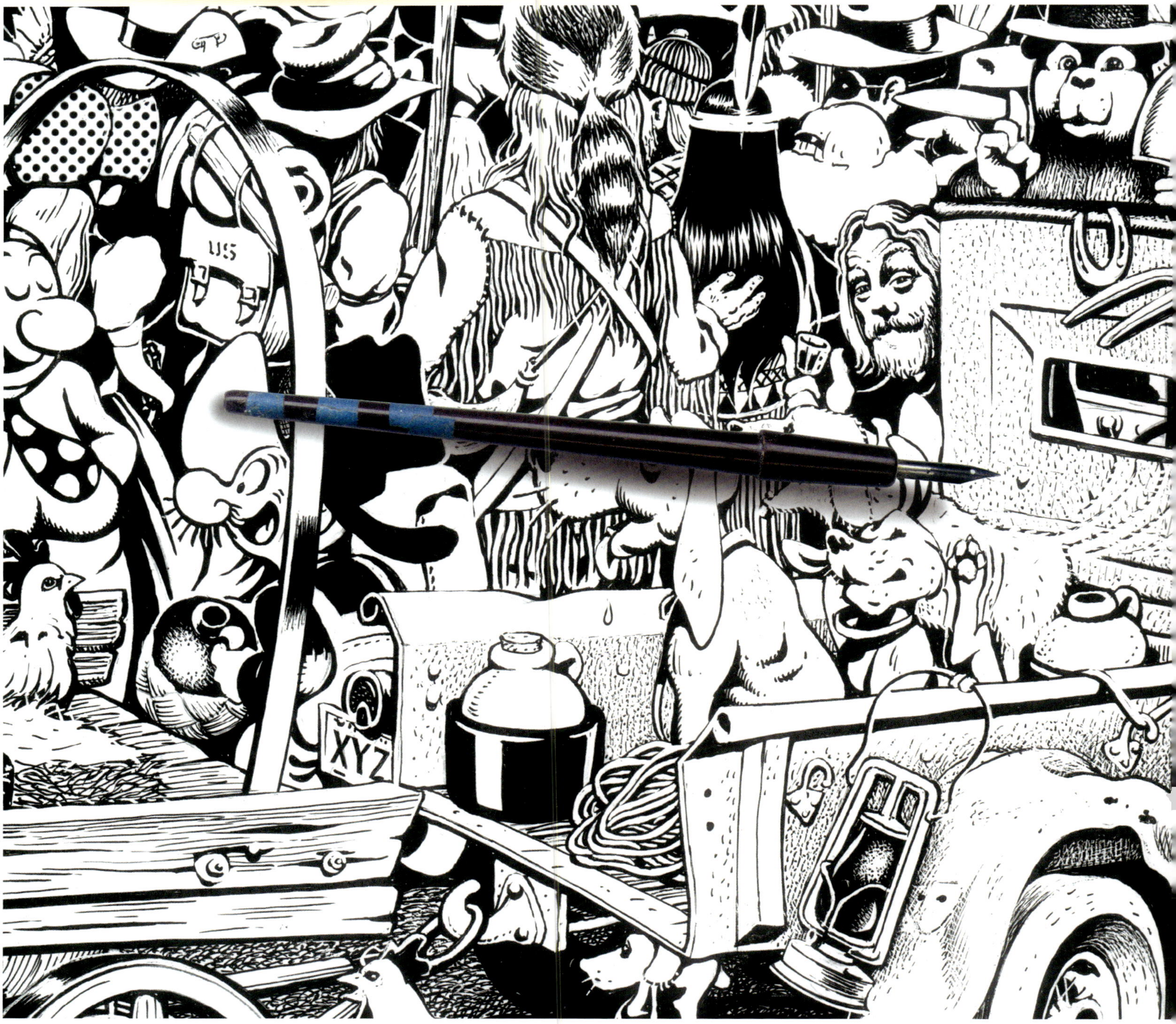

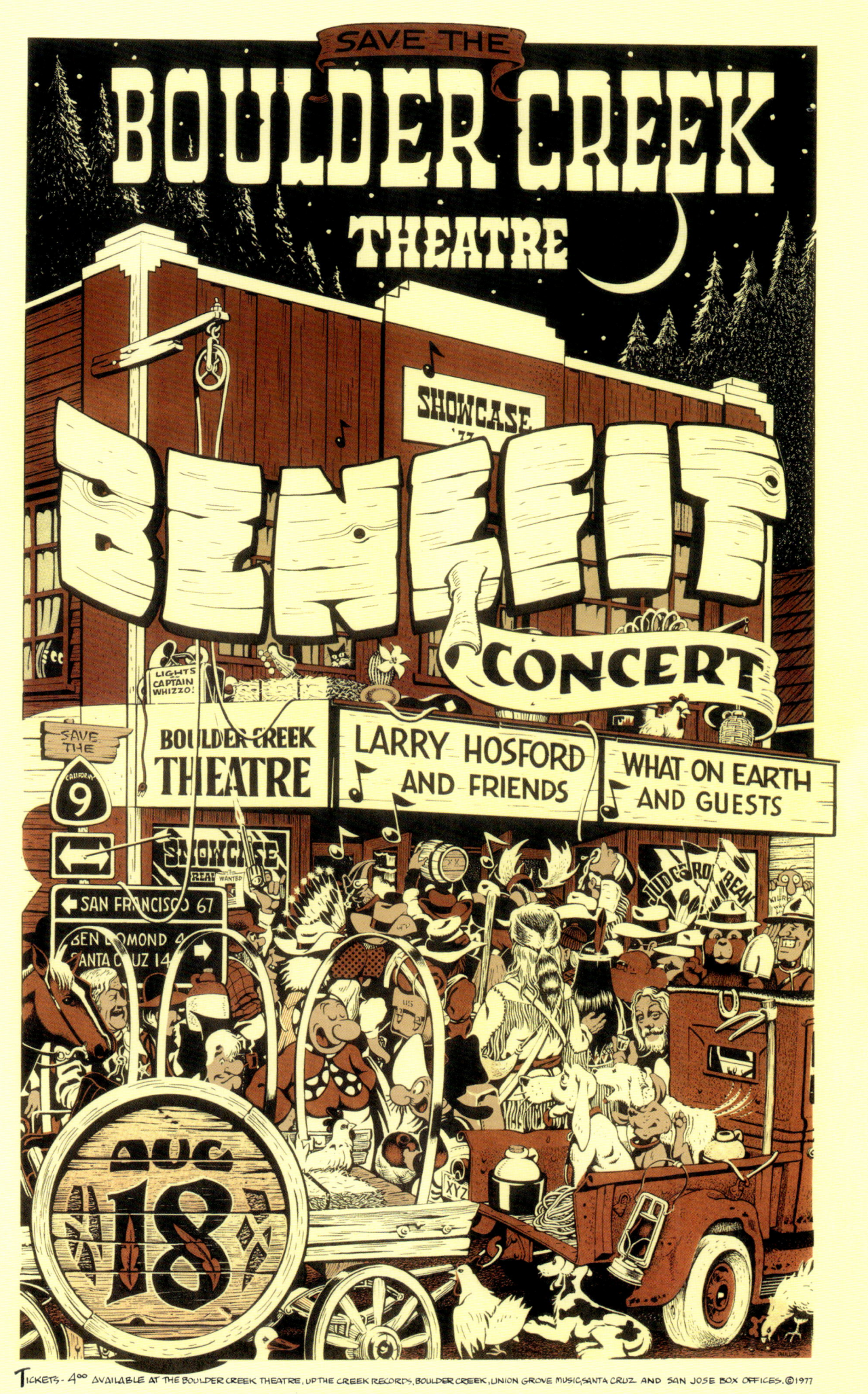

Boulder Creek Theatre Benefit poster, of Rock) 1977, 11"x17" Quality Offset printing.

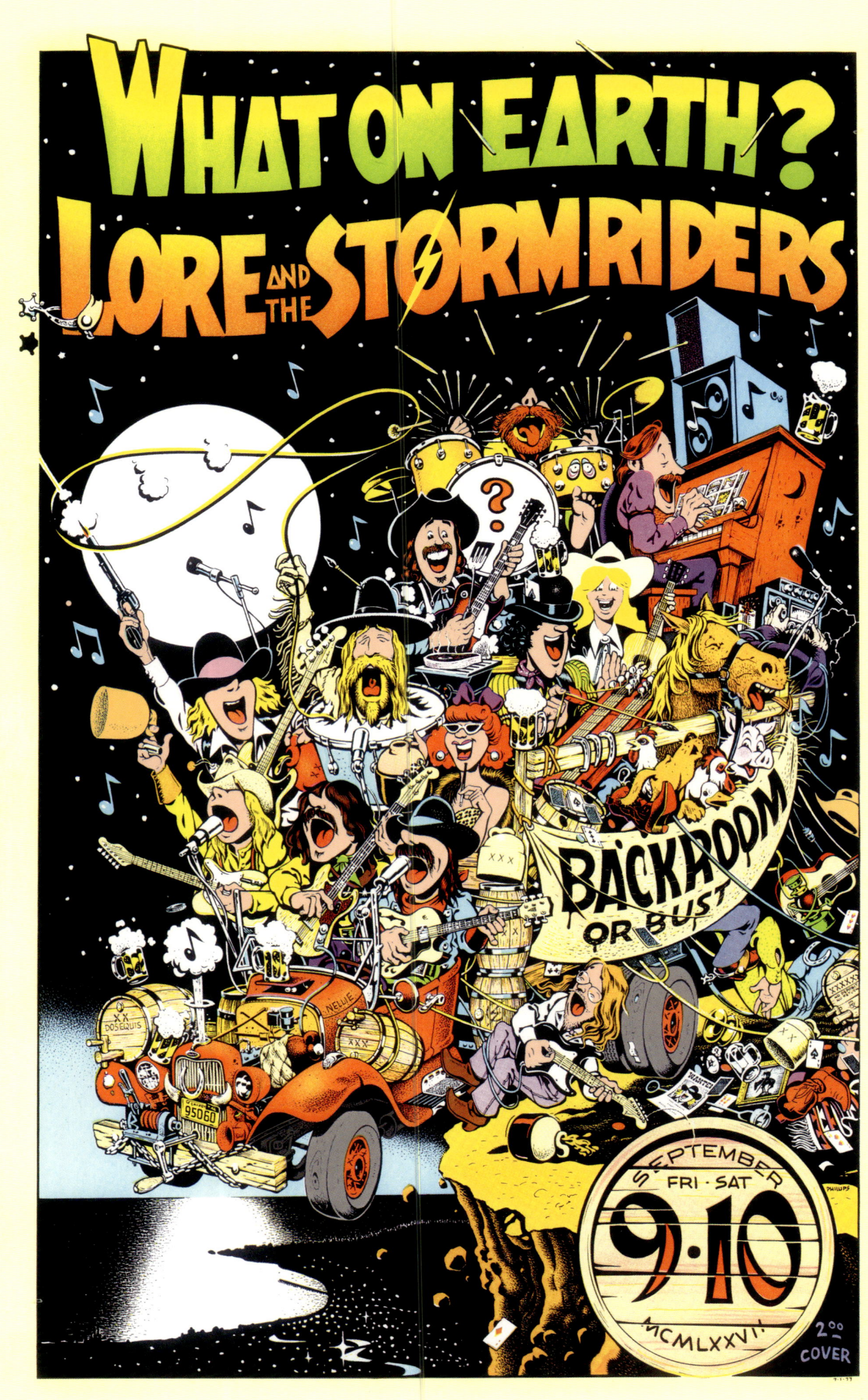

What on Earth - Lore & the Stormriders poster, 11"x17", 1977, numbered on back, Quality Offset printing

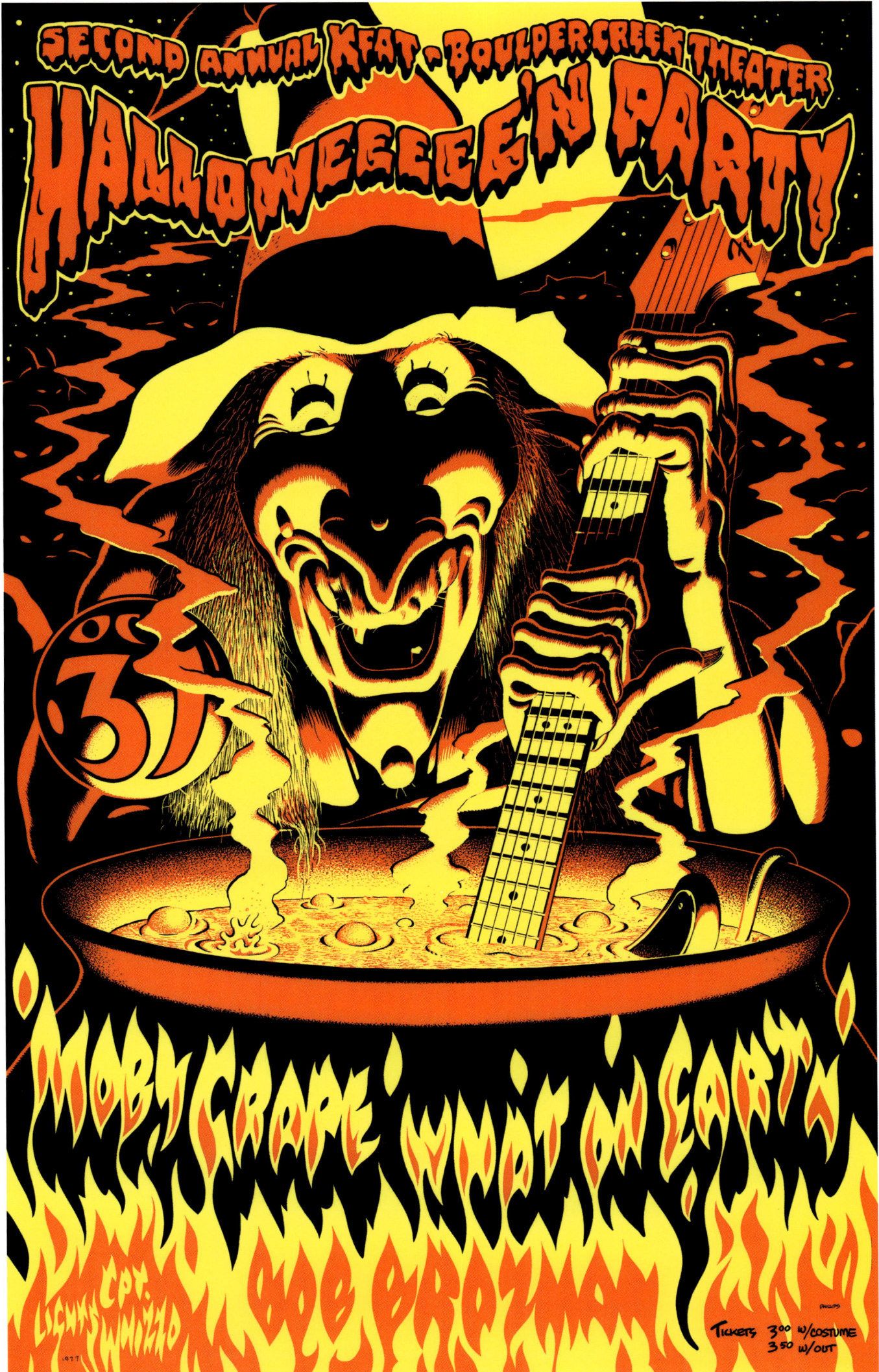

Halloween Party - Moby Grape, What on Earth, KFAT Party poster, 11"x17", 1977, numbered on back, (AOR 4.103) *Quality Offset printing*

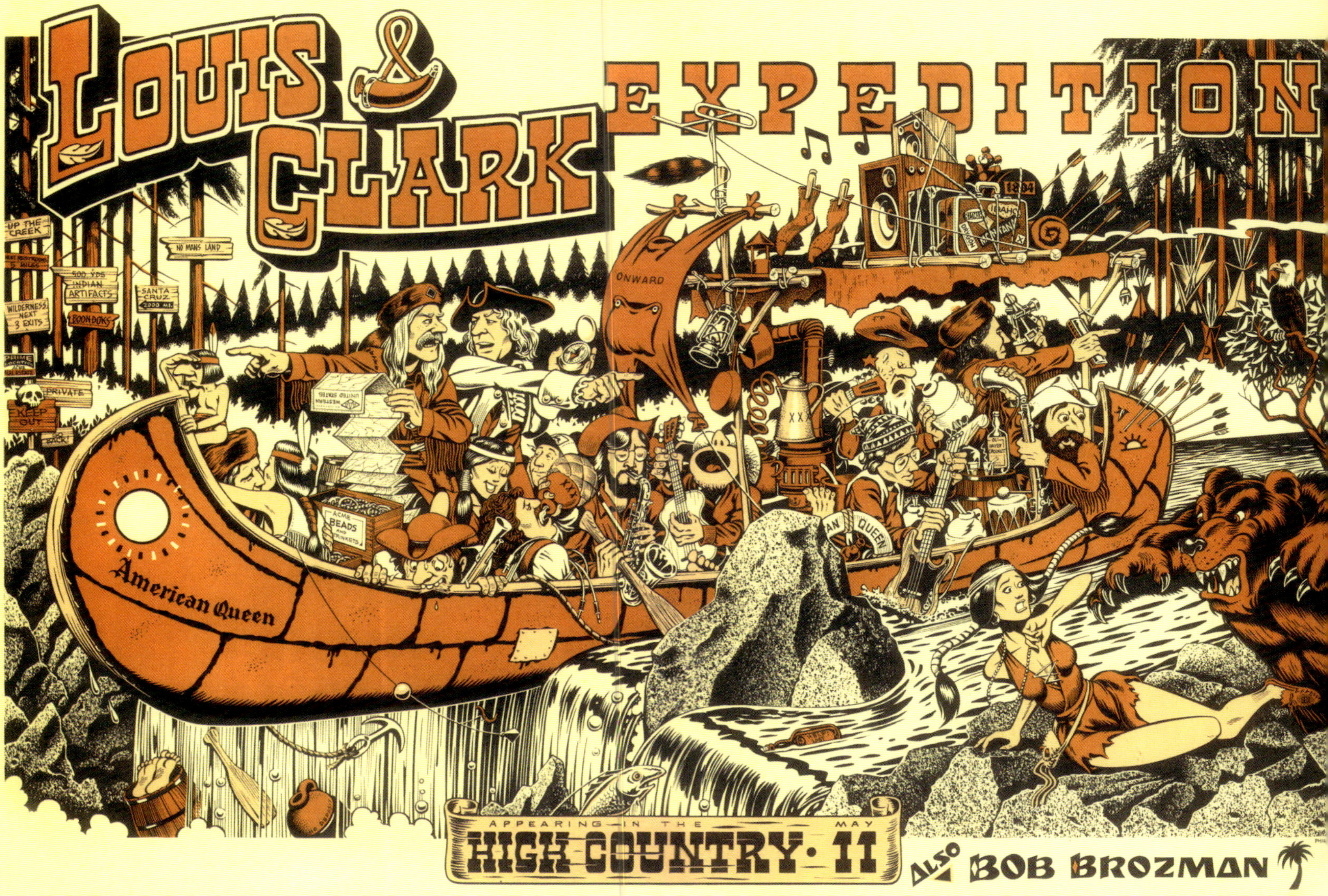

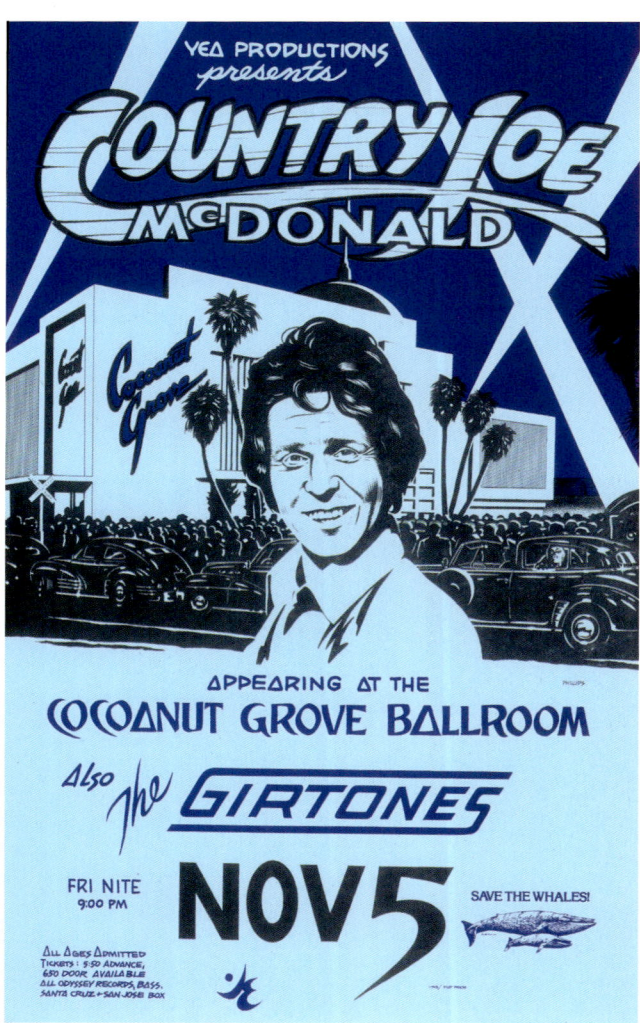

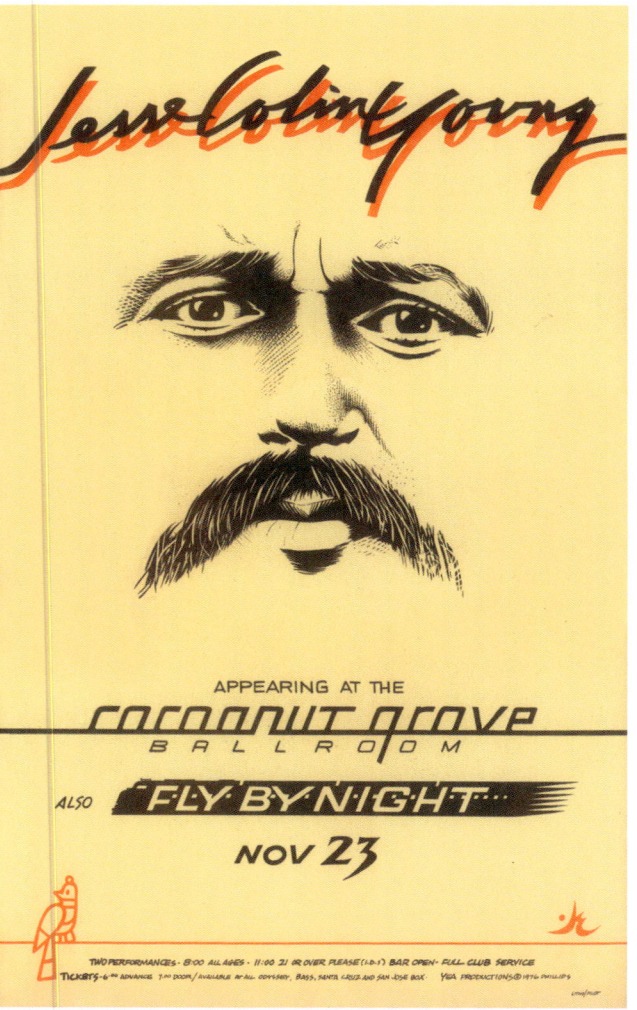

Louis & Clark Expedition
1978,
11"x17", numbered,
#250 edition,
Quality Offset printing.
(Will Simmons loading rifle)

Country Joe McDonald,
1977,
11"x17"
Yea Productions,
Quality Offset printing

Jesse Colin Young,
1977, 11"x17"
Yea Productions,
Quality Offset printing

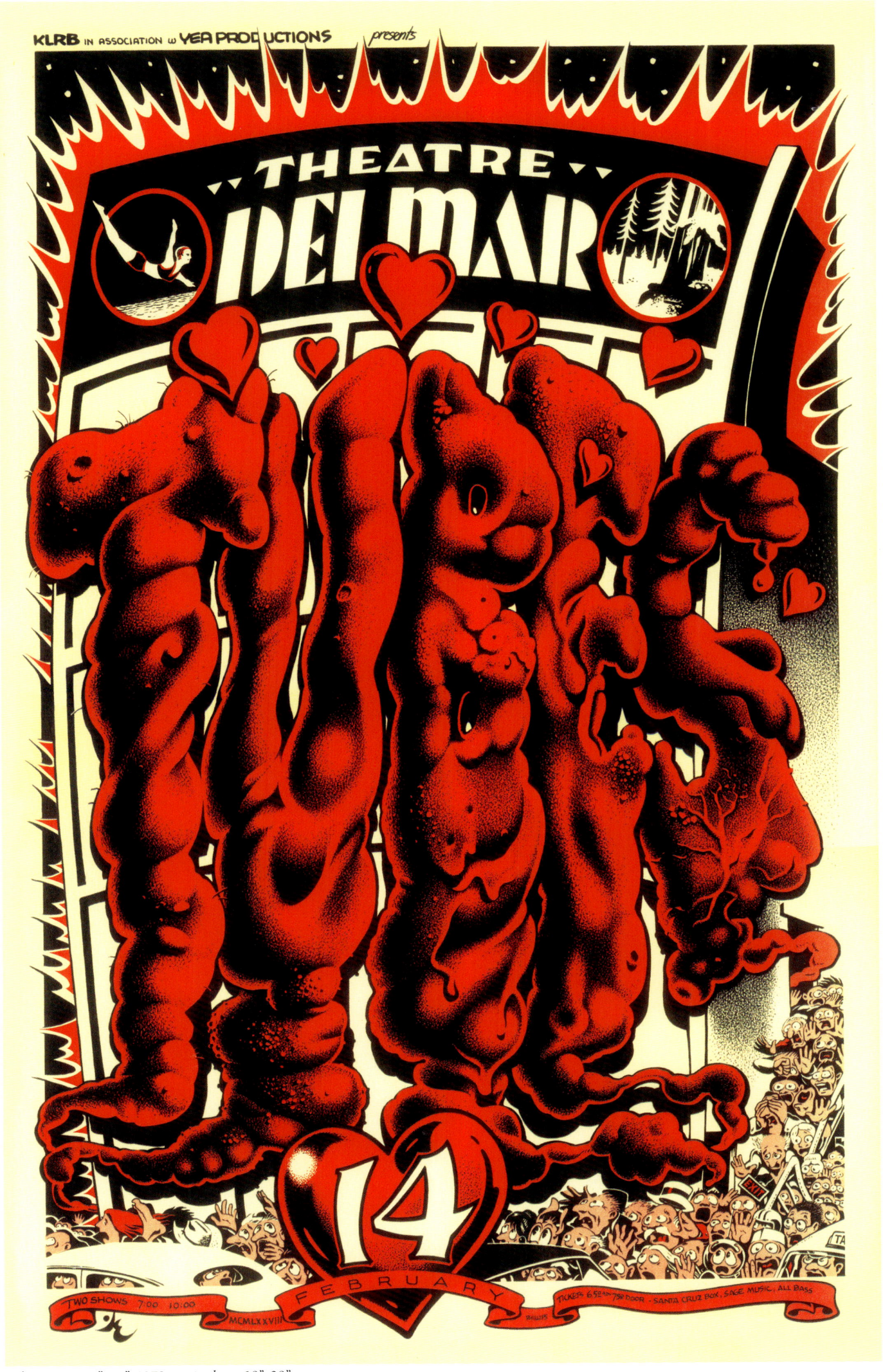

Tubes poster, 11"x17", 1978, original art: 18"x28".

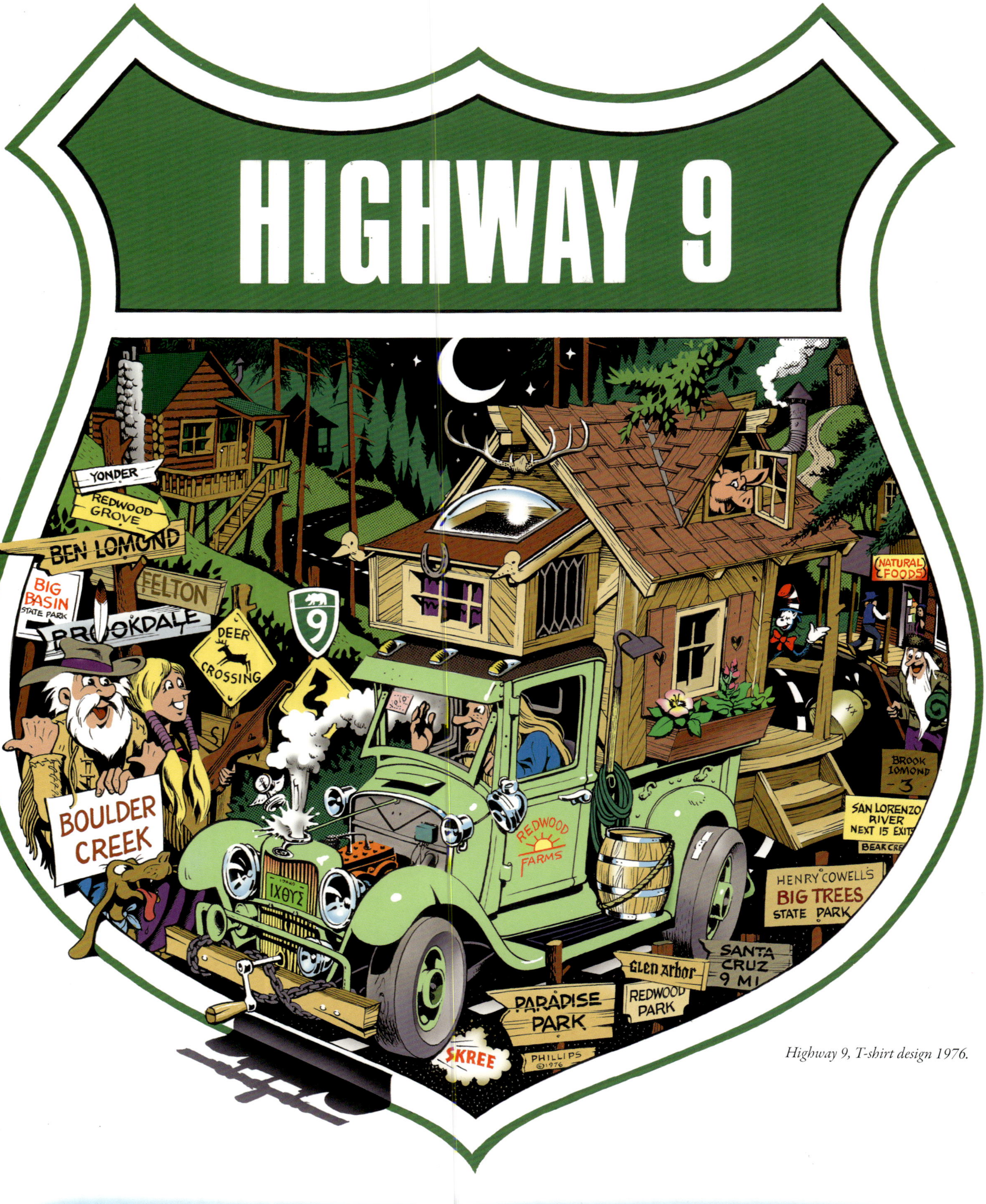

HIGHWAY 9

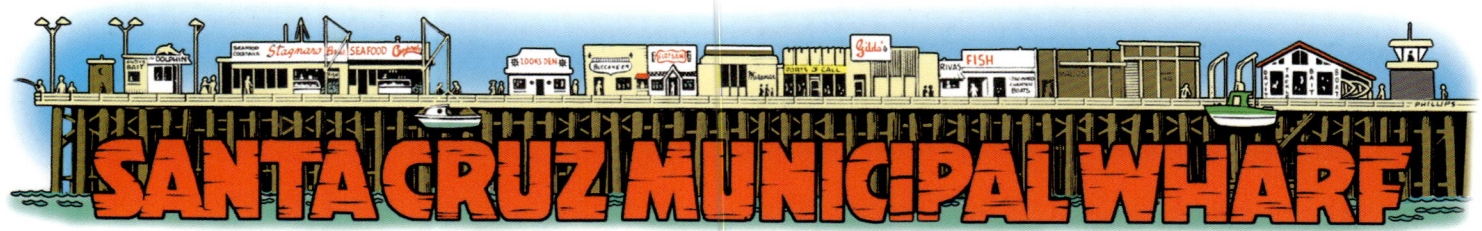

Highway 9, T-shirt design 1976.

Municipal Wharf logo, 1978

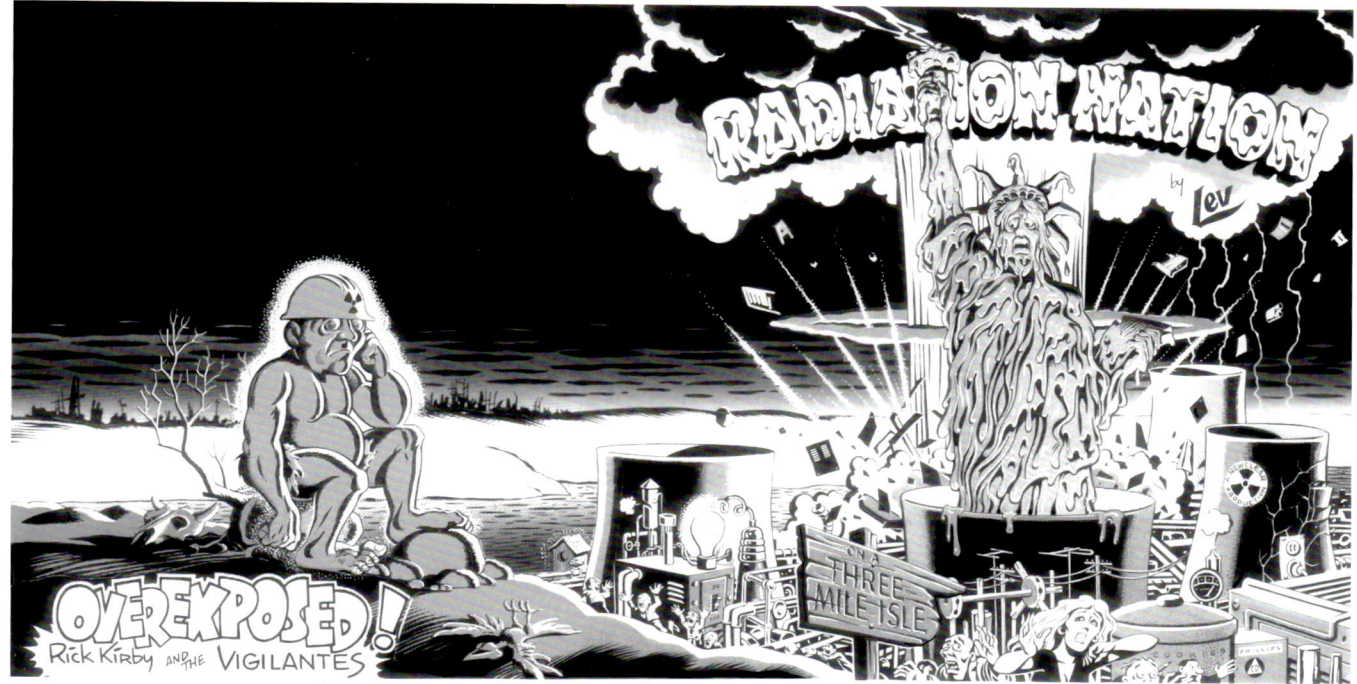

Radiation Nation, 45 record sleeve, front & back, 1976.

Buckle Up, Birthday card, 1977.

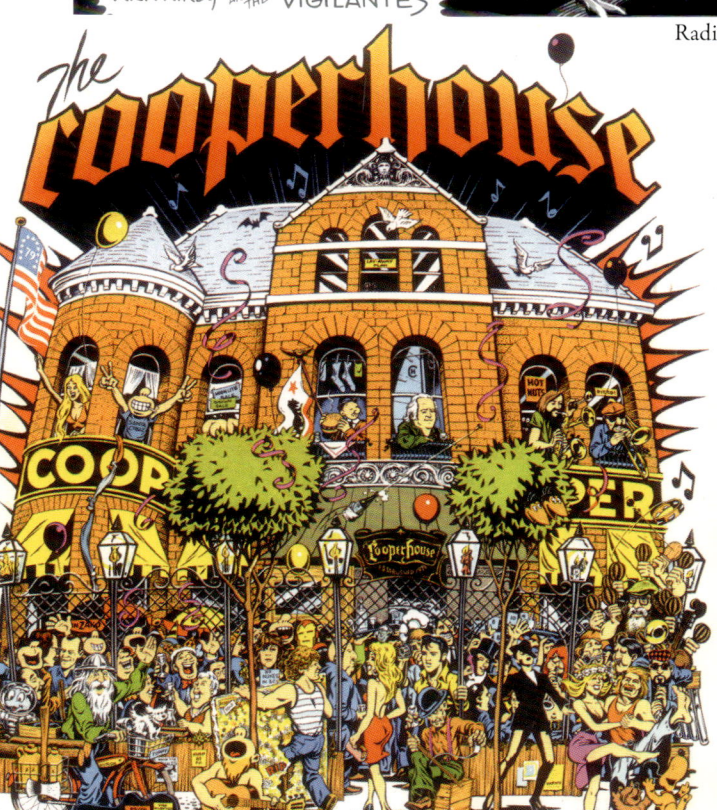

Cooperhouse, postcard, circa 1978.

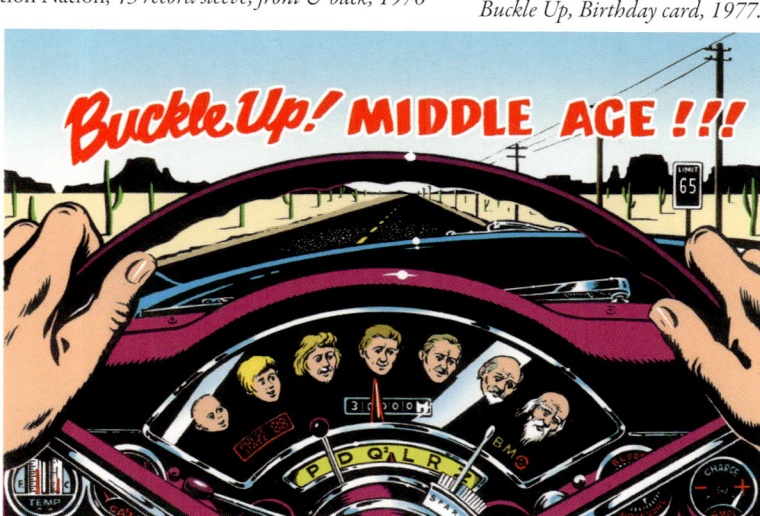

3 logos: for L.Lewis, Jeff Blackburn, Pete Simmons.

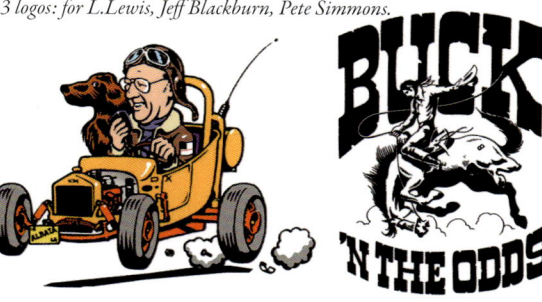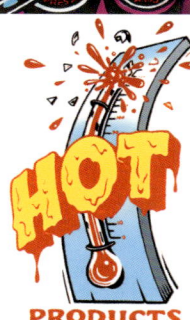

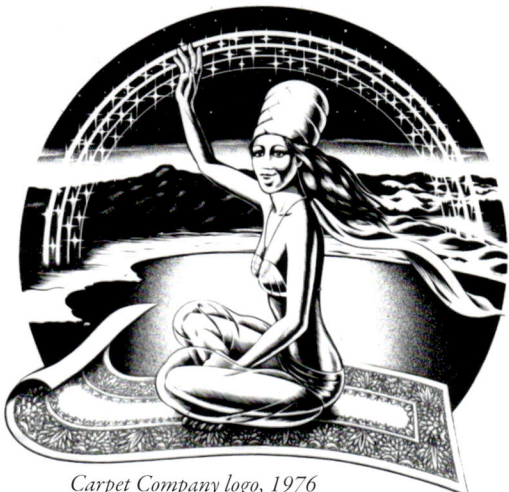

Carpet Company logo, 1976

Back cover Bay Area Music, 1977

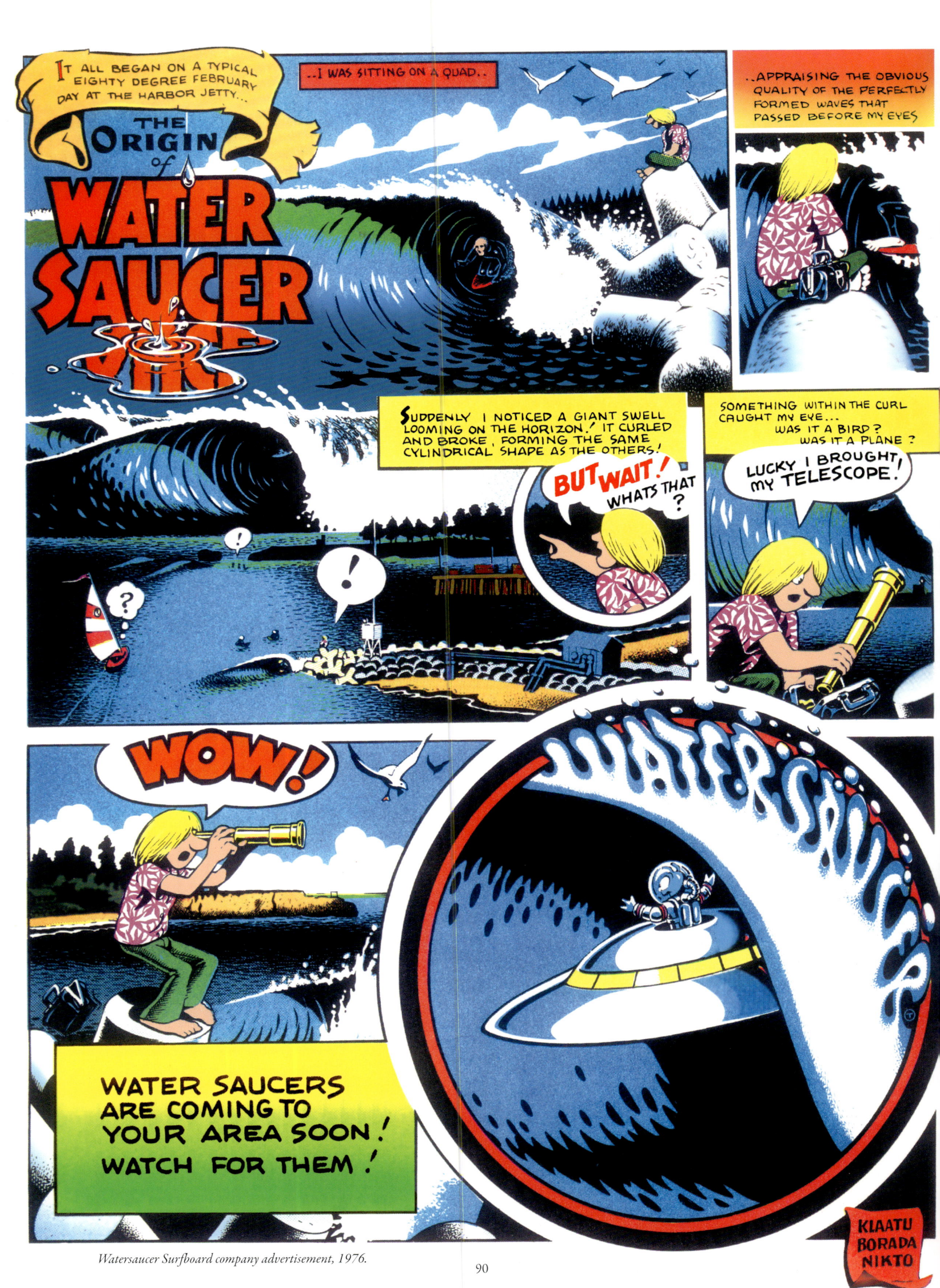

Watersaucer Surfboard company advertisement, 1976.

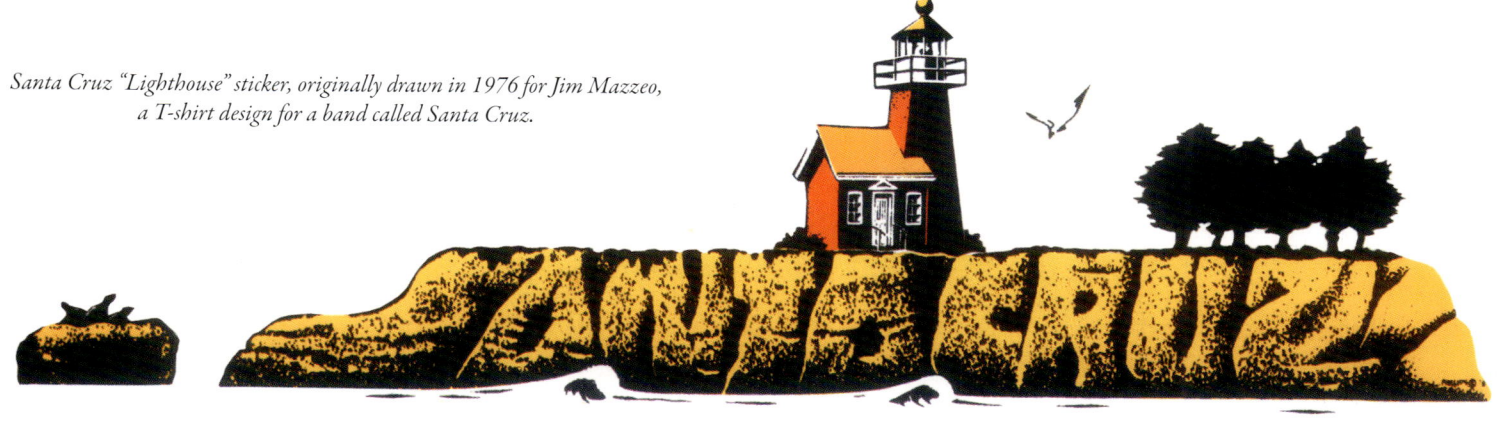

Santa Cruz "Lighthouse" sticker, originally drawn in 1976 for Jim Mazzeo, a T-shirt design for a band called Santa Cruz.

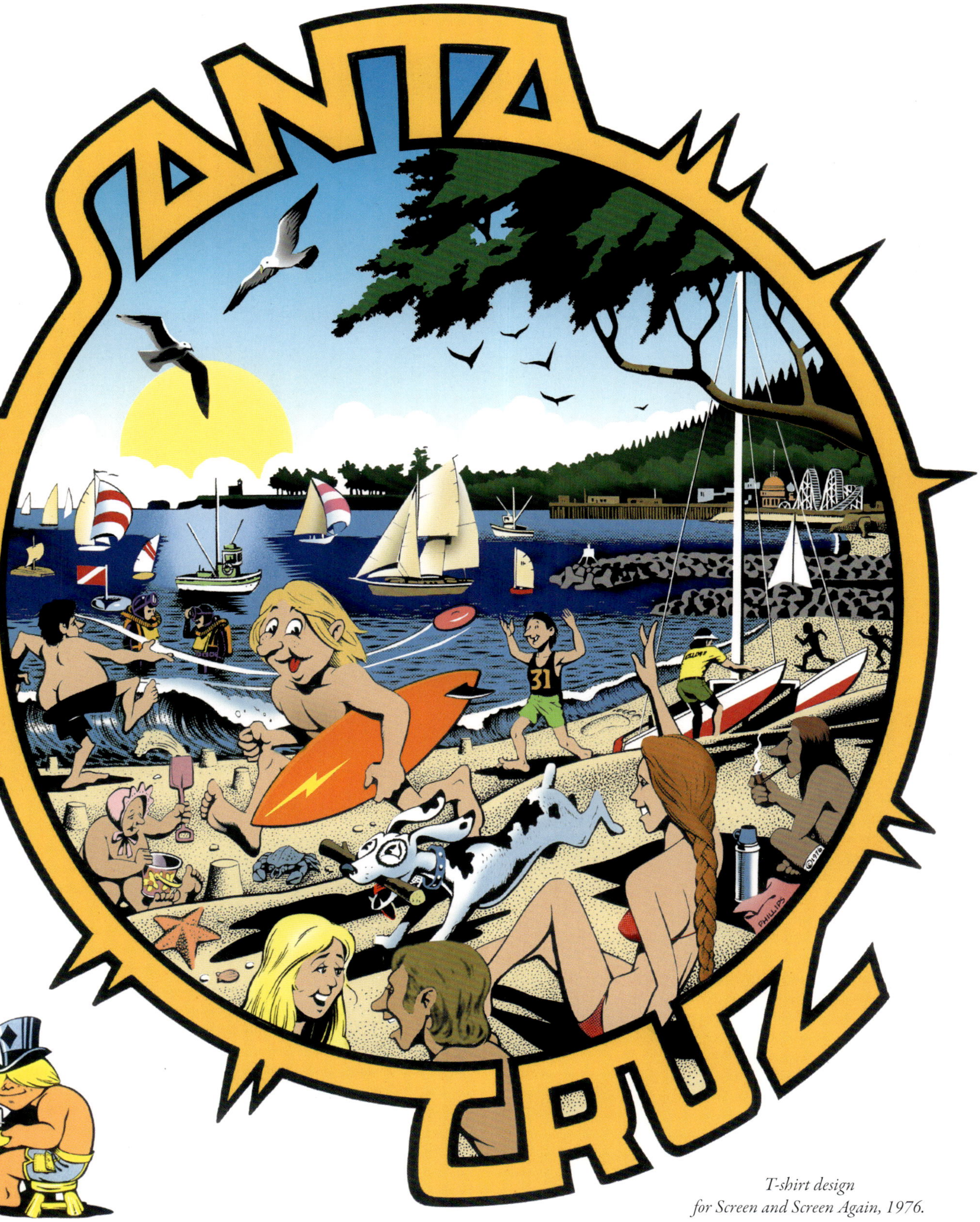

T-shirt design for Screen and Screen Again, 1976.

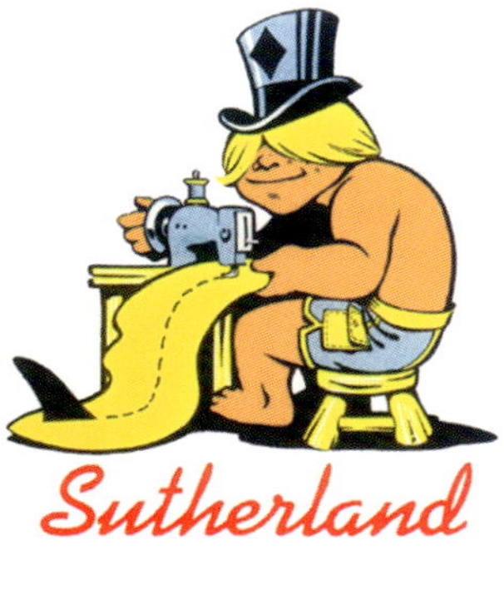

Sutherland

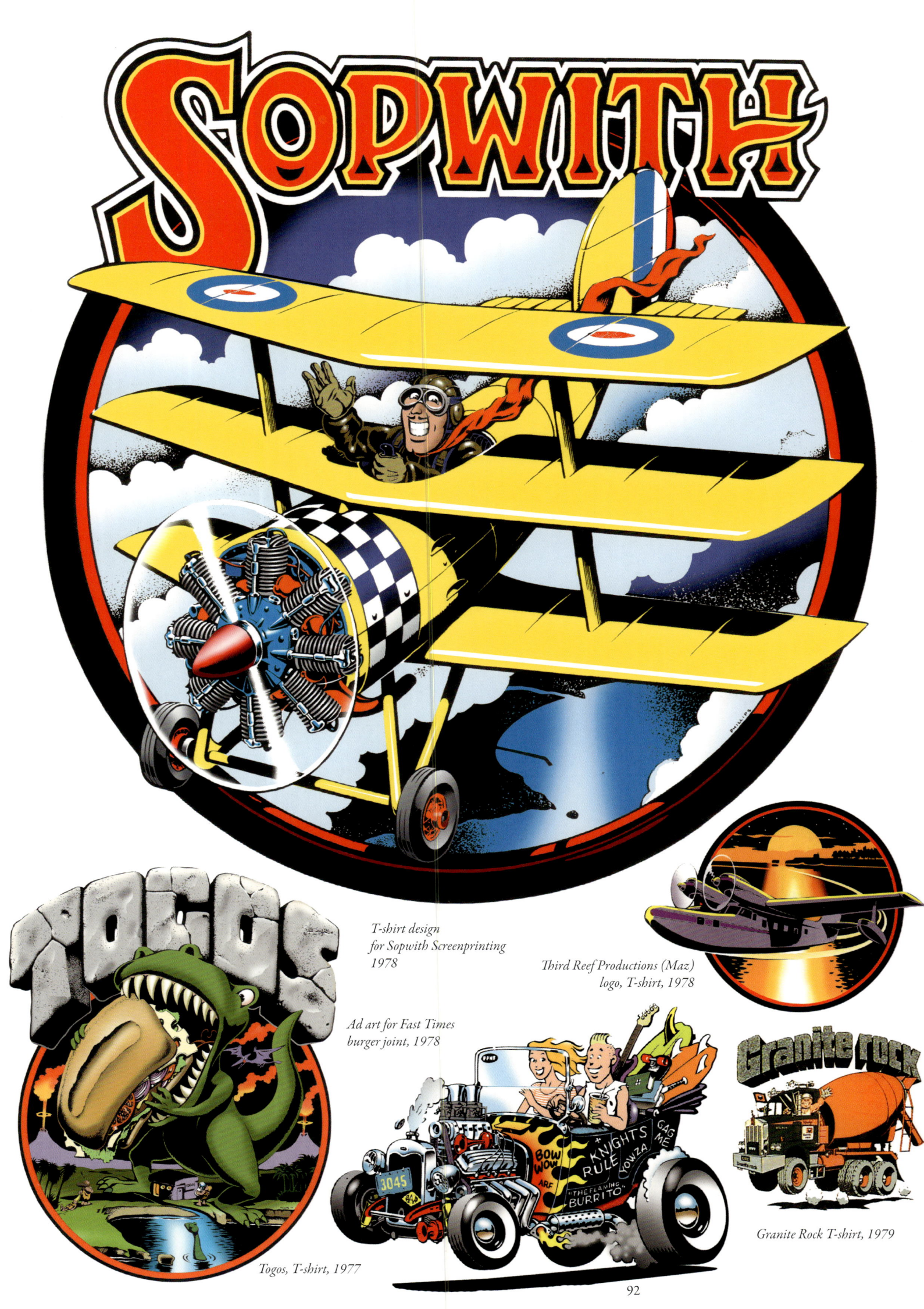

SOPWITH

T-shirt design
for Sopwith Screenprinting
1978

Third Reef Productions (Maz)
logo, T-shirt, 1978

Ad art for Fast Times
burger joint, 1978

Granite Rock T-shirt, 1979

Togos, T-shirt, 1977

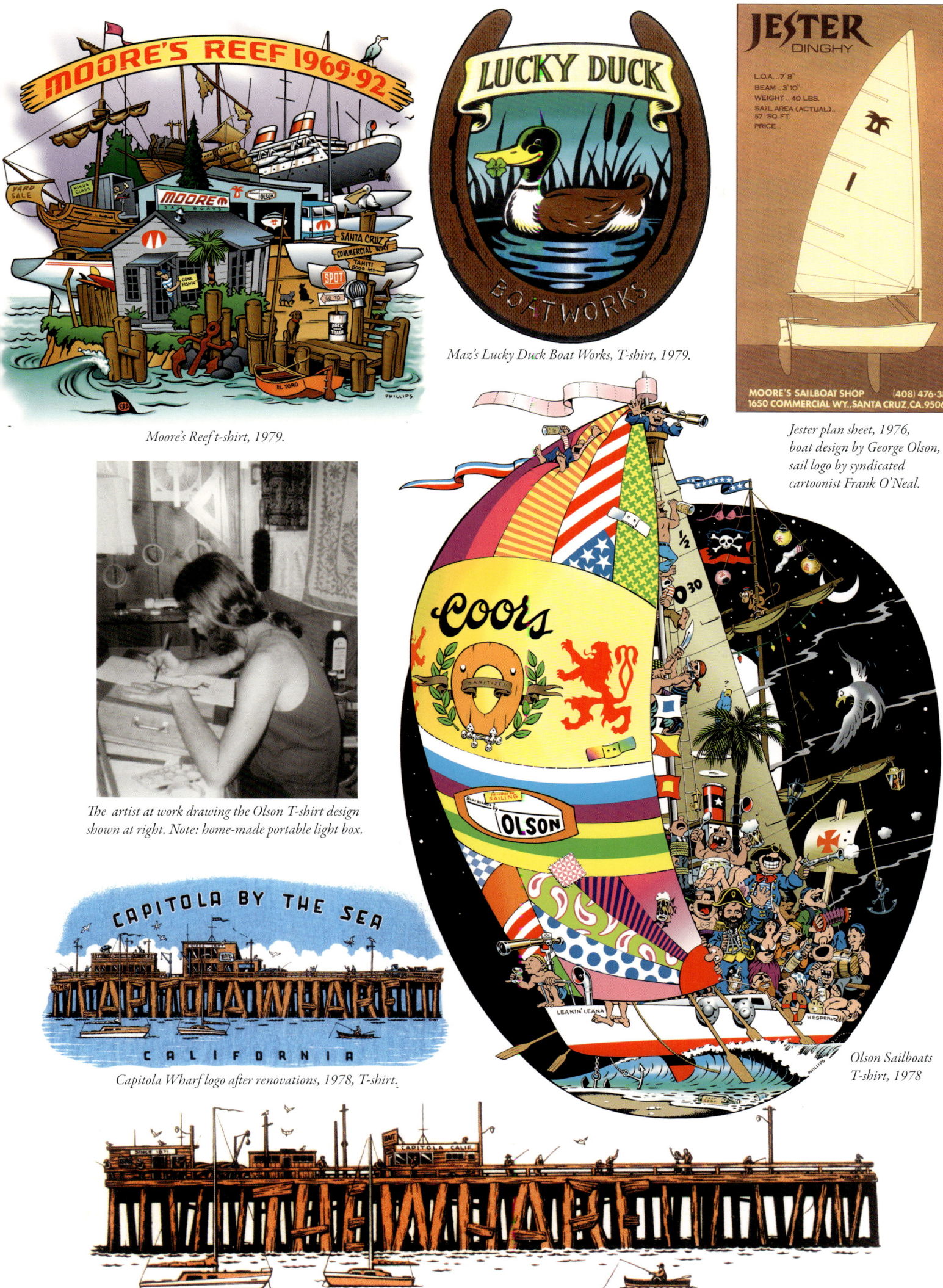

Moore's Reef t-shirt, 1979.

Maz's Lucky Duck Boat Works, T-shirt, 1979.

JESTER DINGHY

L.O.A. ..7'8"
BEAM ..3'10"
WEIGHT.. 40 LBS.
SAIL AREA (ACTUAL)..
57 SQ.FT.
PRICE..

MOORE'S SAILBOAT SHOP   (408) 476-3831
1650 COMMERCIAL WY., SANTA CRUZ, CA. 95065

Jester plan sheet, 1976,
boat design by George Olson,
sail logo by syndicated
cartoonist Frank O'Neal.

The artist at work drawing the Olson T-shirt design
shown at right. Note: home-made portable light box.

Olson Sailboats
T-shirt, 1978

Capitola Wharf logo after renovations, 1978, T-shirt.

Original Capitola Wharf logo, 1976, letterhead.

UCSC

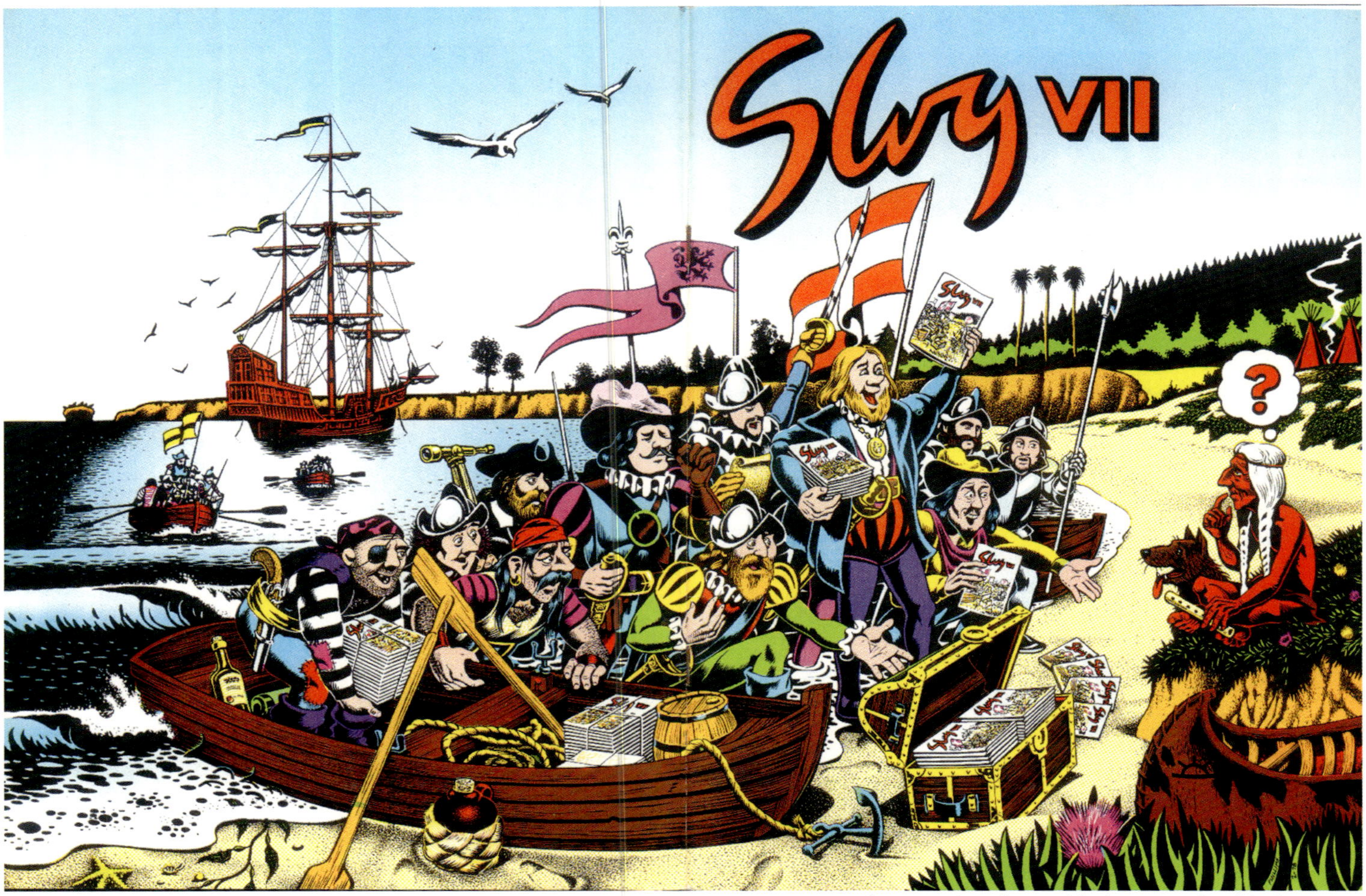

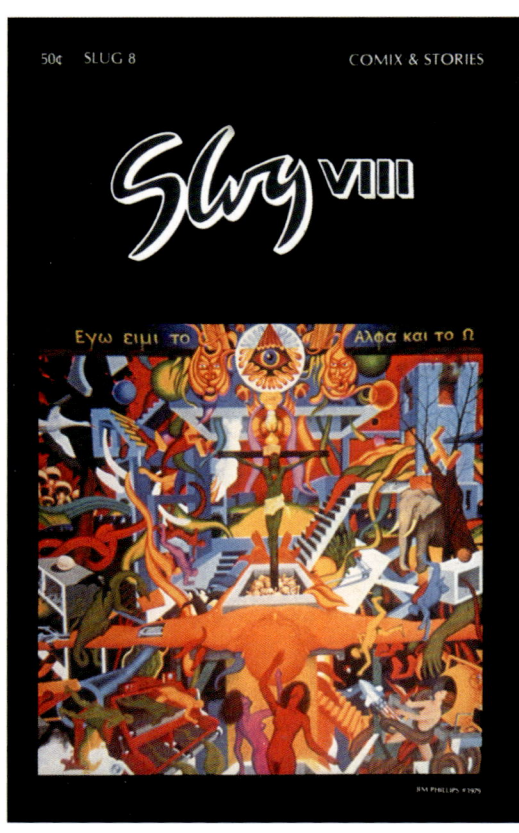

Slug annual #7, front and back cover, 8.5"x11" book, 1978.

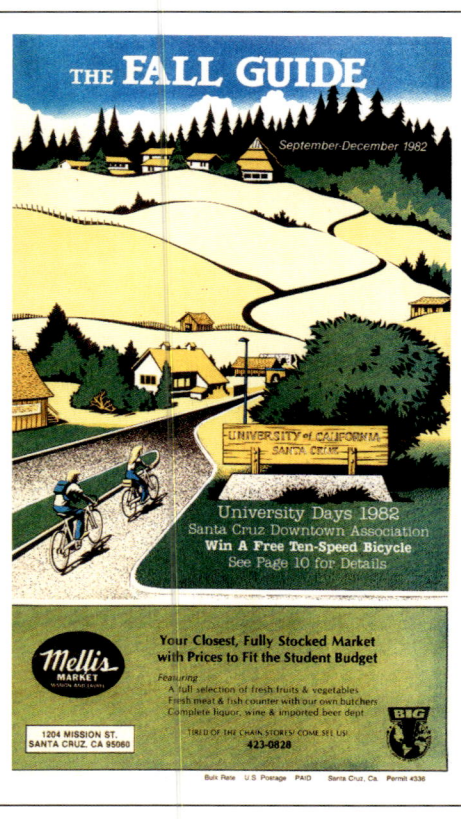

UCSC's Slug *annual #8, 1979.*

UCSC Fall Guide *cover, 1982.*

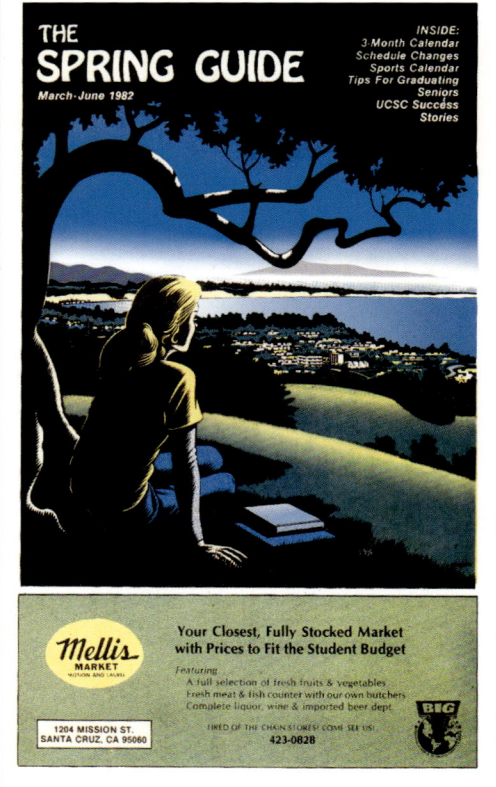

UCSC Spring Guide *cover, 1982.*
Inked from an on-site sketch of Dolly, 12"x15".

Santa Cruz Magazine

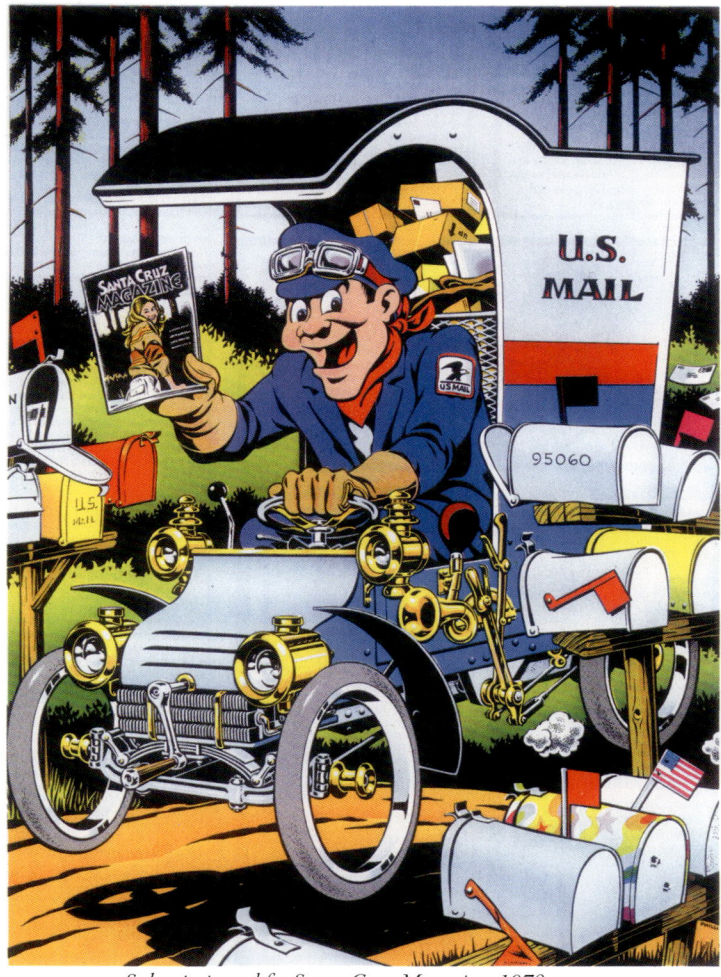

Subscription ad for Santa Cruz Magazine, 1978

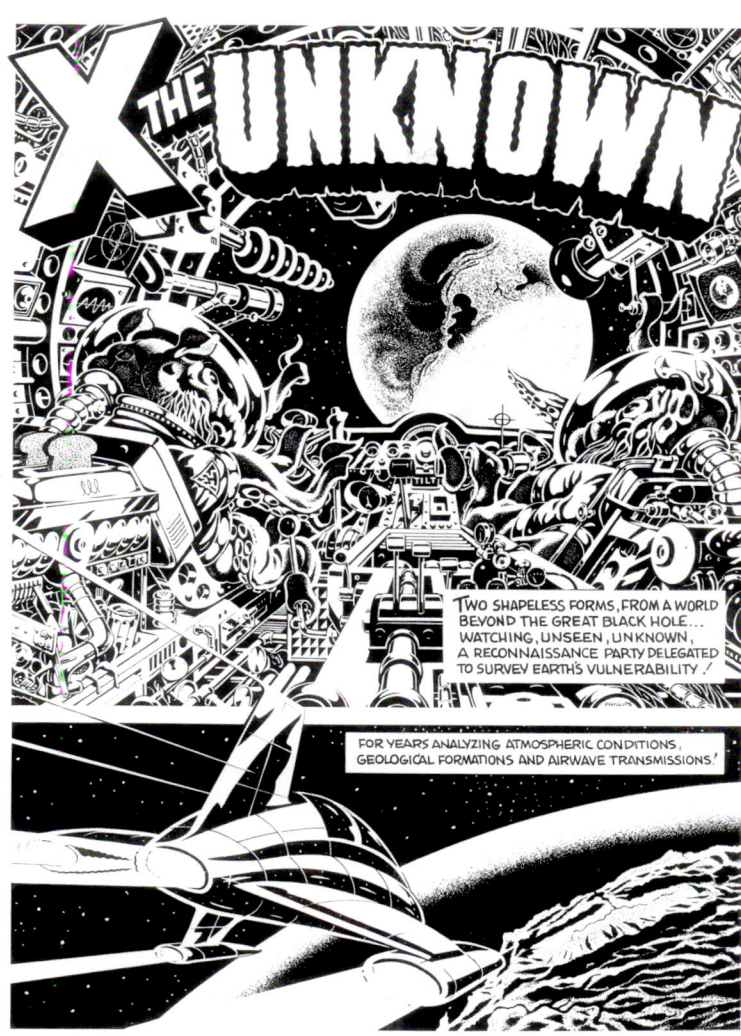

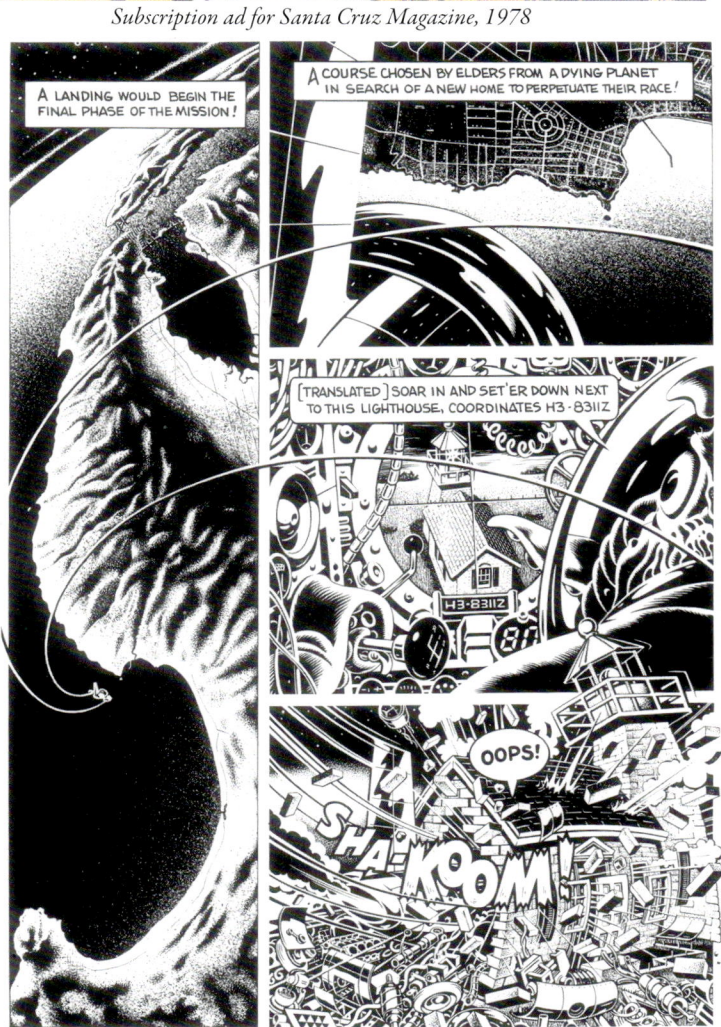

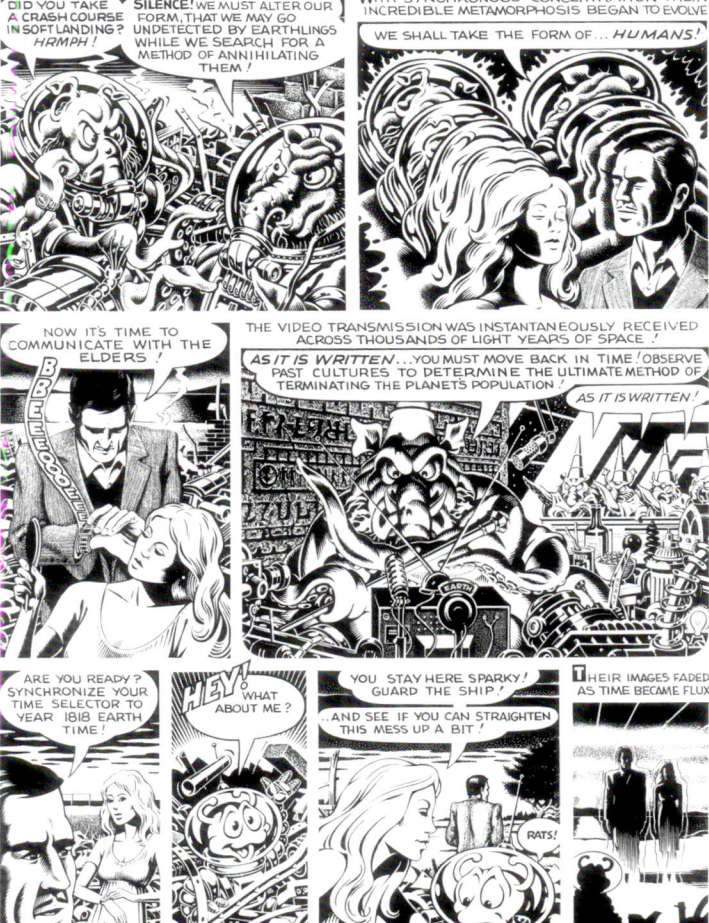

Top right and bottom: X the Unknown, appeared in Santa Cruz Magazine, *1978.*

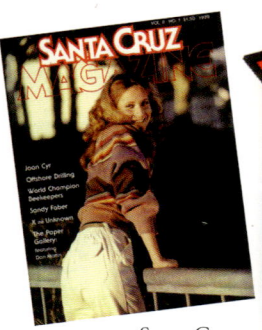

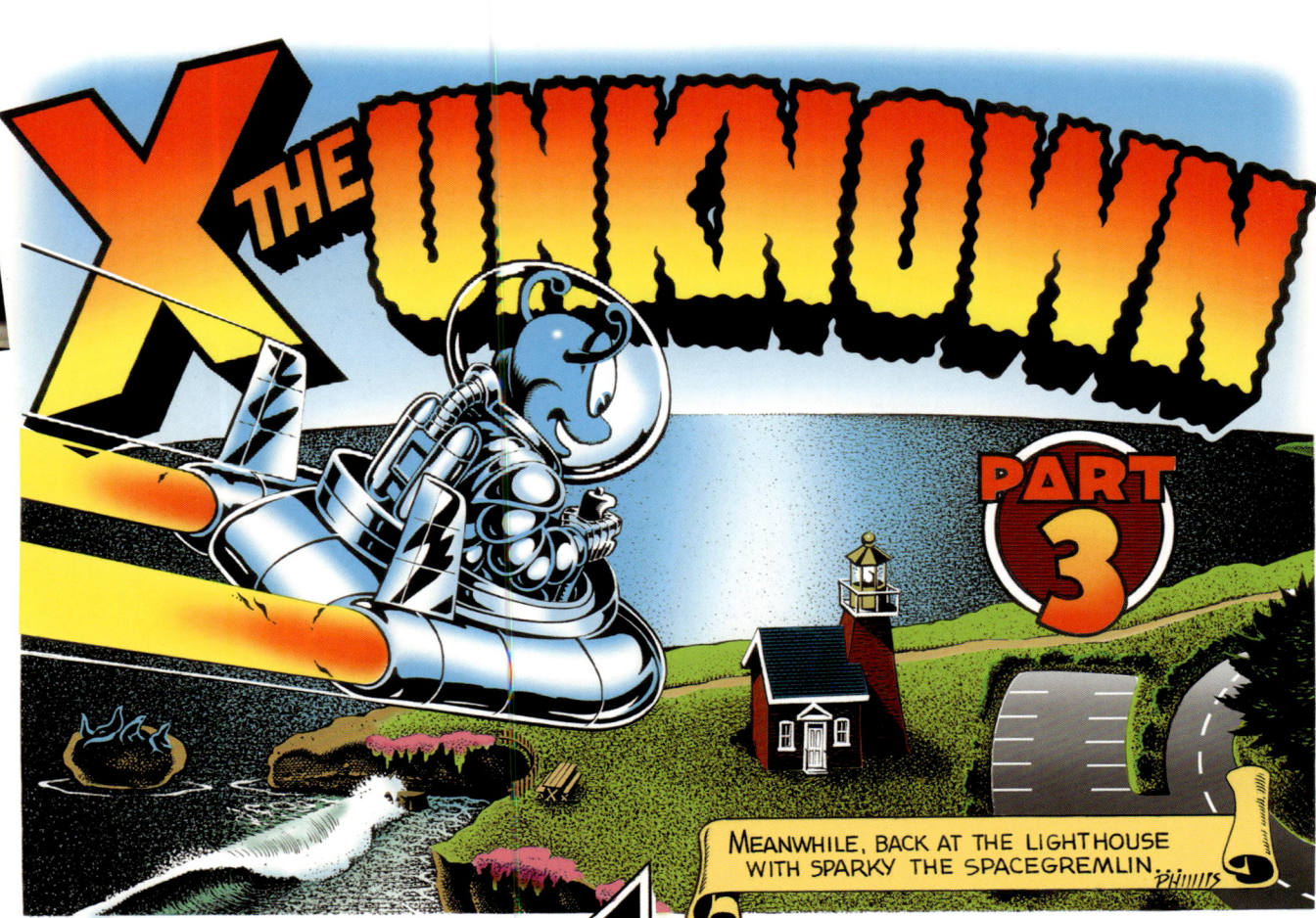

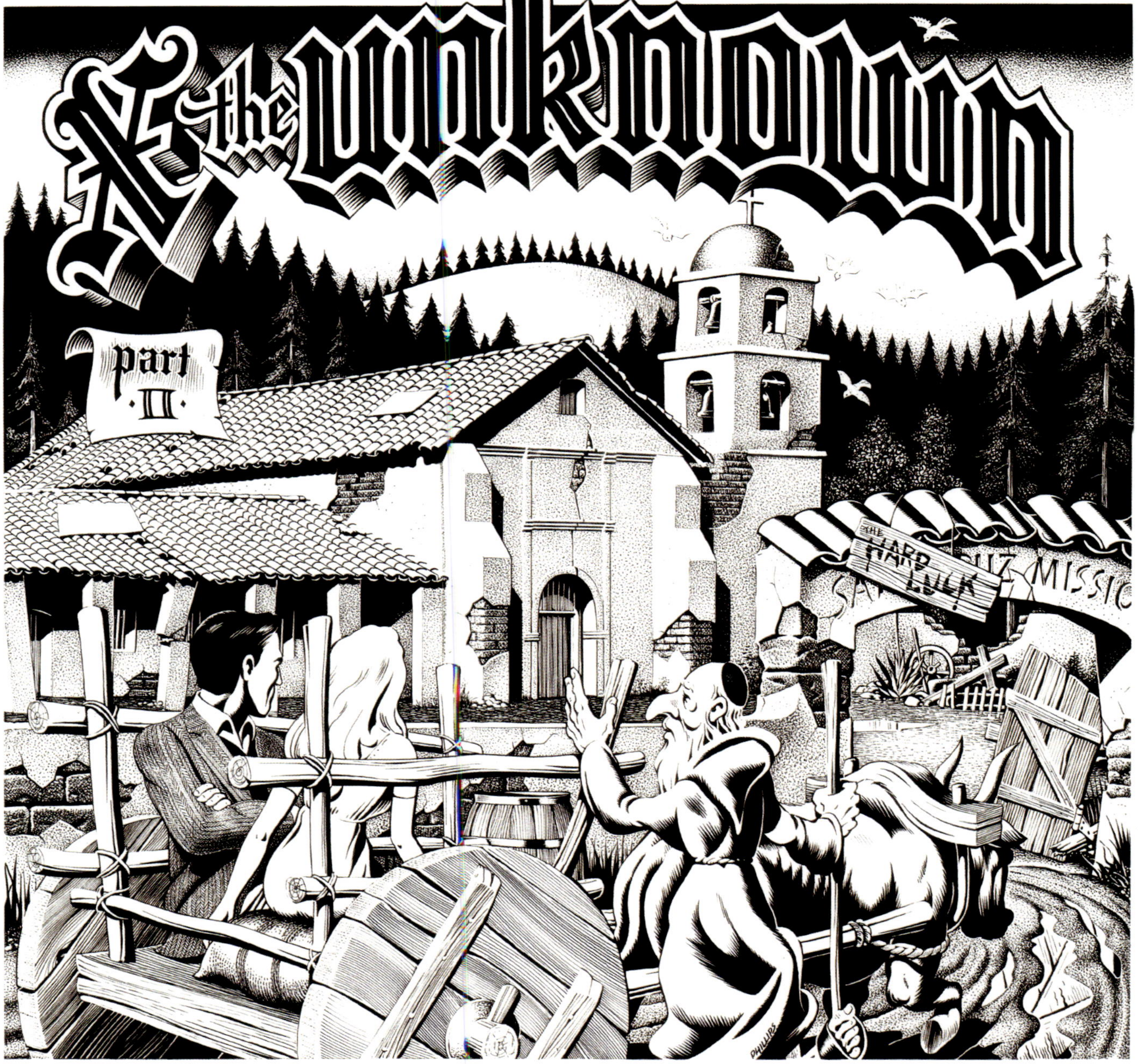

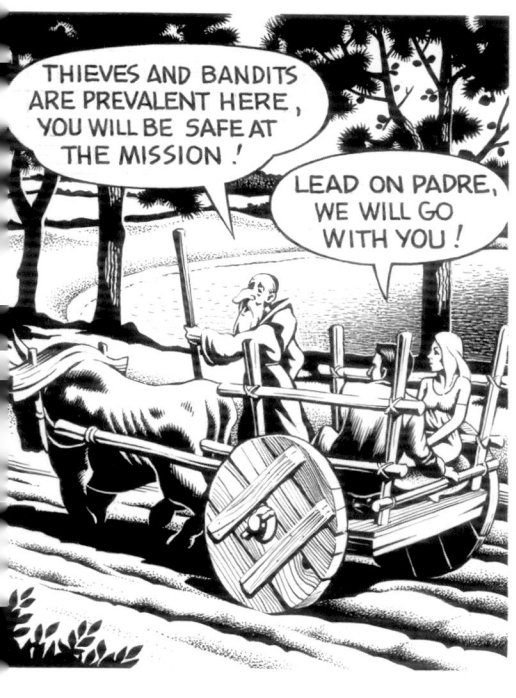

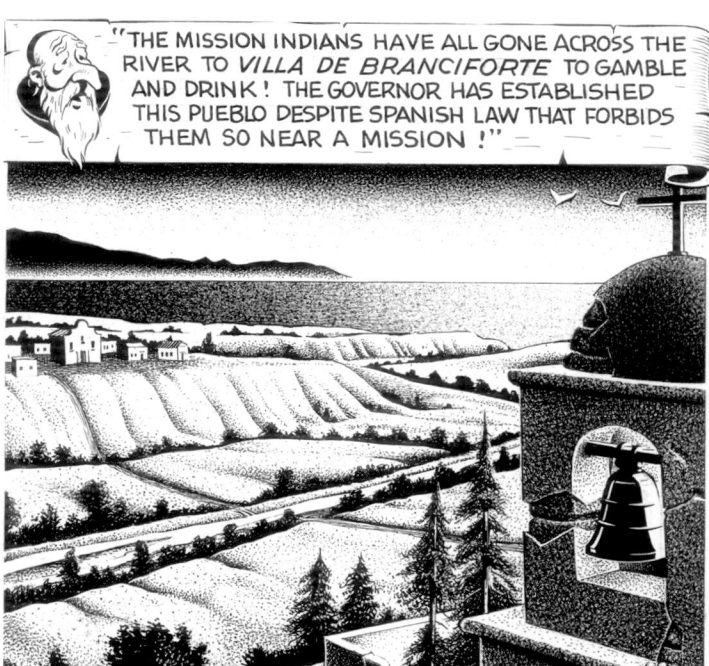

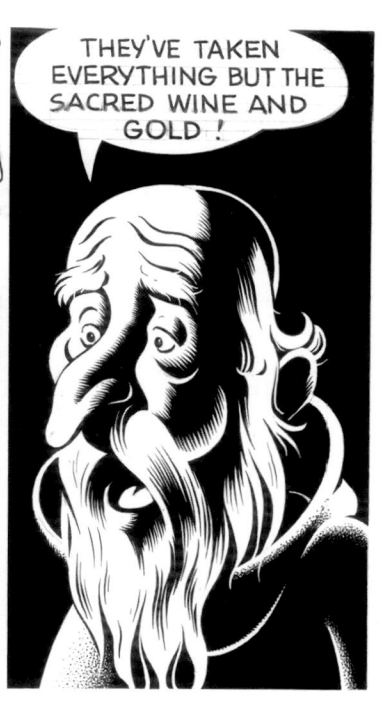

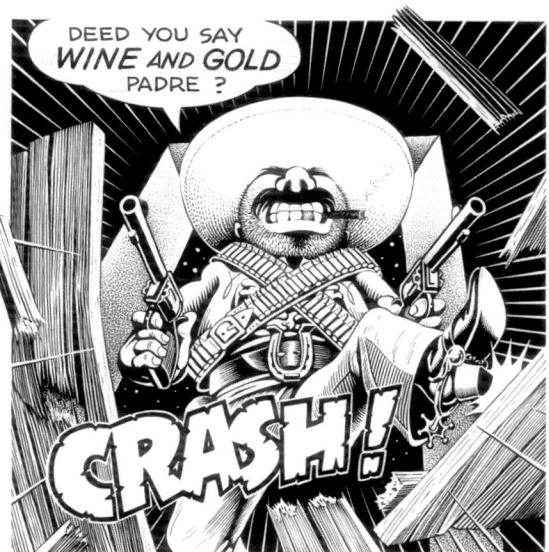

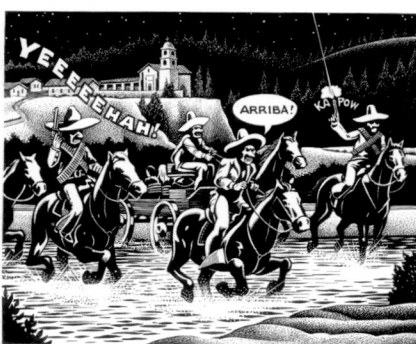

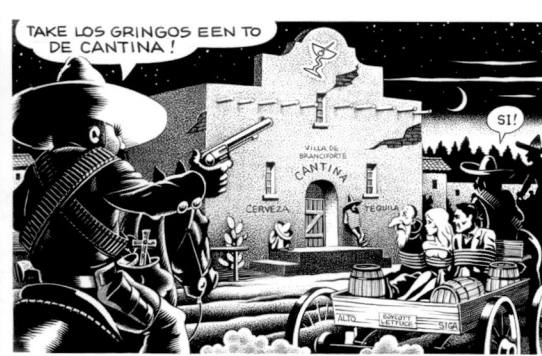

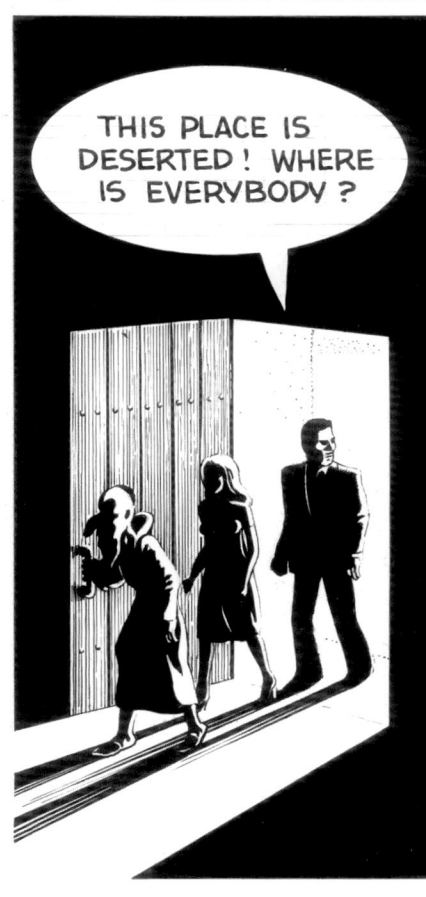

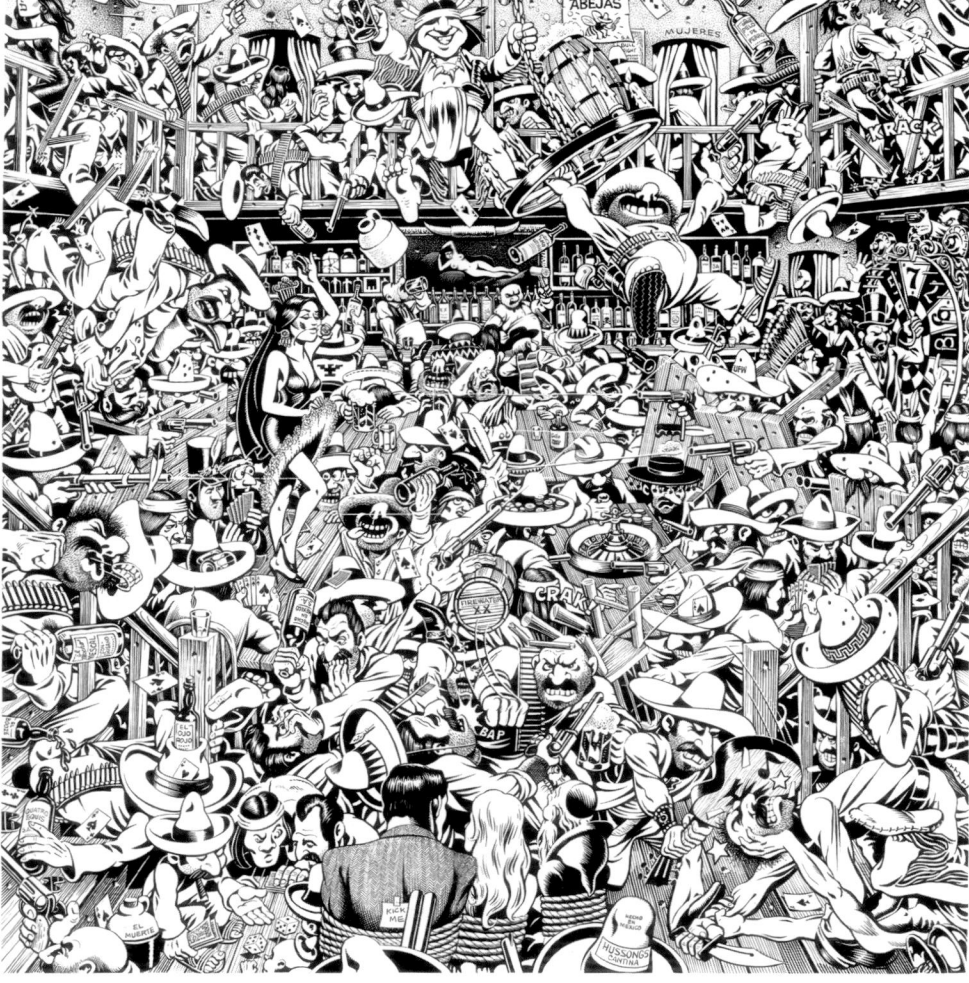

Random panels from the X the Unknown *series.*

Rodeo America T-shirt, 1979.
(image from printed shirt)

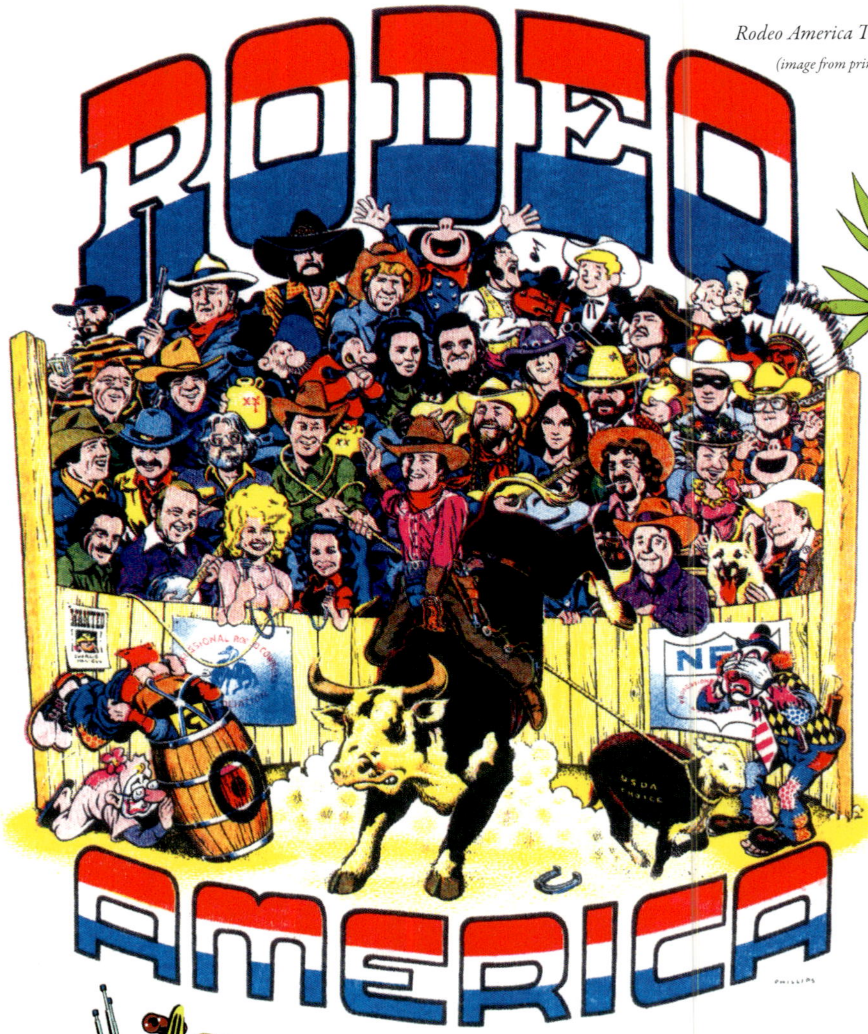

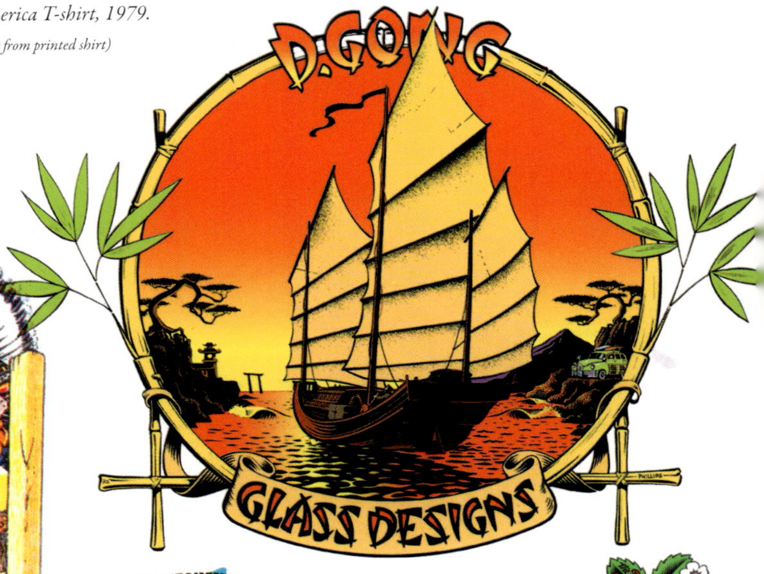

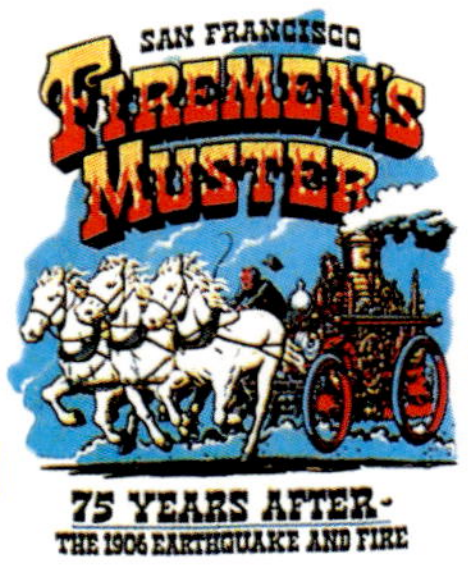

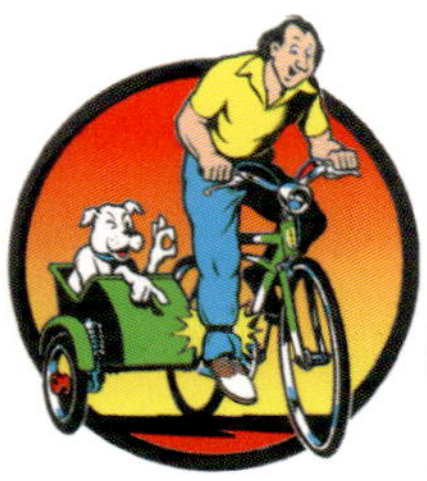

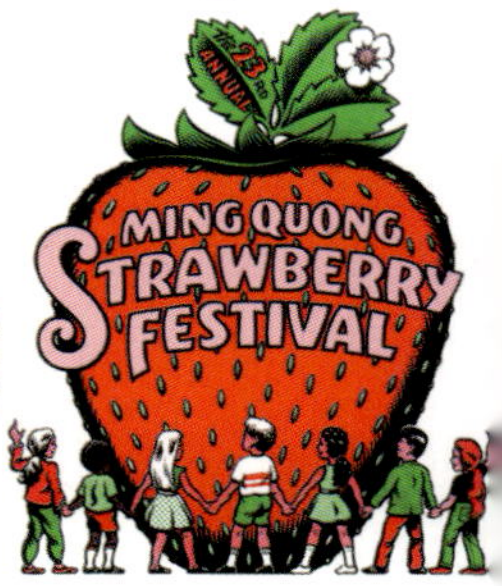

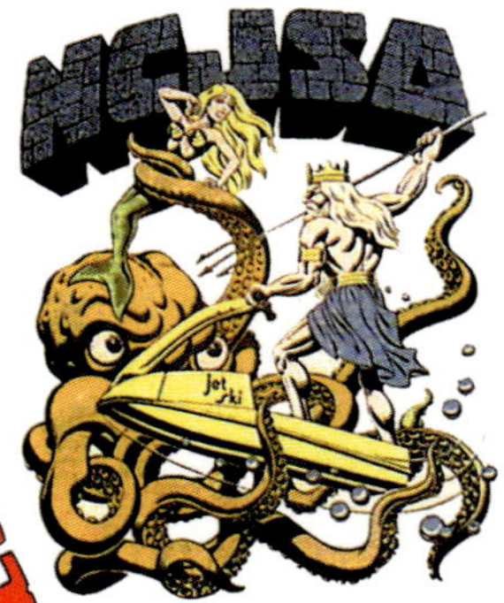

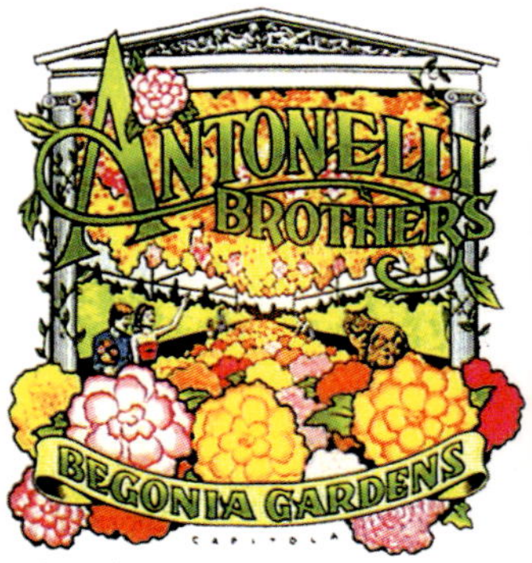

T-shirt designs from the seventies.

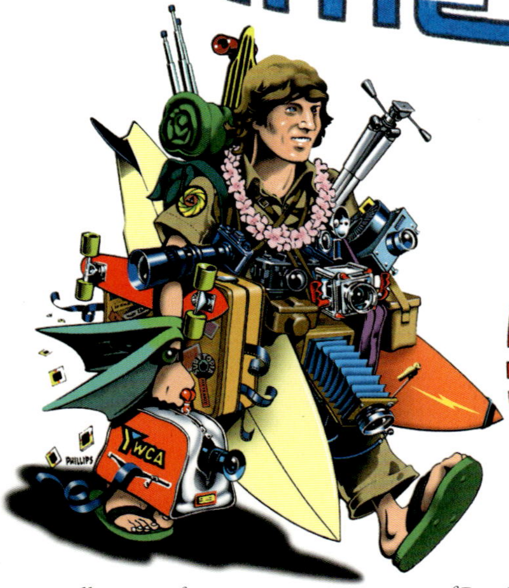

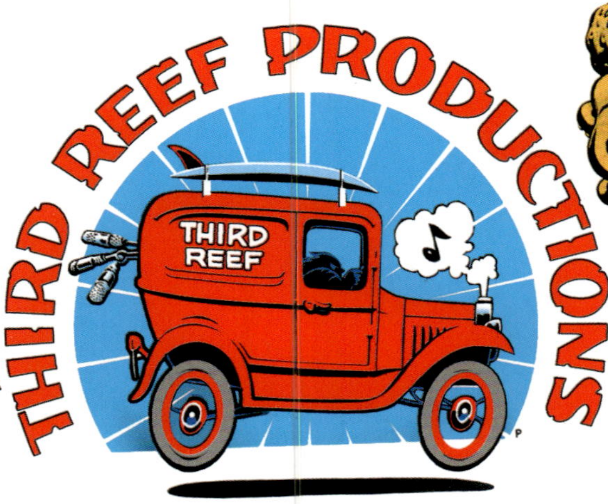

Illustration for magazine story, a portrait of Dan Devine, 1976.

Another logo for Maz, 1978

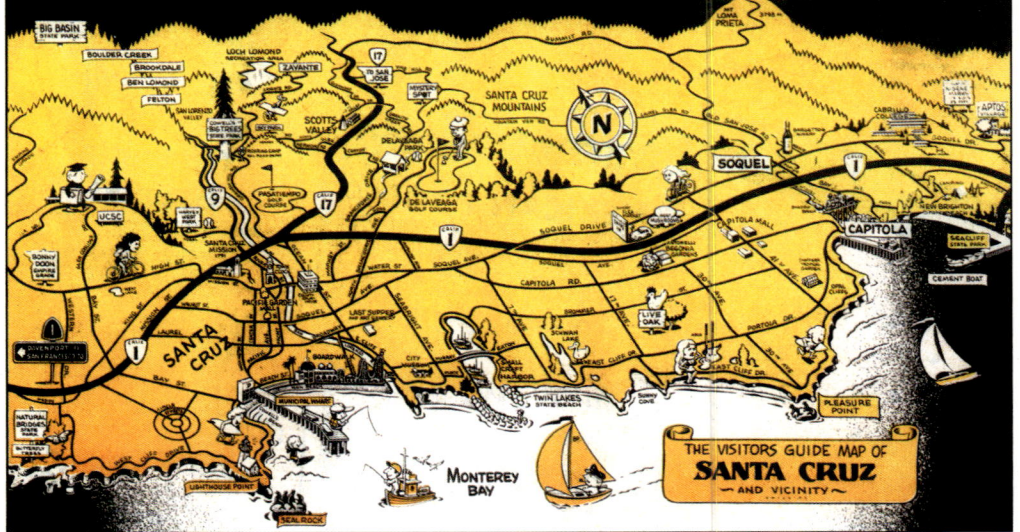

Visitors Guide, map appeared on back cover of each issue, 1980's.

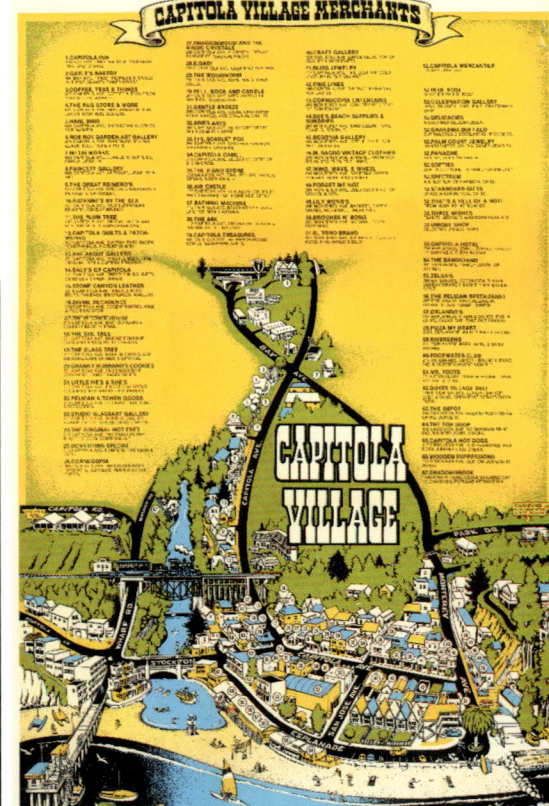

Capitola Village map, signs located around the city, 18"x27", 1978

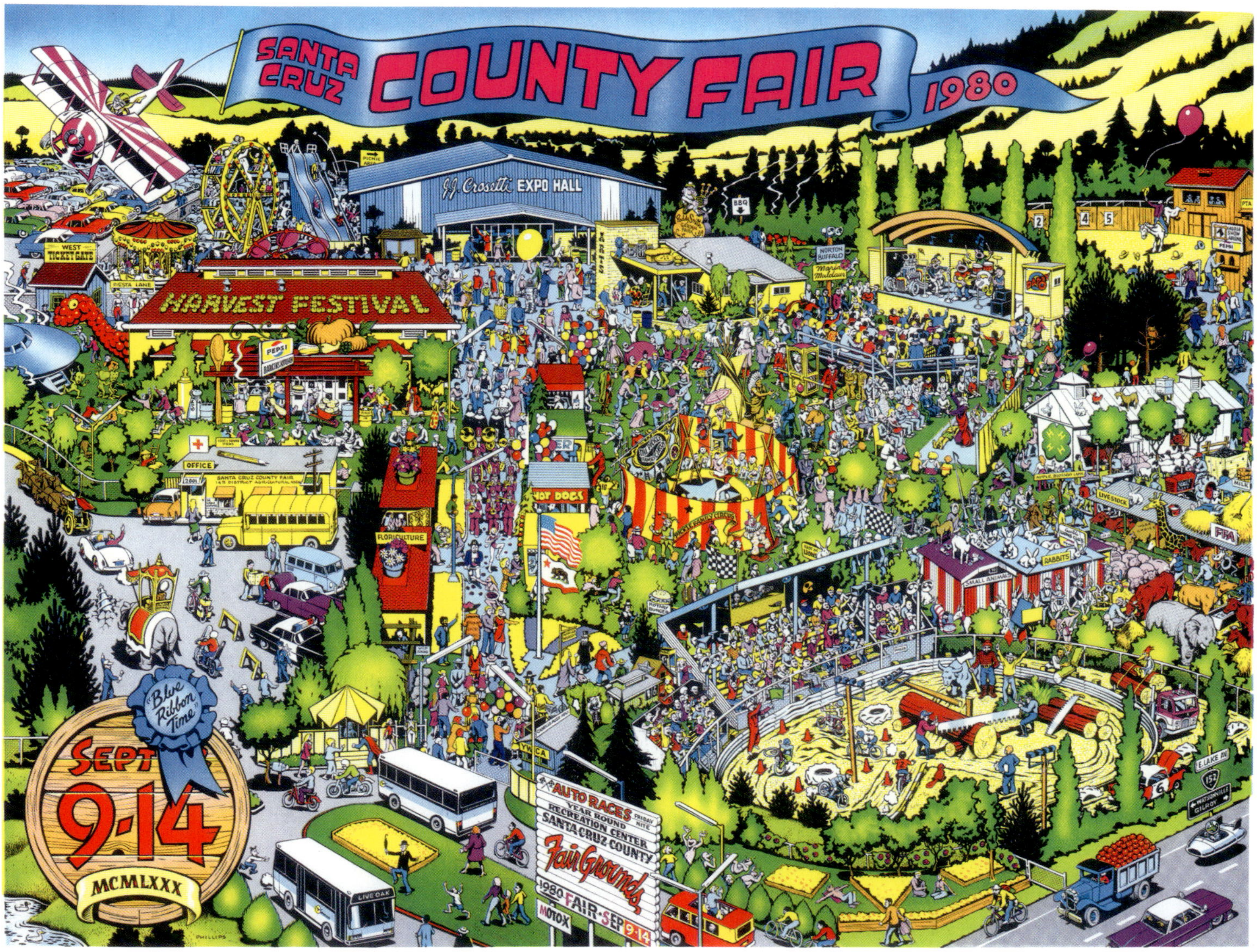

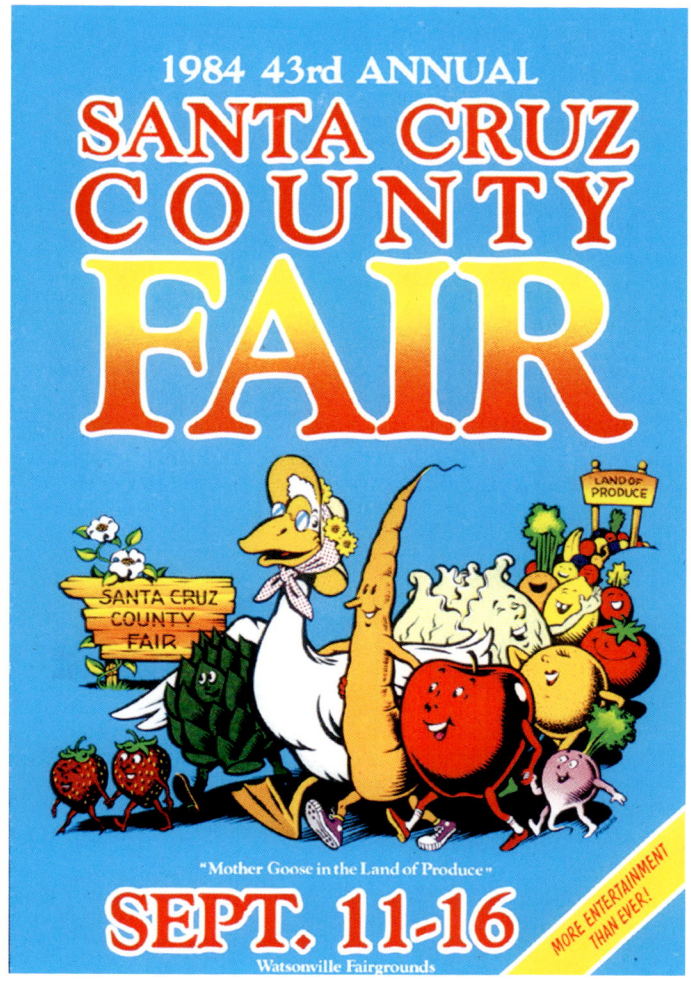

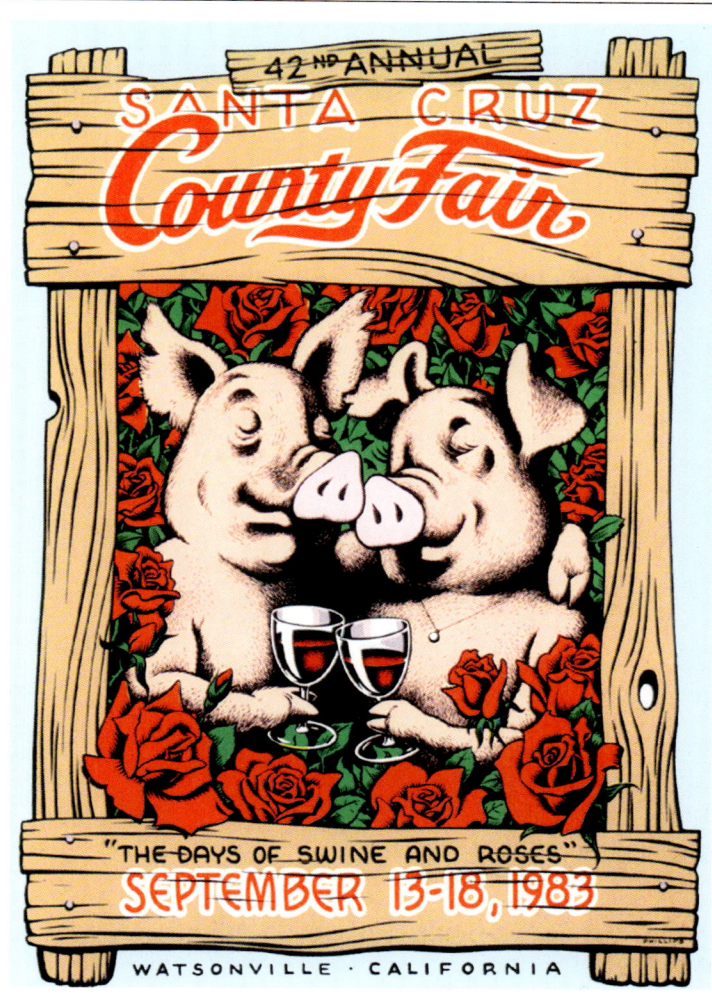

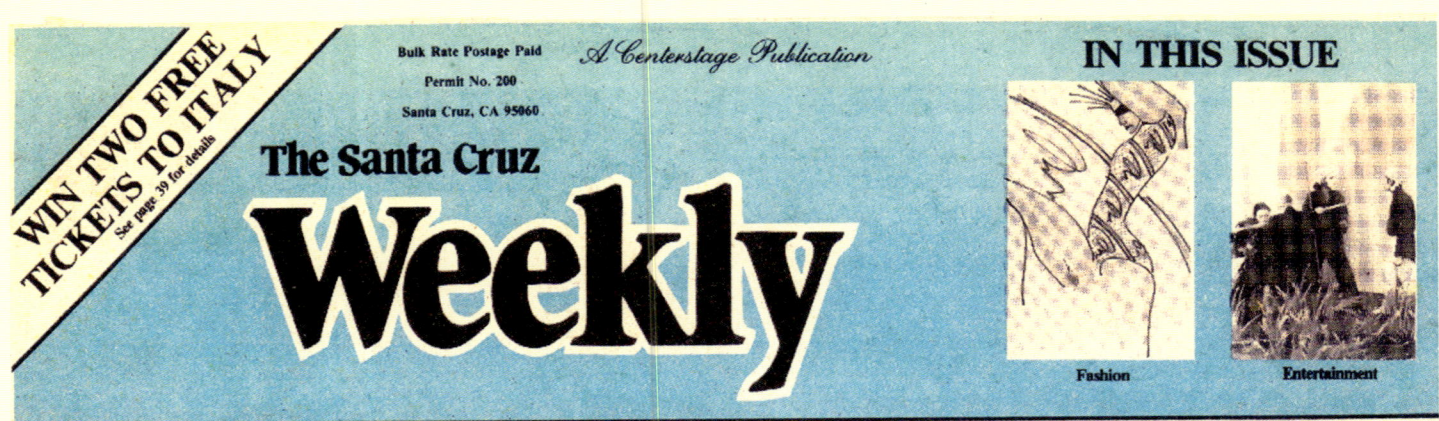

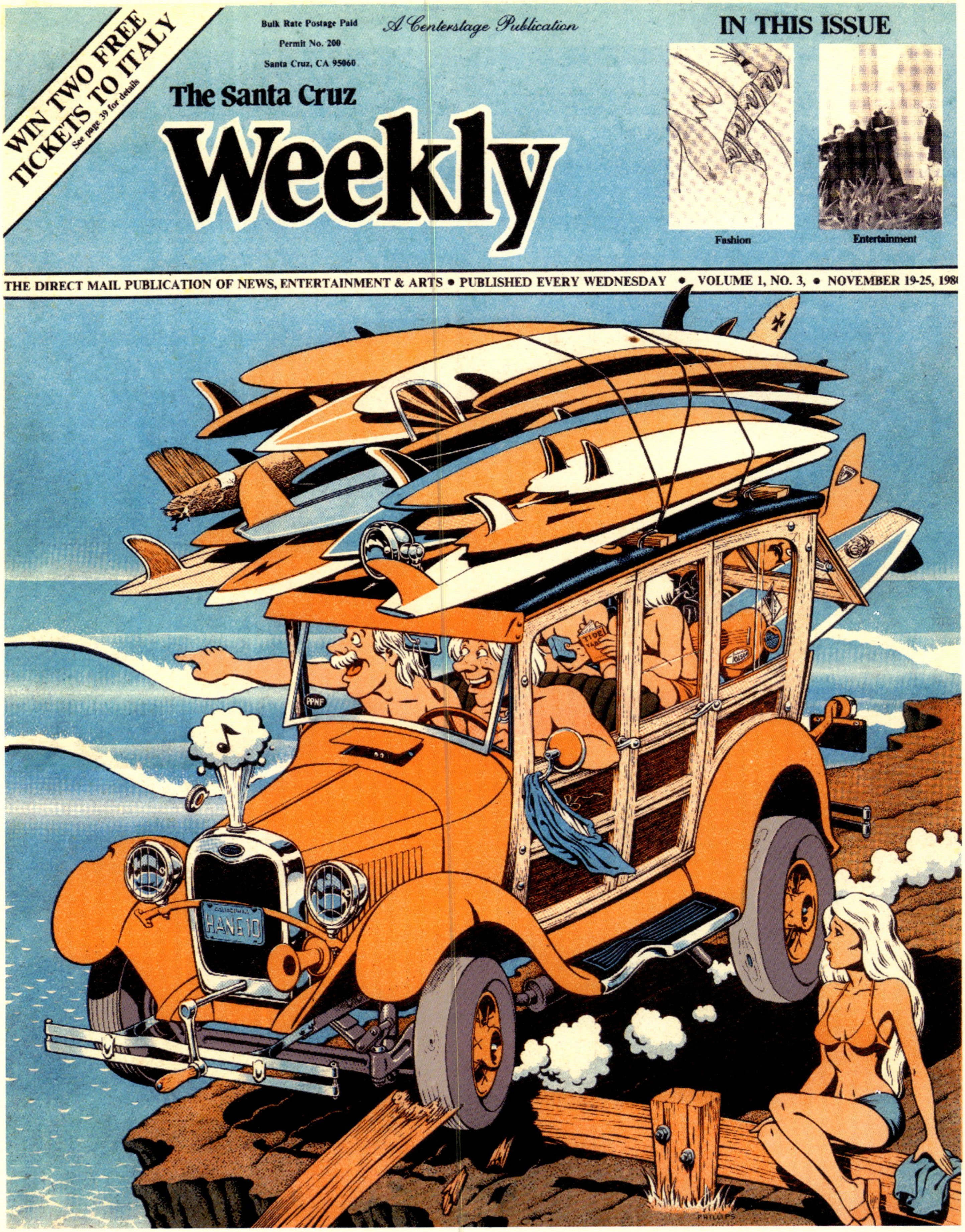

The cover of the November 1980 Santa Cruz Weekly. This woody became the Phillips Studios logo, and has been produced on T-shirts and stickers.

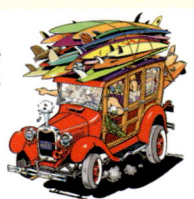

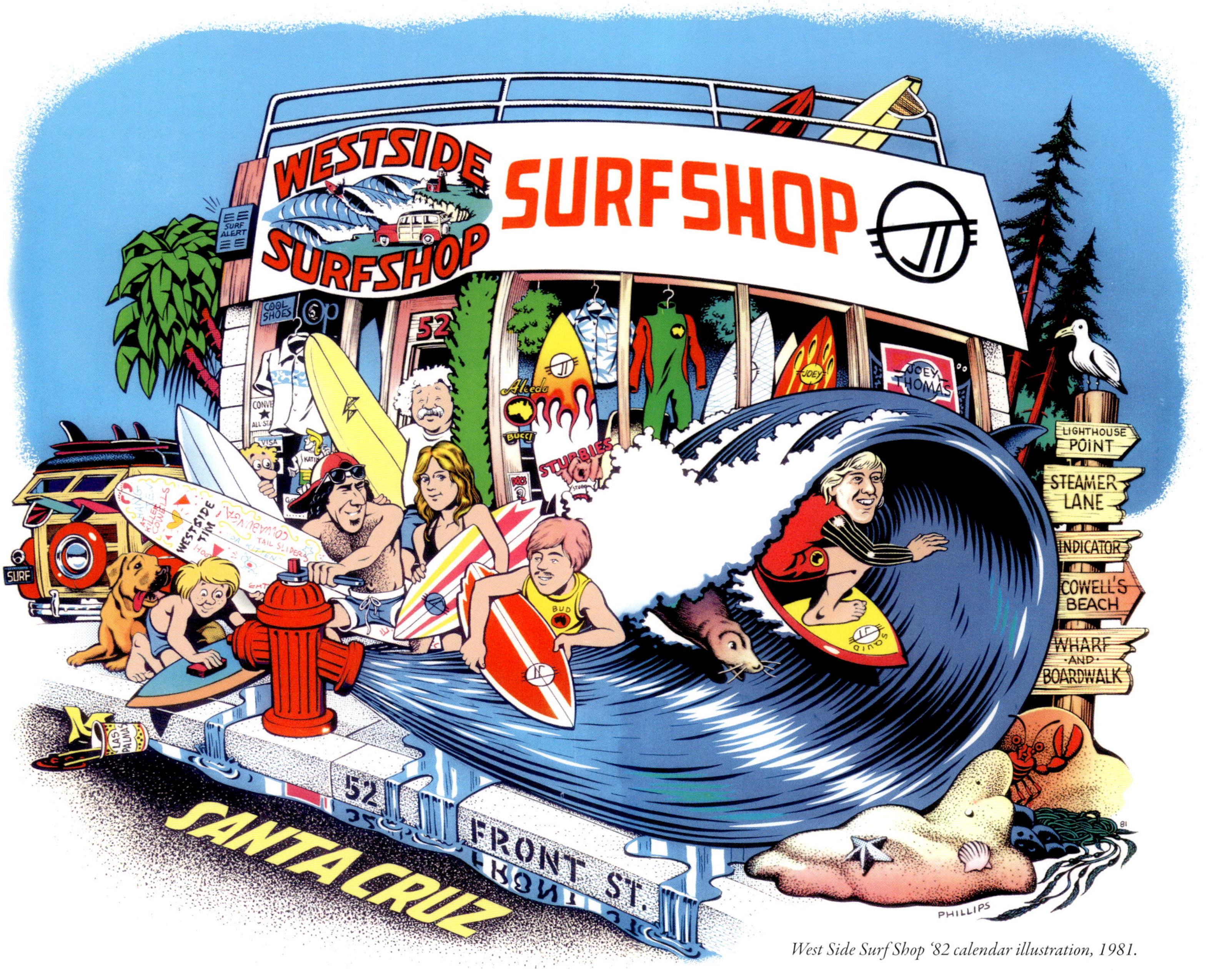

West Side Surf Shop '82 calendar illustration, 1981.

CHAPTER FOUR

THE ROARING 80s: 1979 to 1989

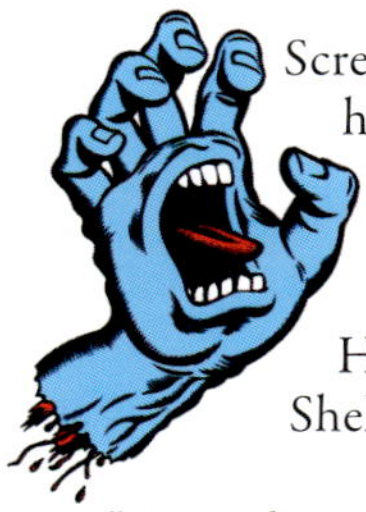

Screaming Hand. The Screaming Blue Hand. A severed hand, dripping gore but very much alive, with an open palm showing an open mouth and teeth and tongue, silent screaming about... something. Gruesome and disturbing but irresistible, Screaming Hand was a little bit Edvard Munch, a little bit Mary Shelley and more than a little bit rock and roll.

"Created in 1985 by illustrator Jim Phillips, the hand served as an overall image for the entire Speed Wheels line, which included Slimeballs, Bullets and OJs. With a bloodstained compound fracture, flapping tendons, and misplaced mouthpiece this aggro amputee became one of the most recognizable skate logos of all time."
- Thrasher Magazine

Screaming Hand popped out of Phillips' head in 1985 and it was more than a little bit responsible for the success of Speed Wheels, one of hundreds of Road Rider brothers and cousins. That simple plastics company called NHS begat Santa Cruz Skateboards, and during the 80s, Santa Cruz Skateboards begat hundreds of thousands of skateboard decks and millions of stickers and hundreds of millions of dollars in sales. Phillips was the primary graphic artist during the Roaring 80s, pumping out logos and ads

and brochures and decks and t-shirts, then starting his own Phillips Studios and eventually hiring more than a dozen young talents to help keep up with the work load.

There was Screaming Hand, but also Slime Balls and Vomit Balls and monsters and skulls and popping eyeballs and gruel and gore, all of this oozing from the Pumpkin Kid, from little Jimmy Phillips, from the son of Edna and Ray, from Mrs. Elliott's and Ralph Gray's favorite pupil, from the kid who got his woody cartoon printed in *SURFER Magazine*. Jim Phillips wasn't a kid anymore in 1984. He was an adult who still thought like a kid, and it was the kids who were buying and the adults who were paying.

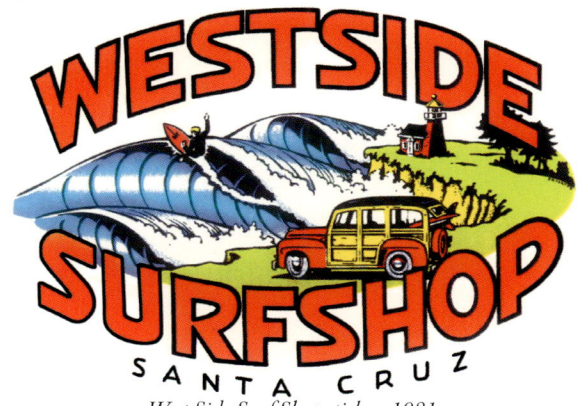

West Side Surf Shop sticker, 1981.

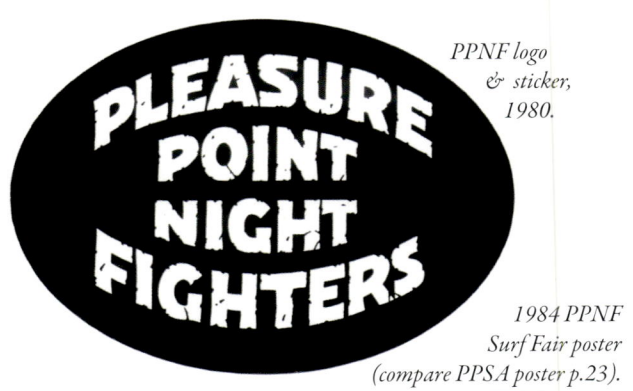

PPNF logo & sticker, 1980.

1984 PPNF Surf Fair poster (compare PPSA poster p.23).

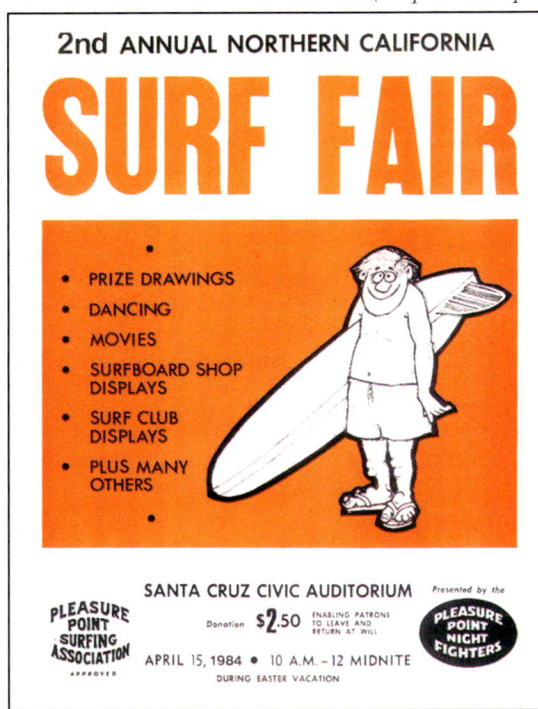

2nd ANNUAL NORTHERN CALIFORNIA

SURF FAIR

- PRIZE DRAWINGS
- DANCING
- MOVIES
- SURFBOARD SHOP DISPLAYS
- SURF CLUB DISPLAYS
- PLUS MANY OTHERS

PLEASURE POINT SURFING ASSOCIATION APPROVED

SANTA CRUZ CIVIC AUDITORIUM

Donation **$2.50** ENABLING PATRONS TO LEAVE AND RETURN AT WILL

APRIL 15, 1984 • 10 A.M. - 12 MIDNITE
DURING EASTER VACATION

Presented by the **PLEASURE POINT NIGHT FIGHTERS**

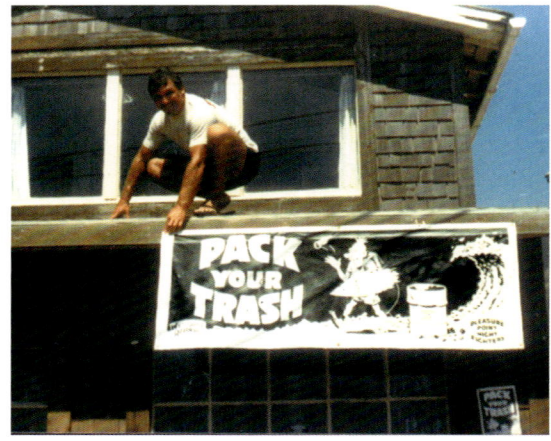

PPNF president Harry Conti hangs a Pack Your Trash banner from the front of PPNF headquarters, 1982.

Pack Your Trash bumpersticker, circa 1981.

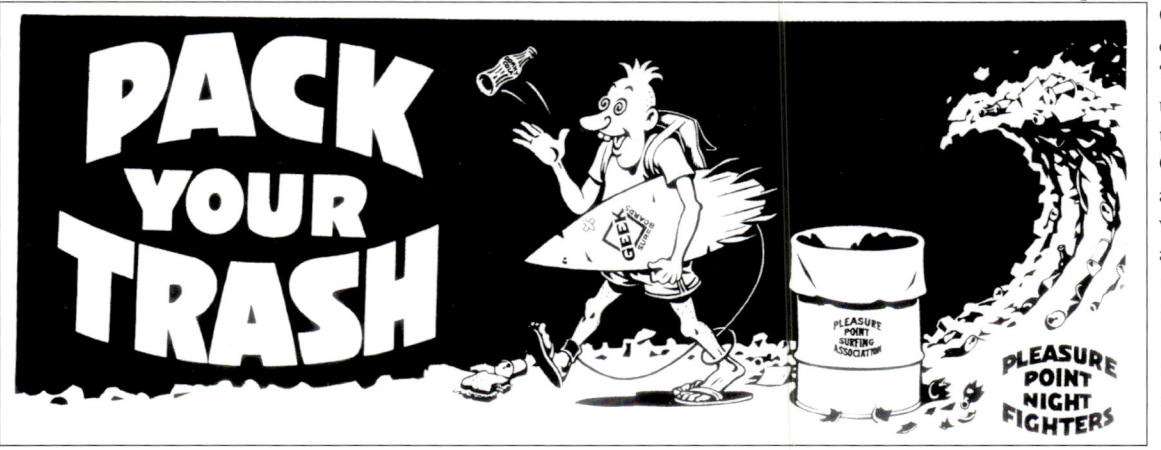

The 80s were nonstop for skateboarding and for Phillips, and the Blue Hand came Screaming out of Phillips' psyche around the middle of the decade. Was it a cry for help? A Rebel Yell? Pleasure or Pain? A reaction to stress and pressure? During the 80s, Phillips put his nose to the grindstone, but he bled green. In two years at the peak of the skateboard boom, Phillips' logos sold an incredible 8 million stickers around the world. NHS and Santa Cruz Skateboards were racking up $50 million in sales. Team riders got a dollar a board. Phillips was on salary and under stress for all of it. When he asked for a nickel a board, he got nixed. It is very possible that Hand is Screaming what Phillips dared not: "ART ROYALTIES!"

The creative and financial pressures bearing down on Phillips weren't the only pressures building up in Santa Cruz County. At the beginning of the Disaster Decade, Santa Cruz was bombarded with low pressure systems as the coast was battered with wind and waves during the deadly El Nino winters of 1982 and 1983. At the end of the decade, pressure along the San Andreas fault let loose deep beneath the Santa Cruz Mountains, and the Loma Prieta earthquake ravaged Santa Cruz and leveled half the town. Phillips and his family and studio survived, but only a few months later, Phillips suffered his own personal aftershock, and severed a 16 year relationship with NHS and Santa Cruz Skateboards for good. Pressure. Screaming. A Severed Relationship. Blood and Gore. Is that what Screaming Hand represents?

Phillips was working full-time for Santa Cruz Skateboards at the turn of the 80s, and picking up other work when it interested him. A glossy monthly called *Santa Cruz Magazine* began in 1979, and one of Phillips' surfing friends, Pat Bisconte, was the Art Director. He asked Jim to create a running three-page, illustrated story. This reminded Jim of the *Surfing Illustrated* opportunity that he blew, back in the early sixties. *Santa Cruz Magazine* had a chance to go big, so he buried himself in *X the Unknown*. It was a story about aliens landing in Santa Cruz, and turning into humans with time-travel abilities. He worked on large boards to get a lot of detail into each panel. Part Two went back to the early days of Santa Cruz and dwelled on historical occurrences. Jim finished the second story, and was on a roll, then started part three, which had his Sparky the Space Gremlin on the splash panel. He wove Sparky into the story. As he began working on the next panel, making up the story as he went along, he got a phone call from Pat, "Sorry man, the magazine folded!"

When *Santa Cruz Weekly* asked for a few covers in 1980, Phillips gave them an image of a woody going over a cliff, which would later become the emblem of Phillips Studios. When he was asked to do a poster for the 1980 Santa Cruz County Fair, Phillips did an elaborate "mob scene" drawing in detail that sometimes only Phillips knew was there. There were several other local cover jobs, for *The Express,* the *UCSC Student Guide, Bay Sports,* and others.

Around 1980, Phillips was asked by an old surfing friend, Harry Conti, to design a t-shirt for a revival of the Pleasure Point Night Fighters: "Jimmy was my hero when I grew up surfing because he had more style than anyone else, and personality," Conti said. "I never knew he was an artist, to tell you the truth! Just watching him in the water, he had a Hawaiian stance, and I never understood his style of surfing until I moved to Hawaii."

Conti wanted to start a surf club similar to the Pleasure Point Surfing

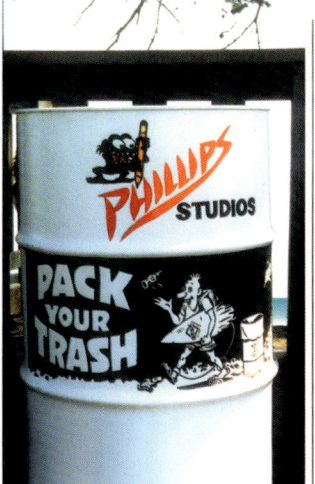

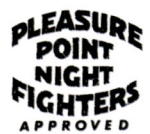

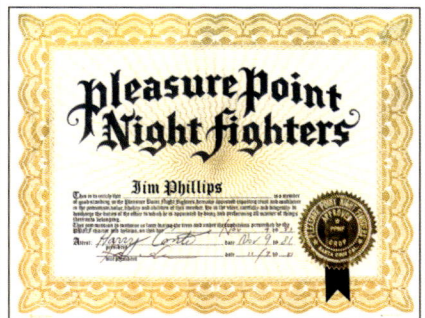

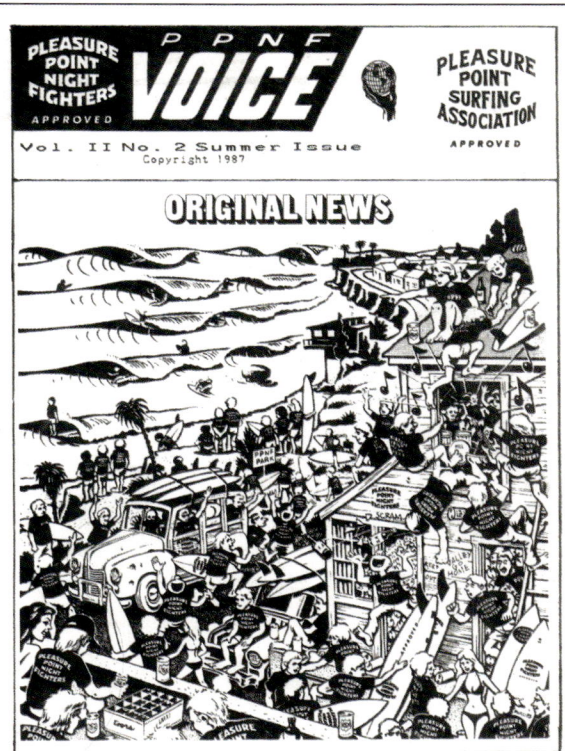

From top: sponsors of trash cans were offered their company logo on the side.

Membership cert.

PPNF Voice Vol2 No2, 1987

Bunny Ball ticket

California stock certificate

Posters: 1981

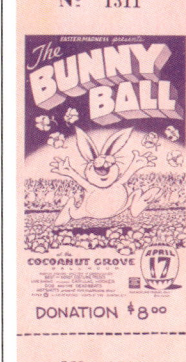

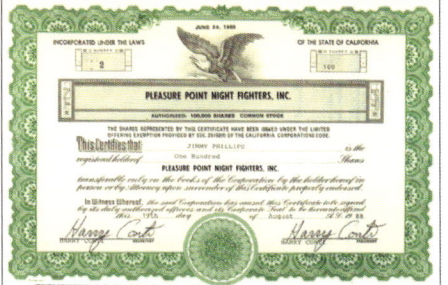

Association of 1963, and he wanted to invoke the name of a Santa Cruz benevolent society that went farther back than that, to the Pleasure Point Night Fighters of the 1920s. The original PPNF were formed then, when the Santa Cruz Fire Department refused to go all the way out to Pleasure Point to fight fires at night. The Night Fighters fought fires and any other battles that presented themselves. When a young girl in Pleasure Point was raped, the Night Fighters drove all the way to San Jose, broke the rapist out of jail, and lynched him. Conti didn't have that sort of thing in mind. He just wanted a surf club that would police the point for trash and improper behavior.

HARRY CONTI: *"I still have that original PPNF artwork. When I got the drawing back, it was this image like the Hulk, Jimmy had put my mug on. I was a garbage-man, had the washboard stomach and all that from packing garbage, so he comes up with this artwork of me breaking out of a brick wall, and I go, 'No, that's not it!. A logo, not an image of me!' So he went back, and the Pleasure Point Night Fighter logo was born."*

Phillips thought Harry's PPNF revivalist ideas were crazy, that no one would ever show for a meeting. "I reminded Harry of the cards and the 'Uncle Fred' incidents, but he talked me into doing the shirt logo, which I made similar to the old PPSA t-shirts." The club gave Jim a genuine California PPNF stock certificate that still hangs on his wall. In 1982 Jim was surfing more than ever because Jimbo was of surfing age, and it was a good thing to revive some of the old brotherhood hanging at the PPNF "headquarters" as Harry called his house overlooking the surf at Pleasure Point.

It would be a connection point for many people from Jim's surfing past.

HARRY CONTI:

"Jimmy was an instigator, but always so clever in staying in the background, like 'Who, me?' He was definitely one of the cleverest ones of the bunch. Most guys here were con artists, in control, and always took advantage of people, but Jimmy never did. He was never one to do that."

Instead of fighting fires or lynching rapists, the 80s version of the PPNF wanted to focus on beach trash and keeping Pleasure Point clean. Conti

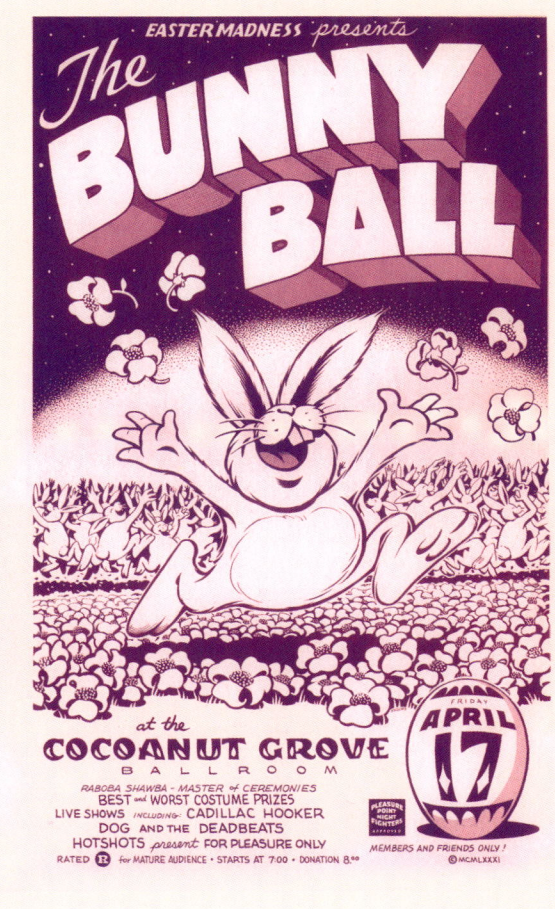

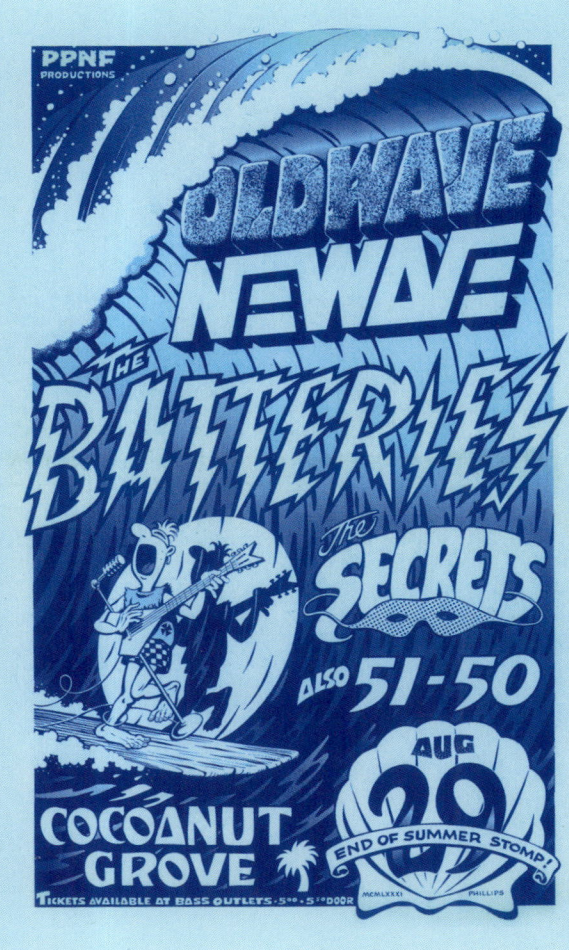

103

commissioned Phillips to do an anti-trash logo, and 20 years after the Pleasure Point Surfing Association entered their "Keep Your Beach Clean" garbage can in the Miss California Parade, Phillips came up with the Pack Your Trash logo. First it was a flyer, but that was just more trash. Jack O'Neill suggested and sponsored a bumper sticker and that was it. You would see Pack Your Trash stickers on many cars for years to come.

The club started a newsletter called the *PPNF Voice,* which turned into four issues of a rough magazine. PPNF threw a couple of rock shows at the Coconut Grove that lost money. They attempted a Surf Fair, like the Pleasure Point Surfing Association had done in the 60s. The first try in 1984 suffered a fatal blow when a terrorist bombed the PG&E Plant at Moss Landing, and the Santa Cruz Fire Department came to the Civic from next door and shut the show down.

What endured from the PPNF are Phillips' designs, the Pleasure Point Night Fighters and PPNF Approved stickers, and the ubiquitous Pack Your Trash. The Pack Your Trash logo shows a

goofy, valley geek walking away from a polluted wave, throwing a beer can over his shoulder. Pack Your Trash has been translated into Spanish, Japanese, Hawaiian, Lakota, and many other languages. It is one of Phillips' designs that you are likely to see anywhere in the world. Frequent travelers aren't surprised to find Pack Your Trash stickers pasted to the side of a hut in feral Indonesia, or flashing from the oar of a paddle in equatorial Brazil. Those Pack Your Trash stickers are on every other car in and around Santa Cruz, and they were the first flares of ubiquity during a decade that would spread the work of Phillips around the world and back again.

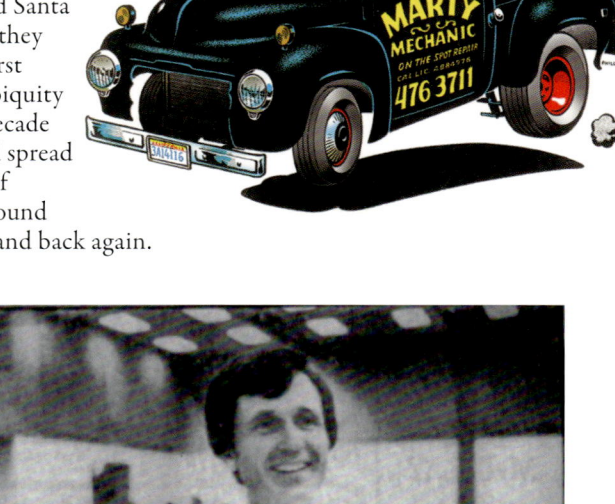

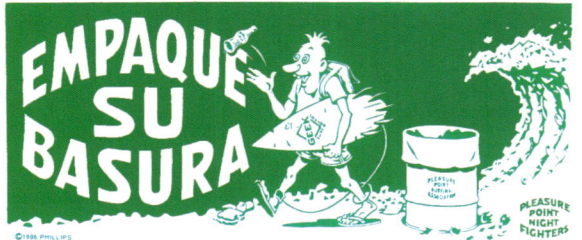

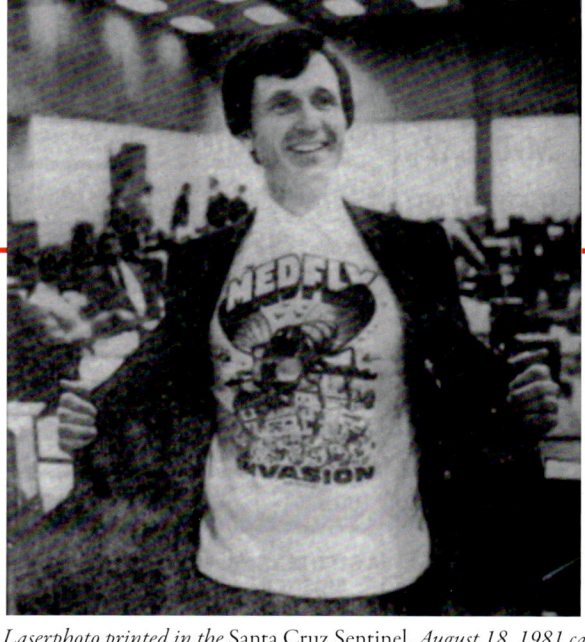

AP Laserphoto printed in the Santa Cruz Sentinel, *August 18, 1981 caption reads "'SACRAMENTO - Assemblyman Walter Herger, R-Marysville, modeled his Medfly t-shirt on the house floor of the state capitol, Monday. Herger was the first politician to put on the shirt in front of news cameras.... designed by local artist, Jim Phillips."*

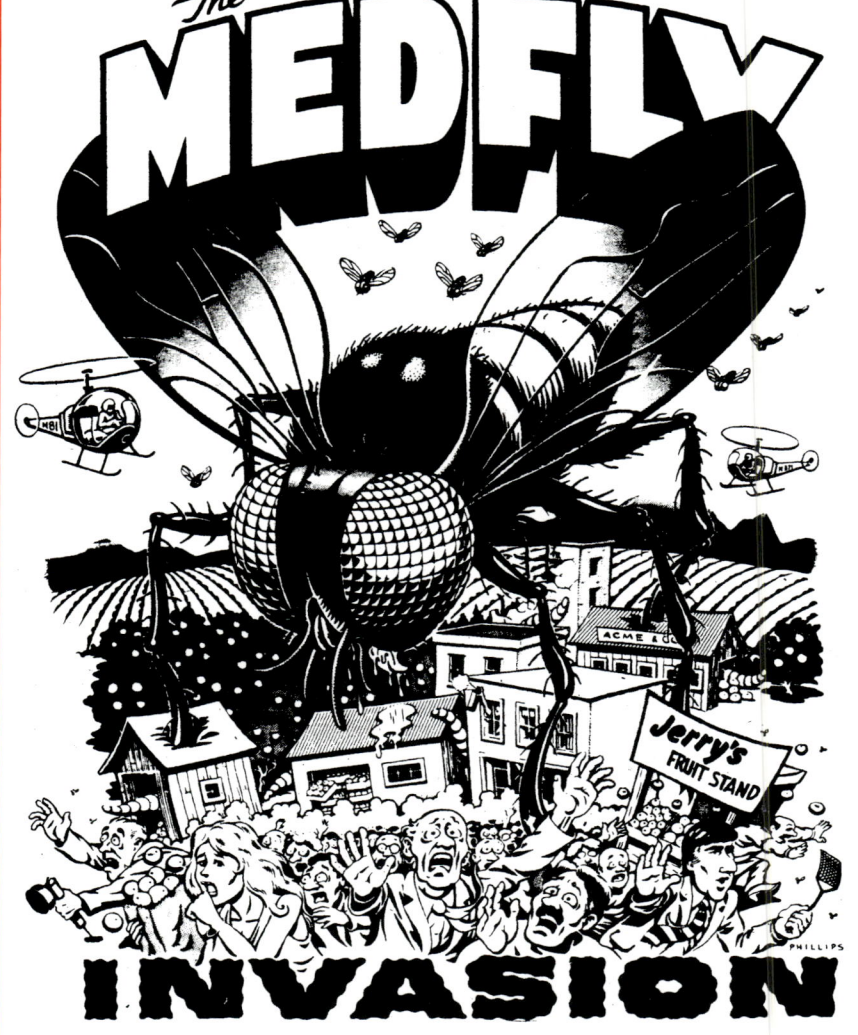

Phillips' Medfly T-shirt was featured on the front page of the Los Angeles Times, *July 22, 1981*

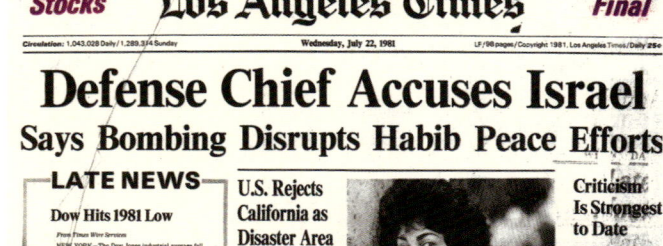

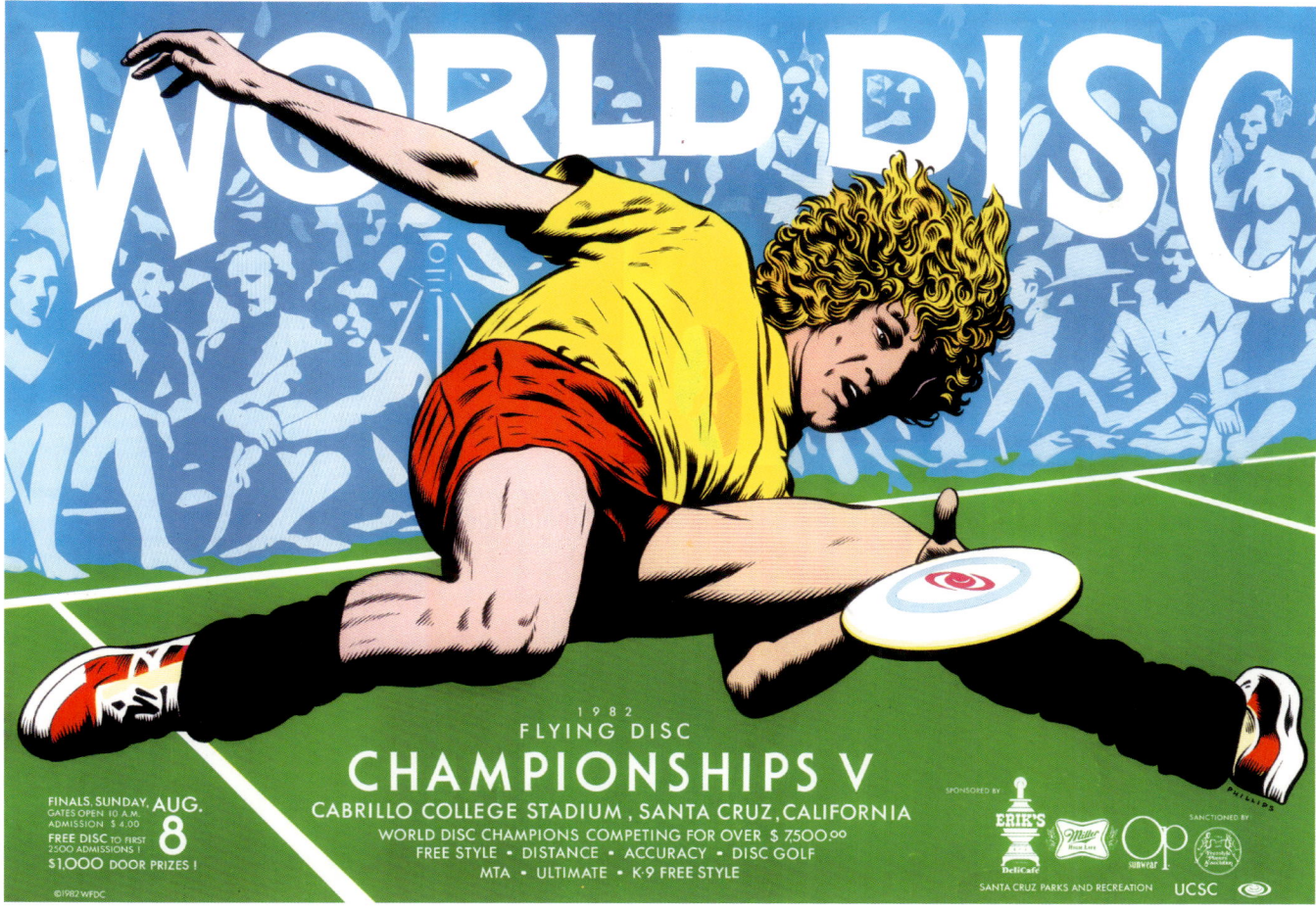

World Disc poster, 16.5"x24.5", 1882

National Horseshoe poster, 22'5"x11, 1983

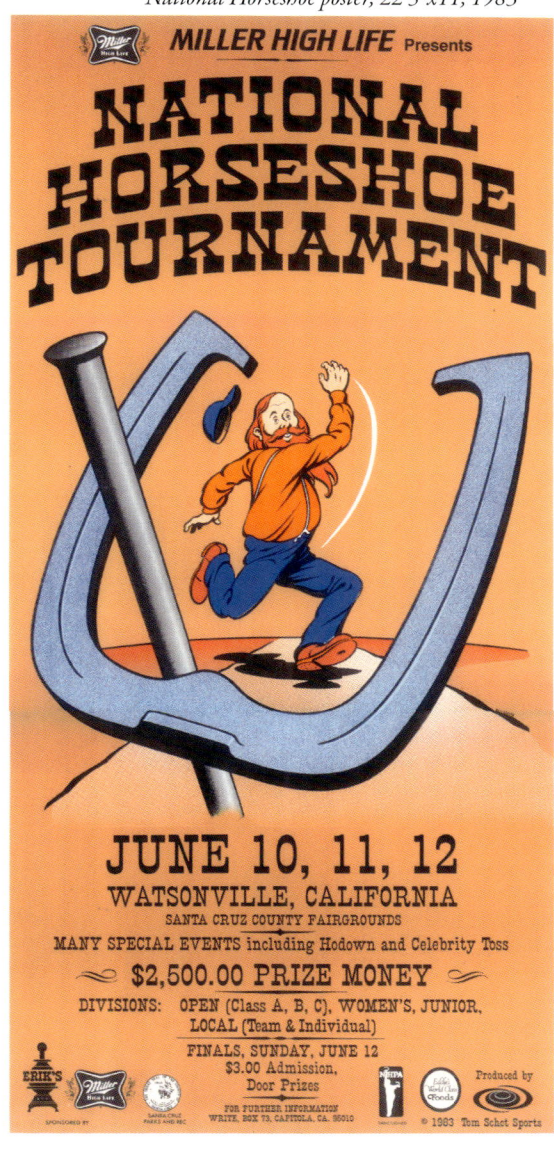

Flora Purim poster, 8.5"x14", 1984,
A Sandy Castle Production (Maz).

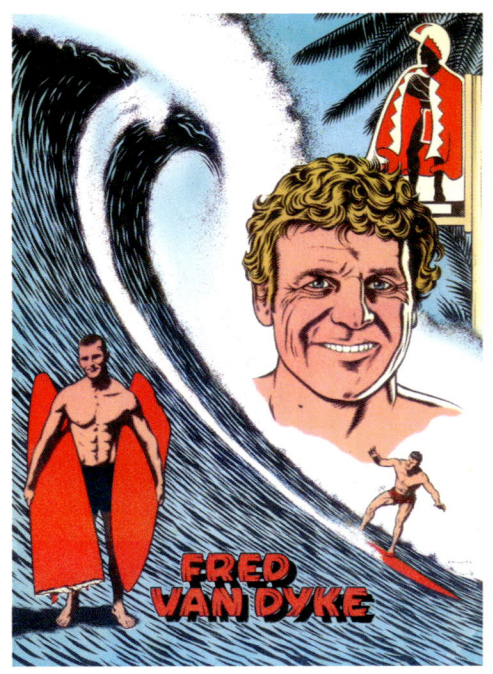
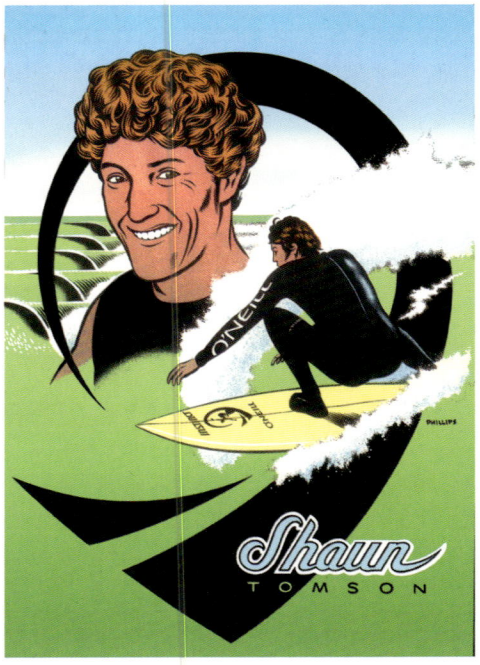
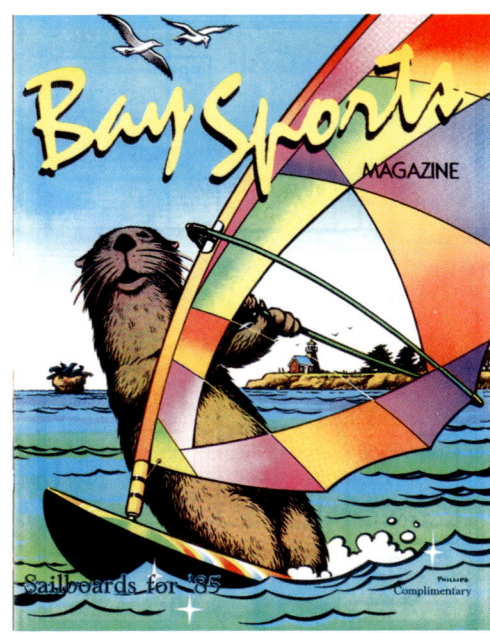

Bay Sports Magazine, *cover illustration, 1985.*

Fred Van Dyke and Shaun Tomson were full page illustrations for Surfin' *and* Ocean Sports, *1982.*

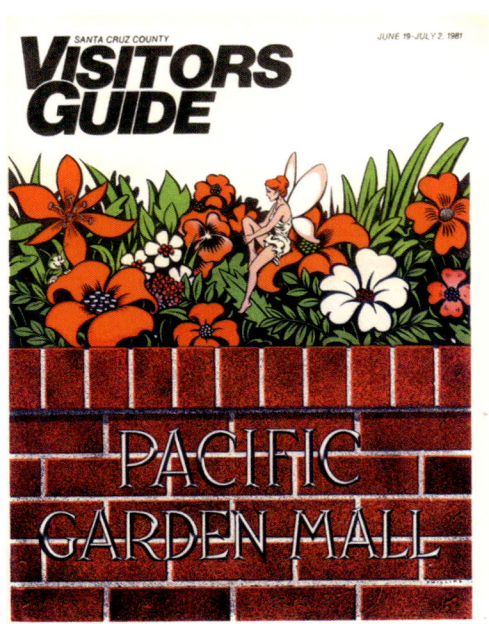
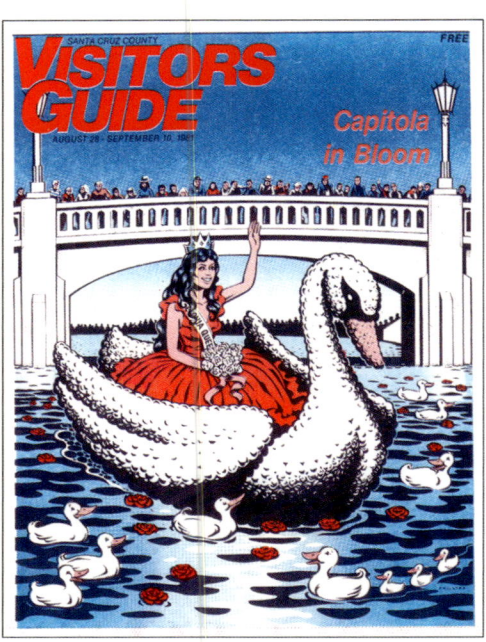
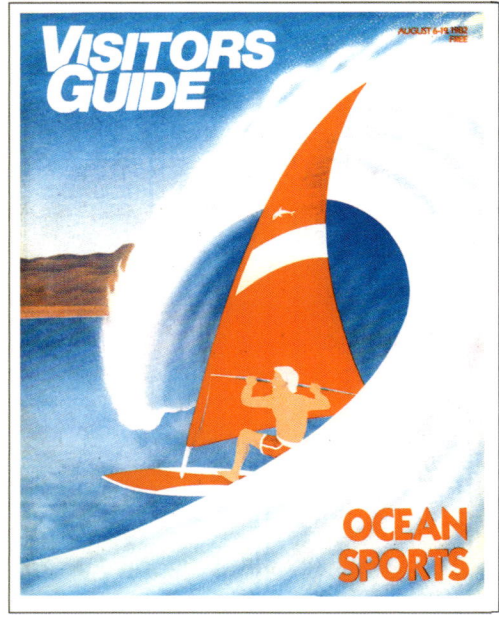

Visitors Guide, *cover illustrations from 1981 and 1982.*

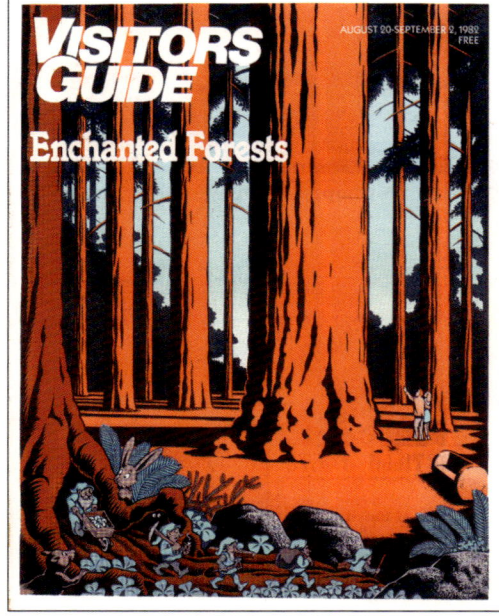
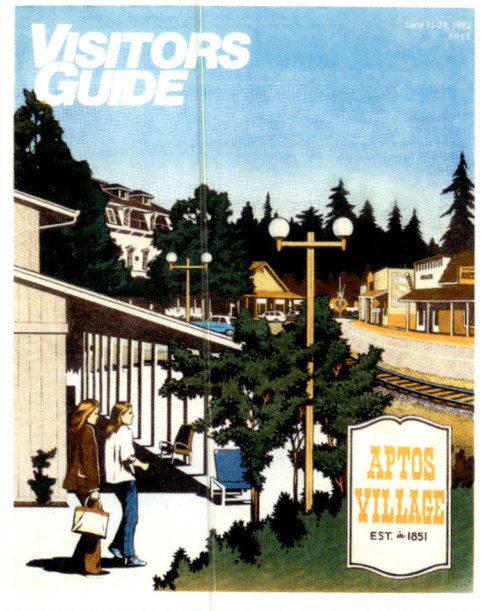
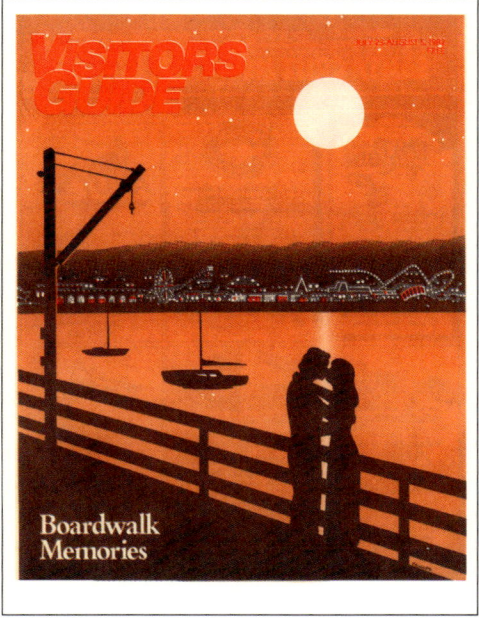

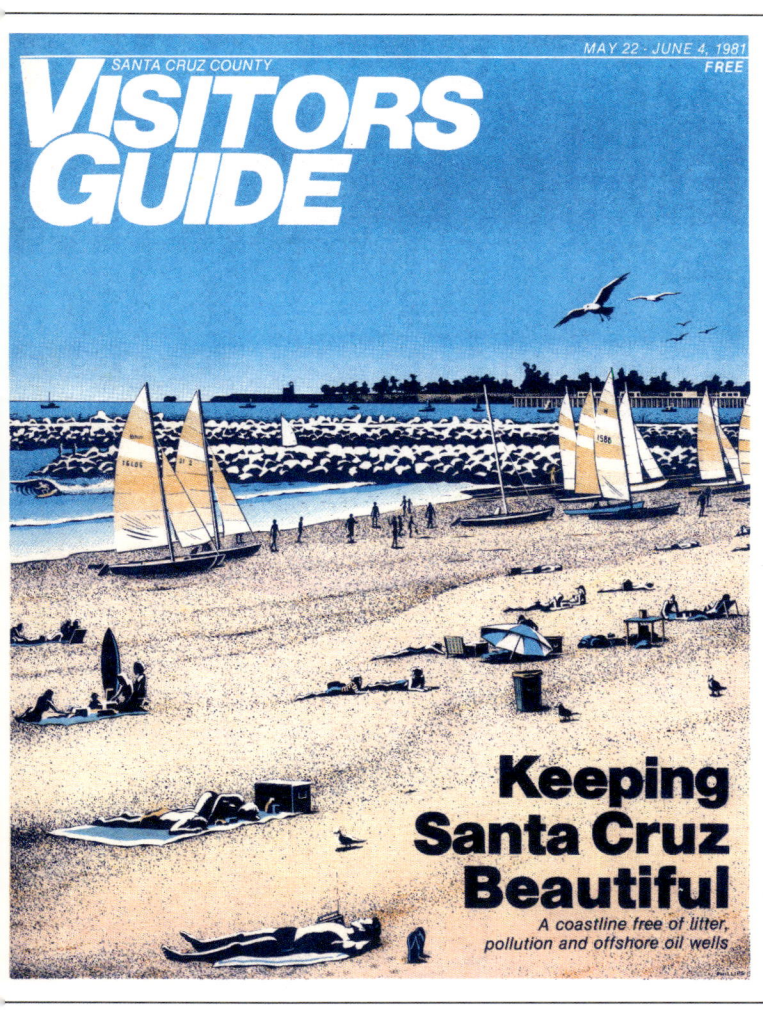

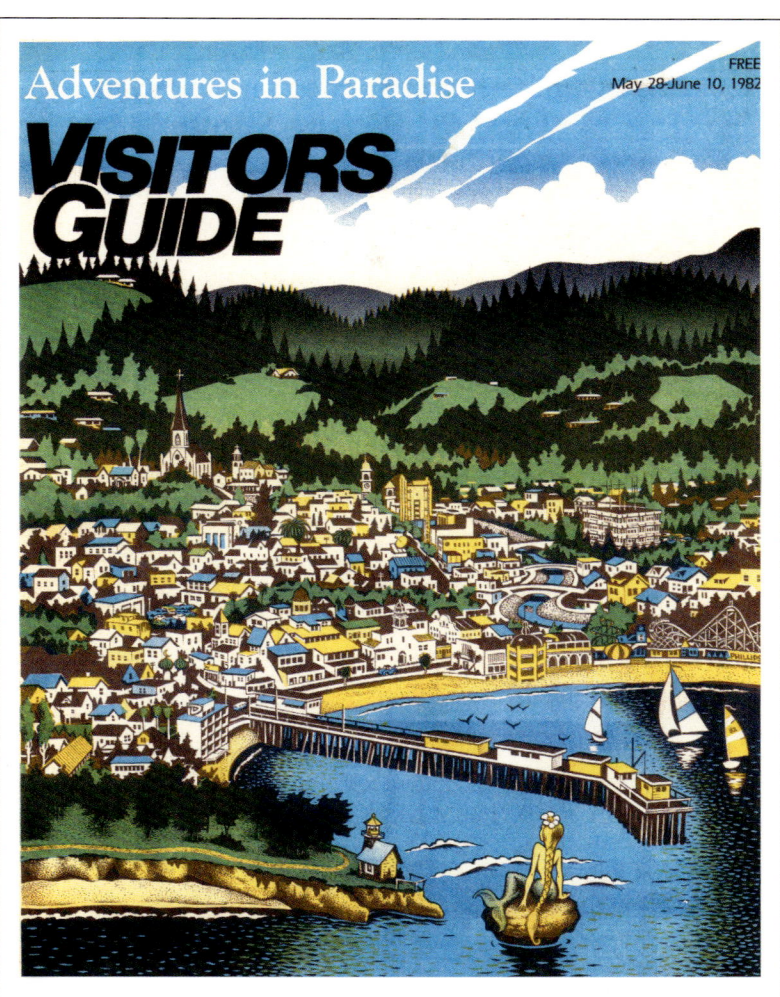

Visitors Guide, *cover illustrations from 1981 and 1982.*

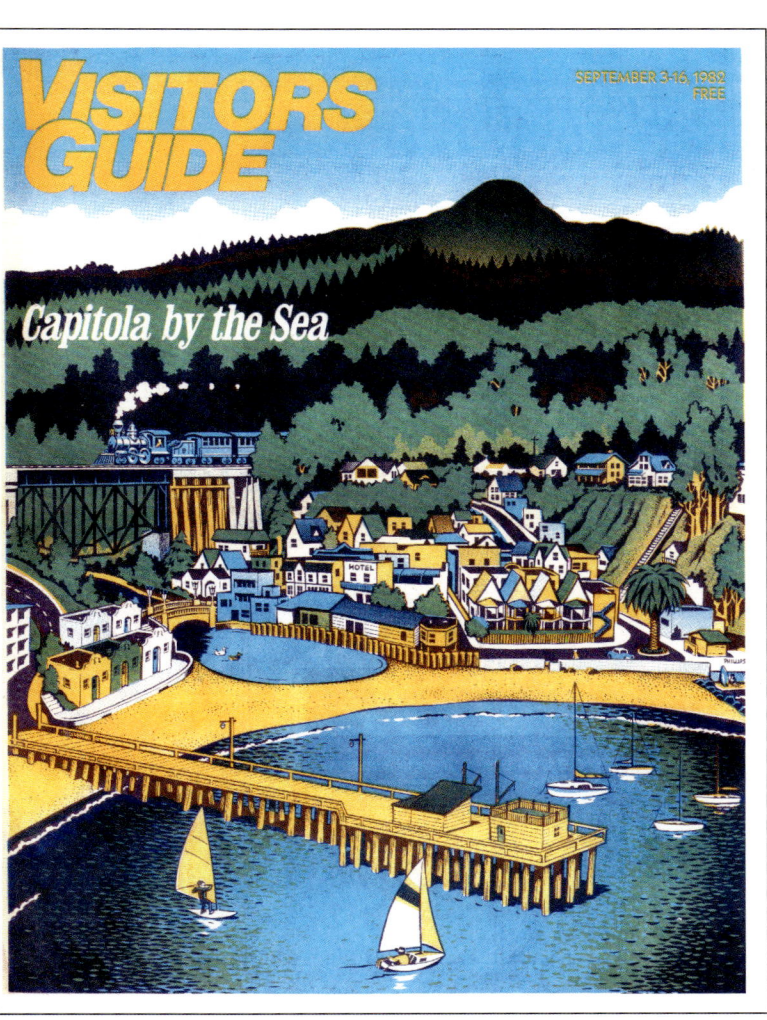

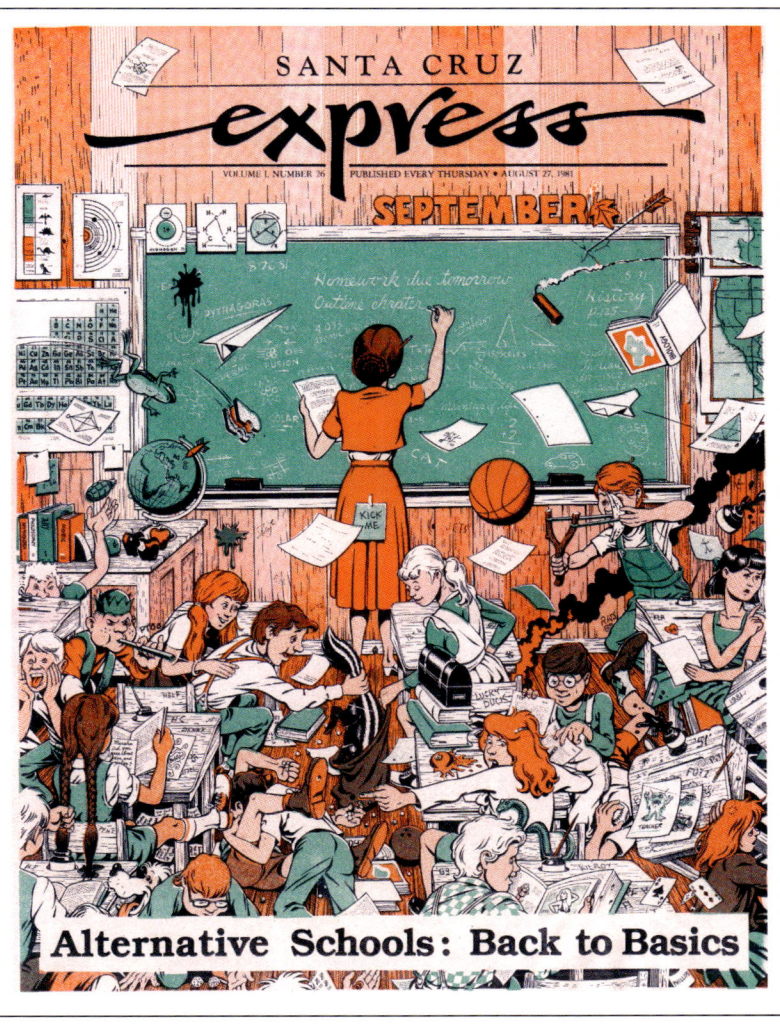

The Santa Cruz Express, *cover illustration, 1981.*

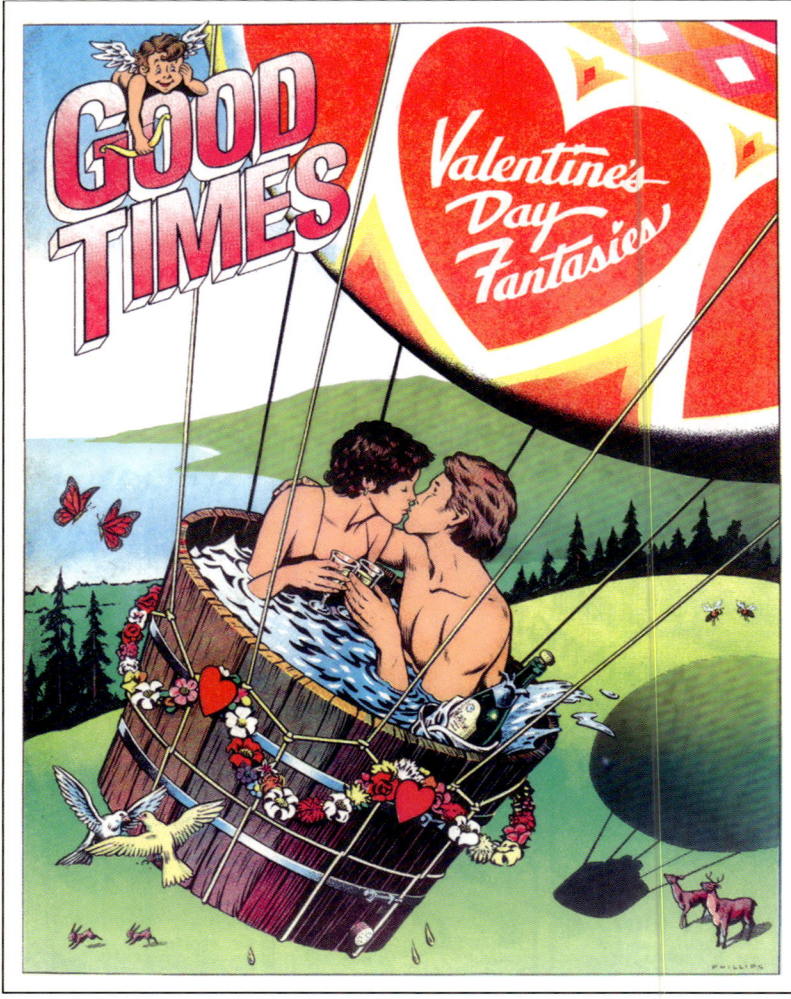

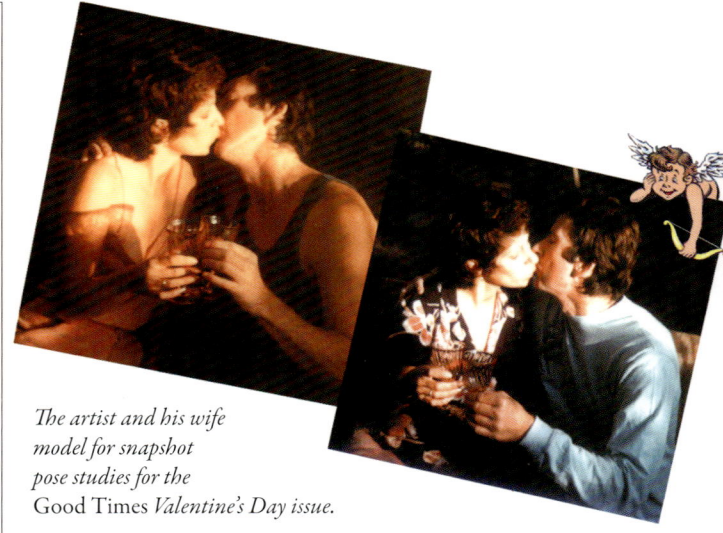

The artist and his wife model for snapshot pose studies for the Good Times *Valentine's Day issue.*

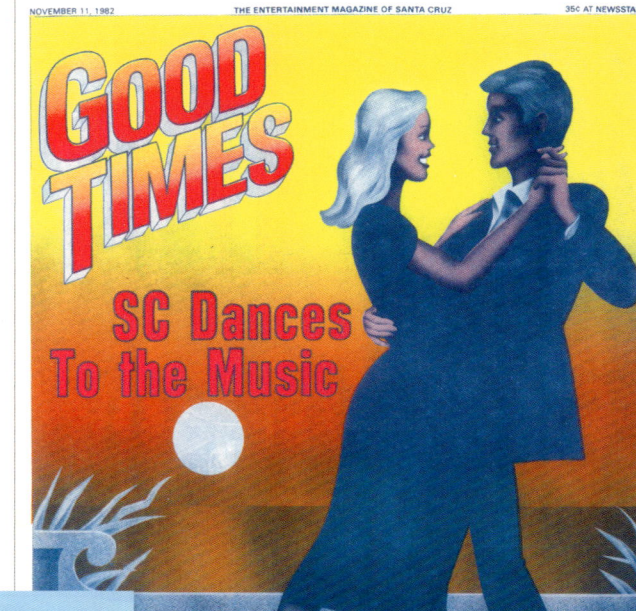

Top: *1992 Valentine's Day cover illustration.*

Left; Good Times *full page ad, 1992.*

Below: *Newspaper rack display board, 1993.*

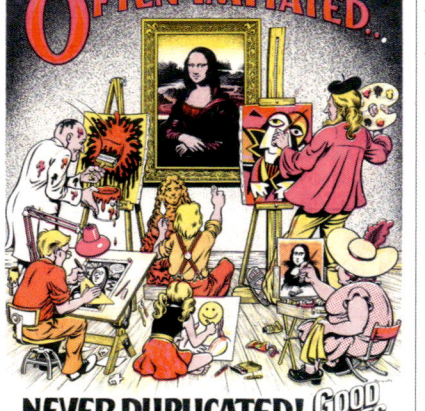

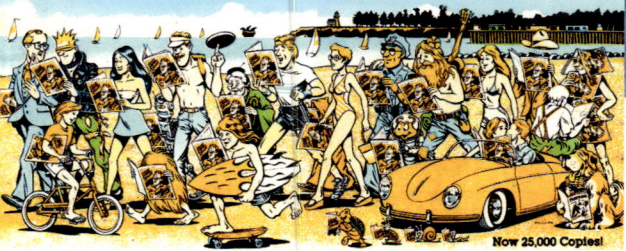

Valentine's Day issue, 1992.

Good Times *covers of 1982.*

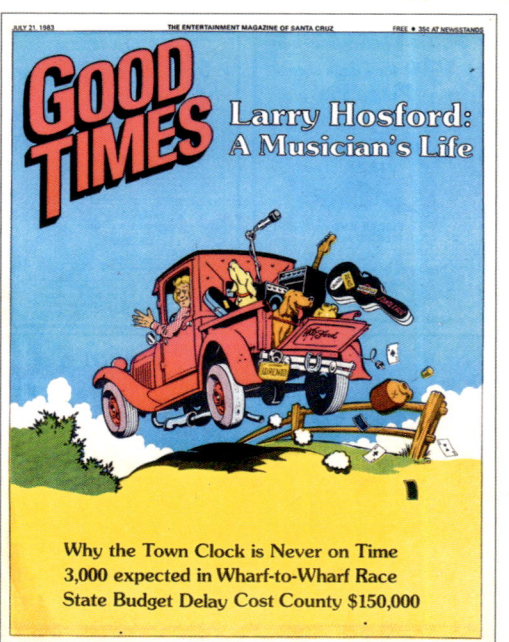

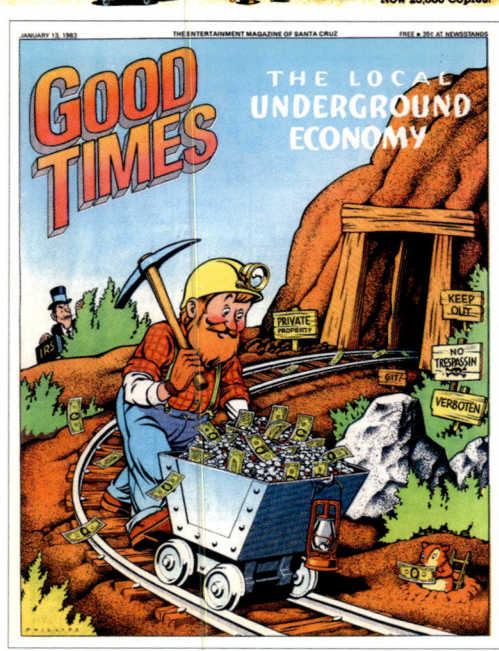

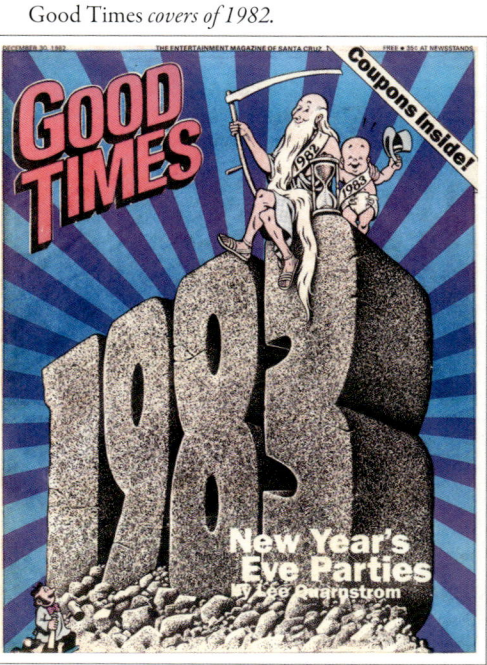

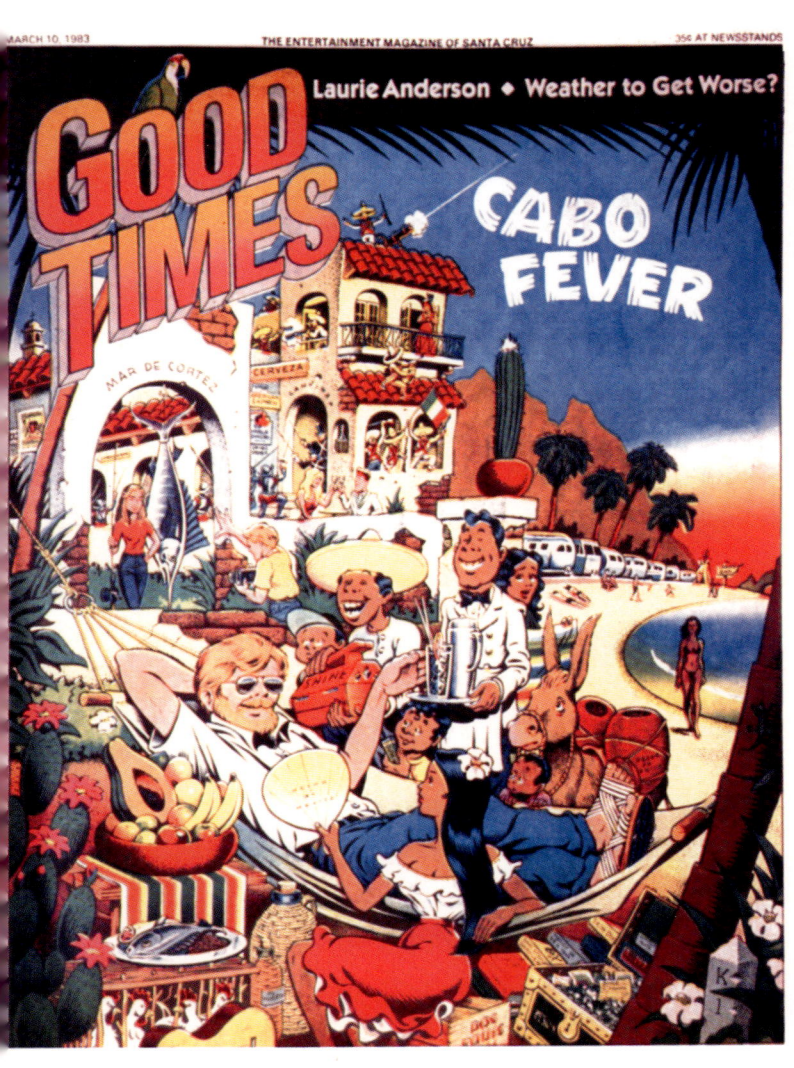

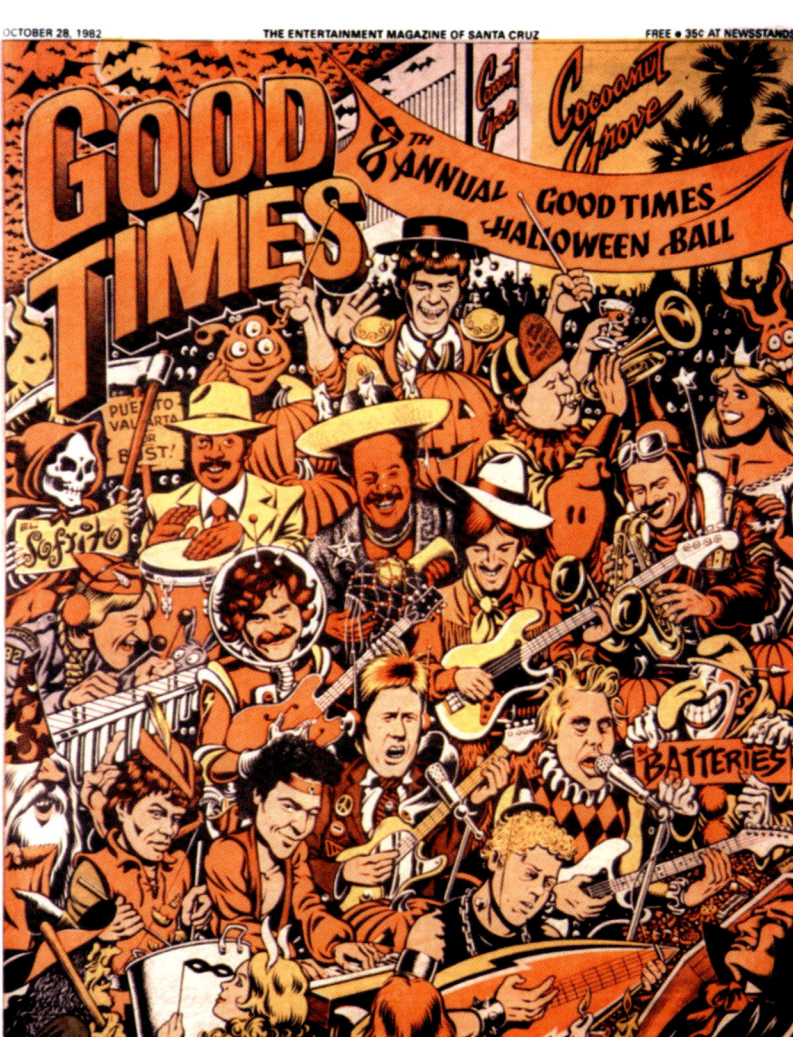

Good Times cover illustrations of 1982 and 1983.

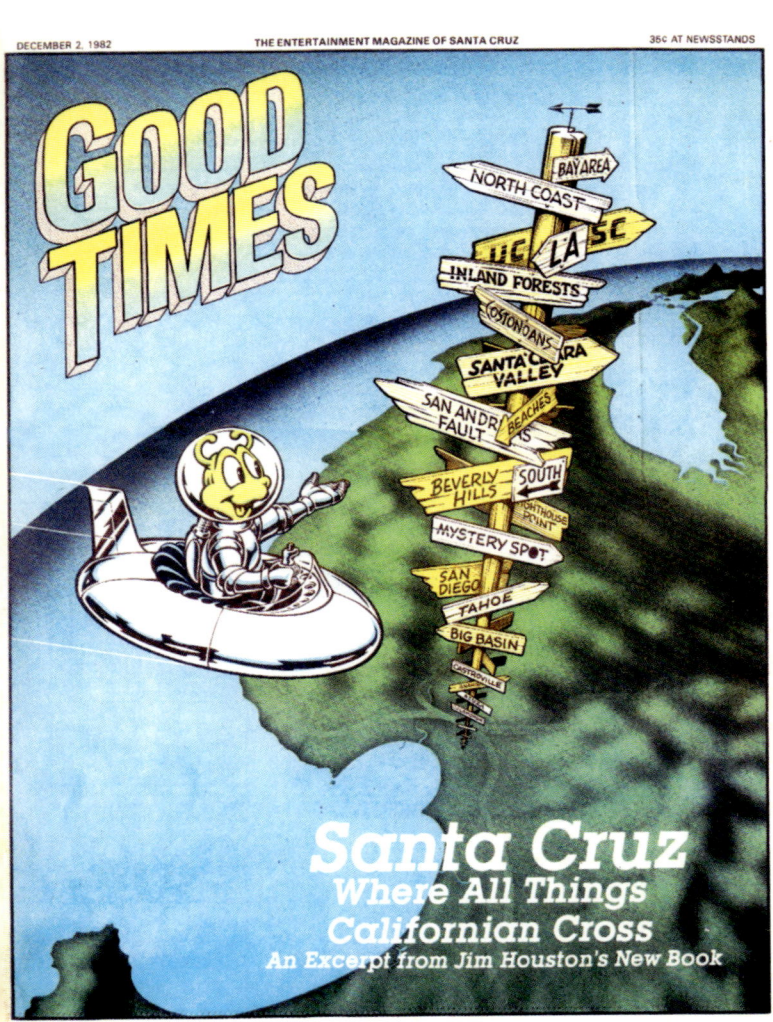

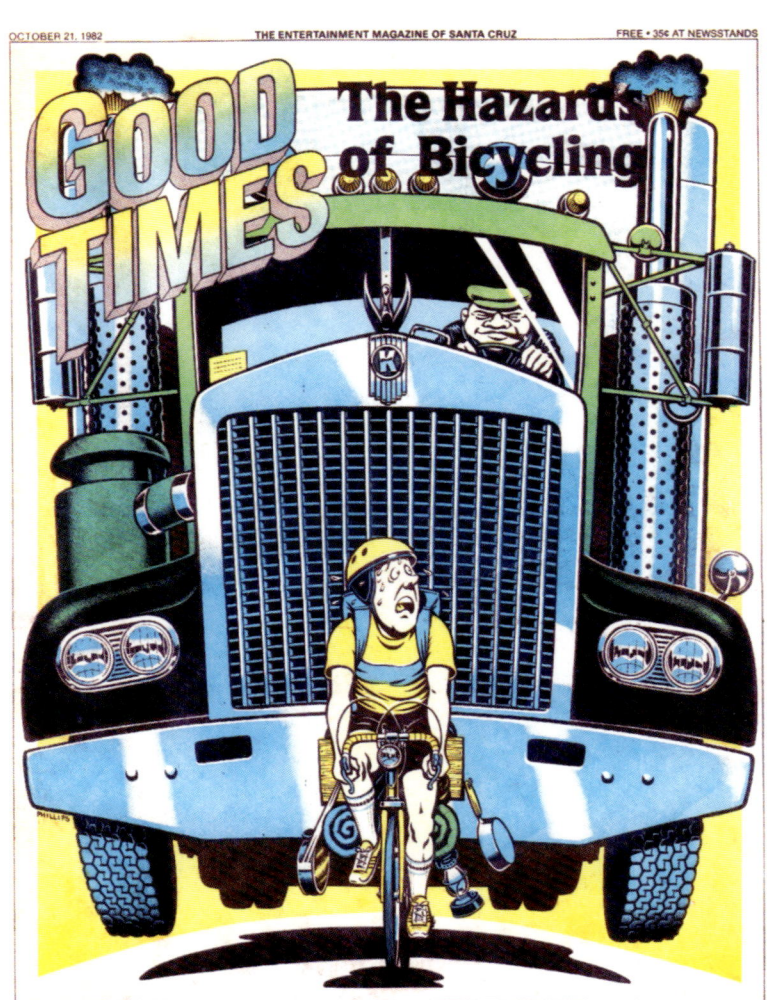

More Good Times *covers on page 140.*

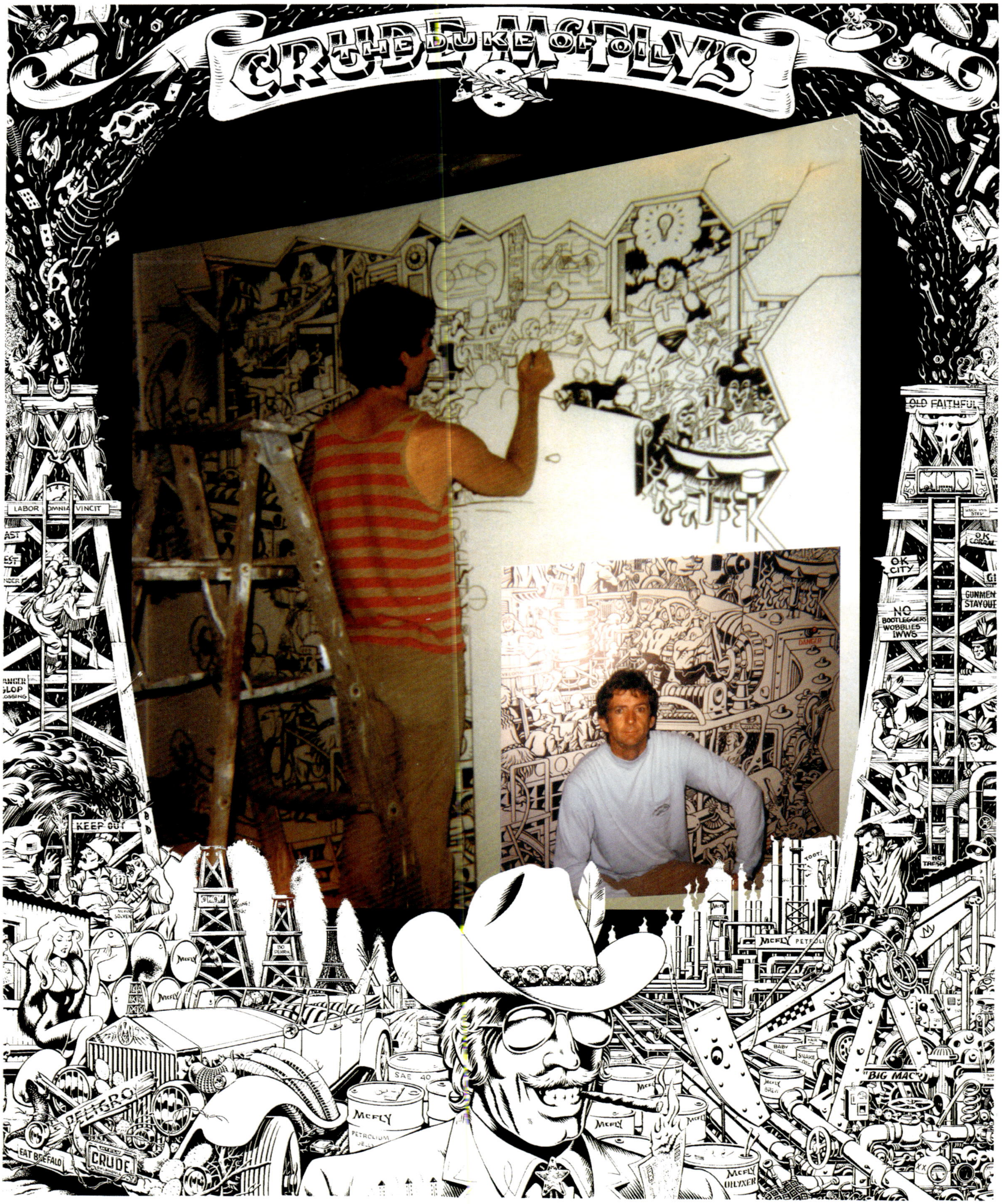

CRUDE McFLY'S — THE DUKE OF OILY'S

Inset: Tracy started a new company in Santa Barbara, 1984. Jim is shown working late at night on a rush trade show display: "The Tracy Factory." In the drawing you can see Tracy running in with an idea.

Border: Crude McFly menu, 1983.
Left: Ad for Coletta Surfboards, 1980.
Right: T-shirt for surfing championships, 1984.

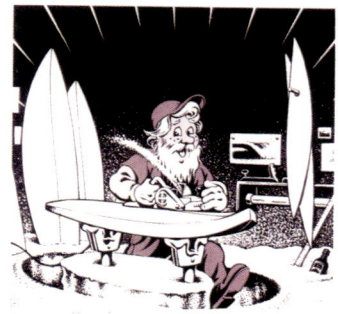

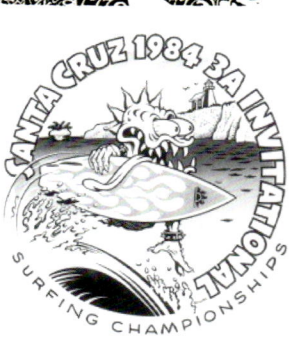

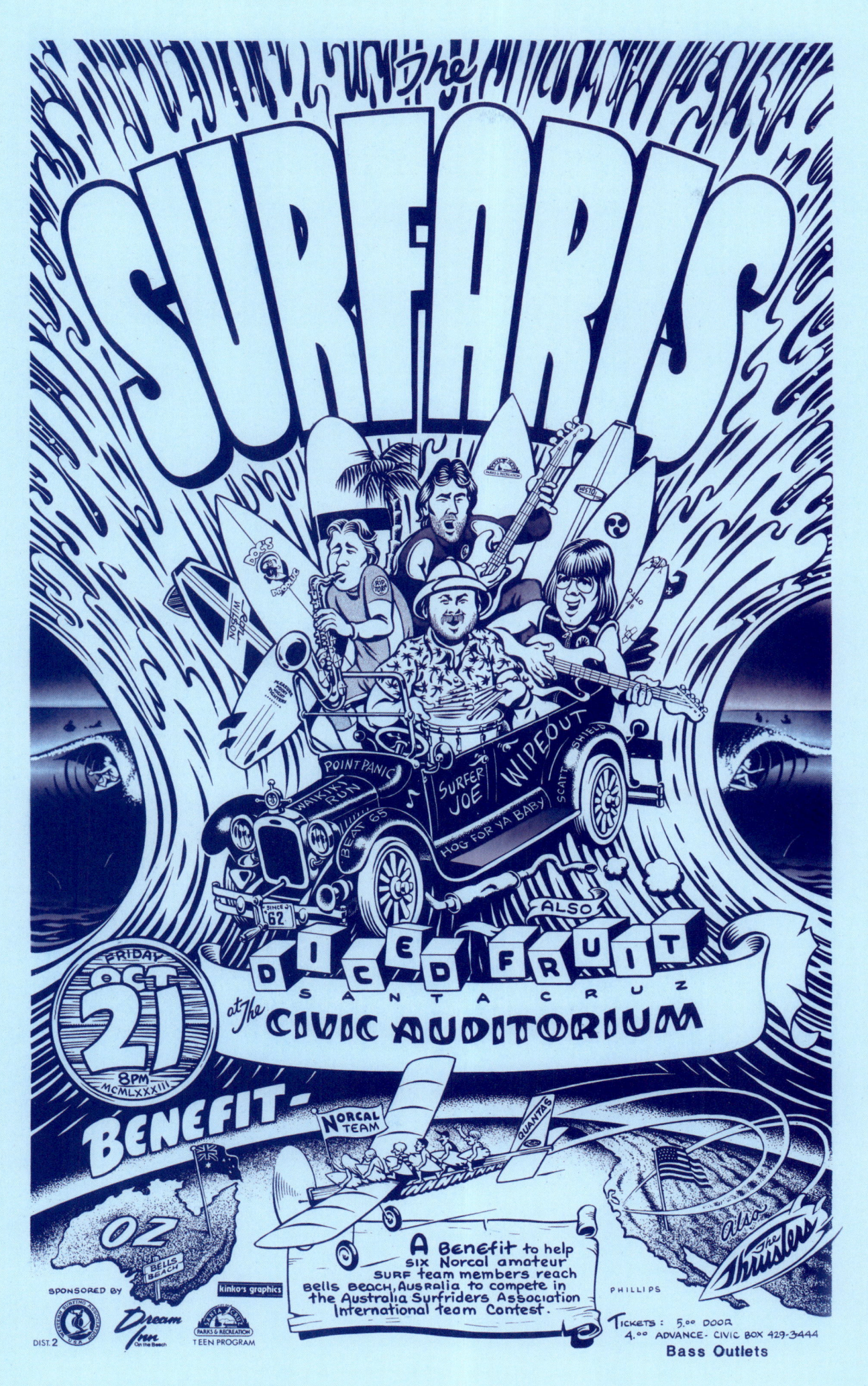

Surfaris poster, 11"x17", 1983, Quality Offset printing

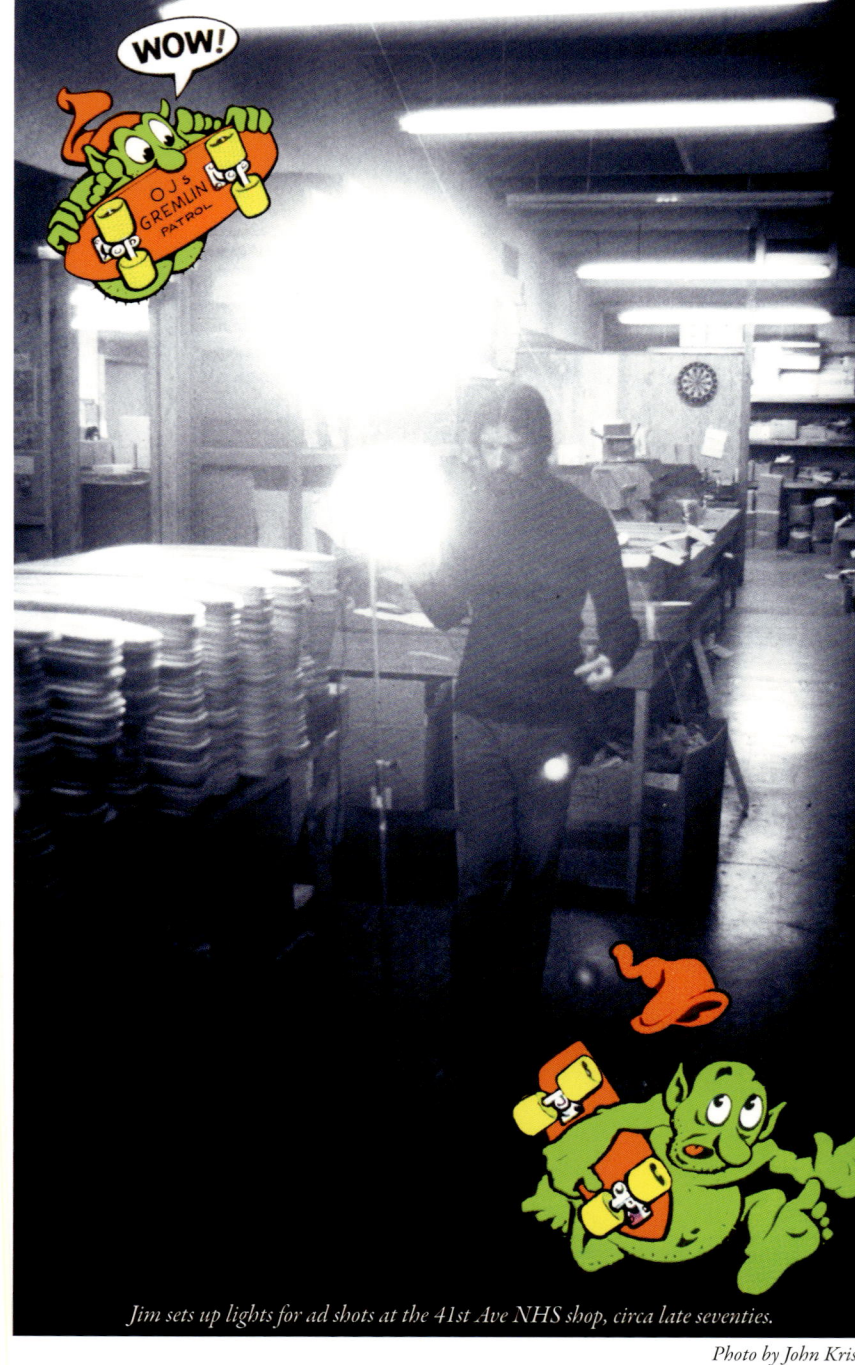

After many Phillips ads and a few Phillips articles, *Good Times* called for some covers. And around the same time, the *Visitors Guide* started requesting covers. These were the main two tabloid newspapers in town. You'd see them next to each other at stores and restaurants, and sometimes they'd both have Jim's cover art, or one this week, and the other on the next. Jim managed to balance them and keep his deadlines. In fact, Jim prided himself at not missing deadlines, a tough standard to live by. The covers gave Jim visibility in town and he wanted to do his best, pouring the midnight oil into most of them. A favorite was the Valentine's Day cover for *Good Times*. Sketched from a Polaroid of Dolly and Jim, he created a couple kissing in a hot tub in a hot air balloon. One of the hottest covers was *Good Times*' Halloween Ball, an illustration of the bands in costume out in front of the Coconut Grove ballroom.

The *Visitors Guide* covers were aimed at tourists, so Jim frequently created covers that featured local scenes, which he was already becoming known for doing. Jim incorporated Santa Cruz scenes in his art frequently then, to give local flavor. The Santa Cruz sticker for NHS was on the back window of half the cars in town, along with a lighthouse sticker he had made as a logo for the group, Santa Cruz. You would think he would have received one of those plaques that the Chamber of Commerce hand out. On one issue of The *Visitors Guide*, Jim did a caricature of Santa Cruz, and one of Capitola. It's not easy to draw a whole town on the kind of budget these papers offered. Jim would show his versatility by doing art that "normal" people could appreciate, conservative fare that visitors could handle. It is sometimes harder to give art pizzazz without using all the tricks, like sight gags or lurid content.

Good Times asked for a cover illustration for an article about Cabo San Lucas. Brooke Shields was hanging around down there, and Cabo was becoming the hip place to take a vacation. In all innocence, Phillips did a drawing that blew up into something else: A drawing of a guy, an American, lying on a hammock living the life in Cabo. Locals were waiting on him, a waiter with a drink, and a pretty senorita fanning him. Brooke was in the background, getting her picture taken with a sailfish. Well, all hell broke loose! Jay Shore, the editor, called and told Jim that there was a protest demonstration downtown about the cover. There were about a dozen or so militant, non-Latino women walking up and down Pacific Avenue in front of the *Good Times*' offices, chanting and carrying signs. The next issue of *Good Times* had a lengthy editorial written by Jay that defended the art and explained why the protesters were misguided. By doing art, you can become a visible target, and a potential platform for opportunists to advance a philosophy, whether justified or not. You can do art, but you can't always get someone to look at it. At least people were looking at it.

Through the mid-eighties, Santa Cruz Skateboards had roped a whirlwind, and Jim Phillips was trying to draw it from the inside out, from the eye, with a million things swirling around him. He was going nonstop for Santa Cruz, working in fevered peace and quiet in his Live Oak home, but he couldn't keep up with the demand. He worked like a madman day and night.

Jim sets up lights for ad shots at the 41st Ave NHS shop, circa late seventies.

Photo by John Krisi

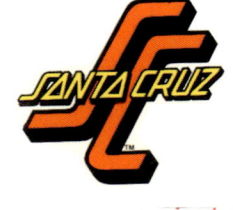
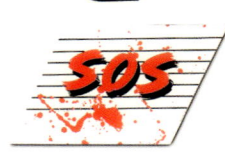

Left: Steve Olson deck & action skating shot, 1979. Courtesy of Ted Terrebonne.

Above: SC logo, concept by Jay Shuirman, 1998, and SOS sticker.

Right: Two Duane Peters Decks circa 1979 - 1980. Photo courtesy of Chris Chicarella.

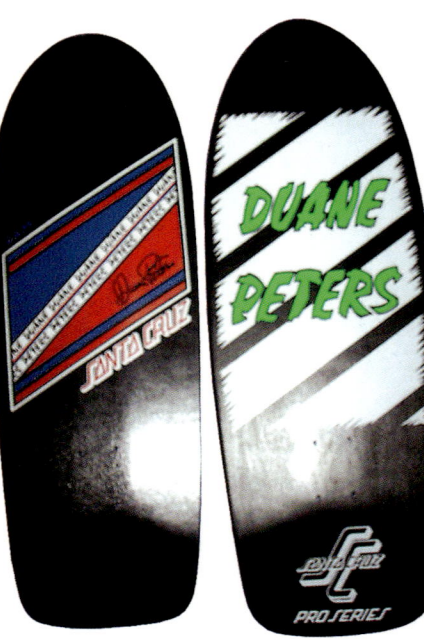

SANTA CRUZ SKATEBOARDS

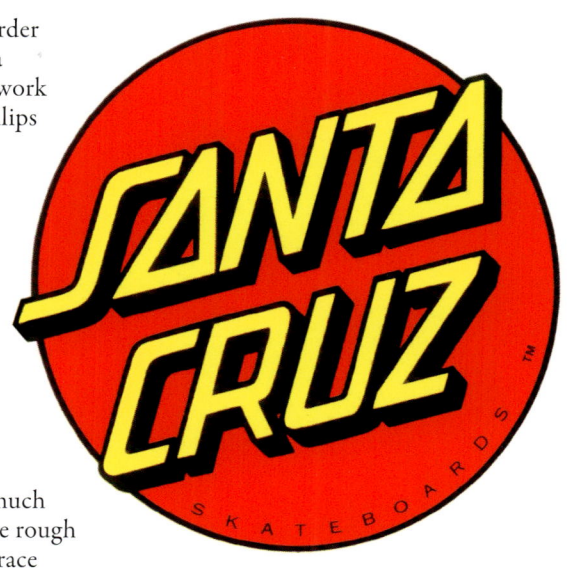

Mike Moore interviewed Jim Phillips about this era for International Longboarder Magazine, Canada. "Besides creating great products, Santa Cruz also developed a reputation for incredible artwork and graphics. The man behind most of this artwork was Jim Phillips. Our resident cartoonist, Mike Moore was able to interview Phillips and find out more about his career with NHS/Santa Cruz."

MM: How did you come to work for NHS?
JP: In 1974, I got a call from Jay Shuirman and Rich Novak, old surfing friends, about doing some ads and t-shirts. My first skate art was for Road Rider Wheels, t-shirts and stickers of my winged wheel logo. It was a natural idea, to put the wings on the wheel.

MM: What is your process in creating a skate graphic?
JP: It was a perfect job for me, working with a target age of 13, because kids like cool stuff. I was once a diehard kid, and I know what they like, it never changes, monsters and creepy stuff. Everything I liked seemed to work, so it was easy. I would just get inside myself and make what I felt was cool, unless there was too much management direction. I'd sketch around with pencil and paper, I would trace the rough pencils with blue pencil onto a quality artboard that was translucent enough to trace through. Then I'd ink the blue contour outlines with black India ink using a crowquill and then use sable brushes for spotting and shading. I worked as large as possible, but your arms are only so long.

MM: As far as pro models go, did the skaters request things?
JP: It got so that to secure better "team" riders the company would assure them they could get whatever they wanted. I would listen to the skaters' ideas and present drawings. Some of their ideas were really stupid! Some of the ideas were anarchistic anti-art like Grosso's silly rag-doll faces. I knew the success of our business meant our designs had to be good, so I assumed a lot of pressure trying to keep the graphics good. I would often try to steer the skaters toward a better part of their idea or into something else. Sometimes a skater's input gave us somewhere new to go, and it often wound up being an entirely valid idea, I'm thinking of the Ray Meyer "Businessman" deck with skateboard poses of Ray in his business suit and briefcase.

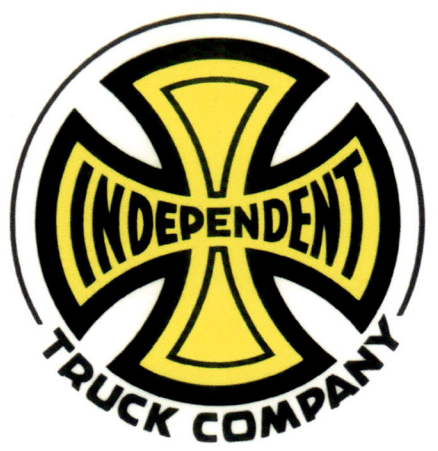

MM: Did you come up with everything yourself?
JP: Often I would be allowed, but it's a cosmic law that whoever has the money wants to direct stuff. Sometimes I'd talk them into a design, like the Slasher. I knew it would sell but had to talk the bosses into it. When I first showed them the Independent iron cross they said no, but I brought in a *Time Magazine* cover showing the Pope wearing iron crosses, so they thought then that it was OK. It's still one of the best selling logos.

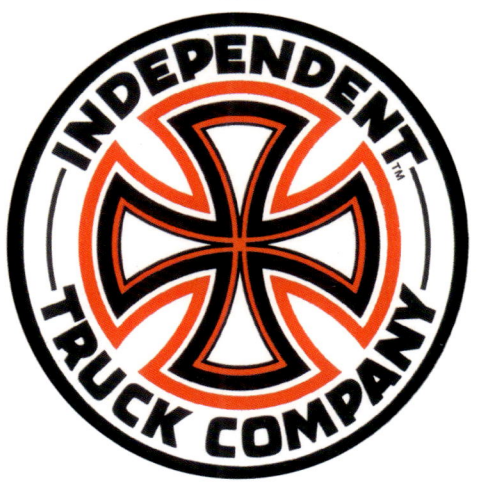

MM: In your history as a skate artist, are there any stand out moments you'd like to share?
JP: One day, I was in a gas station with the family car, and I was washing the windshield. A skateboarder came barreling across the station and ollied over the island that I was pumping from. But he didn't pull it, and he slammed into our car. I looked at the car, and then at him as he picked up his skateboard. I said "You slammed my car!" He looked at me, and said, "Oh no! No way... You're not gonna pin anything on me!" I said, "I should be able to see your license!" He said, "No way man! No way you're gonna make me!" I was feeling a little cocky, and wondered to myself if I could pull it, when I yelled, "Listen! You obviously don't realize who you're dealing with! I created Screaming Hand!" I held up my left hand, making it look like my famous Speed Wheels logo. The kid looked stunned. "You made Screaming Hand?" I looked into his eyes, "Yeah!" The next instant, he whipped his wallet out, and handed over his license, looking at me in awe. I handed it back, saying, "That's OK, I just wanted a little respect!" He yelled to his friend who was watching from across the street, "He made Screaming Hand!" The friend yelled back, "No way, he made Screaming Hand?" The first kid said, "Yeah, he made it!" Second kid: "Totally cool!" They skated off, yelling they would always buy Santa Cruz skateboards. I looked for a dent, couldn't find anything.

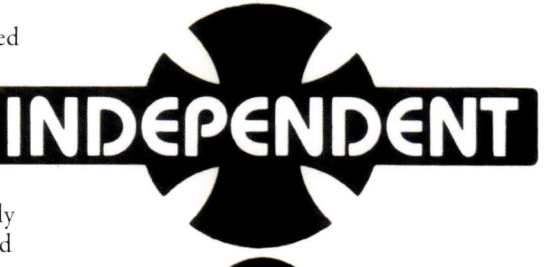

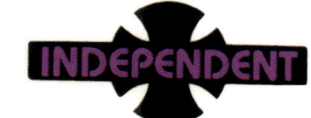

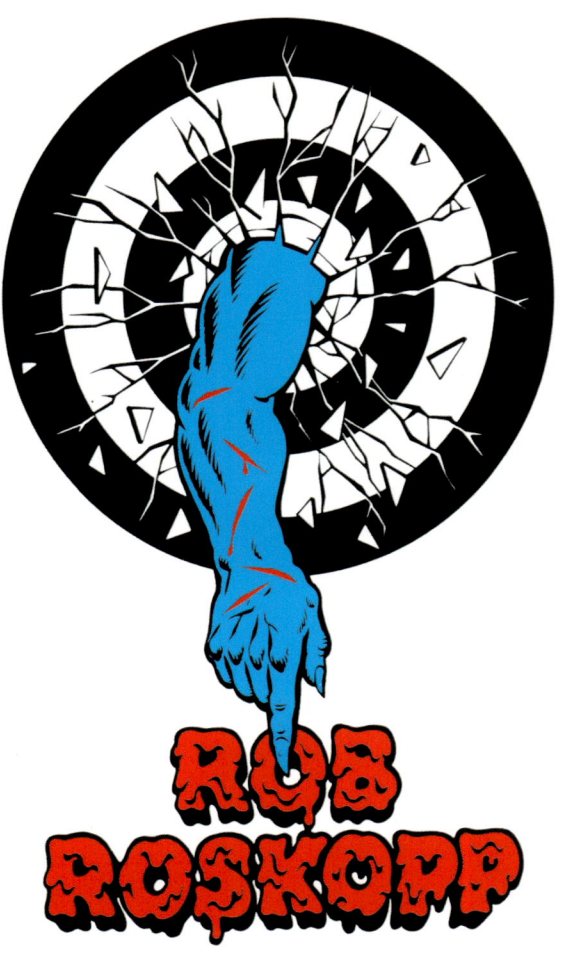

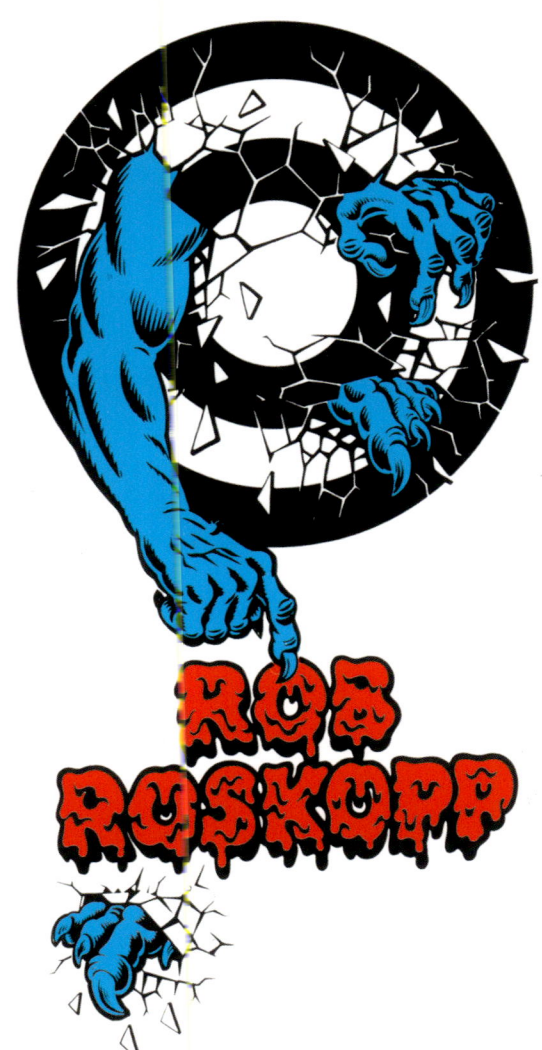

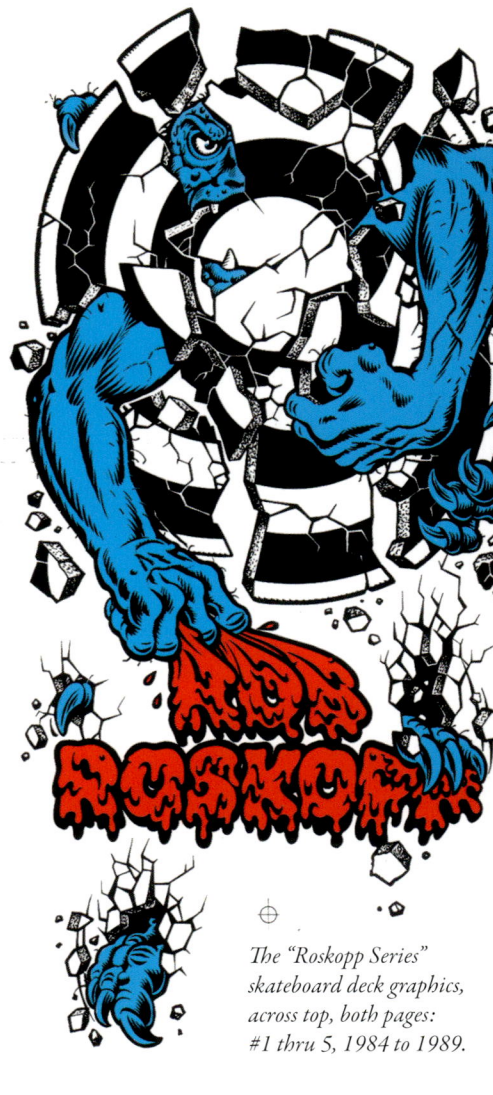

The "Roskopp Series" skateboard deck graphics, across top, both pages: #1 thru 5, 1984 to 1989.

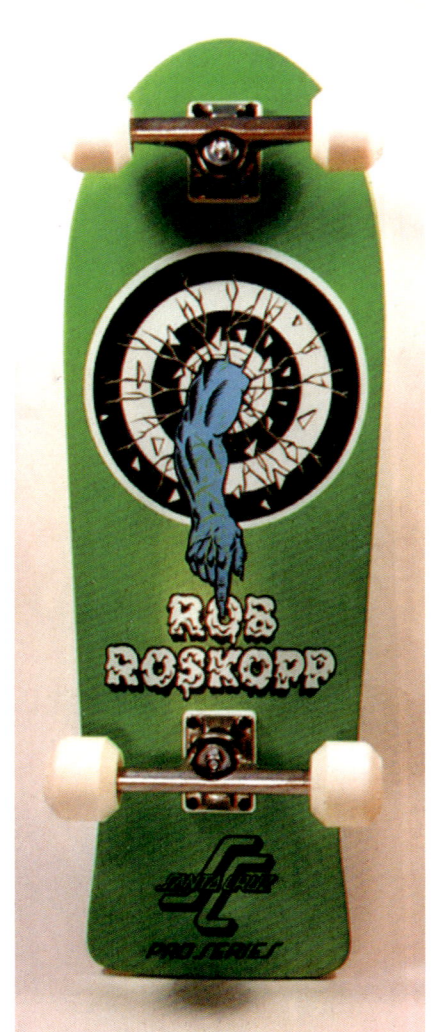

ROB ROSKOPP: *"Jim Phillips was the most influential artist of 80's skate art. His art set Santa Cruz Skateboards apart from every other skate company and was a huge factor in their overall success. Jim incorporates the Santa Cruz lifestyle and his own into every piece he creates."*

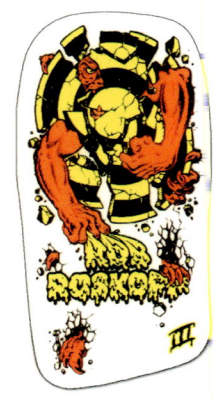

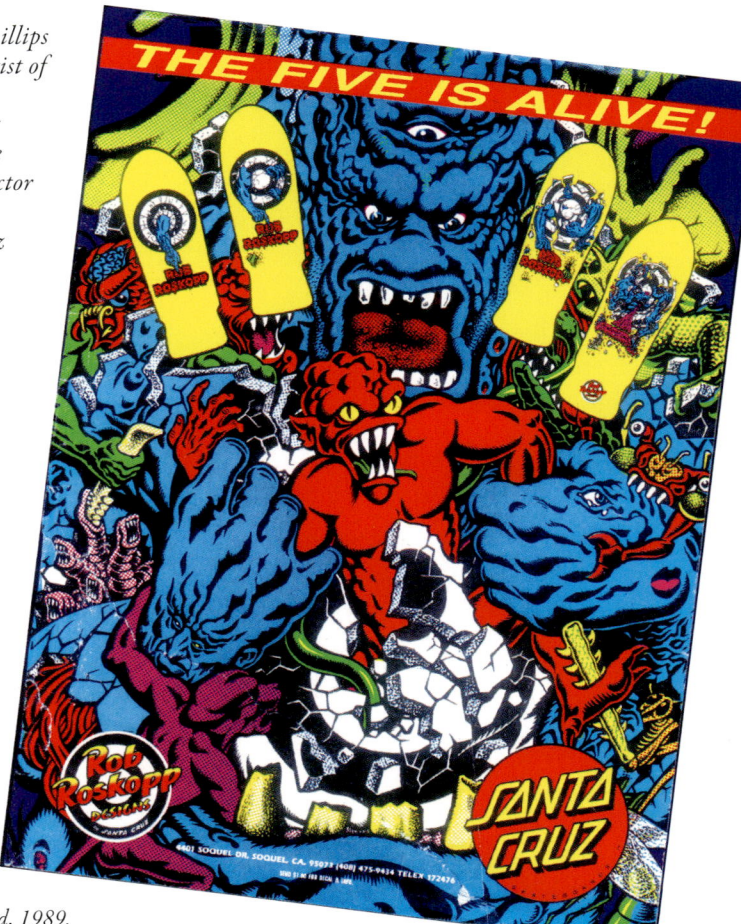

Bottom left:
*Roskopp #1 loaded deck, debut in June 1983.
Above: #3 sticker 3 1/2"x2",
Lower right: Thrasher Magazine ad, 1989.*

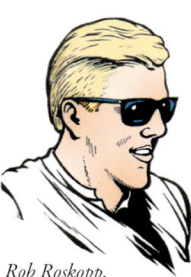

*Rob Roskopp,
from Road Rash comic.*

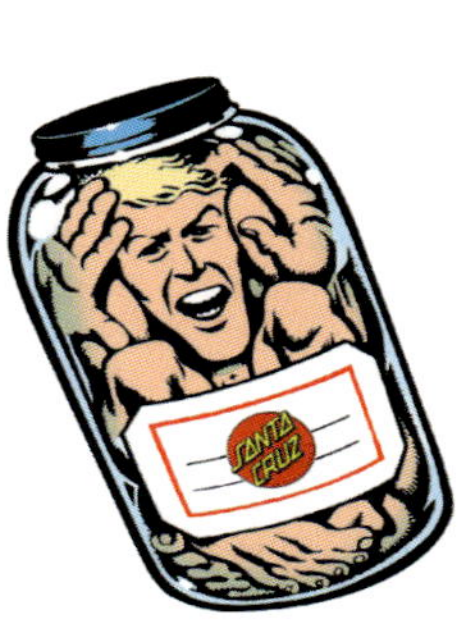

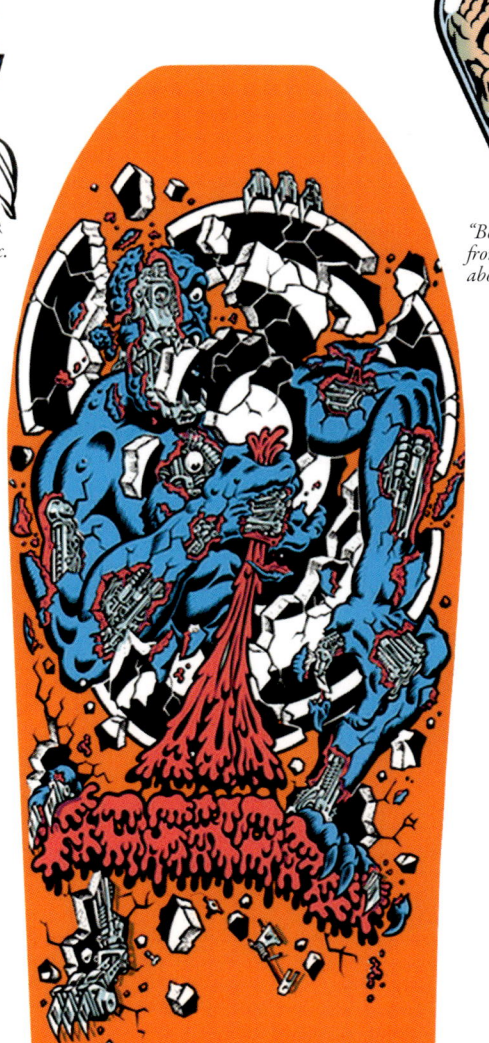

"Body Jarred"
from Pro Motion *magazine
about the "body jar" move.*

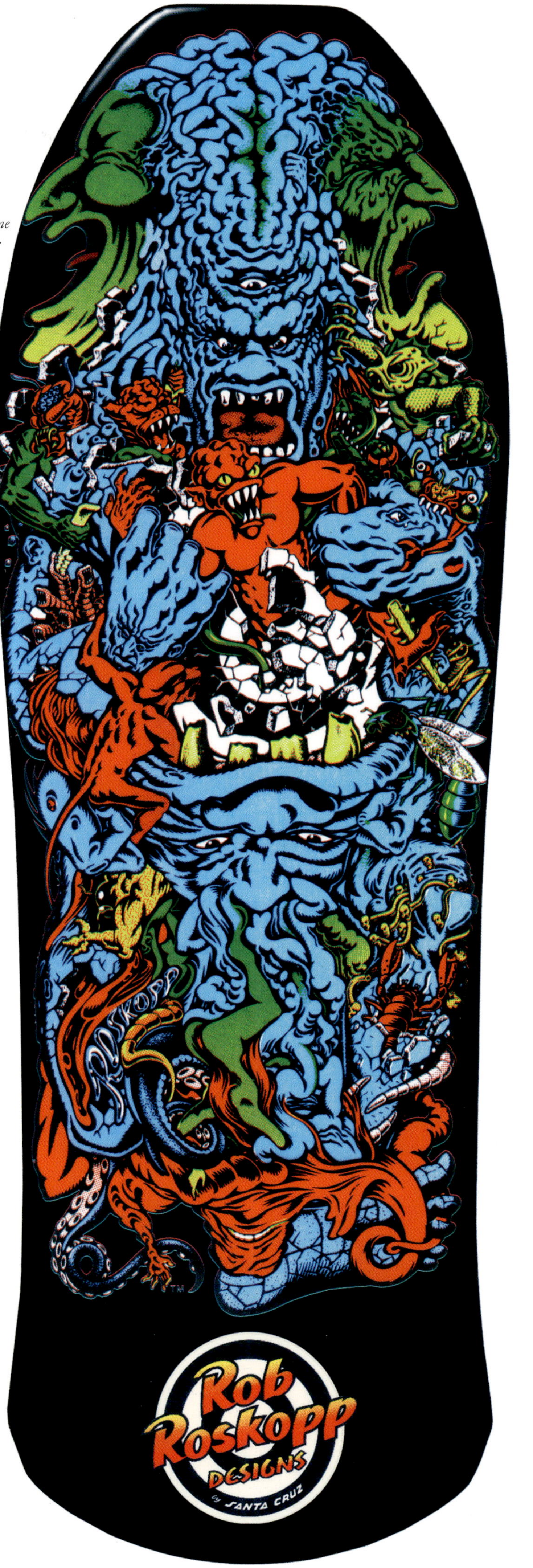

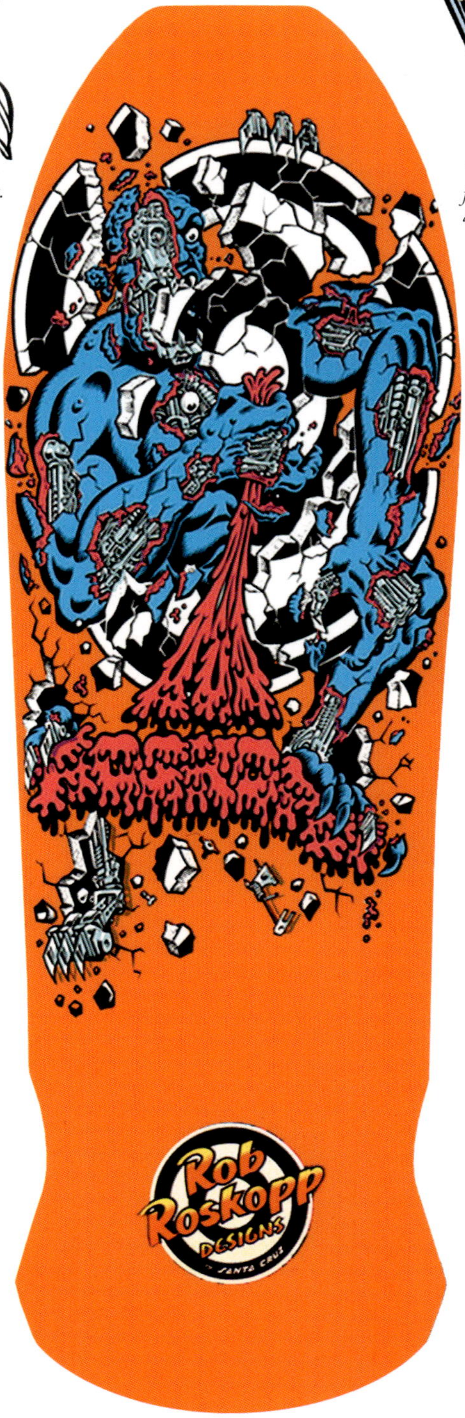

Above: Roskopp #4, 1997; right: #5, 1998.
Below: series stickers 5"x3"(#1), 5.5"x3.5"(#2&3).

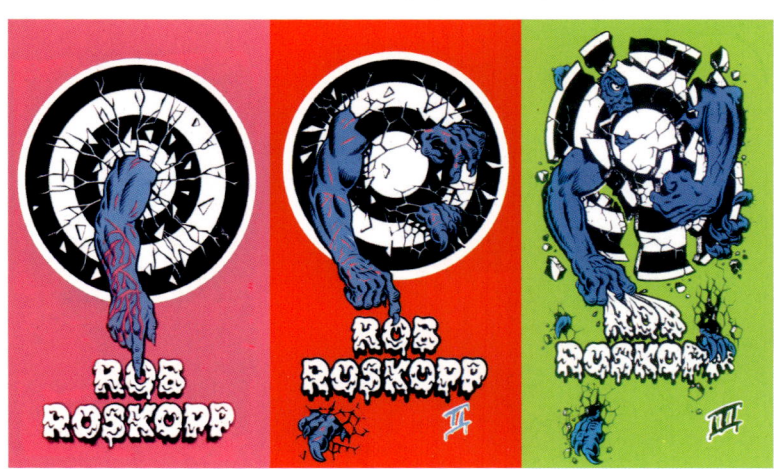

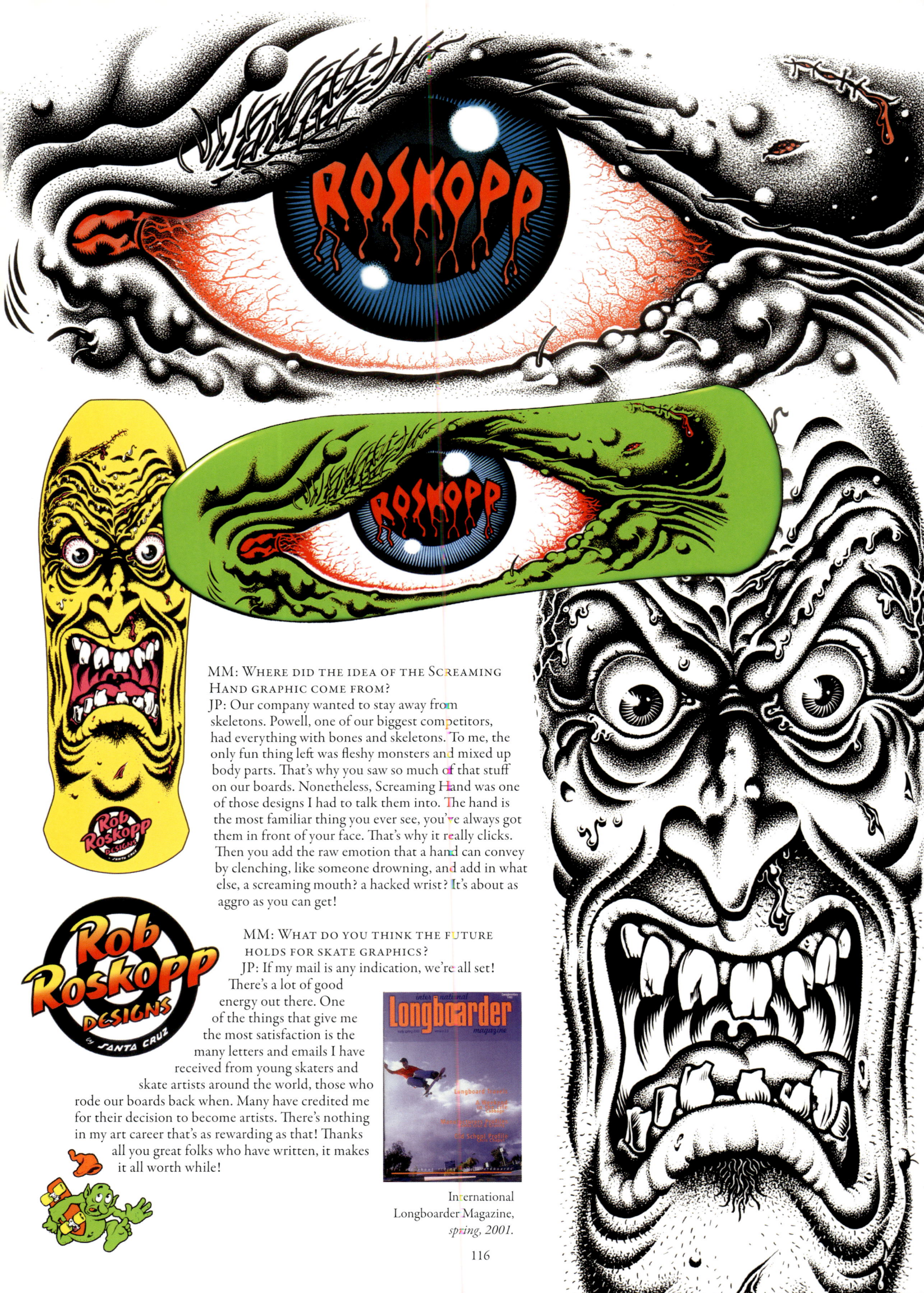

MM: Where did the idea of the Screaming Hand graphic come from?

JP: Our company wanted to stay away from skeletons. Powell, one of our biggest competitors, had everything with bones and skeletons. To me, the only fun thing left was fleshy monsters and mixed up body parts. That's why you saw so much of that stuff on our boards. Nonetheless, Screaming Hand was one of those designs I had to talk them into. The hand is the most familiar thing you ever see, you're always got them in front of your face. That's why it really clicks. Then you add the raw emotion that a hand can convey by clenching, like someone drowning, and add in what else, a screaming mouth? a hacked wrist? It's about as aggro as you can get!

MM: What do you think the future holds for skate graphics?

JP: If my mail is any indication, we're all set! There's a lot of good energy out there. One of the things that give me the most satisfaction is the many letters and emails I have received from young skaters and skate artists around the world, those who rode our boards back when. Many have credited me for their decision to become artists. There's nothing in my art career that's as rewarding as that! Thanks all you great folks who have written, it makes it all worth while!

International Longboarder Magazine, *spring, 2001.*

116

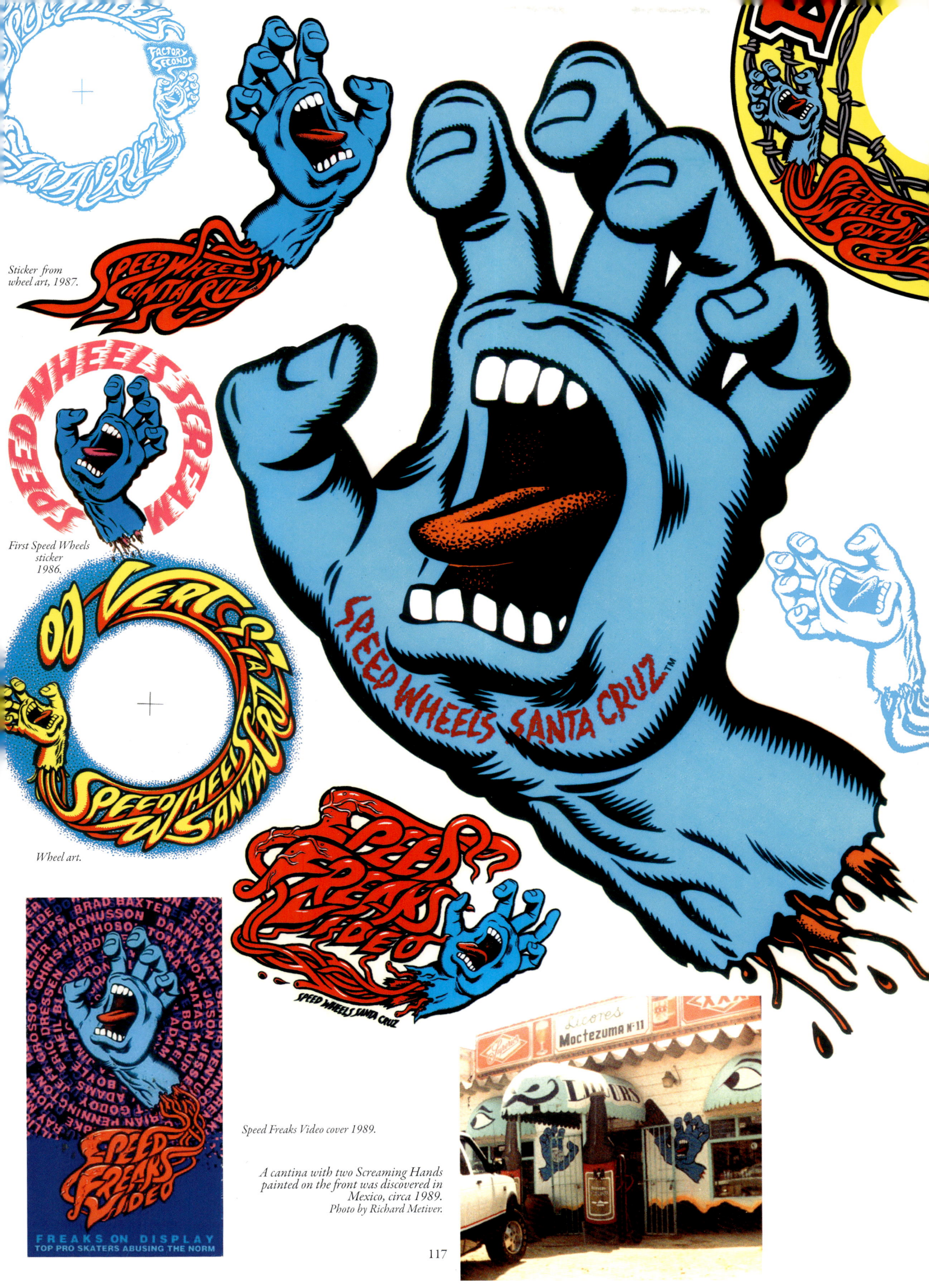

Sticker from wheel art, 1987.

First Speed Wheels sticker 1986.

Wheel art.

Speed Freaks Video cover 1989.

A cantina with two Screaming Hands painted on the front was discovered in Mexico, circa 1989. Photo by Richard Metiver.

FREAKS ON DISPLAY
TOP PRO SKATERS ABUSING THE NORM

117

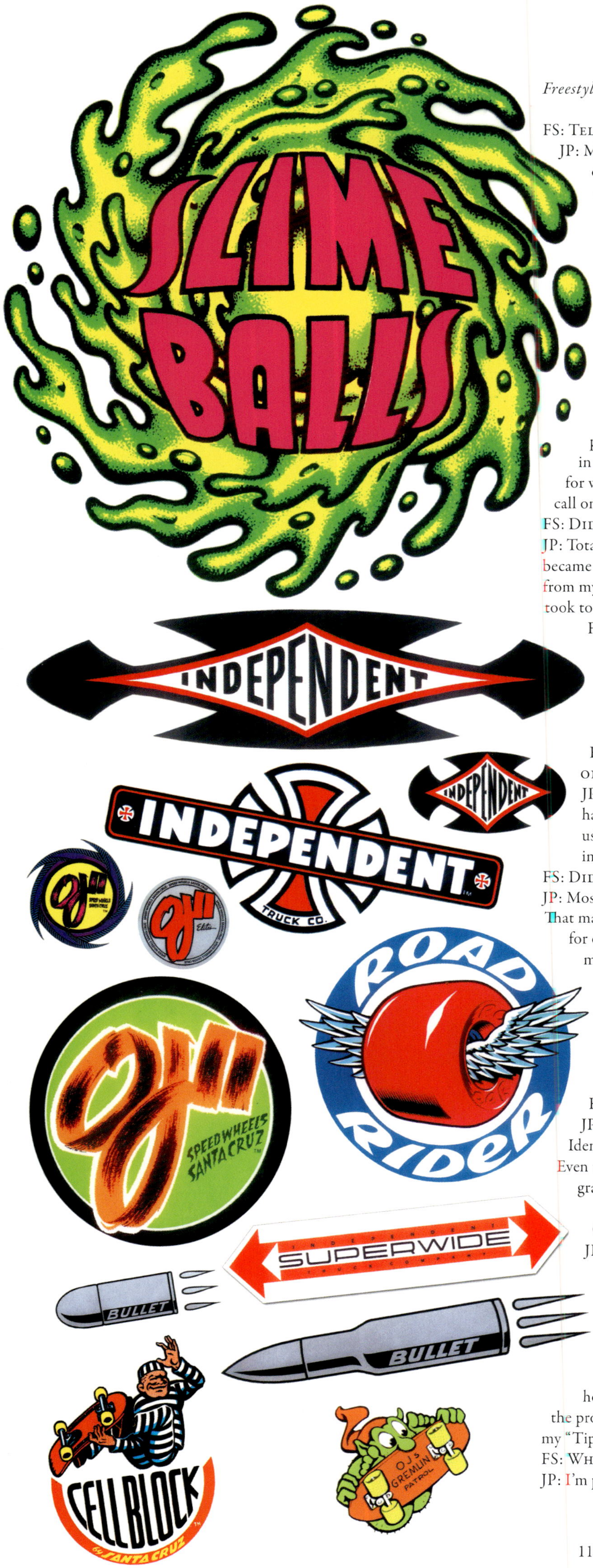

Freestyler Magazine interview, Italy, by Fenton Savastano

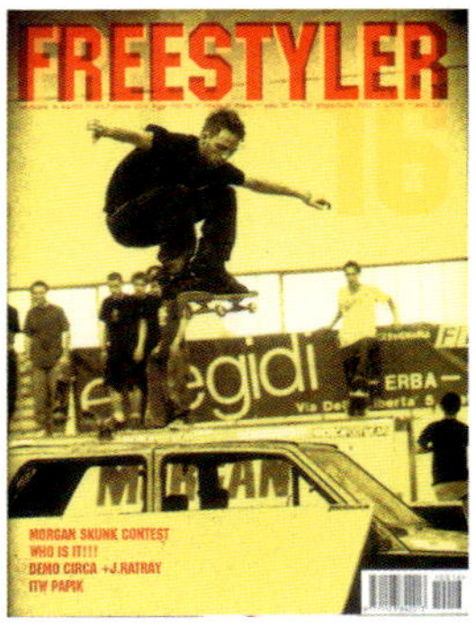

FS: TELL THE READERS A BIT ABOUT YOURSELF.

JP: My first published artwork was a woody, a winner of a surf car cartoon contest in the spring issue of Surfer Quarterly 1962. Since then, it has been my pleasure to earn a living with my drawings of the activities that I enjoy, surfing, skateboarding, and rock and roll.

FS: WHAT'S YOUR RELATION WITH SKATEBOARDING?

JP: Actually, skateboarding for me began in 1952 at age 8 when I used a plank with metal rollerskate wheels and a wooden box nailed on front with handles. There weren't many sidewalks near where I lived but I grew up a few blocks from Pleasure Point in the late 60s, one of the best surfing areas in the world. So I began surfing avidly in the late fifties. Along with surfing, my skateboarding had a revival as "sidewalk surfing," the same type plank and nailed-on metal wheels, but without the box. Friends that I made in those early years, while skateboarding and sitting on our surfboards waiting for waves, were to later become pioneers in the urethane wheel revolution and call on me to create the visual art for Santa Cruz Skateboards.

FS: DID YOU SKATEBOARD?

JP: Totally, and with the development of the urethane wheel in '73, skateboarding became alot more fun. It helped that I was able to obtain skateboards very cheaply from my work at Santa Cruz, so I got to be an avid skateboarder. My son Jimbo took to skateboarding then, so we got to do alot of father and son skateboarding.

FS: WHO WERE THE SKATE COMPANYS?

JP: I worked for many companies under NHS Inc. such as Santa Cruz Skateboards, Independent Trucks, Road Rider Wheels, OJ Wheels, Park Rider Wheels, Speed Wheels. The owners of NHS, Novak, Haut & Shuirman, were originally resin distributors to local surf shops, that's how they got wind of the urethane.

FS: IN THE 80'S, DID YOUR SKATE GRAPHICS REFLECT WHAT WAS GOING ON IN SKATEBOARDING AT THE TIME?

JP: I think so. It had to, that's what was required. The graphics on decks happened after punkrock skaters like Steve Olson and Duane Peters allowed us to push the boundaries that the industry had set out. That opened it up to images that exceeded any reality or limitations.

FS: DID THE SKATERS ASK FOR A SPECIFIC SUBJECT FOR THEIR BOARD?

JP: Most of them did. Santa Cruz wanted to offer everything to attract top riders. That made a big challenge for me, to interpolate their ideas and make them viable for our process; But I enjoyed working with the skaters quite a bit, and prided myself in making something they each really liked.

FS: WHICH IS THE BOARD THAT YOU HAVE DESIGNED THAT YOU LIKE THE MOST?

JP: I like the "Skull", and sales back me up on that. It was one of the decks where I was cut loose to make anything I wanted without restrictions. If you look closely; the Skull is made from hundreds of tiny skulls, ghouls and monsters.

FS: WHAT DO SKATEBOARD GRAPHICS HAVE IN COMMON?

JP: The common property that a skateboard graphic provides is identity. Idenity to a skater, a company, an artist, a philosophy, or certain image. Even those who resist graphics and ride "blanks" are identifying with anti-graphics.

FS: IS IT EASY TO MAKE A LIVING OUT OF ILLUSTRATION IN CALIFORNIA?

JP: Actually it was like falling off a log for me, because I drew cartoons and skated and surfed all my life, and it all sort of just came together. I feel that I have been blessed with a gift.

FS: WOULD YOU SUGGEST IT TO ANYONE?

JP: I receive many emails from around the world from young people asking about a career in art, what to expect and how to start. I never downplay the rigors of it, however I would never want to change occupations. I discuss the pros and cons of a career in art or skate graphics in some length in my "Tip Talk" column in the archive section of my skateboard website.

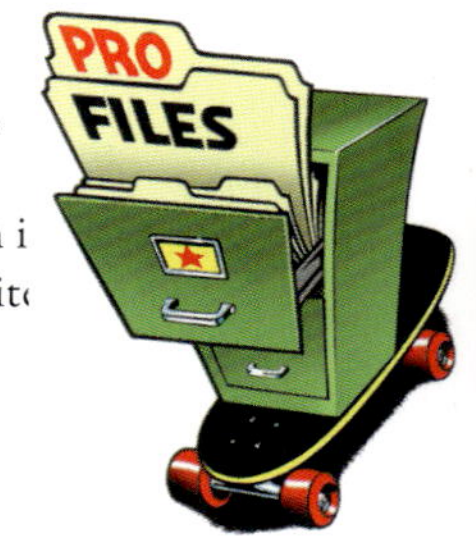

FS: WHAT DO YOU THINK OF SKATEBOARDERS?

JP: I'm proud to have had the privilege of representing some of the world's best skaters with graphic art.

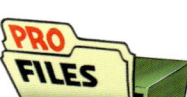

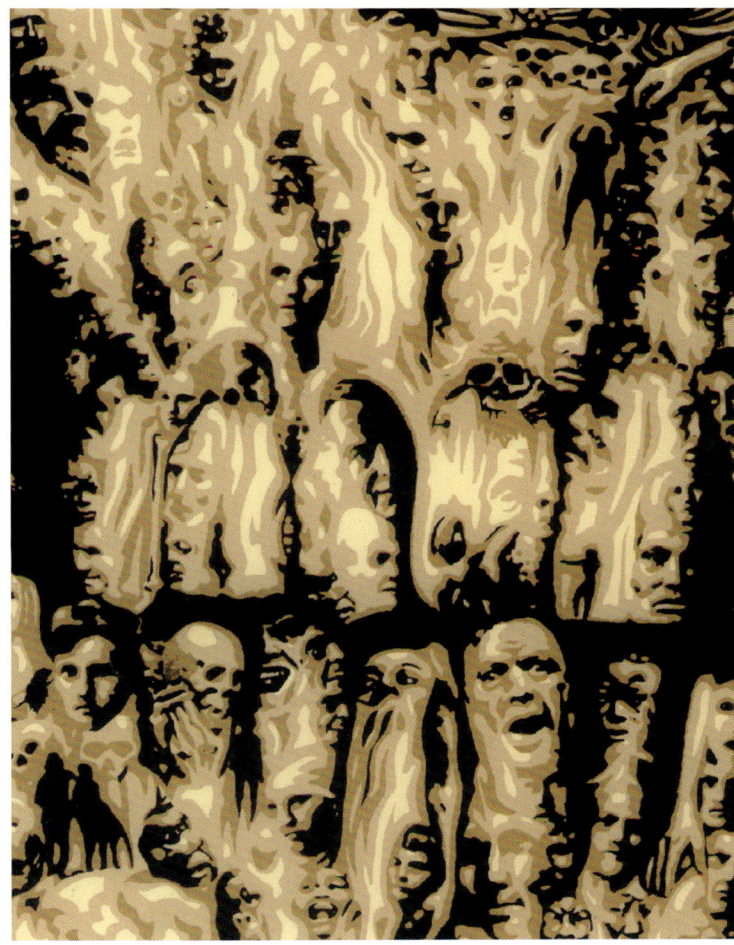

Through the mid-eighties, Santa Cruz Skateboards was going nonstop. Dolly was indispensable to Jimmy in many ways. One way was her typing and office skills. Typesetting is vital for advertising, and Jim didn't learn to type like his father. Dolly landed a secretarial job right out of high school at the Raytheon plant in Waltham, Mass. where her father worked. After a few years she moved to a better paying office job at Geoscience in Cambridge, until a Mr. Jim Phillips came along and convinced her to give notice. Eventually, her skills turned out to be useful for his ad work, especially in the skateboard era, because that's where the computers came in.

DOLLY PHILLIPS: *"Jimmy was going to Aptos Post for typesetting prior to 1985, when owner Steve Manusos showed him a Macintosh computer, when the Macs first came out. When Jim saw what it could do, he was convinced it was something we needed. After much convincing at NHS, we got our first system, a 512k Mac, with only half a megabyte of memory. Still, that was a big improvement over specifying type and then driving to Aptos to drop off and then pick up the typeset copy. It was a struggle at first, learning the new computer language and all the complexities of the technical applications, but when we finally adapted, it was a powerful addition to our capabilities."*

Dolly and computers were a bonus, but still not enough. Phillips Studios sprouted under the NHS umbrella. Jim rented the house next door that his stepfather owned, and put in drawing tables and light tables. Jim had just produced a skateboard comic book for NHS, using young artists as well as Jimbo and himself, so he picked one of the artists that contributed. His first studio apprentice, Justin Forbes, was gifted for his age, and knew how to draw so Jim didn't have to waste time showing him the basics. After seeing them in action, Jimbo quit his job and came in. Everybody called him Jimbo now, to distinguish his name from Jim Sr. The work kept coming and Jim kept hiring, keeping a dozen young skater artists busy.

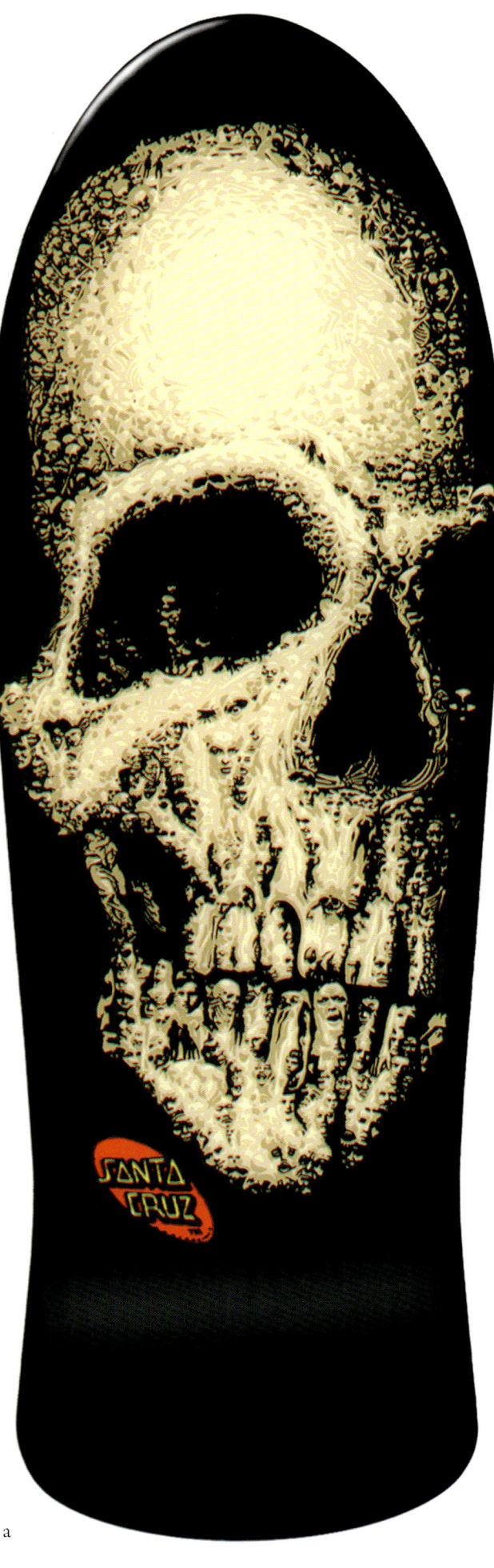

The Skull deck, and Skull deck detail, 1989.

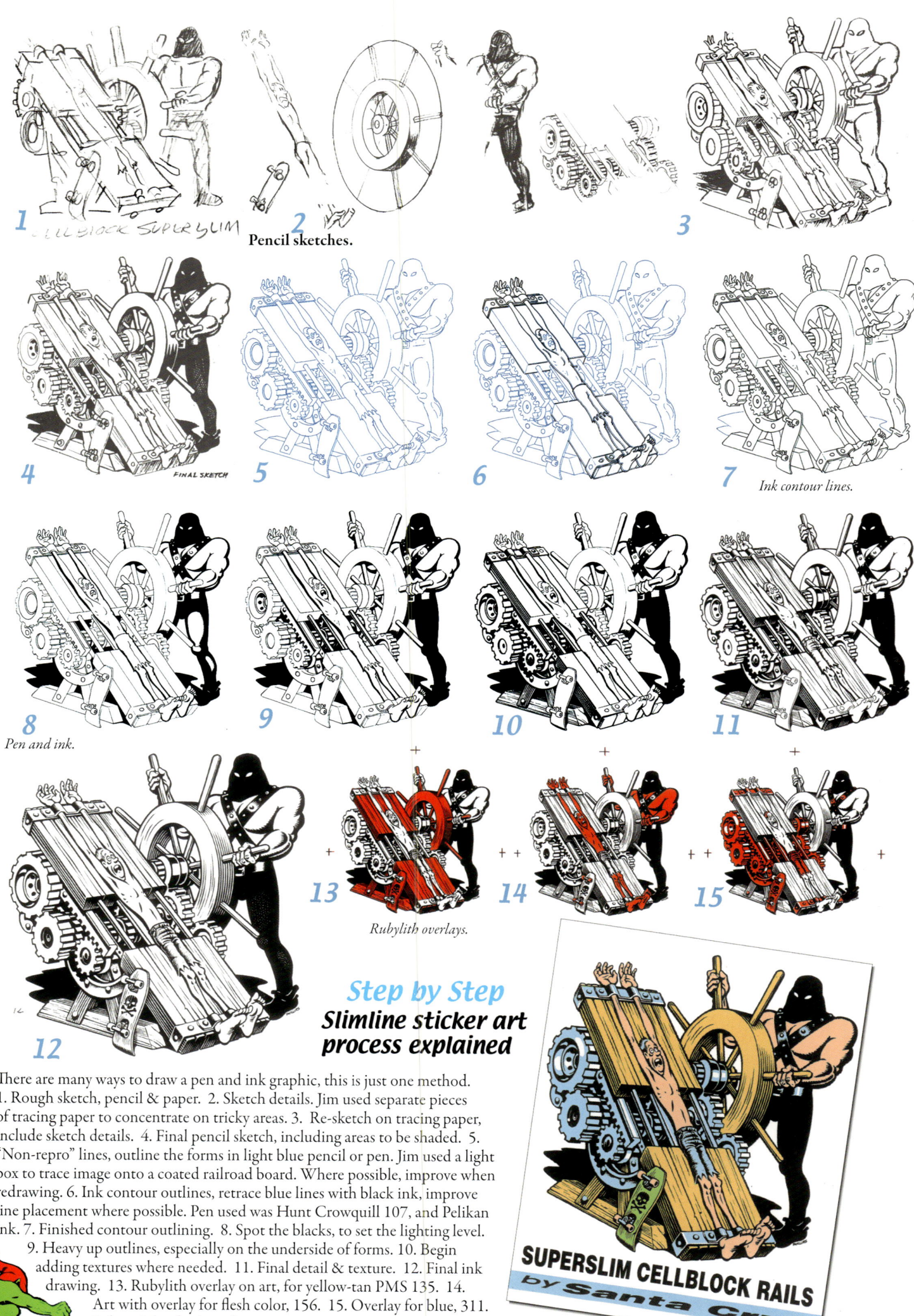

1 CELLBLOCK SUPERSLIM

2 Pencil sketches.

3

4 FINAL SKETCH

5

6

7 Ink contour lines.

8 Pen and ink.

9

10

11

12

13 Rubylith overlays.

14

15

Step by Step
Slimline sticker art process explained

There are many ways to draw a pen and ink graphic, this is just one method.
1. Rough sketch, pencil & paper. 2. Sketch details. Jim used separate pieces of tracing paper to concentrate on tricky areas. 3. Re-sketch on tracing paper, include sketch details. 4. Final pencil sketch, including areas to be shaded. 5. "Non-repro" lines, outline the forms in light blue pencil or pen. Jim used a light box to trace image onto a coated railroad board. Where possible, improve when redrawing. 6. Ink contour outlines, retrace blue lines with black ink, improve line placement where possible. Pen used was Hunt Crowquill 107, and Pelikan ink. 7. Finished contour outlining. 8. Spot the blacks, to set the lighting level.
9. Heavy up outlines, especially on the underside of forms. 10. Begin adding textures where needed. 11. Final detail & texture. 12. Final ink drawing. 13. Rubylith overlay on art, for yellow-tan PMS 135. 14. Art with overlay for flesh color, 156. 15. Overlay for blue, 311. Below right, final product.

SUPERSLIM CELLBLOCK RAILS
by Santa Cruz

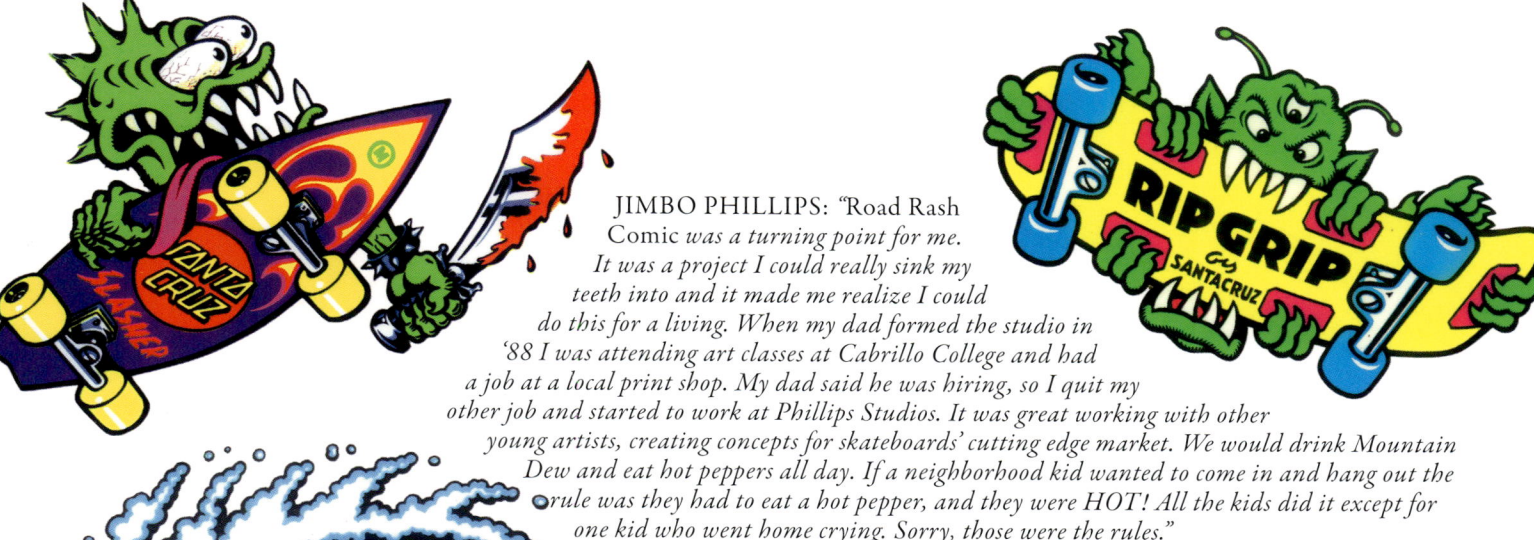

JIMBO PHILLIPS: *"Road Rash Comic was a turning point for me. It was a project I could really sink my teeth into and it made me realize I could do this for a living. When my dad formed the studio in '88 I was attending art classes at Cabrillo College and had a job at a local print shop. My dad said he was hiring, so I quit my other job and started to work at Phillips Studios. It was great working with other young artists, creating concepts for skateboards' cutting edge market. We would drink Mountain Dew and eat hot peppers all day. If a neighborhood kid wanted to come in and hang out the rule was they had to eat a hot pepper, and they were HOT! All the kids did it except for one kid who went home crying. Sorry, those were the rules."*

JIM RAUN-BYBERG: *"I think when I saw Jimmy then he said he needed some help. I realized the flight was 'overbooked' for him, knowing him as well as I do. All of a sudden he's in the saddle, steering, directing like 12 young artists, and he expressed to me that he needed some help, not only in doing the catalogs and ads, but also in kind of being his safety net, and when he needed me, I was right there for him."*

ERIC CARDINALE: *"It was a great opportunity as a young artist coming into a big studio doing some big projects. I was really taken by Jim letting me come in and work on some amazing projects that I later saw in magazines like Thrasher. Seeing some of the art I helped with on stickers and t-shirts was really an ego booster to help me get inspired to do more art, and get into the graphic art business. Being a skater myself it was fun to be able to work on skateboards and to be part of something that was really happening and still is. The studio had a bunch of characters working there, everyone was really lively. It was Mountain Dews and chili peppers, that was our diet, it was the artists' food. That's what the artists ate to get inspired and to do better art, incredible artists there, all feeding off each other and it was really inspiring."*

JIMBO PHILLIPS: *"Graphics had a pretty big influence on board sales because kids want a board that looks rad as well as works rad. No matter how cool the shape, I don't think a kid's gonna want a board with something he doesn't like on the bottom. Kids are into gnarly stuff, and the gnarlier the better. There was an endless amount of things to draw as well as ways to draw them, especially in this field where there are few limitations. Sometimes the rider knew what he wanted, and we'd go off from that, or sometimes we had to give them ideas."*

ANDREAS GINGHOFER: *"Some of the things that influenced our work sometimes was horror magazines or movies, violence, a dead animal in the road, or even watching your friend barfing from partying too much."*

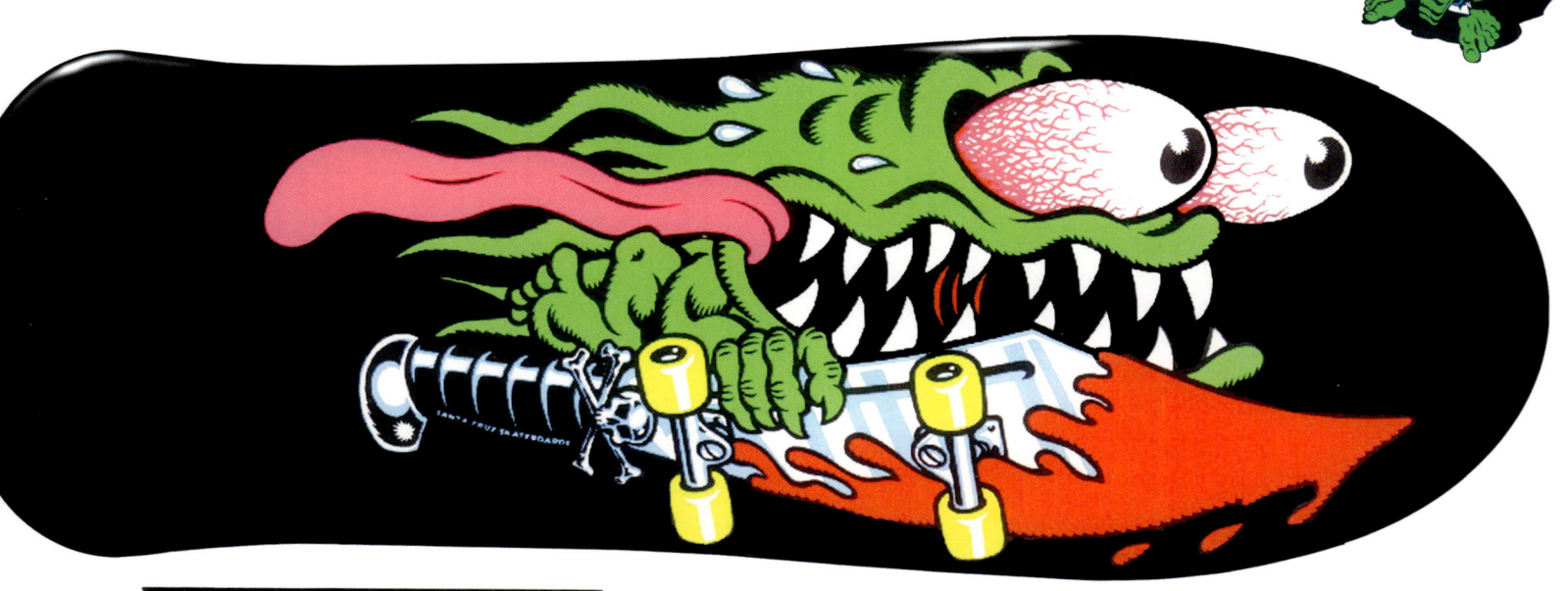

Slasher series, Keith Meek model.

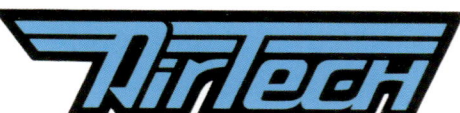

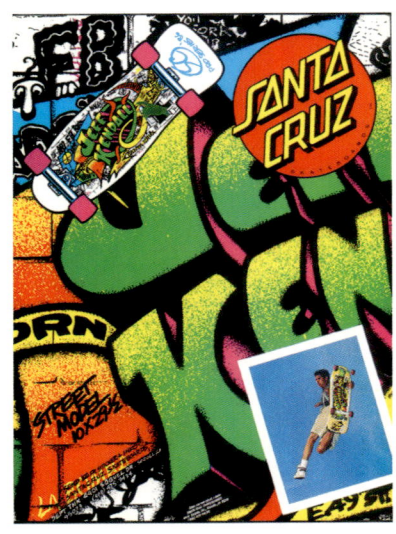
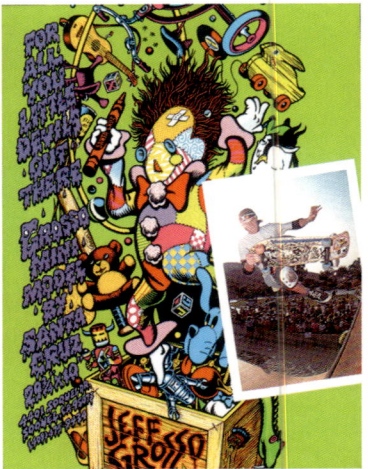
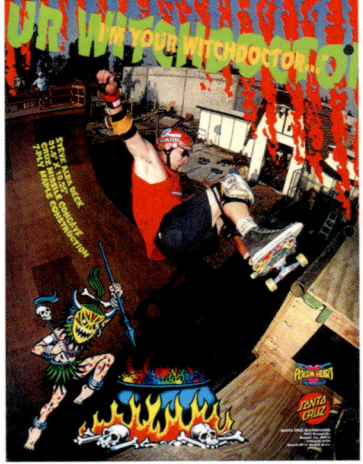
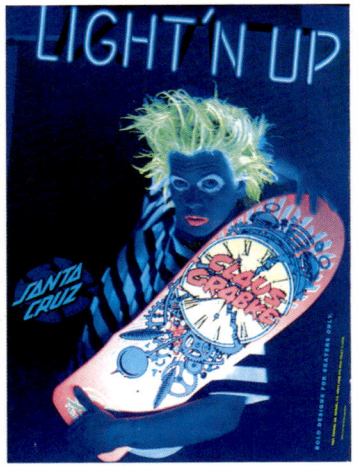

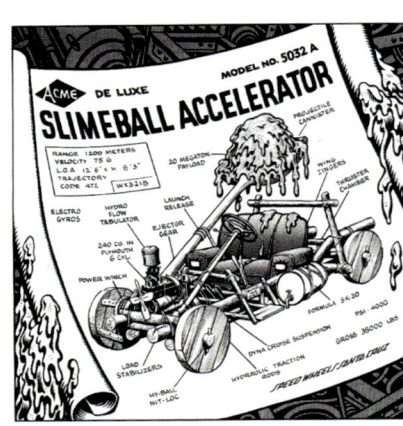
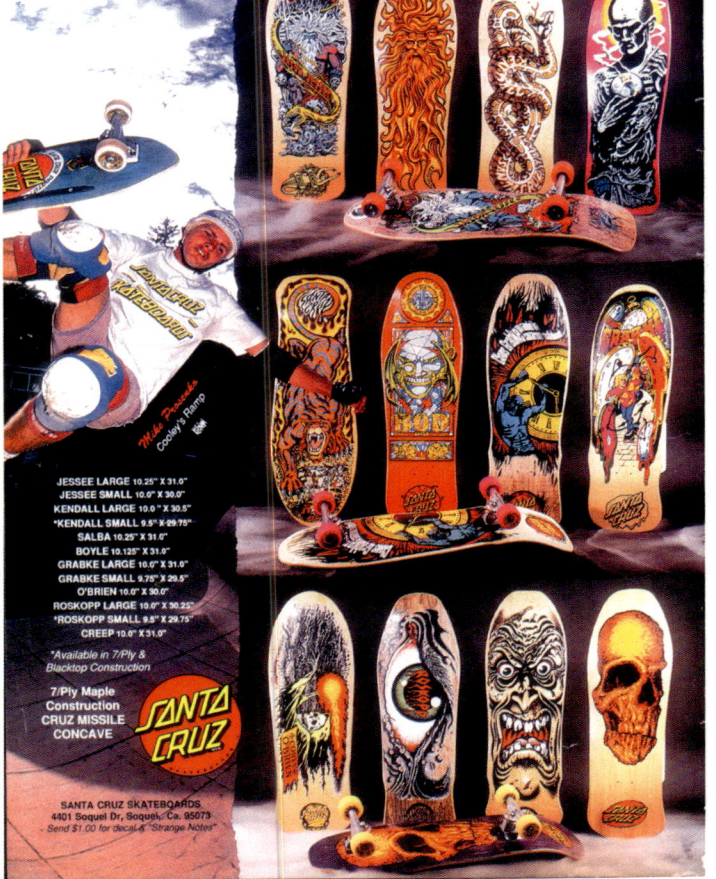
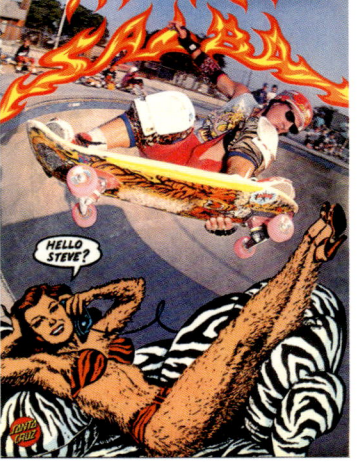

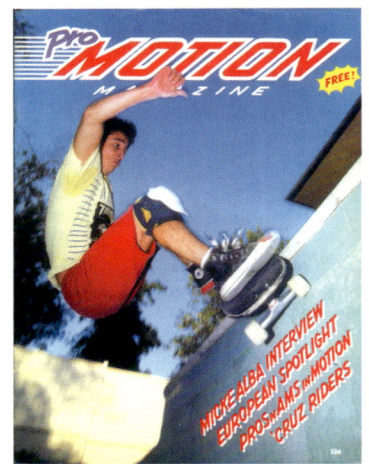
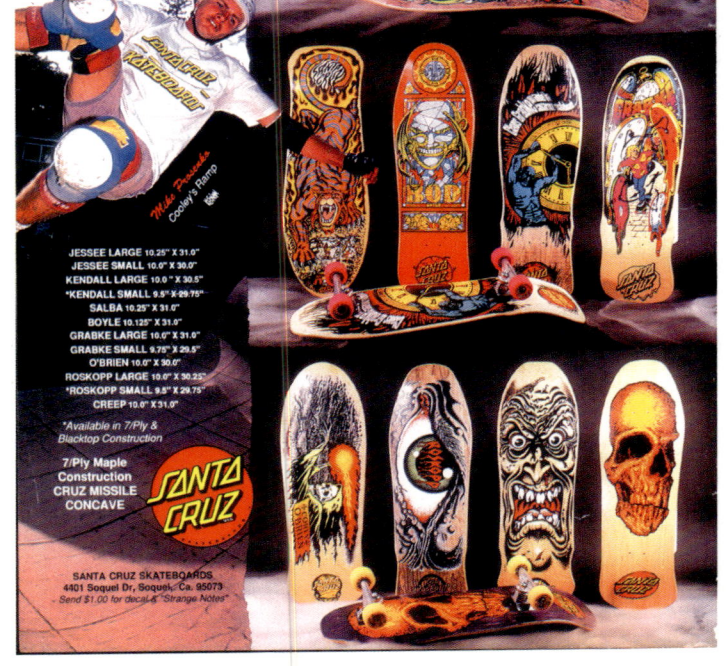
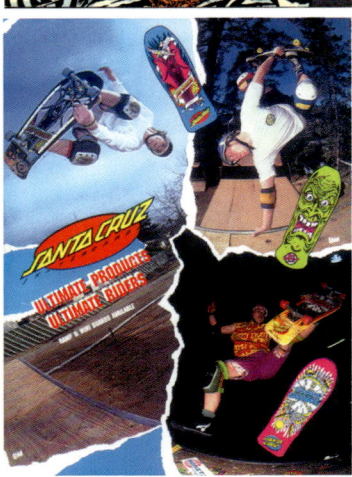

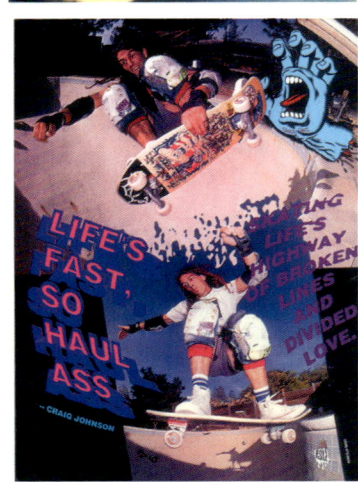
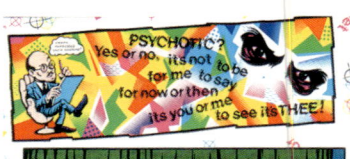
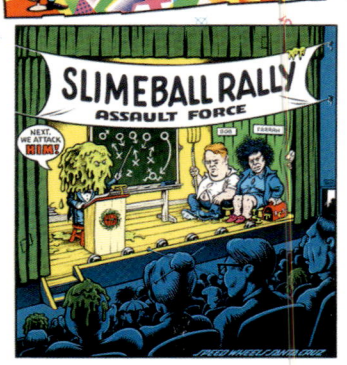
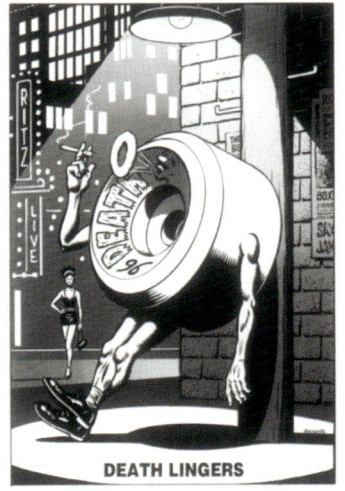
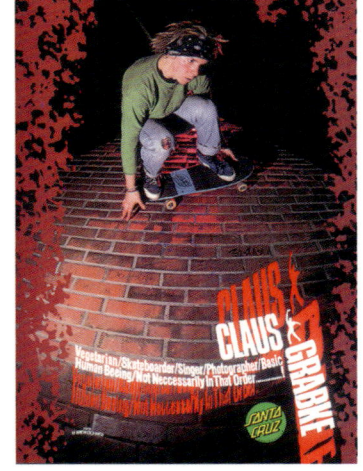

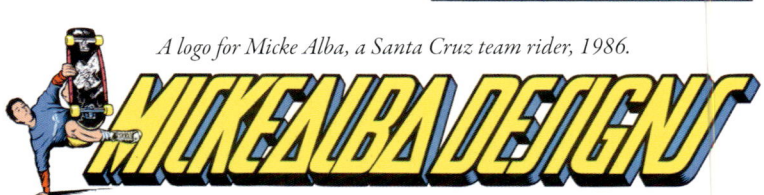

A logo for Micke Alba, a Santa Cruz team rider, 1986.

Phillips designed and composed hundreds of magazine ads for Santa Cruz Skateboards and Speed Wheels Santa Cruz from 1976 to 1990.

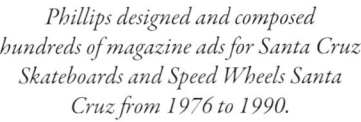
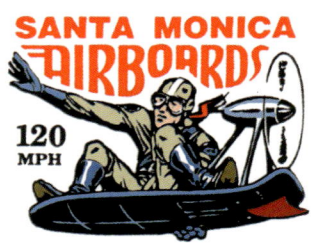

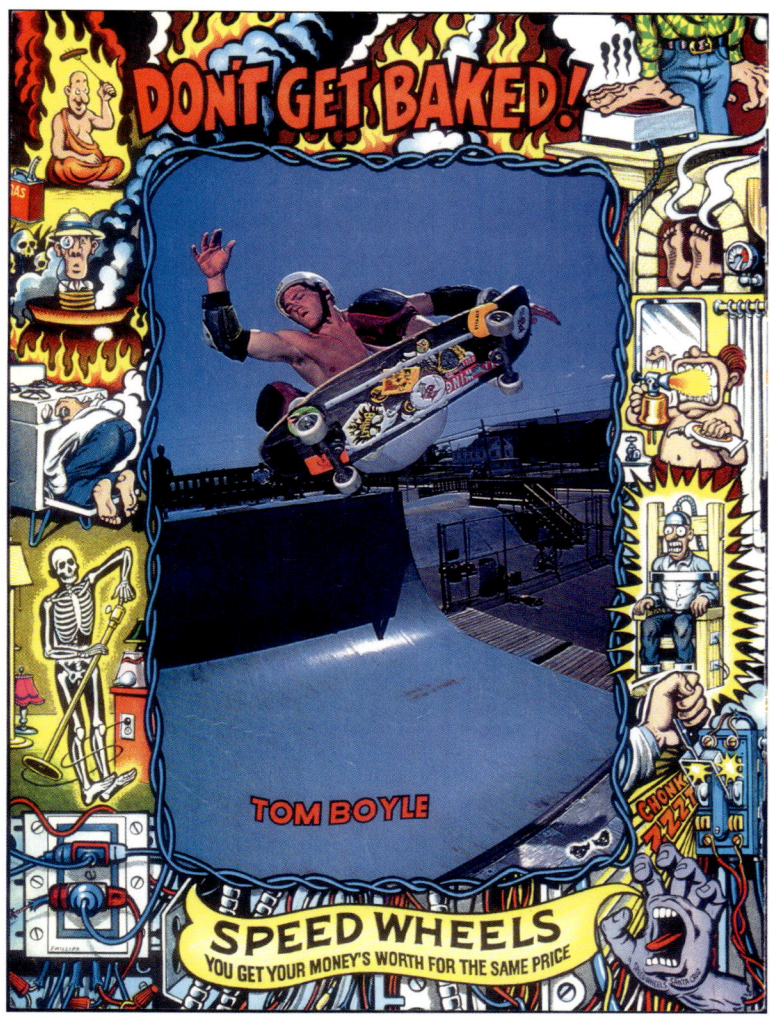

Phillips was directed by Rich Metiver for these hilarious Speed Wheels ads, 1986-87.

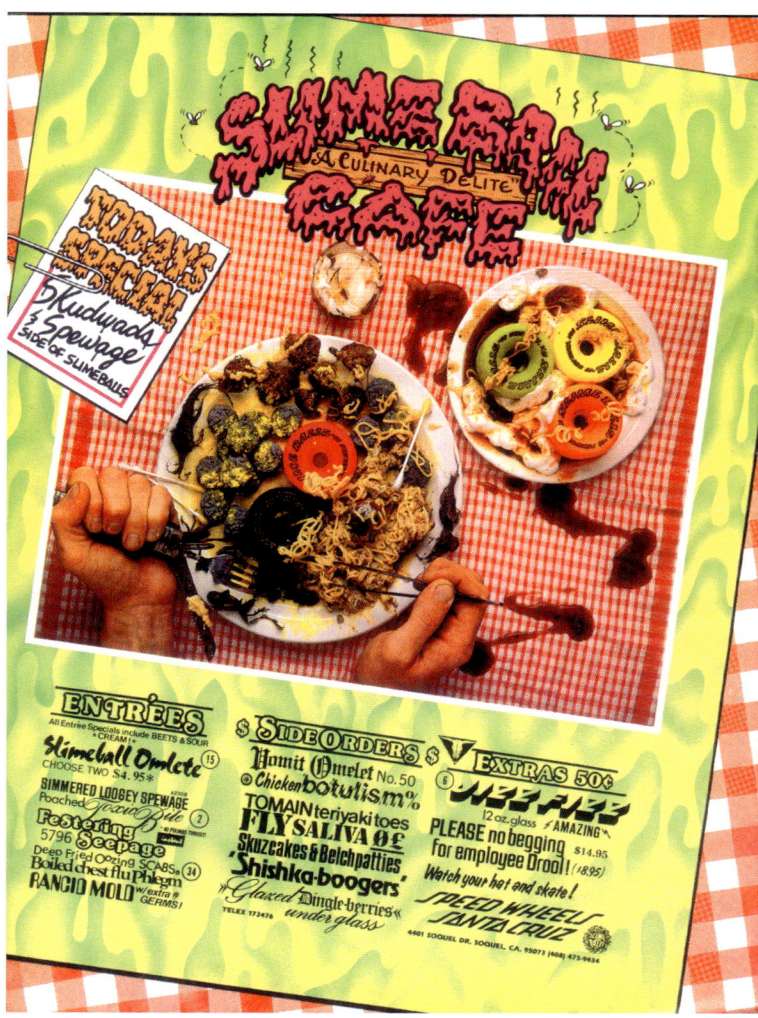

This Slimeball Cafe type was the first job that was done on the Phillips' Macintosh computer in 1985. That file created havoc for the Linotronic printers, but pressure lettering came through.

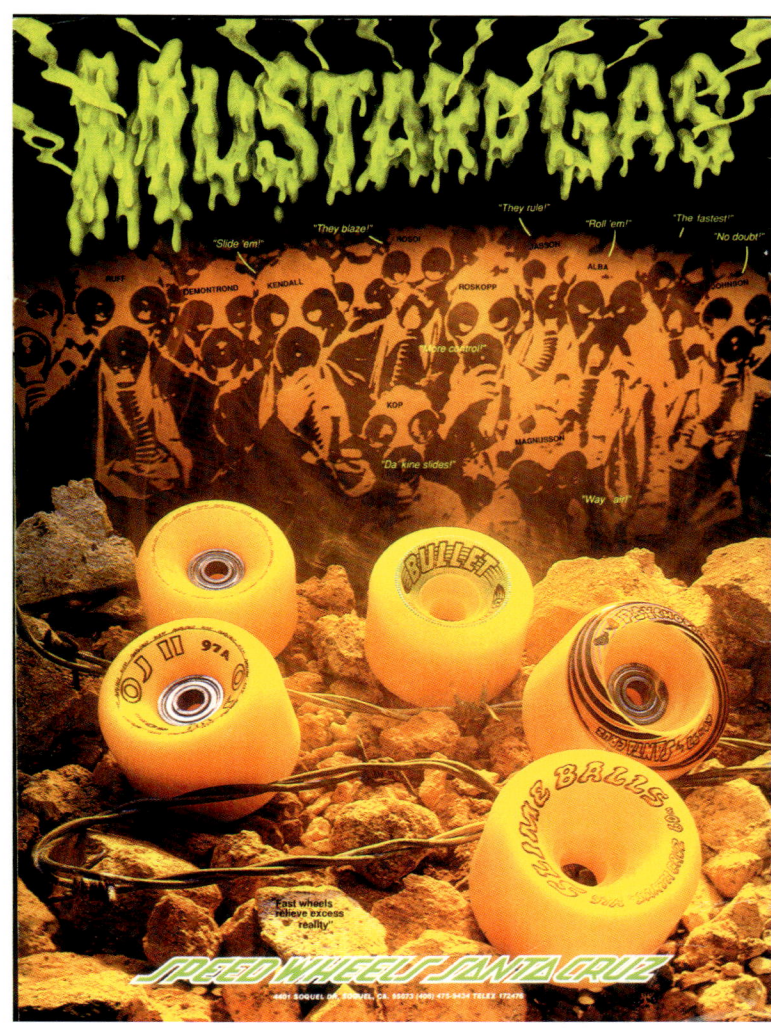

Photo by Rich Metiver.

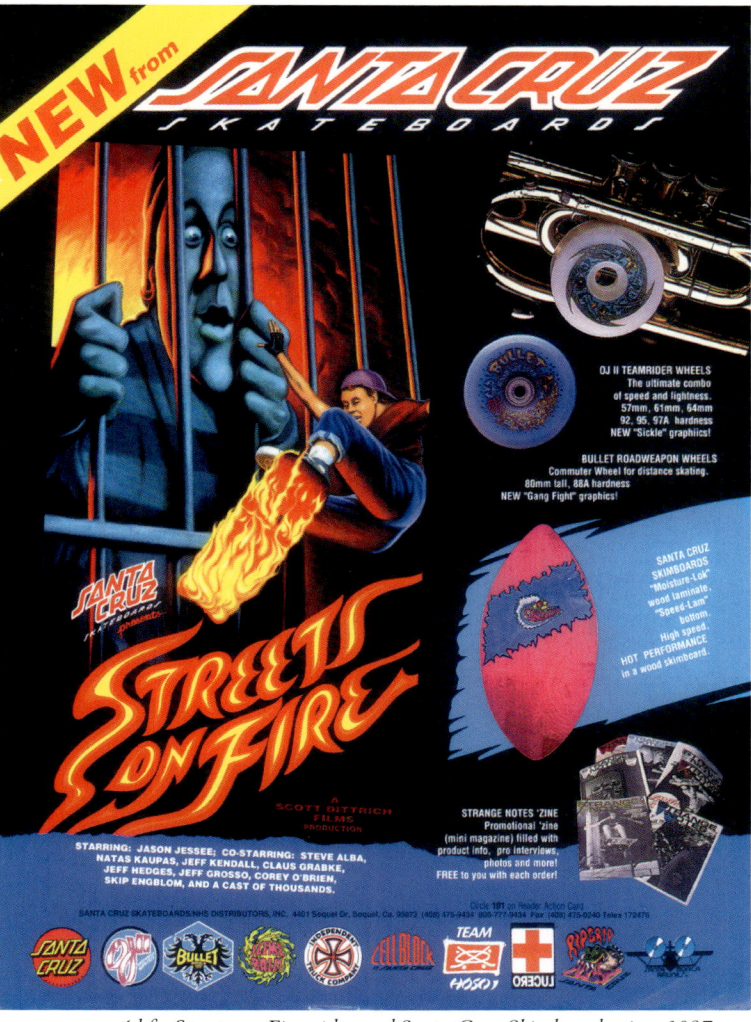

Ad for Streets on Fire *video and Santa Cruz Skimboards, circa 1987.*

KEVIN MARBURG: *"Maybe little kids liked barf and guts, but the older kids liked more simpler graphics stuff, or anything to do with Satan, beer or sex. Sometimes they'd just tell us what they wanted and sometimes we had to give them ideas."*

John Munnerlyn was an artist working unhappily in the Santa Clara Valley in 1987 when he heard the call from Santa Cruz. "My connection is that I was good friends with Bob Denike who was vice-president of NHS," Munnerlyn said. "Bob told me their artist was doing a comic book. That's when Jimmy was putting together *Road Rash*. Bob gave me his number and I called Jim and submitted something under the pseudonym Johnny Mojo." Munnerlyn's comic strip *Teenage Elvis* appeared in the first and only issue of *Road Rash*. Phillips Studios was cranking full speed at the peak of the Roaring 80s.

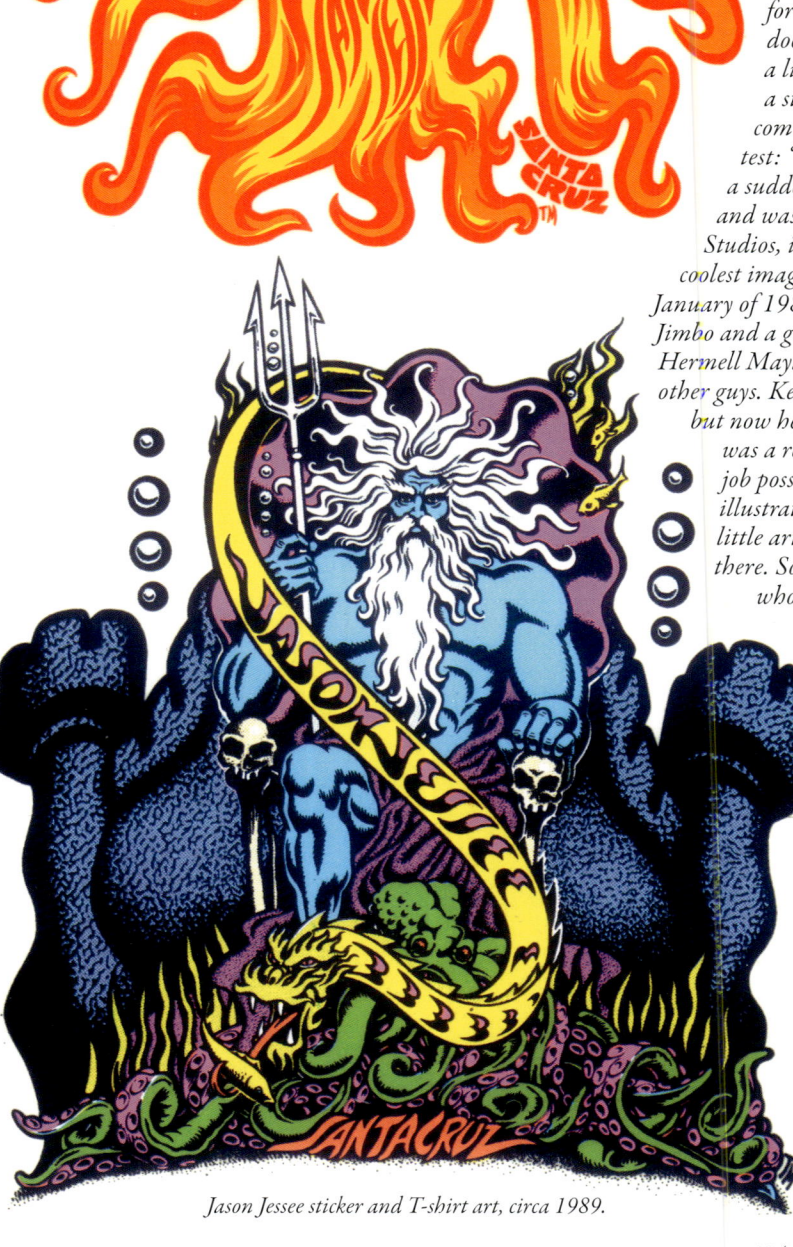

JOHN MUNNERLYN: *"A few months after the comic I called Jim and applied. He had a few guys working for him in the house next door. They kind of gave me a little test. I had to design a sticker to see what I would come up with. I passed the test: 'You can draw.' And all of a sudden I quit the job I hated and was working for Phillips Studios, in Santa Cruz, doing the coolest imaginable graphic art. This was January of 1988 and it was Jimmy and Jimbo and a guy named Justin Forbes and Hermell Mayang and there were a couple of other guys. Keith Meek had been a pro skater but now he was doing illustrations and it was a really good crew. To me it was the best job possible. I'd been doing boring technical illustrations and stuff. Now I was working in this little arty studio that was totally happening. Super casual and fun to work there. So much fun, it was a blast. There were a bunch of us living over the hill who would carpool there. I remember Justin Forbes and I getting there early and looking at Jim's drawing table and we could see he had been up late, working on something. More than once we were blown away by what he had done and how fast he had done it. Our jaws would be hanging because his stuff would blow you away, the detail and the speed and the humor. I was in the center of the world then. We had this great little thing happening for a while, cruising along super busy."*

KEITH MEEK: *"The first time I met Jim I was a silkscreener at NHS. I ended up working for him and that was really cool, I had always wanted to be a graphic designer. Working at Phillips Studios was like going to college, he had so much knowledge, and he was so good, it was great. I learned so much there, it wasn't stale, it was a lot of fun. I have a lot of good stories, like the cow head and all that stuff. I remember everyone sitting there drawing and someone would whisper "Dew break," and then everyone would yell "Dew run" and we'd get out the hot peppers and Mountain Dew and go out and skate around and then come back in, all sweaty, and start*

Jason Jessee sticker and T-shirt art, circa 1989.

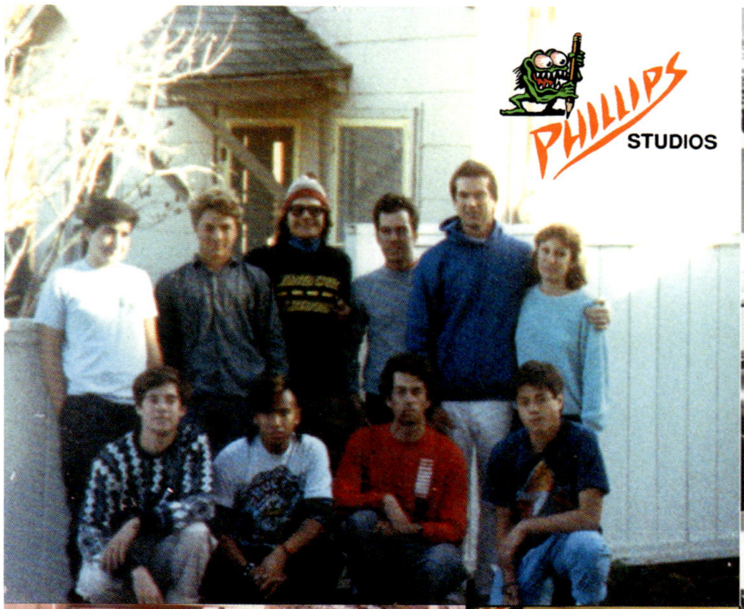

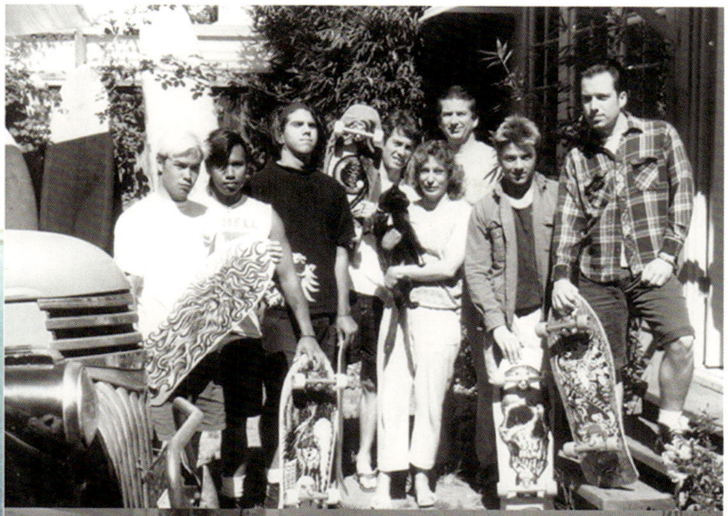

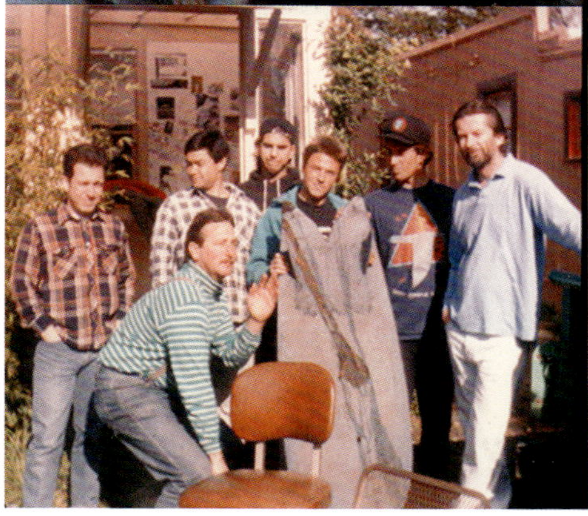

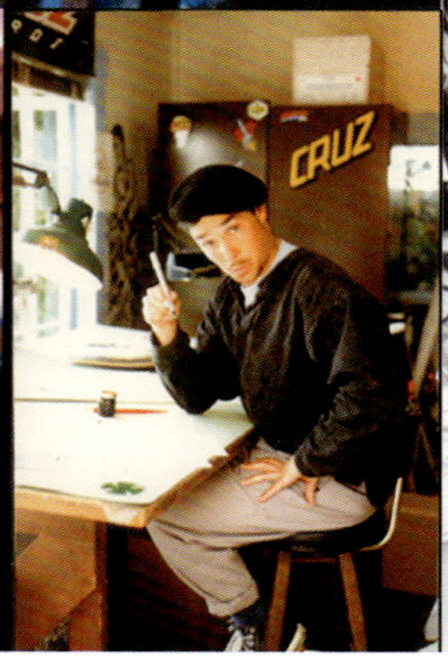

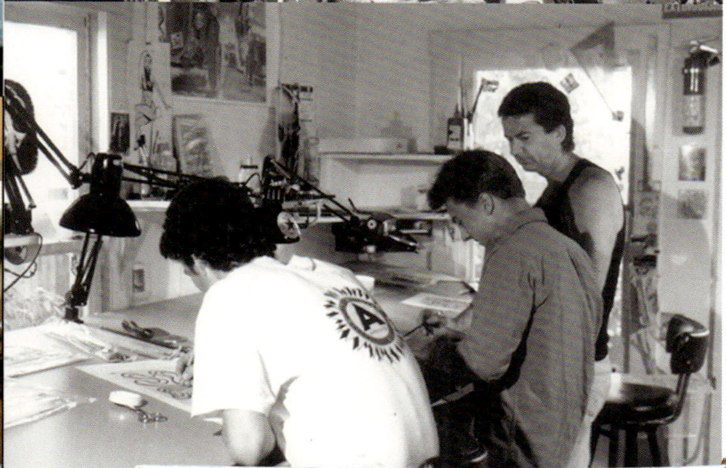

Phillips Studios, Top left photo, 1997: Eric Cardinale, Andreas
Ginghofer, Justin Forbes, John Munnerlyn, Jim & Dolly.
Bottom row: Josh Evenson, Hermel Mayang, Jimbo Phillips,
Joe Staley, posing in front of studio A.
Top right photo 1998: Keith Meek, Hermel Mayang, Kevin Marberg,
Jimbo Phillips, Dolly holding Blackie, Jim, Andreas Ginghofer, John Munnerlyn.
Bottom left photo, 1999: Jim Byberg hams it up for the boys.
Bottom center: Meekster the artiste.
Bottom right: Jim anwers questions from Andreas, Jimbo in foreground.

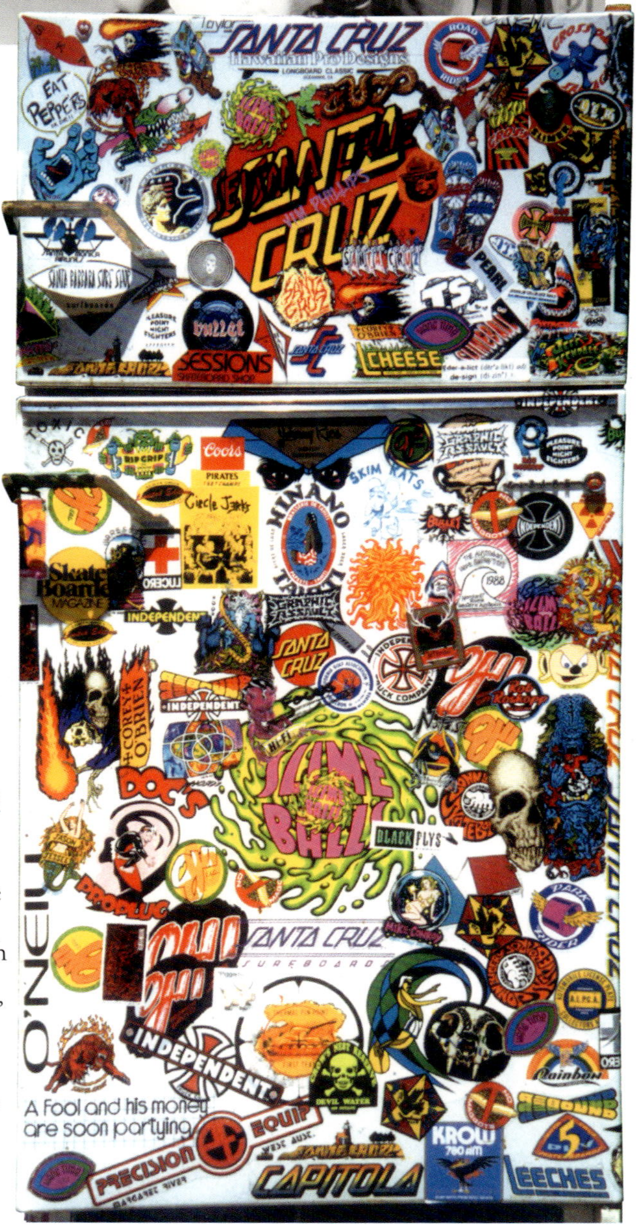

Right: Studio refrigerator covered in stickers.

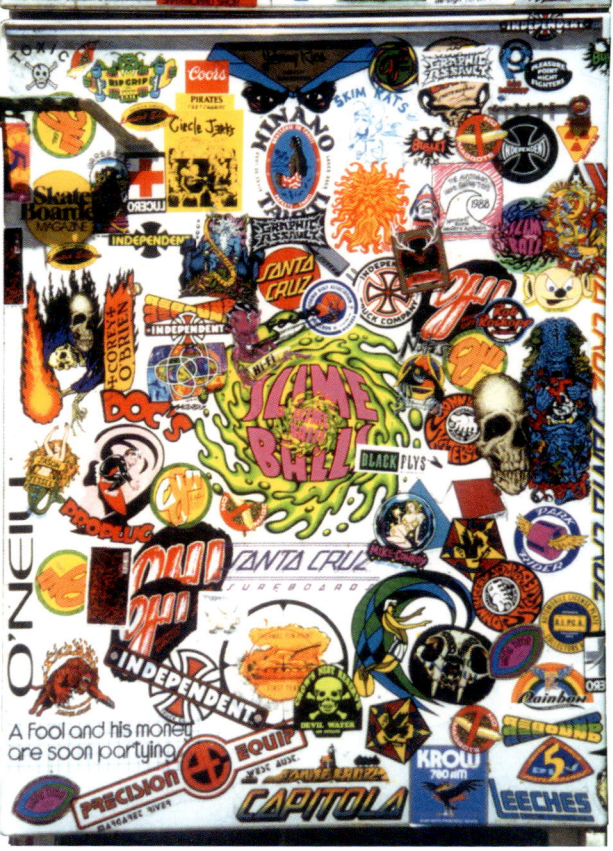

working again. I've surfed a lot with Jim and Jimbo down at Shark's Cove.
I have the utmost respect for Jim, and the whole Phillips family.
His push got me going in the art business."

Munnerlyn remembers drinking a lot of Mountain Dew while working at
Phillips Studios: "It was our drink of choice." He remembers Phillips' art
book collection and his skull collection and he remembers getting amped
on Mountain Dew and a lot of creative freedom during an era of gross out
art: "It was pretty extreme," Munnerlyn said. "There were skulls with eyes
popping out and rotted-out faces. At some point we buried a cow's head in
the backyard and really let it ferment, then we dug it up and cleaned it up and
added it to the skull collection. I guess it was that kind of atmosphere that
inspired Slime Balls and Vomit Balls. Kind of got silly after a while. I worked
my way into little spot art here and there. He would give us jobs and the more
he trusted us to do a good job the bigger jobs he would give us. It was getting
to the point where it was too much work for one guy to do. Managing a bunch
of young guys was not the greater side. Jimmy had always worked on his own.
I had to go through the same thing many years later, and it can be frustrating."

Phillips Studios was equal parts bliss and frustration. The bliss was having
unlimited amounts of work and creative freedom. The frustration came when

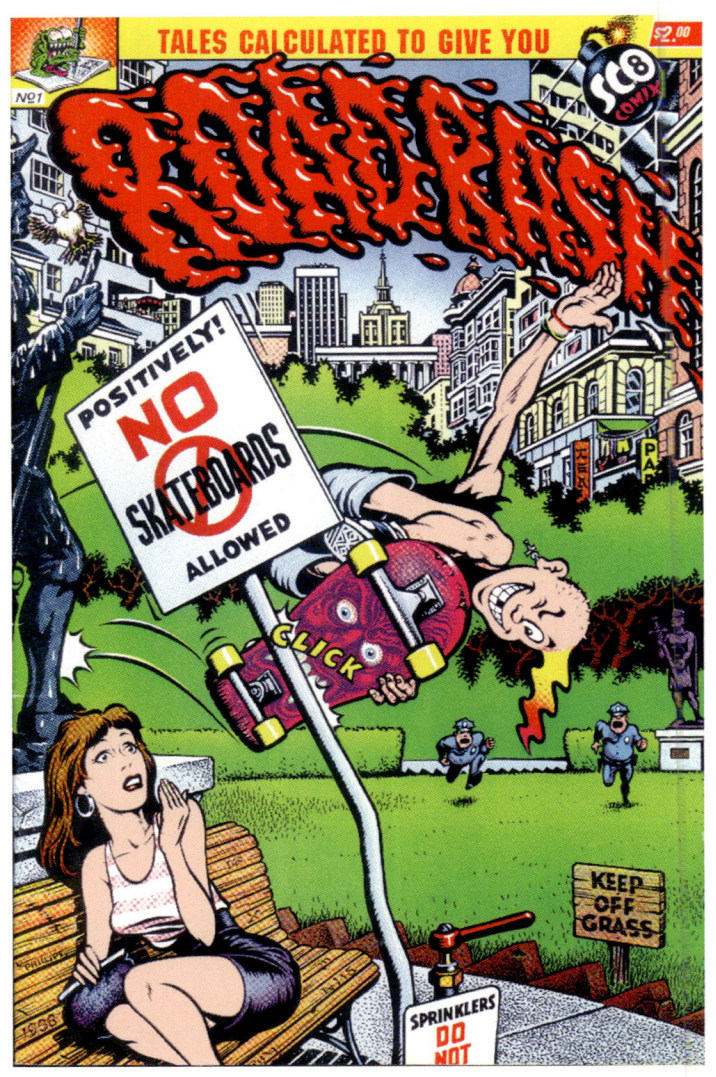

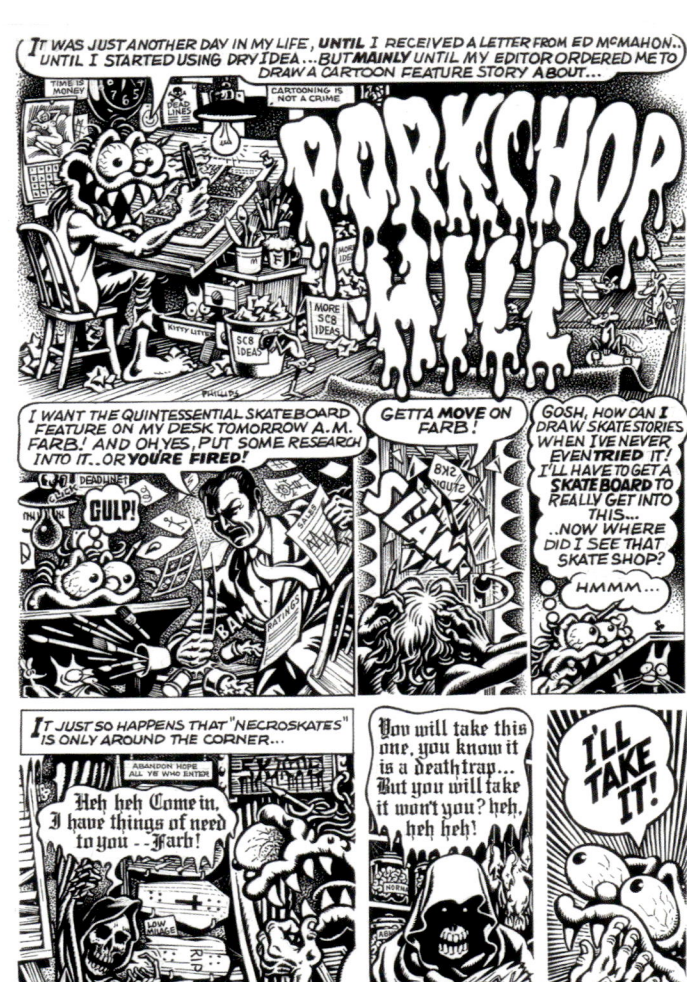

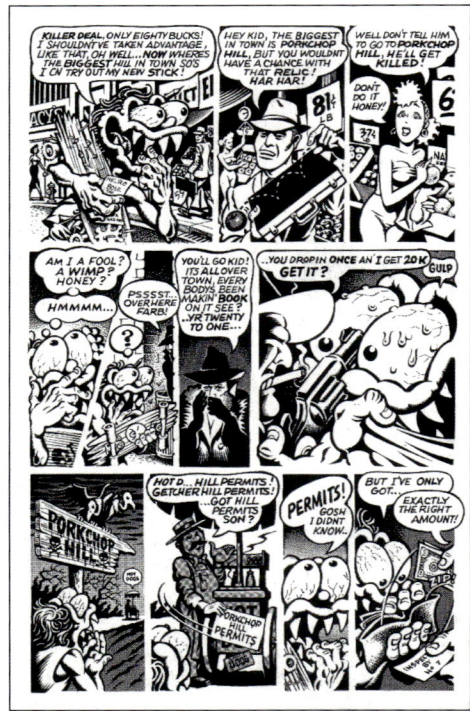
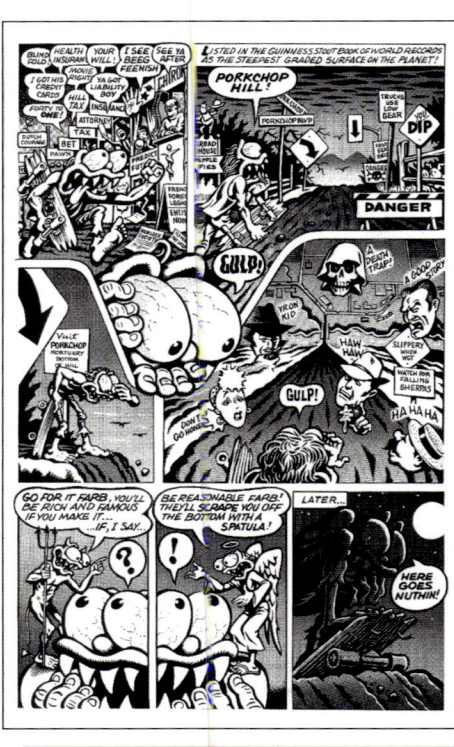
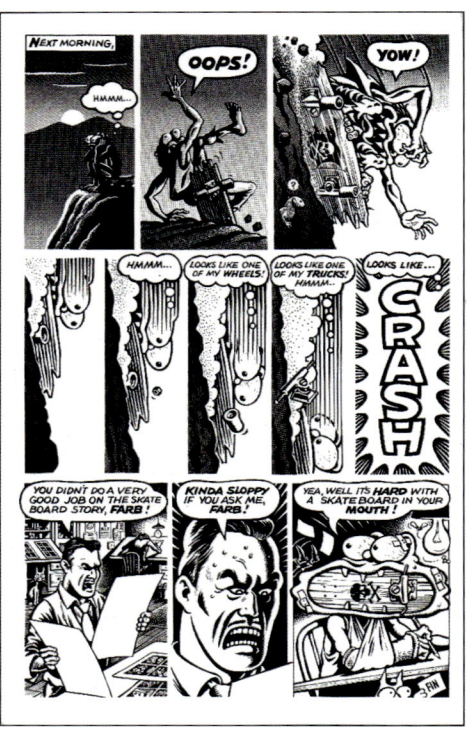

Road Rash *comic book, May, 1988.*

*Right: Escher inspired
'Metamorphosis'
on Ray Meyer
freestyle skate deck, 1999.*

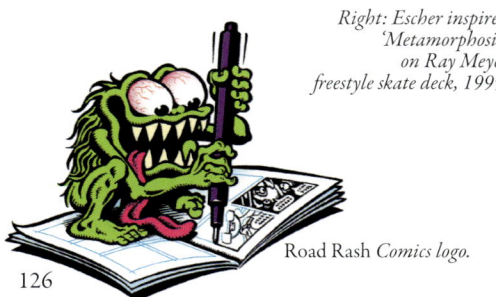

Road Rash *Comics logo.*

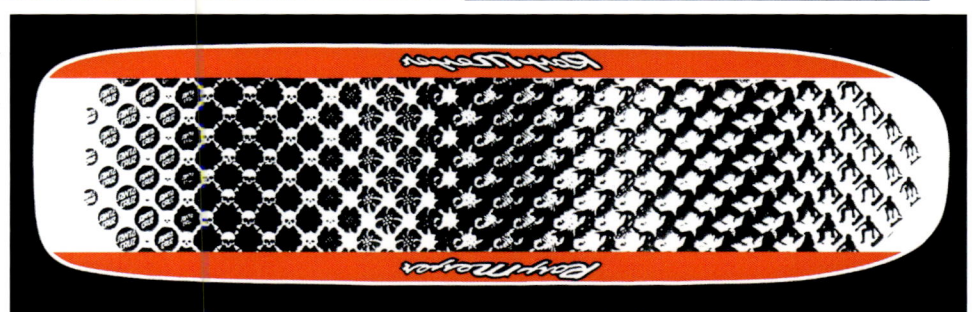

he left his studio to deal with the management. A tremendous amount of work was produced in those few years between 1987 and 1990, but a lot of it took some convincing. Screaming Hand is a perfect example. Powell, one of their biggest competitors, had Bones wheels, and everything was bones and skeletons. Phillips explained that, to him, the only fun thing left was fleshy monsters and mixed up body parts. Nonetheless, Screaming Hand was one of those designs Jim had to talk them into. Phillips explains that the hand is the most familiar thing you'll ever see, because they're always right in front of your face. That's why it really clicks. Then you add the raw emotion that a hand can convey by clenching, like someone drowning, and add in what else, a screaming mouth? A hacked wrist? It's about as aggro as you can get! A recent Mountain Dew ad in a surf magazine had a mouth on the can top just like Phillips' Screaming Hand. A million dollar advertising budget and they couldn't think of anything better.

John Munnerlyn remembers the Loma Prieta earthquake, and other subsequent divisions. He and Jim Byberg had just left Phillips Studios in Kevin Marburg's 1965 Ford Falcon to drive over the hill when the earthquake hit. It was a whopper and they knew without knowing that Highway 17 would be closed. So they turned back, and spent a disaster night Chez Phillips: "We had dinner with Jim and Dolly and Jimbo and watched the news on Jim's battery-powered TV," Munnerlyn said. "Kevin and I slept on the floor in the studio and in the middle of the night an aftershock hit. It was pitch black and we both went for the front door and ran head-on, like Laurel and Hardy."

The Loma Prieta earthquake hit in October of 1989, and it changed Santa Cruz dramatically. Historical buildings downtown that would have taken an Act of Congress to remove were removed by an Act of God. Businesses were relocated. Streets that had flowed north to south reversed direction. Looking back on the earthquake in the fullness of time, if you are looking for a dividing line between Santa Cruz Viejo and Nouveau Santa Cruz, the Loma Prieta earthquake is a pretty obvious fault.

Things were already getting shaky in the relationship between Phillips Studios and Santa Cruz Skateboards. Although Phillips was mostly left alone, he was growing tired of arguing with the "suits" for approval of designs that went on to make millions for The Company, but comparatively little for Phillips. Santa Cruz Skateboard sales topped out at $40 million in 1988 and Phillips's vivid graphics and logos were responsible for a big chunk of that change.

JIM RAUN-BYBERG: *"Phillips kind of went against the grain a number of times, and eventually it got to Novak. But I think that the brilliance of what Jimmy and Dolly and I did, was that we let these guys kind of express themselves in more ways than drawing on paper. We felt that it was important that they not only worked there, just chained to their drawing tables, but had the freedom to express themselves in a lot of different ways, outside of pen and ink, to keep the creative juices flowing."*

JOHN MUNNERLYN: *"Unfortunately it didn't go on forever but got kind of ugly at the end. Jimmy seemed to be butting heads with Novak and everyone at NHS. They wanted him to move his studio into the cannery building they had bought on Seabright Avenue. Jimmy was concerned about losing his creative environment, he said he didn't want to work in a fishbowl. He enjoyed being separate from the rest of the company which was more of the accounting and sales and shipping and less creative stuff. At some point, I think it was around January of 1990, it came to a head. Jimmy came back from an NHS meeting all bent out of shape and asked each one of us what we were going to do. Well my checks were being signed by NHS and I wanted to keep my job, so I said I would go to the Cannery. Another guy said that, too, and we were both fired. I ended up working at NHS until 1999, until I got tired of it."*

Phillips is on good terms with Santa Cruz and Rich Novak now, and time heals all wounds. He is diplomatic when he talks about Phillips Studios at the end of the 80s: He admits that the studio management took up a lot of his time.

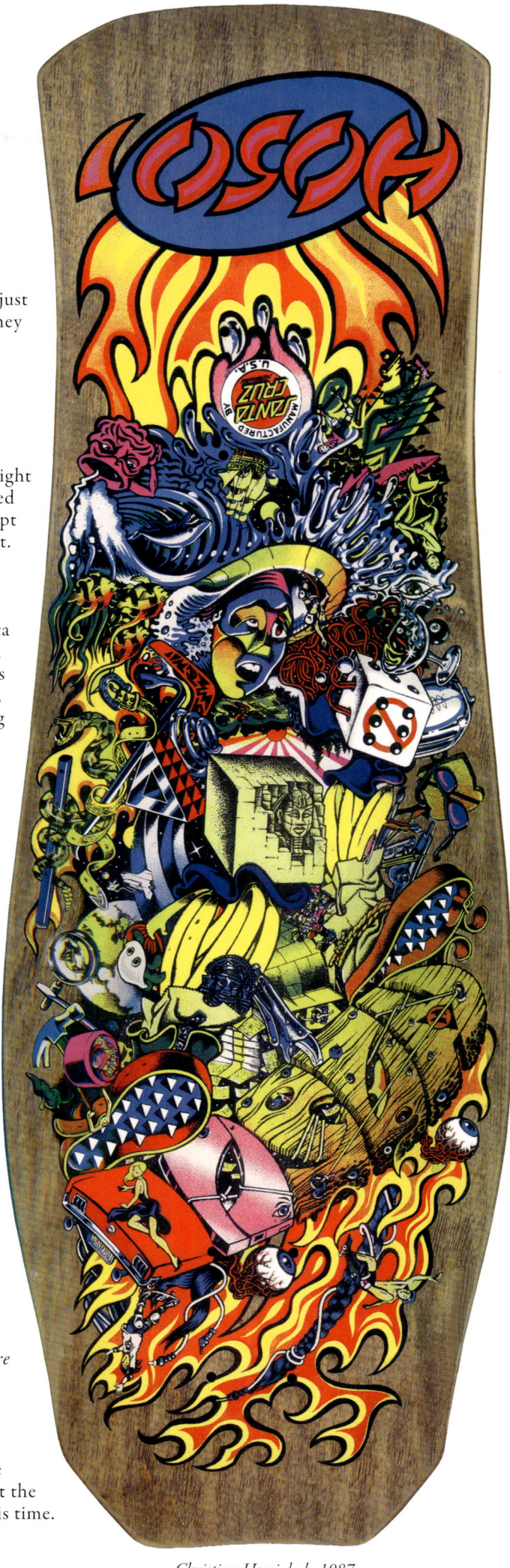

Christian Hosoi deck, 1987.

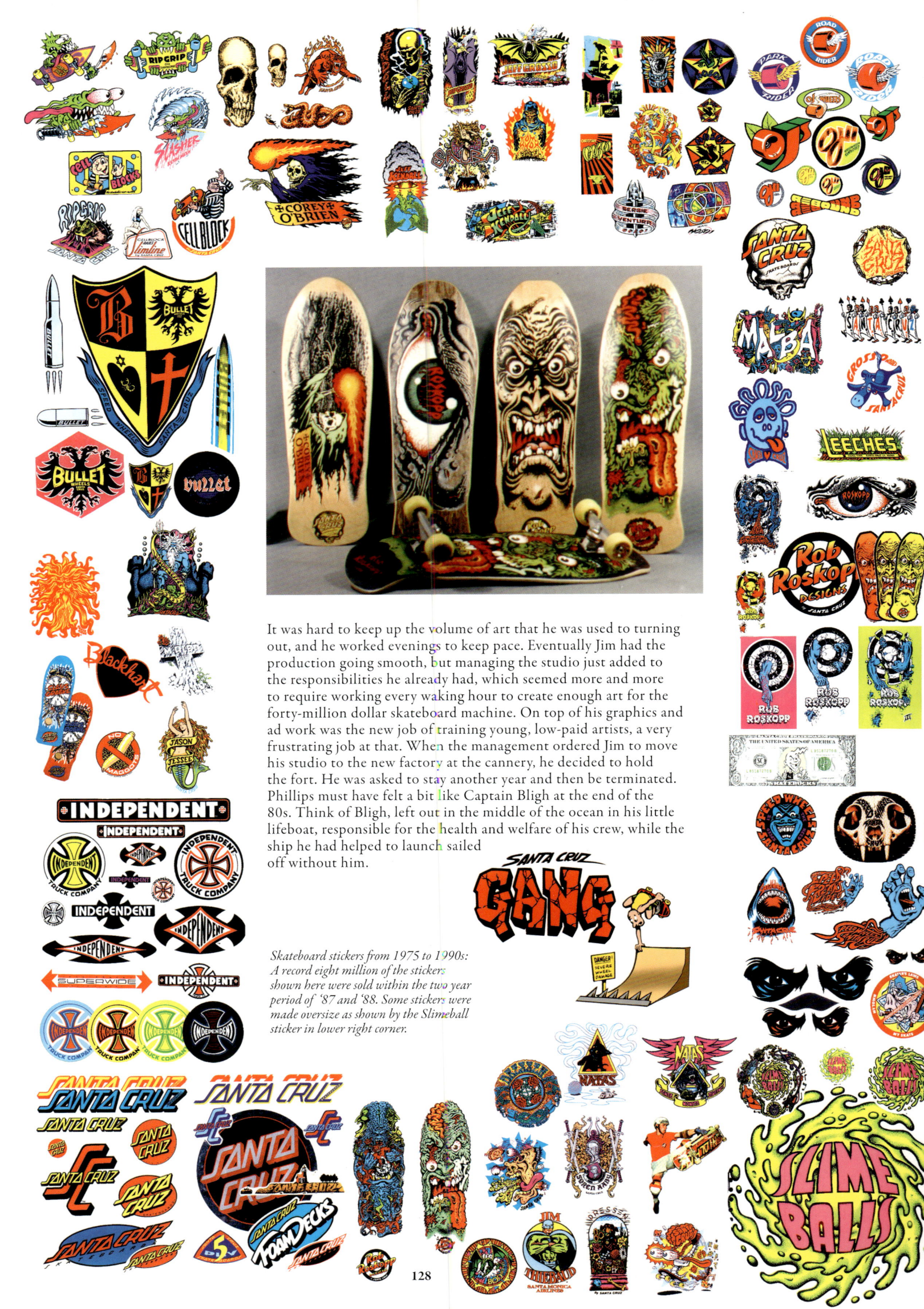

It was hard to keep up the volume of art that he was used to turning out, and he worked evenings to keep pace. Eventually Jim had the production going smooth, but managing the studio just added to the responsibilities he already had, which seemed more and more to require working every waking hour to create enough art for the forty-million dollar skateboard machine. On top of his graphics and ad work was the new job of training young, low-paid artists, a very frustrating job at that. When the management ordered Jim to move his studio to the new factory at the cannery, he decided to hold the fort. He was asked to stay another year and then be terminated. Phillips must have felt a bit like Captain Bligh at the end of the 80s. Think of Bligh, left out in the middle of the ocean in his little lifeboat, responsible for the health and welfare of his crew, while the ship he had helped to launch sailed off without him.

Skateboard stickers from 1975 to 1990s: A record eight million of the stickers shown here were sold within the two year period of '87 and '88. Some stickers were made oversize as shown by the Slimeball sticker in lower right corner.

128

The March 1988 Cracked Magazine had a cover illustration showing Santa skateboarding, and his skateboard had one of Jim's stickers. Phillips Studios sent in a comic photo of Jimbo reading a Cracked Magazine while skating a ramp, which they then printed. That began a relationship with John Severin and the staff of Cracked. Phillips saw it as a way to promote skateboards to the core age level. He created the header logo at right, and a half dozen pages for Cracked plus several collaborative pages for his studio artists also were published.

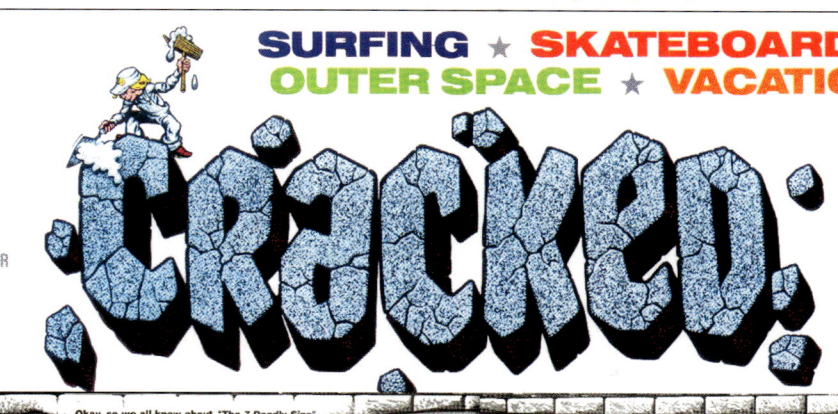

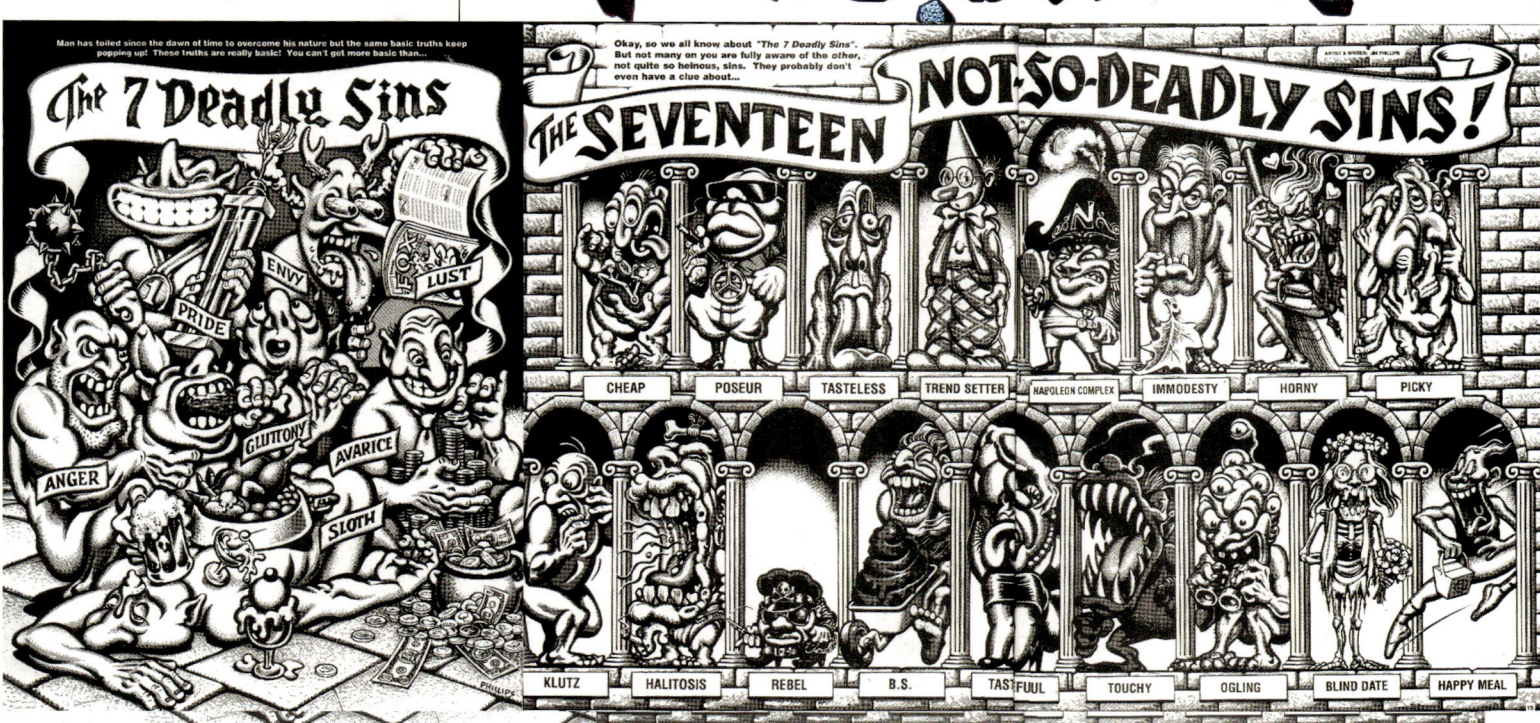

Cracked #258

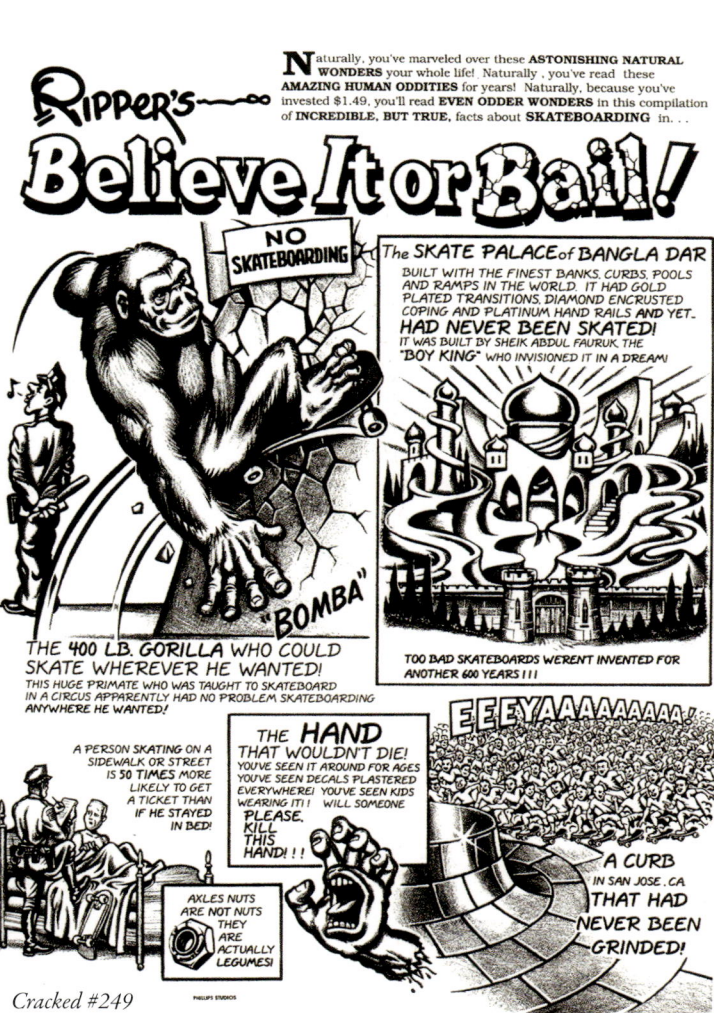

Cracked #249

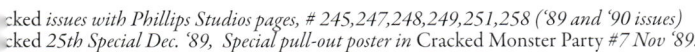

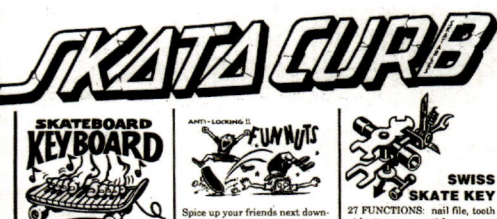

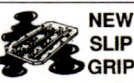

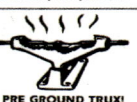

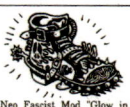

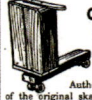

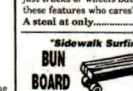

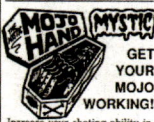

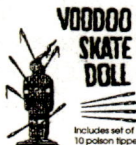

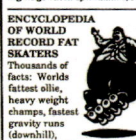

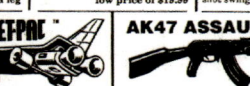

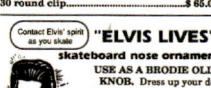

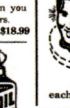

129

Cracked #247

27

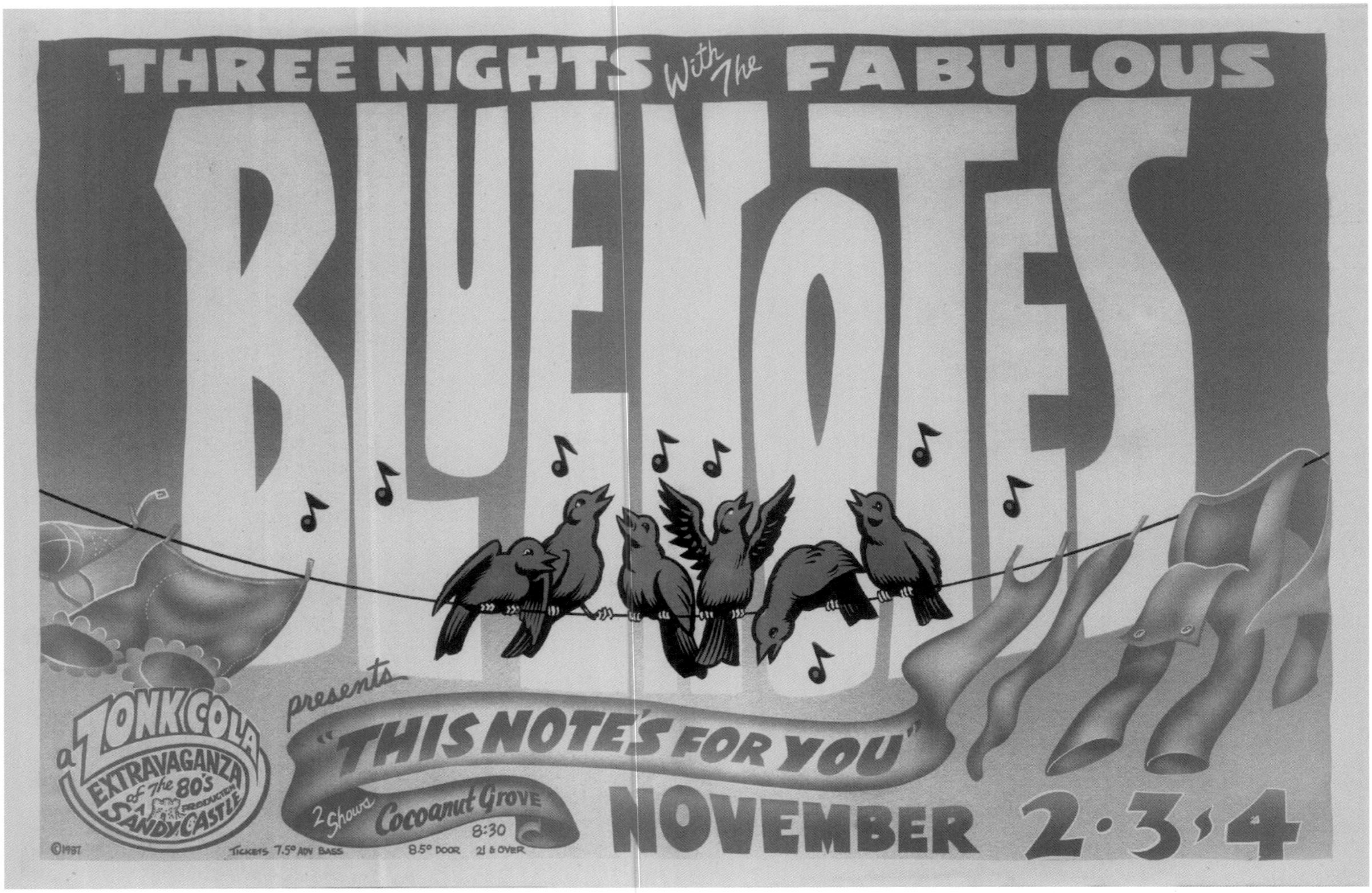

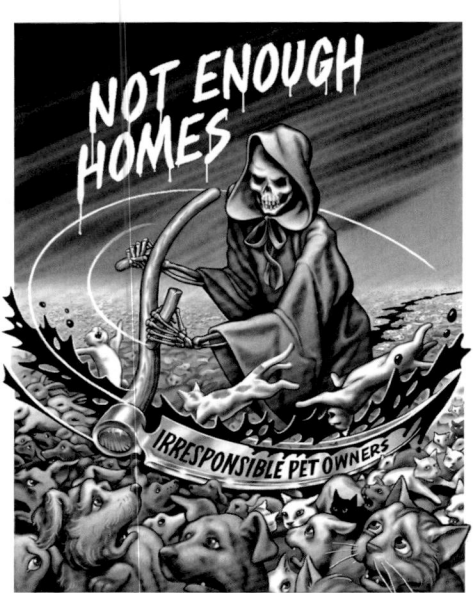

Blue Notes - (Neil Young's band), 1987, 11"x17", a Sandy Castle Production (Maz), Quality Offset printing

Santa Cruz Sentinel

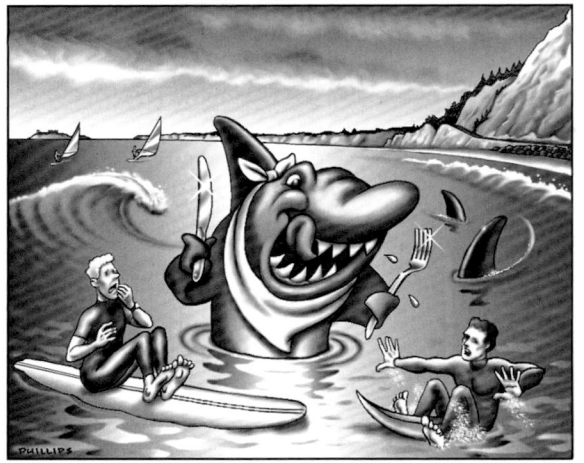

Have you guys seen a chumline go by here?

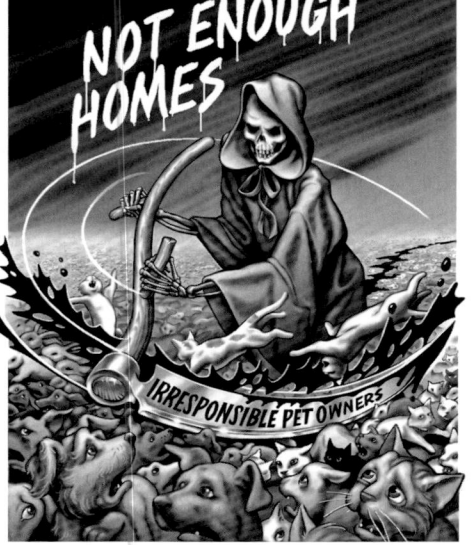

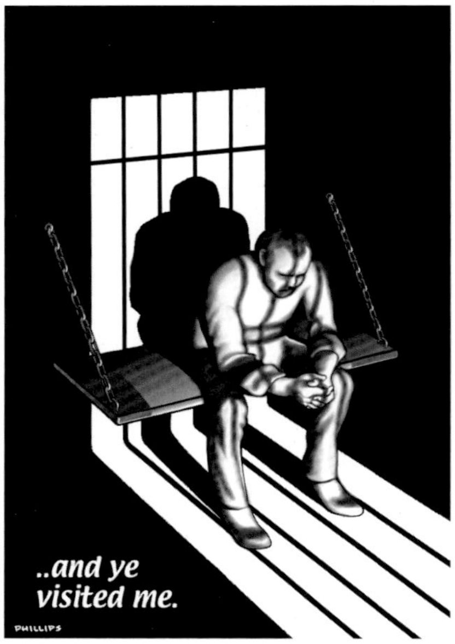

Jim received a thank you card from the SPCA when this cartoon was published.

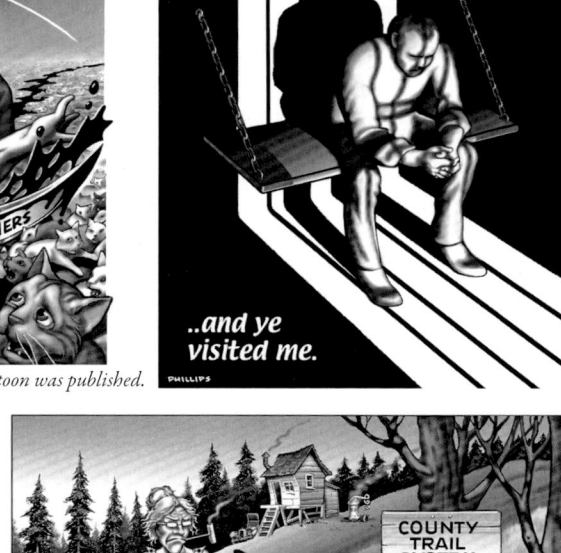

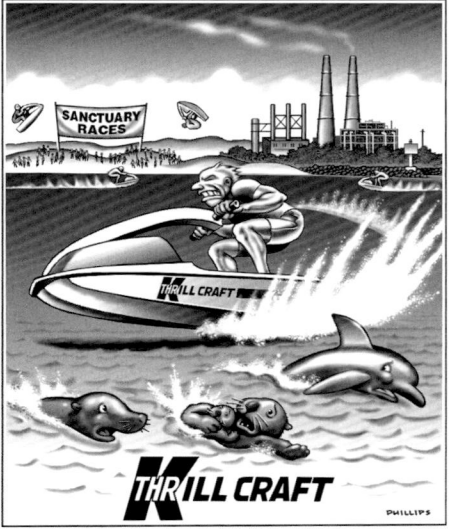

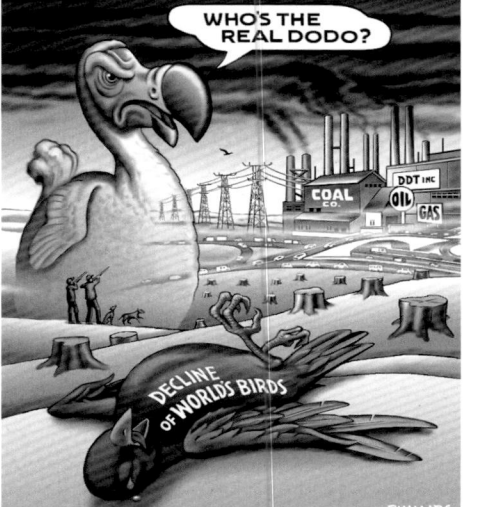

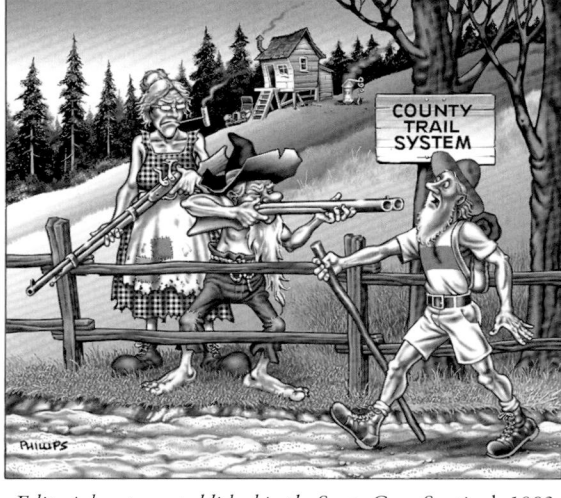

130

Editorial cartoons published in the Santa Cruz Sentinel, *1993*

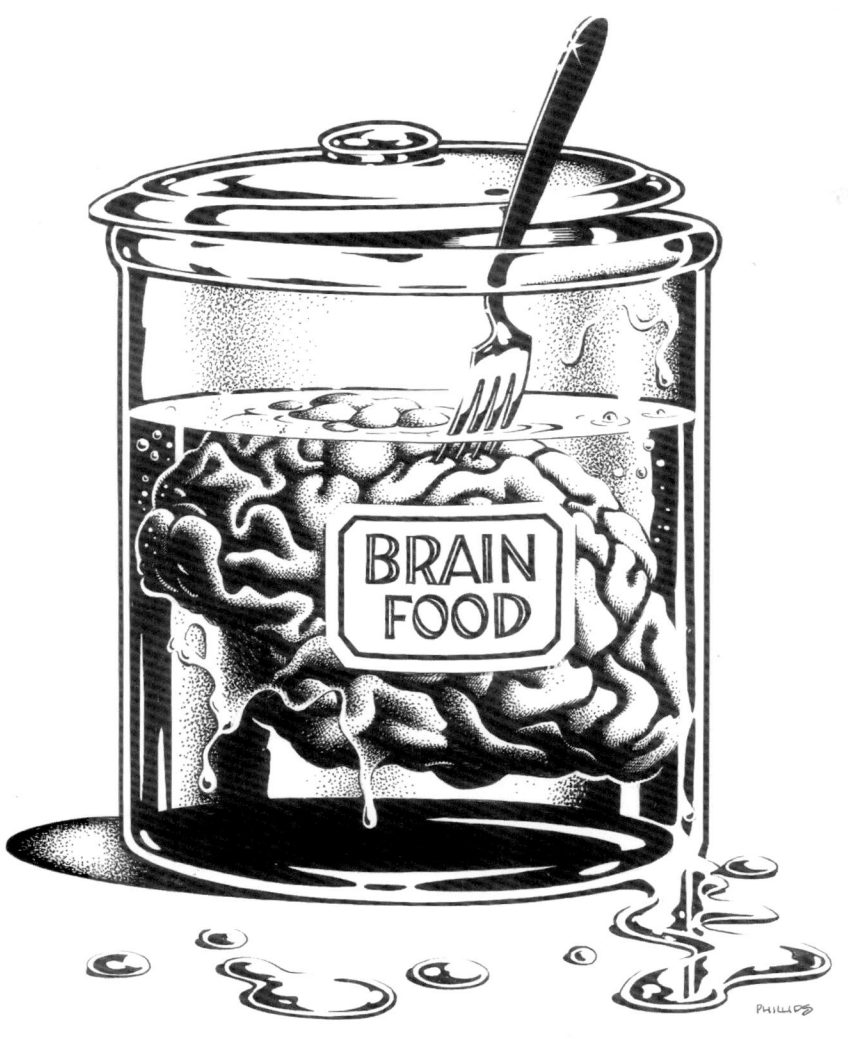

Brain Food, book illustration, circa 1976.

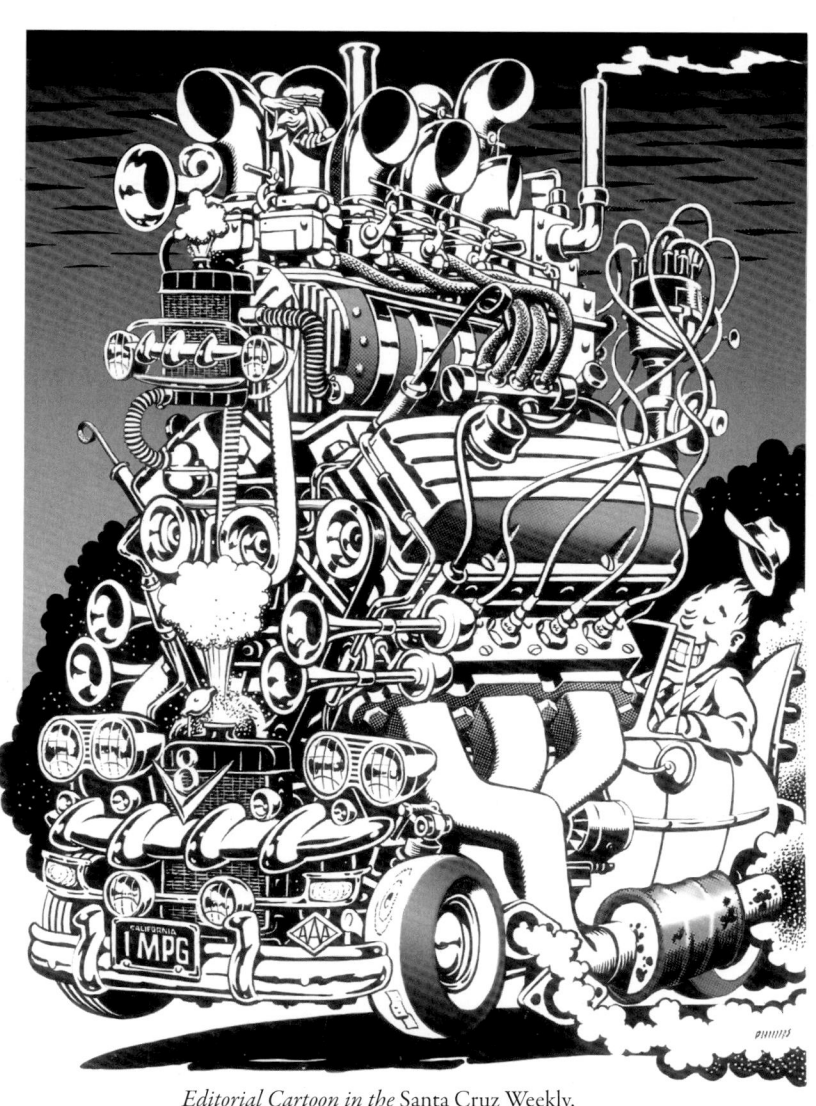

JUST THINK SON, SOME DAY ALL THIS WILL BE YOURS!

Editorial Cartoon in the Santa Cruz Weekly,
on plans to install off shore drilling wells at Año Nuevo, 1980.

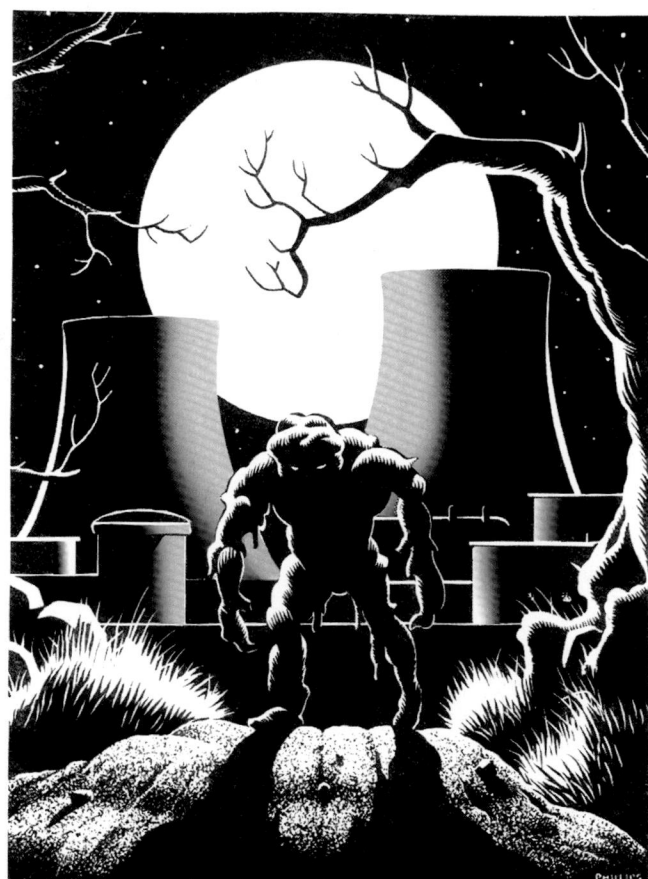

*"More Nukes", 1976. One of many Jim did for "Stan's Crazy Signs,"
5"x7" cards sold in area stores during the mid 70s.
Original art, collection of Larry Williams.*

Editorial Cartoon in the Santa Cruz Weekly,
about concerns over gas consumption in America, 1980.

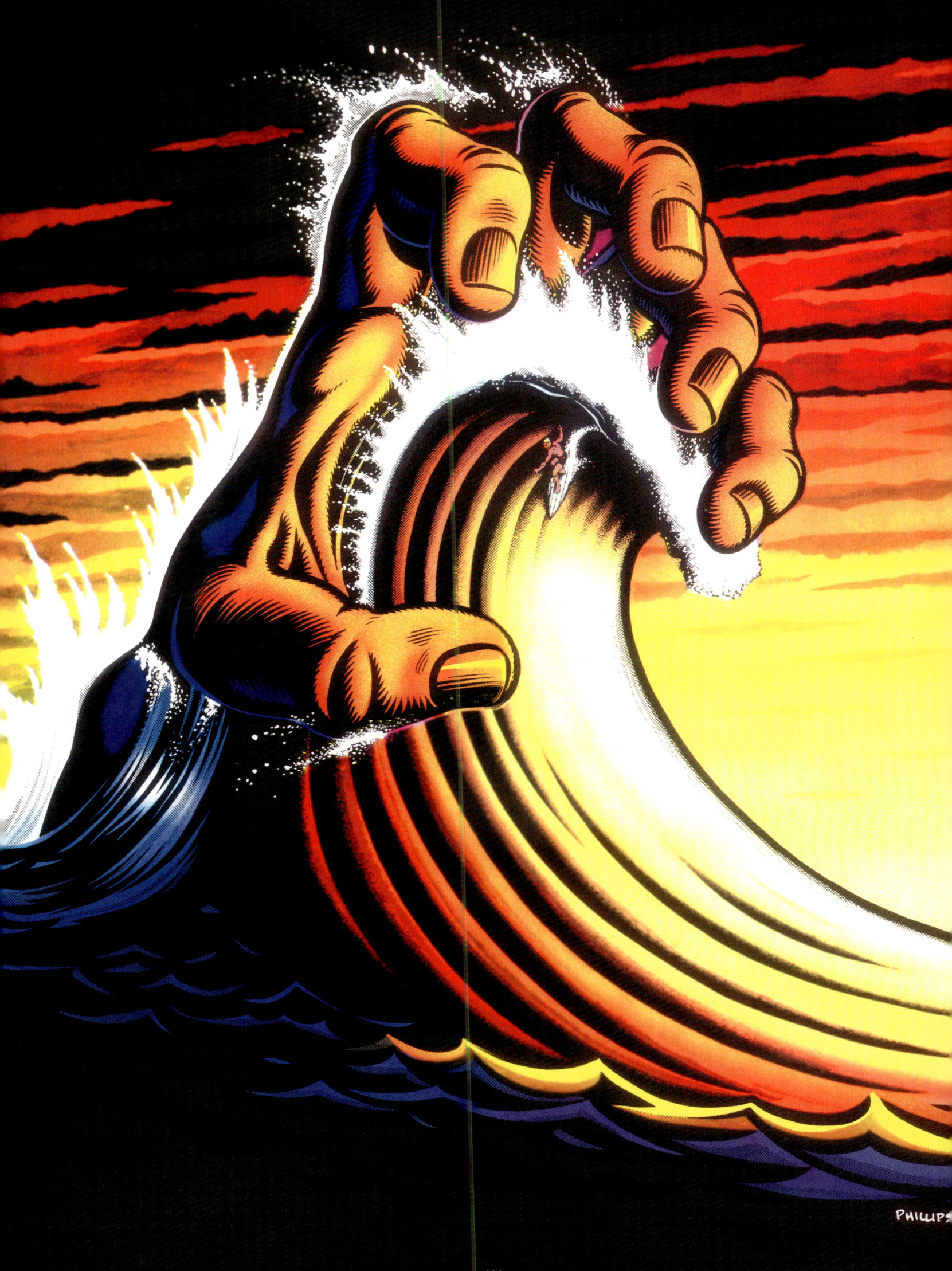

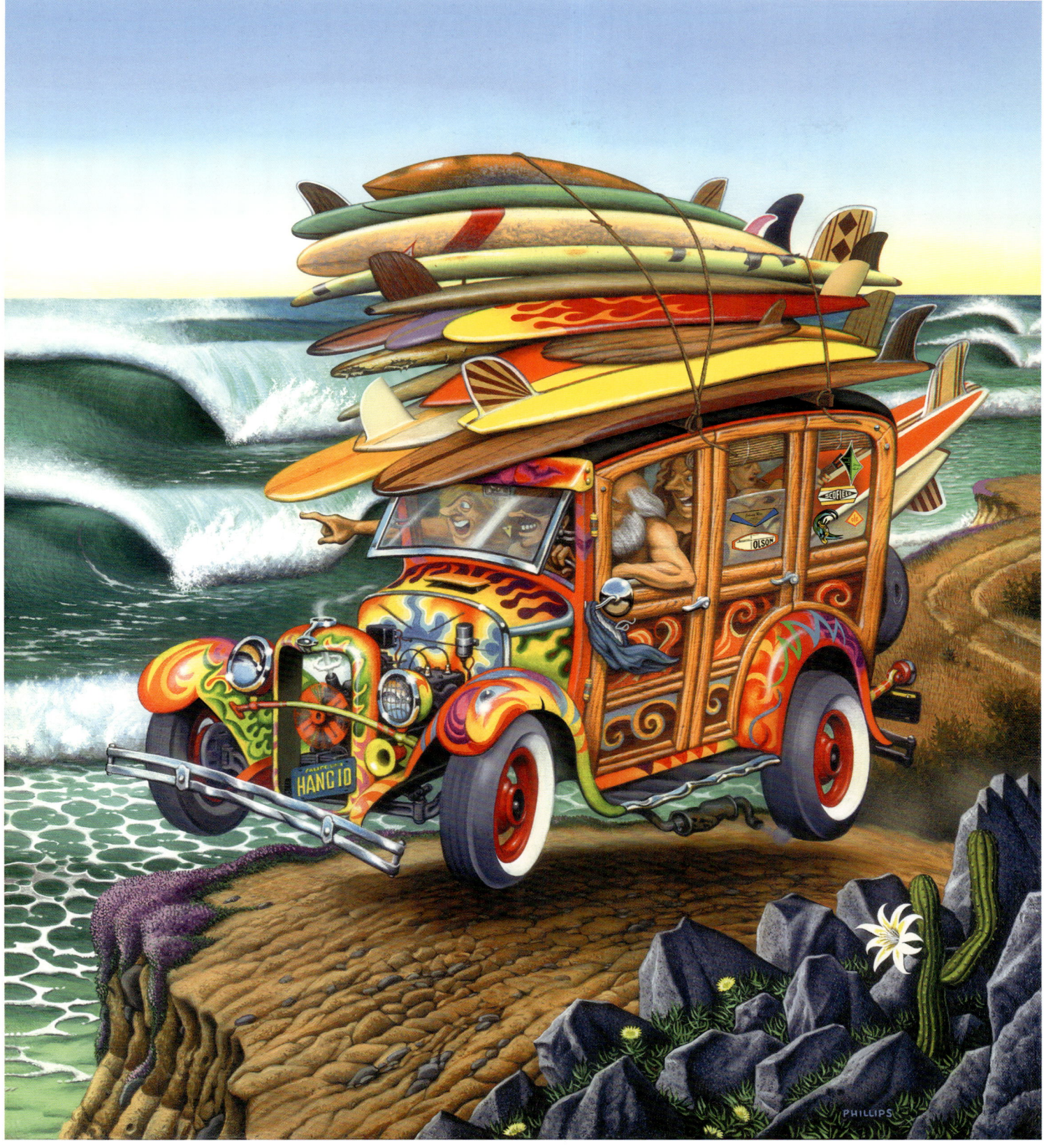

Opposite page: Hand Wave, *pen & ink on Grafix board, 22"x16", 1990. Above:* Woodystock, *oil on canvas, 22" x 20", 1991.*

CHAPTER FIVE

BACK TO THE FUTURE:
1989 to 2002

Jimmy Rocks Digital

Phillips works best on his own. He isn't designed to be a team player or a manager. He is happiest when he is working, alone, in peace and quiet, listening to KUSP on the radio, late at night, not distracted, getting it done, focusing all that undistracted detail and color and energy into his art.

For an extended metaphor, when Phillips cut away from NHS and Santa Cruz Skateboards in 1990, he had to watch from his little boat, alone, as those ships sailed off into the 90s, still making millions from his designs, using artists he had trained in his studio. Was he a little bitter? Maybe, but he didn't really have time for it. He had work to do and so he started paddling.

As always, there was work to be had. The 90s brought in the computer revolution and forced every artist of every kind to determine which way they were going to go. Were they going to stick with traditional, manual mediums of pen and ink and canvas and ignore the future, or did they have the brains and

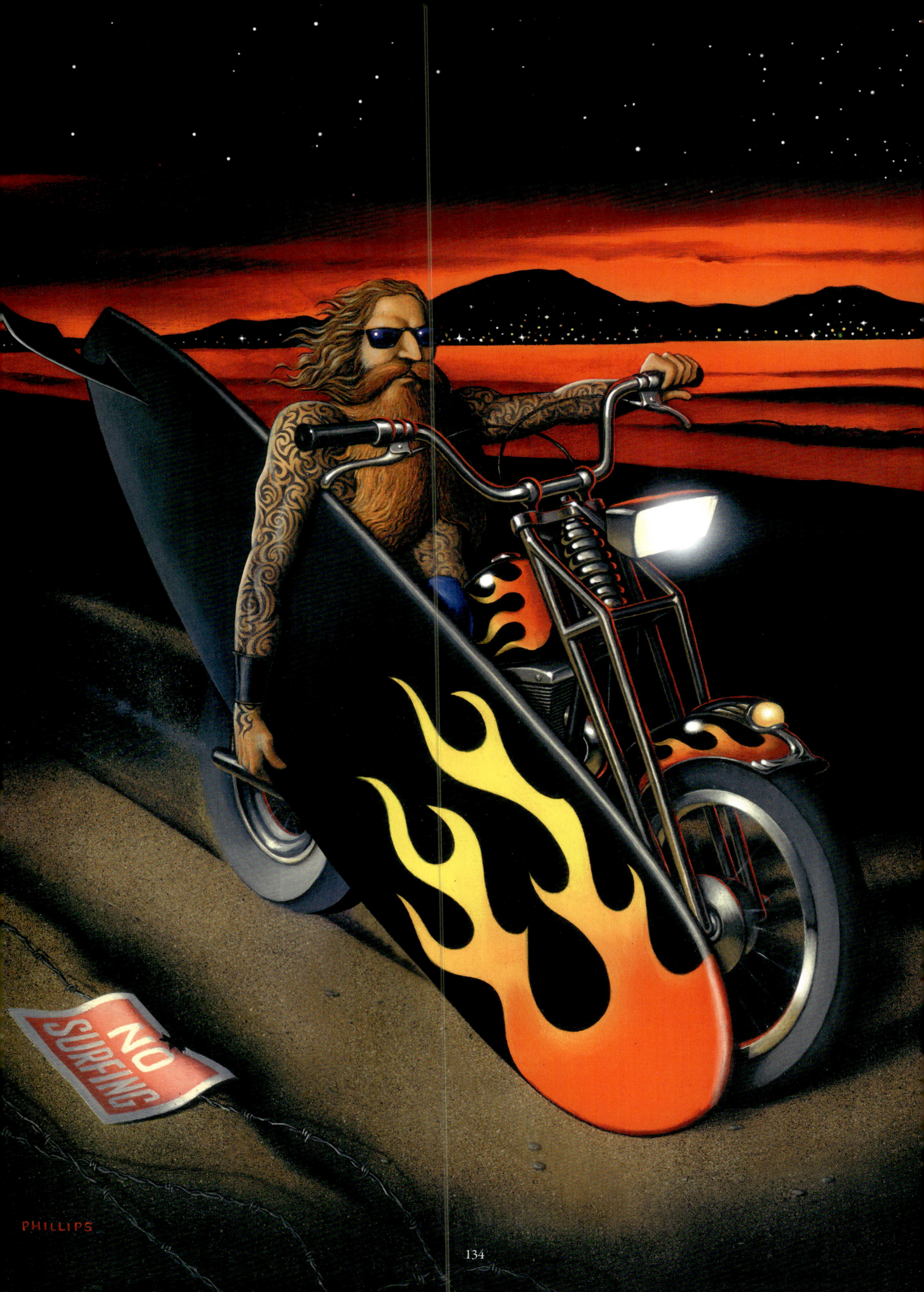

PHILLIPS

money and energy to dive into computers, one of the most powerful tools ever created by a tool-loving race? Phillips looked at the computer revolution as a giant wave he wasn't sure he wanted to ride. He took a few tentative strokes, and then he went for it.

Phillips was singing *On My Own* at the beginning of the 90s and he was back to basics: His lovely house, his devoted wife and his loyal son Jimbo by his side. Phillips' Studios was a one-man show again, but he kept the rental on the studio next door, which was still plastered with stickers and graffiti, and perhaps a few cow skulls still buried in the backyard. He was a little relieved to be out of the grind, but a little concerned about finding another line.

At the turn of the decade the Action Sports Trade Shows were booming. These were biannual bazaars down in southern California at Long Beach and San Diego, where all of the surf/skate/snowboard crowd gathered to schmooze and buy and sell and figure out clever ways to sell t-shirts to the Vals in shopping malls. Phillips drove down to the *Action Sports Retailer Expo* in September 1990 to drum up some business. That Expo was a wash except for meeting the *Surf Crazed Comics* guys, Roy Gonzales and Salvador Paskowitz, who ran Hand Wave in their first issue. *Hand Wave* was originally an illustration for a story by Kookson, which was rejected by both surf magazines, despite Kookson's assurances that he knew the editors.

ROY GONZALES: *"I'd seen Jim's stuff for many years. Every time I'd go up to Santa Cruz he'd be doing the artwork for the concerts and the surf contests and I dug it. Jimmy was like* Mad Magazine *style where Griffin was more Disney style. I liked Jim's surfing stuff because it was totally correct. It was obvious that the work was done by a surfer. I was jazzed when he submitted some work to Surf Crazed Comics because I dug his stuff. We didn't have any distribution at first and then ASR got a hold of it and Hollywood came knocking and pretty soon it took off and I lost control and bailed out for Costa Rica and Maui."*

Surf Crazed was cool, but what intrigued Jim was the way they were coloring the line art: on a Mac! The Phillips got a Mac back when it was introduced in the mid 80's, but mostly for the typesetting capabilities. But this was color, and it was perfect to color cartoons. Salvador filled Jim in on what it took to get set up and he did it. That first color Mac had only eight megabytes of RAM but it was dynamic. With a Mac, he could use millions of colors, and SEE them as he used them. He no longer had to wait for bluelines, or worry about their unpredictable results. That Mac allowed mixtures and shading that would be unimaginable to achieve by hand methods. On the down side there were all the complications that were totally disconnected with actual art. But computer pains are too well known to get into that.

With everything associated with computers there is a steep hill to climb at first, but once you get to the peak of that hill, life gets easier. In 1991, Phillips fired up his colorized Macintosh for his first project. He took the woody-off-the-cliff illustration he had done for the *Santa Cruz Weekly* cover back in 1980, and set to work coloring it in. Phillips had been using that out of control woody as a logo for Phillips' Studios, and as a kind of visual motto for how he felt most of the time: stoked! He

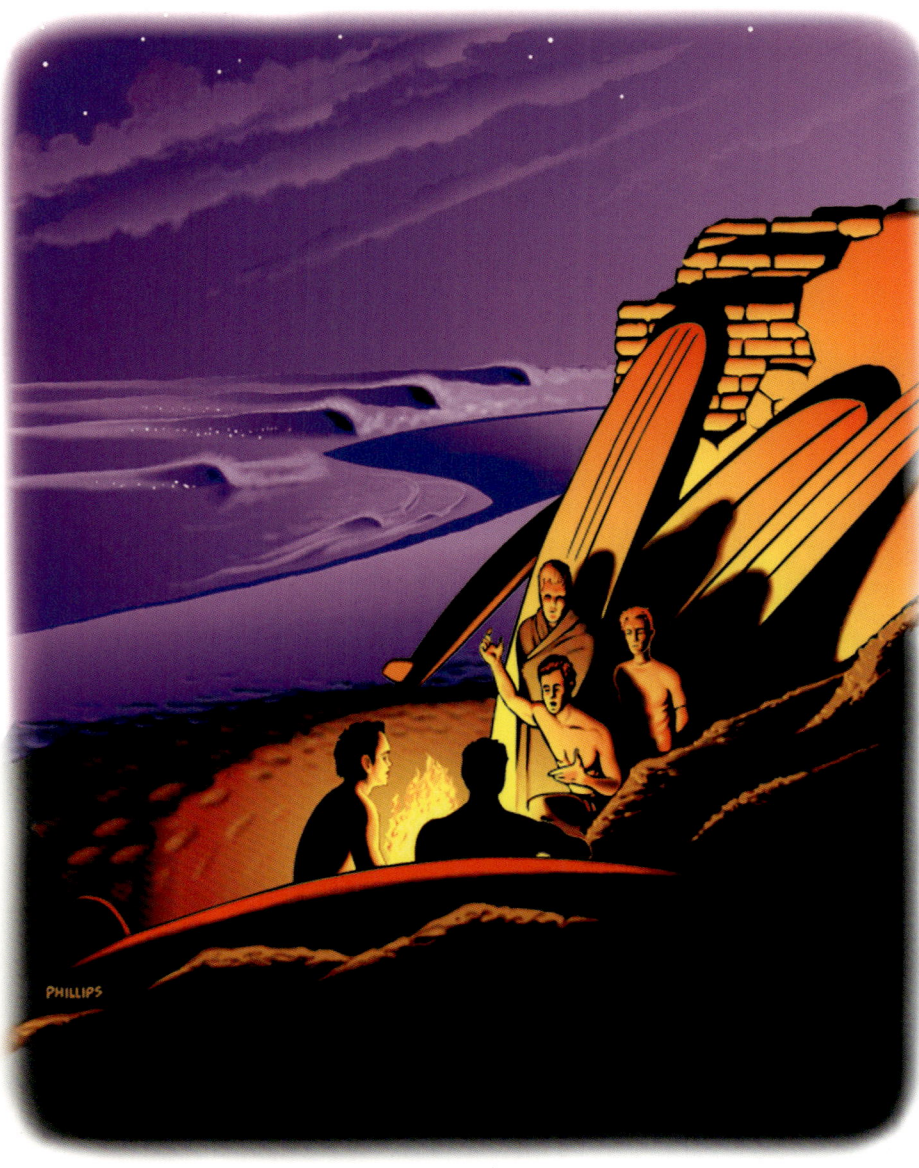

Opposite page: No Surfing, *oil on canvas, 28"x22", 1991. Collection of Bruce Bard.*
Above: Malibu Beach Scene, *appeared full page in* The Surfer's Journal. *Vol. 1, No. 1, 1992.*
Below: Lance's Car, *another illustration for* No Pants Mance *by Denny Aaberg, TSJ, 1992.*

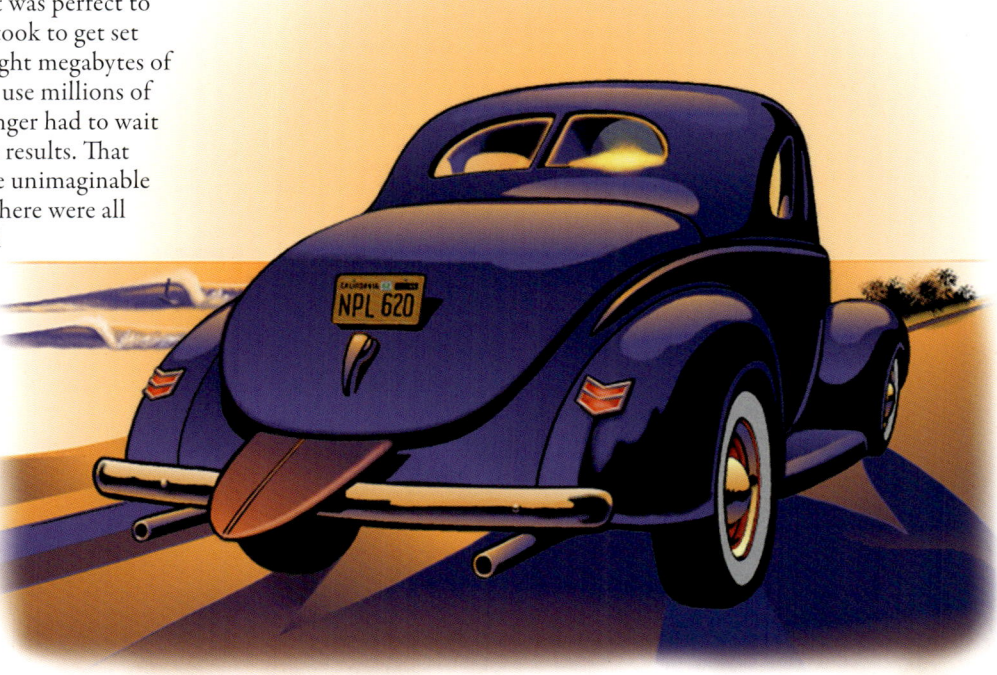

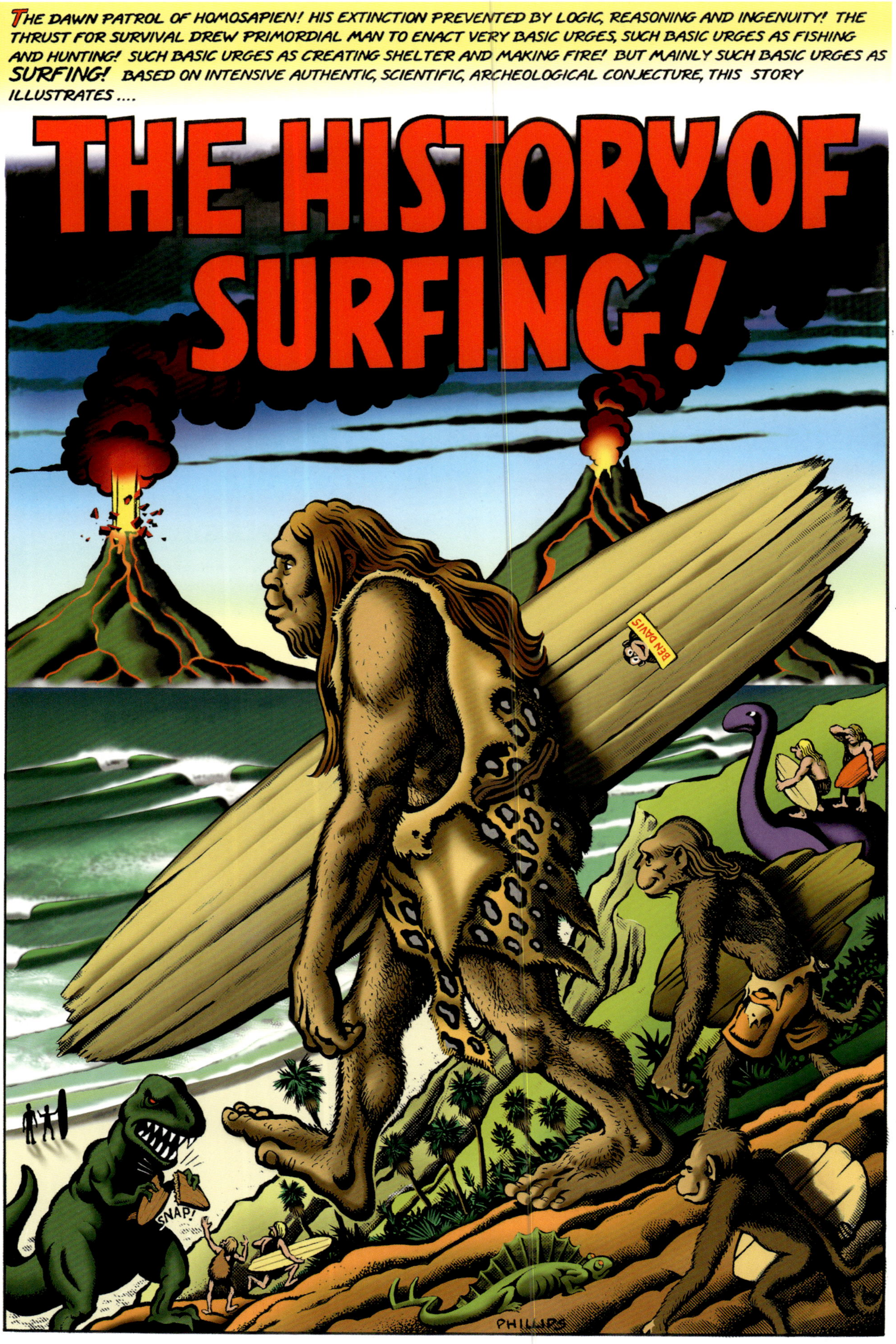

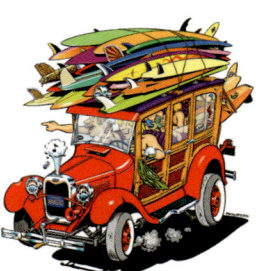

THE DAWN PATROL OF HOMOSAPIEN! HIS EXTINCTION PREVENTED BY LOGIC, REASONING AND INGENUITY! THE THRUST FOR SURVIVAL DREW PRIMORDIAL MAN TO ENACT VERY BASIC URGES, SUCH BASIC URGES AS FISHING AND HUNTING! SUCH BASIC URGES AS CREATING SHELTER AND MAKING FIRE! BUT MAINLY SUCH BASIC URGES AS SURFING! BASED ON INTENSIVE AUTHENTIC, SCIENTIFIC, ARCHEOLOGICAL CONJECTURE, THIS STORY ILLUSTRATES ....

THE HISTORY OF SURFING!

PHILLIPS

This page and 137: The History of Surfing *appeared in* Surf Crazed Comics *No. 2, 1992.*

Opposite page, lower right: Sharky.
Appeared in Surf Crazed Comics *No. 5, 1993*

used that woody logo to learn how to use this powerful new tool, but found out right away that the ancient wiring in his Live Oak bungalow wasn't ready for the 21st century. He called in an electrician for an upgrade, and that guy was hovering around Phillips and at his feet as Phillips fumbled and cursed his way into the computer age. As the electrician was drilling, Phillips got a call from Jeff Girard, the art director at *The Surfer's Journal. TSJ* was a new glossy surf magazine started by Steve Pezman who had been involved with *SURFER* and *Skateboarder* from way back. They wanted two illustrations for their premier issue in January of '92, for a story about Lance Carson by Denny Aaberg, *No Pants Mance.* The assignment was Jim's first commercial job with the new computer, with the computer barely wired up.

MICKEY MUNOZ: *"That night shot of Malibu with the guys sitting around the campfire with the boards leaning up against the Malibu wall and the waves going off in the background is one of the most endearing descriptions of surfing to me. That painting of Jimmy's summed up surfing as well or better than a radical surf shot of a 360 aerial. When you sum it up that is what surfing is all about: Being with your pals and talking about it and planning the next surf adventure and dreaming of waves and hanging out at the beach and the warmth of the fire and the starlight and the beautiful waves coming in. That really is the process of surfing - riding the waves are the icing on the cake. It's what leads up to it, and transpires after it, that really counts. To me that painting represents the circle of surfing, surfing your life!* "

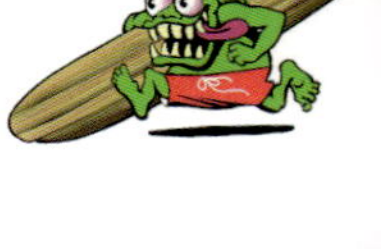

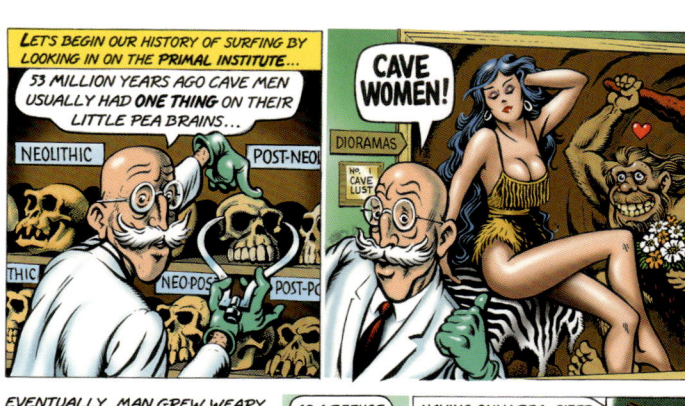
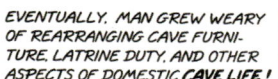
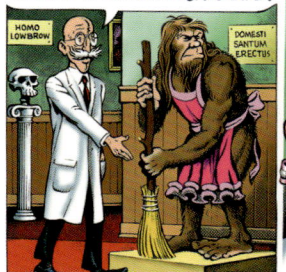
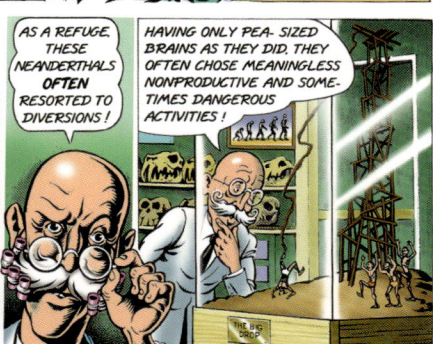
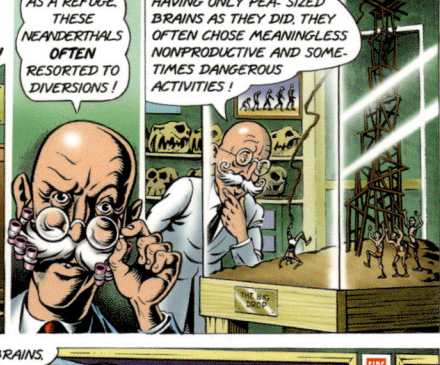
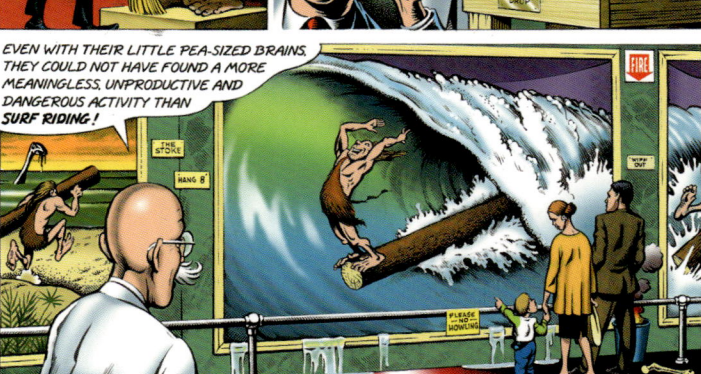
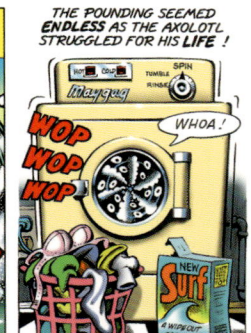
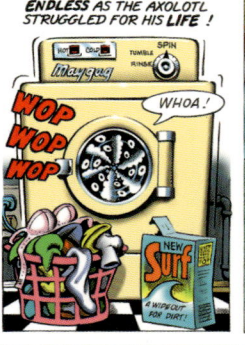
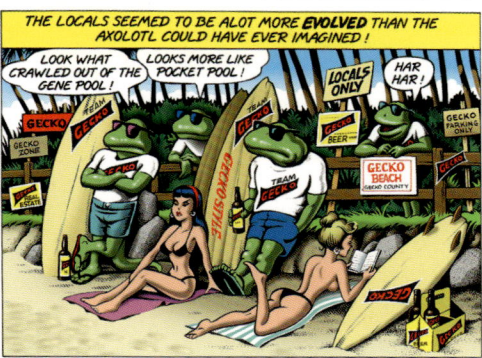
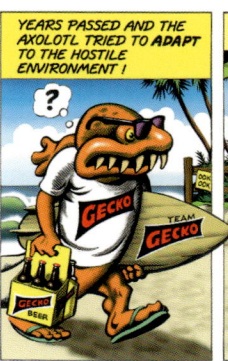
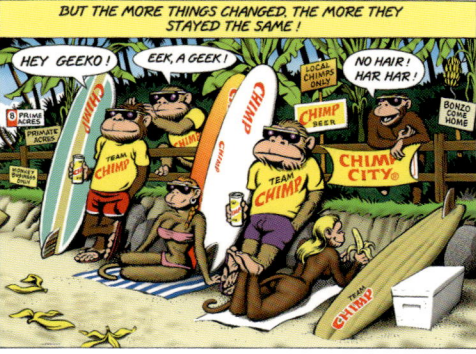
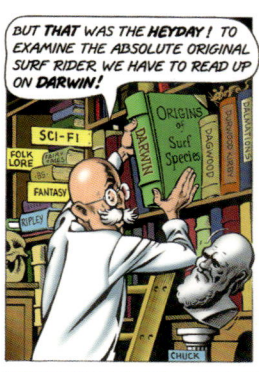
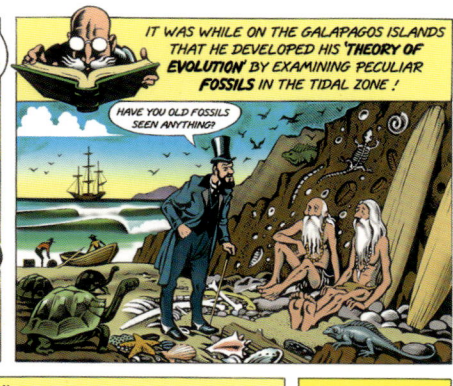
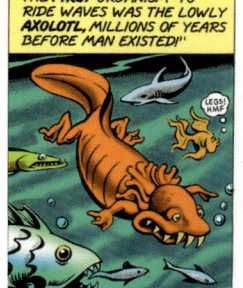
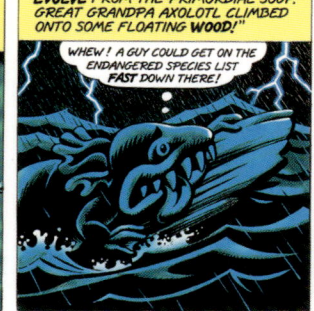
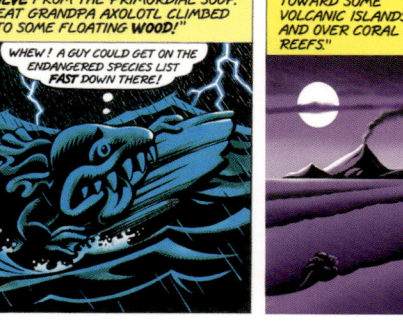
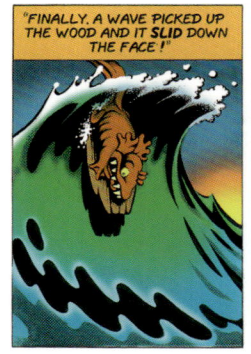
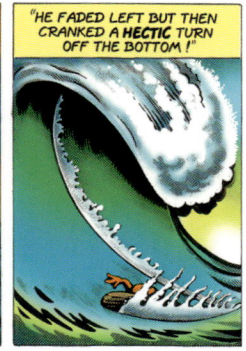
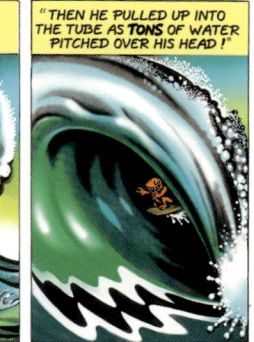
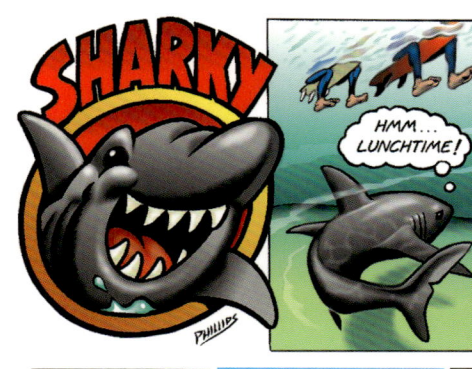
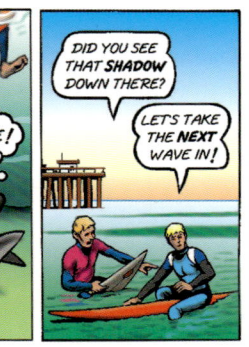
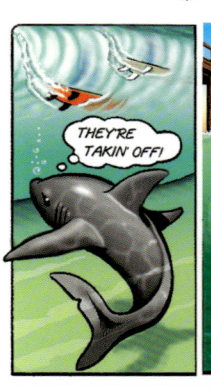
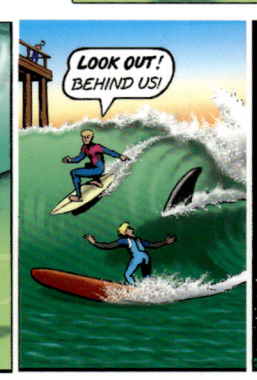
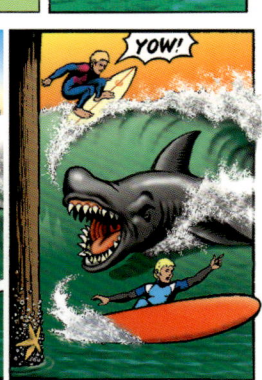
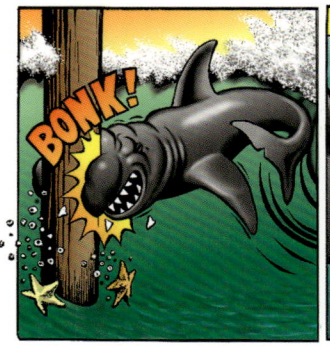
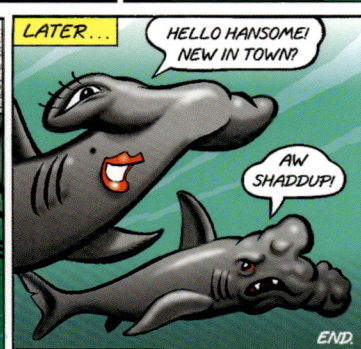

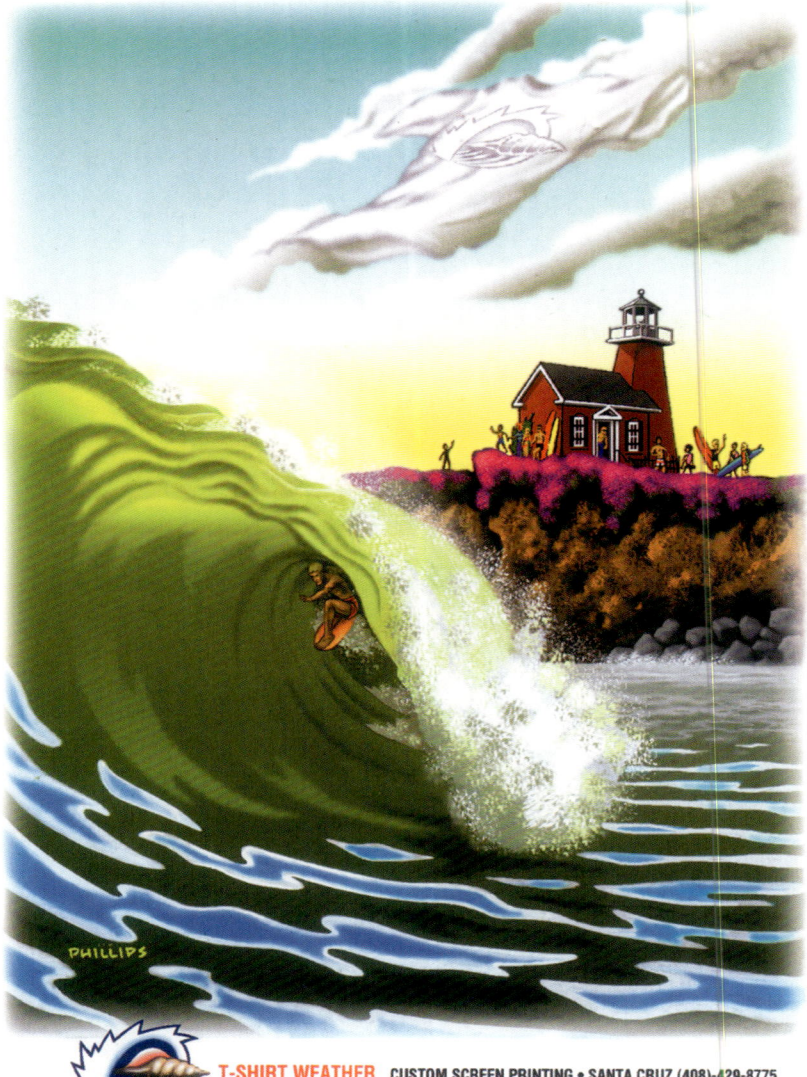

BILL DAWSON: *"My involvement with Jimmy began when I first moved to Santa Cruz and was sharing a house with a common friend of ours, Brian McMahon, in a cabin up in Nisene Marks. On the ceiling were these boards from a wall at 7th Avenue. There was a giant painting of Jesus with the yin and yang symbol below. It was really powerful, and it was the first time I had ever heard of Jim Phillips. Later I lived in another house where Jimmy had painted the living room on this beautiful wood paneling, and around the whole room were characters from comic books: Batman and Spiderman, Superman with long hair, rolling jays. I knew Jimmy's work and I had seen it around town. I met Jimmy in 1991. I had bought the back cover ad space for the longboard club contest at Steamer Lane and so I went to another common friend of ours, Willie Simmons, and asked if he'd call Jimmy about the artwork. His back cover Steamer Lane art was way better than anything they had done for the rest of the contest ads. We did some t-shirts of it and it became the unofficial shirt of the contest. Right after that, we started going surfing together: get up at dawn and go down to Shark's Cove and go surfing. Then I began to wonder what we could do with all this art. I didn't have a print shop, but I had a lot of knowledge in printing and embroidery, and foolishly thought that if we worked hard in the surfing industry, and made some good art, and went to the right places, and did the right things, like having Mickey Munoz international spokesman, we could go somewhere."*

MICKEY MUNOZ: *"I always liked it up north. The northern people were always very cordial. I'm trying to remember when I first met Jimmy. I'd known about his art for many years but it wasn't until the early 90s that I met him at a surf contest at Steamer Lane. It was shortly after that we hooked up on the Pack Your Trash business, so we were in contact a lot more after. I became the sort of ambassador for Pack Your Trash because I had contacts around the world. Unfortunately that business didn't prevail but it was good for awhile and it's still a great idea."*

Pack Your Trash went to the Action Sports Expo of '92, rented a booth, and brought along a few Johnny Rice surfboards to display. They established their line of shirts in thirty surf shops up and down the California coast. At first, Willie Simmons was a partner and salesman, and opened many surf shop accounts, but he got drafted for a Jackson Browne world tour. Bill organized many trash cleanups over the years, and even presented a PYT shirt to Leon Panetta and Sam Farr at the dedication of the Monterey Marine Sanctuary. But to make a long story short, it is hard to get people too interested in trash, even though it's a huge problem in our society.

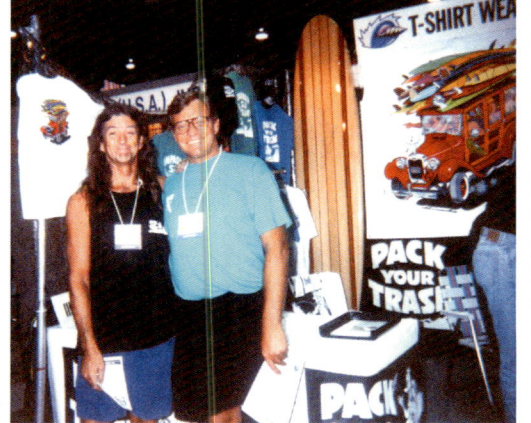

T-SHIRT WEATHER CUSTOM SCREEN PRINTING • SANTA CRUZ (408) 429-8775

Top: T Shirt Weather ad, 1992.
Center: Phillips and Bill Dawson at '93 ASR show.
Below: Ohkuni logo for Kobe Yamauchi's
Sweet Bean shop in Kamakura, Japan

The skateboard revolution entered a new phase and rolled on without Jimmy Phillips. He had severed all ties with NHS and Santa Cruz, and while those companies were losing market share to companies like World Industries and Powell Peralta, they were still generating millions from Speed Wheels and Slime Balls and Independent Trucks and a lot of products branded by Phillips' designs.

In 1992 Jim got a call from Bill Dawson, who ran a contract t-shirt printing company in Santa Cruz called T Shirt Weather. Dawson ordered an ad for the back cover of the Longboard Union surf contest program, and in his conversations with Phillips the word "marketing" came up more than once. He made a t-shirt of the program ad art, a wave in front of the lighthouse, where the contest was held. Sales were good for that shirt, so Dawson brought out a few other of Jim's shirt designs. They produced Jim's "Woody" t-shirts, and then started printing Pack Your Trash t-shirts. Since they were popular and sold well back in the 80s, and there were a lot of bumper stickers still running around town on cars, they included Pack your Trash in the line. Bill and Jimmy were stoked and surfing Shark's Cove every morning at dawn.

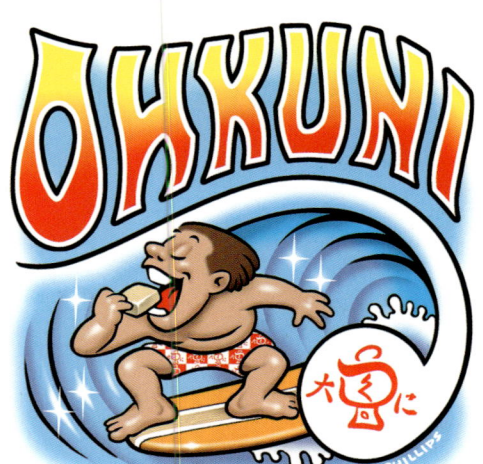

BILL DAWSON: *"We went to the ASR show in San Diego and took Jimmy's wonderful art, and Pack Your Trash t-shirts. We were just walking around the show when we found the Ocean Pacific booth had a surfboard leaning up in front of their display doorway. On that surfboard, down to one of the boogers in the monster's nose, was an exact copy of one of Jimmy's skateboard designs."*

Mickey Munoz connected Phillips with some very good friends in Japan. Mickey introduced Jim to some of the Degawa team who had been to Santa Cruz to surf at the Steamer Lane contests. Kobe Yamauchi, from Kamakura, a team

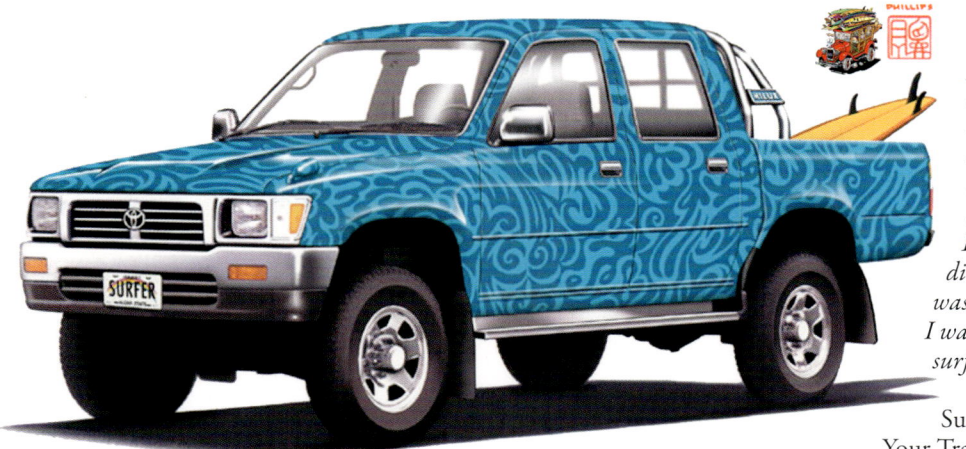

Comprehensive sketch of "magic bus" style pick-up for Toyota of Japan, 1995.

JIRO HANAUE: *"I tried to remember the first time I met Jim. Maybe, Mickey Munoz took me to Jim's place when we surfed for Team Degawa at the Memorial Day contest around 1990. Long before I met Jim, I had known him from his surf art in Surfer Magazine and a friend of mine, Skip Engblom. But one of the best days with Jim was we did dawn patrol at Shark's Cove with Bill Dawson. It was a cold and dark morning but we surfed pretty well. I was so stoked and impressed by Jim's graceful style of surfing on his 8'11" Haut."*

member who is also an artist, took interest in Jim's art. They have since become close friends and keep in touch by daily email. Jiro Hanaue is another Degawa team member who comes to visit the Phillips family most every year.

KOZABURO "KOBE" YAMAUCHI: *"The first meeting with Jim was one of the grooviest experiences in my life. It happened in May 1993. Bill Dawson introduced me to Jim. I surfed with Jim and Bill Dawson at Shark's Cove. I was so impressed by Jim's surfing performance. That was real soul surfing. After surfing, me and Bill were invited to a barbecue dinner at Jim's house. We had a really good time with Jim and Dolly. He showed me various rock posters and surf art that night. I felt on this first meeting that we had been old friends."*

Surfers in Japan were very receptive to the Pack Your Trash t-shirts that Jim and Bill marketed. Munoz also introduced Jim to Degawa team owner Michio Degawa, who owns one of the largest surf shops in Japan, and Michio hired Jim for additional t-shirt designs. Toyota of Japan came to Degawa for help to market their Sports Pickup to surfers. He recommended Phillips. Toyota's first request was for a comp for a 'Magic Bus' psychedelic paint job. Jim had always believed cars should be decorated. He turned in some comps and even suggestions of how to dip a car in swirling color. Apparently those ideas were reconsidered, because then they said they just wanted a logo saying "Sports Pickup," for which they insisted on paying a substantial amount. Jim's Japanese was somewhat limited, so when the request for a Japanese television Toyota commercial came down, he wasn't sure exactly what was happening. But sure enough, Brentwood Pictures came up from southern California to film it. They filmed Jim at the beach and in his studio. Jim used Japanese phrases, and professed inspiration by Hokusai, but none of that got used. They did use shots of Jim with Rosie, Jim's old pickup truck, stacked with his surfboard collection. They sent one of the tapes that aired on Japanese TV: It had six slick high-tech ads for Toyota cars, and then Jim.

Filming of TV commercial for Toyota of Japan, 1995.

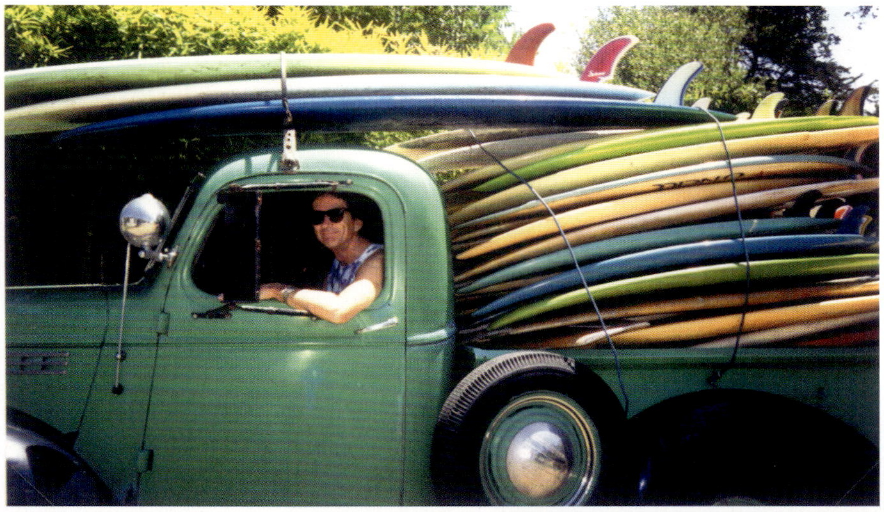

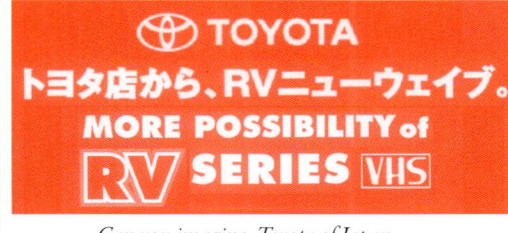

Can you imagine, Toyota of Japan filming a Chevy pick up for a Japanese TV commercial?

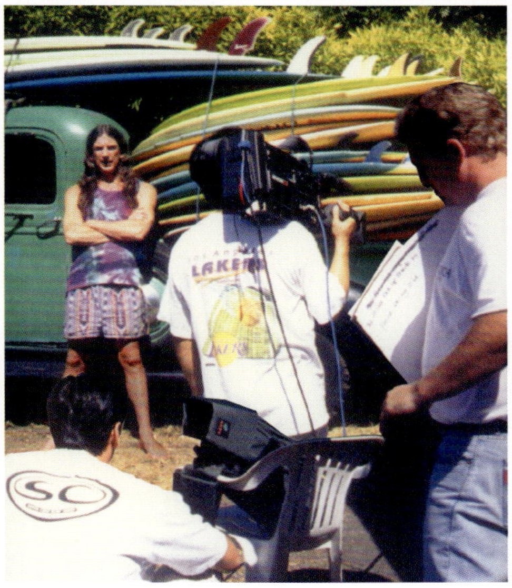

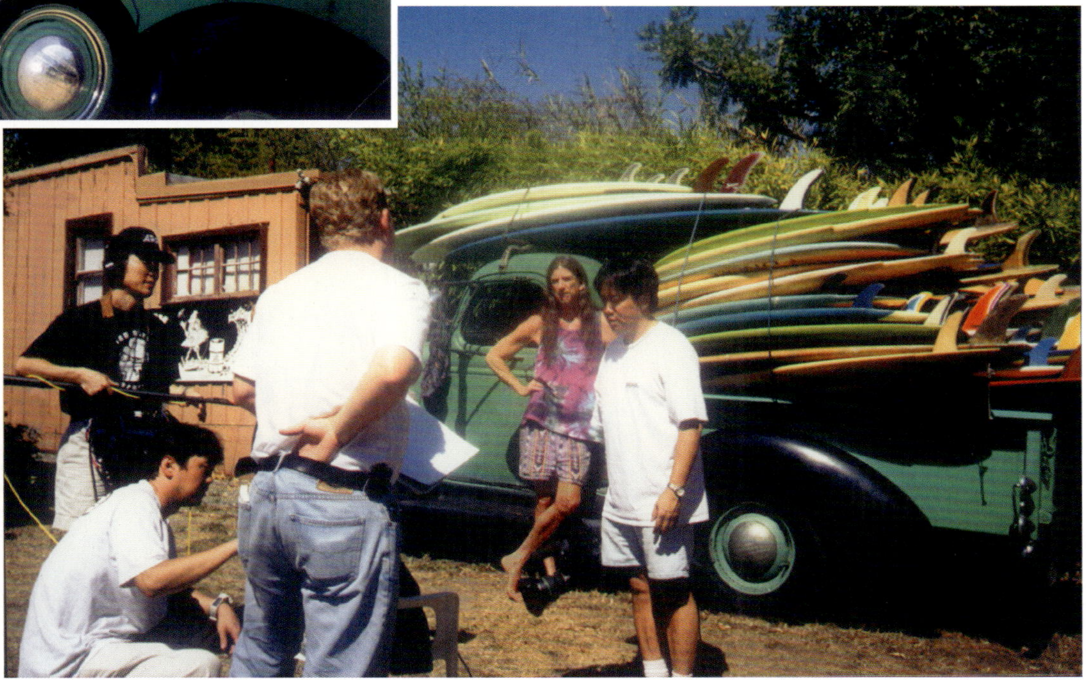

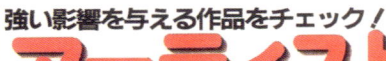

アーティスト

・ムーブメントに参加し、ヒッピーカルチャーに影響を与えた偉人だ。彼の息子と活動している。サンディエゴ在住のハリー・デイリーは、絵画、グラヴィティ

数々の時代を作って
きたアーティスト

Jim Phillips ジム・フィリップス

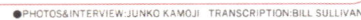

●PHOTOS&INTERVIEW:JUNKO KAMOJI TRANSCRIPTION:BILL SULLIVAN

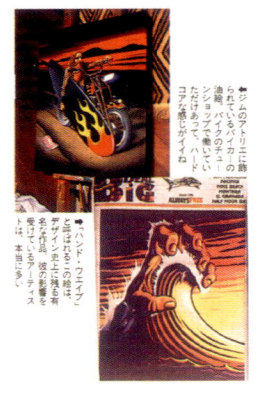

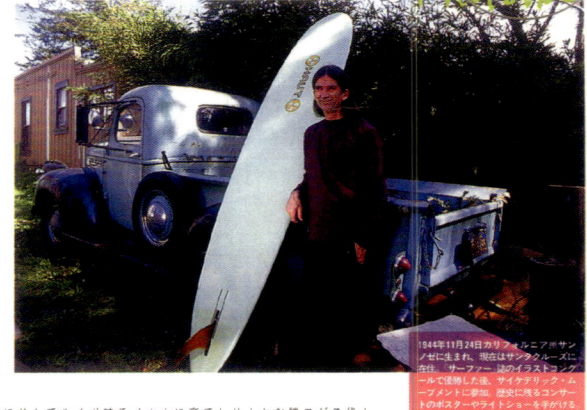

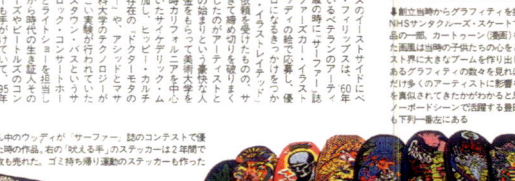

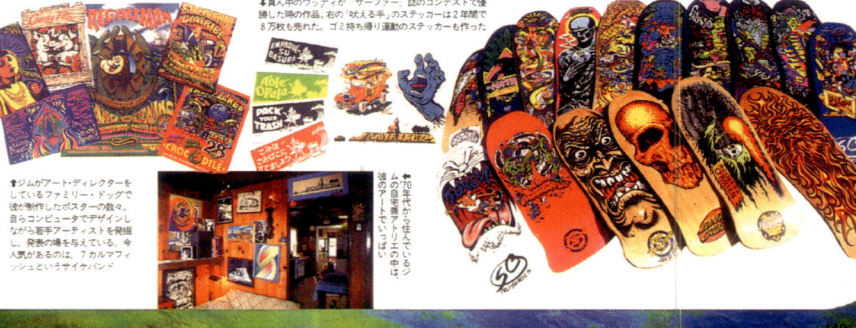

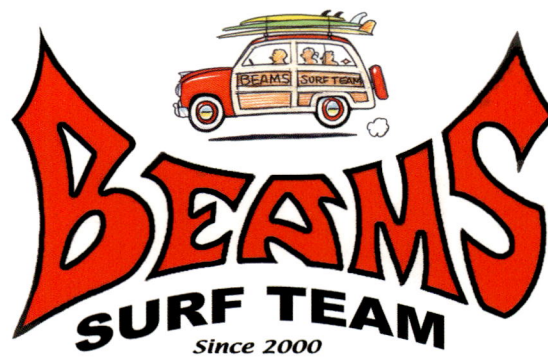

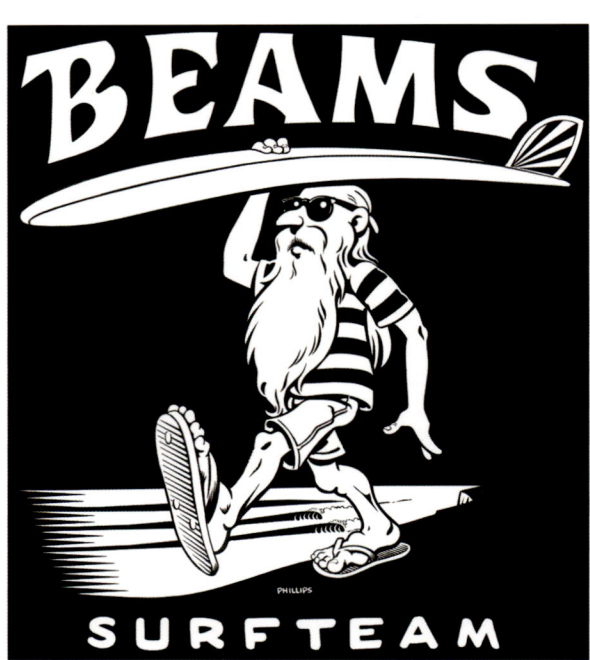

Club T-shirt design, 2001.

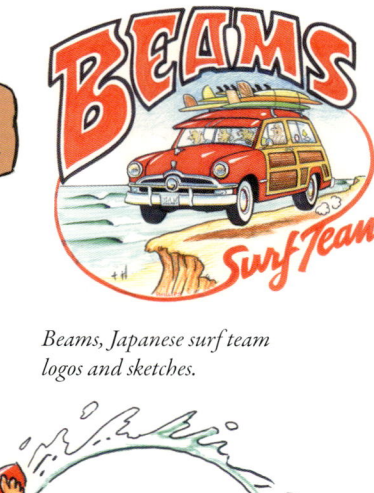

Beams, Japanese surf team
logos and sketches.

Above: A page from Fine *magazine,*
1997, one of several articles
on Jim's art in Japanese
magazines.

Left: Fine *magazine*
issue cover.

Below left: *Japanese*
PYT sticker.

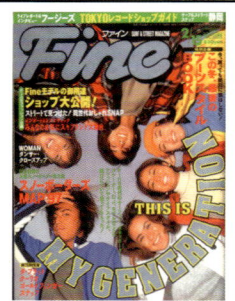

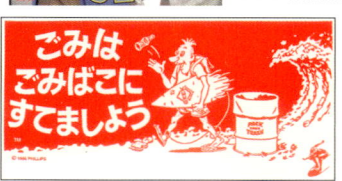

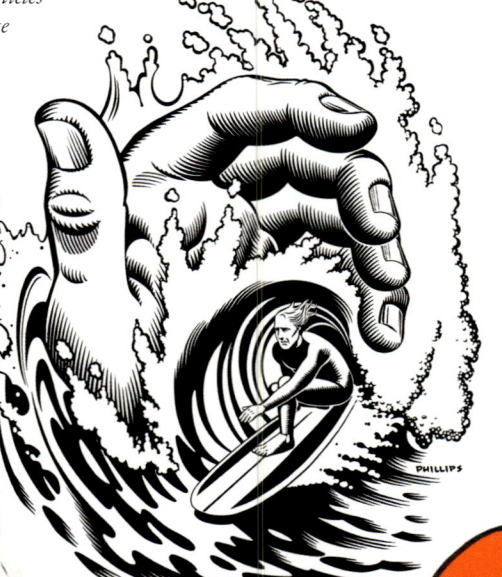

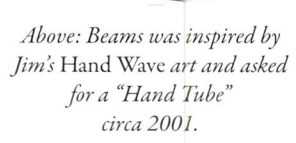

Above: Beams was inspired by
Jim's Hand Wave *art and asked*
*for a "*Hand Tube*"*
circa 2001.

Suketchi.

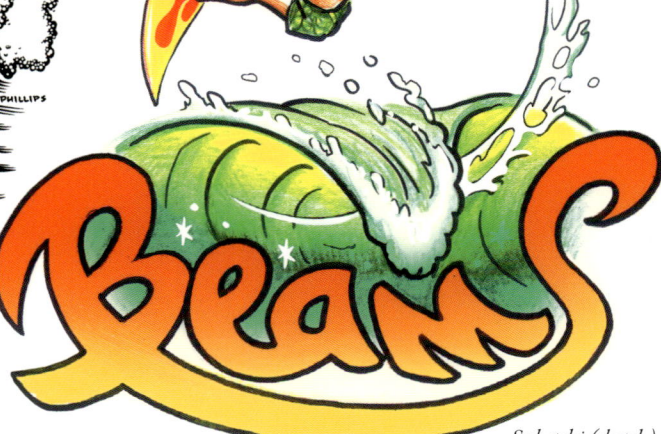

Suketchi (sketch).

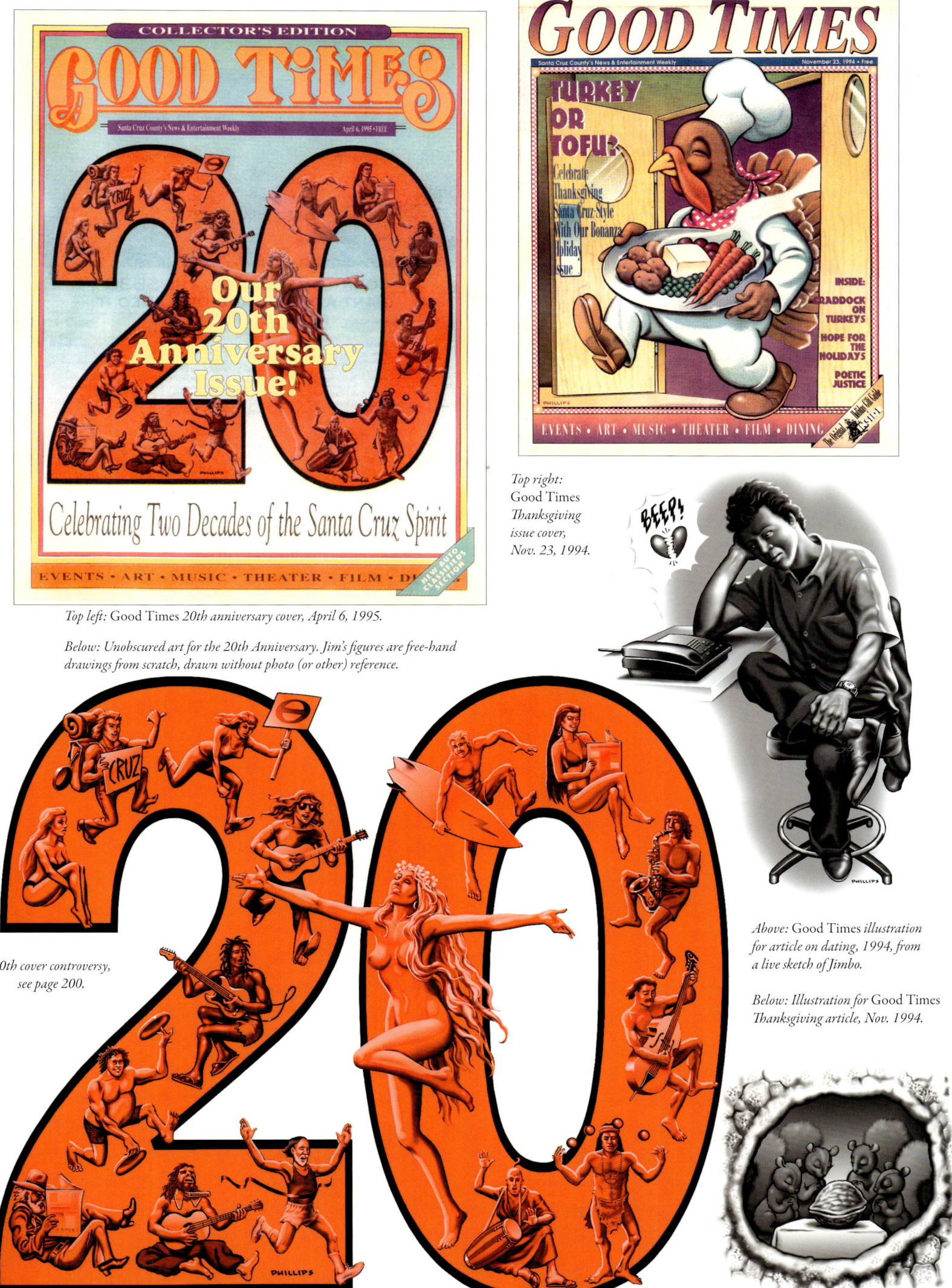

Top left: Good Times *20th anniversary cover, April 6, 1995.*

Below: Unobscured art for the 20th Anniversary. Jim's figures are free-hand drawings from scratch, drawn without photo (or other) reference.

Top right:
Good Times
Thanksgiving
issue cover,
Nov. 23, 1994.

20th cover controversy,
see page 200.

Above: Good Times *illustration for article on dating, 1994, from a live sketch of Jimbo.*

Below: Illustration for Good Times *Thanksgiving article, Nov. 1994.*

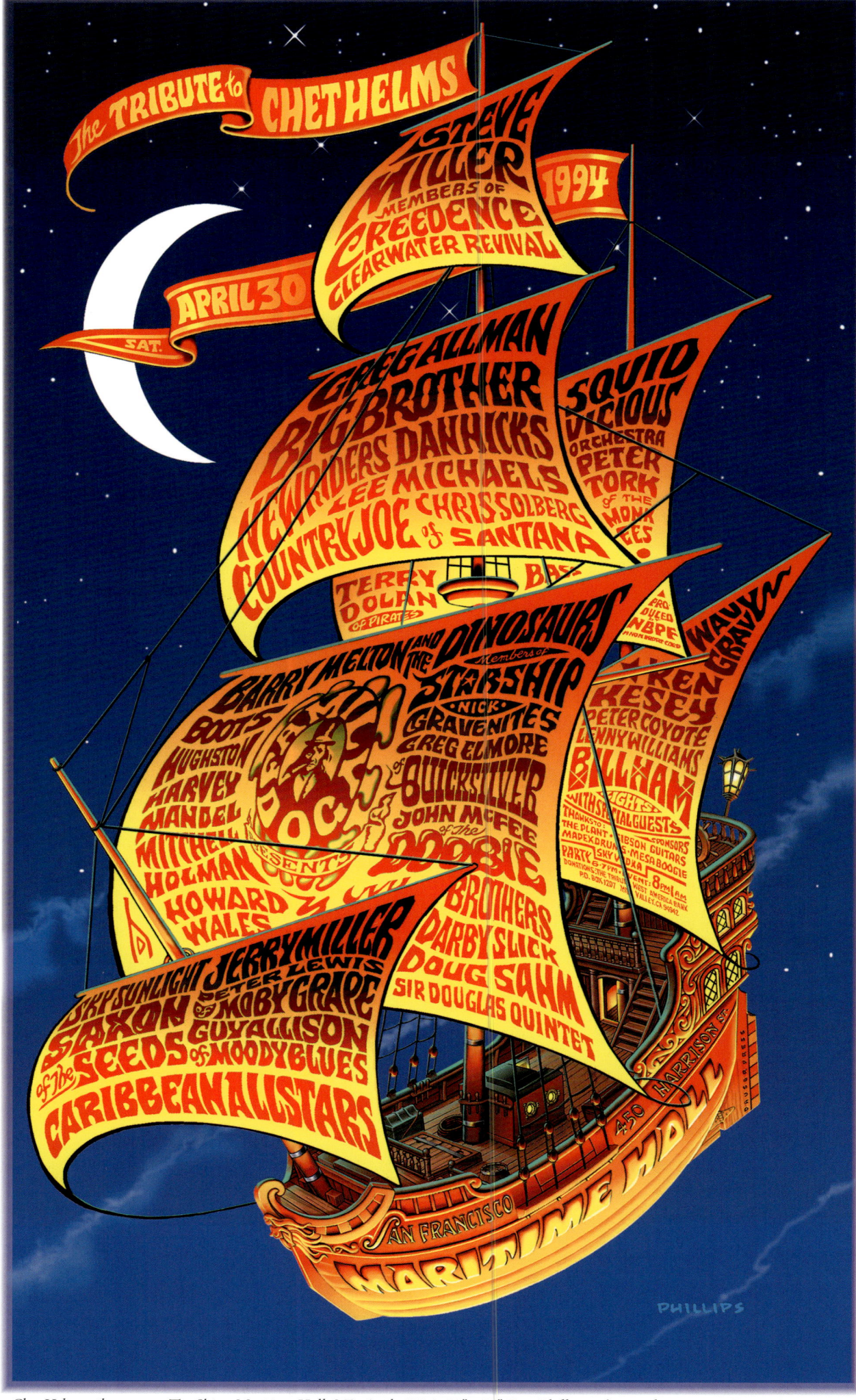

In 1986, Abbeyville Press published a 13" by 11", 500-page, ten pound book called *The Art of Rock*. The author, Paul Grushkin, wrote in a copy that Phillips received for his contribution, "To Jim Phillips, whose art opened my eyes!" Jim's works in the book include: the Moby Grape "Witch" poster, the Santa Cruz Civic Tubes poster and the Boulder Creek Theater Benefit.

PAUL GRUSHKIN (from Art of Rock): *"Throughout California, a number of regionally based artists created works in a variety of identifiable styles. One such...was Jim Phillips, who made his home near Santa Cruz, on the coast south of San Francisco. His graphic work garnered local acclaim: it appeared frequently on concert posters, in newspaper ads, and on magazine covers. His cartoon-style drawings were always distinctive, and many believe Phillips is one of a number of obscure artists deserving much wider recognition."*

While Phillips' Santa Cruz posters might have been underrepresented, in the end that book rekindled an interest in rock art that helped him work his way through the 90s. Jim had been getting some interest in his Witch posters from people who had seen the book and tracked him down. In October of 1993 he bought a booth at Wes Wilson's 2nd Annual Rock Art Expo & Ball at the Hall of Flowers in Golden Gate Park in San Francisco. Mouse, Kelley, Singer, Conklin and many of the other great psychedelic artists were

Chet Helms tribute poster, The Ship, *Maritime Hall, S.F., April, 1994, 17" x 25". First Phillips rock poster by computer, Dauser Press.*

there. At the show, Jim displayed what few old posters from the Santa Cruz series that he had left, not having done any recent editions since '84. At the show, one collector came by and paid a couple hundred dollars each for three of his posters. That was a hook, but his inventory suddenly seemed extremely limited.

RUSTY GOLDMAN aka PROFESSOR POSTER: *"Jimmy Phillips is a prince disguised as a cartoonist. He was my next-door neighbor at the first Wes Wilson Poster Show at the Hall of Flowers. We got very close during the show, and I told him I recognized his talent immediately. I asked him if he would be so inclined as to put his impressions of who and what Professor Poster is on a card. And I asked his fee. He looked at me with the nicest eyes and said, 'Professor, let me just ride your coattails!' And that was such a wonderful compliment. Well, he did a very nice drawing of a steamer trunk full of posters with a top hat and a cane, and that was just me. I use it on my cards and website to this day."*

In March of 1994, Phillips began a relationship with Bruce Dauser, a printer who had seen those posters in *The Art of Rock* and stopped by Phillips' booth at the '93 Hall of Flowers show.

BRUCE DAUSER: *"The thing was, before Jimmy and I met at that show, probably 2 or 3 years before that, I'd seen a bunch of his Santa Cruz work that was printed over at Quality Printers through Derek who worked there. For probably, say, at least for 3 years I kept saying, 'I've gotta get a hold of this guy Jim Phillips; we've gotta do a poster.' Then this thing with Chet came up, and that just worked out ideal."*

"Bruce Dauser was one of the original Haight Ashbury hippies, hanging out with Janis Joplin at 1090 Page Street," Dolly explains. He had connections. Dauser had gotten word that Boots Hughston was promoting a Chet Helms Tribute Benefit, and needed a poster.

BRUCE DAUSER: *"Albert Nieman called me and said that they needed another poster done. I think he heard it from Chet, not from Boots Hughston originally. And then I talked to Chet about it, and I said, 'You know, I think I have an artist that will do this.' That's when I called Jimmy and Chet said, 'Okay, go with it.' Albert had gone to SF State back in '65, and bumped into all these people hangin' there, and then migrated over to the Haight Ashbury. He knew Chet and all the people. In '66 he opened New Reflections on Cole St., and a few months later I became a partner in that. When that store opened there were only maybe three or four stores open in the Haight at that time."*

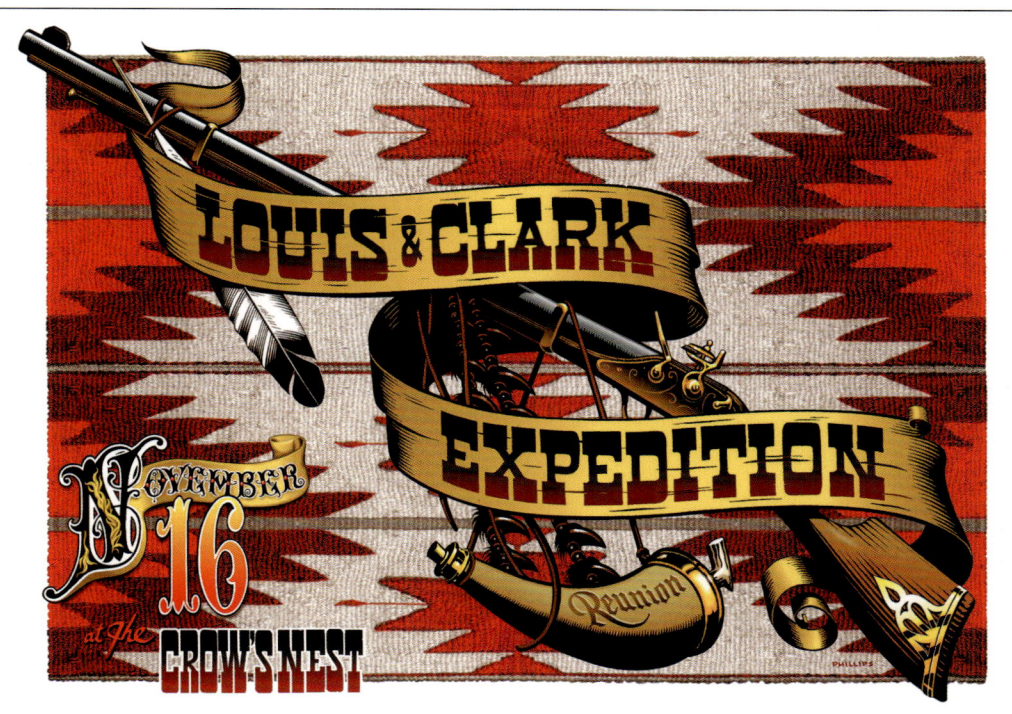

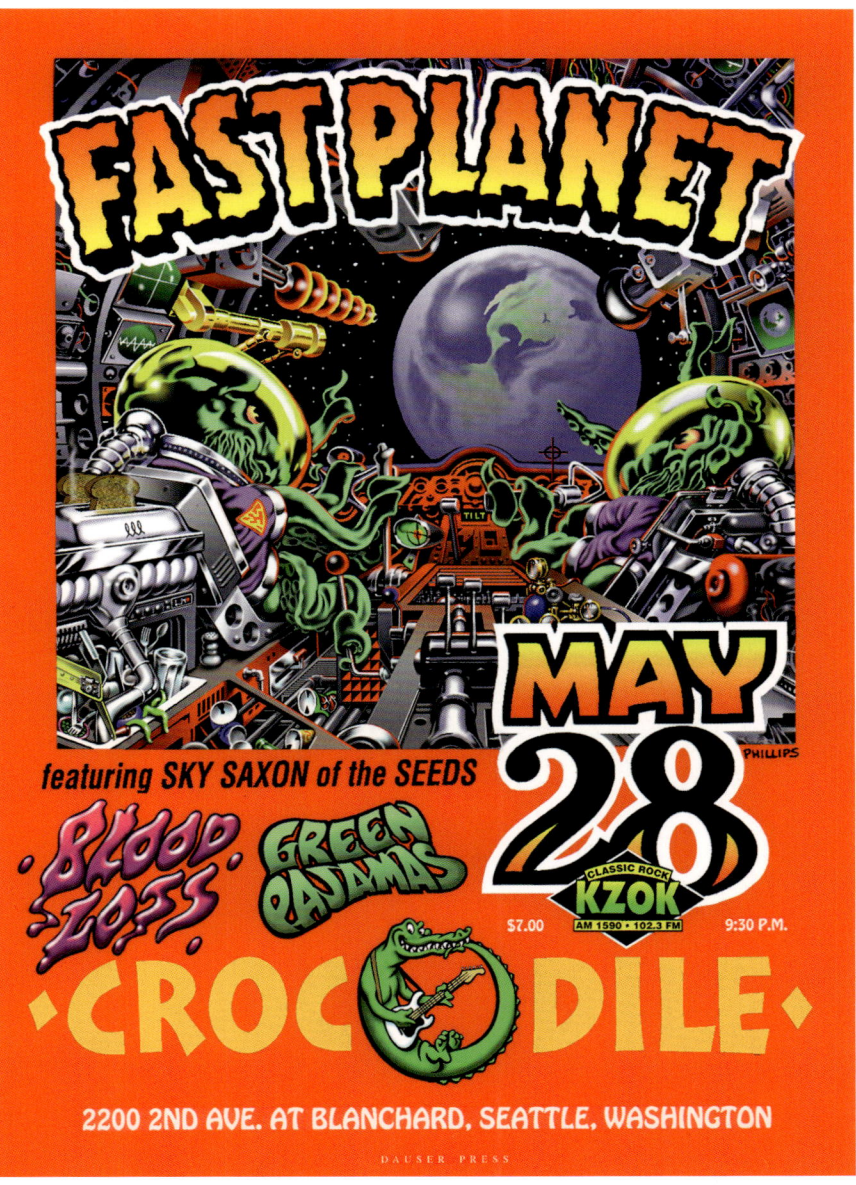

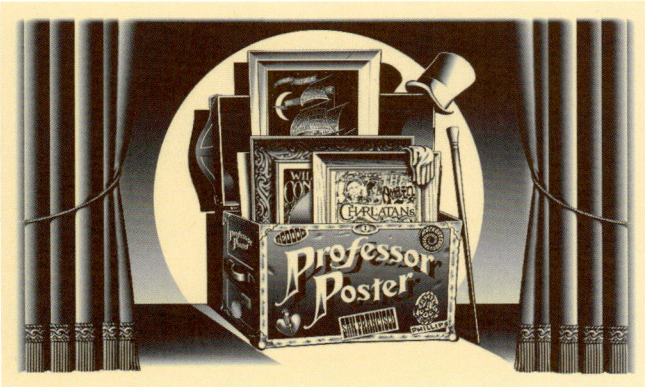

Professor Poster's calling card, 1994.

Louis & Clark Reunion, *Crow's Nest, 11"x16" 1994. Numbered edition of 300, Quality Offset printing.*

Fast Planet, *featuring Sky Saxon of the Seeds, at the Crocodile Lounge, Seattle, Wa. 1994, 12"x 8 1/4". Printing: Dauser Press.*

143

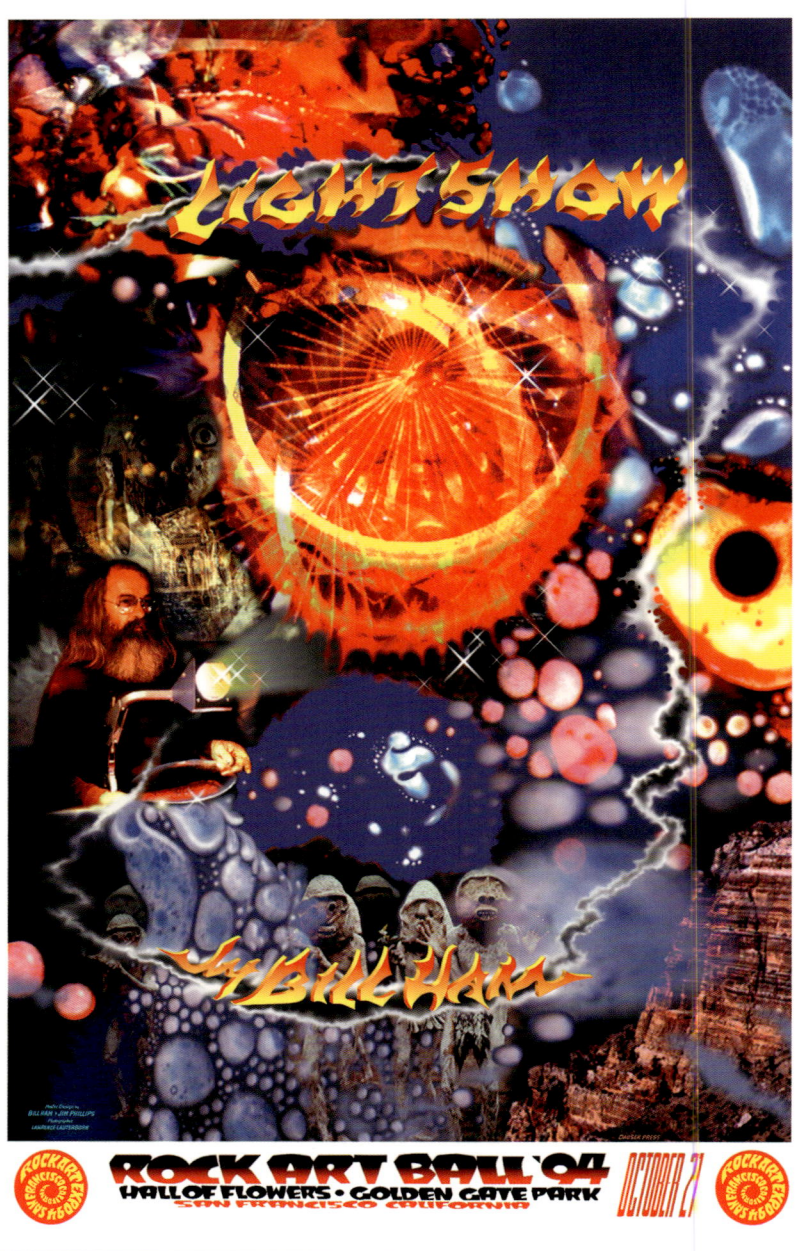

Top: Bill Ham Light Show *poster, 1994, 15"x22". Printed & produced by Dauser Press.*
Below: Bill Ham Dance Machine, *show cancelled, poster unpublished.*

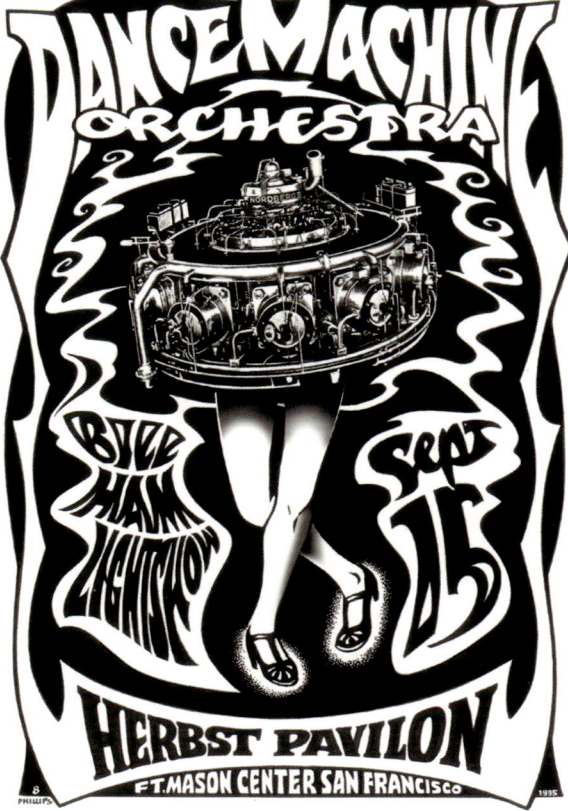

Bottom: *"Theda," Bill Ham show at Herbst Pavillion, 1995, 6"x10". Printed & produced by Dauser Press (show cancelled).*

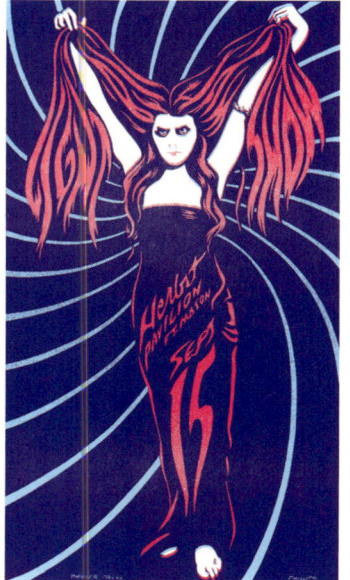

Wes Wilson and Alton Kelley were already doing posters for the show, but rock superstar Steve Miller had just signed on and Boots wanted a poster including the Space Cowboy for the complete lineup. Stanley Mouse was scheduled to do a poster for that show, but Bill Graham Presents offered him work for the Fillmore's grand reopening the same night as the Helms show. It must have been an offer he couldn't refuse. At any rate, it allowed an opportunity for Jim to get involved in posters again.

As it turned out, the cover of SF Chronicle Datebook used Mouse's design but he eventually turned out a Tribute poster after all, with a parody theme. It also turned out later that Steve Miller was ill and unable to attend, so it was sort of a fluke that Phillips was the one chosen to do the poster. Phillips was ubiquitous again, as that poster was hung up all around San Francisco as the basic advertising unit for the show.

STANLEY MOUSE: *"There is a new consciousness, in life and in art. History will reveal this. Jim Phillips is riding the crest of this wave."*

Phillips' concept for the Chet Helms poster was a Ghost Ship, sailing through the heavens, with an incredible array of talent on the sails: Steve Miller, Creedence Clearwater Revival, Gregg Allman, Big Brother, Dan Hicks, Lee Michaels, Country Joe, Santana, The Doobie Brothers. A night of a thousand stars, sailing through the stars. At the time of the Tribute poster, it was the largest computer project Jim had worked on. He had only 8 MB of RAM memory, since it was quite expensive back then, a primitive operating system and the early software versions of the day, such as Photoshop 2.

Perhaps needless to say, Phillips had many late-night crashes. Late on the last night of the Helms poster, he accidentally trashed the sails with all the names on them! It represented two days of meticulous hand lettering by computer. At 3 AM, he lost the sails. Devastated, and shaky, he called Bruce to tell him he had trashed the file and that it was all over. Bruce told Jim to forget about it and just go to bed, that he would recover the next day. Bruce called the printer in the morning and pushed the schedule back a day. The following day Dolly helped Jim redraw the names and sails with ink on paper. After scanning that, he had to connect the file with the sails to the ship's hull which were on two separate files, but it failed repeatedly because of the limited memory. It took 6 hours of trying and retrying until Jim finally drastically reduced the poster size and filesize.

BRUCE DAUSER: *"It was 6:30 AM when finally it did go through, and worked. I think I was out of there at around 7 AM getting the film in, so that they could run the film out the same day. John from Post Digital was gracious enough to understand it was a benefit, so instead of charging us double for the rush, he saved us a day on the film. That was how we made up that day and recovered the time he lost the night before. Jim was basically fooling the system. He figured out what no one else figured out, that you could go down to 150 resolution and still get by with it, because of the limited memory he had. When he kept trying to paste the ship to the sails, which you had to do to put them back together, the time bar would go across, and then we'd wait a long time, and then it would crash. It got late but we kept trying for hours, and every time we tried, our eyes closed and we'd want to go to sleep. So finally he lowered it all the way down to 133 dpi, and it worked beautifully."*

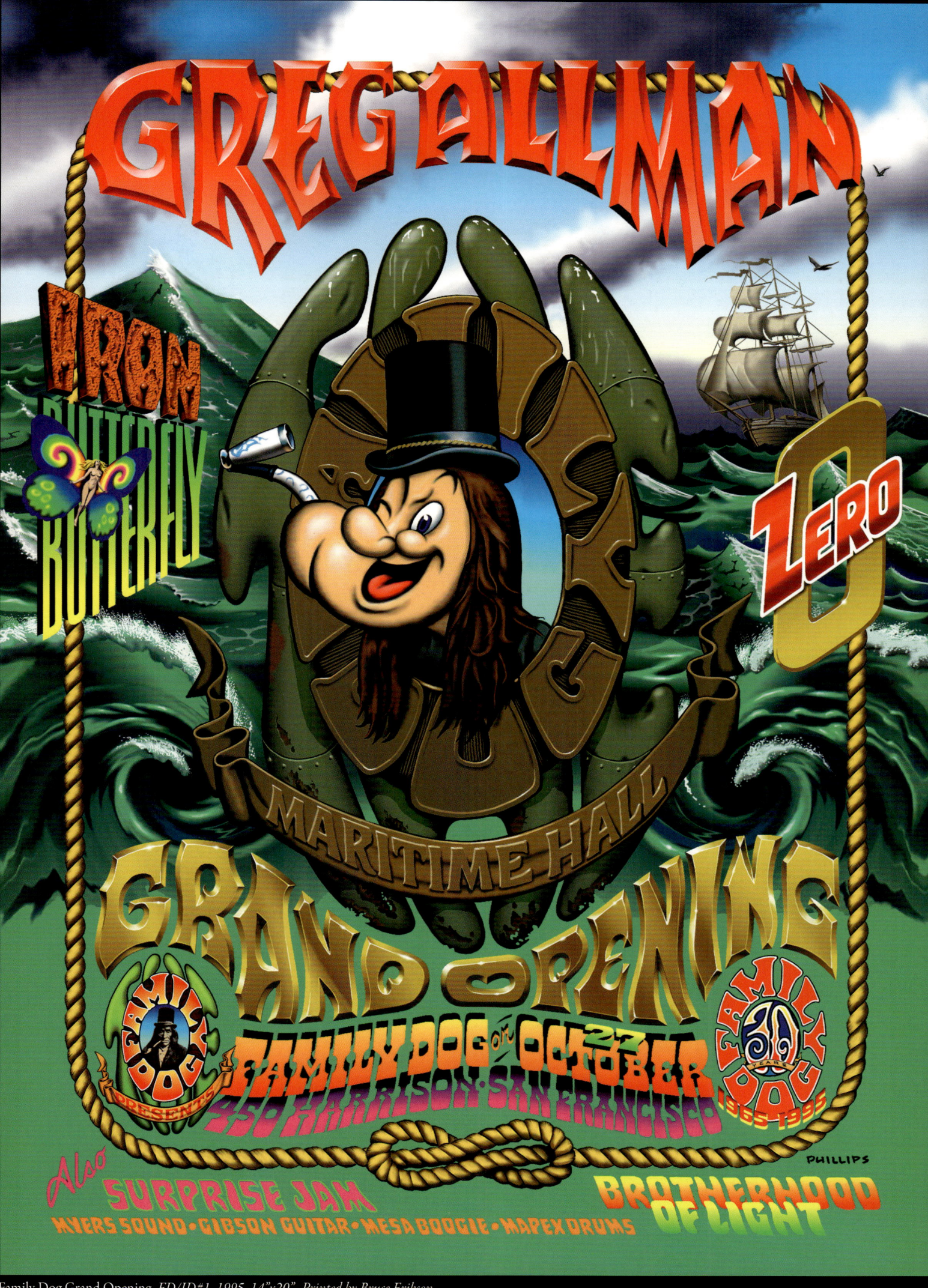

Family Dog Grand Opening, *FD/ID#1, 1995, 14"x20". Printed by Bruce Erikson.*

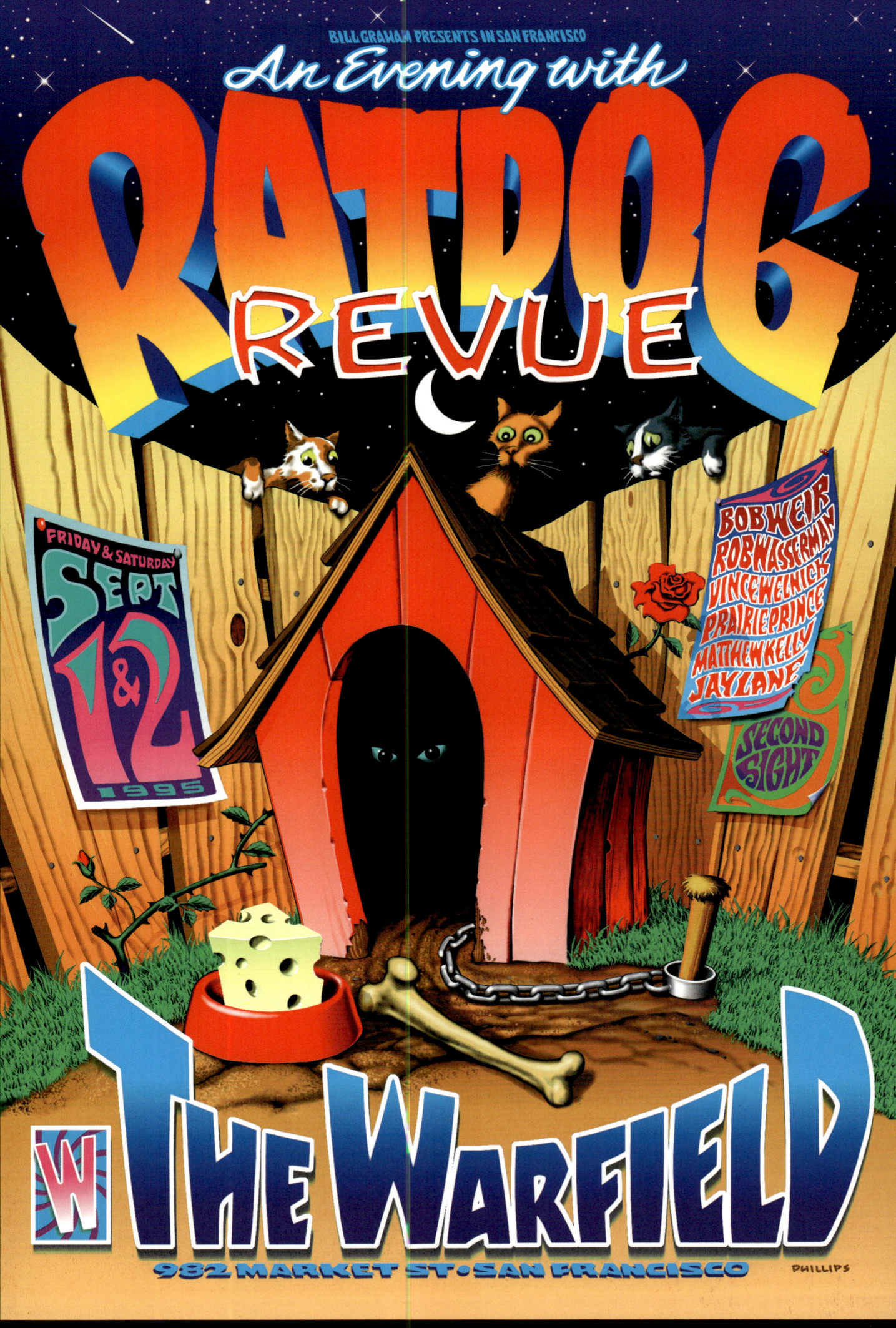

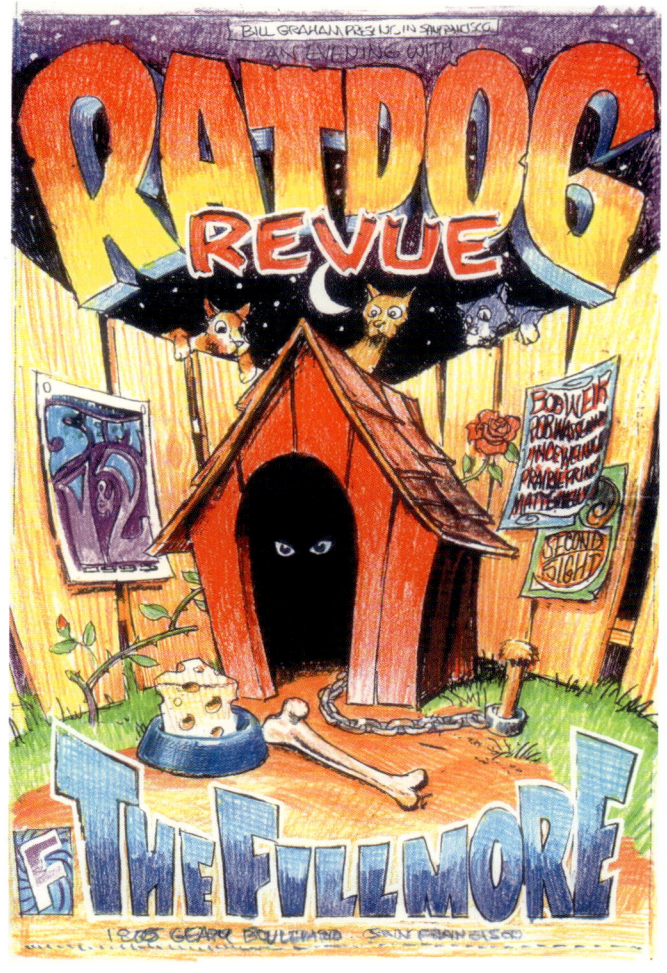

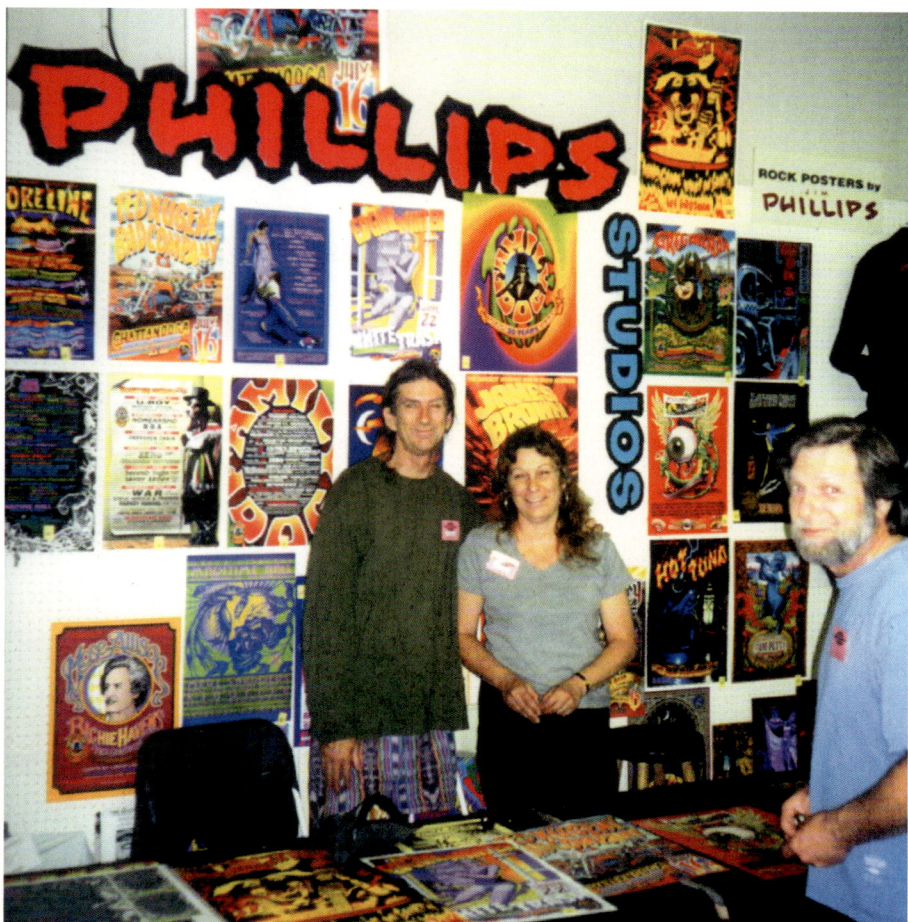

The Chet Helms Tribute was a success. It was a night of several dozen stars from the 60s, the ones with their names painstakingly lettered into the poster, which was also a hit, and sold like hotcakes. Almost as soon as Phillips set up a table in the downstairs lobby to sell the posters, the overhead lights went out. Jim looked at Mouse, over at the next table, who just shrugged. It was too dark to see the wares. Then Jim remembered that he packed a small Tensor light, so he got it out and mounted it below the Tribute poster that was hanging on the wall. It was like a beacon. People couldn't keep their eyes off of it. They lined up to buy it, signed by the artist. The line stayed until four a.m. and that made the hippie/capitalist/artist a believer about the viability of the collectible rock poster market.

The computer eventually came to be a common method of creating rock posters, pushing former methods into the "old world." Phillips was ahead of his time, and somewhat surprised that the San Francisco artists were mostly unequipped with computer capabilities. Eventually, other poster artists climbed aboard, with a few on Phillips' encouragement.

Bruce Dauser introduced Jimmy to Bill Ham, one of the pioneers of psychedelic light shows in San Francisco during the mid-sixties. He looked the part, with his long, white flowing beard and hair. He lived in one of a row of tall old Victorian houses on Pine Street. "The first time I visited his house," Phillips said, "I noticed the house where I lived back in '67 was right next door." Jim spotted a psychedelic window he had painted, that had survived 27 years. Jim looked through that house, since it was empty and owned by Jamie, Bill's landlord, but none of the murals he had done for Michael Brown or any other evidence of his earlier stay was evident, except the window. Jamie was remodeling the house and just about to replace the window, so he gave it to Jim, who managed to photograph it before it accidentally shattered in his garage.

Opposite page: Ratdog poster, BGP#127, 1995, 13"x19". Printing: Great Impressions.

Above: Ratdog rough sketch submitted to BGP, note venue change.

Top right: Rock Art Expo T-shirt (black shirts), 1994.

Bottom left: Derek Knepper, and the four-color press he operated at Quality Offset, holding the first Helms tribute poster.

Bottom right: Jim and Dolly at a rock poster expo, 1996. Bruce Dauser looks on at right.

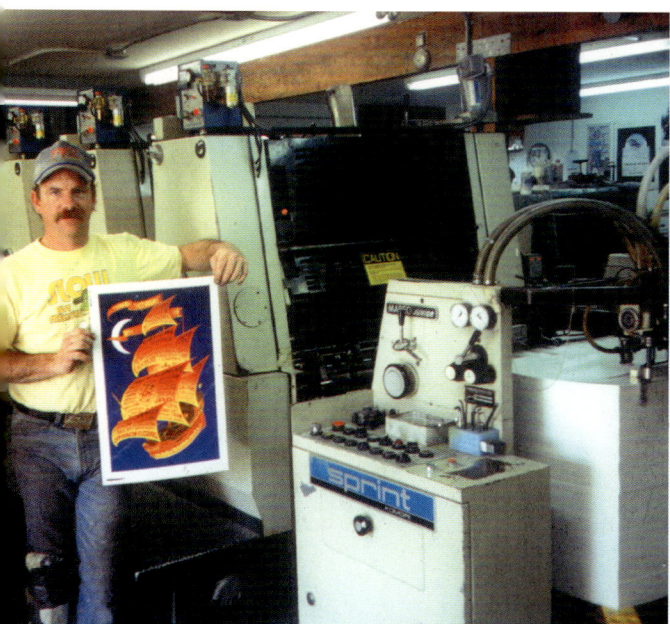

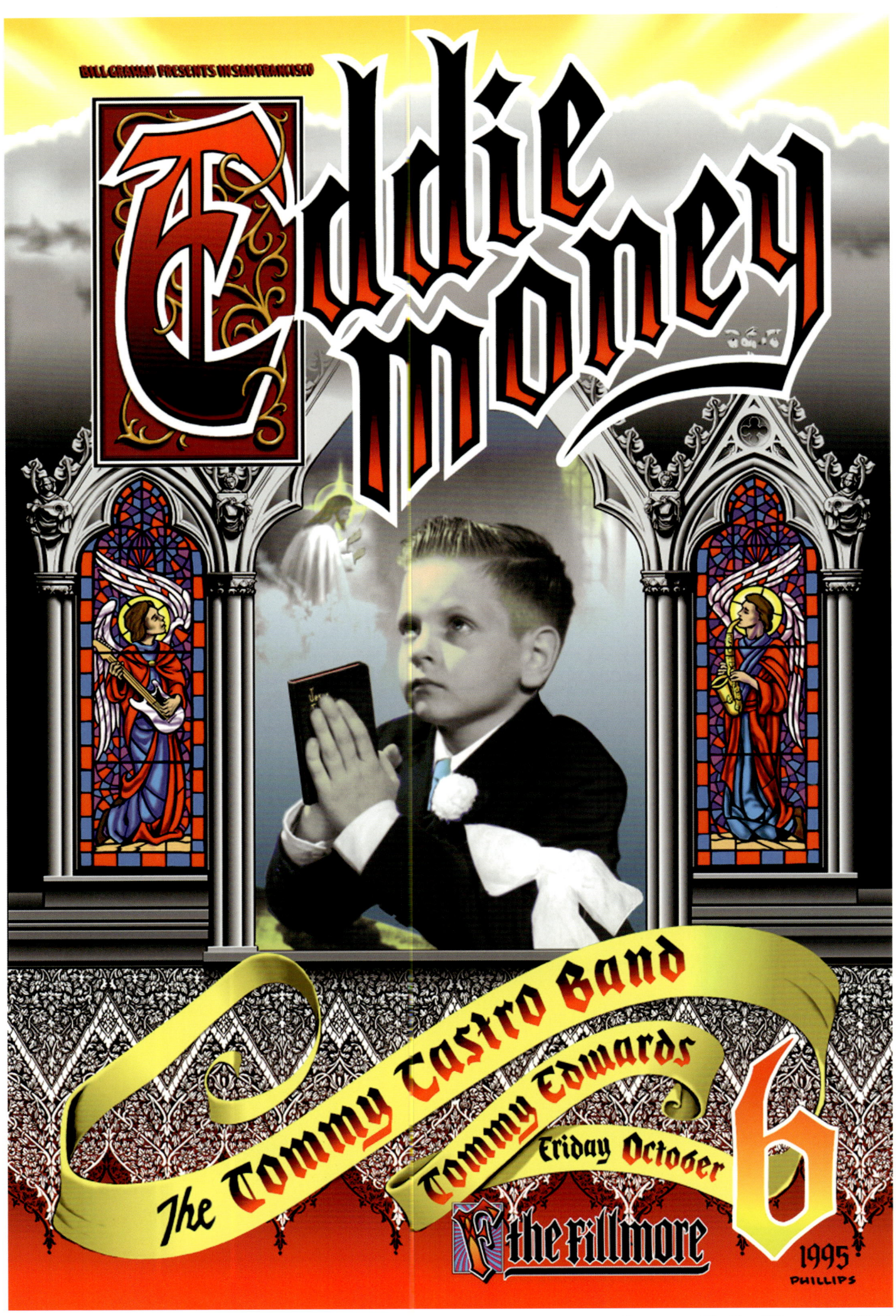

Eddie Money *poster, #F200, 1995 13"x19". Printing: Great Impressions.*
The photo of Eddie praying to the Lord was from his first communion.

Opposite page: Hot Tuna *Fillmore poster, #F207,*
BGP, 1995, 13"x19". Printing: Great Impressions.

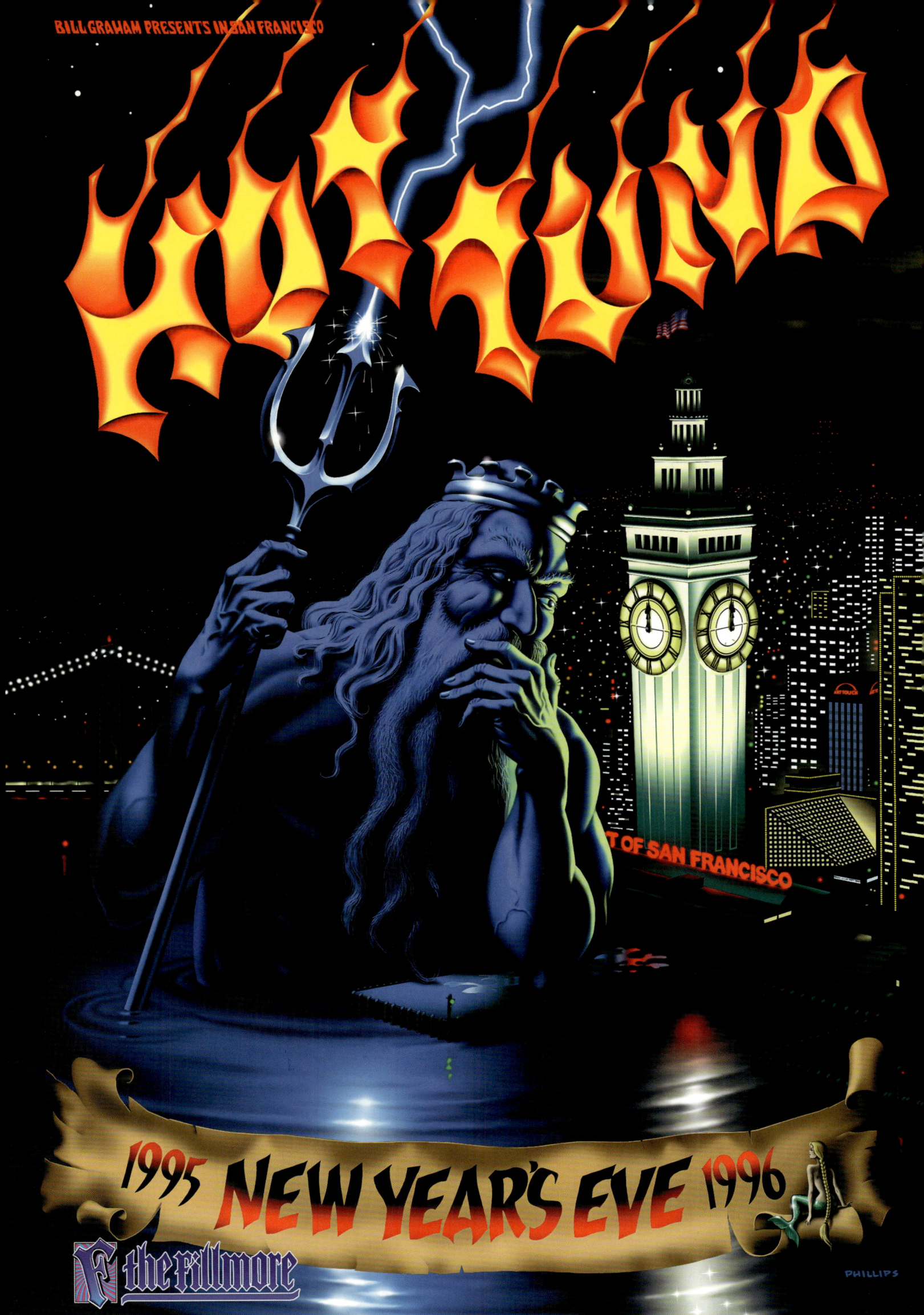

Art directed posters for Maritime Hall

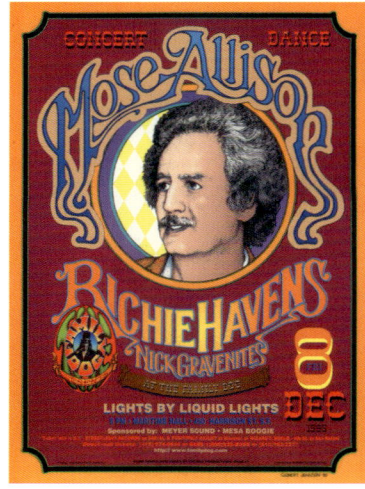
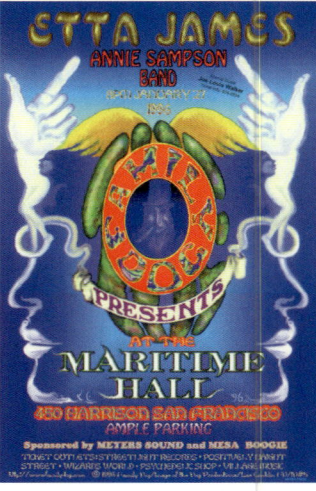
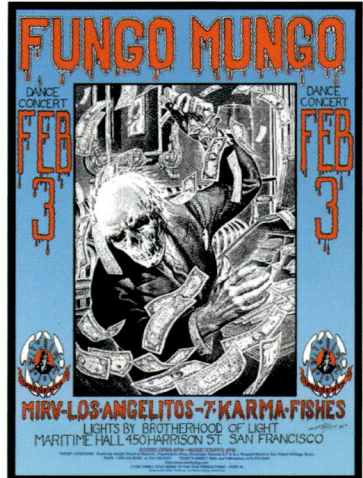
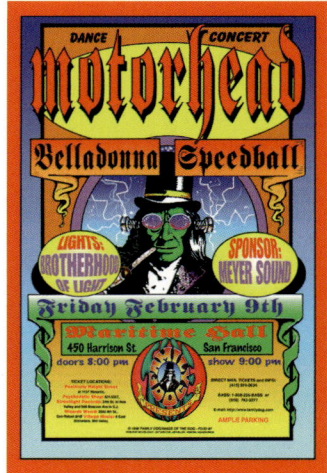

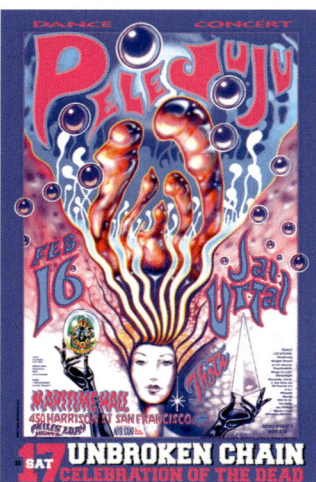
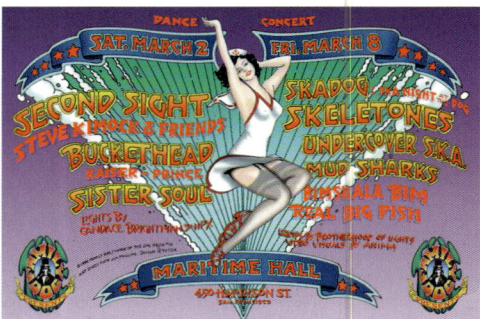
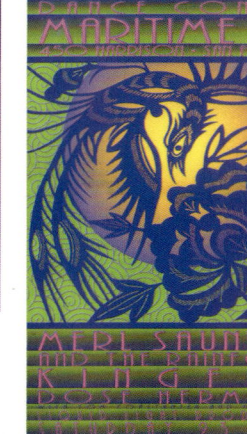
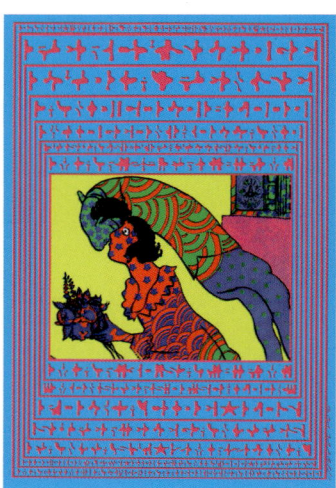

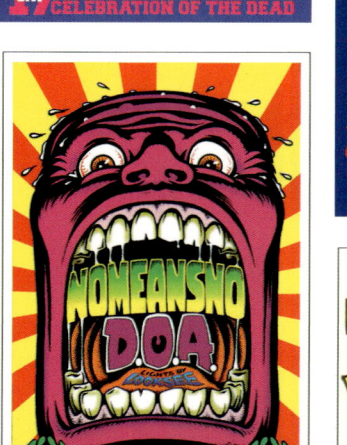
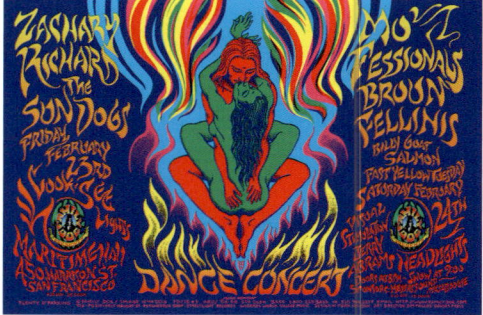
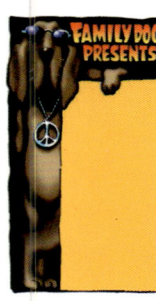
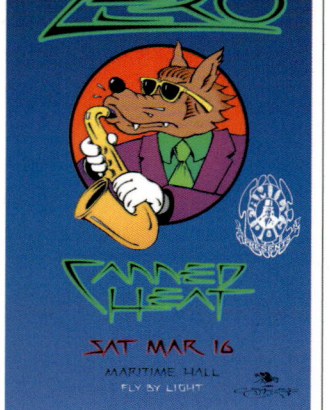
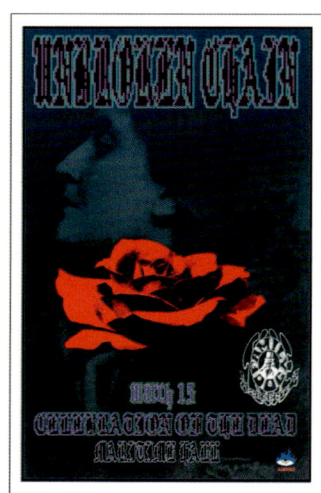

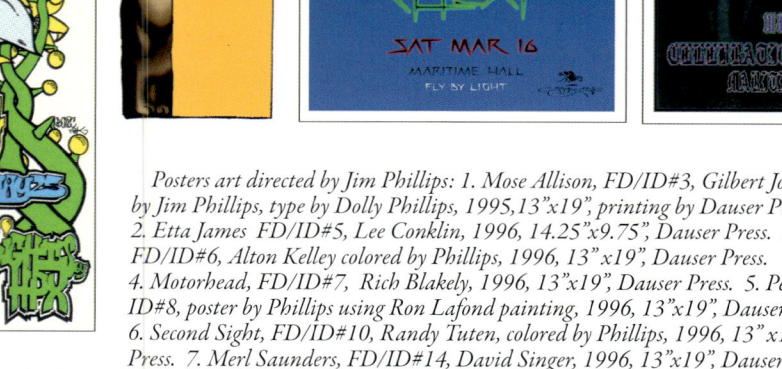

Jim Phillips was Family Dog art director at Maritime Hall during 1996 and 1997. He commissioned art work for these shows and worked with many noted Bay Area rock poster artists, often providing the colorization.

Posters art directed by Jim Phillips: 1. Mose Allison, FD/ID#3, Gilbert Johnson, colored by Jim Phillips, type by Dolly Phillips, 1995, 13"x19", printing by Dauser Press. 2. Etta James FD/ID#5, Lee Conklin, 1996, 14.25"x9.75", Dauser Press. 3. Fungo Mungo FD/ID#6, Alton Kelley colored by Phillips, 1996, 13"x19", Dauser Press. 4. Motorhead, FD/ID#7, Rich Blakely, 1996, 13"x19", Dauser Press. 5. Pele Juju, FD/ID#8, poster by Phillips using Ron Lafond painting, 1996, 13"x19", Dauser Press. 6. Second Sight, FD/ID#10, Randy Tuten, colored by Phillips, 1996, 13"x19", Dauser Press. 7. Merl Saunders, FD/ID#14, David Singer, 1996, 13"x19", Dauser Press. 8. Percy Sledge/Cold Blood, FD/ID#15, Victor Moscoso, colored by Phillips, 1996, 13"x19", Dauser Press. 9. Zachary Richard FD/ID#9, Mark Henson, colored by Phillips, 1996, 13"x19", Dauser Press. 10. No Means No, D.O.A., #FD/ID 16A, Jimbo Phillips, 1996, 14"x22", serigraphed by Jimbo Phillips. 11. Sublime/Voodoo Glow Skulls, #FD/ID 17B, Boot Hughston (Boots Jr.), 14.5"x23", silkscreen printed by Boot & Jimbo Phillips. Bottom center, Family Dog business card and ad by Phillips. 12. Zero/Canned Heat, FD/ID#13, Stanley Mouse, 1996, 13"x19", Dauser Press. 13. Unbroken Chain FD/ID#12, Mouse, 1996, 13"x19", Dauser Press.

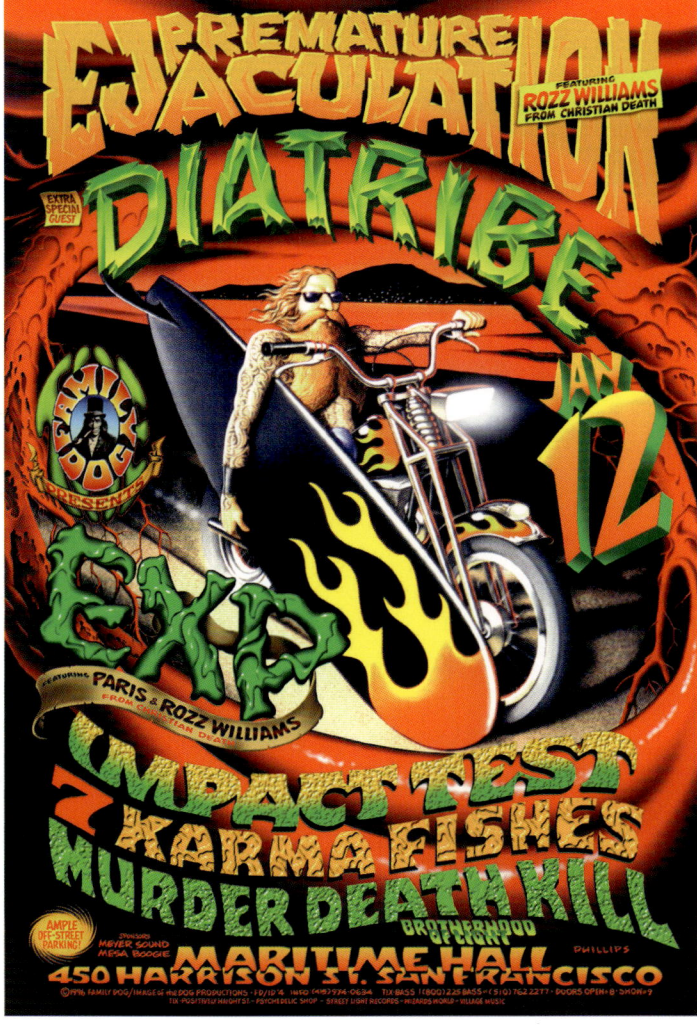

Diatribe poster, FD/ID#4, 1996 14.25"x9.75", Dauser Press.

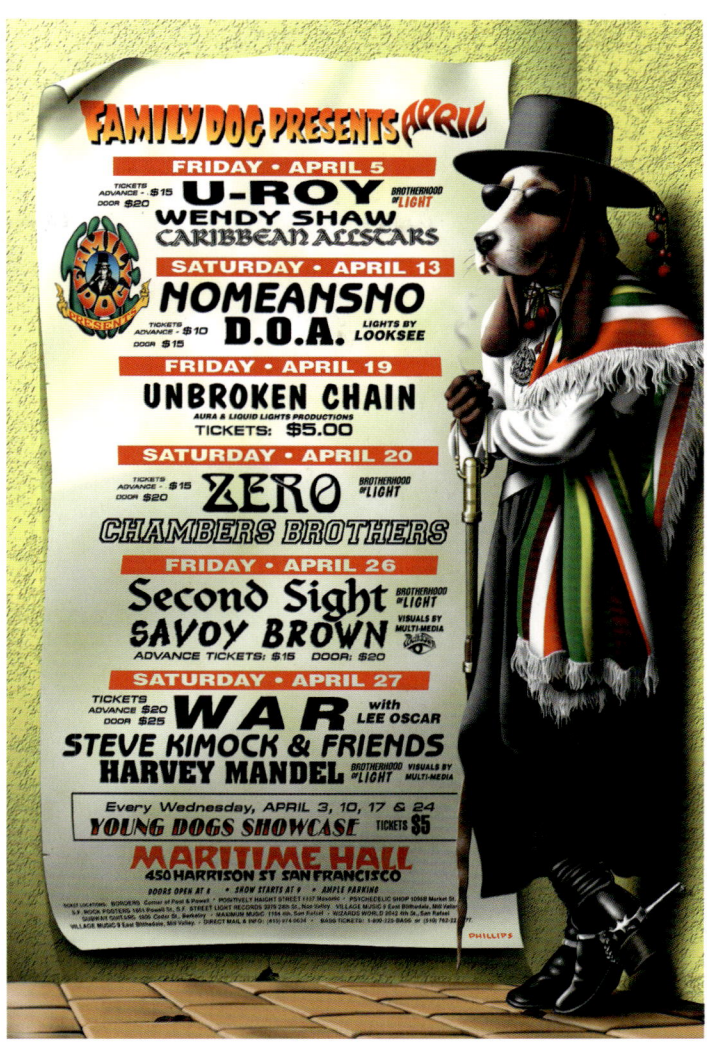

"April Dog" FD calendar poster, FD/ID#16, 1996, 13"x9", Dauser Press.

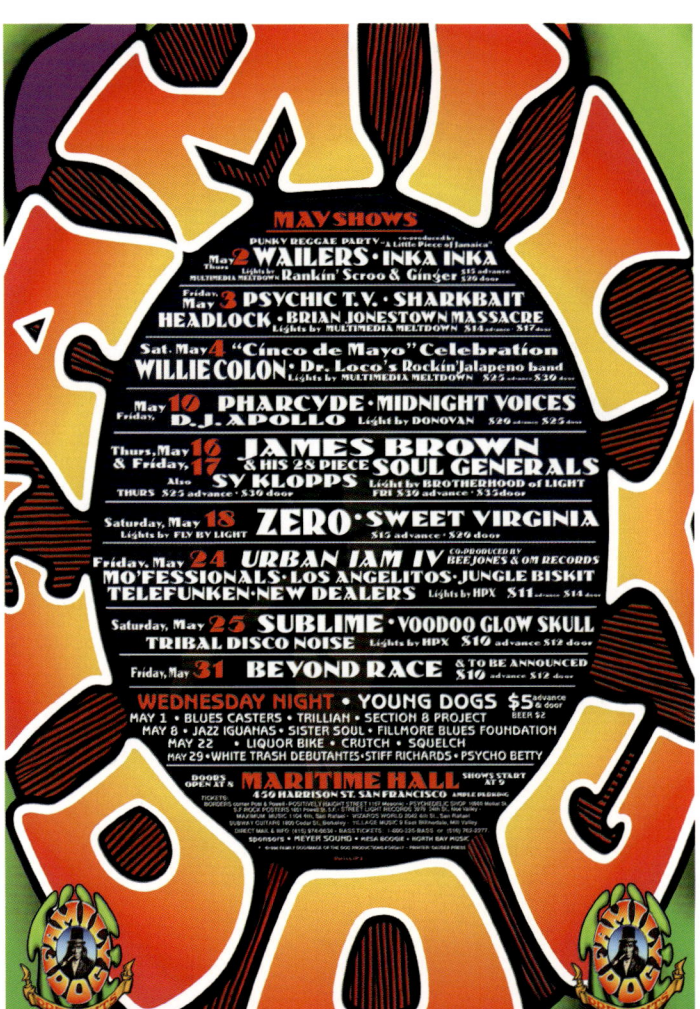

May calendar poster, FD/ID#17, 1996, 13"x19", Dauser Press.

151

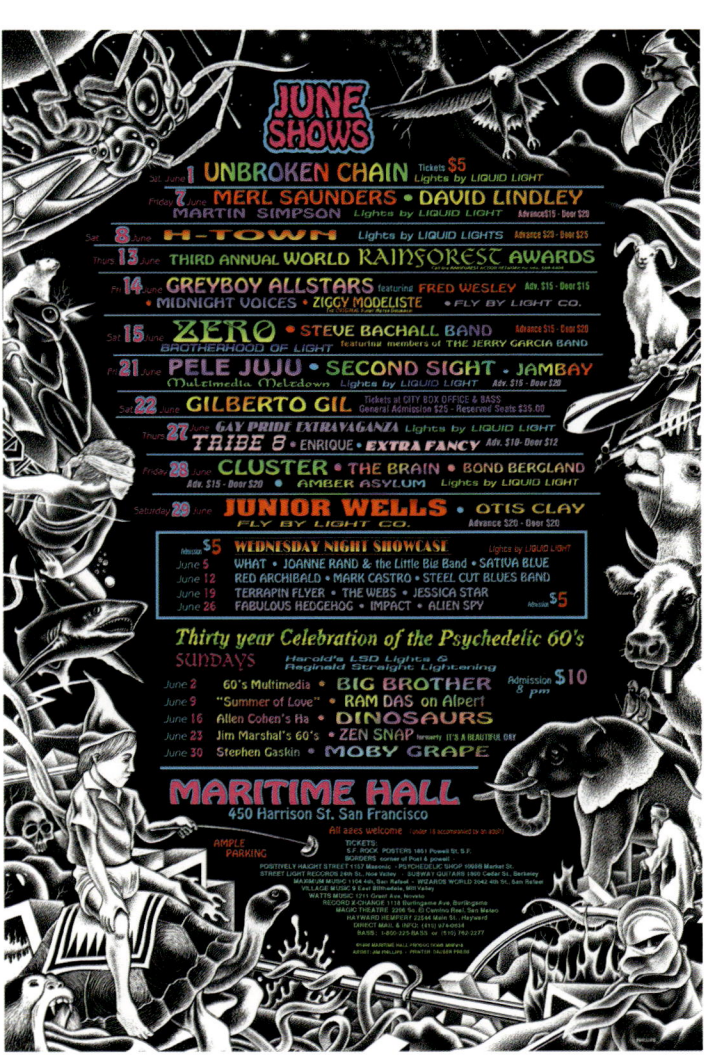

June calendar poster, MHP#18, 1996 , 13"x19", Dauser Press.
First Maritime Hall poster after MH/Family Dog series.

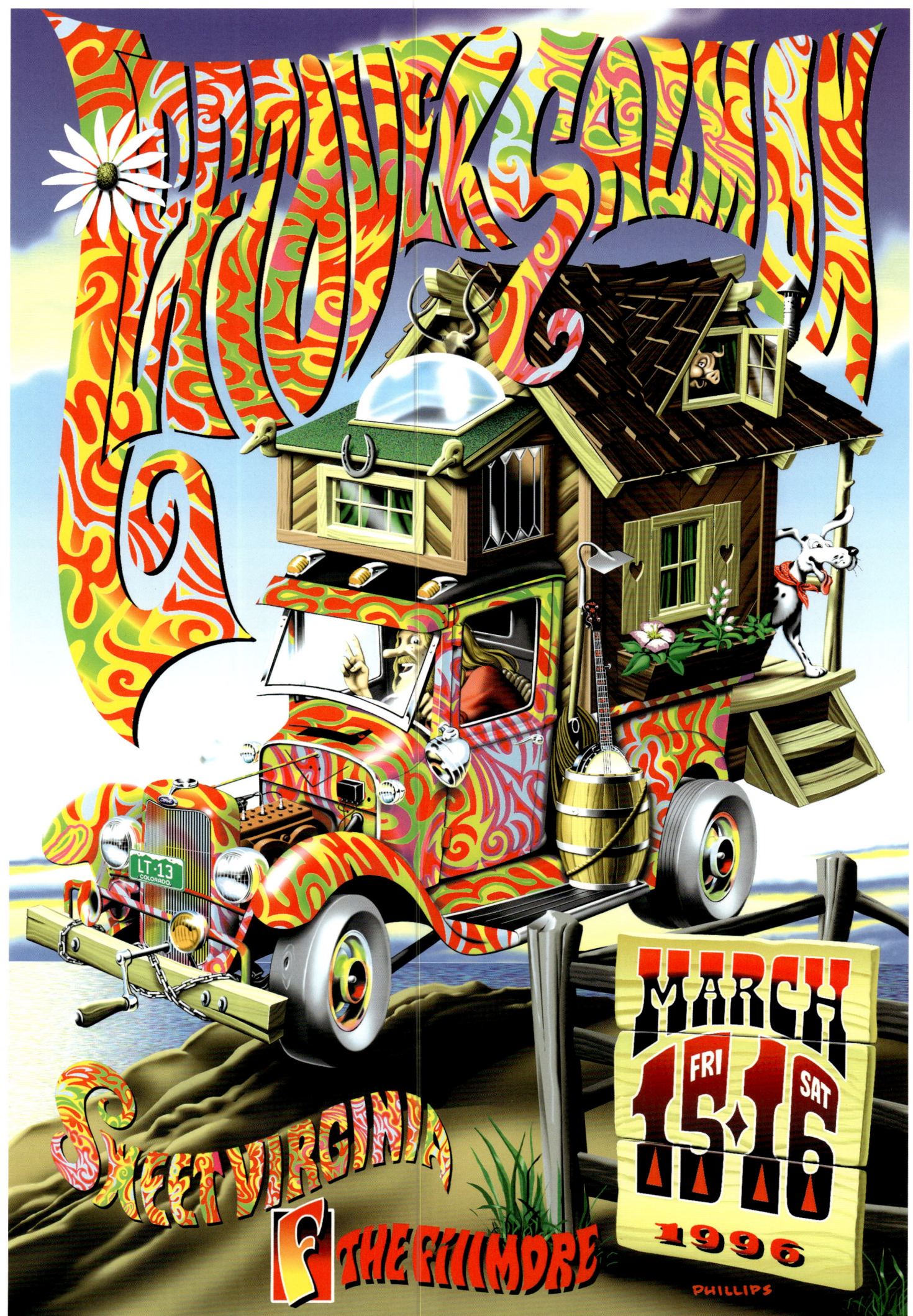

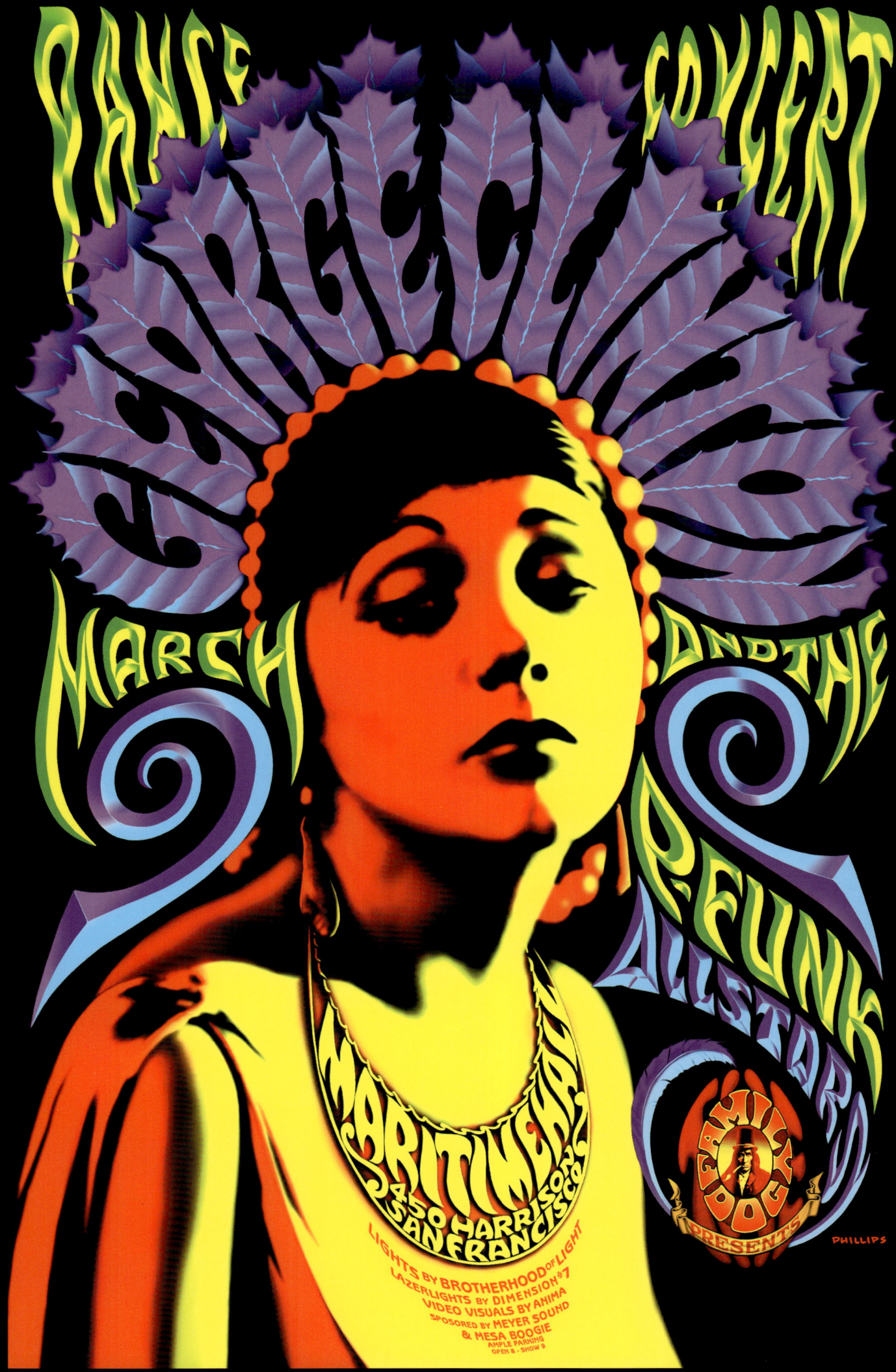

George Clinton & P-Funk Allstars *poster, FD/ID#11, 1996, 13"x19.5". Printing: Dauser Press.*

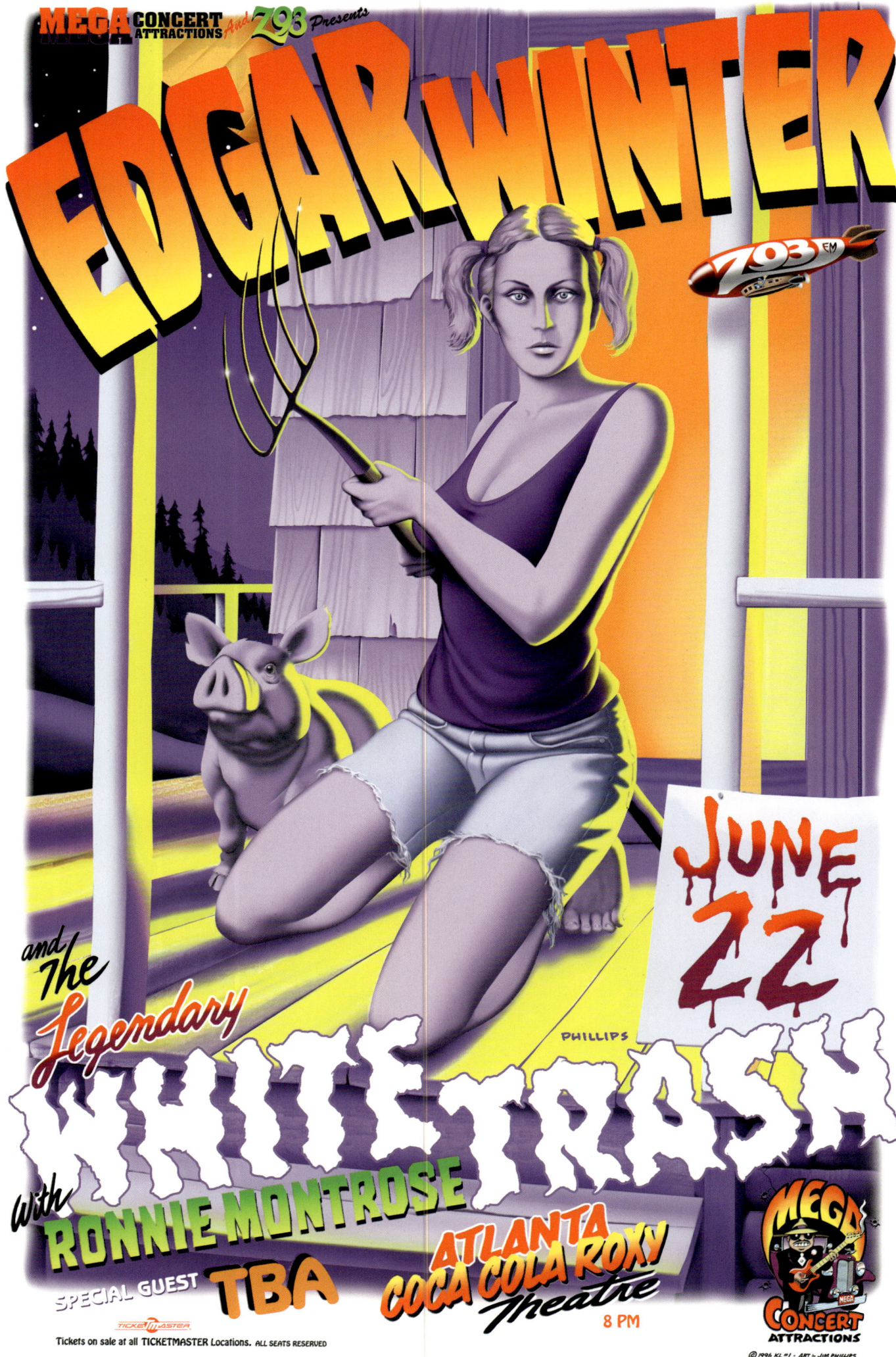

Edgar Winter, White Trash poster, 1996, #KL1, 13.5"x20", Quality Offset printing
Bill Dawson's daughter Dai modeled for the figure painting. Mega and Z03 FM logos are bonus Phillips designs.

© 1996 KL #1 · ART by JIM PHILLIPS

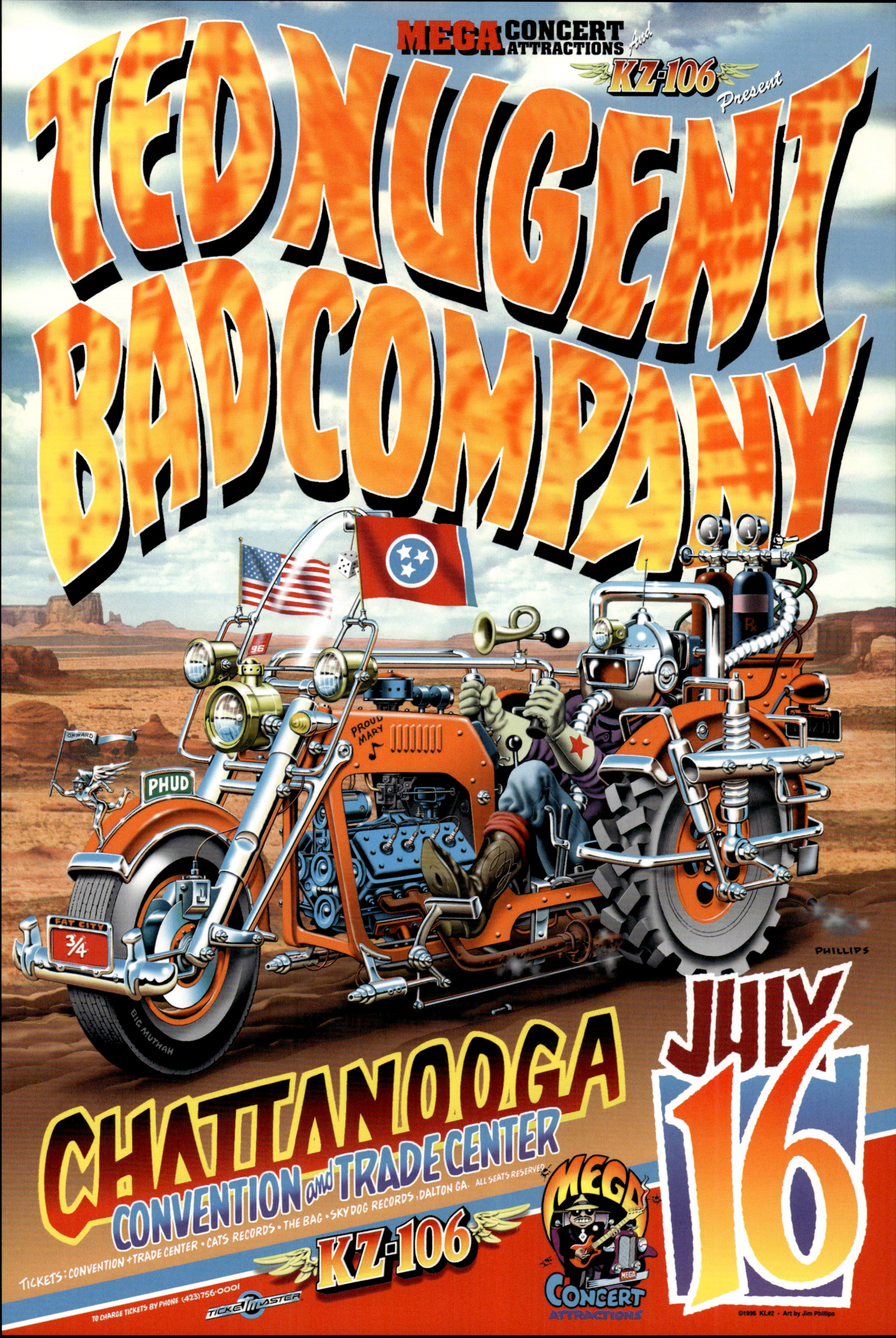

Ted Nugent, Bad Company *poster, 1996, #KL2, 17 3/4" x19", Quality Offset printing.*

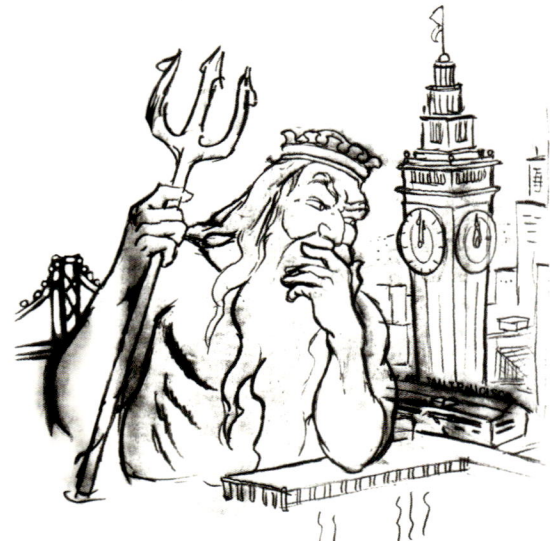

Rough Sketches

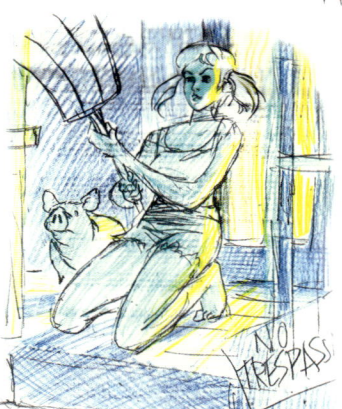

Below: Edgar Winter (p.154) sketch, notice it has Hot Tuna and Fillmore. This was the first concept of that poster. BGP asked for a southern girl defending her home (but no guns). They later changed direction and asked for another idea.
Jim suggested Neptune (top & p. 149), but not before he crumpled it up and threw it in the wastebasket in a fit of frustration. It was retrieved and faxed to BGP next morning and approved.
Left: A preliminary Hot Tuna sketch.

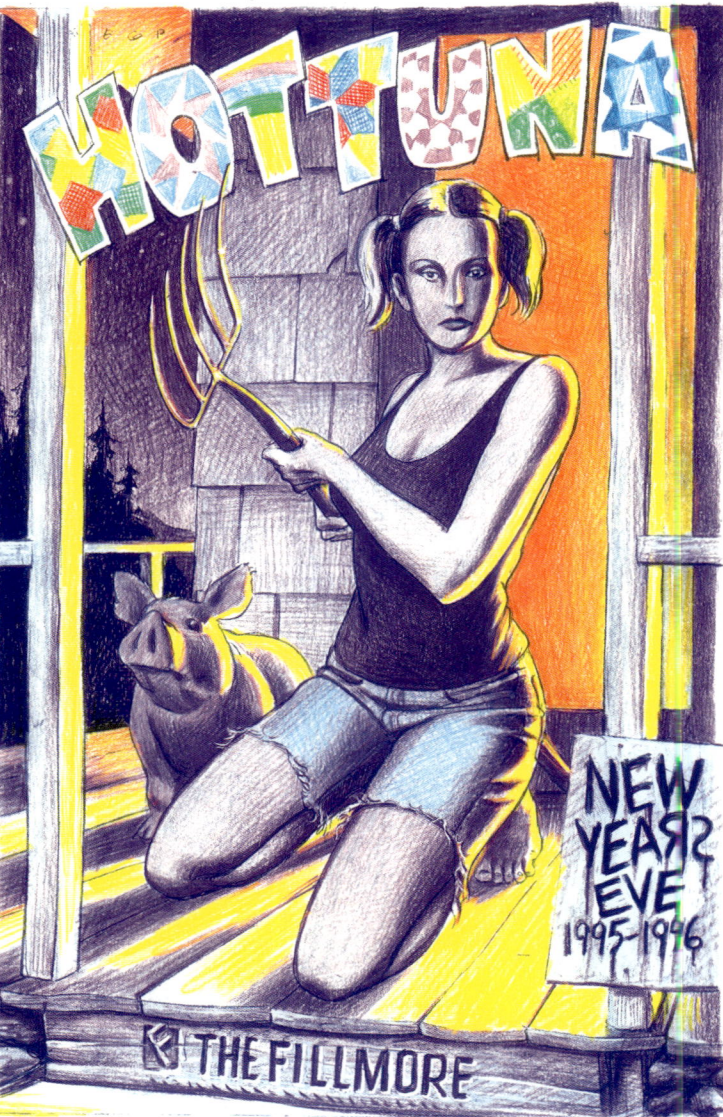

Bill Ham's house is a classic artist's pad, paint spattered here and there from his abstract expressionist tempera on paper paintings, and figures made of wire and colored rags in various poses. Downstairs he has a studio for his lightshow inventions and equipment. He has a light machine in a large cabinet with frosted glass on the front panel. When he turns it on, some kind of mysterious device effectively casts continuously changing colored light shapes on the glass.

BRUCE DAUSER: *"Bill Ham is the grand-daddy of the liquid light. He was doing Light Sound Dimension, LSD, back before he did the light show cabinet for the Trips shows and the Red Dog in Virginia City in the very early 60s. Everyone says that Red Dog was the first psychedelic happening, but what Bill was doing with all those fantastic jazz musicians, thinking sound and light and doing meditative and happening sessions, came earlier. It was after that he was asked to do the lights at the Family Dog Avalon Ballroom. He's the one who hung the screens and put it all together, started that whole San Francisco dance/lightshow thing off at the Avalon. Bill and Alton Kelley were two of the original three members of the Family Dog 'family' and Bill was managing the Family Dog House and he was the manager of that property in fact. And he had the 'Pine St. Thing' going on too; that's what we called it. Now, Bill lives in a beautiful old house directly across the street from where it began. It's a three-story Victorian sitting up on top of the hill on Pine Street, where you can look out onto this expanse of the city. The studio itself is an artist's studio, a comfortable, relaxing place to be, great vibes and great jazz always on the radio, and then he's got his light studio down below."*

Ham asked Phillips to create a poster for his light show and concert-the Rock Art Ball-which would follow Wes Wilson's October '94 Rock Art Expo, at the Hall of Flowers. Bill came down to Jim's Santa Cruz studio, and they stayed up all night working it on the computer with slides of his lightshow works.

BILL HAM: *"I found the Art Rock Ball to be an opportunity to recreate a sight-specific environment performance light show. For me it was going back to the S.F. rock/dance lightshows that I participated in and helped to create. A Dance implies people turning around, and when you turn around you're looking at the walls, which we flooded with color and imagery enveloping the bands and audience participants. The process of doing my original form of light show was to play spontaneously with live music in a meditative situation. We had posters from those shows, but I had never been able to work on a full color poster until I did one with Jim. I enjoyed working directly with him, and the rock poster show provided a sort of impetus for a self-financed poster and Bruce Dauser was an important element to that. The poster I did with Jim was the first opportunity for me to do a poster that began to relate to the light show aspect of the event more directly. I was happy to meet Jim after all those years. It's been a very good friendship. We've had several projects that haven't quite worked out and some that have and we look forward to keeping on."*

Wes Wilson asked Phillips to design the staff shirt for the Rock Art Expo. Together with his Helms Tribute poster it was good to have new items for his second poster show. Phillips' table was back-to-back with Bill's and they enjoyed good-natured camaraderie. Bill's light show at Expo was fantastic, projected in 360 degrees on every wall. Jim and Dolly danced to the great 60s rock bands such as Country Joe McDonald, Nick Gravenites and many other old favorites. They had a ball, and their poster sales held promise. Bill remained a close and loved friend along with Bruce and many other of their then-new acquaintances.

In August of 1995 Boots Hughston of Maritime Hall asked Jimmy to do the Grand Opening poster for the Family Dog's new venue, with an October 27 show date, 30 years to the day from the opening of the Avalon Ballroom. During the mid-60s the Family Dog was a San Francisco hippie commune headed by Chet Helms, who held concerts at the Avalon Ballroom.

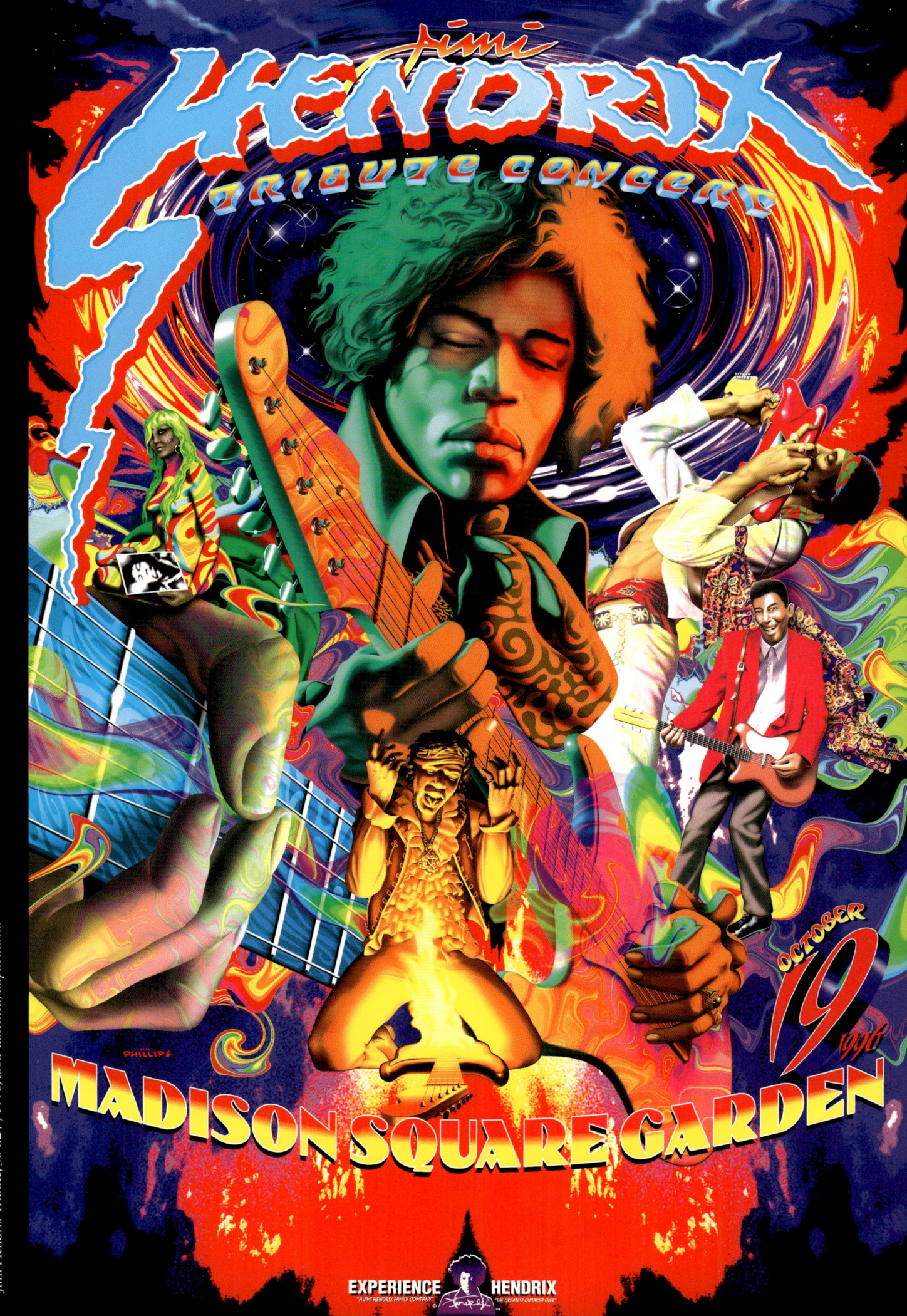

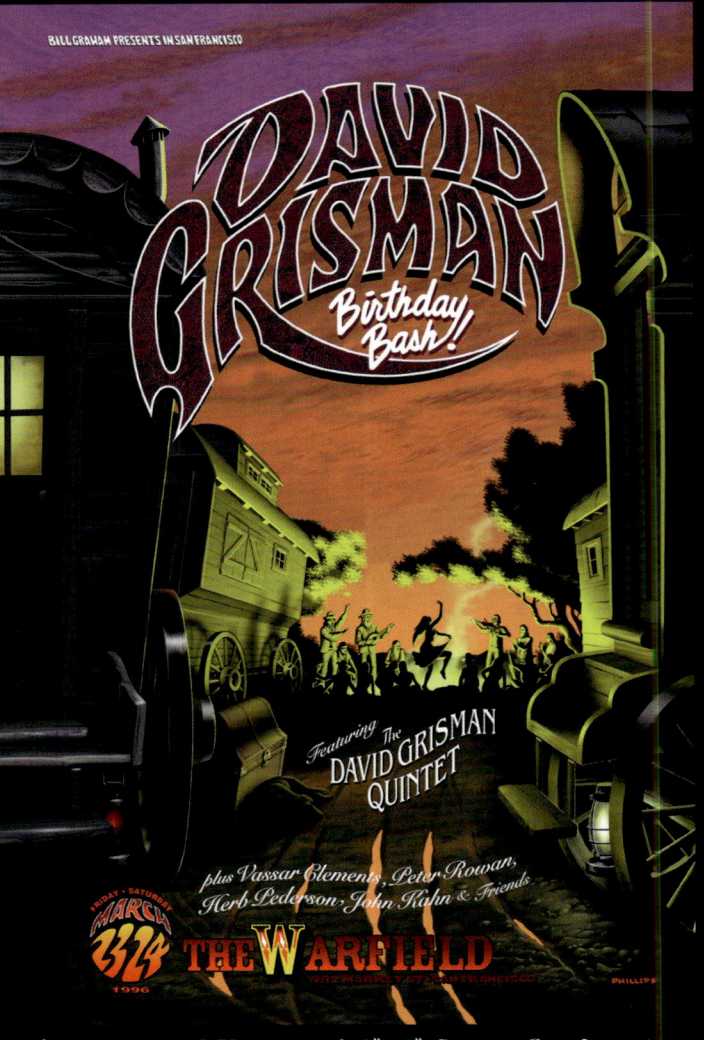

David Grisman *poster, BGP#139, 1996 13"x19". Printing: Great Impressions.*

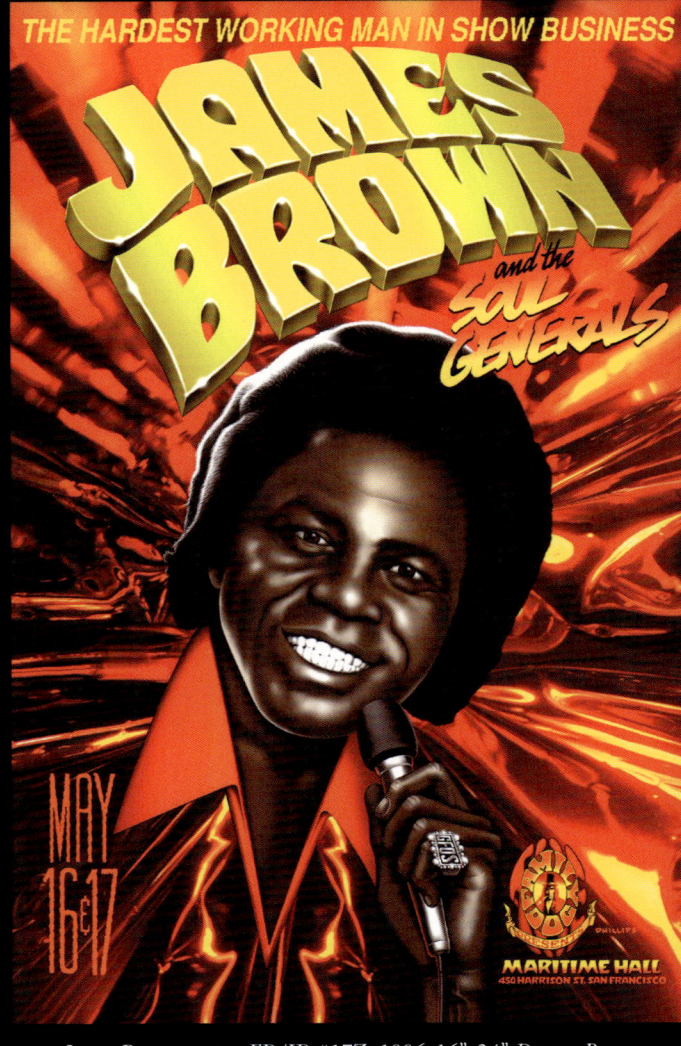

James Brown *poster, FD/ID #17Z, 1996 16"x24", Dauser Press.*

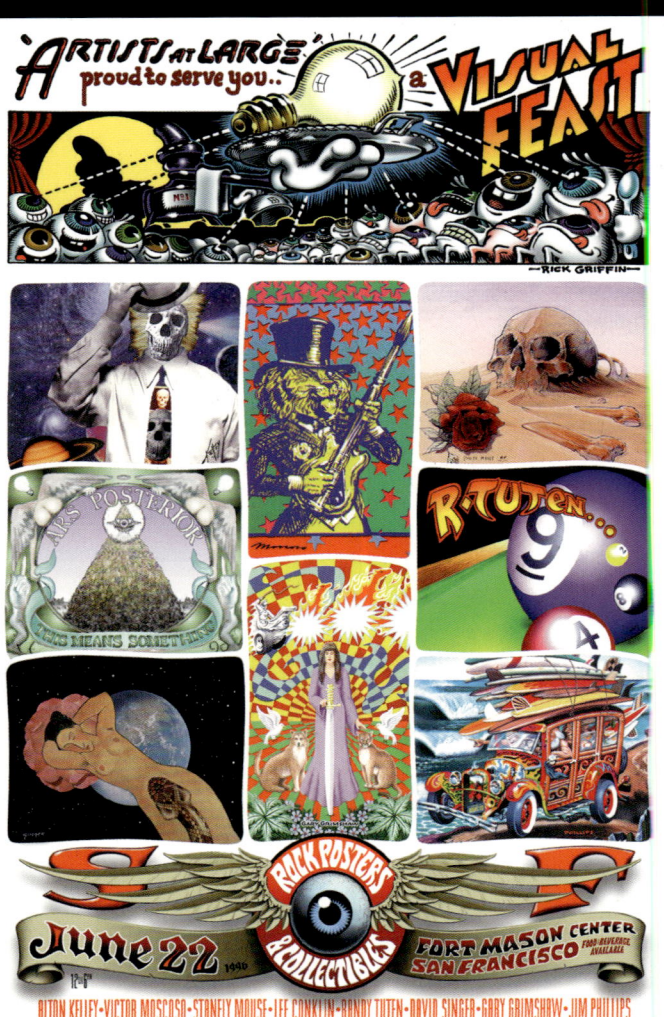

SF Rock Posters Artist Show *poster, 1996 13.25"x19.5", Dauser Press.*

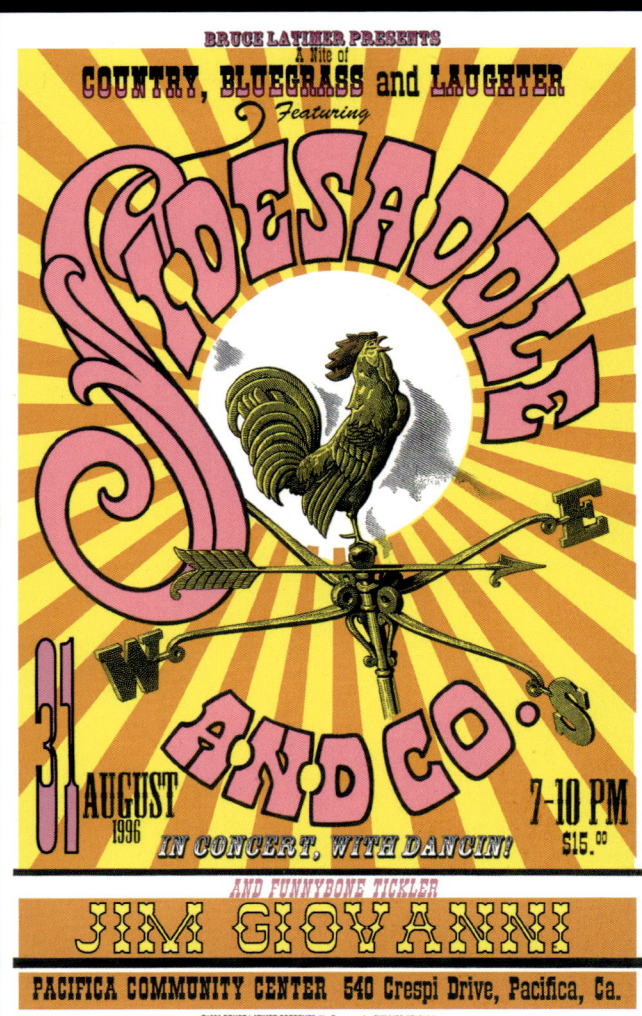

Sidesaddle/Bruce Latimer, *1996, show cancelled - unpublished.*

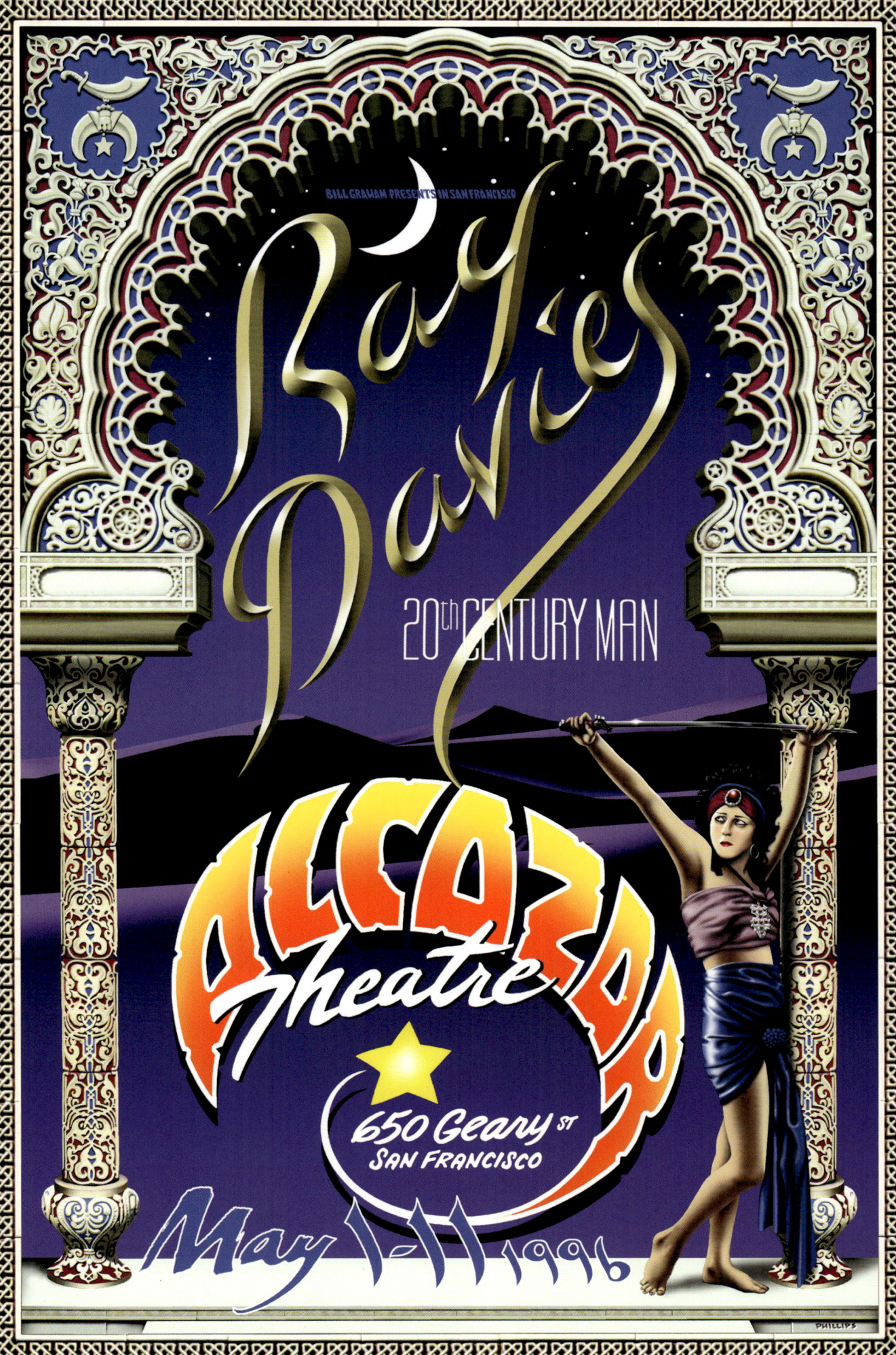

Ray Davies, BGP#142, 1996, 13"x19". Printing: Great Impressions.

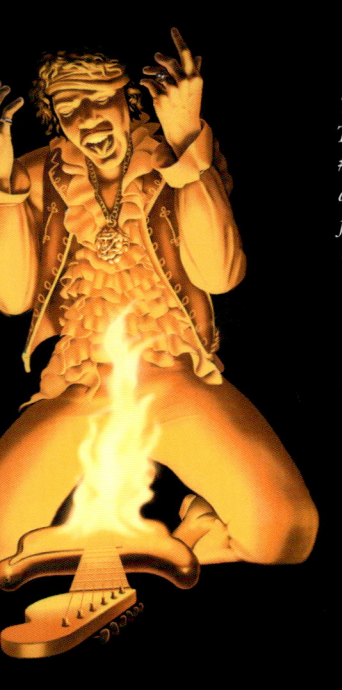

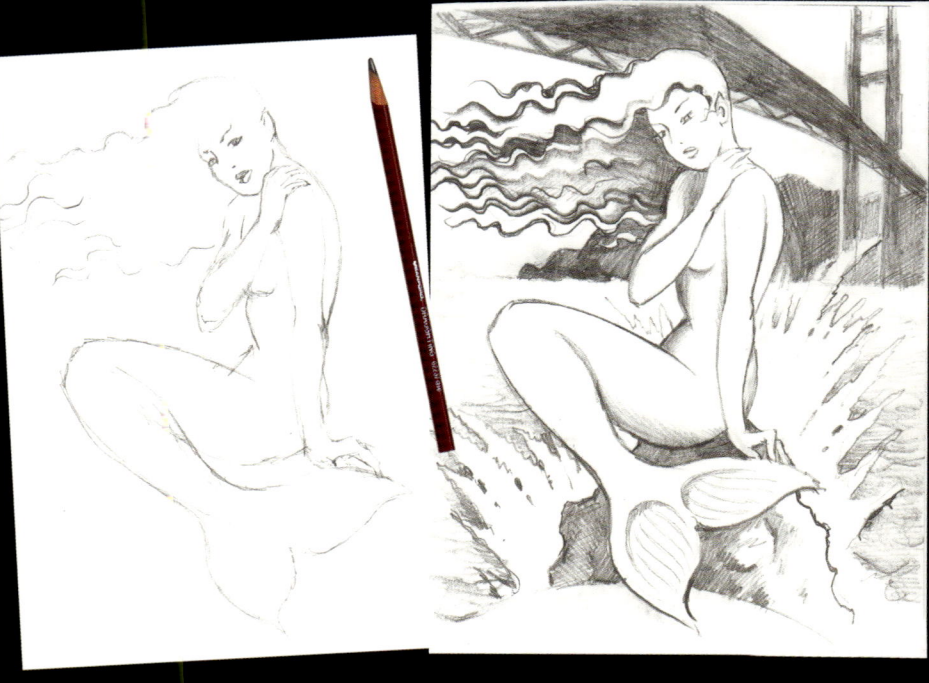

Top right: Tom Petty #2 sketches drawn freehand by Jim "flat on his back" after his release from the hospital with a broken pelvis.

The Maritime Hall was a huge seaman's hall on Harrison Street, with a good-size stage and auditorium, and lots of stairs. The show was scheduled for October, with Gregg Allman as the opening act for Iron Butterfly. Boots asked for Popeye on the poster. Jim countered that Popeye was owned by King Features Syndicate, one of the largest comics agencies, and that their characters were jealously guarded by attorneys. Boots insisted, citing the Family Dog Tribute to Dr. Strange poster, the Captain Marvel Kesey poster and other traditional psychedelic usage of established images. Phillips freely admits that his own artistic path was littered with such usage, and he began to think how to accommodate Boots' wishes, feeling obliged because of the honor of being chosen to do the grand opening of the return of the Family Dog. Phillips computer-painted a takeoff on the original Family Dog logo, drawing Popeye as a hippie with long hair with the stove pipe hat and odd-looking pipe. Phillips likes to involve humor in his work whenever he can, because it makes people feel good to laugh. He made a pencil sketch of it and showed it to Boots, who gave the go-ahead with the artwork. They eventually decided that it wasn't Popeye after all, but his hippie brother, Deadeye.

Once again, Phillips was rolling in Phase Next of his brilliant career. Just after the grand opening poster was commissioned, Bill Graham Presents called for a Ratdog poster, and then an Eddie Money poster. There were 13 owners at BGP, and so all of Jimmy's designs had to run a gauntlet of tastes, which always complicates things exponentially. One or more of the owners could always raise some sort of restriction or objection. Precious art time would tick away while they decided, with Jim reluctant to progress not knowing whether the job faced a setback. Jim's Edgar Winter in Atlanta poster was originally a Fillmore Hot Tuna poster that was redirected.

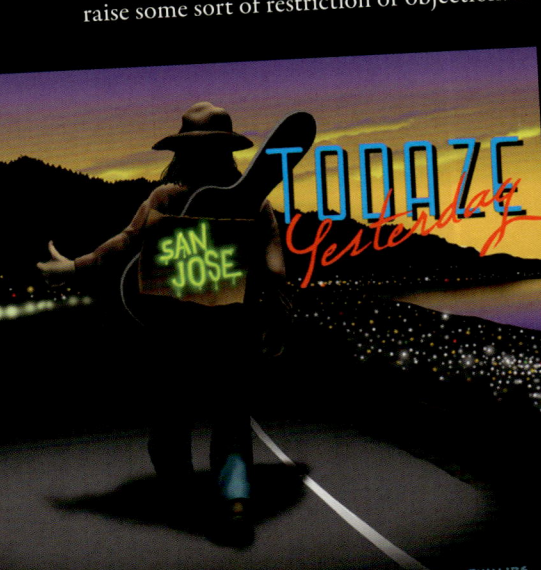

Before you knew it, Phillips had a job again, as the Family Dog art director, managing posters and artists. Phillips worked closely with Chet Helms and instead of hogging the glory, he shared the wealth, creating a series of posters by the best artists of rock history, including Mouse, Kelley, Moscosso, Singer, Tuten, Conklin, and many others. Phillips would color some of the other artists' posters on his computer, and design his own, sometimes filling in at the last minute when an artist flaked. Once again Phillips had a pen to the grindstone and was burning the midnight ink. BGP demanded more and more posters and he was involved in a back-straining, mind-bending creative tug of war. He did Hot Tuna, David Grisman, Leftover Salmon. The shows were great. Dolly and Jimmy went to every show. Jim did posters for Maritime Hall and the Fillmore. It began to seem that all their friends lived in the city. They were used to heading home at 1:00, and getting home about 3:00. Those long hours became dangerous, especially one rainy night. Jim had worked all night on one of posters and had to get Kelley's Fungo Mungo poster press-sh[...] a printer in San Jose. It was just before he was able to email [...] He delivered it in the late afternoon and headed back on H[...] 17. It was dark and raining, and he got a little sleepy. Throu[...] the watery spray, he saw the lane he merged into wasn't a lan[...] all, but a muddy shoulder. The car hydroplaned into a slow[...] sideways and then backwards, helpless to steer. Fortunately[...] drifted backwards off the shoulder, and it softly hit the guar[...] and stopped. They were grateful to miss the other cars as th[...] hydroplaned backwards. Art can be dangerous.

The artists who design posters for Bill Graham Presents are usually offered tickets to the show, and Phillips made it a habit to attend most of them. The Ratdog Revue was special, because it was the first Grateful Dead incarnation after Jerry Garcia died.

Right: Eyeball, *oil on canvas, approx 12"x10", 1990. Collection of SF Rock Posters.*

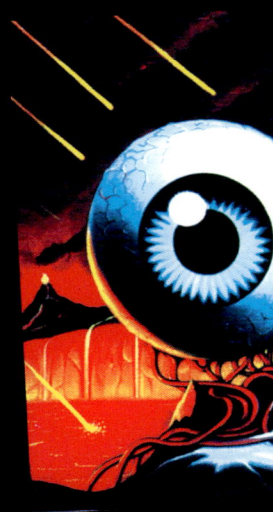

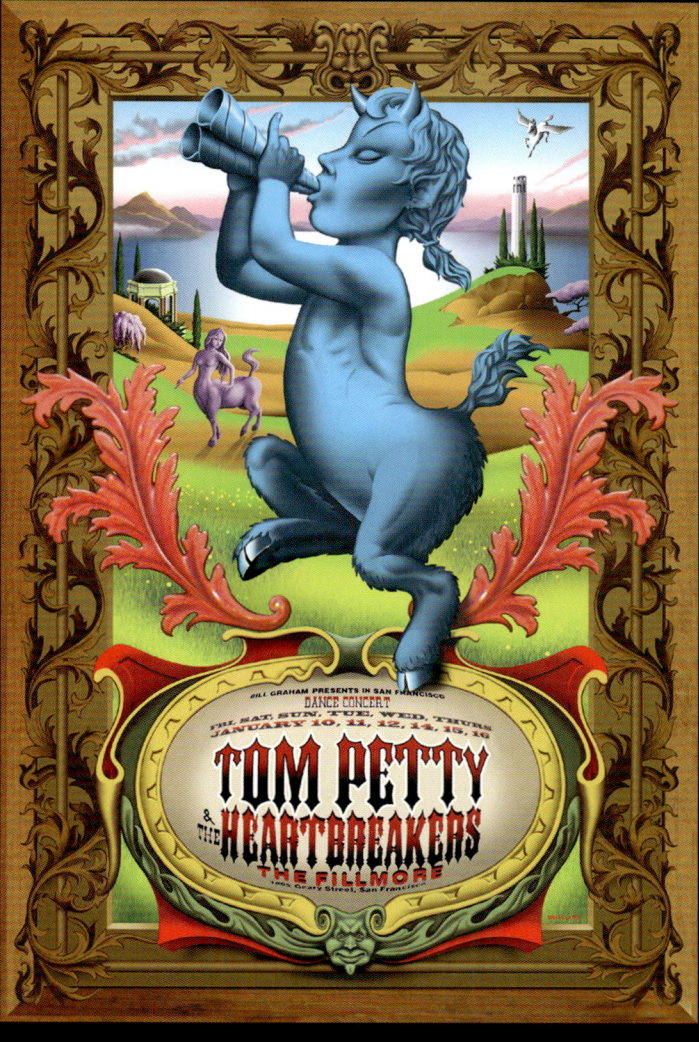
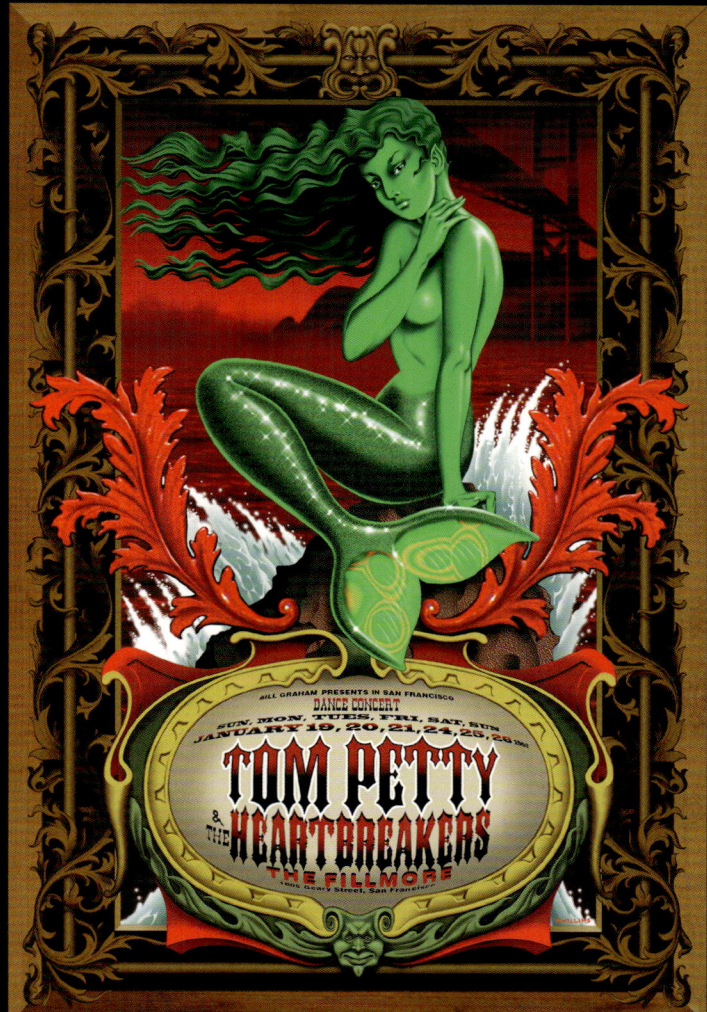
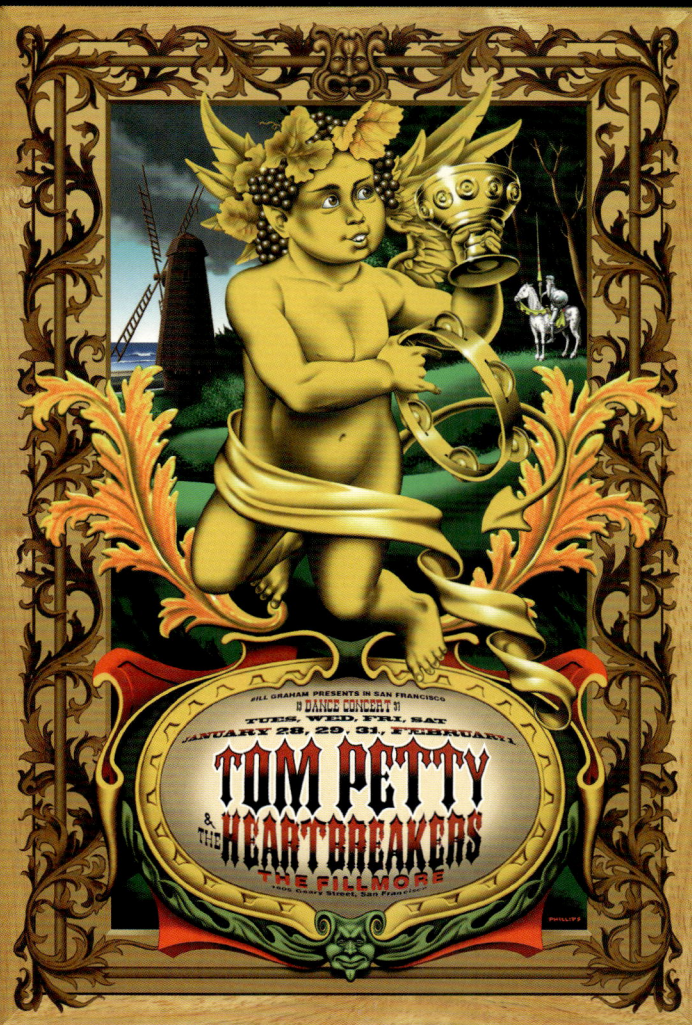
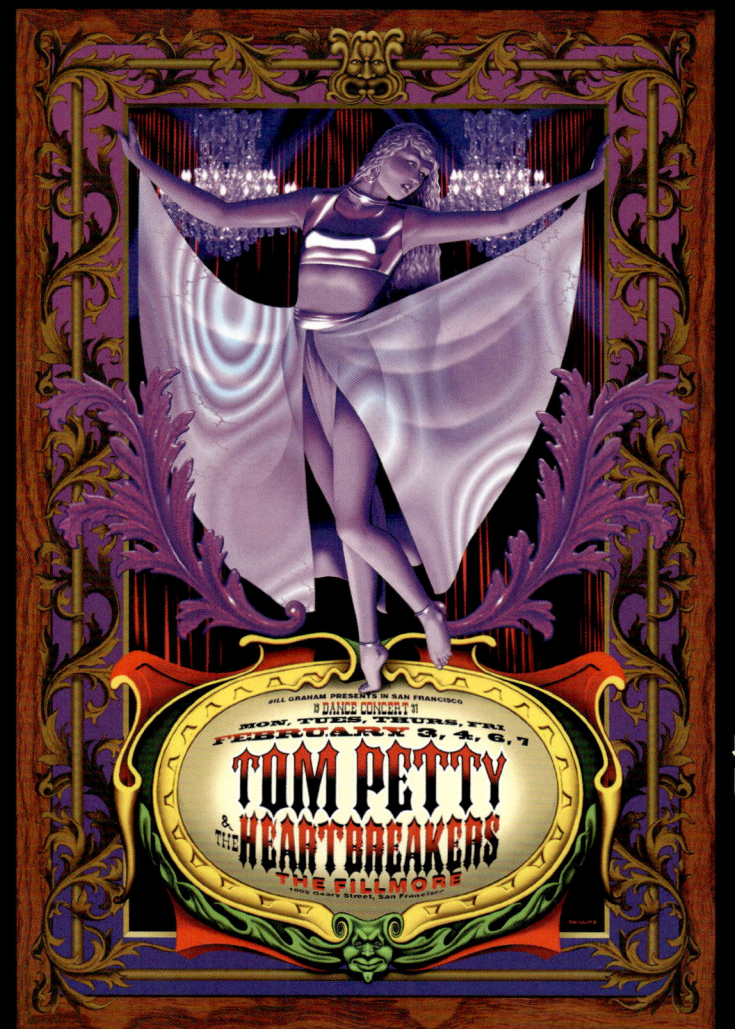
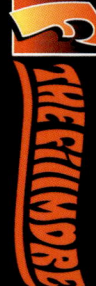

Tom Petty Set, *1997; No.1 (top left & clockwise) BGP #F251; No. 2 BGP #F233; No.3 BGP # F254; No.4 BGP #F255, all 13"x19", printing by Great Impressions.*

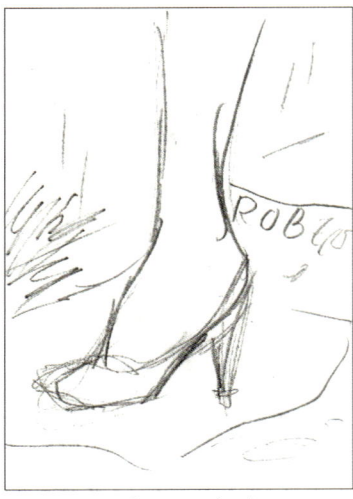

Original concept sketches.

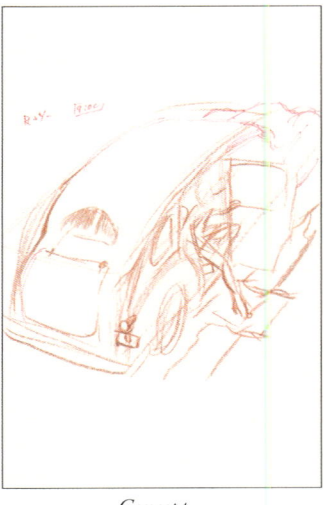

Concept.

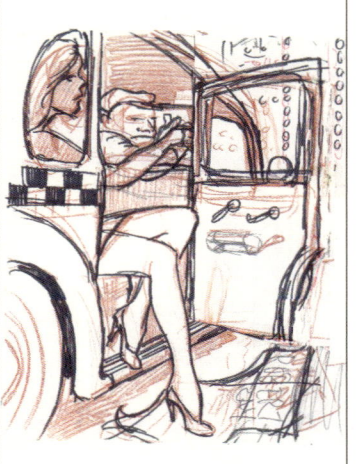

Final concept angle.

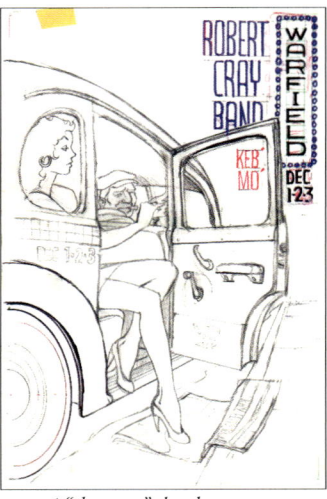

A "clean-up" sketch.

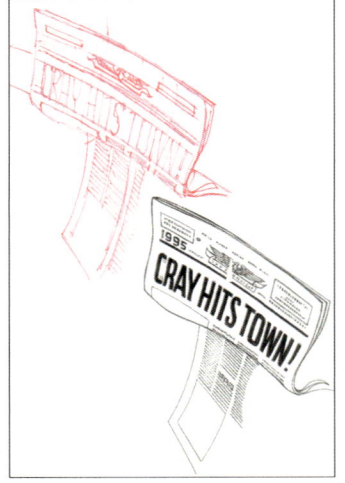

Detail sketch and scan ink.

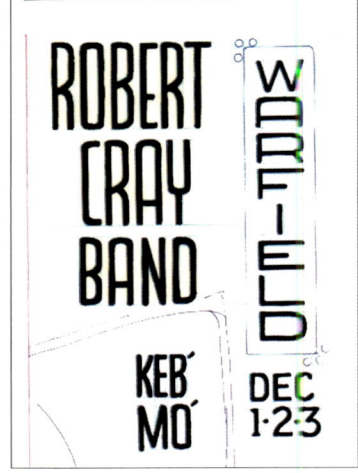

Inked lettering for scan.

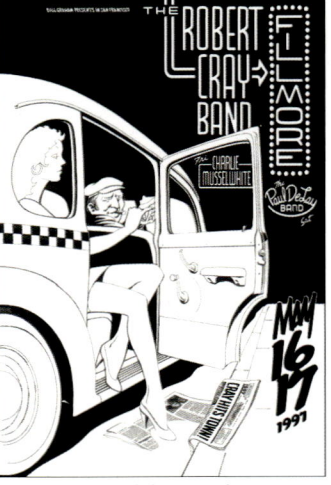

Inked drawing for scan.

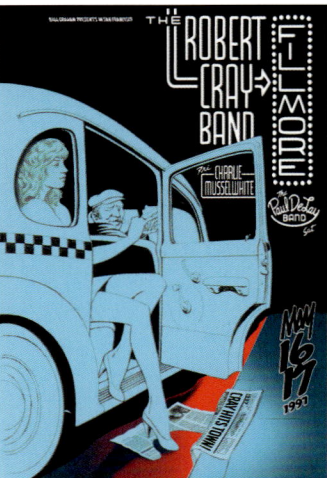

Computer color spotting.

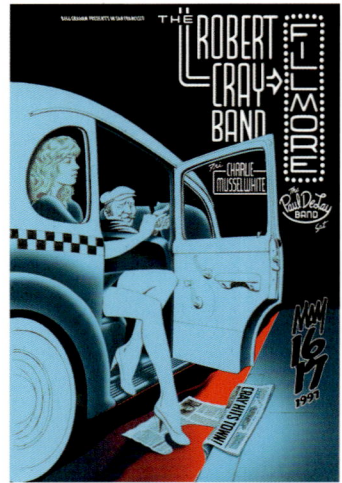

Shading with Photoshop airbrush tool.

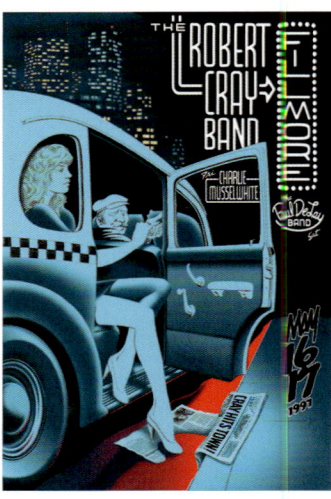

City lights.

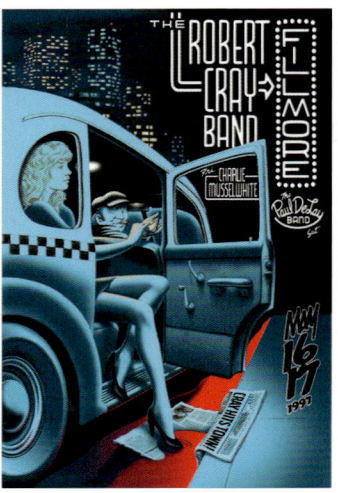

Figure detail.

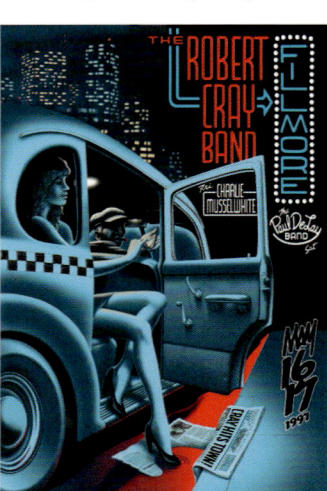

Final figure detail.

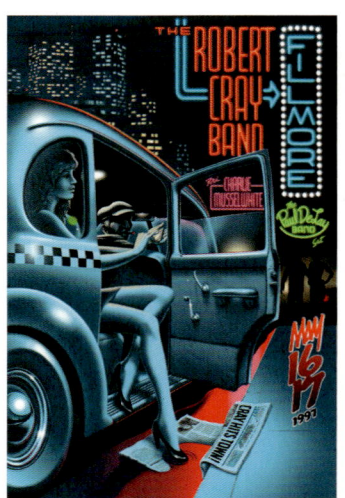

Highlighting, with airbrush tool.

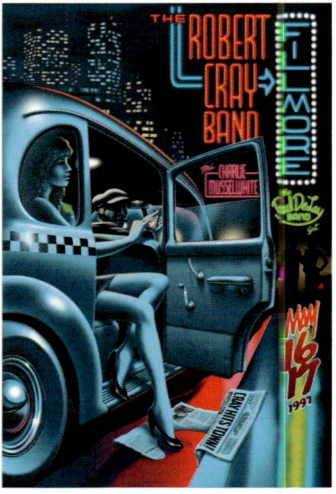

Neon reflections.

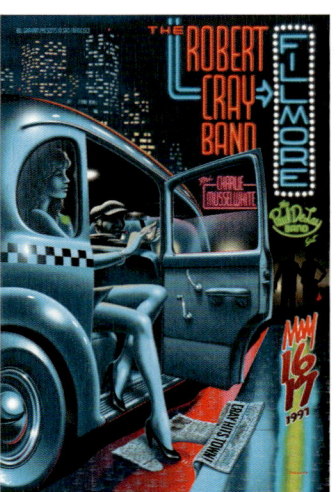

Rain effects.

Cray poster process

Here are "snapshots' of the Robert Cray poster during construction, from concept to finish. It is a totally freehand drawing without use of photo references or typesetting.

Opposite page: Robert Cray poster, #F272, 1997, 13"x19", printing by Great Impressions

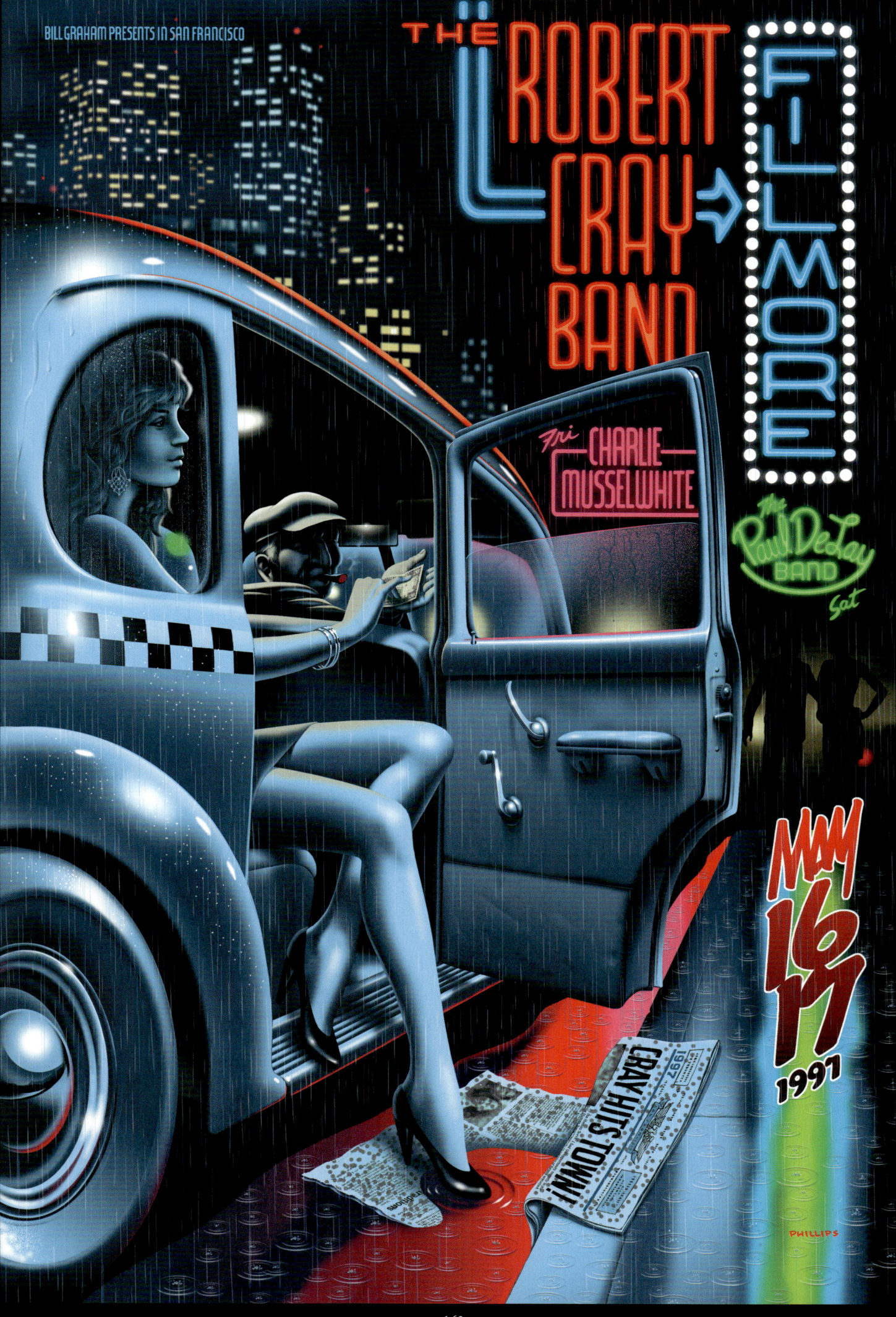

BILL GRAHAM PRESENTS IN SAN FRANCISCO

THE ROBERT CRAY BAND → FILLMORE

Fri CHARLIE MUSSELWHITE

The Paul DeLay BAND Sat

MAY 16 17 1997

CRAY HITS TOWN! 1997

PHILLIPS

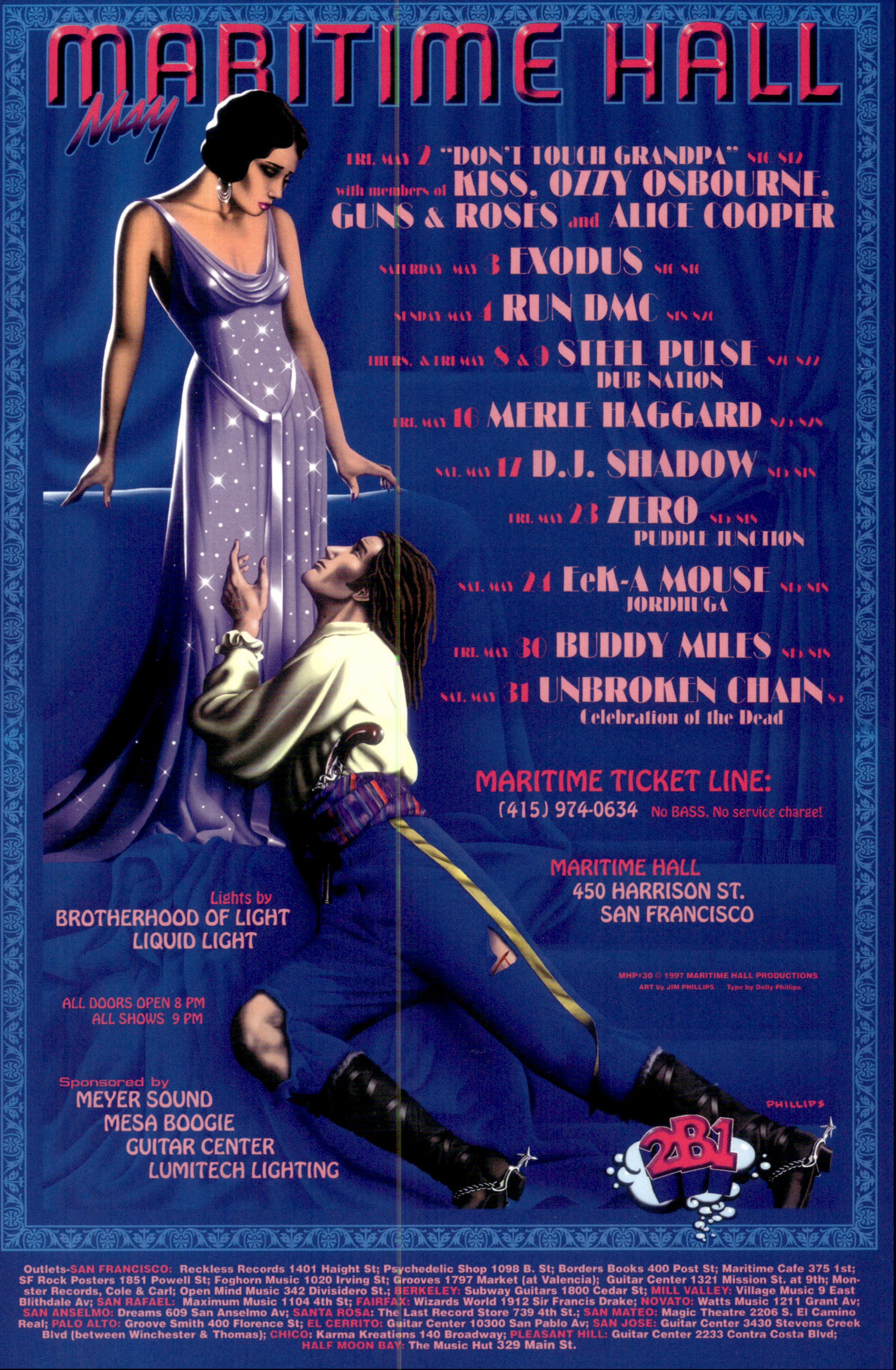

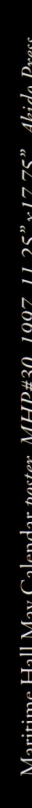

MARITIME HALL

May

FRI. MAY 2 "DON'T TOUCH GRANDPA" $10 $12
with members of **KISS, OZZY OSBOURNE, GUNS & ROSES** and **ALICE COOPER**

SATURDAY MAY 3 EXODUS $10 $10

SUNDAY MAY 4 RUN DMC $18 $20

THURS. & FRI. MAY 8 & 9 STEEL PULSE $19 $22
DUB NATION

FRI. MAY 16 MERLE HAGGARD $25 $28

SAT. MAY 17 D.J. SHADOW $13 $15

FRI. MAY 23 ZERO $13 $15
PUDDLE JUNCTION

SAT. MAY 24 EeK-A MOUSE $13 $15
JORDHUGA

FRI. MAY 30 BUDDY MILES $13 $15

SAT. MAY 31 UNBROKEN CHAIN $5
Celebration of the Dead

MARITIME TICKET LINE:
(415) 974-0634 No BASS, No service charge!

MARITIME HALL
450 HARRISON ST.
SAN FRANCISCO

MHP#30 © 1997 MARITIME HALL PRODUCTIONS.
ART by JIM PHILLIPS Type by Dolly Phillips

Lights by
BROTHERHOOD OF LIGHT
LIQUID LIGHT

ALL DOORS OPEN 8 PM
ALL SHOWS 9 PM

Sponsored by
MEYER SOUND
MESA BOOGIE
GUITAR CENTER
LUMITECH LIGHTING

PHILLIPS

2B1

Maritime Hall May Calendar poster, MHP#30, 1997, 11.25" x17.75", Akido Press.

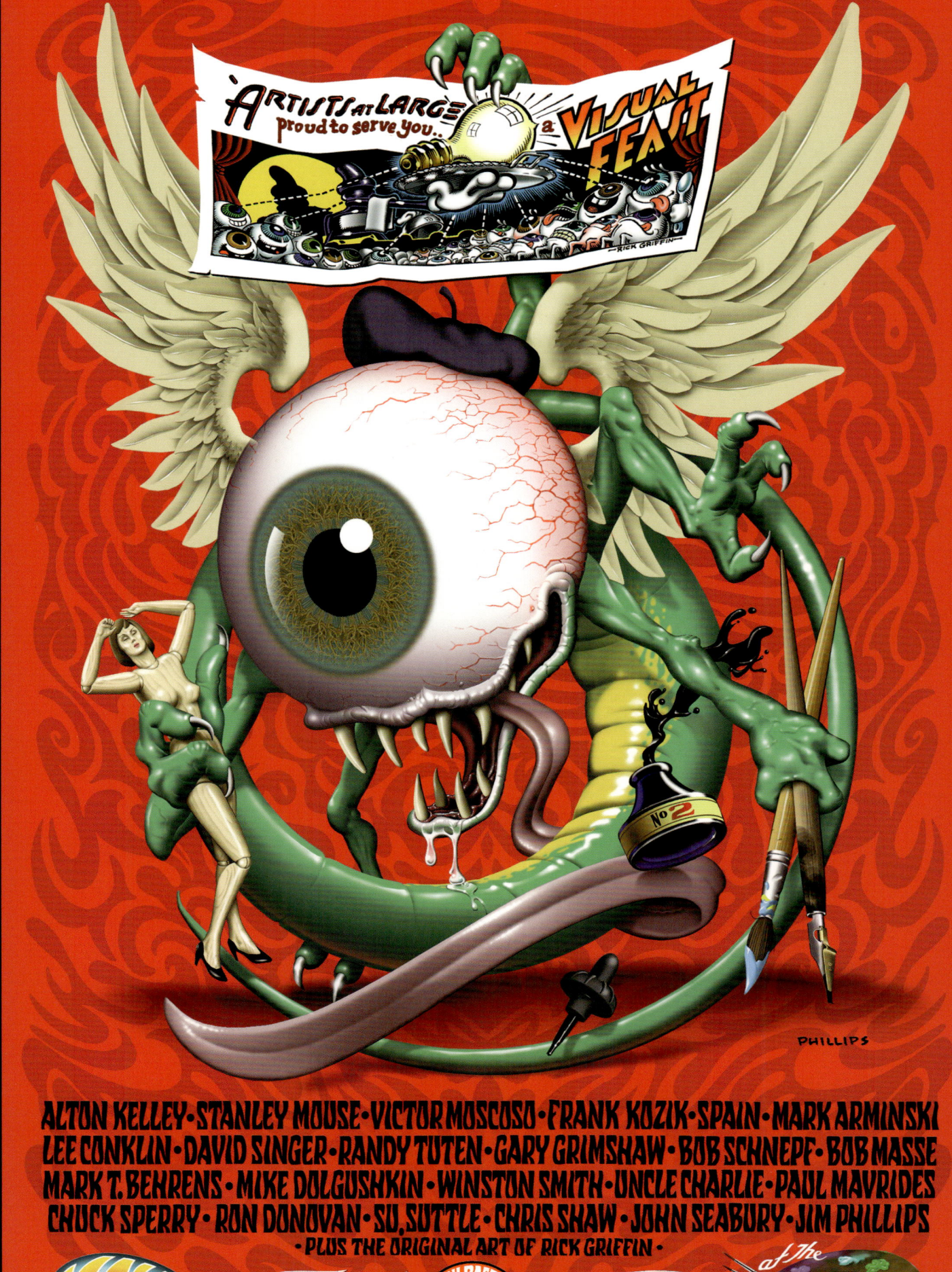

ARTISTS AT LARGE proud to serve you.. a VISUAL FEAST

PHILLIPS

ALTON KELLEY • STANLEY MOUSE • VICTOR MOSCOSO • FRANK KOZIK • SPAIN • MARK ARMINSKI
LEE CONKLIN • DAVID SINGER • RANDY TUTEN • GARY GRIMSHAW • BOB SCHNEPF • BOB MASSE
MARK T. BEHRENS • MIKE DOLGUSHKIN • WINSTON SMITH • UNCLE CHARLIE • PAUL MAVRIDES
CHUCK SPERRY • RON DONOVAN • SU SUTTLE • CHRIS SHAW • JOHN SEABURY • JIM PHILLIPS
• PLUS THE ORIGINAL ART OF RICK GRIFFIN •

MAY 18 1997

ROCK POSTERS & COLLECTIBLES
SECOND ANNUAL ARTIST SHOW IN SAN FRANCISCO
12 TILL 6 $8.00

at The SPECTRUM GALLERY
511 HARRISON ST

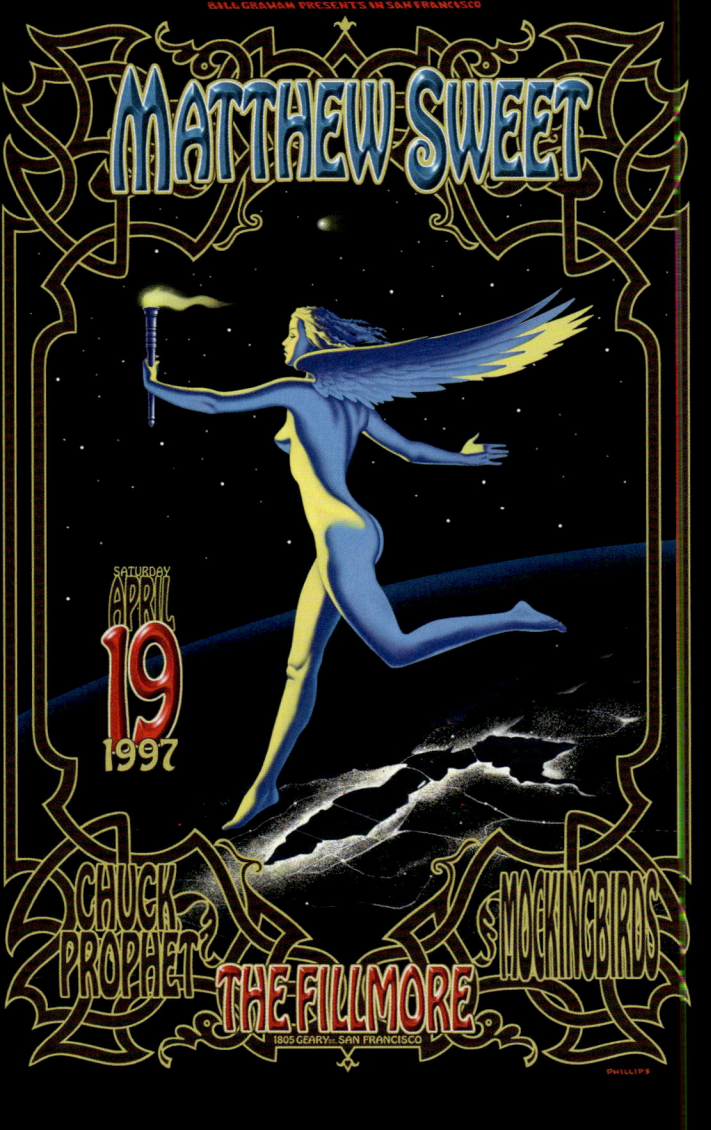

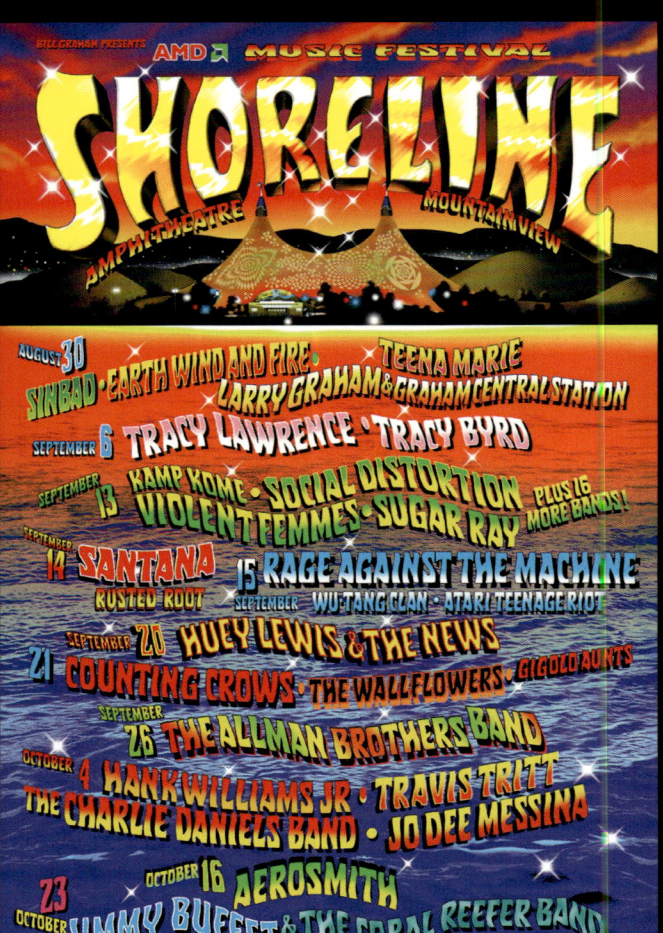

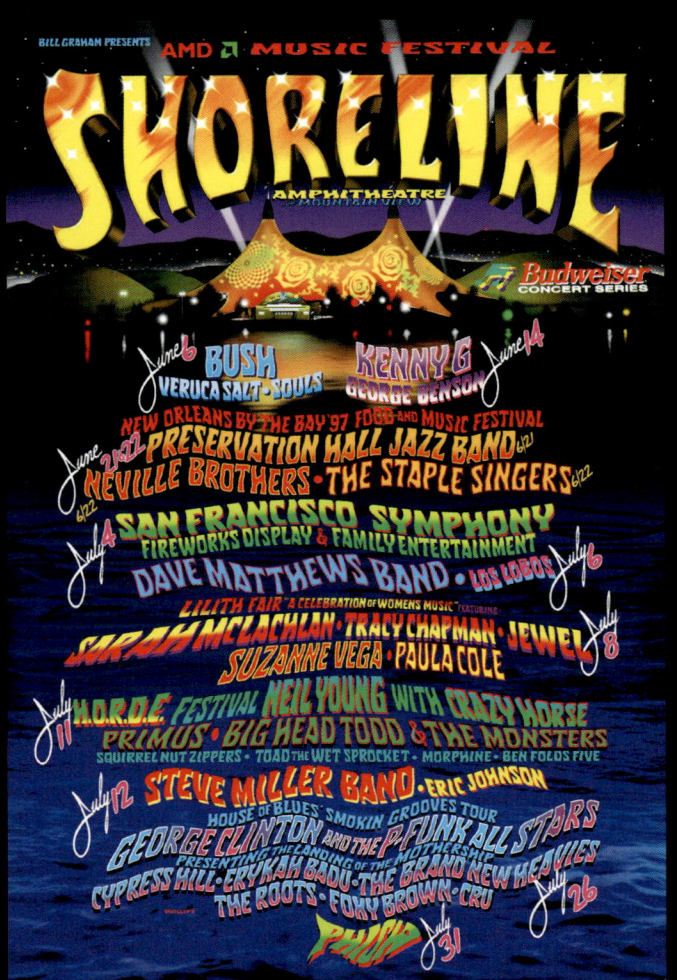

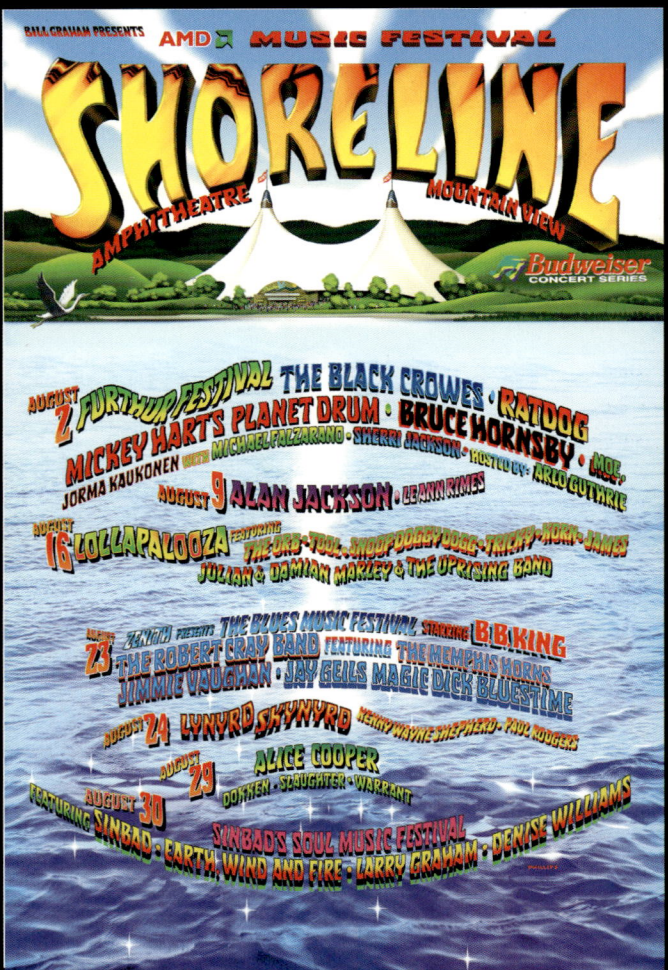

Top left: Matthew Sweet *poster, BGP#F266, 1997, 13"x19", printing:*
Great Impressions; the figure is based on a 1920's Coles Phillips painting.
Shoreline Amphitheatre Series, *1997, 13"x19", printing by Great Impressions*
top, BGP#166; bottom right, BGP#169; bottom left, BGP#174.

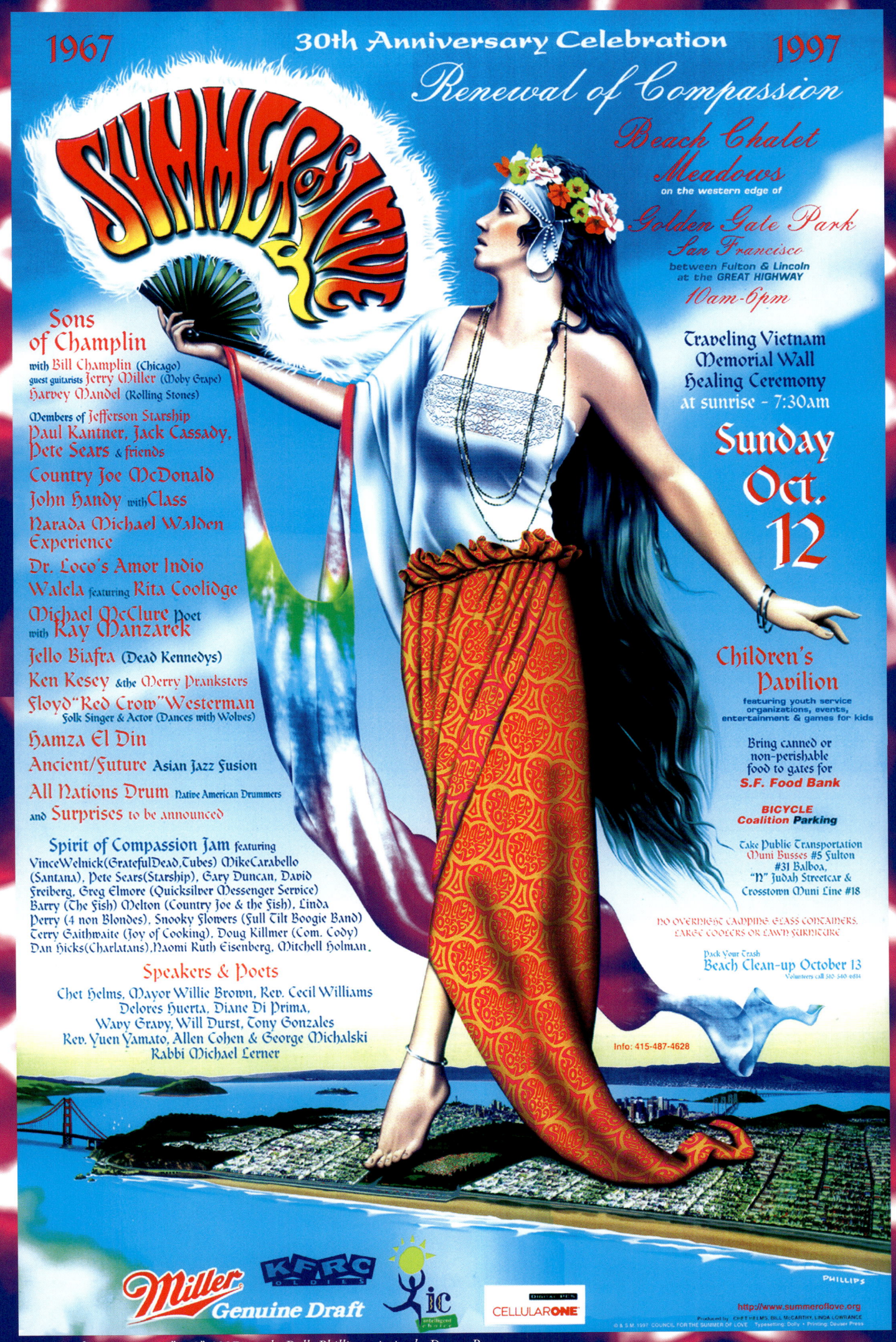

Summer of Love *poster, 20"x13", 1997, type by Dolly Phillips, printing by Dauser Press.*

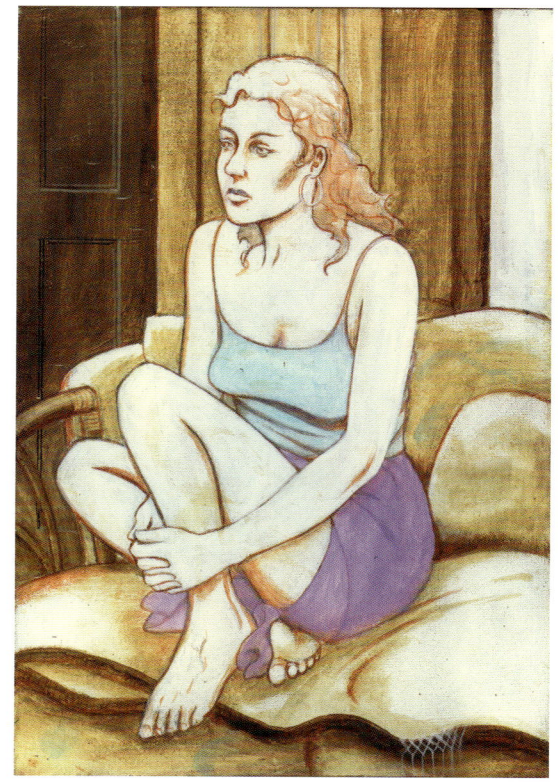

This rendering of young Jimi Hendrix' first guitar was made for the Hendrix family from an old photo that was so blurry it was hard to see him.

Phillips attended the September 95 show, and got another taste of the sheer selling power of Rock Art. "It was a great show!" Phillips said. "But while we lived it up inside during the show I spent all my money on drinks, so when we were walking out, worried about being broke in the city, I said to Dolly, 'Hey, maybe I could sell my signature and pick up a few bucks!' So I waited until they brought the box of the night's posters to the sidewalk to hand out the way they do. I got mine, but whatta rude crush by a bunch of burly guys. Then I noticed six police officers standing over by their van, and wondered if it would be legal. I walked over to them and asked 'Hey, can I sell my signature on the sidewalk?' One of them said, 'Are you the artist?' 'Yeah,' I said. One of the cops reached into their van and pulled out some of my Ratdog posters...of THIS?' he said. I nodded yes.'Well then, will you sign ours?' I said I'd love to, and signed 'To SF's finest!' on each one. They were stoked! Then I turned back to the crowd, all full of confidence, and started to hawk my signature, waving my Sharpy pen, calling 'Signed by the artist, 5 bucks!' It was sort of hard to get anyone's attention near the box and those who heard me looked at me like I was crazed. Then a big Warfield bouncer came over and told me to stop and get out! I said I didn't have to, that it was a public place and 'THEY' said it was OK! I pointed at the six cops standing there looking right at us. But the guy kept yelling at me, and I decided to let it go, not wanting to have word get back to BGP about it. So I walked down the sidewalk a little and it seemed a lot mellower than back at the mob scene. People were walking away looking at the posters, so I started waving my pen and offering my siggy again. It was darker, so some people were frightened, thinking I was a Market Street loony. I looked around and there were other loonies. A guy with a poster stopped and begged me to sign, saying he didn't have any money. I signed the back. No one else believed I was the artist, so we turned the corner with nothing to show for all my pen waving and huckstering. We walked to the lot in back of the theatre, where, at the gate, I was panhandled by a street beggar. 'Here,' I said, giving him my last dollar, '...now you've got more money than me!' and walked into the lot. There were thirty or so people waiting, I found out, because a car was blocking the entrance to the garage. Then I looked and saw that it was OUR car! And then when I went to open the door I discovered that I had locked my keys inside! The attendants called for a locksmith, saying they couldn't open it themselves. It seemed like forever for the locksmith to arrive. There we were, standing around with all these people holding posters...so I told Dolly, 'Hey, what the heck, I'm gonna work the crowd!' So I held up my pen and announced again, 'Ratdog posters signed by the artist - five bucks!' People finally went for it! I signed them on a hood of a car. Some people questioned who I was, thinking I was scamming, so I took out my driver's license, and that made more people want the signature. A few people examined the license, looked at me, and then walked away saying they still didn't believe it! By the time I was making a little cash, a street hustler came by selling two wrinkled Ratdog posters, I gave him four bucks each for them. After working the parking lot and the lock guy still hadn't showed up, I walked over to the gate and started getting people that were still streaming down the sidewalk from the Warfield. I was getting a lot of customers but had to show my license every time, so I just started waving IT! After a few minutes, the guy who had panhandled me before, who was still standing there, leaned over to me and said 'Hey man, you're doin' better than I am!' and after watching my technique some more, whispered: 'I'm gonna get me a pen too!' I'm sure he worked some of the later shows."

The locksmith truck finally showed up so everyone could get their cars out. Jim and Dolly drove off the lot with 50 bucks cash. "We felt safer not being broke, and it was an experience not to be missed."

The work just kept coming. While working on Fillmore rock posters for BGP, Arlene the Art Director asked Phillips to do a four-poster series for Tom Petty and the Heartbreakers. Phillips was jazzed, and gave Arlene the Art Director a shopping list of 25 subjects to choose from. The BGP staff chose Pan, Mermaid, Bacchus and Temptress. Phillips designed the first one, Mermaid, and then the project went on hold when Tom Petty injured his hand slugging a wall.

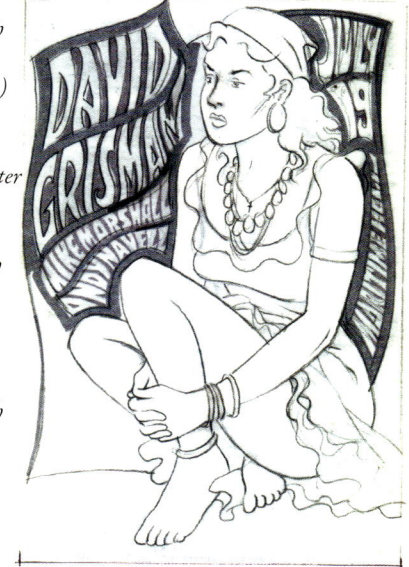

Top: Original sketch on canvas of a live model (Dolly) 20" x 14", used as basis for the David Grisman poster at right.

Center right: Sketch from painting as layout for Grisman poster.

Below: Rough sketch for BGP Warfield Grisman poster (page 158).

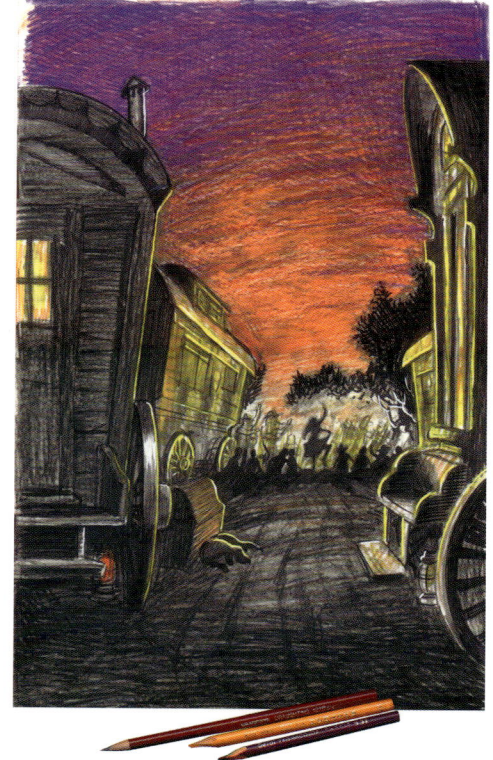

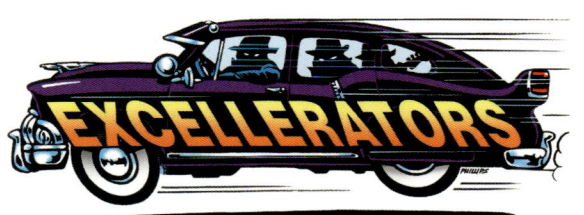

The Excellerators, a logo for another Willie Simmons' band.

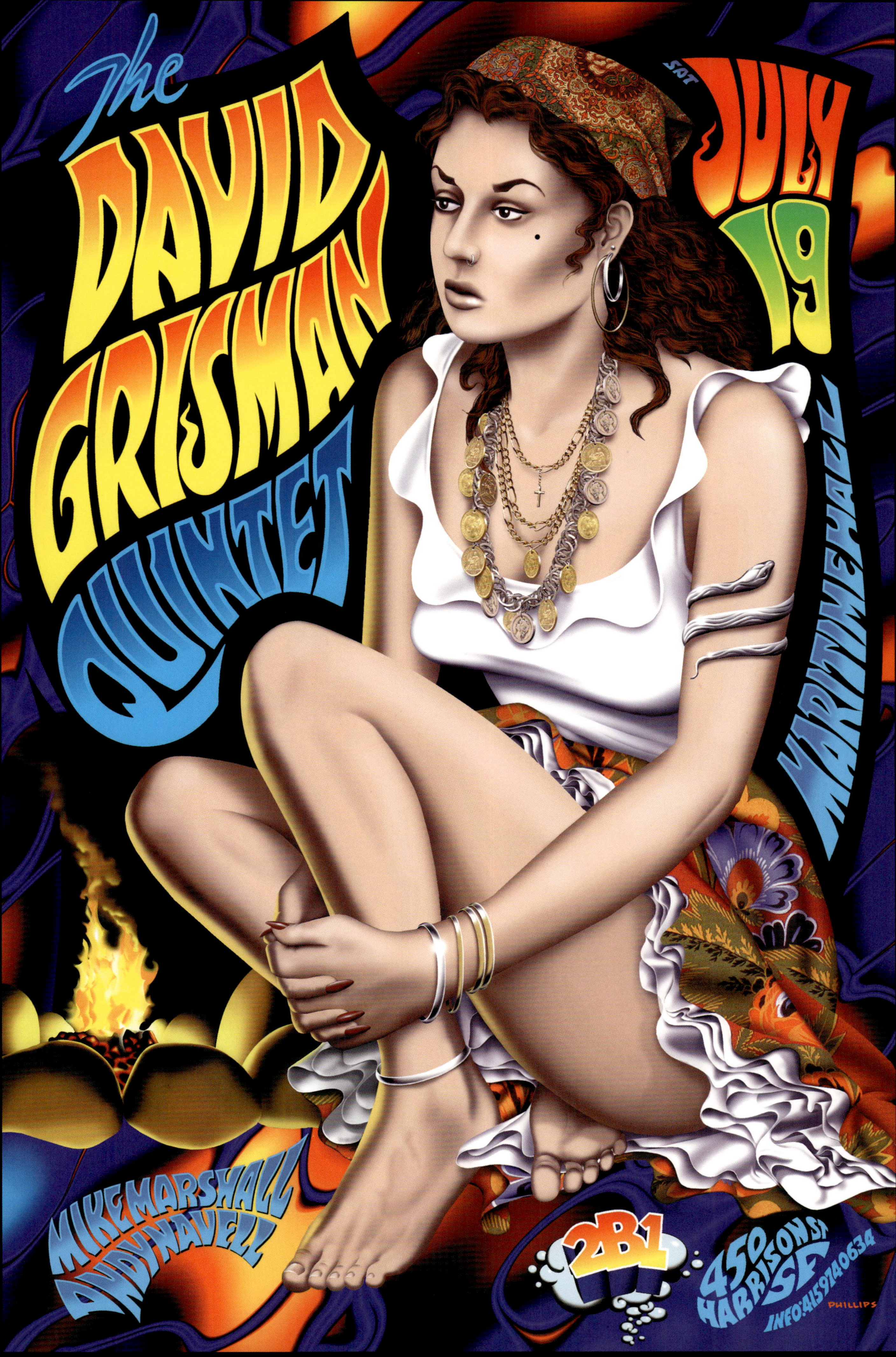

The David Grisman Quintet

The David Grisman Quintet
Mike Marshall
Andy Navell
Sat July 19
Maritime Hall
2B1
450 Harrison SF
Info: 415 974 0634
Phillips

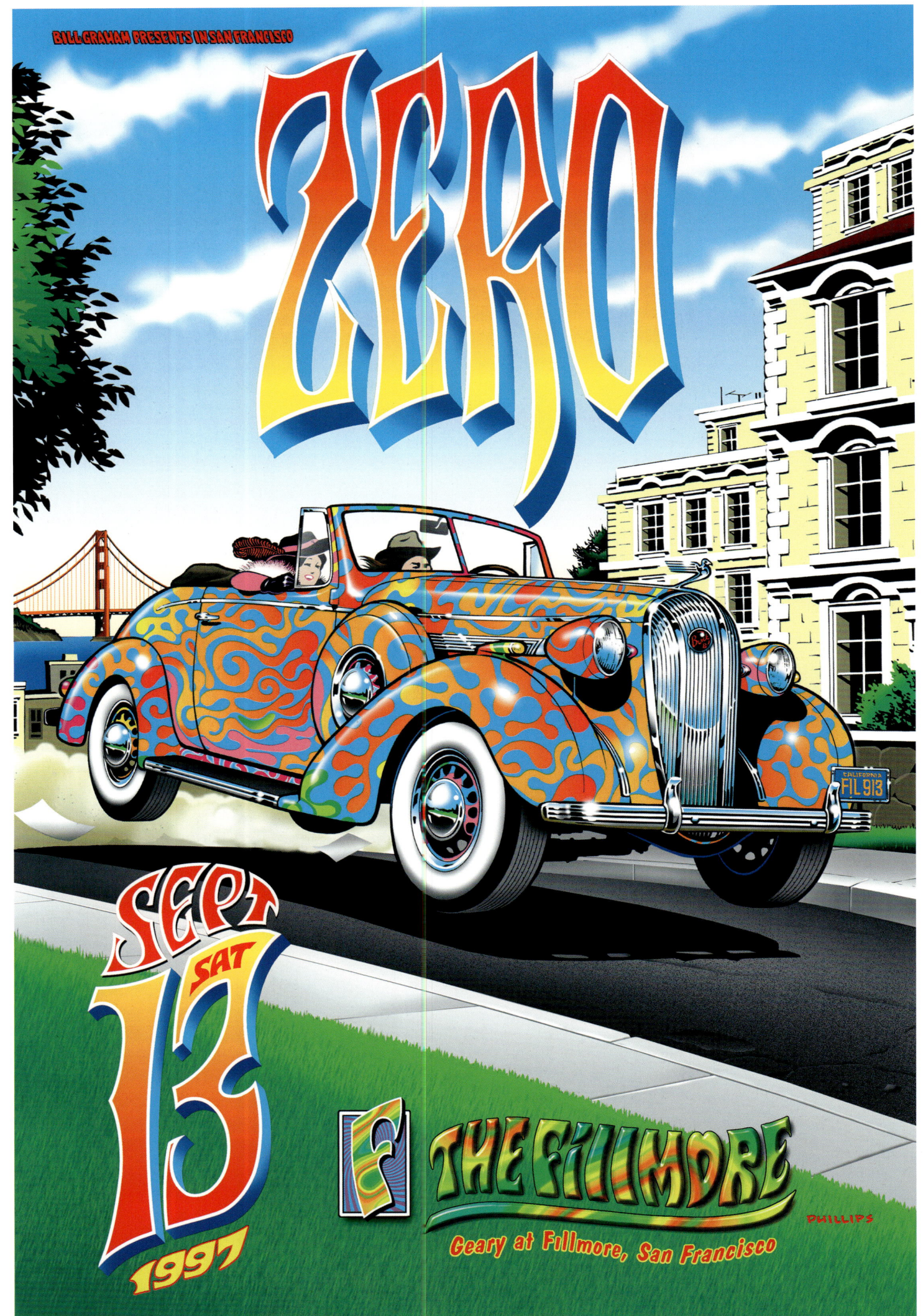

Zero poster, BGP #289, 1997, 13"x19", printing: Great Impressions.

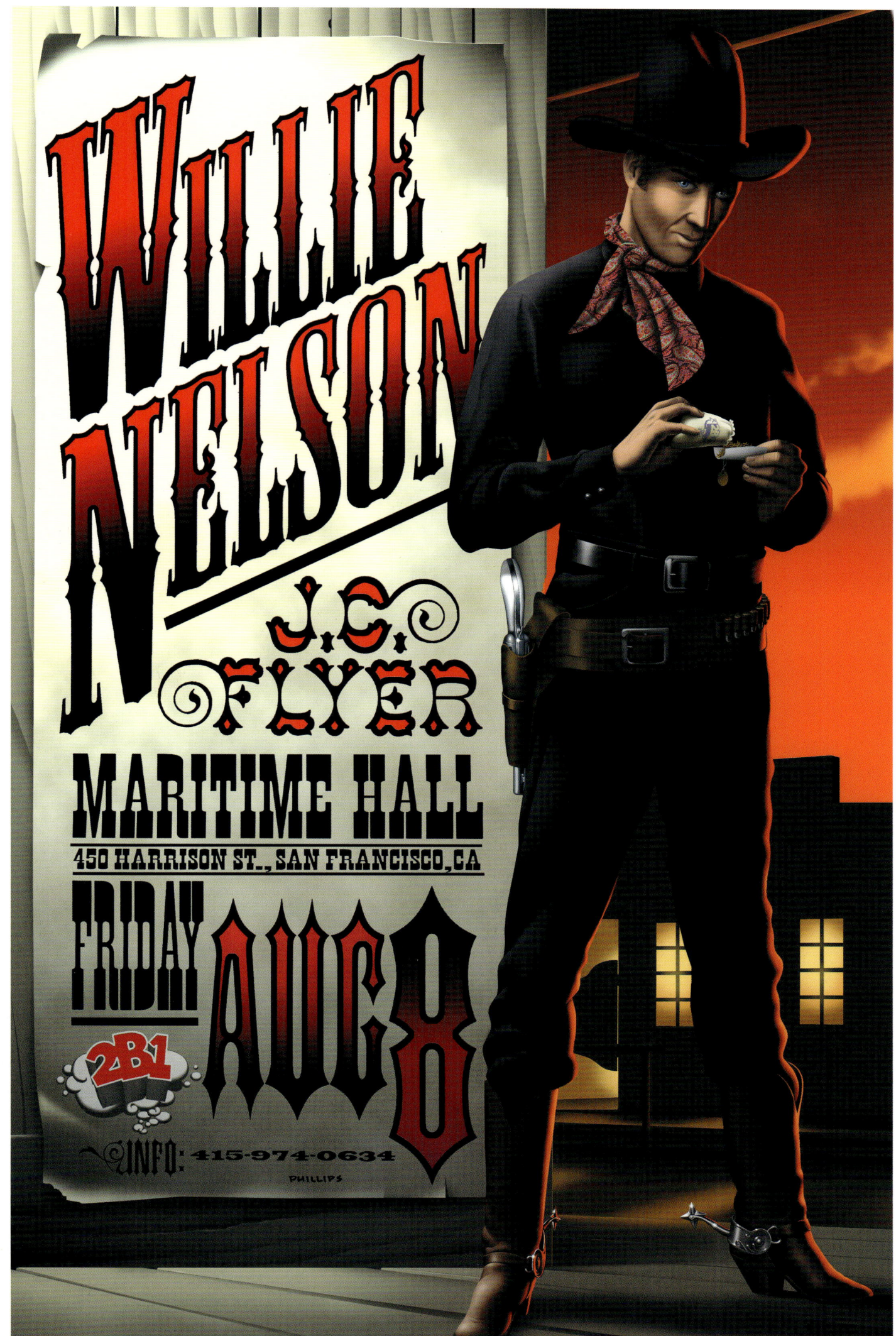

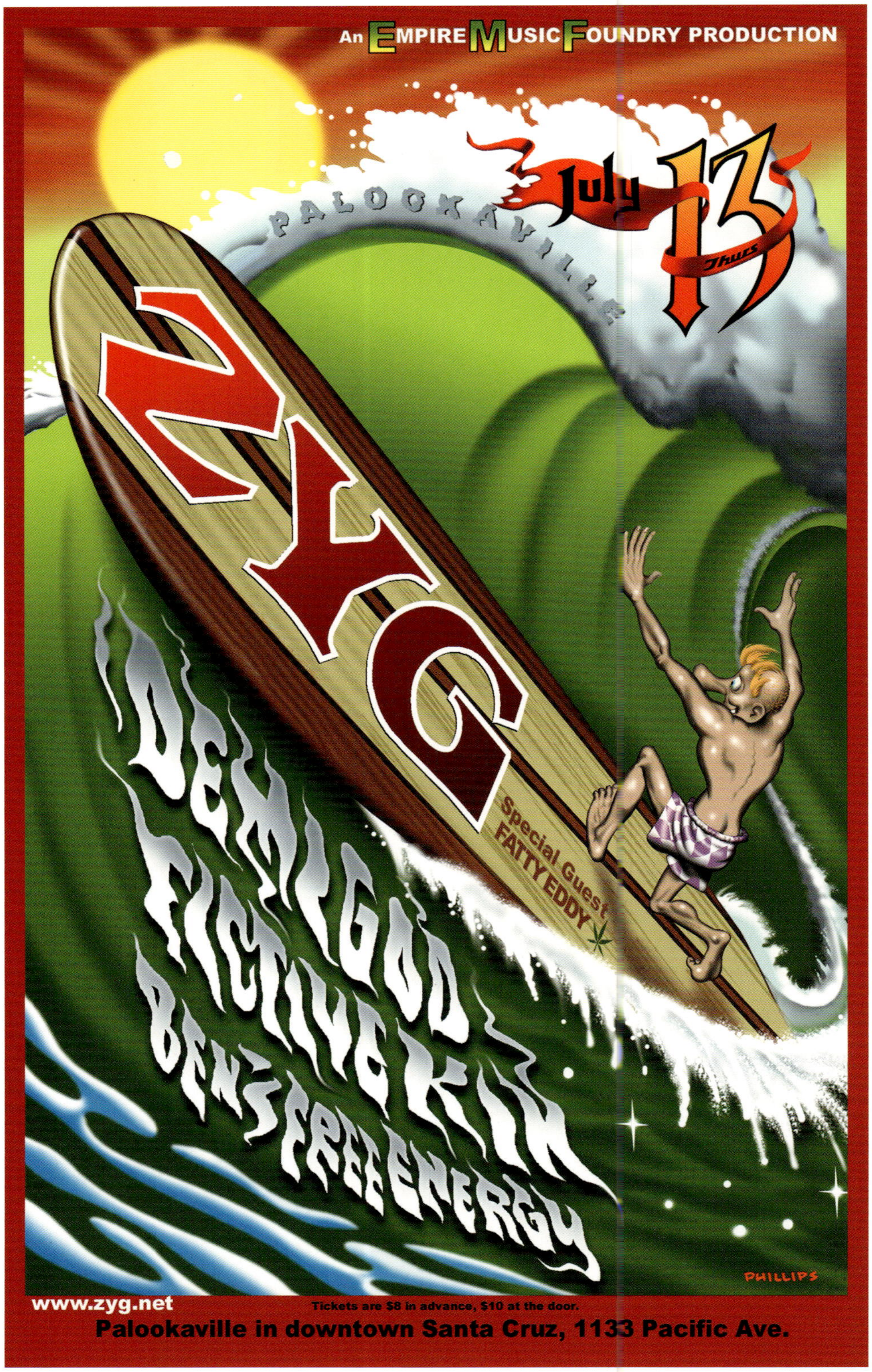

An EMPIRE MUSIC FOUNDRY PRODUCTION

PALOOKAVILLE
July 13 Thurs

ZYG
DEMI GOD
FICTIVE KIN
BEN'S FREE ENERGY

Special Guest
FATTY EDDY

PHILLIPS

www.zyg.net   Tickets are $8 in advance, $10 at the door.
Palookaville in downtown Santa Cruz, 1133 Pacific Ave.

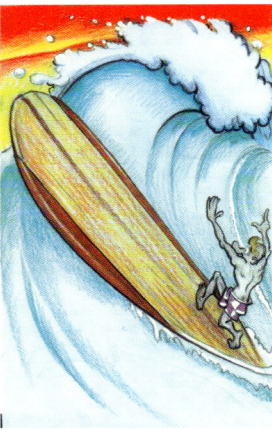

Top right:
Pencil for
Zyg.

Opposite page: Leftover Salmon/String Cheese Incident
poster, BGP#183, 1997, printing: Great Impressions.
The owners at BGP insisted that Jim include a love-in next
to the Golden Gate Peace sculpture in Golden Gate Park
that was a controversy in the news then.

Left: ZYG, 2000, 17"x11", Post Digital printing, limited
to 100. Zyg was a garage band a few doors
down from Jim's Studio.

Below: Schwa rave card, 4.5"x3.5", 1997.
In the late 90s small gang-printed cards began to be an
economical way for shows to advertise. Sparky the Space
Gremlin makes another appearance.

Bottom: Leftover Salmon *card, 4 1/4" x5 1/2", 1997.*

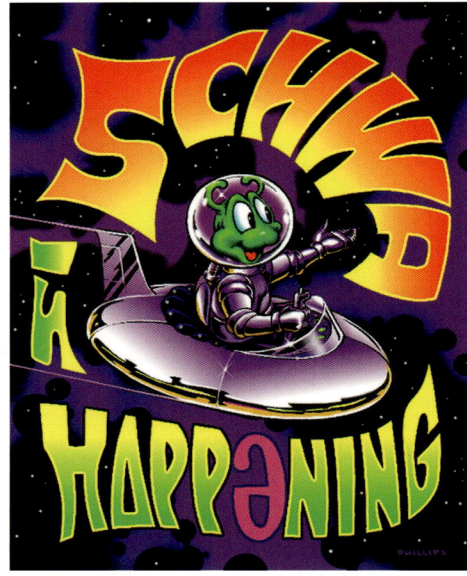

ARLENE OWSEICHIK: *"Of all the poster artists I have worked with,
Jim seemed to have made the quickest transition from manual to digital
art. One day he's sending us art boards, the next day it's digital files on
disk, without any sacrifice of his made-by-hand style. He is a real pro.
We turn to Jim when we have a high profile poster for someone who will
appreciate traditional, i.e. old Fillmore, style poster art. Jim's posters are
always intricate, charming, have great lettering, and tell a story."*

GRANT MCKINNON: *"At San Francisco Rock Posters and Collectibles
we celebrated our 10th anniversary in September of 2002. We were in the
Cannery for a year and then moved to our current location on Powell Street.
It's been my pleasure to know Jim for 8 or 9 years now and I had admired his
work for many years before that, mainly seeing it on posters and in The Art
of Rock. Jim only got three posters in there and I definitely think he should
have had more. Here in the shop, I'd say Jim is fourth or fifth on the list
in sales. I push his art because he designed our new winged logo and our
matches. Jim's new Fillmore series sell really well: Tom Petty,*

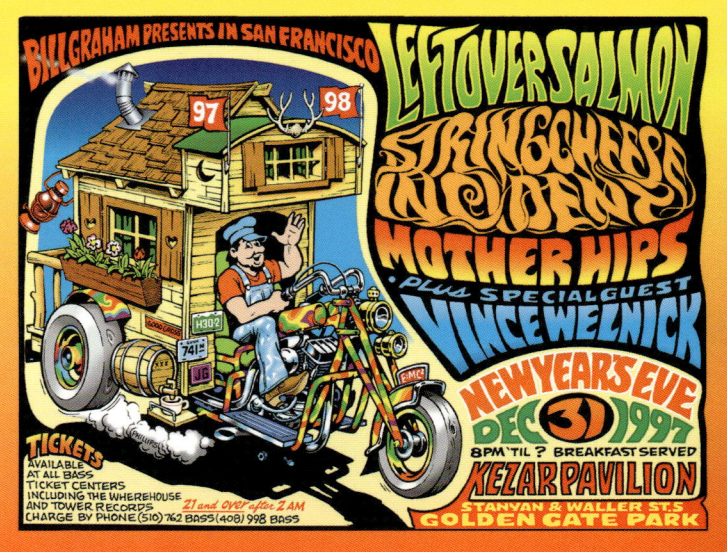

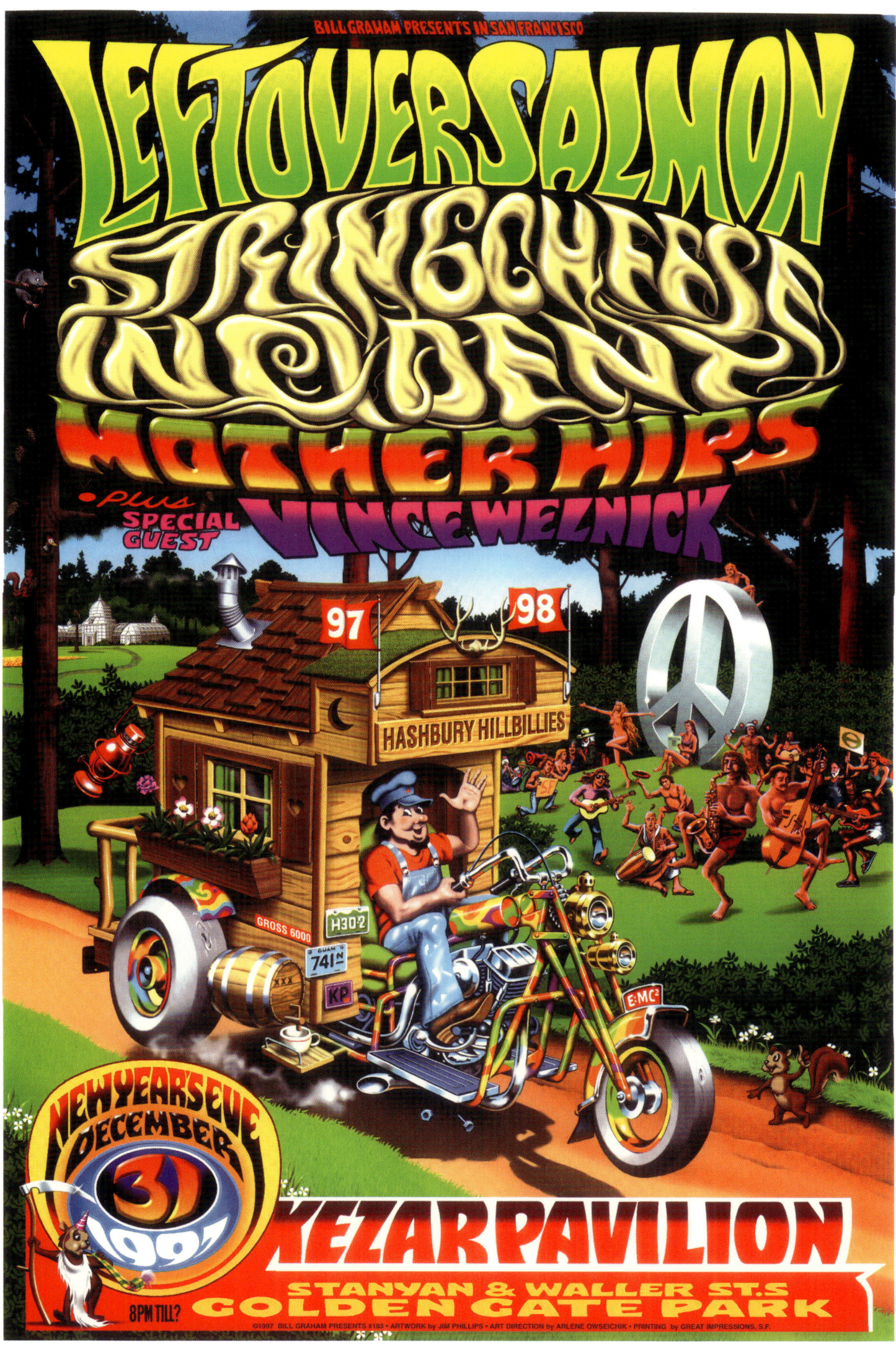

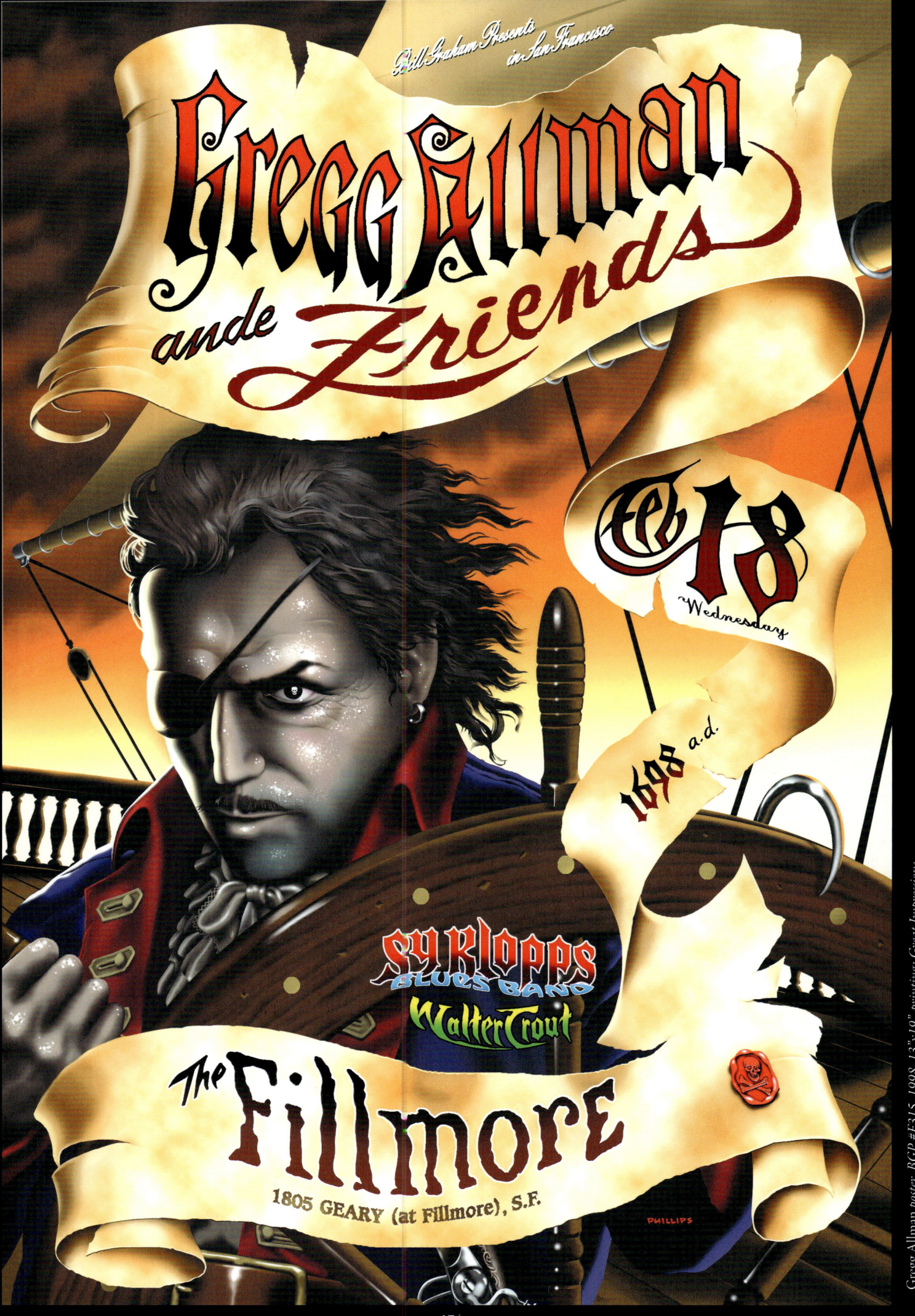

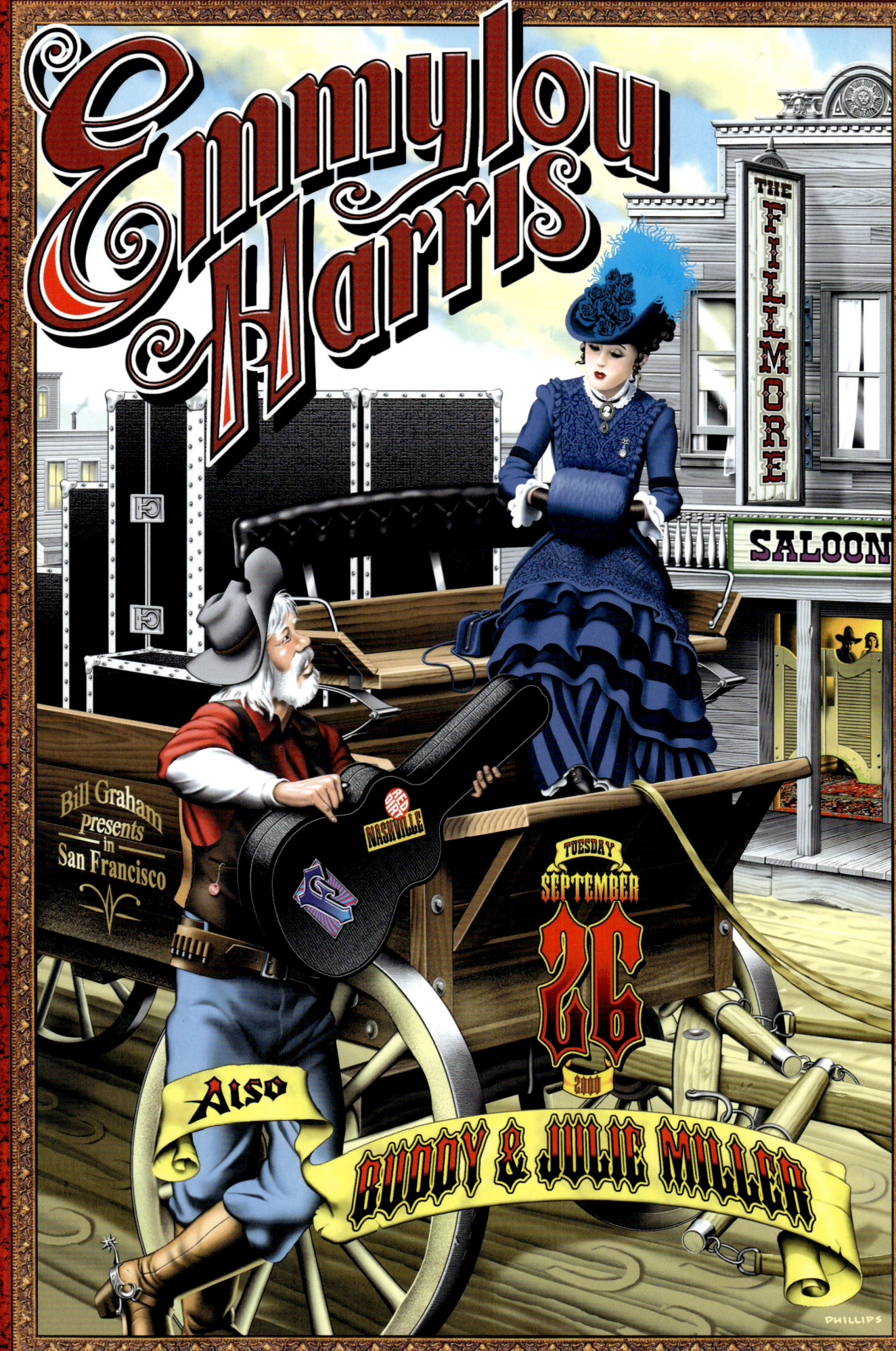

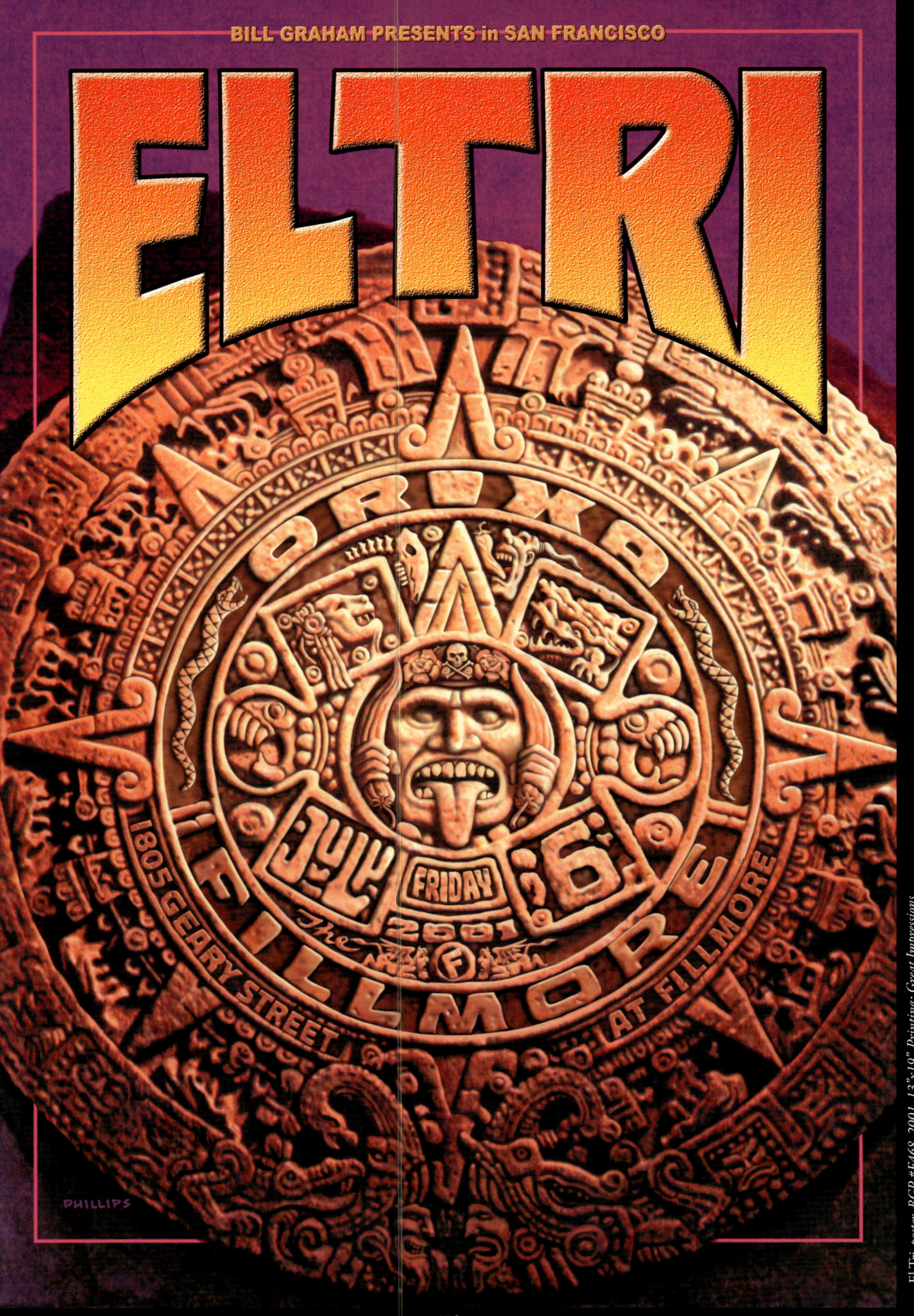

El Tri *poster, BGP #F468, 2001, 13"x19". Printing: Great Impressions.*

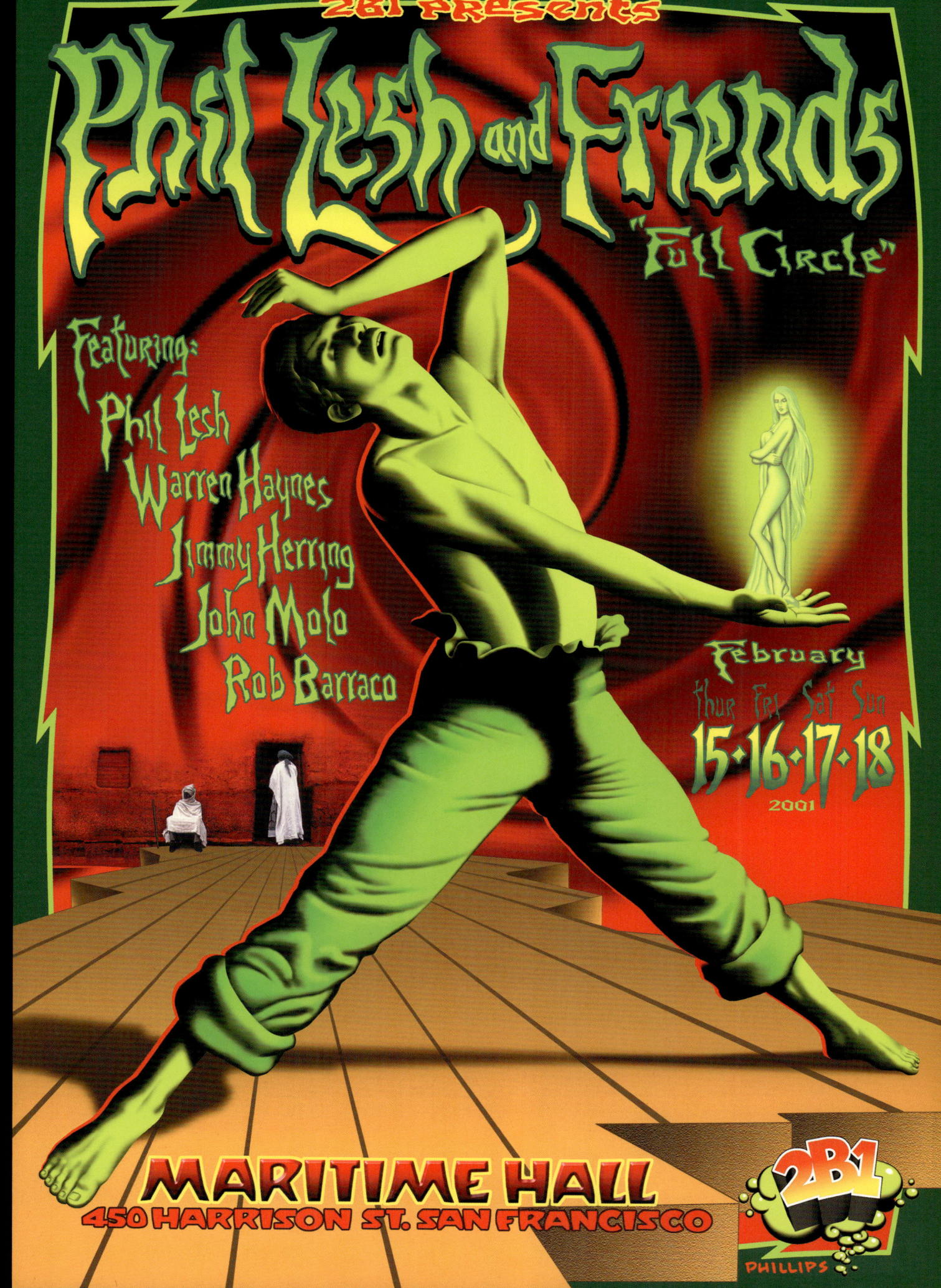

Phil Lesh, MHP#112, 2001, 12"x18". Printing : Akido Press.

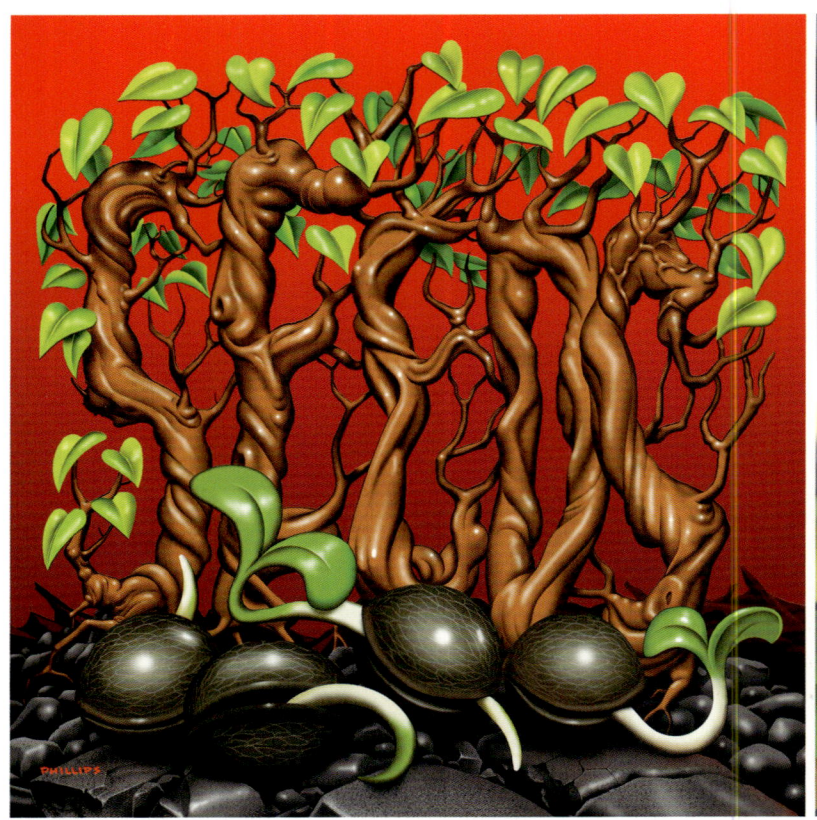

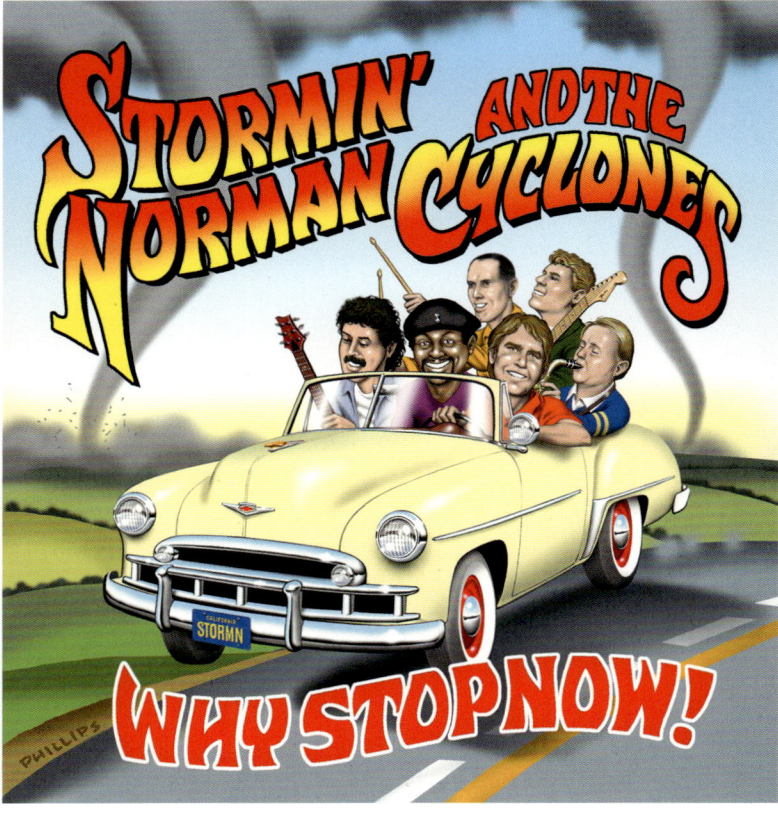

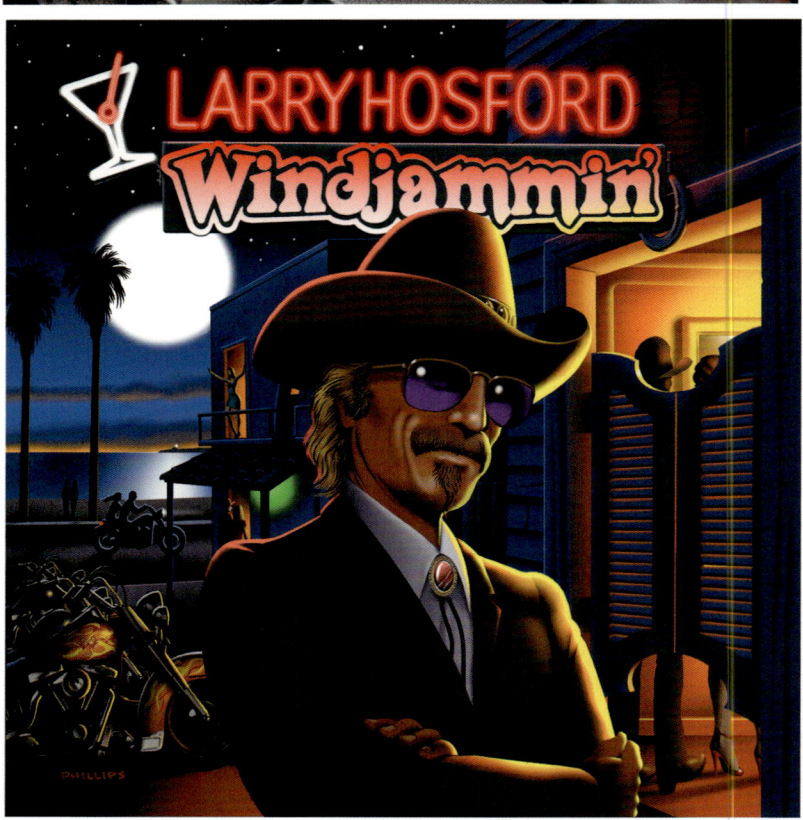

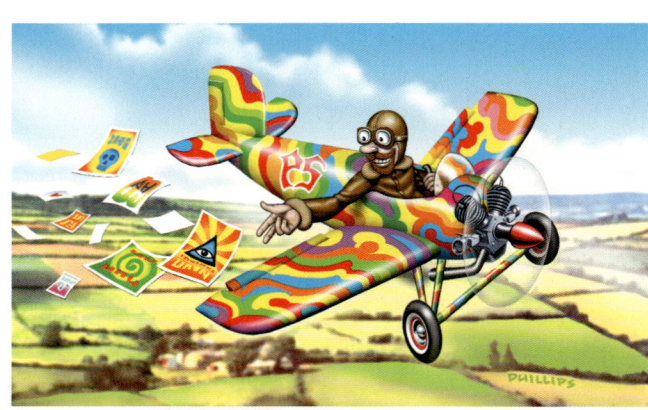

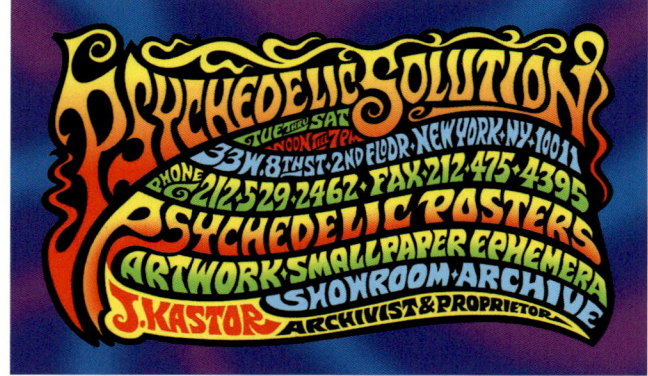

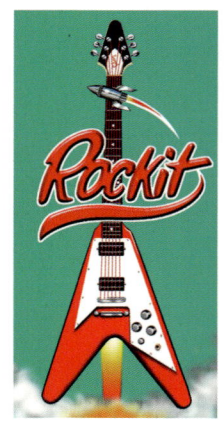

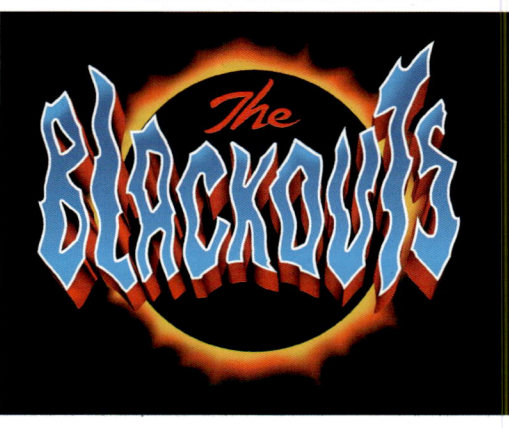

Seeds, Stormin' Norman, & Larry Hosford CD covers, circa 1999.
Calling card: Psychedelic Solution, front & back. Bottom: Three logos for
Will Simmons: Rockit Collectibles, Blackouts, Wild Card.

Matthew Sweet. The older stuff is a little slower because it is more valuable. My personal favorite from the old days is the Moby Grape Halloween poster. That's a fabulous piece of artwork and it sells for about $300. Of his more recent work, I would probably say it's a four-way tie for the Tom Petty series. Tom Petty played for four weeks at the Fillmore and I went to several of those shows. Those were great shows, they were the funnest thing I'd been to in my life. I got a different Phillips poster each time and all my friends were freaking out. 'I know this guy. He's a friend of mine.' We probably framed 10 or 15 or 20 of them just in our store. I think Jim has some of the most fluid art I have ever seen. To me it is as strong as Rick Griffin's art in the smoothness and the flow. He has a strong sense of color and a strong sense of depth perception. Jim had a great sense of balance, except when he fell off the ladder."

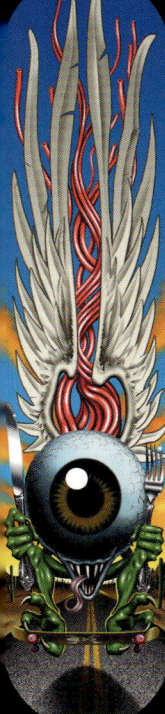

Festus.

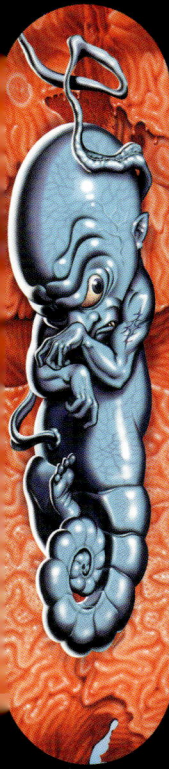

Grip Tape

Next three pages: A series of skateboard graphic grip tape, 1999.

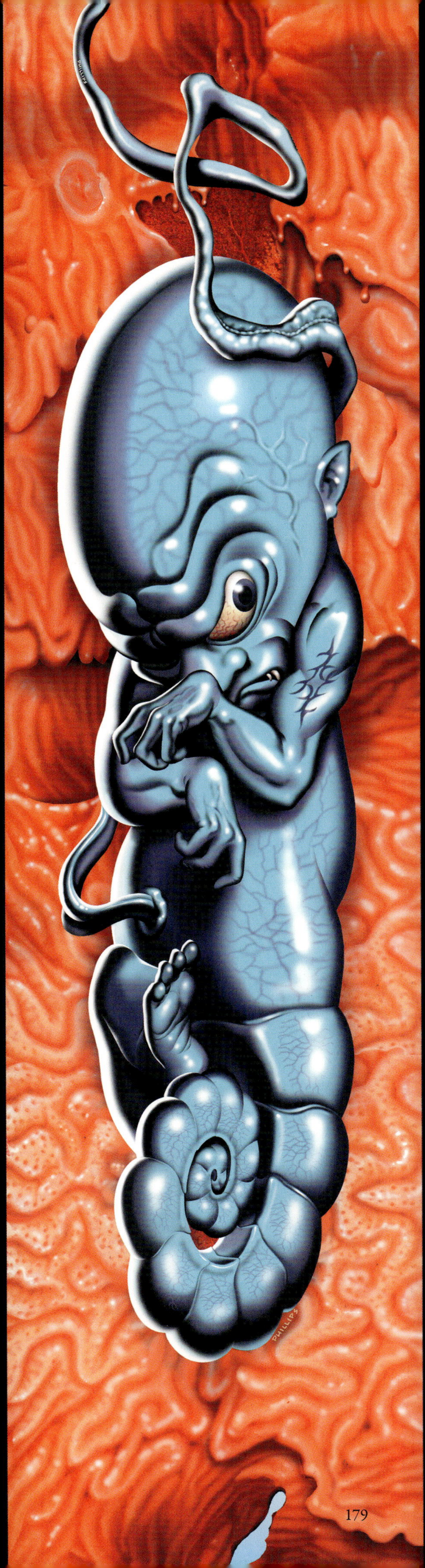

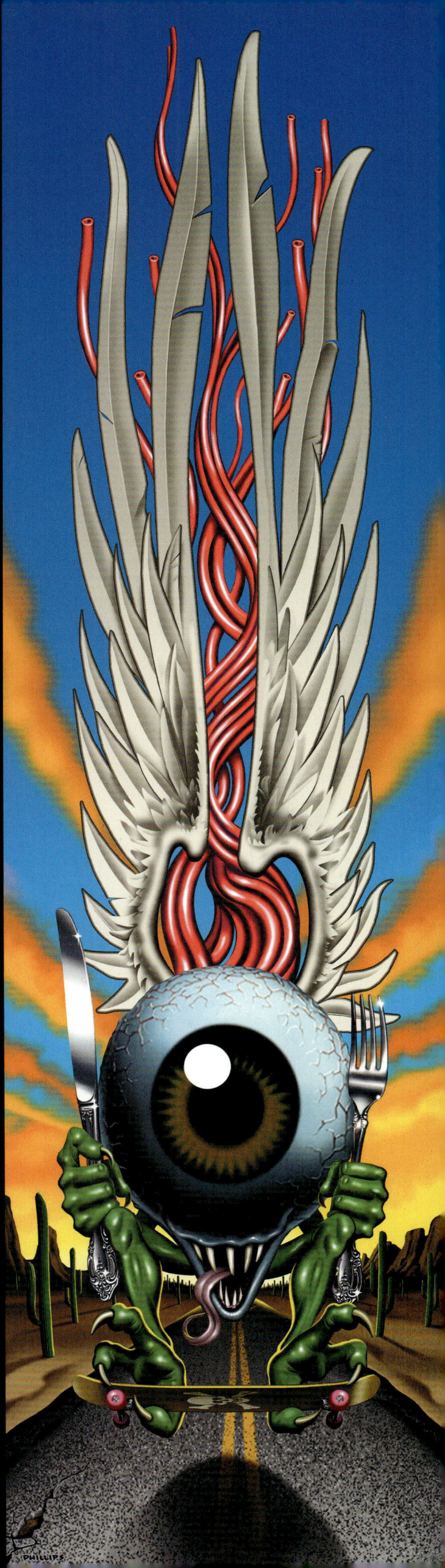

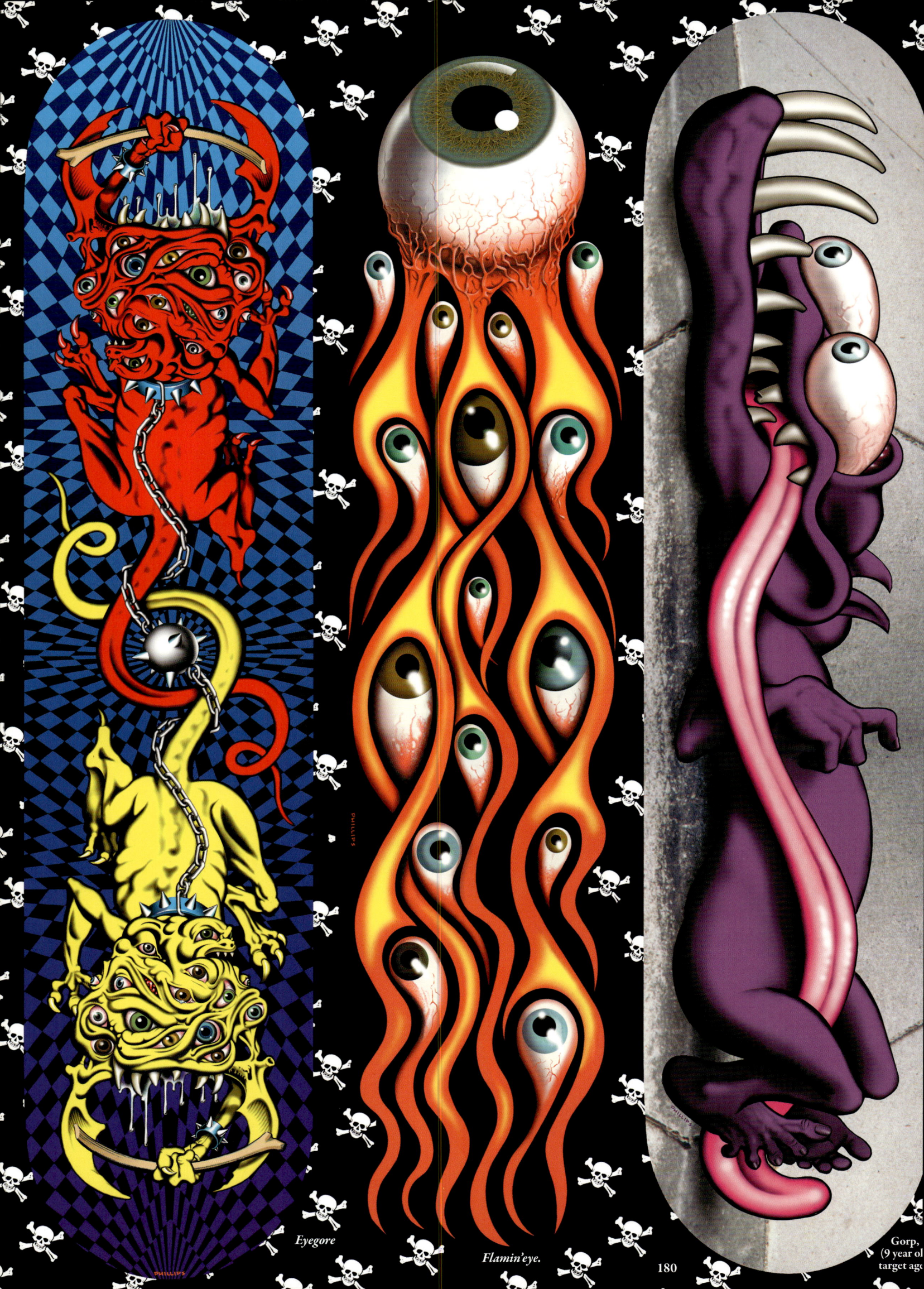

Eyegore

Flamin'eye.

180

Gorp,
(9 year ol
target ag

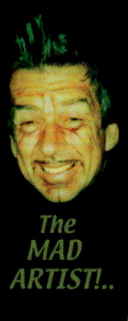

The
MAD
ARTIST!..

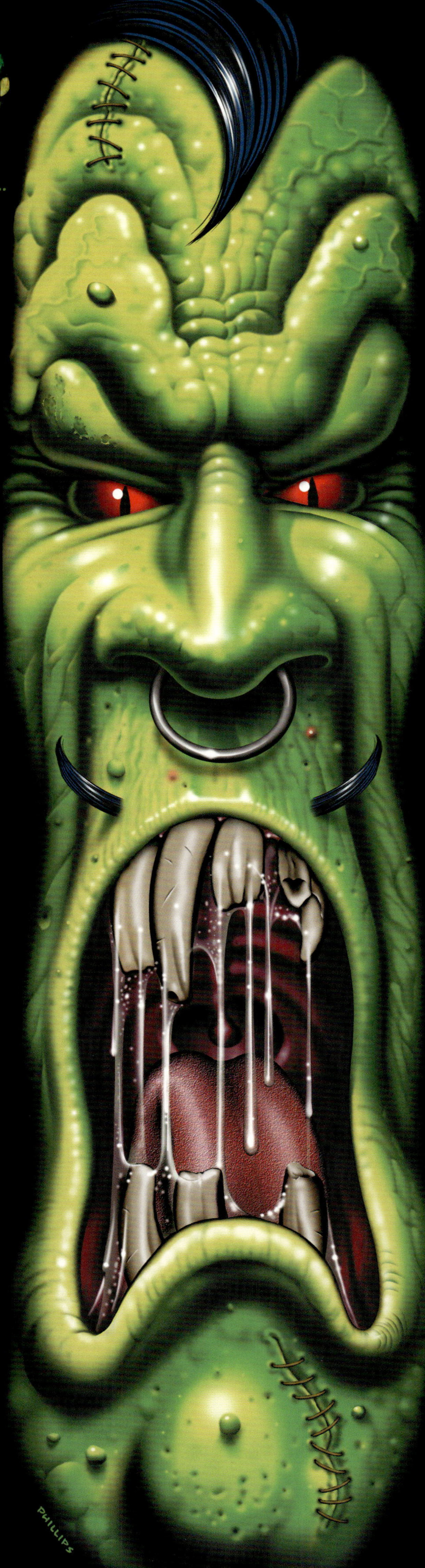

PHILLIPS

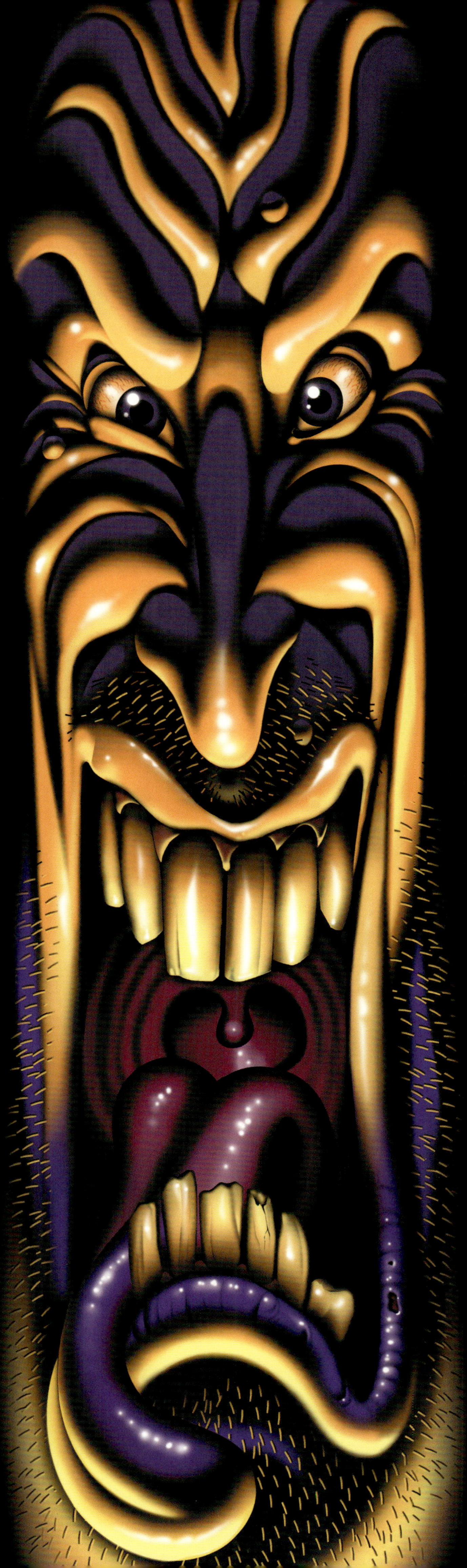

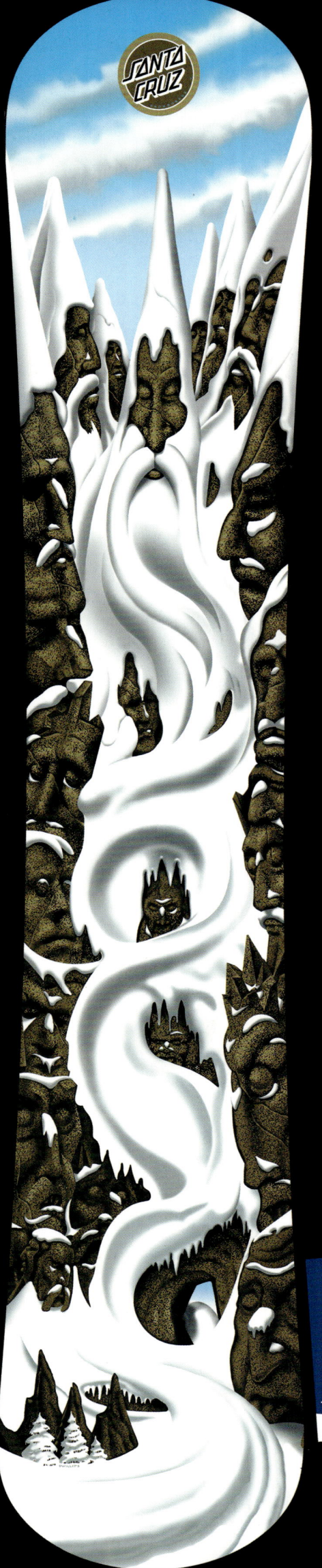

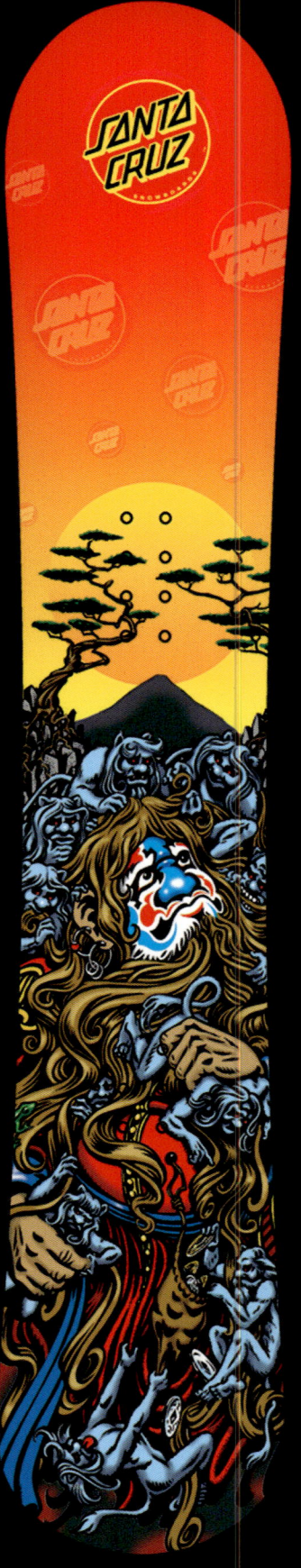

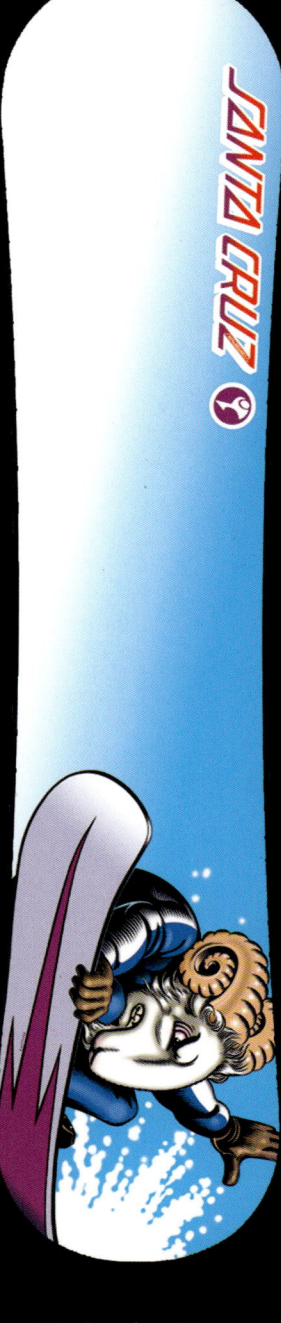

*Top; Snowboard designs
for Santa Cruz, 1999.*

*Lower center:
PYT snowboard sticker, 2000.*

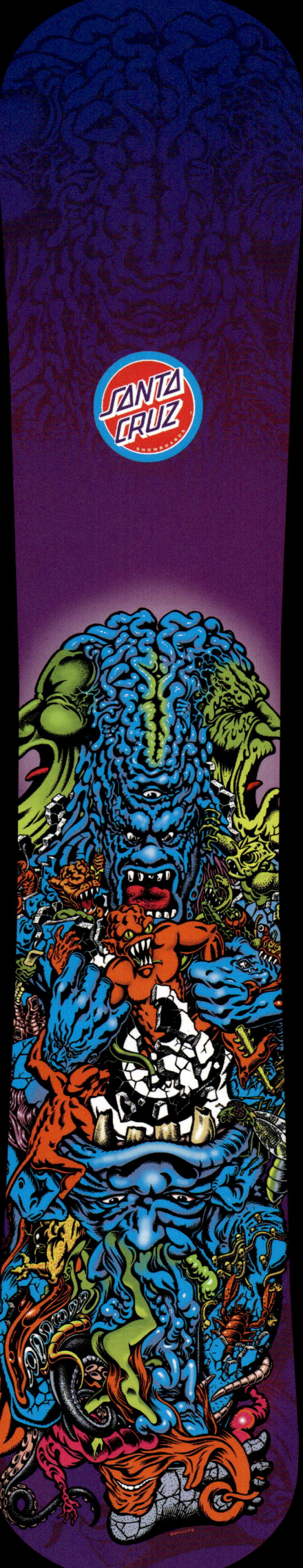

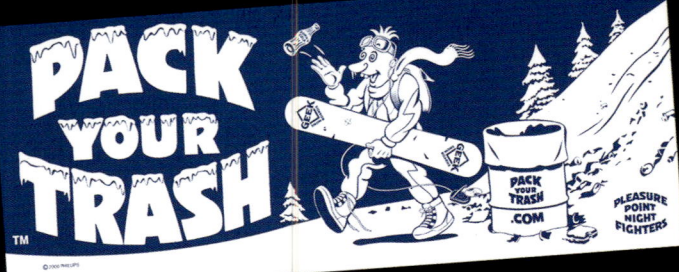

SNOWBOARDING

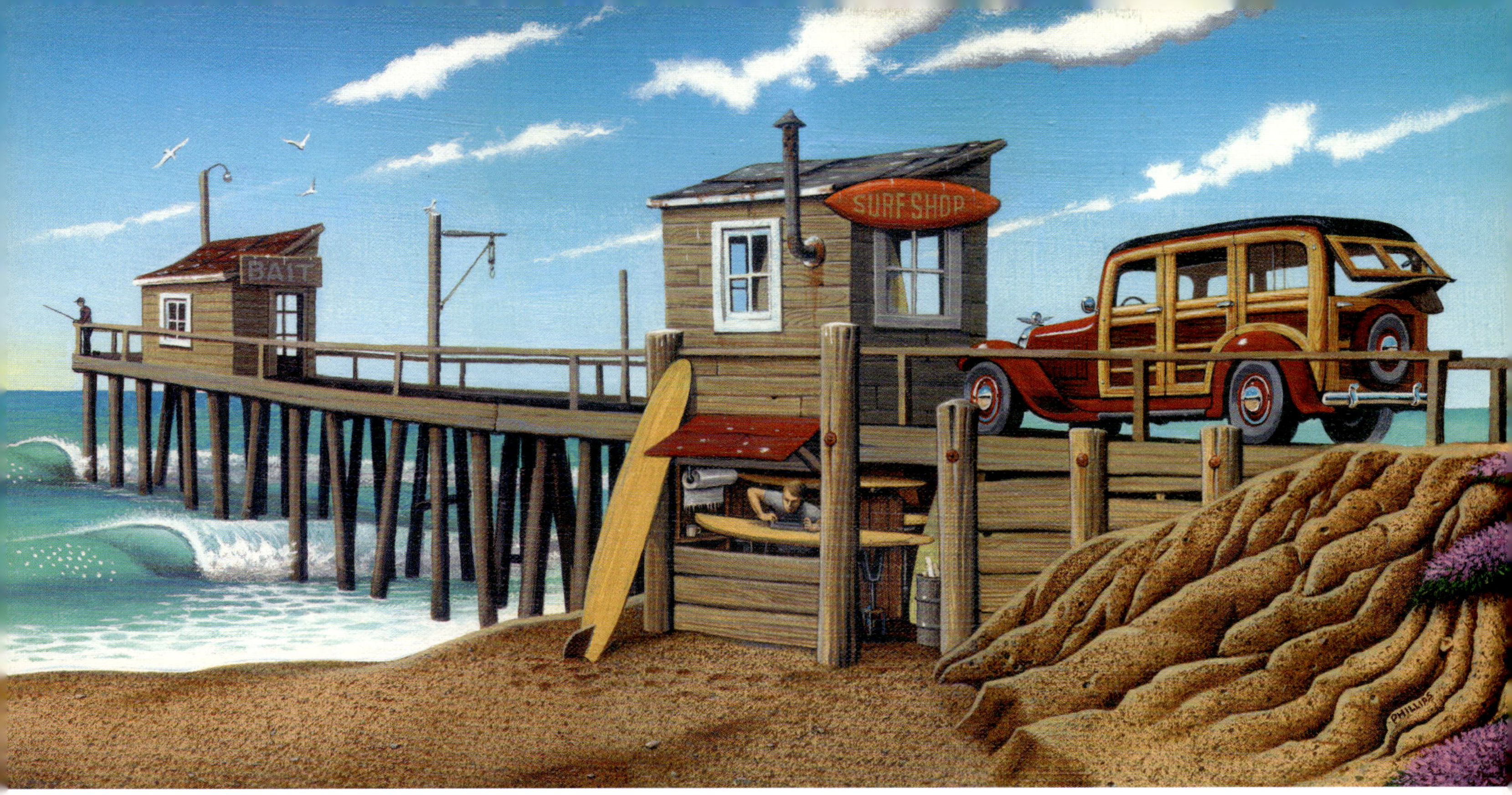

Top: The Wharf, *acrylic on canvas, 1992, approx 14"x22". Collection of Briar Buckhauser.*
Below: The Wharf 2, *acrylic on canvas, 1999, 12"x24", a revisit of the first wharf painting. Collection of Rich Novak.*

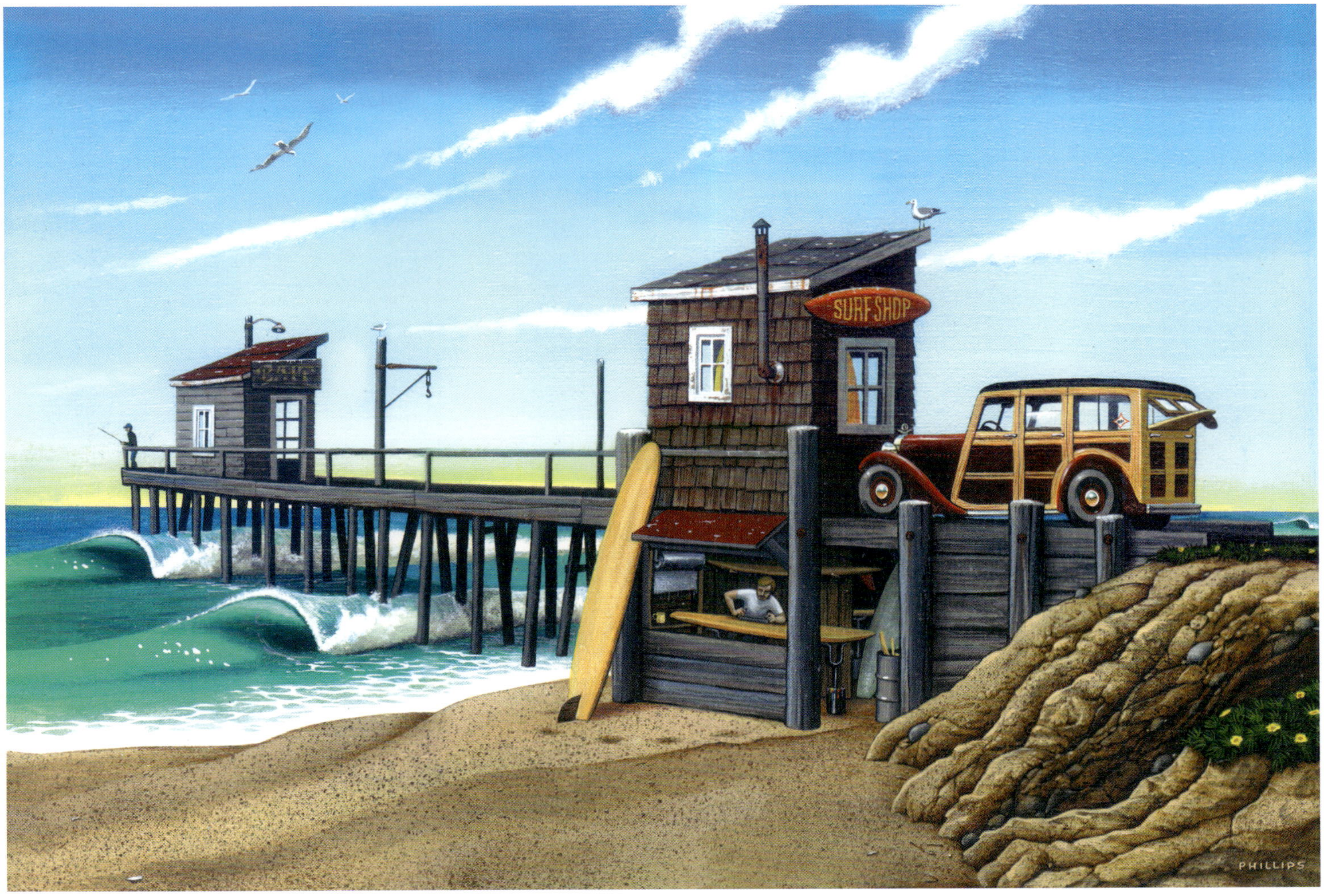

Phillips had never injured his hand slugging any walls, strangely enough, but in December of 1996 he was badly injured when his ladder slipped while trimming trees over his backyard deck. He broke his pelvis in several places and was put in traction for a week with 25 pounds hanging from a bolt running through his shinbone. The King of Physical Gross Out art was grossed out. On New Year's Eve '96, Phillips underwent a five-hour surgery

to place 12 pins, a plate and a broken-off drill bit. A day or two later, Phillips got a call from Arlene saying that Tom Petty's hand was better and he was ready to play a show, and would Jimmy be able to give them the poster with a new date by the next day? No problem. The show must go on. Jim didn't want to lose the poster, and said he could do it. He called Dolly from his hospital bed, and directed her to do those very tricky alterations over

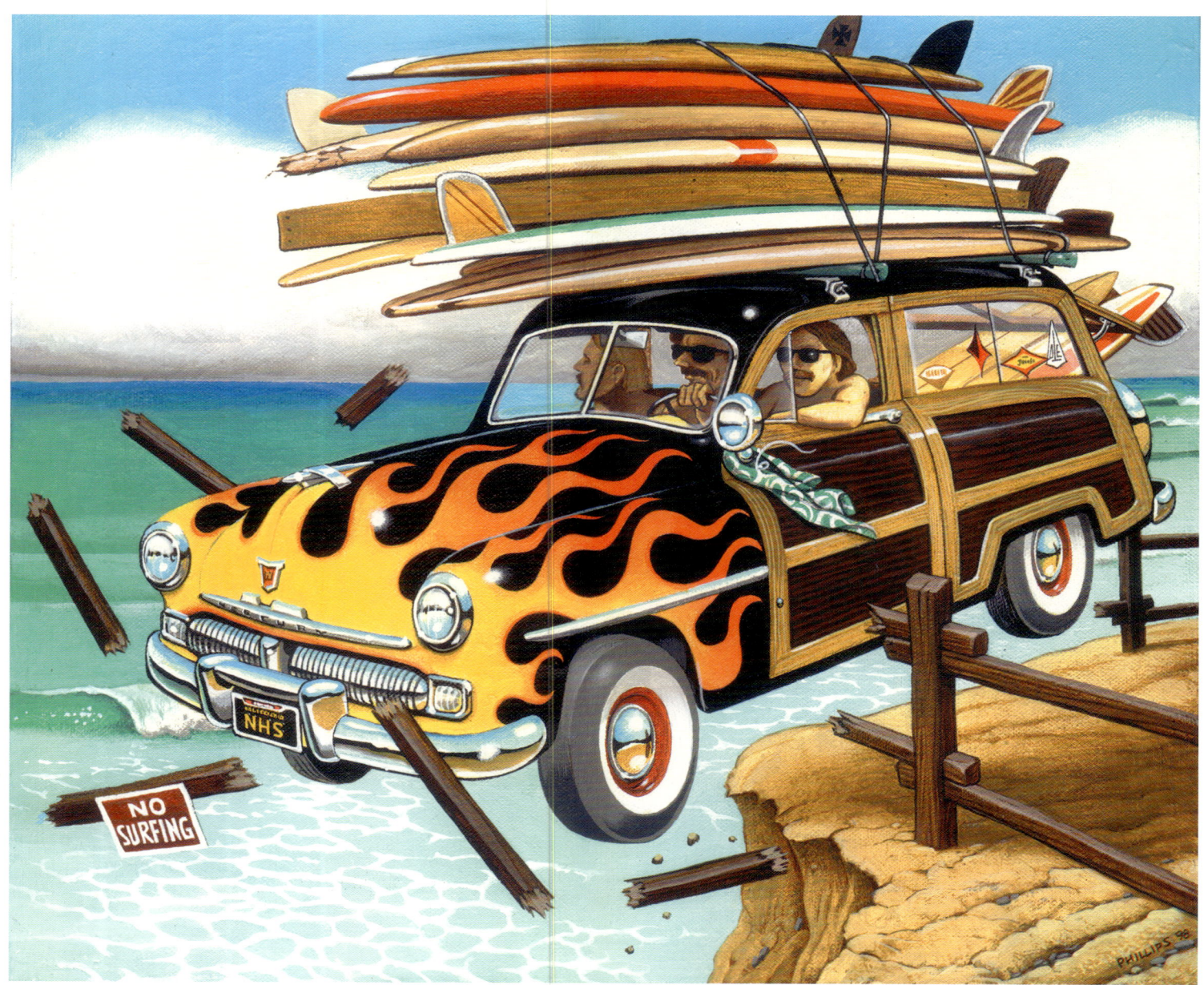

Top: Merc Woody, *acrylic on canvas, 1998, approx 16"x20".*
Bottom: History of Surfing *redux, acrylic on canvas, 1999, 20"x14".*

The collection of Rich Novak

the telephone. She e-mailed the final art to BGP. Another week later he was released, getting a ride home, flat on his back in Bill Dawson's pickup camper shell. At home, Big John set up a bed in the living room, and Jimmy laid flat on his back, just happy to be alive and home. A day or two later, Arlene called and asked if he would be able to continue the series, and if so, they would need the art in 6 days. Jim didn't want to let the Petty set go, and assured her he could do it even though he hadn't even tried sitting up yet, and knowing doing the poster would require sitting at the computer for days. Dolly brought him some paper and he immediately started sketching, flat on his back. He promised a mermaid. He sketched different poses until he found something in the fourth that had appeal, and there was no doubt about whether to use it. The next step was to actually try sitting. He used one more day to rest before starting, using up the cush time he usually saved for finish. The next day he hobbled on one leg to his computer chair and found he could sit. Not only that but he endured the 8O hours needed to complete a poster. The work helped Jim keep his mind off his injury. He started right away on some other posters, and then soon after, created the other two Petty posters.

ARLENE OWSEICHIK: *"Jim is truly a great artist. His professionalism is illustrated in his recounting of the Tom Petty poster series saga. I see now what a challenge it was for him to complete the project. He rose to the occasion, and, as a result, there exists an outstanding and timeless set of posters."*

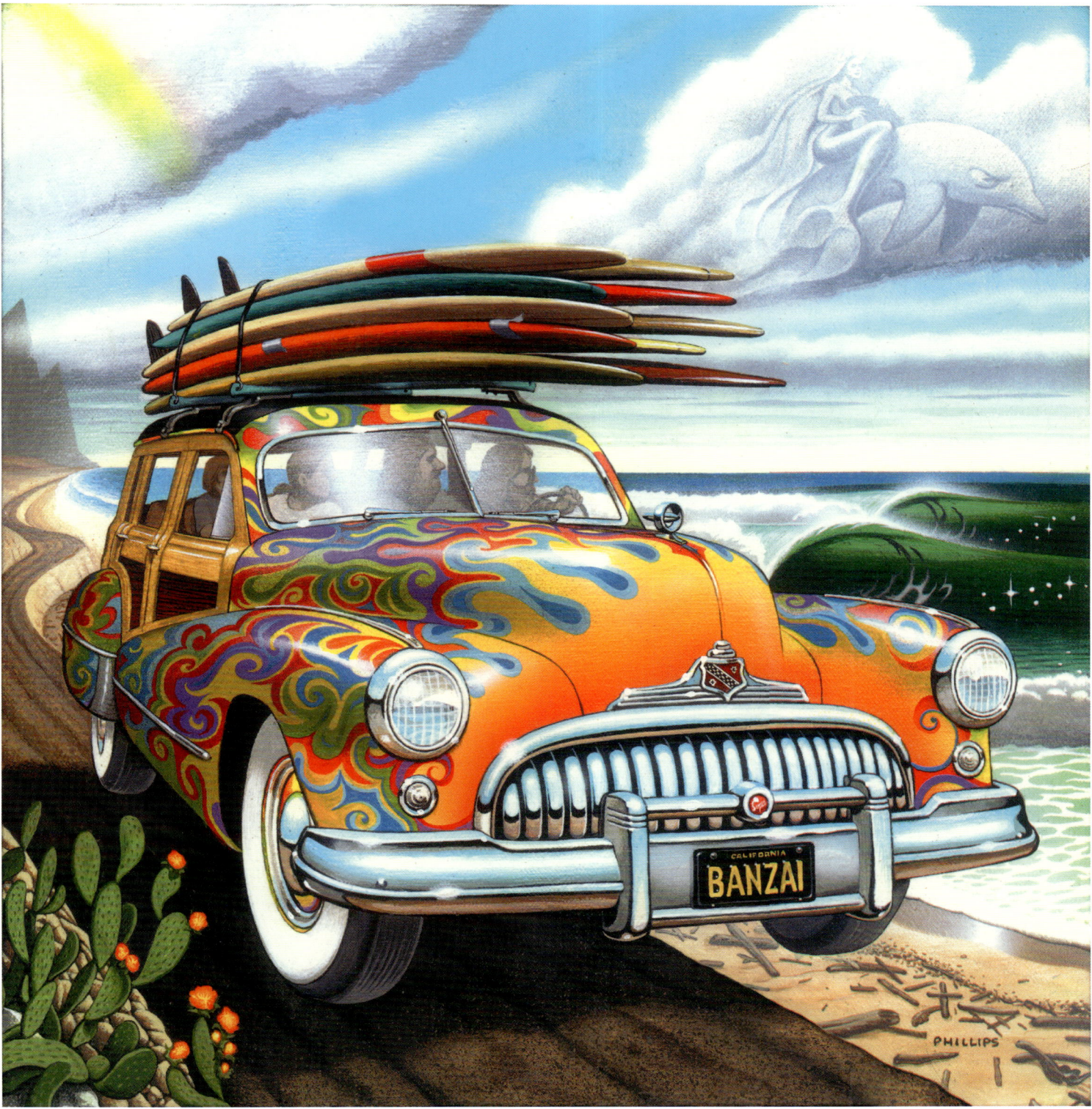

Banzai Buick, acrylic on canvas, 2000, 14"x14".

Always on the lookout for new opportunities, Phillips reconnected with Bill Dawson who was forced to move to Bakersfield when Pack Your Trash folded. They teamed up to make t-shirts and stickers from Phillips' Family Dog logo, and Dawson moved to Berkeley to be closer to the City and help Phillips market t-shirts at the Maritime Hall shows. Phillips was a 20% partner and all lights were green, until vendors reported back that most people were unfamiliar with the Family Dog. "It had been thirty years since the Avalon days, a person could be 40 and not remember the shows", Bill Dawson said, "We overestimated the public's memory span. The Family Dog kind of fizzled on us." In late 1996, Chet Helms left the Family Dog and Phillips went with him. That freed them to plan for the Summer of Love thirty year anniversary in Golden Gate Park scheduled for October 1997. Although the Hall of Flowers Rock Art poster show had collapsed, the rock poster industry grew to be a viable market.

Of all Phillips' 90s-era rock posters, you have to dig the one for James Brown. The hardest working man in the illustrating business worked up a cold, cold sweat making a poster for the hardest working man in show business, and it turned out to be a money maker. The night James Brown played Maritime Hall with his 28 Soul Generals was a fantastic show. For Jim and Dolly Phillips it was great to see one of their favorite singers from their teenage days, and James was still in great form. Jim had done a special show poster because Family Dog was doing monthly calendar posters then. Professor Poster took the initiative, arranged the printing production and offered Jim half interest to do the poster art. Jim worked hard at James Brown's portrait, trying to do justice to the Godfather of Soul. Professor Poster had obtained permission from management and bodyguards for Jim and Dolly to meet with James, show him the new poster, do some signing, and have a group portrait taken with him. However, Dolly was suffering from a pinched nerve in her neck, and they were unable to stay after the show and meet James Brown as they had wanted to. A few weeks later, the Professor presented

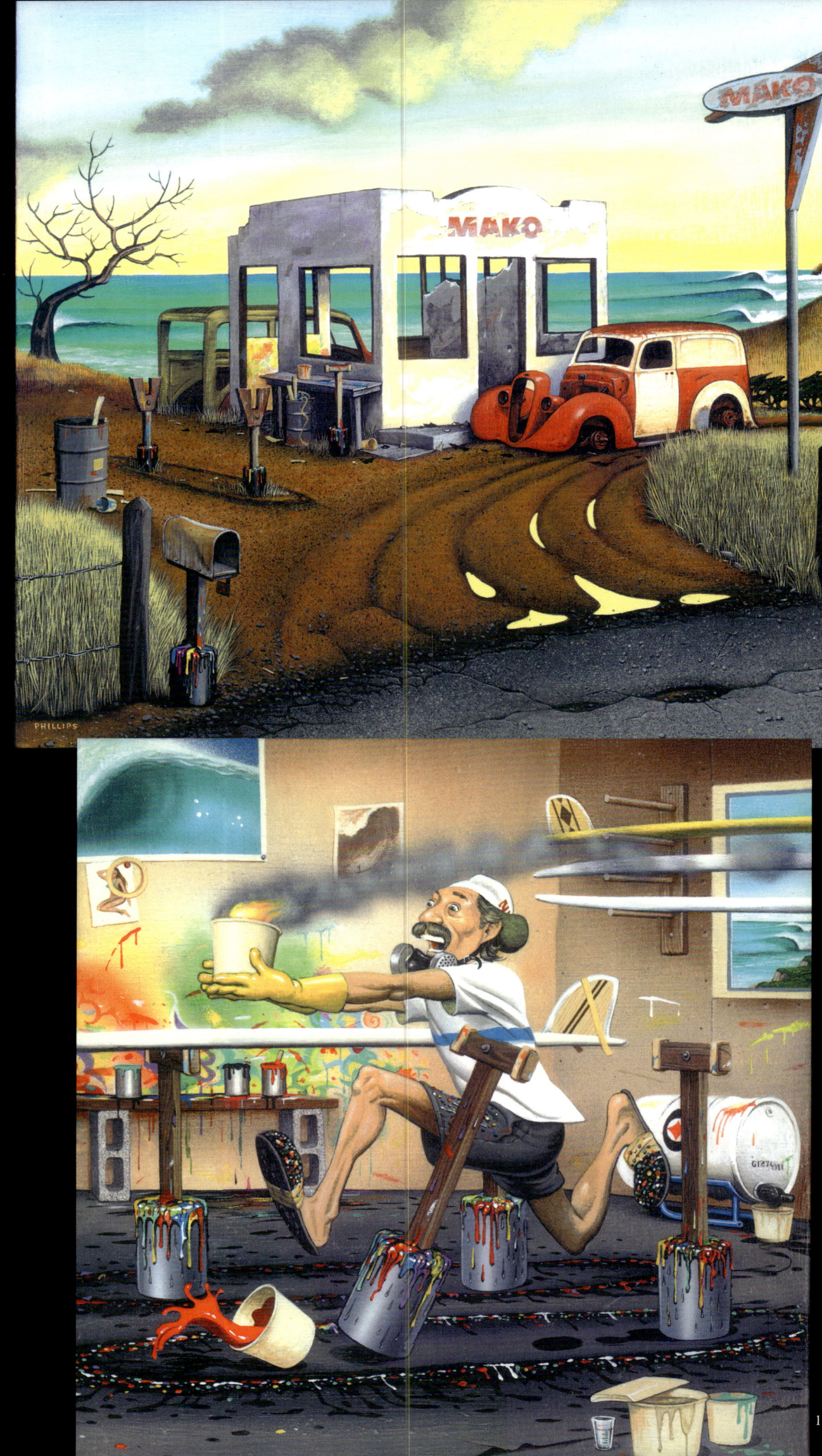

Top: MAKO (The Last Surf Shop), acrylic on canvas, 1999, approx 14'x 20', inspired by the Mako surfboard shop of Santa Cruz circa 1959.
Bottom: Hot Batch, acrylic on canvas, 1999, approx 16'x 20'. A bucket of excess resin, when mixed "hot" can smoke and ignite.

186

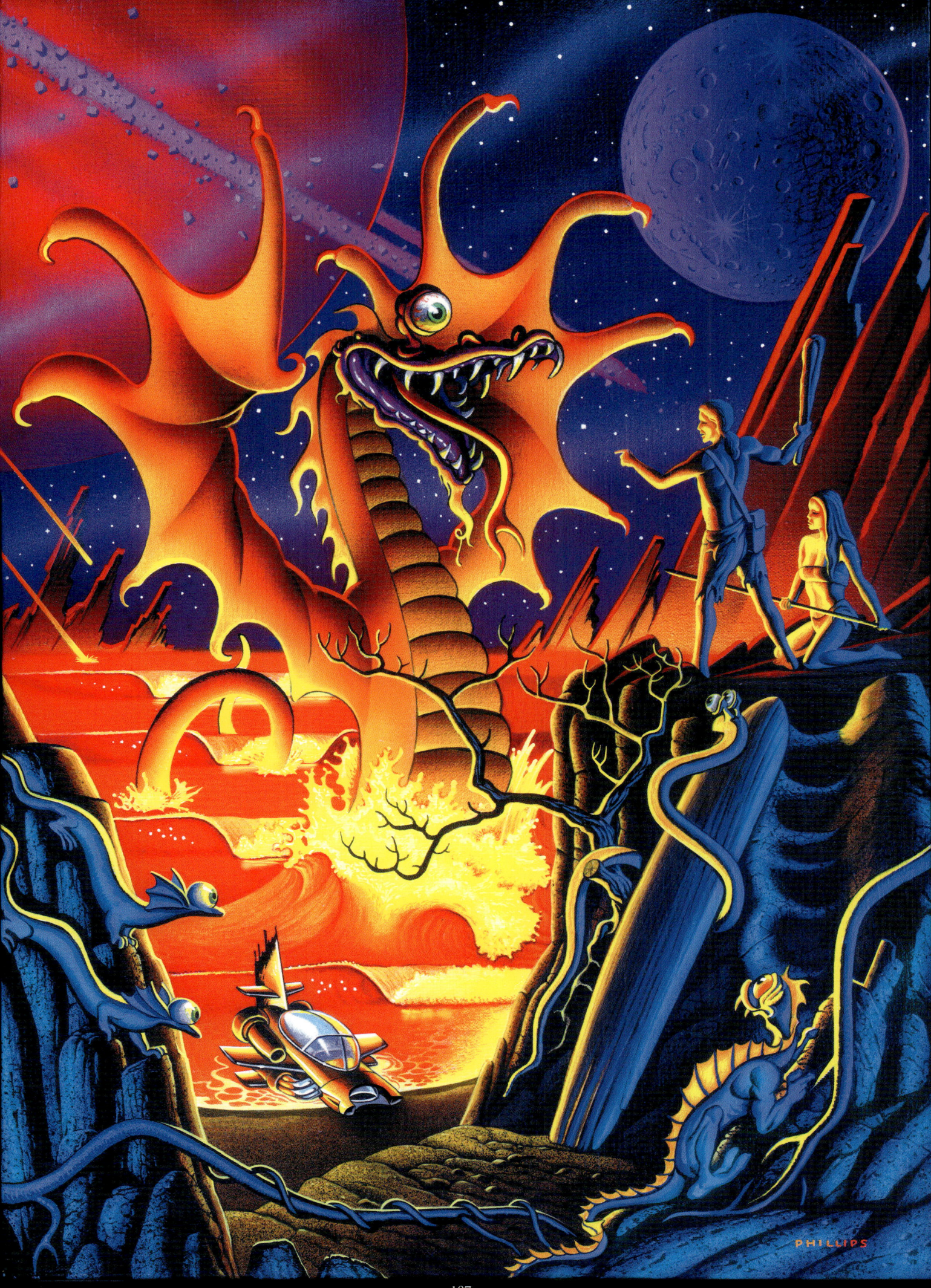

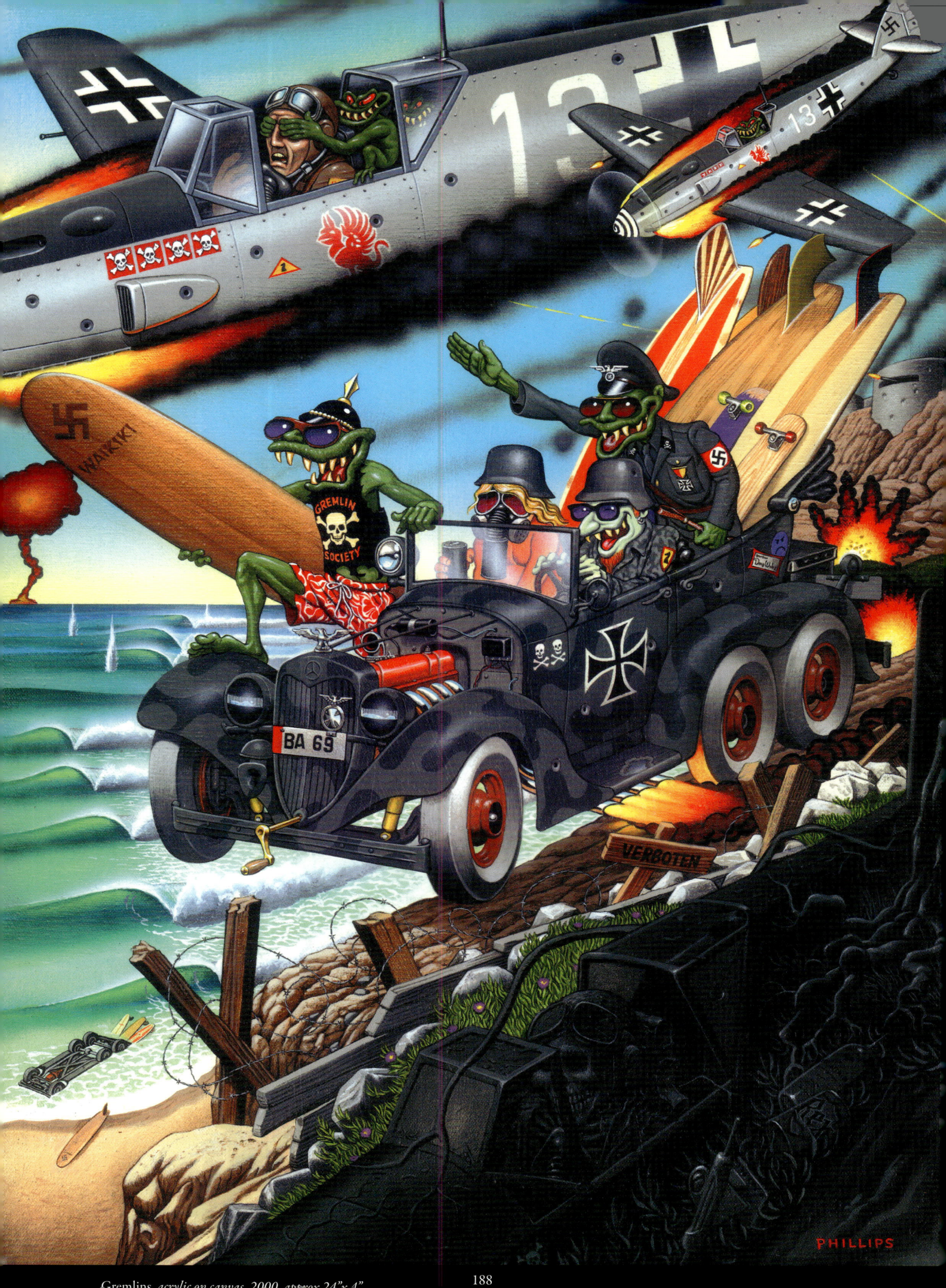

Gremlins, *acrylic on canvas, 2000, approx 24" x 4"*

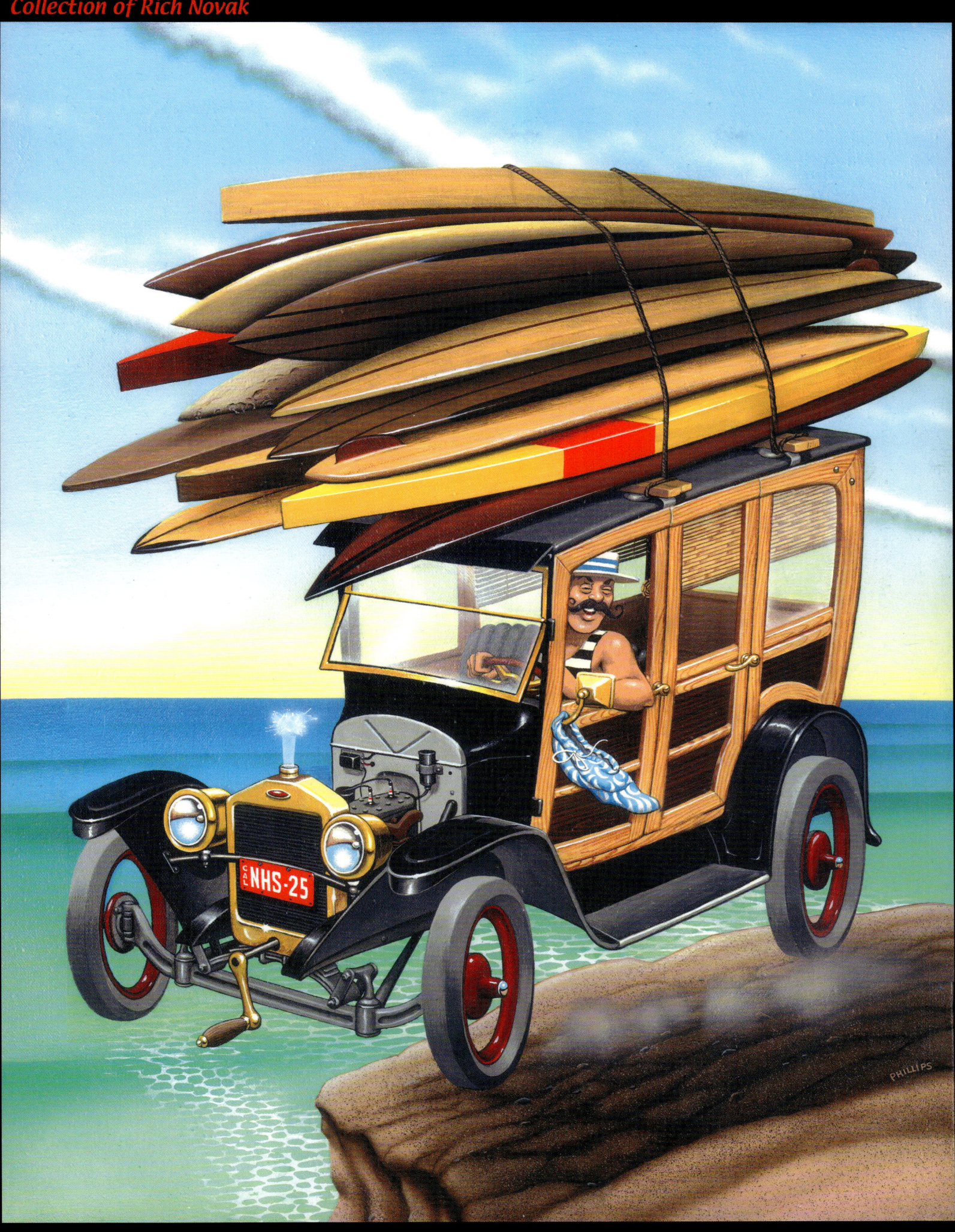

Woody T, *"a barbershop Woody,"* acrylic on canvas, 1999, approx 18"x24".

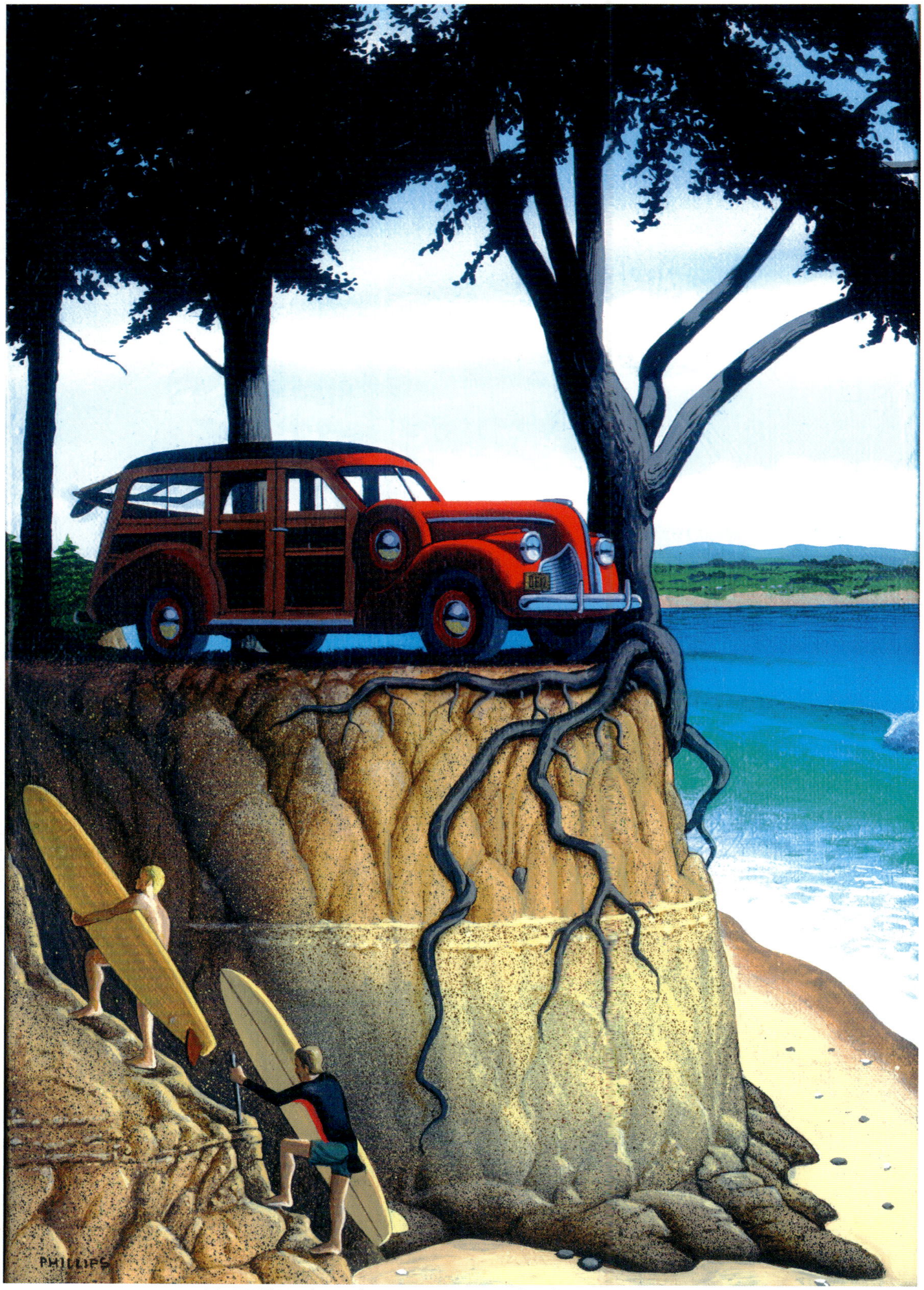

Jim with a framed photo of himself in trademark top hat with his arm around the hardest working man in show business.

Work was slow in 1998. It was slow all year, ever since Jim fell off of the treadmill he was running, up and down the coast, with the San Francisco poster scene. His absence from local work had left a void. Jim did a CD cover for Larry Hosford, and a poster for Stormin' Norman, and poster orders from the web. Dolly began to look around at what was available in local employment, and went to NHS to see Rich Novak. When she told him she was looking for work he asked what Jimmy was doing. Rich told her he had all the work Jimmy wanted to do! He called and Rich said, "Jimmy, I just want you to paint!" On December first, Jim picked up where he left off with his last series of paintings: The Woody series. He went out to the garage and picked out one of the hundred canvases he had stretched at Maz's Lucky Duck boat shop back in the 80s. He found a canvas with an old sketch on it, a flamed '49 Merc woody loaded with surfboards crashing through a fence, going over the cliff. Jim was happy to get back to painting as he had been using the computer for several years.

That woody painting blossomed into a series of surf paintings, with Phillips free to choose any subject and any medium he wanted. By January of 1999, Jimmy was starting on number three of the series, Mako, a wistful painting featuring an abandoned surf shop. As he continued on with the series, Jim was finally away from the stress of deadline work, and thankful for not much more than to sit for hours and paint with triple-zero brushes, listen to music, and talk with Dolly.

Mostly Jimmy and Dolly are just living, quietly and happily, with the radio on and the front door open, enjoying the peace and quiet and sunshine of their quiet Live Oak neighborhood in a Santa Cruz now brimming with people. Jimbo, Jenny, Cassidy Noel and Colby James live next door. Music, family, warmth, Phillips has what he has wanted all along.

The Wild Hook, *acrylic on canvas, 2001, 20"x12". Collection of Rich Novak.*

Bottom: a few logos for Bruce Hammonds, 2001.

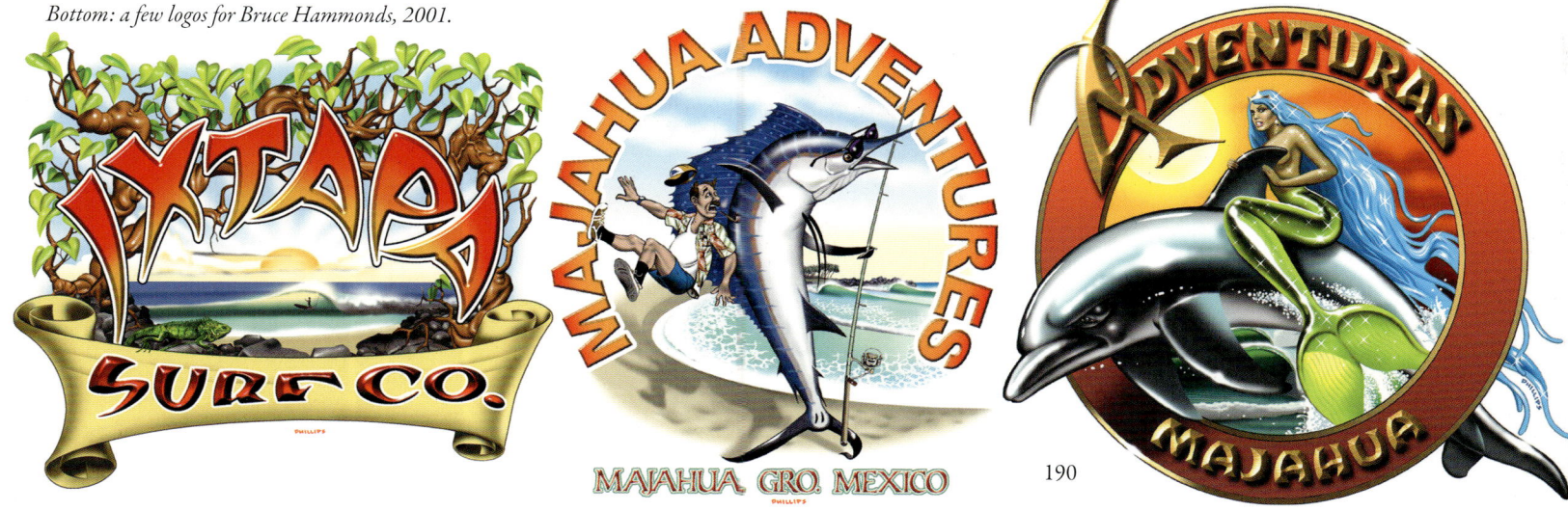

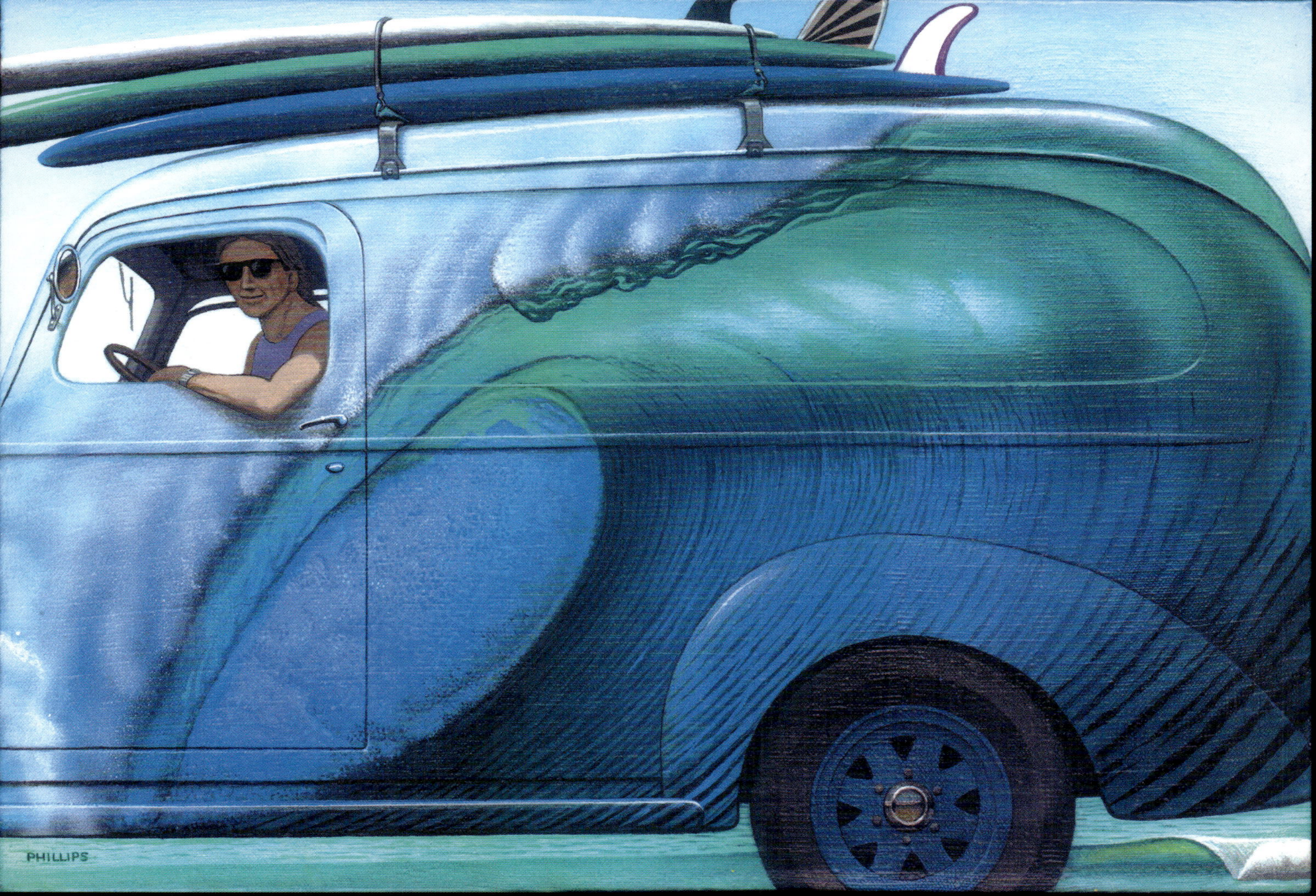

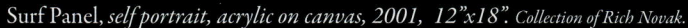

Surf Panel, *self portrait, acrylic on canvas, 2001, 12"x18".* Collection of Rich Novak.

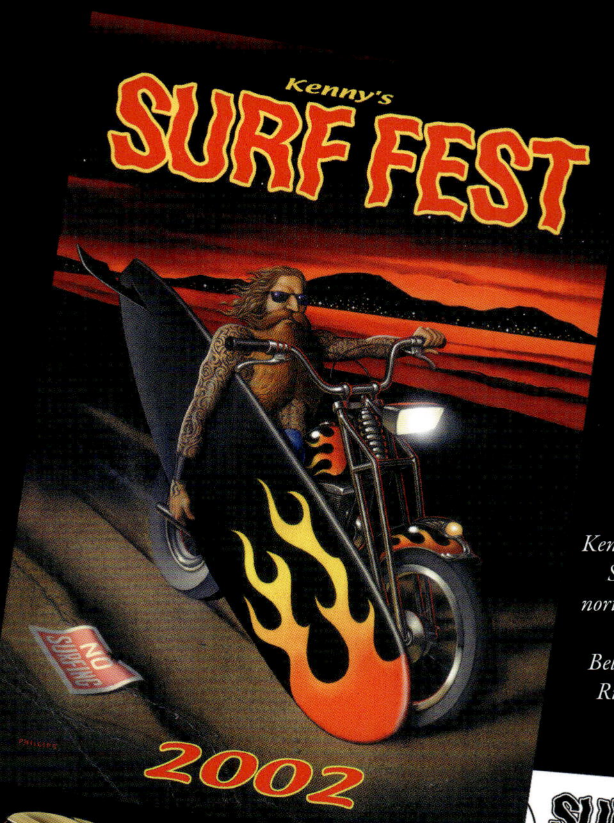

Post cards for
Kenny Stocks' annual
Surf Fest on the
northern coast ,6"x4".
Left: 2002,
Below: back of card.
Right: 2001 card.

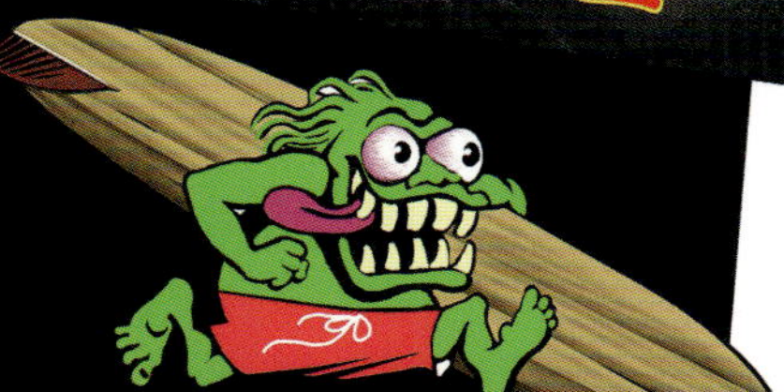

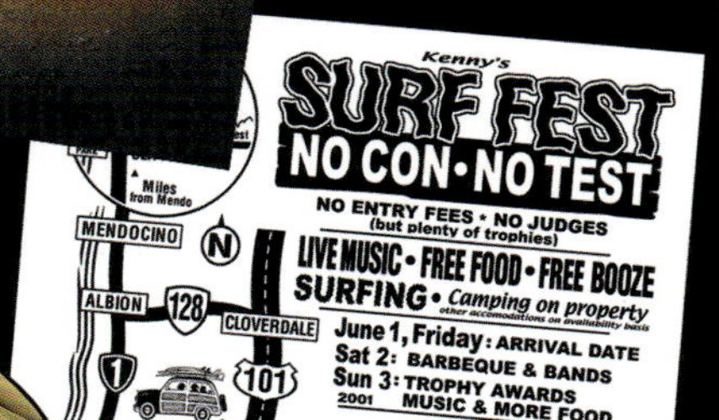

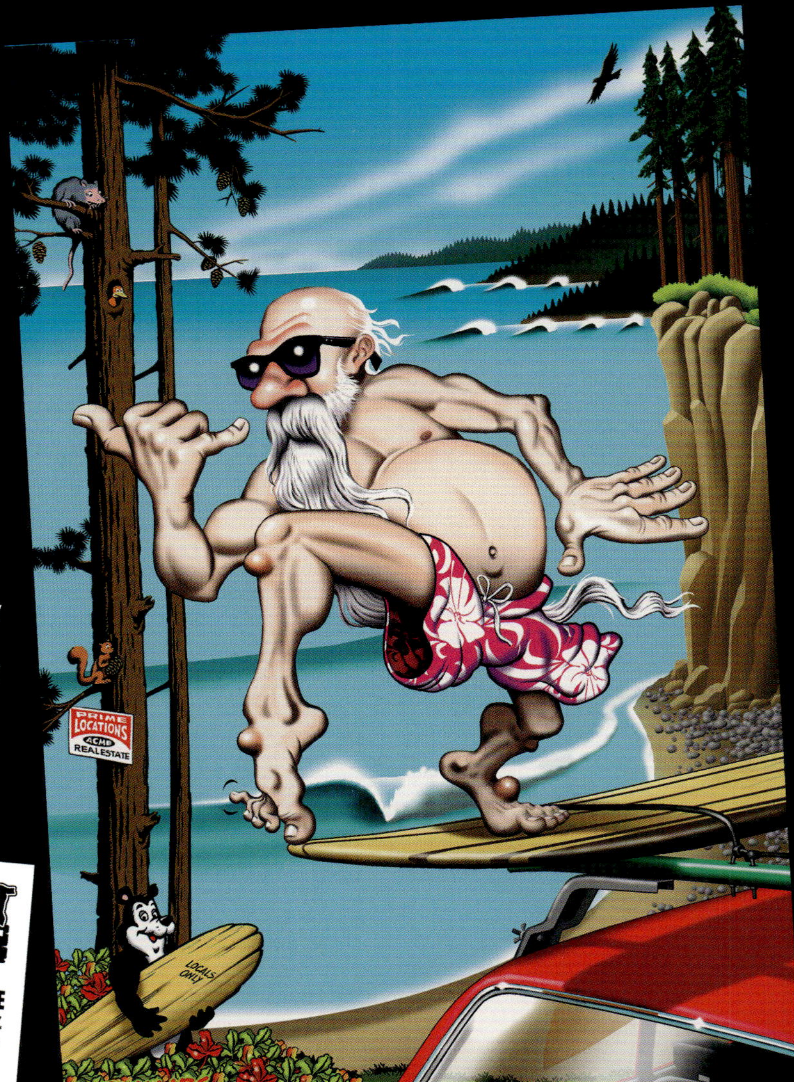

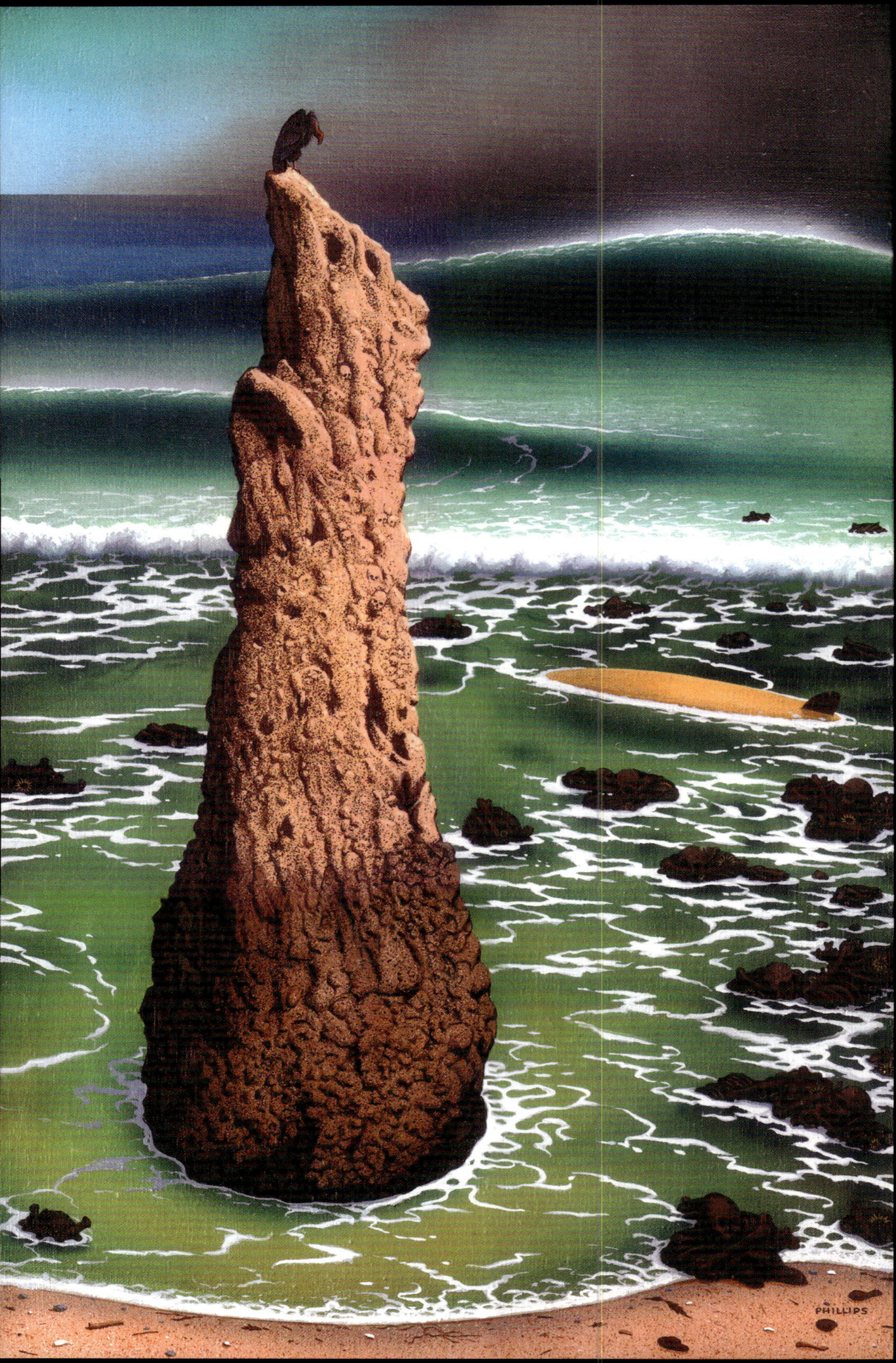

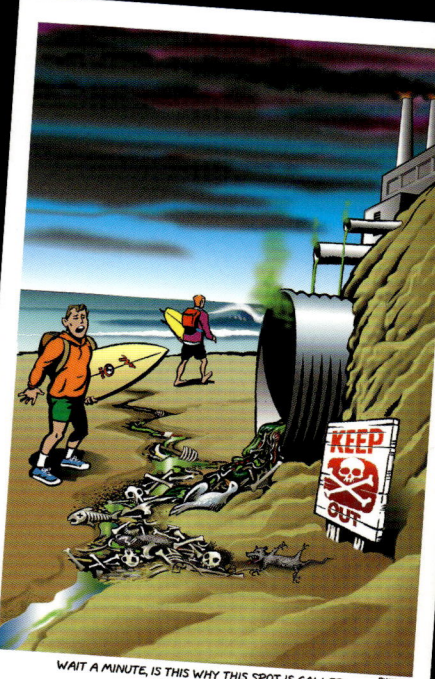

WAIT A MINUTE, IS THIS WHY THIS SPOT IS CALLED "KILLER PIPES"?

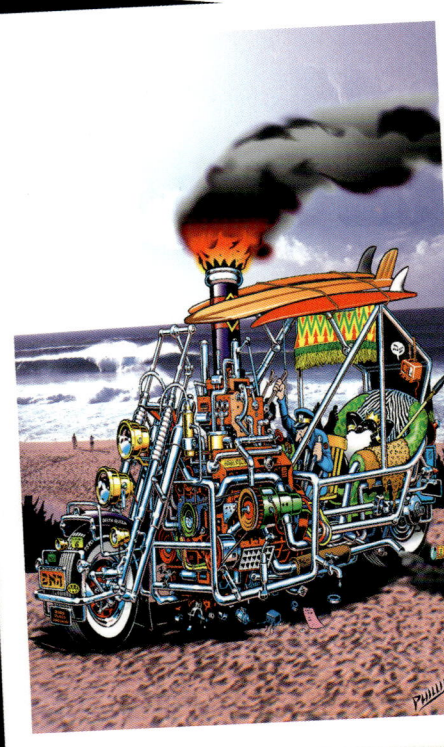

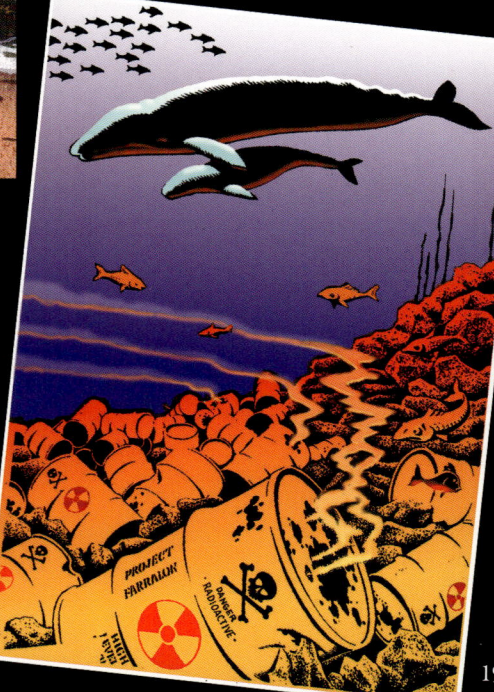

The Boneyard, *acrylic on canvas, 2001, 16"x24". Collection of Rich Novak.*

Hawaiian PYT translated by Rell Sunn for Jimmy

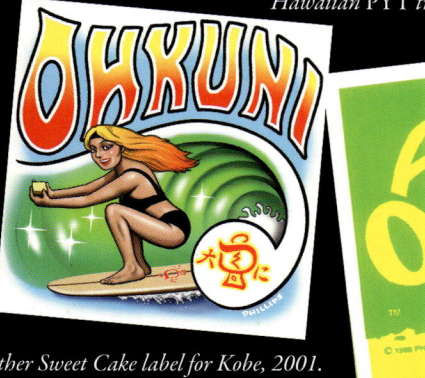

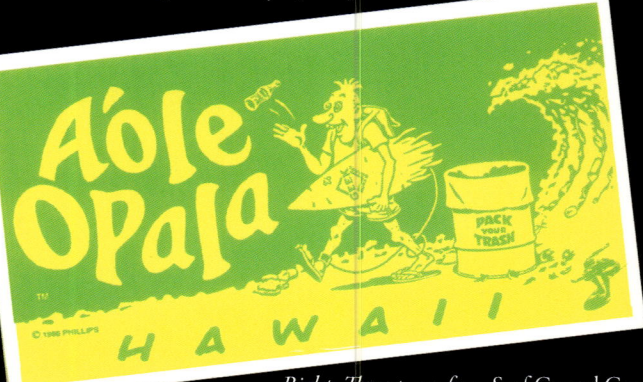

...nother Sweet Cake label for Kobe, 2001.

Right: Three pages from Surf Crazed Comics.

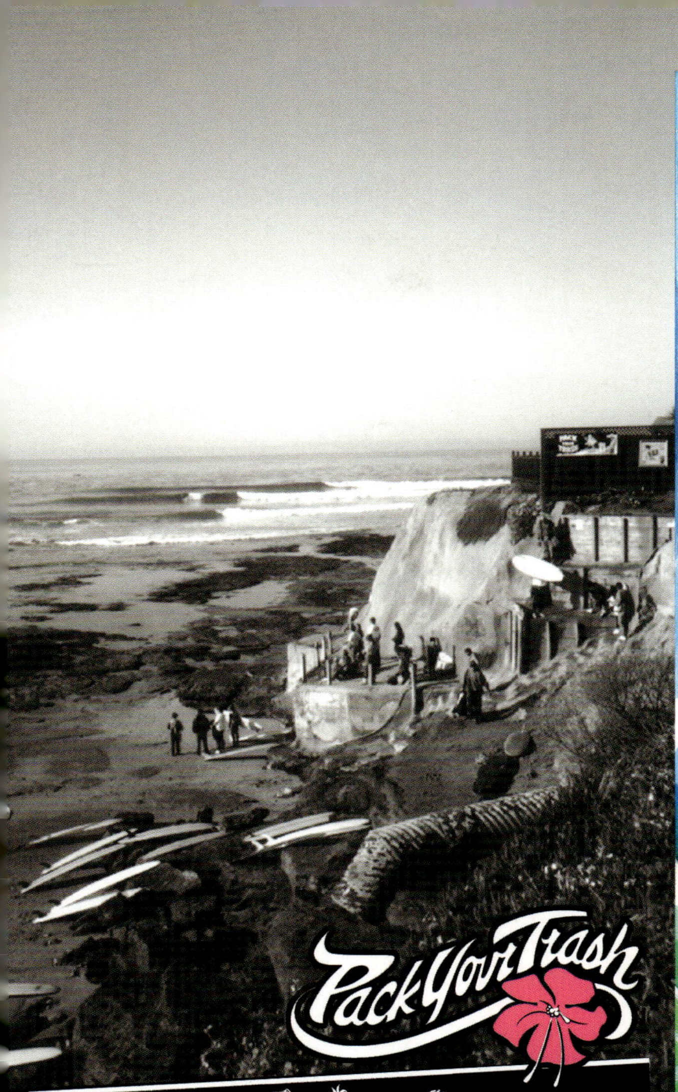

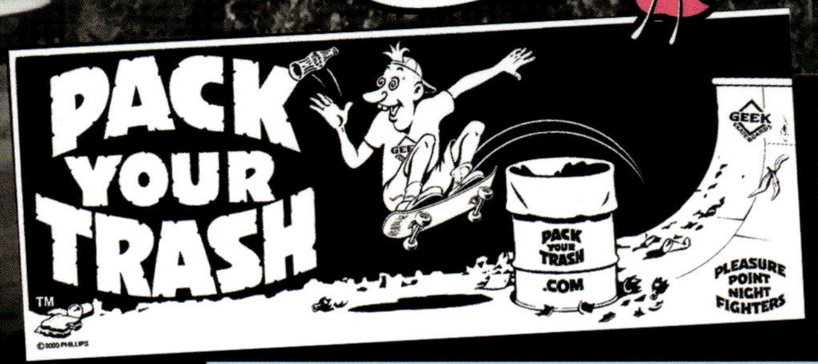

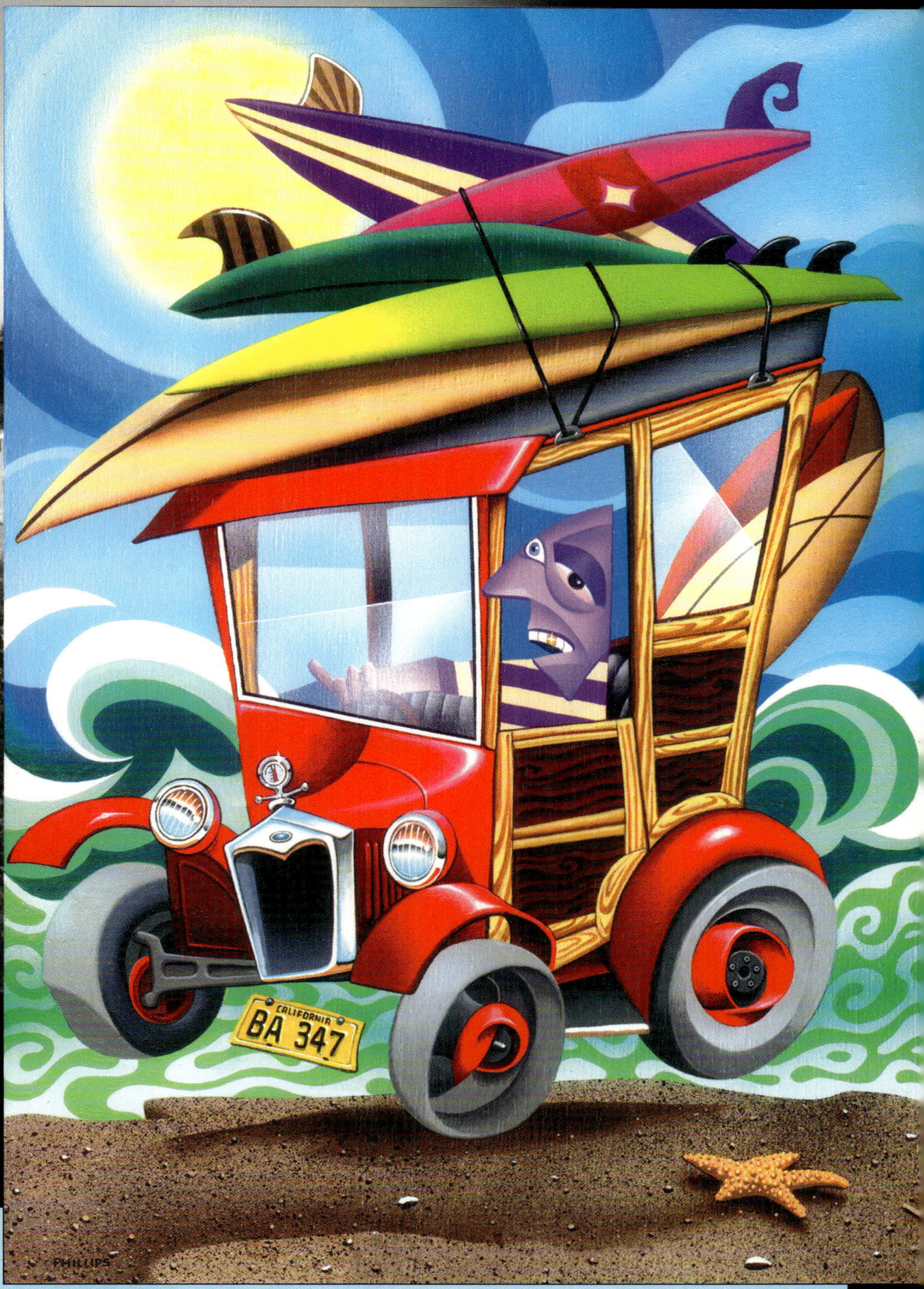

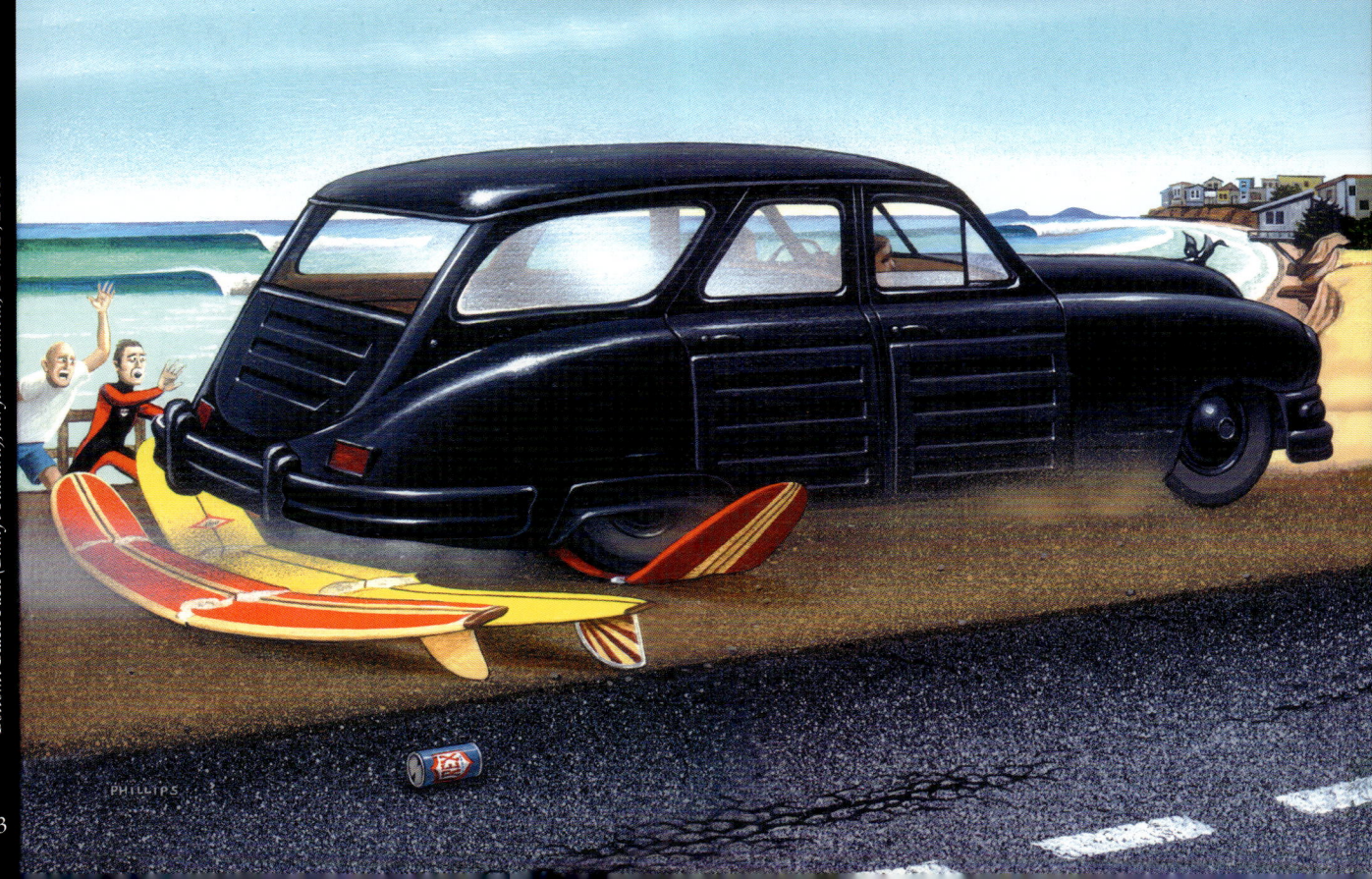

Collection of Rich Novak

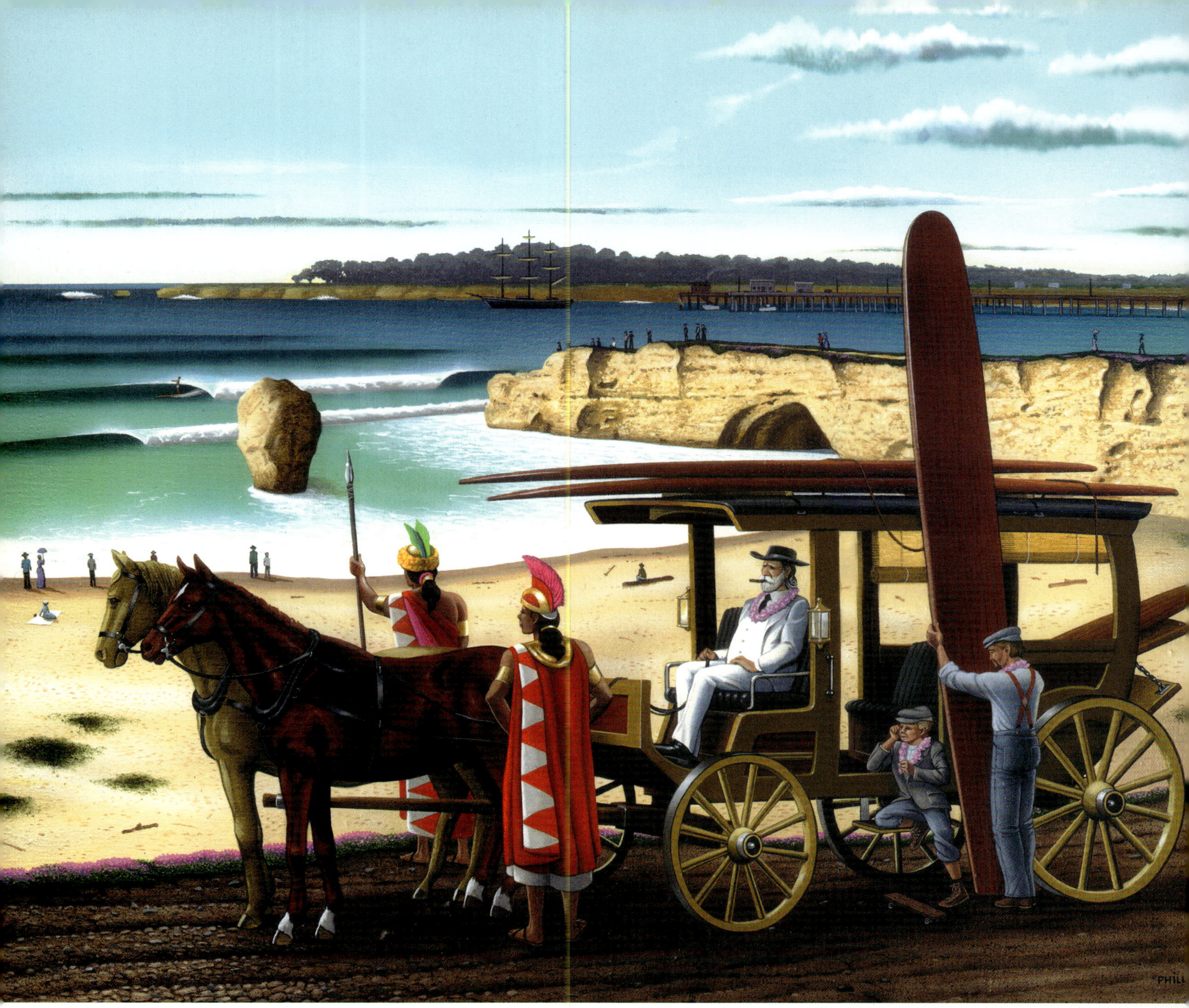

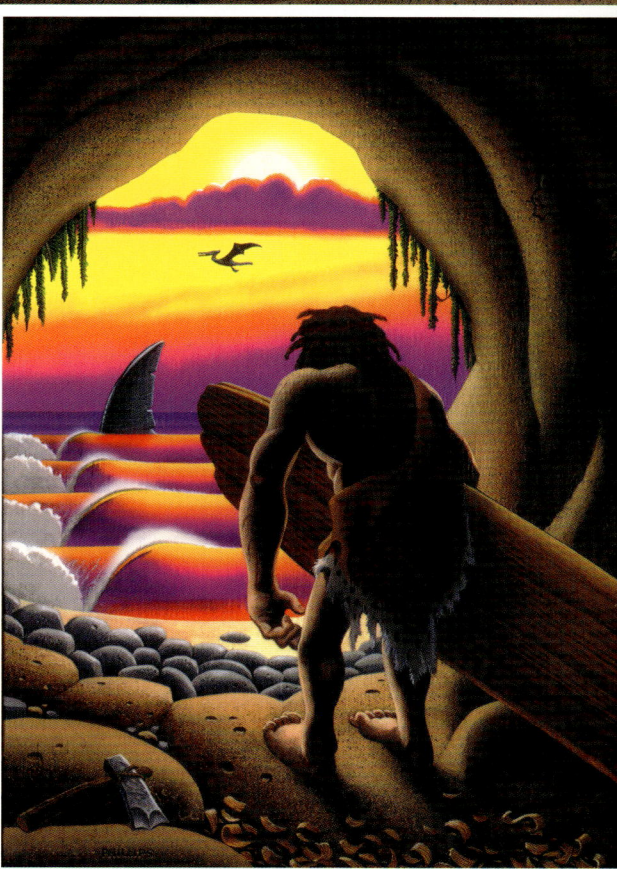

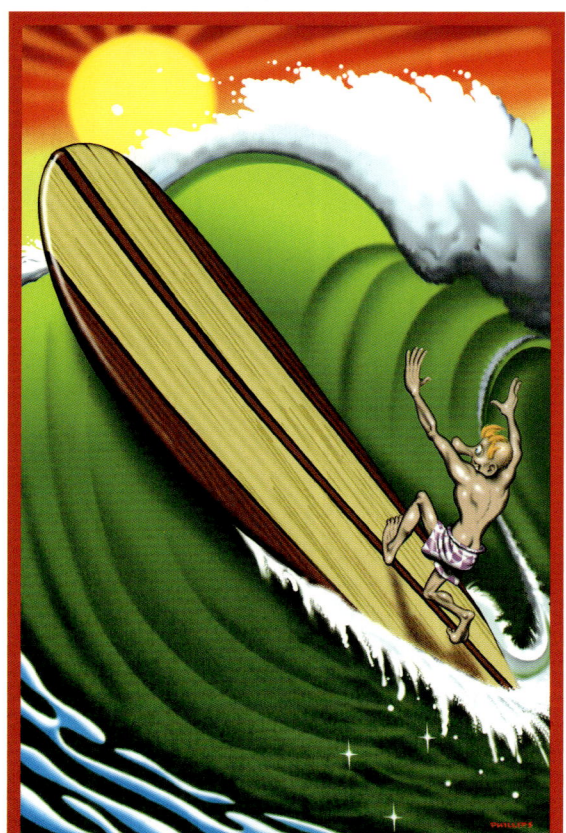

Above: Three Princes, *illustration for an article on the history of Santa Cruz, a depiction of the first surfers in California, appeared in* Surfer's Journal *Vol.1, No.2, 2002, acrylic on canvas, 24"x18".*
Collection of Rich Novak.

Left: Zyg *poster artwork sans lettering, see p.172.*

Right: Cave Surfer, *"The first surfer," acrylic on canvas, 2001, 12"x6".*
Collection of Rich Novak.

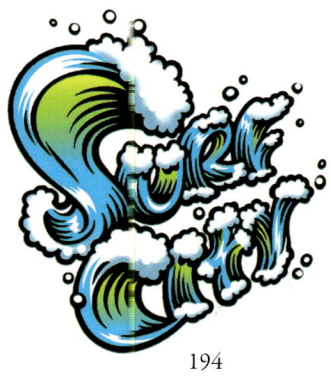

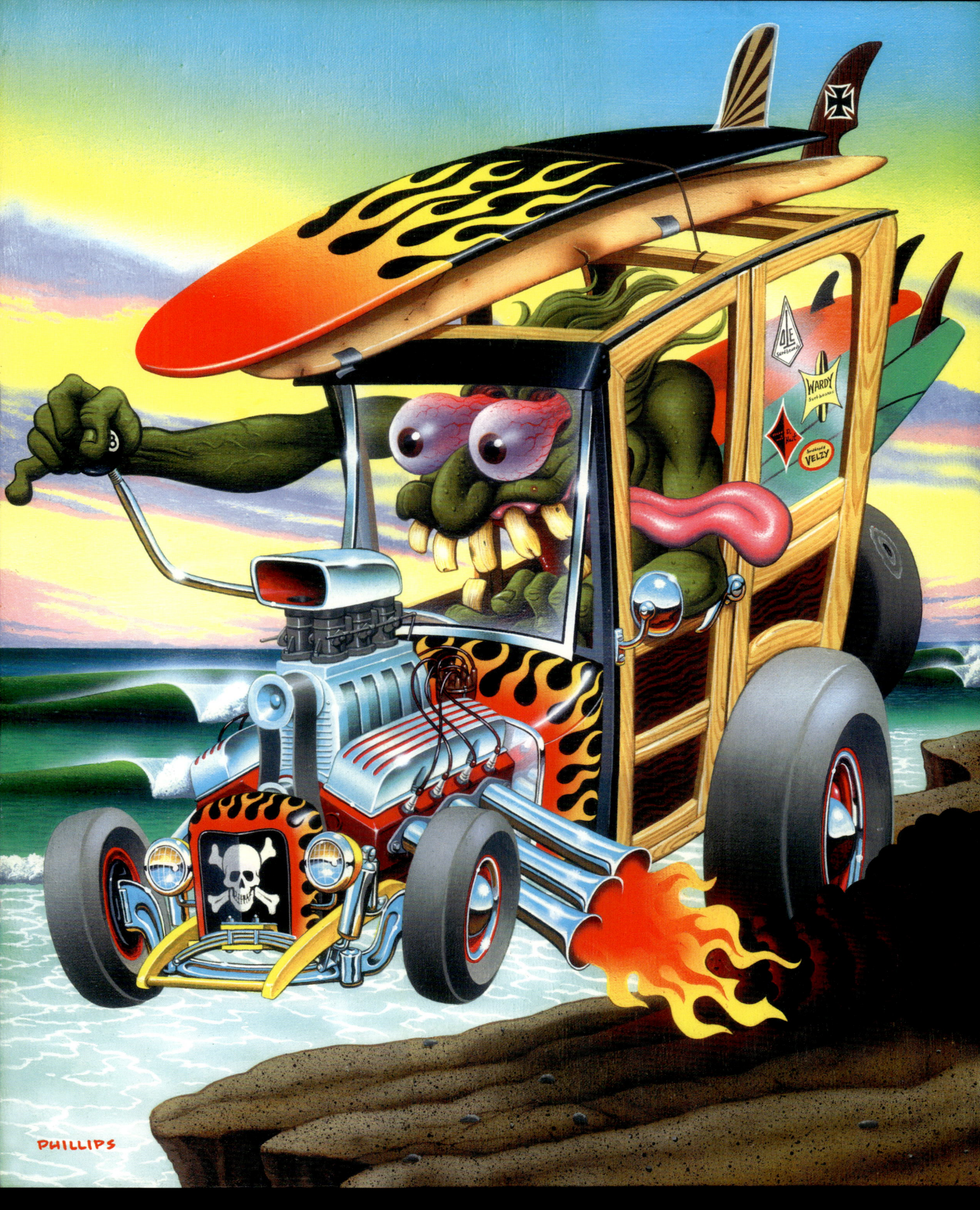

Hotrod Woody, *2001, acrylic on canvas, 20"x24". Inspired by Mouse/Big Daddy Ed Roth.*

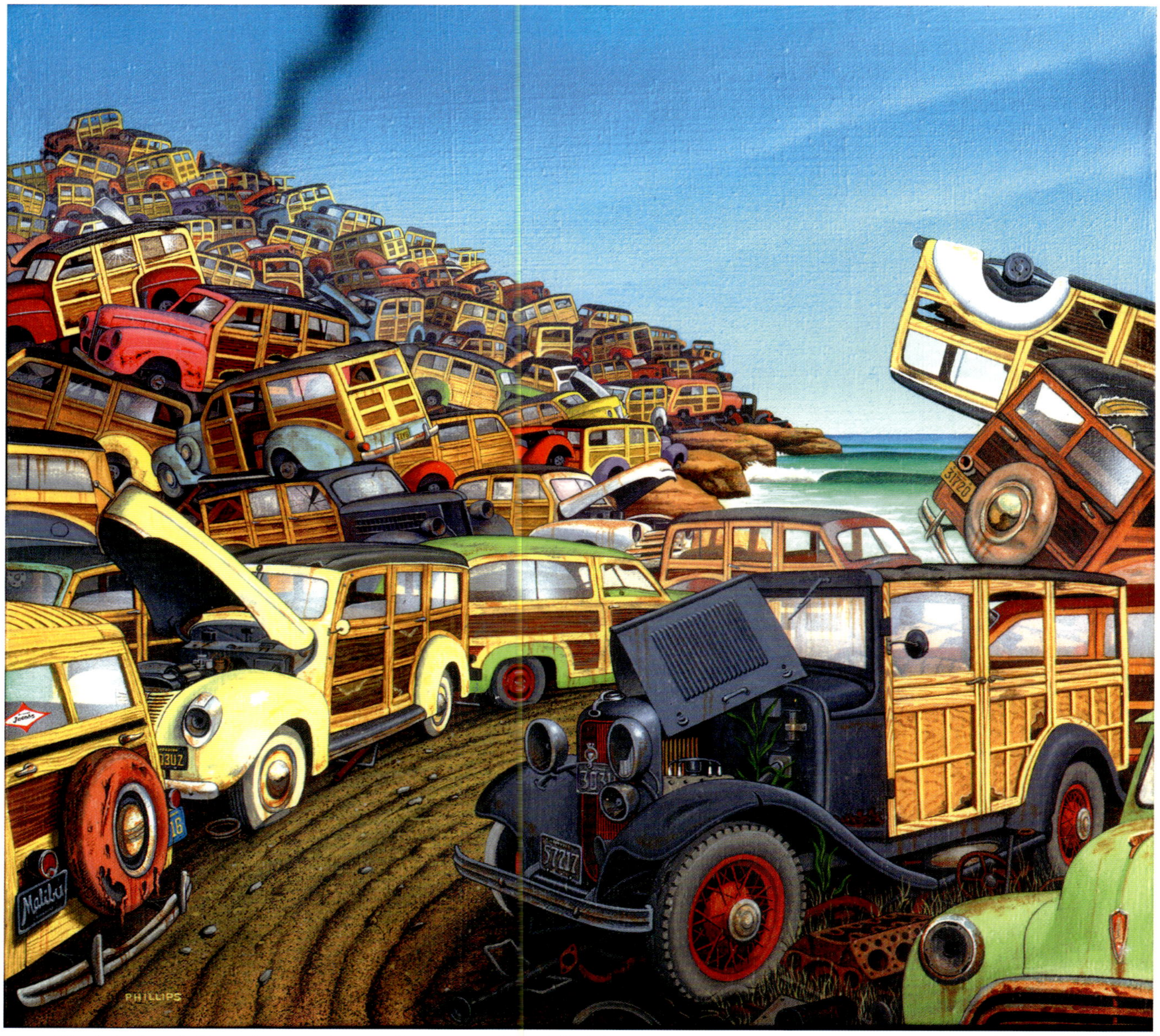

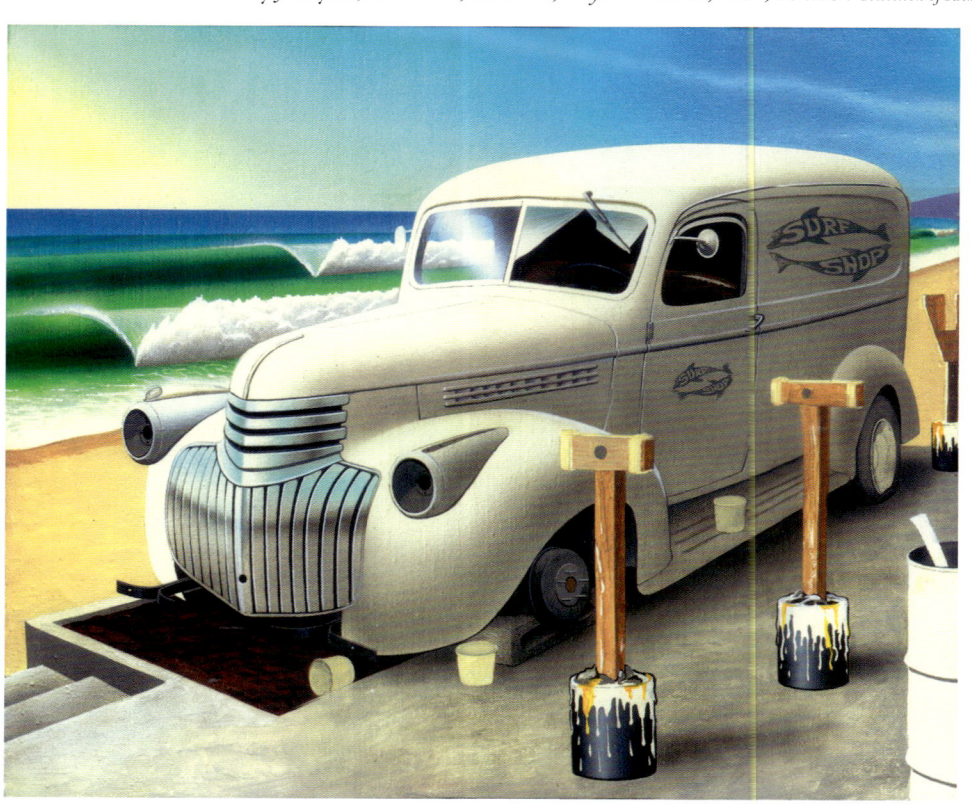

Woody Junkyard, *50 woodies, count 'em, acrylic on canvas, 2001, 16"x18".* Collection of Rich Novak.

MUSIC, FAMILY, WARMTH
La Dolce Phillips in the 21st Century.

"History is in the art.
Civilizations will crumble, but art is left behind."
- Jim Phillips

If Jim Phillips' line about "civilizations crumbling" is true, what will people think when the California bay area is destroyed by an earthquake or a tsunami, and all that survives is the art contained in this book? Archaeologists who find this collection floating in the surf line or glowing and throbbing in the rubble will come to the inescapable conclusion that the last 40 years of the 20th Century were pretty stoked.

Here in the first years of the 21st Century, Jim Phillips has a nice little niche for himself in Santa Cruz. The little house in Live Oak is now covered with ivy and shaded with trees and while the outside is still free of psychedelia, the inside is awash in color: The cupboards are painted up, and patched with a Screaming Hand sticker or a Sylvester the Cat sticker here and there. There is art on the walls: Hicks, Picasso, some Jimbo Phillips. The bathroom

El Truck, *acrylic on canvas, 16"x20", unfinished. This painting was in process when this book was published.*
Not yet collection of Rich Novak.

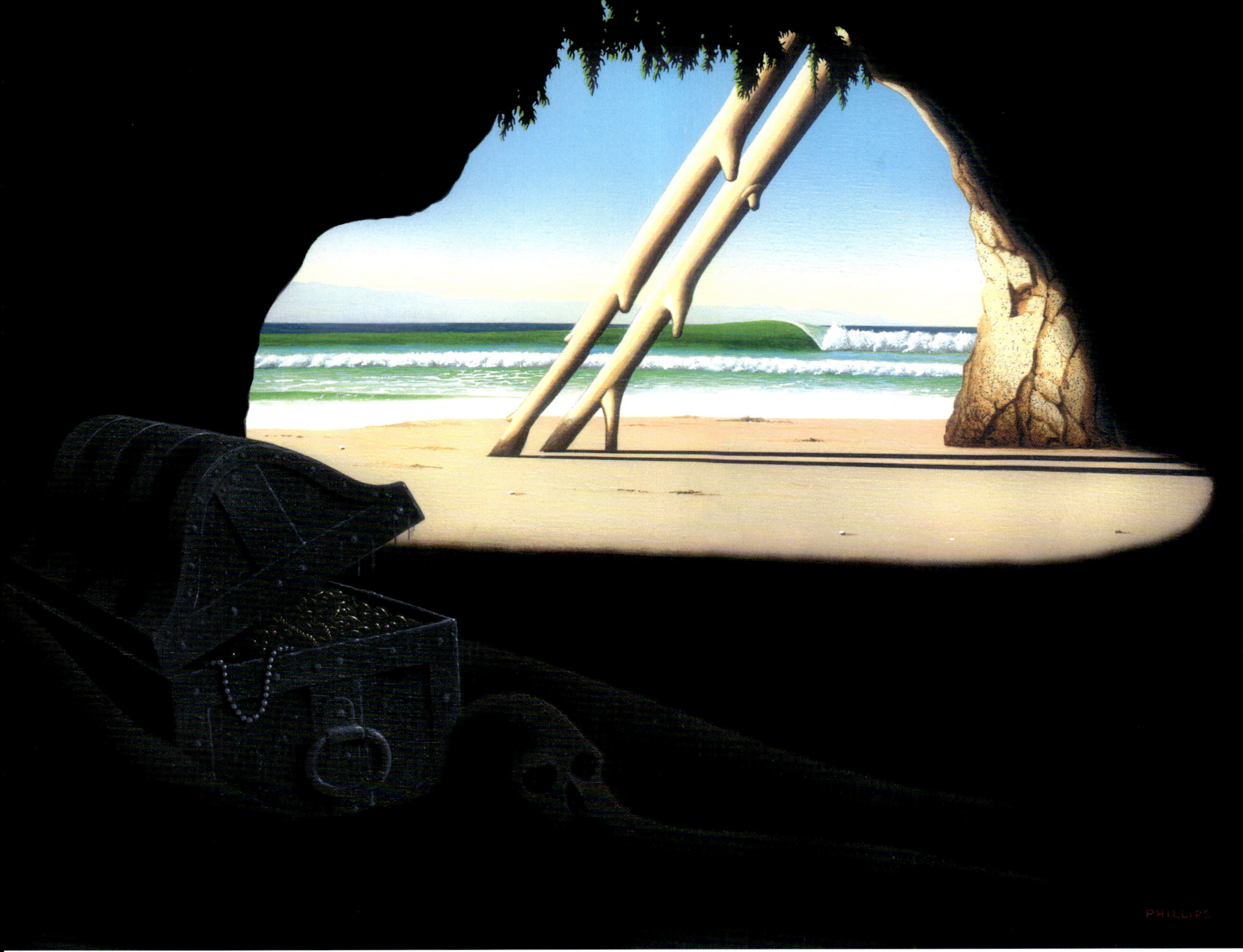

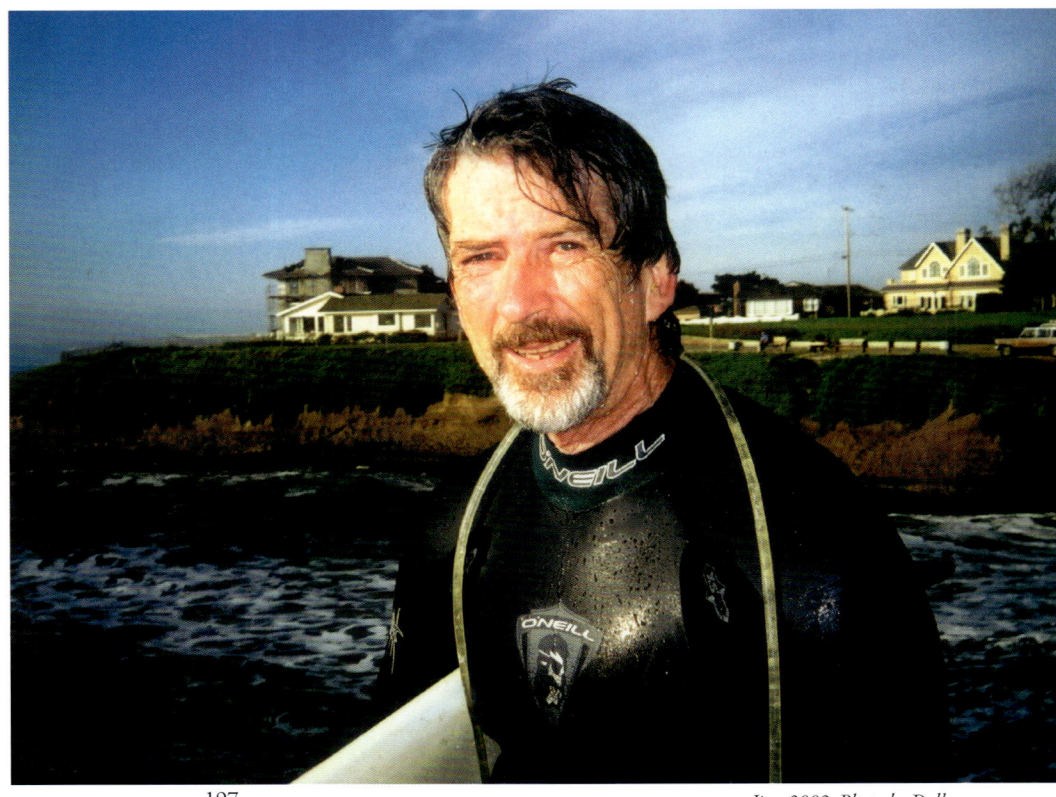

door is covered with poster prints of old San Francisco, and hidden away in the archive room is a King Tut's Tomb of stickers and drawings and scratchboards, 40 years of art recording the civilization of the San Francisco Bay Area.

Phillips has fans and friends around the world, from Japan to France, and tries to answer everything. Freelance projects and favors come in over the phone or on the fax or email. He accepts or rejects them according to his mood and whether the sky is foggy or the surf is good or bad.

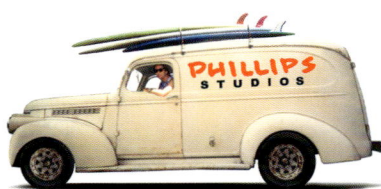

Jim, 2002. Photo by Dolly .

UNIVERSITY OF SAN FRANCISCO
SAN FRANCISCO 17, CALIFORNIA
March 26, 1954

ARTMENT OF EDUCATION

Mr. James Phillips
309 26th Avenue
Santa Cruz, California

My dear Jim:

I have owed you a letter for some time. You know when some one writes you a letter you should reply at your first opportunity. I received your note some time ago and have not had time to type out my reply.

I enjoyed your letter very much. I like to get letters from you and Ann because you write such nice letters.

Is it still kite season down at Santa Cruz? It is here. Two little children were trying to get their kite up into the air in the lot next to our house the other day. I gave them some help and they let out a lot of twine and the kite was almost out of sight when the wind fell and down came the kite in a big tree near by. They tangled the twine all up and that was the last I saw of them.

How is your face? If Dr. Hoffman is taking care of you I know that you are all recovered. Dr. Hoffman is a wonderful doctor and a great friend of all of ours.

How about the demerits? Have you beaten Ann's record yet? That was a fine record she made and it will be hard to beat.

Say, have you saved enough for the basketball yet? I want to get down to play with you when you get it. Basketball is lots of fun and practice will make you a good basket shot. I used to be a good basketball plyer.

We are planning to get down to see you folks for Mother's birthday.

It has been raining here for some time but it has now turned cold so i can't work in the garden.

Well, I will close now. Grandma joins me in sending all of you all of our love.

Grandpa.

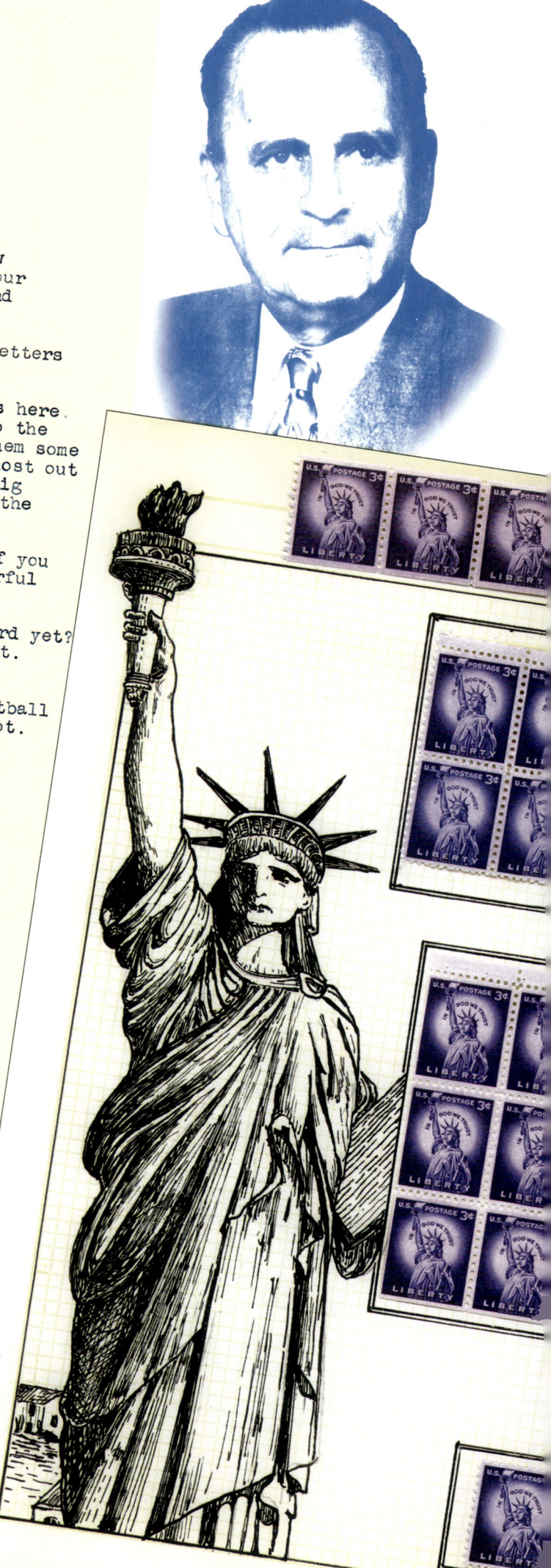

Above: A letter to 10 year old Jim from Grandpa.
Above left: Jim's grandpa, Henry C. Hall.
Right: One of many illustrations from Hall's stamp album,
showing his drawing and pen & ink skills.

Nov. 20, 1977

Dear Mr. Phillips:

I must apologize for the long delay in acknowledging receipt of your letter and cartoons way back in September. The sheer magnificence of your cartoon detail floors me. I can only say that I wish I was young enough to start over again by stealing as much of your technique as I could absorb. The wild motorbikes I especially like. Hopefully, we'll be seeing art like yours on the covers of national magazines before long. I mean mags like Readers Digest, which claims to be a voice of the times.

I fail to see any Walt Disney influence in your work, unless it is in the clean cut lines and readable compositions you put together, but , then I'm a poor judge of drawing. I only know what I like, without quite knowing the psychological reasons.

I met Bob Carlson a few years ago when I was in Aptos overnight. Knew him from my Disney studio days. He was then doing animated things for Peanuts. Yes, he is a fine guy. Deserves to be working on animation that is more suited to his skills than the simple camera trick stuff he was doing then.

You mention that you are looking for some biographical material about me and my duck work. The current (Nov.) issue of PSA CALIFORNIA in-flight magazine has an article with good illustrations about me. So full of gushy praise for my work that I winced with embarrassment.

Again I apologize for being so slow at answering mail. Yours was not an easy letter to answer. I stand in awe of such skillful use of pen and ink.

                    Sincerely

                    Carl Barks

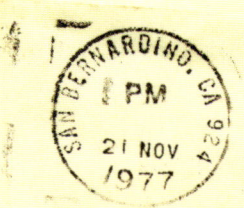

Mr. Jim Phillips
1410 Webster St.
Santa Cruz, CA.
95062

Carl Barks worked for Disney Studios; he wrote and drew Donald Duck *comic books. He is reponsible for the* Donald Duck *family as we know them, and was a major art influence for Phillips. This 1977 letter was a reply to a Phillips fan letter to Barks.*

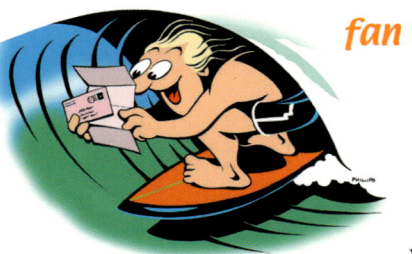

fan mail to Jim

A sampling of the many letters and emails that Jim receives.

Envelope drawing by Radman, received in Sept. 2002, one of many Phillips Studios has received from Rick Augeri in Texas.

Jim,
I stubbled across your web page and I am so stoked to have found it. I just want you to know that you were my idol as a little kid. I am now 21at the University of California San Diego. I'm hoping to enter the world of graphic design, a decision that I'm sure had something to do with the influence you had on me. I am not the artist you are, but I have started doing freelance graphics for Sector 9 and Illenium Skateboards. I washoping you might have some tips for a begginer and I am also curious if youdo any poster prints of your skate graphics. Nathan Reifke

Jim, I've been a fan of yours since I started skating in about 86, and have always dug your artwork. Thanks especially for the production tips, and archives, as they are very inspiring and helpful to a budding young artist!
Take it easy. -Andy, - Australia.

hi mr phillips
my name is rick jaremback, i am an artist from Ft lauderdale Fl. im 20 and im on my way to a carrier in the art world.
ive been skateboarding since i knew how to walk and your art has been a strong inspiration to me.
although my style is very different from yours, you and many artist havehelped me to find my groove in what is "art"
to me its a serious thing which is about the only serious thing in mylife. Just wanted to say thanks.
oh and i am commemorating all the artist that have inspired me. i amgetting half sleeve tattoos on my arms and legs.
from Edward Gorey, Van Gough, local artist, friends and you.
rick

Hi.
ive been meening to write you for a wile now.
ive got an old coppy of art alt. feachuring a bunch of your stuff. i alway seem to go back to it.I remeber drewling over you designs in the 80s when i was skateboardin and the looks on peoples faces when i came to school with a turquios roskop minni design T shirt. there was nothing like that at the time. anyways, verry cool site, i wanted to drop you a line and tell you that you drawings had grate influence on me and still do!
Donny, http://www.dirtydonny.com

I was wondering if Mr Philps was the one that design the Jeff Kendall pumpkin board in 87-88?? Ever since I was growing up around skateboarding. I have always been a fond of his work. Although,there were a lot of other skate companies out there. I choose to continue skating Santa Cruz & Santa Monica Airline boards because of the unique graphic that had..Especially the Roskopp face.. Well done Mr Philps..I hope your legacy continues.. sinerely, Tim Ng

Hi...Great site...great work.
I have been a fan and admired your work since I was probably about 12, I am 28 now. I am a NYC/NJ based artist and run my own studio out here. I am very curious if you would be kind enough to offer a fellow artist some tips on marketing, promoting and how to start off in the world of sk8/surf/snow art.
Jay Alders, www.AldersStudio.com

I grew up skating in the 80s, and your art was one of the very biggest influences on my soft little brain - To this day, I often look to your images for advice and inspiration.
The reason I'm writing to you, is that I am wondering if you have a need for any fresh talent, either in your studio, or on the digital side of things. It would be a real thrill for me to work in any capacity for you, and I've got alot going that you could use in return. I have attached my resume to this message, and you can take a look at my portfolio if you're interested.
Rock On!, DB

It's good to hear that Santa Cruz has bought the graphics. I think it's sadwhat has become of the company, they are just not the same without your graphics. I think the most beautiful graphics you did for skateboards I think you sold your art too cheap ! I have a lot of friends in the art-business, some of them own galleries and the prices they charge are nothing compared to yours. And the fact is that your art is worldwide know and most gallery-art comes and goes with trends and hypes. You should get definately get more recognition. If people talk about skateboard art it's always the same they only mention Cliver and McKee because a lot of people don't even know your name, sad.
I think the name of fame of Santa Cruz was largely build on their graphics, so the sport should built you a statue.
I'm very curious to see your new board-graphics because the graphic side of skateboarding changed a lot, and I think Santa Cruz could assure themself a new place at the top. It's sad that the graphic side of skateboarding has mostly faden away, maybe it was just a part of the eighties, that's why I'm curious. Also your most famous graphics to buyers also perfectly matched the caracteristics of the skaters, all of the SC skaters had a rough/bad image and your graphics helped building their attitude, it's all marketing. I just think there should be a book that covers your entire carreer. Mark

Mr. Phillips,
Too bad that the Grosso was sold, but I hope who ever bought it will appreciate it. I will take the Kendall, and if possible I would like the Jessee Neptune also, and the Corey O'Brien. The Kendall and the Jessee are for me, but the O'Brien will go to a friend of mine who thinks of your art the same way I do. I was talking to him tonight and I made a really good point. These skaters wouldn't be known if it wasn't for your artwork. Most of the people didn't even know what these skaters looked like, but they knew their boards. You and your artwork, in my mind, made the skaters popular. Your artwork is what sold Santa Cruz boards. Jaime said several times that you were responsible for making Santa Cruz what it was. That has to fill you with so much pride. I love to draw and design graphics, but I hardly think I would ever be able to hold a candle to you. If the Grosso, Alice in Wonderland or the Grosso, Toy Box some how become available, please let me know. As they are Jaime's actual first choice. Take care, Chris Chicarella

Mr. Phillips.
It is an honor to email you. I have loved your work since I was a kid. I love your designs for Rob Roskopp decks in the 80's. I was browsing around the net and found your site and couldn't believe my eyes. The designs in your gallery really took be back. To see the Roskopp 4 design again was great, It's got to be my favorite. The detail in the line art is great. Were the Roskopp designs an original idea from you, or was it requested from Rob himself? The fact that the design evolved over the years was a great way to sell more decks. Anyway, I just wanted to finally greet you. If you ever need a new website, PLEASE contact me, I'll hook you up.
Ron Fugelseth, Art Director Oxygen Productions

Hey Jim, You rock dude! Rick Augeri

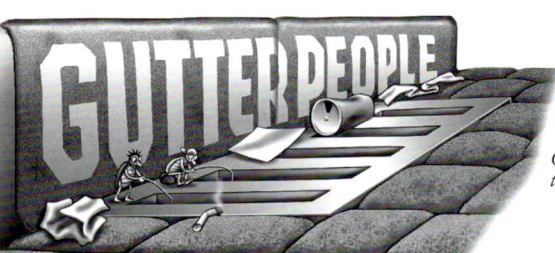

Gutter People: A logo for outreach to troubled youths in detention, 1993.

Jim-

I have never felt more honored to be writing an e-mail in my entire life. Yr work has inspired and dazzled me more than you will ever know and I just found out yr name three days ago. My name is Dennis Franklin and I live in Providence, RI. I am 24 years old. A college graduate (studied industrial design and film) and You are a big reason that art is the most important thing in my life. I grew up in Detroit. and when I was younger nobody skated in Detroit, and if they did they weren't black. I skateboarded and the only reason I wanted to skateboard was because I wanted a SANTA CRUZ deck with yr BADAZZ artwork on the bottom. Now I had seen Powell boards in the burbs and their graphics were nice but your artwork was amazing! The first deck I ever saw with yr work was the Jeff Kendall Pumpkinhead board. I saw that deck at a bike shop and it blew my mind. But I lived in the city, skateboarding was already too pricey for my family as I tried oh so hard to get a Nash executioner. So I knew that getting a Santa Cruz deck was next to impossible. So I waited, patiently I waited and I read Thrasher to look at the ads to see the decks. Then I saw the 5th Roskopp deck, I bugged out! I had to have it. The picture was so small and the chaos called to me. I was going to get this deck at all costs. So to make a long story short..... I conned my mother into buying me a really early birthday gift. really, really early. I loved that deck it had G&S trucks, and OJ2 wheels becuz the screaming hand made me insane. I stared at that deck all the time. slept with it even. Many decks have come and gone my way but my favorite ones have worn yr artwork as a badge of honor (I broke a JESSE sungod deck last year opps!). I practiced drawing because I wanted to draw like you and Derek Riggs(IronMaidenRawks). Okay, I just wanted you to know why I am writing this e-mail. I am really interested in purchasing some of yr original work. I am a very serious collector. I don't really collect much art outside of work I trade with friends. But I would starve if it meant I could afford to buy yr work. You are truly a master and I would love to share yr vision with future generations. My favorite graphic of all time that you did is the Grosso vampire work. Until I went to SkateboardCollector.com I had only seen that deck once in Thrasher and some kid was riding it and I never saw any trace of it again until last week. I was amazed. I actually got to see the entire graphic!!! You are truly a wonderful teacher Mr. Phillips. Although you have never taught me in a classroom setting yr work continues to push me to always strive to be a better artist and to really stretch my imagination. I know this e-mail is approaching the length of a short story, but it's not everyday I get to communicate with a personal hero. the world just got a lot smaller and life just got a helluva a lot better. Thank you so much!!!
Student4Life, Dennis Franklin

Hello. I am an avid fan of your artwork from back in the day.

The stuff you did for NHS was so cool. Your artwork totally defined a era in skateboarding. I was wondering if you had any stickers left? I am looking for the Jason Jessee "Hot Rod" design. I would love to get my hands on anything with this graphic on it. Thanks, Michael Moore

Thanks for the many years of killer skate graphics! My name is Nate Kent. The first skateboard I ever had besides banana boards was the first Salba deck. For the past several years I've been looking for an old deck, or sticker of those graphics (the girl tied in the pot and the two dancing witch doctors). Thanks again, Nate Kent

I am a artist interested in drawing and designing art for skateboards, posters and t-shirts. I was wondering how you got started and if you could give me any tips on getting started. It would be greatly appreciated. I think you are good artist and I've liked your work for many years.
Thank you. Sincerly, - Gabby

Mr. Phillips, I stumbled onto your web site after reading an article in "International Longboarder Magazine". I am proud to say that I was a skate rat from the 70's! and after visiting your web site was taken on a trip down memory lane. I owned many Santa Cruz 70's boards as well as a billion Road Rider and OJ wheels! The Santa Cruz ad with the dog was the absolute best. So good in fact that I had a friend in high school at that time (that was a pretty good artist) draw it for me on one of my school notebooks....whish I still had it! Anyway, what's my point right? I'm sure you get asked this a 1000 times a week but I am wondering if you sell (or know where I can get)any of the old 70's Santa Cruz, Road Rider or OJ stickers, poster's or whatever? No I don't want to sell them on e-bay! Just trying to re-live a fond time. Thanks In Advance For Your Time
- Mark James - St. Petersburg Florida

Dear Mr. Phillips,
My name is Matt and I am a big fan of yours. Art work by you and VC Johnson were probably more influencial in getting me into skateboarding than anything else. I am curious to know if you are doing anything in the skateboard industry these days. Your graphics were and still are amazing. Art work seems to have taken a back seat these days, especially with the lack of rails used today. Do you have any plans to work with Santa Cruz again? I hope that this letter finds you well and I hope to hear from you soon. Happy Holidays. - Matt DeAngelis

I loved the Roadrash cover & Porkchop Hill, and as a kid, of course, I didn't put it together that one person had drawn all these things I liked so much (Slimeballs, etc.) & spent many hours copying the logos with colored pencils, etc...
Anyway, you're one of the greats, Jim. May all the credit come your way, from every direction
- Matt

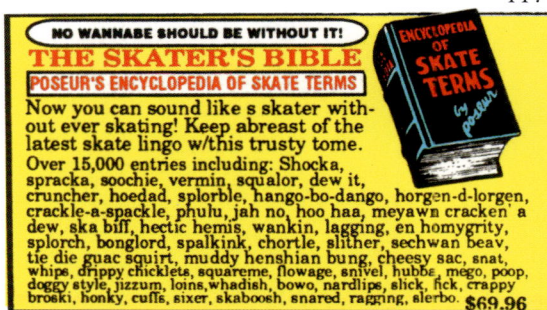

GOOD TIMES LETTERS

This cover art on the Good Times provoked public controversy.

A letter from the Mayor of Santa Cruz, signed by 38 outraged constituents, was followed by weeks of debate in the Good Times *letters column.*

Outraged

We are offended by your 20th anniversary cover (April 6). Exploitation of women's bodies is, of course, a common-place tactic used by the media to sell, and this cover continues what has been for you quite a bad record in this regard.

Most offensive is the "centerpiece" of the "artwork" on your cover showing a naked white woman with long blond hair, her breasts only marginally covered by the word "Our." Further, of the additional three women on the cover, only one (the protester) has any clothing (tight-fitting tank top and pants), the other two clad only in bikinis. Finally, unlike the men, who are all doing something, these woman appear as passive sexual objects (True, one is reading the newspaper, though the paper in no way obscures a view of her body).

Following the same old pattern of profiting via the objectification of women is not our idea of "Celebrating Two Decades of the Santa Cruz Spirit," a spirit which seems antithetical to this kind of activity. Sure, Santa Cruz is not (unfortunately) a "Feminist Utopia" as was suggested in an article a number of years ago in *Ms. Magazine*, but it still seems reasonable to expect more than what we get from this county's oldest and largest circulation weekly.

Get with the times and the real Santa Cruz Spirit, *GOOD TIMES*.

Mike Rotkin, Edward "Ted" Rico, Abra Brayman, Keren Ness, Julie Trupke, Marilyn Garrett, Paul Butler, Matthew Fitt, Kevin Browning, Marjan Tehrani, Keith Kjoller, Sharon Kaplan, Lisa J. Creson, Lynda Aadams, Alba Gafford, L.A. Jordan, Karin Lynn, Rick Warner, Mana Salcedo, Christina Peterson, Eric Swanson, Laurie B. Tanenbaum, Michelle Waters, Nicole Gasparik, Heather Logan, Peter Jerome Simpson, Matthew Rector, Jacek Lentz, Karen DeBraal, Jonathan Paul, Kim Reitz, Sheri Linhares, Kristy Armstrong, Cap Pack, Jane Devlin, Juan Gonzales, Sitara Care, Violet Hales, Maritza Partida, Jan Carey, Nili Ness , Barbara Lopez

Editor's note: From our perspective, Jim Phillips' cover illustration was an excellent representation of an era known for its free-spiritedness.

Nudism is still very much a part of the Santa Cruz lifestyle. It appears in local art, and on our beaches.

It's unfortunate that you saw the women on our cover as sex objects. We didn't, nor did the vast majority of the readers we talked to. We saw free-spiritedness and beauty. You apparently saw sex and exploitation.

Who is truly guilty of objectifying the human form in this case?

We'd also like to see some facts regarding our "bad record." To us, your letter sounds reactionary and puritanical.

GOOD TIMES LETTERS

Thanks

The letter in this week's *GOOD TIMES* (April 20) by Mike Rotkin, et al. in reaction to your 20th anniversary cover proves what many have known for a long time: Feminism has become a reactionary, puritanical, dogmatic, politically correct religion. As a result, it has alienated many former feminists (such as myself) as well as many sympathetic to issues important to both women and men. Books such as Christina Hoff Sommers' *Who Stole Feminism* and Warren Farrell's *The Myth of Male Power* tell part of the reason this has happened.

Thank you for not cow-towing to their hysterical — though predictable — reaction to your cover.

Jerad Lee
Santa Cruz

Ladies first

Outrageous! The first two signers of the letter of protest ("Letters," April 20) about your April 6 cover which objectified women were men! Whatever became of good old-fashioned etiquette? Can't ladies be first in the feminist utopia? Oops, attempts of courtesy may be perceived as chauvinistic backsliding. Hey! This is becoming difficult.

Somebody ought to write a reference book about "Politikette." Then if we have any questions about anything we are saying, seeing, thinking or doing, we can look it up.

Dennis Case
Aptos

GOOD TIMES LETTERS

Get a life

When I read the alarming letter signed by Mr. Rotkin et al, expressing their collective outrage at your 20th anniversary cover (Apr. 6), I immediately went to my recycling bin to make certain my copy also had the images to which they were referring. With the aid of a jaundiced magnifying glass, I was able to discern . . . nothing. Well, perhaps that's too simplistic, but that these good people should become so agitated over an issue of such incredible insignificance is truly mind boggling. If they can't "get a life" maybe they should consider leasing one with an option to buy.

Mick Smallwood
Santa Cruz

Police our pictures

You don't get it, do you? In regards to your 20th Anniversary cover (April 6), you wrote that the cover celebrated free-spiritedness and beauty. Okay. Fine. But why are there only four women, all of them young and of a certain shape? Three are fairly passive, one is protesting. There are twelve men, and they are old, young, fat, thin, six are playing musical instruments, three are involved in sports. There are men of various ethnicities. Where are the fat women, the musical women, women of diverse ethnicities, old women and women athletes?

I like all kinds of women: fat to thin, all colors, old and young, clothed and unclothed. Your response to the "outraged" letter didn't strike me as thoughtful. As a signer of the letter, I am flummoxed by my new title of "puritanical." This is news to me and those who know me. Without giving you the story of my own spirited life in response to your name-calling. I'll simply try to further this dialogue . . . that cover didn't cover men and women equally. All you need to do is look at it, count up the numbers of men and women and compare them. As an exercise, create a cover in your mind of four beefcake white guys surrounded by twelve fat women, women athletes, women of many diverse ethnicities, women playing a variety of musical instruments, old women, and young and have the centerpiece be a naked younger blonde guy. Maybe our point will sink in a little bit.

Karen DeBraal
Santa Cruz

Unfortunate

Bums, long-haired, unkempt, guitar-playing, Frisbee-tossing freaks, a surfer, juggler and a drummer were the "men" portrayed on the cover of your 20th anniversary issue. I was as offended by your portrayal of Santa Cruz men as Mike Rotkin, et al. were of the portrayal of Santa Cruz women. Most offensive is the overt sexuality of the buffed-out, bare-chested free spirits. Further, none of the men are pursuing any worthwhile activity, but seem to be engrossed in only hedonistic pursuits. It is unfortunate that you chose to portray a woman crusading for social change, yet all the men appeared to be self-absorbed, stoned or dim-witted.

I humbly suggest that you avoid future offense to all of us who are repulsed by the objectification of all people. This could easily be achieved by having your artists draw gender-neutral stick figures in their future works. It would be up to the reader to determine the sex of the subject from the context. An added benefit to this would be that the children (who are our future) would no longer feel that certain activities were reserved for only one sex.

Alex Anderson
Santa Cruz

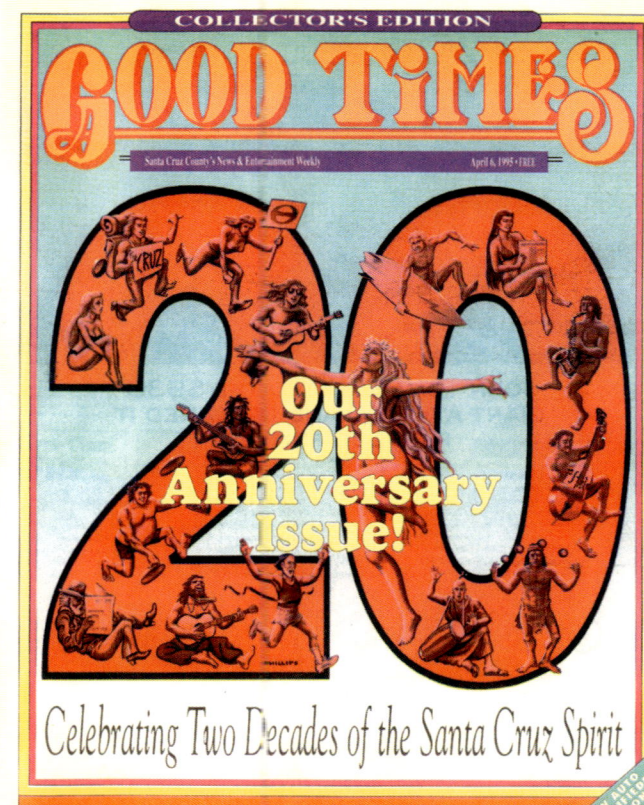

COLLECTOR'S EDITION

Good Times

Santa Cruz County's News & Entertainment Weekly   April 6, 1995 • FREE

20

Our 20th Anniversary Issue!

Celebrating Two Decades of the Santa Cruz Spirit

EVENTS • ART • MUSIC • THEATER • FILM • DI

Good Times *20th Anniversary, refer to page 141.*

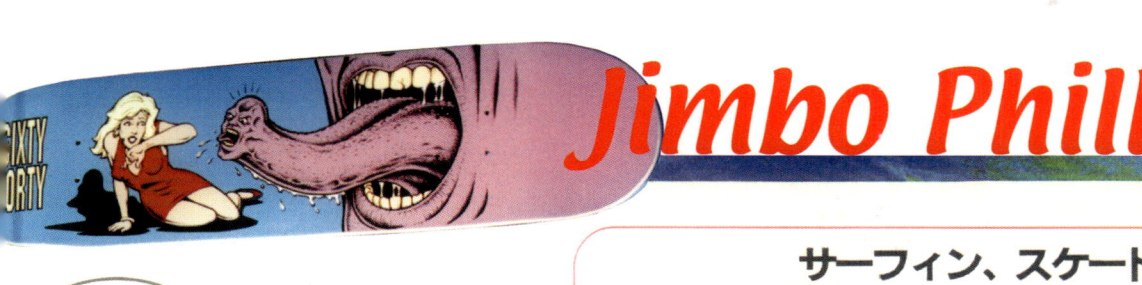

Jimbo Phillips

コミック調の画風が魅力のアーティスト

Jimbo Phillips
ジンボ・フィリップス

カリフォルニア サーファー

カリフォルニア・サンタクルーズ在住のジム・フィリップスは、サイケデリックなペイントなどで活動を続ける新進アーティストだ。ジンボは、アニメーションの世界へサーフ＆スケートスピリットを浸透させよう

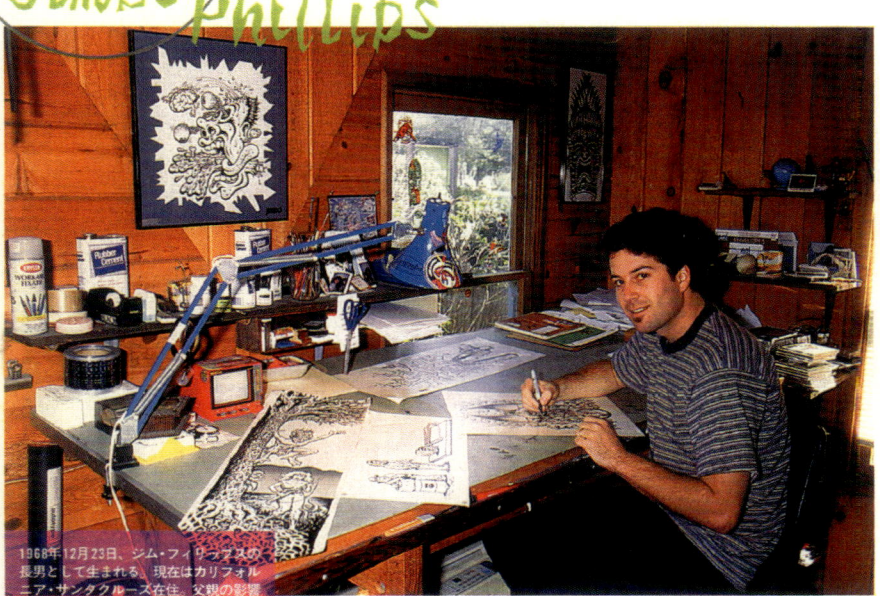

1966年12月23日、ジム・フィリップスの長男として生まれる。現在はカリフォルニア・サンタクルーズ在住。父親の影響で自然と幼い頃より絵を描き始め、サンタクルーズ・スケートでグラフィティを手がけた後、60／40、ファミリー・ドッグのデザイナー、サーフボード・アーティストとして活躍中。

↓地元のプレジャーポイントでサーフィンを楽しむジンボ

↓スケートはプロになりたかったというだけあり、かなりの腕前だ。
↓サンタクルーズのライブハウスで、人気のパンクバンド、アンディサイザンクではドラマーを務める。パンクながらもポップな音が最高

Left: Article on Jimbo in Japanese magazine, Fine, 1997.

↓サーファーたちのオーダーに応じて、サーフボード・アートのデザインも手がけている。彼が描くモンスターやセクシーな女のコは、大人から子供まで大好評で口コミながらも今までに150本ほどの注文をこなしている。自分だけの板を手にして、発注主の男のコも嬉しそうだね。オーダー料は1本＄50〜150

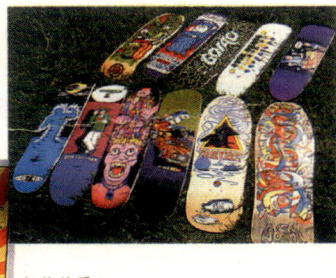

➡ジンボは'80年代にスケートボード・グラフィティのモンスターブームを作った

➡彼が初めて仕事をもらったという、スケートブックコミック『ROAD RUSH』に掲載された作品。人気がコ

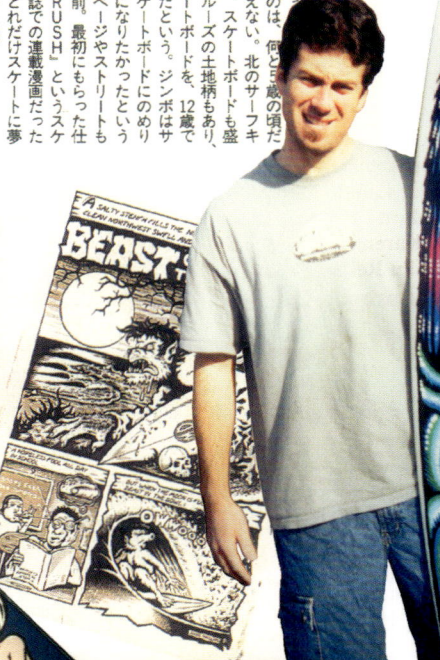

ジンボ・フィリップスは、右の彼を見てわかるように、アーティストにして絵を描き始めたのは、何と3歳の頃。そうして絵を描き始めた彼は、北のサーフキャピタルと呼ばれ、スケートボードも盛んだったサンタクルーズの土地柄もあり、7歳の時からスケートボードを、12歳でサーフィンを始めたという。ジンボはサーフィンよりもスケートボードにのめり込み、一時はプロになりたかっただけあって、ランページやストリートも何気なくこなす腕前。最初にもらった仕事が『ROAD RUSH』というスケートのコミック雑誌での連載漫画だったというから、彼がどれだけスケートに夢中だったかがわかるよね。

その後、地元の大手スケートメーカー、NHSサンタクルーズ・スケートに、父親のジムがアートディレクターを務める老舗の音楽プロモーター、ファミリー・ドッグでポスターやフライヤーのデザイナーとして活躍している。地元シェイパーのスティープと組んで手がけているサーフボードのグラフィティも、なかなかの評判。将来の夢は動きのあるアニメーション・ビデオを作りたいというから、今から楽しみだよね。

親のジムがアートディレクターを担当する他、父親の後を引き継いでグラフィック・アーティストとして参加。'80年代にコミック調モンスターのイラストで、一大ブームを作り出す。昔からスケートをやっていた読者なら、下の写真にある彼のグラフィティのいくつかを覚えている人もいるはず。また、この頃はサーフィンがカルチャーとして認められ始めた時代でもある。ジンボのような少年が生まれた時代でもある。アーティストとして活躍するには最高のチャンスだったわけだ。

今やはりスケートボード・メーカー60／40でグラフィティを担当する他、

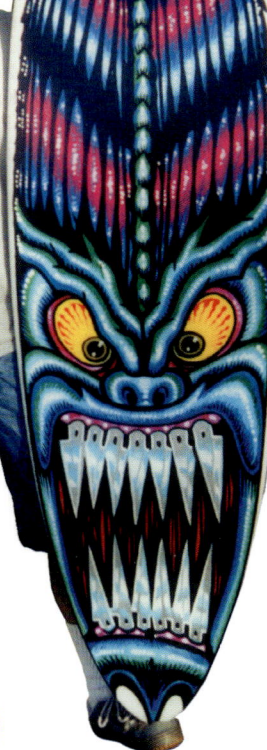

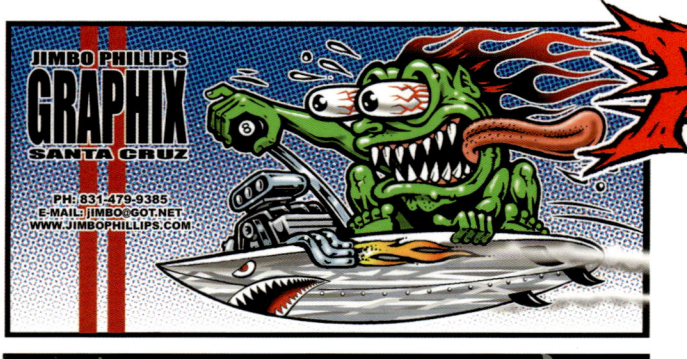

GRAPHIC ASSAULT

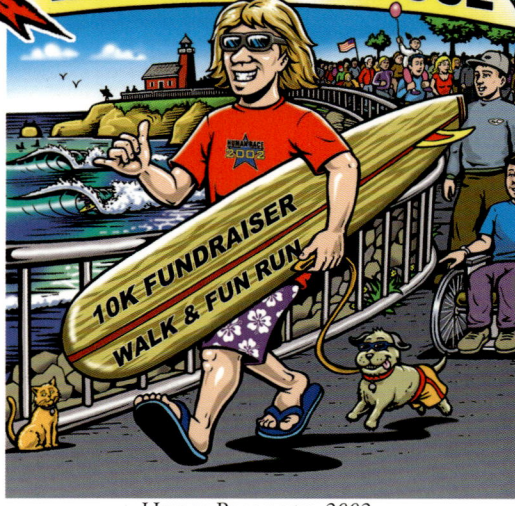

Human Race *poster*, 2002.

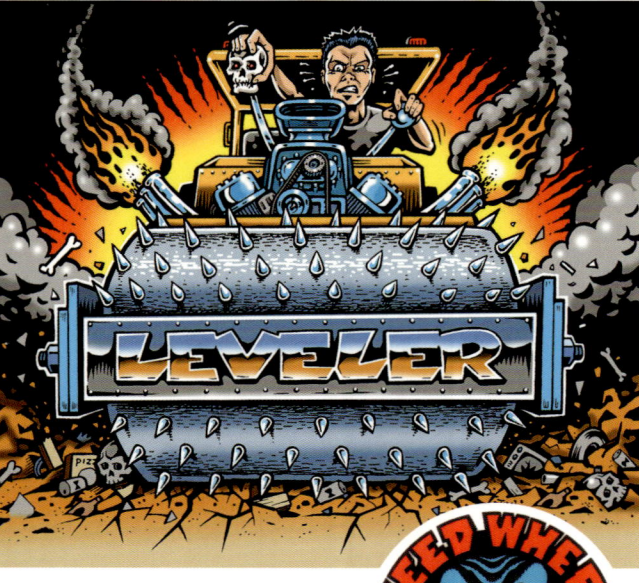

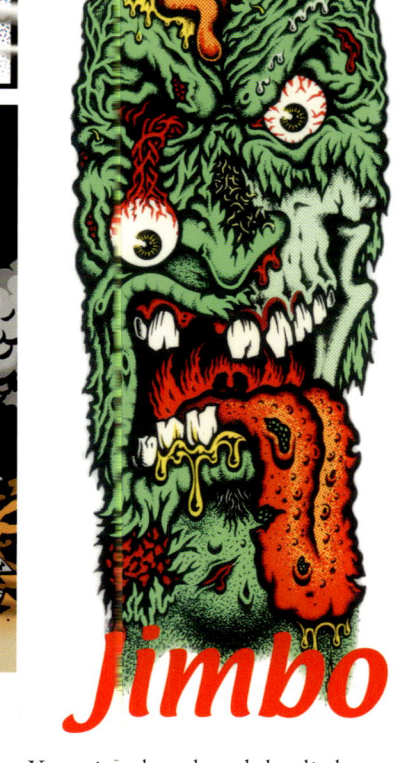

Jimbo

You might have heard that little nugget of American wisdom, "The nut doesn't fall far from the tree." Well in the case of Jim Phillips Jr., that little seed of wisdom sprouts into the truth. Jim Phillips is the tree that Jimbo fell from, and all you have to do is walk out the door of Jim Phillips' house and count 20 paces and you will find the nut. In this case, Jimbo Phillips. Is Jimbo Phillips a nut? Well, no, he's actually a well-rounded and squared-off husband of the former Miss Jennifer Griffin, and father of Cassidy Noe (5) and Colby James (1). Jimbo lives in the house that used to be Phillips Studios and there he continues the work that his father began in the middle of the 20th Century.

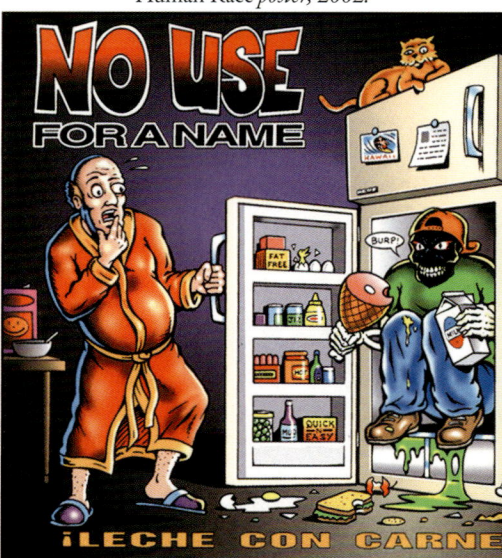

¡LECHE CON CARNE!

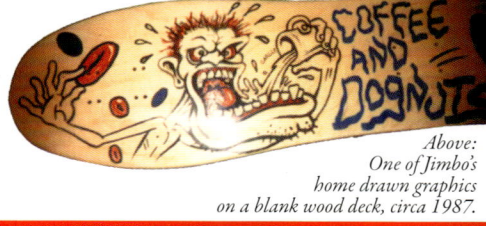

Above:
One of Jimbo's home drawn graphics on a blank wood deck, circa 1987.

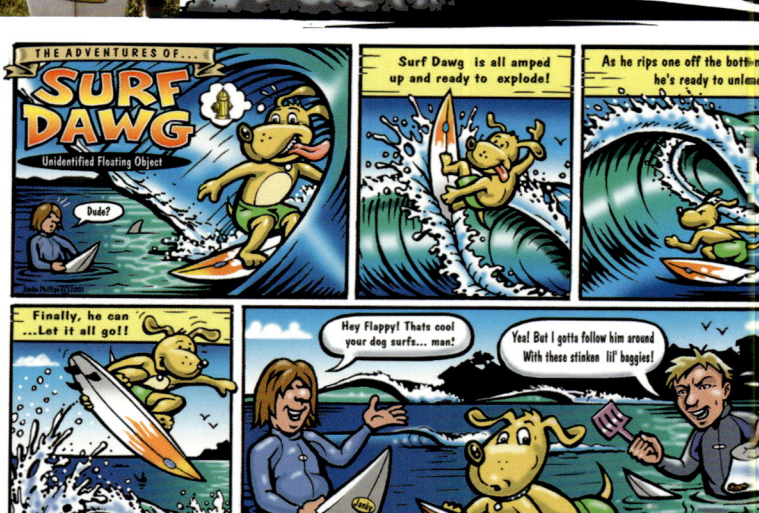

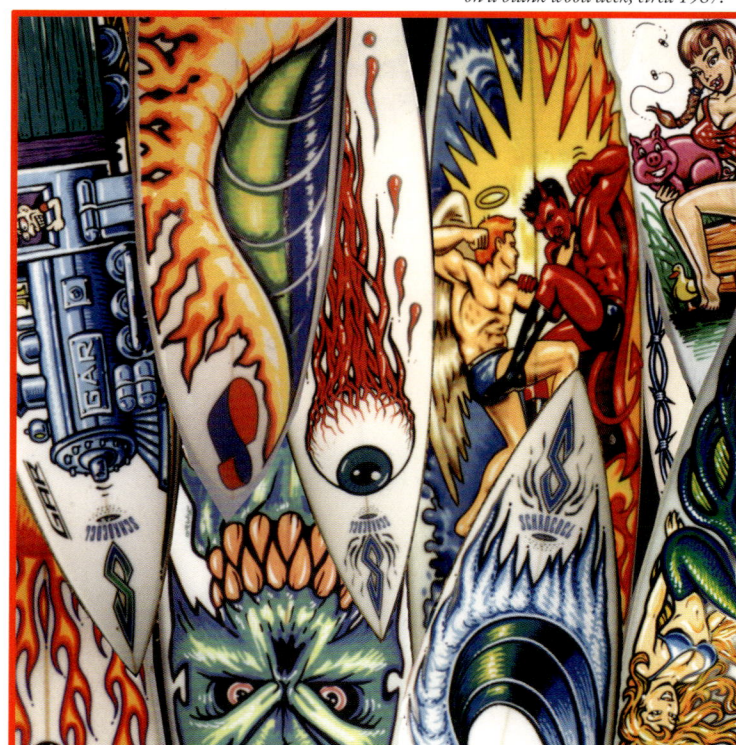

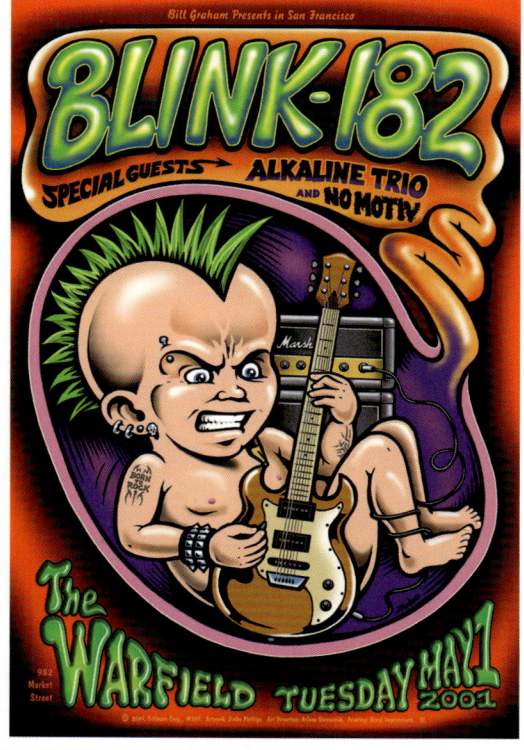

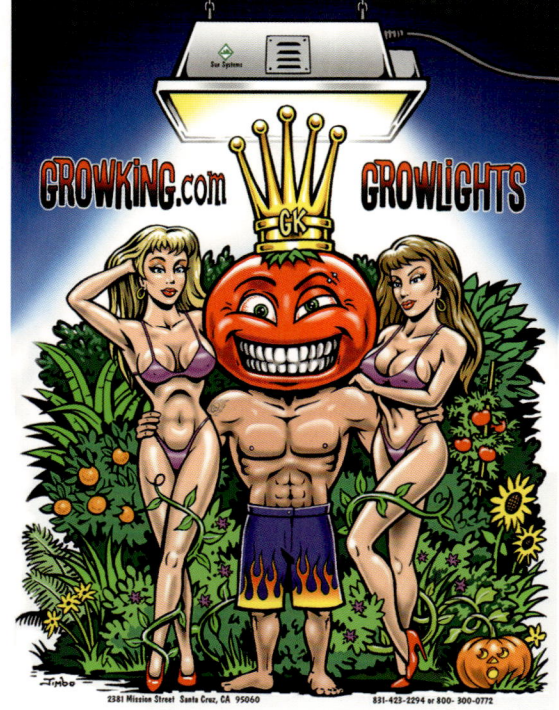

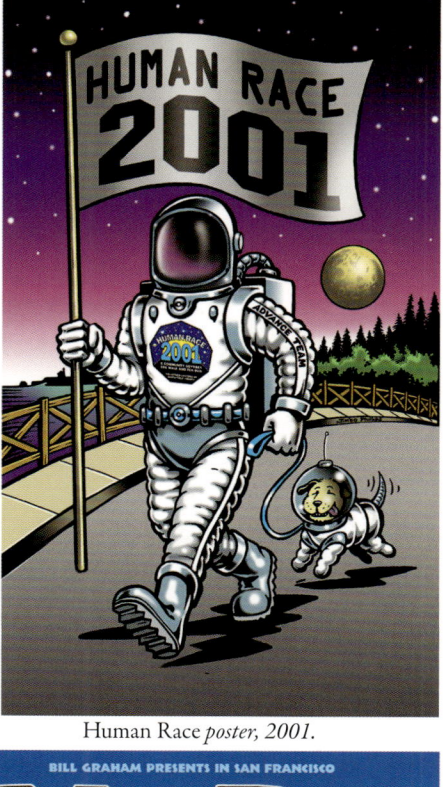

Human Race *poster, 2001.*

But Jim Jr. does have his father's nutty sense of humor and some of his cartooning style. Friends call him "Jimbo" as does anyone else who knows the two. Jimbo Phillips is an artist, surprise, surprise, and a pretty good one. You don't have to look too hard to see the Phillips style and sense of humor in Jimbo's work, and sometimes you have to look hard to tell the two apart. Like pops, Jimbo began scribbling almost instantly. He was born in Melbourne, Florida on December 23, 1968 during his parent's occupational transplantation. Eight years later, Jimbo did his first comic book. It was a space gremlin, named *Bazooka*. Sound familiar?

Back in Santa Cruz, Jim and Jimbo enjoyed a father-son relationship that half of this troubled world can only envy. They collected comic books together, skateboarded together, surfed Sharks Cove together and changed the world of skateboard graphics together. When the golden years hit, he appreciated having a core-age skater around. Jimbo was 13, and helped him stay on the right path. Jimbo would get blank wood decks so he could draw his own graphics. One time he drew a face on the bottom of a deck, and that gave Jim senior the basic idea for the Roskopp "Face" deck. Who

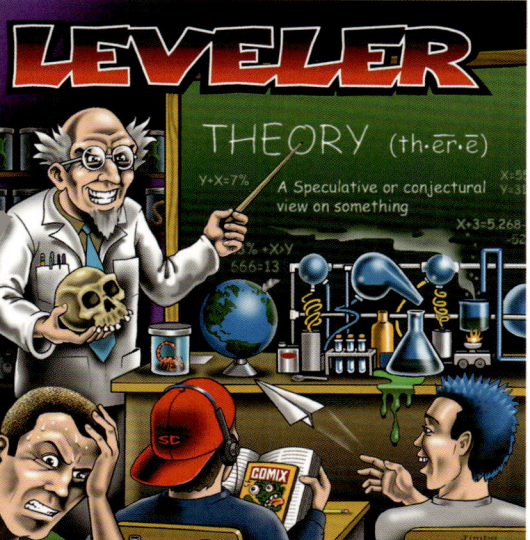

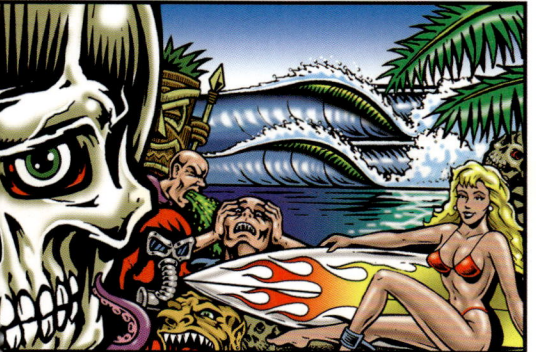

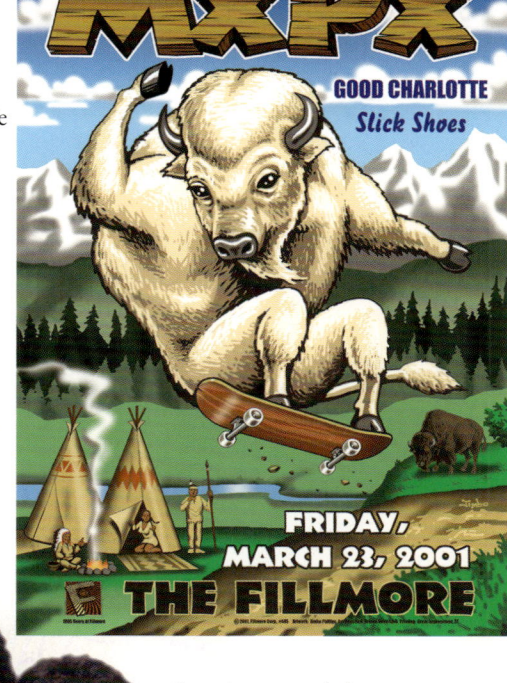

knows how many of those Santa Cruz units sold, but it was a lot. The next year Jimbo was assigned by his father to draw the next stage of the Face, a mutated decaying Dorian Grey version, complete with maggots, eyeball hanging out.

Jimbo turned 32 at the Turn of the Century and he stays busy doing art for local surf shops and bands, enjoys a close relationship with pops. Not just emotionally, but geographically. Jim and Jimbo still live side by side, and share ideas in that quiet corner of Santa Cruz.

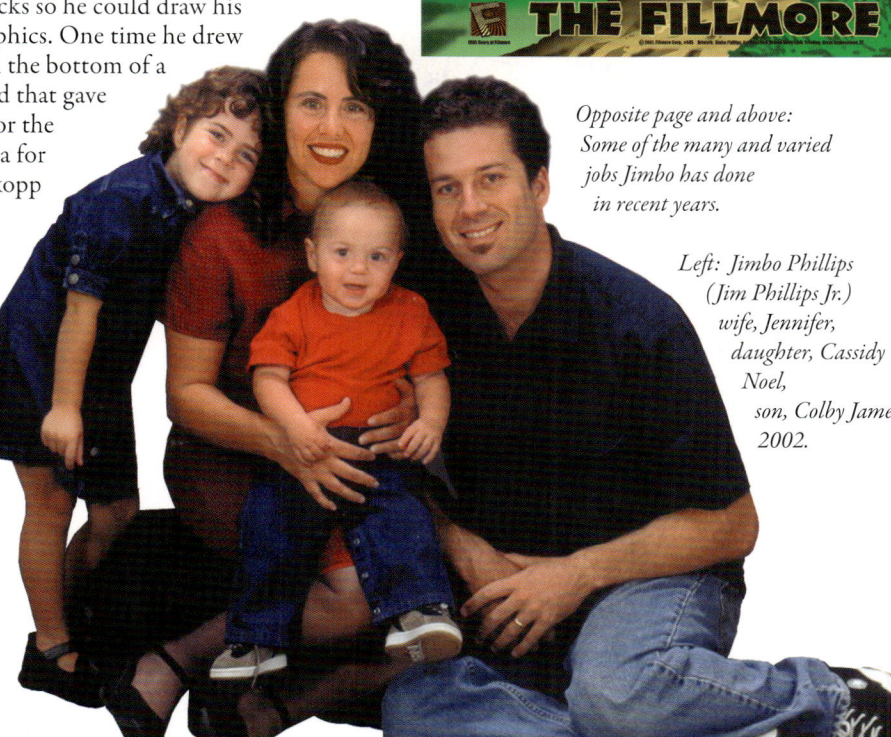

Opposite page and above:
Some of the many and varied
jobs Jimbo has done
in recent years.

Left: Jimbo Phillips
(Jim Phillips Jr.)
wife, Jennifer,
daughter, Cassidy
Noel,
son, Colby James,
2002.

Index

Aaberg, Denny, 135, 136
A and M Records, 80
Abbeyville Press, 142
Action Now Magazine, 71
Action Sports Retailer Expo, 135, 138
Akido Press, 164, 169, 171, 177
Alba, Mickey, 122
Alice in Wonderland, 54
Allison, Mose, 150
Allman, Gregg, 160, 174
Anthony, Earl, 14, 15
Aptos Post (Post Digital), 119
Asleep at the Wheel, 74, 79
Artichokes, 75
Art of Rock, The, 83, 142
Atlantis Fantasyworld, 78
Avalon Ballroom, 33, 156, 185
Baba, Meher, 28
Backroom, 78, 84
Ballentine, Bill, 31
Bank of America, 44, 49
Bard, Bruce, 135
Barks, Carl, 199
Batman, 138, 55.138
Bay Area Music, 89
Bay Sports, 102, 106
Beach Boys, 21
Beams, 140
Beatles, 34, 36, 40
Beecher, Henry Ward, 9
Benson, Gary, 25, 26
Biddle, Bob, 18
Big Brother, 144
Bike Shop West, 44, 49
Bill Graham Presents, 144, 147, 148, 156, 160, 161, 166, 184
Bisconte, Pat, 102
Blackburn, Jeff "Buck", 28, 37, 75, 79, 80, 89
Blackburn & Snow, 23
Blackouts, 178
Blakely, Rich, 150
Blue Notes, 130
Boneyard, 192
Boston, Mass., 33, 36, 37
Boston University, 34
Boulder Creek Theatre, 76, 80, 83, 85
Braddock, Benjamin, 41, 71
Branciforte Jr High, 15
Branciforte Bee, 16, 207
Brentwood Pictures, 139
Brighton, Mass., 36
Brown, Bruce, 53
Brown, James, 158, 185
Brown, Micheal, 32
Browne, Jackson, 138
Buck and the Odds, 75, 89
Buckle Bakery, 57
Bunny Ball, 103
Bullet Wheels, 101
Byberg, Jim, 7, 18, 31, 44, 49, 80, 121
Cabo San Lucas. 112
Cabrillo Junior College, 27, 80, 121
Cadillac Wheels, 42, 69
California College of Arts and Crafts, 27, 28, 29, 80

Cal Litho, 37, 43, 52, 60
Cannery Row, 37
Canned Heat, 150
Canty, Steve, 28, 29, 30, 31
Capitola, Ca., 18, 93
Captain America, 54
Capuzzo, Joe "Cap", 36
Cardinale, Eric, 121
Carson, Lance, 135, 135
Cassady, Neal, 30
Castro, Fidel, 30
Catalyst, 75, 76, 78
Cave Surfer, 194
Chicago, 57, 58
Christian Community, 58
Cinnamon Cinder, 18
Clash, The, 30
Clinton, George, 153
Cocoa, Fla., 33, 39
Coconut Grove Ballroom, 72, 86, 104
Cohen, Allen, 31
Cohen, Harvey, 28, 31
Cold Blood, 150
Coletta Surfboards, 110
Conklin, Lee , 142, 147, 150, 160
Conquest, Dennis, 19, 20
Conti, Harry, 27, 101, 103
Cooperhouse, 89
Cox, Denny, 37
Coyro, Dan, 80
Cracked Magazine, 129, 207
Craviotto, Johnny, 79
Cray, Robert, 162, 163
Creedence Clearwater Revival, 144
Crocodile Lounge, 143
Crossroads, The, 75, 79
Crosstown Bus, , 33, 34, 36
Crude McFly, 110
Crusader Rabbit, 12
Cub Scouts, 13
Cycle Shack, 51
Cymbaline Records, 78
Daddy-O, 79, 99
Dale, Dick, 18
Dali, Salvador, 7, 29
Dauser, Bruce, 143, 144, 147, 156
Dauser Press, 142, 143, 144, 150, 151, 153, 158, 164
Dawson, Bill, 138, 154, 184, 185
Dawson, Dai, 154
Da Vinci, Leonardo, 9, 10
Davies, Ray, 159
Davis, George, 28, 30, 37, 38
Del Mar Theater, 74, 76, 80, 89
Degawa, Michio, 139
Degawa Surfboards, 138, 139
Denike, Bob, 124
Dennis the Menace, 14
Desmond, Steve, 19
Dingman, Rollin, 58
Disney Studios, 12, 15
Disney, Walt, 29, 80, 135
D.O.A., 150
Dogtown Skates, 71
Donald Duck, 12, 38
Doobie Brothers, 144
Doors, The, 34, 35, 36
Dozey Dinkle, 14
Dr. Strange, 160
Ducks, The, 79, 80, 81
Duck's Landing, 79
Durer, Albrecht, 43
Eau Gallie, Fla., 38
EC Comics, 15

Elder, Bill, 15, 64, 80
Eggert, Mr., 15, 16, 64, 74
Elliott Mrs., 15, 16, 101
El Tri, 176
El Truck, 196
Engblom, Skip, 139
Erikson, Bruce, 145
Escher, E.C., 7, 29, 126
Eternal Truth, 59
Evenson, John, 17, 18, 66
Evenson, Josh, 125
Excellerators, 168
Fabert, Jaque, 28, 29
Family Dog, 33, 145, 147, 150, 156, 160, 185
Farr, Rep.Sam, 138
Fast Planet, 143
Felix the Cat, 12
Fenway Park, 33
Fiberglas Works, 7, 42, 43, 44, 45, 46, 49, 53, 54, 69, 72, 80
Fillmore, The, 144, 147, 156, 160, 168
Fineburg, Marjane, 38
Fineburg, Willie, 33, 38
Fine Magazine, 140
Fithian, Steve, 20
Flintstone, Fred
Flash Gordon, 12
Florence, Italy, 9, 36
Forbes, Justin, 124, 125
Freestyler, 118
Fungo Mungo, 147, 150
Garcia, Jerry, 74, 80
Garcia, Jerry Band, 73, 74, 75
Gardner Museum, 33
Garrison, Michael, 4
Gentry, Bobby, 34
Geoscience, 36, 119
Gibson, Charles, 10
Gidget, 19
Ginghofer, Andreas, 121
Ginsberg, Arnie, 34, 36
Girard, Jeff, 136
Golden Gate Park, 172, 173, 185.
Goldman, Rusty, 143
Gonzales, Roy, 135
Good Times, 40 ,76, 78, 79, 80, 108, 109, 112, 141, 172,173, 200, 202
Goodwill, 37
Goofy, 38
Gravenites, Nick, 156
Gray, Freddie, 14
Gray, Harold, 14
Gray, Ralph , 14, 15, 31, 60, 70, 72, 80, 101
Greatful Dead, 160
Great Impressions, 147, 148, 152, 158, 159, 161, 162, 166 , 170, 174, 175, 176
Gremlins, 188
Gremlin Society, 17
Greyhound Bus, 10
Griffin, Rick, 10, 19, 22, 23, 32, 58, 135
Grisman, David, 147, 158, 159, 160, 168, 169
Grosso, Jeff, 113
Grushkin, Paul, 142
Gurno, Leo, 27
Gump, Forest, 2, 36, 42
Guthrie, Arlo, 21
Guthrie, Woodie, 21
Haight Ashbury, 37, 143
Half Moon Bay, 10, 11, 32
Hall, Edna "Grandma" 10,

12, 40
Hall, Edna May, 10, 14
Hall, Gene, 26
Hall, Henry C. "Grandpa", 10, 12, 31, 198
Hall, Mary, 10
Hall of Flowers, 142, 156, 185
Ham, Bill, 144, 156
Hammons, Bruce, 190
Hanaue, Jiro, 138
Hand Wave, 132, 135, 140
Hara, John, 31
Harmony Food, 56
Harris, Emmylou, 175
Harris, Little Joe, 26
Harvard Square, 33, 36
Haut, Doug, 7, 19, 69, 70, 71, 118, 138
Haut Surfboards, 7
Heim, Ian, 33, 34
Hells' Angels, 42
Helms, Chet, 142, 143, 144, 147, 156, 160, 185
Hendrix, Jimi, 157, 168
Henson, Mark, 150
Herbst Pavillion, 144
Herger, Walter Assemblyman, 104
Hester, Henry, 70
Hicks, Dan, 144
Highway 9, 88
Hill, Tony, 25, 27
History of Surfing, 136
Hoffman, Doc, 12
Hoffman, Hienrick, 53
Hollywood and Vine, 80
Hosford, Larry, 75, 80, 89 108, 178, 190
Hot Rod Woody, 195
Hot Tuna, 147, 148, 156, 160
Hughston, Boot, 150
Hughston, Boots, 143, 144, 150, 156
Hulk, The, 55
Hunt Pen Co. 82
Iello, "Joe the Landlord", 33
Independent Trucks, 70, 71, 118
International Longboarder Magazine, 113, 116
Iron Butterfly, 160
Isla Vista, 44
James, Etta, 150
Jan and Dean, 25
Jesus, 28, 30, 31, 32, 36, 37, 38, 40, 53, 58, 60, 61, 62, 63,148
Jiminy Cricket, 15
Johnson, Gilbert, 150
Jones, Ross, 19, 20
Kamakura, Japan, 138
Kampion Drew, 66
Katz, Gabe, 31, 37
Keller, Ernie, 31
Kelley, Alton, 37, 142, 144, 147, 150, 156, 160
Kelly, Sandy, 37, 38
Kerouac, Jack, 21
Kesey, Ken, 30
Ketcham, Hank, 14
Kienholz, Tom, 25, 26
King Features Syndicate, 160
Knepper, Derek, 143, 147
Kookson, Gideon, 135
Krazy Kat, 12
KFAT, 84
KLRB, 76
KRLA, 18
KSBW TV 8, 14

KUSP Radio, 74, 76, 79, 133
Lafond, Ron, 30, 150
Latchman, Mitch, 53
Latimer, Bruce, 158
Lesh, Phil, 177
Leftover Salmon, 147, 152, 160,172, 173
Levine, Wes, 36
Lewis, L., 89
Lighthouse Point, 80
Little Orphan Annie, 14
Live Oak Elementary, 15, 49
Longwenus, Lou, 60
Longboard Union, 64
Lore & the Stormriders, 85
Los Angeles Times, 104
Lothar & The Hand People, 33
Louis and Clark, 86, 143
Lucas, Jerry, 58
Lucas Method, The, 58
Lucky Duck Boatworks, 190, 93
Macintosh, 119, 123, 135
Mad Comics, EC, 15
Mad Magazine, 15, 16, 80, 135
Mahood, Reverend, 38
Mako, 186
Mako Surfboards, 17
Manusos, Steve, 119
Manwarren, John, 28
Marberg, Kevin, 124, 125, 127
Maritime Hall, 147, 150, 151, 156, 160, 164, 185
Mayang, Herme, 124, 125
Mazatlan, Mexico, 30
Mazzeo, Jim, 18, 19, 28, 31, 32, 33, 75, 92, 98, 105, 130 34, 36, 76, 79, 91, 130, 190
McCormack, Geoff, 43, 44, 72
McCracken, Jim, 33, 34, 36
McCracken, Joann, 34
McDonald, Country Joe, 80, 86, 156
McGuire, Dave, 27
McGuire, Mr., 41, 42, 69, 71
McMahan, Brian, 28, 31, 138
Medfly, 104
Meek, Keith, 121, 124, 125
Metiver, Rich, 117, 123
Metzger, Rick, 25, 26, 28, 30, 34
Mexico City, 30
Michaels, Lee, 144
Mighty Mouse, 12
Mighty Snail, 82
Mikus, Tony, 26
Milan, 9
Miller, Steve, 144
Miss California Parade, 23, 104
Moby Grape, 79, 80, 84, 142
Money, Eddie, 147, 148, 160
Monterey, Ca., 37
Monterey Bay, 9, 10
Monterey Marine Sanctuary, 138
Monterey Naval Postgraduate School, 37
Monroe, Keith, 26
Moore, Mike, 113, 116
Moore's Reef, 93
Morrison, Jim, 34, 36
Moscoso, Victor, 147, 150, 160
Moseley, Bob, 79
Moss Beach, Ca., 32
Motorhead, 150
Mountain Dew, 121, 124, 125
Mouse, Stanley, 142, 144, 147, 150, 160, 195
Muldaur, Maria, 72
Munch, Edvard, 101

Rosie.

206

Background: "Rollin" as Santa in this ad art. Santa Cruz Plastics was formed thru NHS to continue serving surf shops with materials in the late 70s.

Municipal Wharf, 88
Munnerlyn, John, 124, 127
Munoz, Mickey, 136, 138, 139
Murphy, 23, 58
Museum of Fine Arts, Boston, 33
Meyer, Ray, 113, 126
Nasworthy, Frank, 41, 42
National Horseshoe, 105
Nelson, Randy, 49
Nelson, Tracy, 42, 43, 44, 49, 50, 51, 110
Nelson, Willie, 171
New Reflections, 143
New Testament, 58
New World, 187
Niagara Falls, N.Y., 36
Nieman, Albert, 143
NHS, 7, 69, 70, 102, 112, 113, 118, 119, 124, 127. 133
No Surfing, 135
Northern California Surfing Invitational, 25
Novak, Rich, 7, 22, 69, 70, 71, 113, 118, 127, 184, 186, 189, 190, 192, 194
Nugent, Ted, 155
Oakland, Ca., 11, 28, 30, 33
Ocean pacific, 138
Oceanside Surfboards, 33, 39
OJ Wheels, 68, 101
Olson, George, 7, 22, 69
Olson, Steve, 25, 71, 93 118
Olson Surfboards, 7, 25, 28, 69
O'Neill, Jack, 22, 104
O'Neill's Surf Shop, 22, 42, 64
Oracle, 31, 32, 37
Otto Meyer, 40
Otto's Surf Shop, 40
Overlin, Jim, 40
Overlin Surfboard Shop, 39, 42, 43
Owseichik, Arlene, 168, 183, 184
Pack Your Trash, 44, 71, 104, 138, 139, 140, 182 , 185, 192, 193
Palace, The, 28
Palm, Al, 19
Panama, 11
Pannetta, Leon, 138
Parker, Ron, 24
Partlow, Gary, 16, 17
Pasadena, Ca. 18
Paskowitz, Salvador, 135
Patton, Gary, 53
Paulson, Einer, 30
Paulson, Iris, 31, 38
Pele Juju, 150
Pescadaro, 10, 12, 17
Pescadaro Elementary, 10
Peters, Duane, 71, 118
Petty, Tom, 161, 168, 178, 183
Pezman, Steve 136
PG&E Power Plant, 104
Phillips, Cassidy Noel, 202, 203
Phillips, Colby James, 202, 203
Phillips, Coles, 166
Phillips, Dolly, 33, 34, 36, 37, 38, 40, 55, 58, 71, 78, 79, 112, 119, 125, 127, 139, 143, 144, 147, 150, 160, 168, 183, 184, 185, 190
Phillips, Edna May, 12, 38, 40, 101
Phillips, Jenny, 202, 203
Phillips, James J. "Jimbo", 38, 71, 119, 121, 125, 127, 129, 135,

141, 150, 201, 202, 203
Phillips, Raymond L., 10, 11, 12, 101, 119, 190
Phillips-Rusnak, Ann, 10, 11, 15, 16
Phillips & Son, 53
Phillips Studios, 101, 102, 119, 121, 123, 125, 127, 129, 135
Phillips, Walt, 22
Picasso, Pablo, 21, 37
Pilot Press, 74, 75
Pine St., 156
Pleasure Point, 12, 16, 18, 25, 26, 69, 70, 103, 118, 193
Pleasure Point Night Fighters, 23, 26, 101, 102, 103, 104
Pleasure Point Surfing Assn., 25, 26
Pope, 7, 71, 104, 113
Popeye, 80
Post Digital, 144, 172
Powell Peralta, 71, 116, 127
PPNF Voice, 103, 104
Prochnow, Bill, 80
Professor Poster, 143, 185
Pro Motion, 115
Purim, Flora, 105
Purple Haze, 75
Puff the Magic Dragon, 18
Puisseaur, Dave, 25, 26
Quality Offset Printing, 74, 75, 76, 80, 83, 86, 111, 130, 143, 154, 155
Quality Products, 69, 70
Radiation Nation, 89
Raitt, Bonnie, 72
Ratdog, 146, 147, 160, 168
Rat Fink, 17
Ray's Photo Engraving, 60
Raytheon, 119
Red Blanchard Show, 12
Red Dog, 156
Renaissance Fair, 58
Rice, Johnny, 29, 138
Richard, Zachary, 150
Richardson, Bob, 21
Richmond, Ca., 11
Righetti, Don, 55
Road Rash, 115, 121, 124, 126
Road Riders Wheels, 7, 42, 68, 70, 71, 101, 118
Rock Art Ball, 156
Rock Art Expo, 142, 147
Rockit Sports, 178
Roderick, Tony, 69
Ron Jon, 38
Rose, Mitchell, 28, 29, 31
Rosie, 139
Roskopp, Rob, 71, 114, 115, 203
Ross, Jones
Roth, Big Daddy Ed, 10, 17, 195
Russell, Rod "Stickman", 27, 28, 38
Saint Anthony, 43
Saint Josephs Church, 18
Salinas, Ca., 14
Salt Lake City, 11
Samuels, Jeff, 4
San Francisco, 33, 37
San Francisco Chronicle, 144
San Jose, 10, 25, 160
San Jose State University, 49, 67
San Mateo, 10
Santa Barbara, 110
Santa Claus, 14
Santa Cruz, 7, 10, 18, 91

Santa Cruz Civic Auditorium, 77, 76, 79, 80, 104, 142
Santa Cruz County Fair, 99, 102
Santa Cruz Fire Department, 25, 103
Santa Cruz Express, The, 107
Santa Cruz High, 18, 19, 20
S C Horsemens Assn., 15
Santa Cruz Lighthouse, 91
Santa Cruz Magazine, 102
Santa Cruz Sentinel, 55, 76, 79, 130
Santa Cruz Skateboards, 7, 69, 70, 71, 101, 102, 116, 118, 119, 127, 133
Santa Cruz Skimboards, 123
Santa Cruz Snowbaords, 182
Santa Cruz Surfboards, 7
Santa Cruz Surf Shop, 65 69
Santa Cruz Weekly, 100, 102, 130, 135,
Saunders, Merle, 150
Savastano, Fenton, 118
Saxson, Sky, 143
Screaming Hand, 101, 113, 116, 117, 127, 196
Screen and Screen Again, 91
Scofield, Steve, 53
Scofield Surfboards, 40
Seattle, Washington, 143
Second Sight, 150
Seeds, The, 143, 178
Seventh Avenue, 138
Severson, John, 19
Severin, John, 129
SF Rock Posters, 158, 160, 160
Shaggy Fish, 79
Shark's Cove, 197, 203
Shelley, Kent "Webster", 18
Shields, Brook, 112
Shore, Jay, 112
Shoreline Amphitheatre, 166
Shuirman, Jay, 7, 69, 70, 71, 113, 118
Schwa, 172
Sidesaddle, 158
Simmons, Pete, 78, 89
Simmons, Willie, 78, 79, 86, 138, 168, 178
Simran, 56
Singer, David, 142, 147, 150, 160
Sioux City, Iowa, 37
Skateboarder Magazine, 69, 70, 71
Skull deck, 119
Slasher, 113, 121
Sledge, Percy, 150
Slimeballs, 101, 125, 128
Snail, 82
Solar Surfboards, 7
Soquel Elementary, 12
Sonday Funnies, 58
Sound Light Demension 156
snowboarding, 182
Sparky, the Space Gremlin, 78, 102, 109, 172
Speckman's Junkyard, 18
Speedball Pen Co., 12
Speed Freaks Video, 117
Speed Wheels, 101, 113, 117, 118
Spiderman,138
Sri Yukeswar, 28
Staff of Life, 44
Staley, Joe, 125
Stanford University, 10

Stan's Crazy Signs, 130
Steamer Lane, 9, 138
Stearns, Dave, 18
String Cheese Incident, 172, 173
Stocks, Kenny, 53, 191
Stormin' Norman, 178, 190
Straight Theater, 37, 38
Sultzer, Davey, 17, 18, 21, 23, 28, 38
Summer of Love, 167
Sundaze, 40
Sunset Beach, 10
Superman, 12, 38, 40
Surfaris, The, 111
Surf Crazed Comics, 135, 136, 137, 192
Surf Fair, 23, 26, 101, 104
Surfer Magazine, 19, 22, 58, 69, 70, 101, 118, 36
Surfin' and Ocean Sports, 106
Surfing Illustrated , 23, 58, 102
Surfing International, 23
Surfers Journal, The, 135, 136, 194
Sunn, Rell, 192
Swami Satchidananda, 52
Sweet, Mathew, 166
Tequila, Mexico, 30
Third Reef Productionsk, 92
Thomsen Fiberglas, 29
Thomsen, Jeff, 19, 29, 31, 33
Thompson, Don, 27
Thrasher Magazine, 101, 114
Three Princes, 194
Time Magazine, 71, 113
Tomson, Shaun, 106
Toyota of Japan, 139
Tracy Factory, 110
Tracy Inc, 45, 46, 47, 49, 50, 58, 80
Treasure, The, 197
T-shirt Weather, 138
Tubes, The, 76, 77, 79, 80, 87, 142
Tuten, Randy, 147, 150, 160
Twin Lakes Beach, 80
Twin Lakes Church, 62
UCSC Student Guide, 102

Vallentines Day, 108, 112
Van Dyke, Fred, 23, 106
Van Dyke, Gene, 23
Van Dyke, Peter, 23
Venterini, Gary, 26
Ventures, The, 18
Vickers, Sandy, 32
Virginia City, 156
Visitors Guide, 106, 107, 112
VooDoo Glow Skulls, 150
Vomit Balls, 101, 125
Waikiki, 10, 18
Waltham, Mass., 36, 119
Warfield Theatre, 168
Warhol, Andy, 10
Watersaucer, 90
Wes Behel Volkswagon, 54, 55
Westside Surfshop, 101
Whittenberg Door, 60
Wild Card, 178
Wild Hook, 190
Williams, Caitlin, 37
Williams, Gene, 19
Williams, Larry, 52, 131
Williams, Reggie, 37
Winter, Edgar, 154, 156, 160
Wilson, Wes, 142, 143. 144, 156
What On Earth?, 75, 76, 78, 79, 80, 84, 85
Wonder Woman, 55
Woody Junkyard, 196
Woodystock, 132
Woody T, 189
Wood, Wally, 15, 64
World Disc, 105
X-Games, 42
X The Unknown, 102
Yamauchi, Kozaburo "Kobe", 138, 139, 192
Yea Productions, 72, 74, 76, 79, 80, 86
Yoe, Craig, 58
Young, Jesse Colin, 80, 86
Young, Neil, 34, 76, 79, 130
Yogananda, Parmahansa, 28
Zap Comics, 58
Zero, 150, 170
Zyg, 172, 194

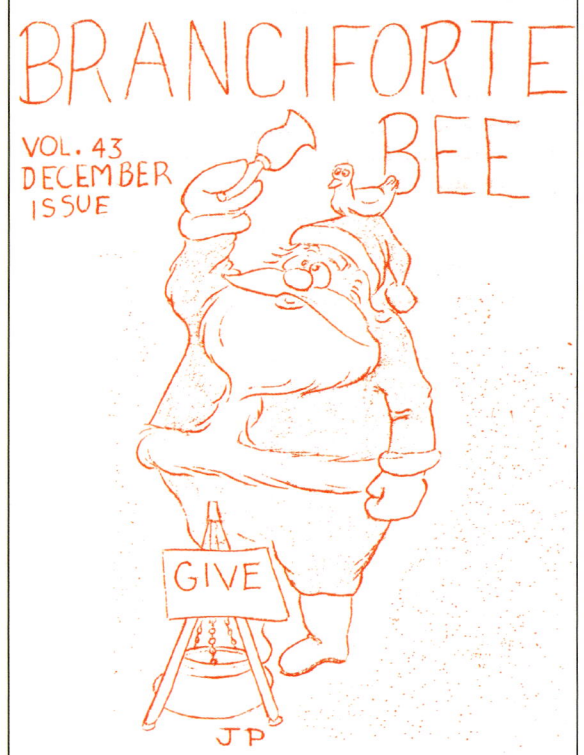

Backgroung: Surf Santa Cruz, 1979 t-shirt design.

Cover of Branciforte Bee, *Branciforte Jr. High, 1958.*

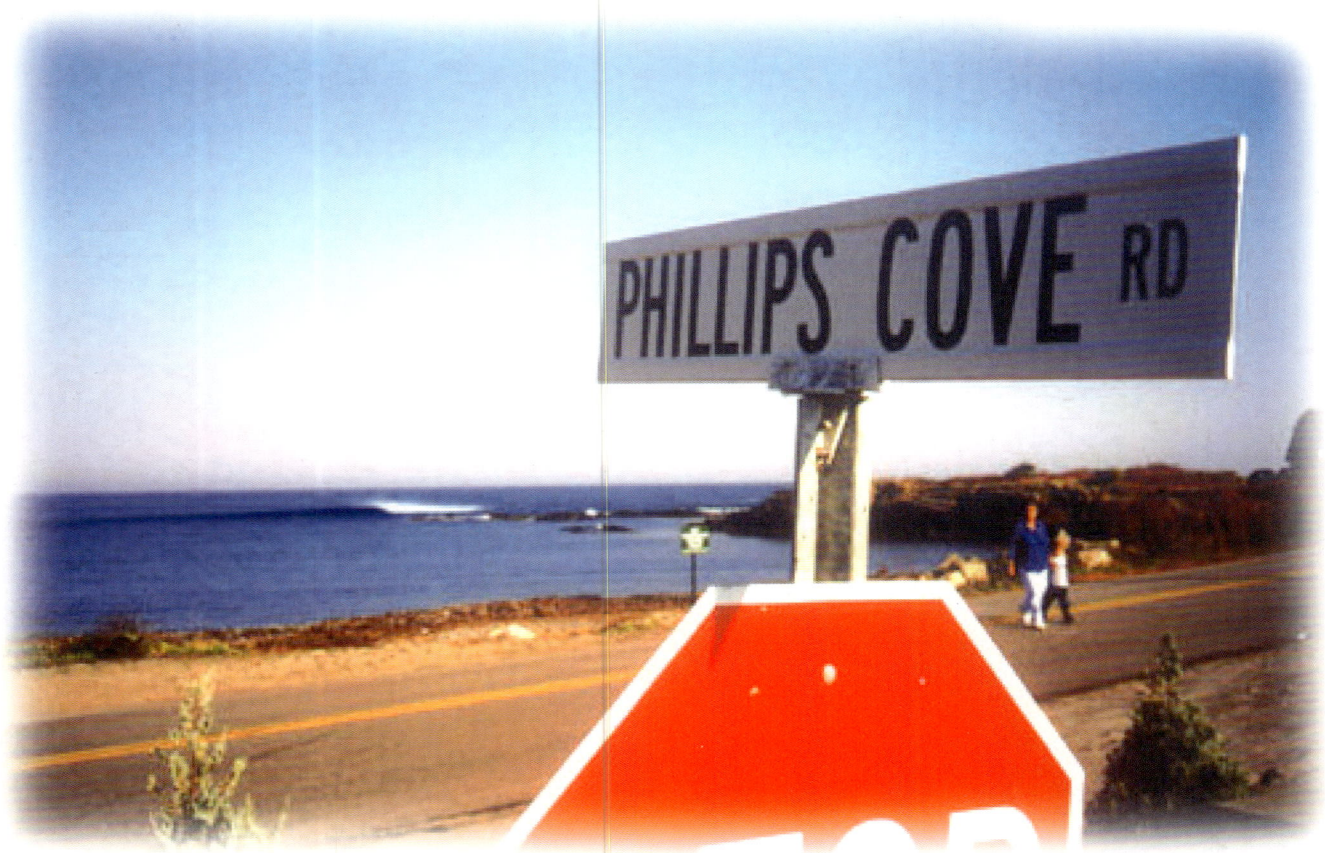

actual sign

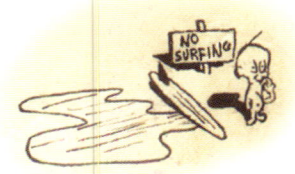